INTRODUCTION TO
AMERICAN CONSTITUTIONAL STRUCTURE

By

William Funk
Jeffrey Bain Faculty Scholar &
Professor of Law
Lewis & Clark Law School

AMERICAN CASEBOOK SERIES®

Mat #40616953

610 Opperman Drive
St. Paul, MN 55123
1–800–313–9378

Printed in the United States of America

ISBN: 978–0–314–18350–7

For Renate, because she has to put up with me;
For my children, because I love them;
And for my ConLaw class of the Fall 2007,
because they were the guinea pigs

*

Preface

More than a half century ago, Professors Noel Dowling at Columbia and Paul Freund at Harvard separately invented the modern Constitutional Law casebook. Today, the Dowling book continues in its sixteenth edition under the names of Professors Kathleen Sullivan and the now deceased Gerald Gunther. What characterized the modern Constitutional Law casebook was its focus on the Supreme Court and judicial review, beginning the book with *Marbury v. Madison*, and its coverage—both the structural constitution and selected rights provisions, normally substantive due process, equal protection, and the First Amendment. Today, while there are a few exceptions, this model has endured.

Typically well over 1,000 pages, these books are not even designed for a one semester course and usually even two semesters cannot cover the entire book. Moreover, today they are not well suited for an introduction to the Constitution. They reflect their pedigree in books written at a time when most beginning law students had "pre-law" backgrounds in college and progressed directly to law school. Thus, they presume a fair acquaintance with American history and government, which today's entering students are much less likely to possess.

This book is specifically designed to be used in a one semester introduction to the Constitution. Its design is at once both unusual and traditional. It is unusual in at least two ways. First, unlike most Constitutional Law casebooks, this book is limited to the structural constitution. That is, it is limited to the powers of the three branches of the federal government, their interaction, and their relation to the powers and responsibilities of the states. Moreover, it is also consciously limited in length, so that it can be fully covered in one semester, even while it does not radically edit cases. Second, unlike virtually all other Constitutional Law casebooks, it does not assume that the students are knowledgeable concerning American history or government. Today, the last time many entering law students were exposed to any American history or government was in high school. Foreign students are even less likely to have any background in American history or government. This book addresses that lack in three ways. First, it begins with the entire Constitution, from Article I to the Twenty Seventh Amendment, accompanied by comments and questions to expose students to the "forest" of the Constitution as a prologue to the particular "trees" that the book will later focus on. Second, it supplies a rich historical narrative both for the original Constitution as well as for many of the cases that follow, thereby furnishing a context for the students. This is supplemented with an appendix that provides a time-line connecting historical events, cases, and Chief Justices. The first chapter also includes an introduction to theories of constitutional interpretation and their characterization. In addition, to further bring cases alive, pictures and short biographies of current and famous former justices are provided when they first appear in cases. Third, the book consciously strives to anticipate and answer the questions beginning law students are likely to have and which are likely to make legal study more intimidating than necessary. For example, what is a "plaintiff in error" or a "writ"? What is the difference between a "concurring opinion" and an "opinion concurring in the judgment"? What is the difference between a "concurrent resolution" and a "joint resolution," and how is the latter different from a normal "bill"?

Although this book is novel in these respects, it is traditional in its coverage of the normal first semester of Constitutional Law. After the introductory chapter, *Marbury v. Madison* is the first case ushering in the subject of judicial review, albeit after an extensive narrative on the structure of the federal and state court systems and on Supreme Court procedure. The chapter on legislative powers focuses on the Commerce Clause, although some of the other Section 8 powers are included, and there is also significant coverage of the recent developments regarding Congress's powers under Section 5 of the Fourteenth Amendment, which is followed by a chapter on the Dormant Commerce Clause. The chapter on executive powers and the separation of powers includes all the canonical cases, while bringing the present "war on terror" into the mix.

The book's goal is to make the structural constitution both exciting and accessible to the modern student who never knew a life before the internet and cell phones. I hope it succeeds, and I invite your comments and suggestions.

WILLIAM FUNK
Jeffrey Bain Faculty Scholar &
Professor of Law
Lewis & Clark Law School
funk@lclark.edu

April, 2008

Summary of Contents

Table of Contents

Page

Table of Cases

The principal cases are in bold type. Cases cited or discussed in the text are roman type. References are to pages. Cases cited in principal cases and within other quoted materials are not included.

INTRODUCTION TO
AMERICAN CONSTITUTIONAL STRUCTURE

Seated: Justice Anthony Kennedy, Justice John Paul Stevens, Chief Justice John Roberts, Justice Antonin Scalia, Justice David Souter. Standing: Justice Stephen Breyer, Justice Clarence Thomas, Justice Ruth Ginsburg, Justice Samuel Alito.

Chapter 1

INTRODUCTION

A. THE CONSTITUTION

A constitution is the law that establishes the government of a nation, a subdivision of a nation, or even a supra-national organization. Constitutions are usually called constitutions, but not always. For example, the constitution of the United Nations is called a charter, the constitution of Germany is called the Basic Law, and the first constitution of the United States was called the Articles of Confederation. Constitutions are usually texts, but not always. For example, the United Kingdom is famous for having an "unwritten constitution," which is the body of law that establishes its system of government. A constitution usually contains not just the positive authorities of government–what the government is authorized to do–but also restrictions on the government–what the government is forbidden from doing. These restrictions are what in the United States we call constitutional rights. Under many constitutions, however, citizens are not just protected from what government might do to them, they are also granted certain positive rights–rights that entitle them to receive certain things from the government, such as, for example, a free public education. The United States Constitution does not contain such provisions, although some state constitutions and several foreign constitutions do. Thus, the United States Constitution does not ensure that persons receive an adequate education, housing, health care, clothing, or nutrition.

The United States Constitution is the oldest written national constitution in continuous use. Proposed on September 17, 1787, to the thirteen original states, it was ratified on June 21, 1788, when the ninth state ratified it. Government under the Constitution began on March 4, 1789, when the House of Representatives and the Senate met in New York City. George Washington, elected the first President in February, 1789, was inaugurated in New York City on April 30, 1789, at the Federal Hall on Wall Street, at which point there were only 11 states in the union.

Congress proposed twelve amendments to the states in September, 1789, ten of which, popularly known as the Bill of Rights, were ratified in December 1791. Since then, the United States has ratified 17 other amendments, the most recent in 1992, although that amendment was one of the original 12 proposed in 1789.

This constitutional law book, like virtually all constitutional law books, does not attempt to cover the entire Constitution. Because it focuses on the structural elements of our governmental system as contained in the Constitution, this book does not cover those parts of the Constitution that are considered the "rights" portions, such as the Bill of Rights and the Equal Protection and Due Process Clauses of the Fourteenth Amendment. Those constitutional rights are covered in other books and courses. Still other provisions of the Constitution rarely are considered in any law school course for various reasons. Nevertheless, what follows is an outline of the entire Constitution, including all those provisions that arise or not in other courses. One should have a view of the forest before delving into particular trees in depth.

This summary is not a substitute for reading the actual Constitution, which is found in Appendix I. Rather it is an outline to assist in reading it, with some comments and questions to focus attention on certain aspects.

The Preamble

The preamble is not "law," as the rest of the Constitution is. Like statements of purposes that often introduce statutes passed by legislatures, however, one may look to the preamble to inform the meaning of the constitutional text. For example, the language of the preamble, "we the people," was used to counter the southern states' position prior to the Civil War that the United States was created by the states coming together, suggesting that they could leave if they wished. The preamble, their opponents argued, stood for the proposition that the United States was created by the people, not by the states. Whatever the merits of this argument, it took the Civil War to resolve the issue.

Article I

Article I relates to Congress and the legislative powers of the United States. Section 1 states that all legislative powers "herein granted" are vested in Congress. Thus, we must look to the rest of the Constitution to find what legislative powers are indeed granted. Section 2 is limited to matters pertaining to the House of Representatives, including the election of its members. Note that it uses the term "electors"; that is the term used at the time for those who would vote to elect a person. The requirement for a decennial census comes from Section 2's demand that representatives (and direct taxes) be apportioned among the states on the basis of population. Note also that it is the House of Representatives that impeaches someone.

Section 3 is limited to matters pertaining to the Senate, including the selection of Senators. Under the original Constitution, Senators were not elected by voters, but instead were chosen by the state legislature.

This reflected the concept that Senators represented the state, whereas Representatives represented the people. The Senate is the court that tries an impeachment case after the House has impeached someone. A conviction requires a two-thirds vote, unlike the impeachment itself, which only requires a simple majority. Impeachment only means removal from federal office (and disqualification for holding a federal office later); it does not by itself have other legal effect. Neither a Senator nor a Representative holds a federal office. Thus, a person might be impeached and convicted and still be elected to the House or Senate, and indeed there is currently a member of the House of Representatives who was earlier impeached and convicted and removed from being a federal judge. Note that this section describes the only duty identified in the Constitution for the Vice President, and it is unclear what else the Constitution allows the Vice President to do.

Section 5 relates to the internal workings of the House and Senate. It is important that each house is the judge of the elections, returns, and qualifications of its own members. Thus, disputed House and Senate elections are decided by each house, not by the courts. Moreover, each house has the power to establish standards and maintain discipline with respect to its members and, therefore, may punish or even expel a member.

Section 6 contains the congressional privilege against arrest when going to or returning from Congress, except for "treason, felony and breach of the peace," and against being questioned "in any other place" regarding their speech in either house. The former privilege is effectively meaningless today, inasmuch as the Supreme Court has interpreted "treason, felony and breach of the peace" to refer to all criminal law, *see Williamson v. United States*, 207 U.S. 425 (1908), limiting the privilege to arrest in civil suits, something that was common in 1789 but does not exist today. The "Speech and Debate Clause," however, remains alive and well and will be considered in Chapter 5.

Section 6 also prohibits a member of Congress from being appointed to a federal office whose pay was increased during that member's term in office. Moreover, it absolutely prohibits a person from being both a member of Congress and a federal officer at the same time. This is an important element in separating the executive and legislative powers. Compare this with the United Kingdom where the Prime Minister and other cabinet members must be members of the House of Commons.

Section 7 provides the procedural rules for making laws, including provision for Presidential veto and "pocket veto" (when the President neither signs nor returns a bill to Congress within ten days and Congress is not in session). Note that the ten days does not include Sundays.

Section 8 is a major section that will be considered in this book. It contains the list of almost all the things about which Congress can make laws.* Later in this book we will deal with some of them, notably the Commerce Clause, the Taxing and Spending Clause, and the Necessary and Proper Clause. Among the more obscure authorities is Congress's power to grant letters of Marque and Reprisal. These were authorizations by Congress to private persons to attack and capture property belonging to foreign nations or citizens of foreign nations, which the persons could then keep as a reward. In the absence of such an authorization, persons engaging in such activity would be guilty of piracy. This was a way to privatize war-making in the 18th century.

Section 9 contains a list of laws that Congress is specifically prohibited from making. The first clause, albeit indirectly, prohibited Congress from restricting the importation of slaves for twenty years. The second clause prohibits Congress from suspending the privilege of the writ of habeas corpus (Latin for "you have the body"), except in cases of rebellion or invasion where the public safety requires it. The writ of habeas corpus has been much in the news with respect to unlawful combatants held at Guantanamo. A "writ" is a formal written order issued by a body with administrative or judicial jurisdiction. The writ of habeas corpus is an order issued by a court to an official holding a person in custody, demanding the official to justify why the person is being held. The third clause prohibits Congress from passing bills of attainder or ex post facto (Latin for "after the fact") laws. A bill of attainder is a law in which the legislature finds a person to be a criminal and punishes that person in some way. An ex post facto law is a law that criminalizes action after the fact, so that a person could be prosecuted for something that was lawful when done.

Clause four refers to a "capitation" or other direct tax. In the 18th century, governments obtained their revenues from customs duties (fees paid for the privilege of importing goods), excise taxes (a tax on some transaction—today, gasoline or cigarette taxes are examples), property taxes (a tax paid on real property—e.g., land—or personal property—e.g., an Iphone), or a capitation or head taxes (a fixed tax levied on each person). The former two were the principal sources of revenue and were known as indirect taxes; the latter two were known as direct taxes and were viewed with some skepticism at the time. Requiring them to be proportional to population was intended to ensure that the national government would not discriminate against some states in favor of others. In 1895, the Supreme Court declared a federal income tax unconstitutional as a direct tax not levied in proportion to population. *Pollock v. Farmers' Loan & Trust Co.*, 157 U.S. 429 (1895). The 16th Amendment in 1913 in effect overruled that case and authorized a non-proportional income tax.

Section 10 goes further and specifies what laws states may not make. Note that sandwiched between the prohibition on passing bills of

* Article IV, Section 1, and Article IV, Section 3, clause 2 also authorize Congress to make laws dealing with particular matters.

attainder and ex post facto laws and the prohibition on granting titles of nobility, both of which Section 9 also prohibited to Congress, is a prohibition on impairing the obligation of contracts, which is not prohibited to Congress.

Questions

1. "Legislative powers" may be vested in Congress, but what are "legislative powers"? Congress often demands information from executive officials, and sometimes issues subpoenas (a particular form of legal demand) to executive officials to appear or bring certain documents. Is demanding such testimony or information a "legislative power"? Did you see anything in Article I that would authorize such action?

2. What benefit did slave states receive in terms of their representation in the House of Representatives?

3. Why do you think Senators were to be chosen in a different manner than members of the House of Representatives?

4. If a person believes he has been wrongfully convicted by the Senate after impeachment, wrongfully declared the loser of an election by the House or Senate, or wrongfully expelled from the House or Senate after being elected, what sort of relief might that person seek?

5. On what basis may the House or Senate expel a member?

6. What do you think the exception of Sundays in counting the ten days for a pocket veto says about the Founders' religious views and their reflection in law?

7. In light of Section 8's authorizations to Congress, what kind of role do you think the Founders had in mind for Congress to play in matters of foreign affairs and war making?

Article II

Article II relates to the President of the United States. Section 1 begins by vesting the "executive power" in the President and then provides the means by which the President and Vice President are elected. This section is the source of what we call the Electoral College, although that term is not used in the Constitution, the entity that actually elects the President and Vice President. Note that it does not provide for a general election to determine who the "electors" are but leaves to the state legislatures to determine the method of appointing the "electors." Clause 3 provided how the electors would vote for the President, with the person coming in second being elected Vice President. In the election of 1800, however, Thomas Jefferson and Aaron Burr, both Republicans, tied in the vote for the President, leaving the decision to the House of Representatives, which was controlled by members of their opposing party, the Federalists. This was not what the Framers had intended, largely because the Framers had simply not foreseen the birth of political parties. As a result, the 12th Amendment was adopted, changing the method by which the Electoral College votes for President. Note that only a "natural born citizen" is eligible to be President. Sorry, Arnold. Clause 6, relating to what happens if the President or Vice President leaves office, dies, or is disabled, has been largely supplanted by the 25th Amendment, but it is still Congress that by law determines the order of succession in case of a vacancy in the offices of both the President and Vice President. *See* 3 U.S.C. § 19. Note also that during the period for which he was elected, the President's pay cannot be increased or decreased, and he is prohibited from receiving any other financial benefit from the federal or state governments. Finally, note that the President's oath of office is to protect the Constitution of the United States, not to protect the United States.

Sections 2 and 3 contain a list of powers and duties of the President. Note that there is a specific authorization to the President to require principal officers in the executive departments to provide an opinion in writing on any matter relating to their offices, but there is no specific authorization to the President to be able to direct them to do anything else. Moreover, there is specific authorization for the President to appoint ambassadors, other public ministers and consuls (the term "public ministers and consuls" refers to officers involved in foreign affairs below the rank of ambassador), and all other principal officers of the United States (with the advice and consent of the Senate), but there is no specific authority for the President to fire an officer once appointed.

Section 4 specifies that the President, Vice President, and all civil officers of the United States may be removed from office by impeachment for and conviction of treason, bribery, or other "high crimes and misdemeanors." While treason and bribery are well understood, the phrase "high crimes and misdemeanors" is not. There is some historical basis for interpreting "high" to refer to crimes and misdemeanors against the government, which would be consistent with treason and bribery. Some commentators have suggested that abuses of office that do not rise to the level of a criminal offense may still be "high crimes and misdemeanors." Others, however, have argued that only "serious" crimes can be "high crimes and misdemeanors." The impeachment of Andrew Johnson charged him with removing the Secretary of War in violation of the Tenure in Office Act, which required any removal of a cabinet member to be approved by the Senate. No one suggested, however, that this was a criminal offense. Of course, Johnson was not convicted, but whether what motivated the nineteen Senators who voted "Not Guilty" was the fact that the alleged act was not a criminal offense or some other reason is not known. The two articles of impeachment passed by the House with respect to President Clinton both involved criminal offenses, perjury before a grand jury and obstruction of justice. He too was acquitted in the Senate. Only seven persons have ever been removed from office by impeachment, all of them judges, one of whom was elected to Congress three years later and as of this writing has served as a representative from a Florida district for the past sixteen years.

Questions

1. Under the Constitution, could a state legislature provide that the governor of the state should appoint the state's electors without any state election?

2. Why do you suppose the Constitution prohibits Congress from adding to or subtracting from the President's pay during his term of office?

3. In light of Sections 2 and 3's authorities and duties of the President, what kind of role do you think the Founders had in mind for the President to play in matters of foreign affairs and war making?

4. Section 3 states that the President "shall take care that the laws be faithfully executed." How do you suppose the President is to do that? And what does it mean?

5. If the President believes that a bill presented to him by Congress for his signature would be unconstitutional, is he required to veto it?

6. If there is a law that the President believes is unconstitutional, may he decide not to enforce it? Is he prohibited from enforcing it? Or, is he required to enforce it?

7. How is it that a person who was impeached by the House and convicted by the Senate and thereby is barred from holding "any office of honor, trust, or profit under the United States" can thereafter be a member of the House of Representatives?

Article III

Article III relates to the federal judiciary. Section 1 vests the judicial power of the United States* in a Supreme Court, but it leaves to Congress the determination of whether or to what extent to have lower federal courts. The Framers were not sure that lower federal courts would be necessary; they believed that state courts would be able to decide most, if not all, the cases that might arise under federal laws. Section 2 then describes what the federal judicial power extends to, that is, what matters can possibly be brought before federal courts. There are two general categories—cases** and controversies. Scholars disagree over the

* When the Constitution refers to the "United States," it refers to the national government, not the several states. Thus, the judicial power "of the United States" refers to the judicial power of the federal government. Also, when the Constitution refers to the "laws of the United States," it refers to federal laws, not state laws. Similarly, in Article II, Section 2, where the Constitution gives the President the power to grant pardons for offences "against the United States," it means the President can grant pardons for federal crimes, not state crimes.

** Section 2 refers to "cases, in law and equity." In English law (and therefore colonial law) at the time, court cases could be either cases in equity or cases at law. Cases at law were brought in "common law" courts, presided over by judges but whose decisions were made by juries. Cases at equity were brought in the courts of chancery, whose decisions were made by judges, not juries, who derived their authority from the king. Typically, in civil cases, courts of law would provide money damages as a remedy, whereas courts of equity would enter injunctions. These were at the time of purpose in the Constitution of distinguishing between cases and controversies, but it is an issue for scholars only, as no one has ever found that, whatever the distinction, it makes any legal or constitutional difference. Within these two categories the Constitution lists a number of different types of cases and controversies, for each of which there is a reason why a federal court, rather than a state court, might be a better forum. In this course we will see cases almost exclusively brought under the authority to hear cases "arising under" the Constitution or "laws of the United States." Section 2, Clause 2, identifies two of the types of cases or controversies over which the Supreme Court would have original jurisdiction—that is, in which the original trial would be in the Supreme Court itself. The clause then states that the Supreme Court would have appellate jurisdiction over all the other mentioned types of cases, but it says that Congress may make "exceptions" to that appellate jurisdiction. That is, Congress may say that as to some of the types of cases, or perhaps some subset of a type of case, the Supreme Court will not have appellate jurisdiction.

Section 1 of Article III also provides that federal judges shall hold their positions "during good behavior" and shall not have their pay diminished. The removal limitation is substantive; it does not describe what procedure is required. Both the removal and pay provisions were clearly designed to provide a measure of insulation to judges from retribution from the political branches for unpopular decisions.

Article III, Section 2, Clause 3 is one of the few "rights" provisions in the original Constitution, requiring a jury trial for all crimes and requiring the trial to be in the state in which the crime was committed. This provision applies only to federal trials, not state trials.

Section 3 is a response to British actions against the colonies, where treason could be charged fairly easily. "Attainder of treason" related to an old British practice of punishing not just the traitor but all his heirs as well.

Questions

1. May the President remove a Supreme Court Justice he believes is not acting in "good behavior"? May Congress impeach and convict (and thereby remove) a Supreme Court Justice it does not believe is acting in "good behavior"? What is "good behavior" anyway?

2. Article III refers to Congress being able to make exceptions to the Supreme Court's appellate jurisdiction, but it does not specifically provide for exceptions to lower federal courts' jurisdiction over the types of cases and controversies within the judicial power of the United States. Nevertheless, federal courts have *never* been authorized to hear all the cases within the judicial power of the United States. What authority in

the Constitution two separate court systems existing side by side. Subsequently in the United States most states and the federal government have merged both cases at law and cases in equity into the same court system. Thus, today, cases in law and equity means all cases.

Article III would justify withholding some of that power from federal courts?

3. Why do you suppose the Framers would want to enable federal courts to hear controversies between citizens of different states, controversies to which the United States might be a party, or controversies between states?

Article IV

Sections 1 and 2 of Article IV relate to the relationship between states. The Full Faith and Credit Clause assures that court judgments and other public acts by one state will be recognized by other states. Thus, for example, if a person is found liable for a tort and ordered to pay damages to the plaintiff, the plaintiff could use that court judgment in another state to collect upon the defendant's assets without having to bring another tort suit against the defendant. Added to the Full Faith and Credit Clause is a provision authorizing Congress to prescribe both the way one would have to prove the existence of the public acts, records, or judicial proceedings of the other state in order to have faith and credit given to them and the effect such public acts, etc., would have. This is one of the few provisions outside of Article I that gives Congress the authority to make laws.

Section 2 begins with the Privileges and Immunities Clause. It assures that when a citizen of one state travels to another state that citizen does not lose the "privileges and immunities" of citizenship. The clause does not, however, specify what are "privileges and immunities" of citizenship. The extradition clause requires a state to return escaped criminals to the state from which they escaped. Finally, section 2 concludes with what is known as the Fugitive Slave Clause, which likewise requires a state to return to the rightful owner a slave who escaped to that state.

Section 3 allows for the admission of new states into the union. In addition, this section contains the Property Clause (Section 3, Clause 2), that specifically authorizes Congress to dispose of property belonging to the United States and to make all rules regarding the territory and property of the United States. This effectively grants Congress plenary power to make rules and regulations regarding what happens to or on federal property. Thus, for example, under this clause Congress can allow for grazing on federal lands or prohibit it, authorize mining on federal lands or prohibit it, create federal parks or give the land away. This is another of those few provisions outside Article I authorizing Congress to make laws. Note that there is no specific provision for Congress to acquire property for the United States.

Section 4 is called the Guarantee Clause. By its terms the "United States" guarantees "a republican form of government" to every state. How that is to be done is not specified. Nor is it clear what is meant by a "republican" form of government. We know the Framers wished to preclude a state from instituting a monarchical form of government, but many scholars believe that they equally wished to preclude a state from adopting a pure form of democracy, wherein the people would make their own laws, as opposed to electing representatives who would make laws on their behalf. This clause also promises that the United States will protect states from invasion as well as from domestic violence if the state requests the aid.

Questions

1. Does the Full Faith and Credit Clause require South Carolina to recognize marriages legally performed in Massachusetts between two persons of the same sex? If so, does the Defense of Marriage Act passed by Congress, stating that no state need recognize a marriage between persons of the same sex, eliminate that requirement?

2. In 1803 the United States concluded a treaty with France for the purchase of the Louisiana Territory for $15 million. This purchase doubled the territory of the United States at the time and included all of what is now Arkansas, Missouri, Iowa, Oklahoma, Kansas, Nebraska, Minnesota south of the Mississippi River, much of North Dakota, nearly all of South Dakota, northeastern New Mexico, northern Texas, the portions of Montana, Wyoming, and Colorado east of the Continental Divide, and Louisiana on both sides of the Mississippi River. President Jefferson doubted the constitutionality of his purchase, but he did it anyway, letting pragmatic concerns overcome his principles of limited federal power. Can you think of a way this purchase may be justified constitutionally?

Article V

This article relates to amendments to the Constitution. It specifies two different methods by which an amendment may be proposed. First, and the way that every amendment has in fact been proposed, Congress by a two-thirds vote can propose new amendments to the states. Congress has only proposed six amendments that were not ratified. Interestingly, the very first amendment proposed by Congress is one of those. What we refer to as the First Amendment was actually the third amendment proposed by Congress. Another of the failed amendments was a proposed Thirteenth Amendment passed by Congress on March 2, 1861. It was an attempt to keep the southern states from seceding by banning any amendment to the Constitution that would interfere with slavery within any state. President Lincoln, in his inaugural address two days later, stated he had no opposition to the proposed amendment. The South seceded anyway, and only two states ratified the proposed amendment. It is ironic that it is the actual Thirteenth Amendment that in fact abolishes slavery. A proposed amendment stating that "equality of rights under the law shall not be denied or abridged by the United States or by any State on account of sex" failed to achieve ratification by the necessary three-fourths of the states by 1982.

The other method for proposing an amendment is if the legislatures of two-thirds of the states call for a constitutional convention, which convention can then propose amendments. This is, of course, the method by which the original Constitution was proposed to the states.

However the amendments are proposed, Congress can specify whether states can ratify the proposals through legislative action or through state conventions.

Originally, there were two limits on what amendments could be adopted. The one that remains today forbids any amendment of the Constitution that would deprive a state of its equal suffrage in the Senate without its consent.

Questions

1. What if a state legislature ratifies a proposed amendment, but before the amendment receives approval from three-fourths of the state, a new legislature is elected and repeals its ratification? What should be the effect of the repeal? This is no idle question; this has occurred on more than one occasion.

2. What if legislatures of two-thirds of the states called for a convention to propose a balanced budget amendment to the Constitution, could that convention, after it was convened, propose other amendments in addition to or in place of the balanced budget amendment?

3. Could an amendment amend Article V to rescind the limitation on amendments?

Article VI

Clause 2 of Article VI is the Supremacy Clause. It states that the Constitution, laws, and treaties of the United States are the supreme law of the land. Note that this clause does establish a hierarchy among the Constitution, laws, and treaties. This is because this clause is aimed at the states; it is to establish that federal "law," whether the Constitution, laws, or treaties are supreme over state law. It also requires state judges to follow these federal laws rather than conflicting state laws. Note also that only laws "made in pursuance" of the Constitution are supreme, but that treaties already made before the Constitution, because they were made under the authority of the United States, are supreme.

The third clause of Article VI requires all federal and state officers and all federal and state legislators personally to swear (or affirm)* to support the Constitution. Finally, this clause also contains a "rights" provision, forbidding any religious qualification for holding any office under the United States. Note that this does not prohibit a state from requiring its state officers to be members of a particular religion.

* The alternative of "affirmation" in place of an "oath" was an accommodation to those religious groups, like the Quakers, who for religious reasons could not swear an oath.

Questions

1. Could a state require candidates for the House of Representatives from that state to be members of a particular religion?

2. If the Supremacy Clause does not establish a hierarchy among the Constitution, the laws, and the treaties of the United States, how do we know that the Constitution is supreme over federal laws? And which is the higher authority between treaties and laws?

Article VII

Article VII governs the ratification of the original Constitution. When nine states ratified the Constitution, it would go into effect. Of course, it would only be in effect in those states that actually ratified it.

First Amendment (1791)

The First Amendment contains the two Religion Clauses–the Establishment Clause and the Free Exercise Clause–as well as the Free Speech Clause and the Free Press Clause. It also addresses the right to peaceably assemble and the right to petition the government. Note that the limitation of the First Amendment is on laws passed by Congress; it says nothing about what states can do. At the time, all the states already had their own bills of rights, so that there was no felt need to protect people from their own states in the new Constitution; the federal Bill of Rights was to protect persons (and states) from the new national government. Also, the Establishment Clause forbids laws "respecting an establishment of religion," not laws "establishing a religion." At the time of the First Amendment, three states had established religions,* and this clause was to assure that the new national government could not disestablish those religions.

Second Amendment (1791)

Written in the passive voice, this amendment by its terms is not limited to protecting against actions by the federal government, but it, like the rest of the Bill of Rights, was not intended to restrict state governments. The major question posed by the language of this amendment is the significance of the opening language: "a well regulated militia, being necessary to the security of a free state...." One interpretation is that this amendment is not intended to create an individual right to keep and bear arms, but instead is intended to protect the states against the possible disarming of their militias, rendering the states defenseless against insurrection, invasion, or tyranny. Another interpretation is that it creates an individual right, but only an individual right to keep and

* An "established religion" refers to an official connection between a particular religion and the government. For example, in all of the three states that had an established religion, the government taxed on behalf of the official state religion. Great Britain then and now has an established religion–the Anglican Church–so that the head of the church, the Archbishop of Canterbury, is appointed by the monarch and serves in the House of Lords.

bear arms as part of a state militia. A third interpretation is that it creates an individual right to keep and bear arms but only to keep and bear those arms that may be useful to service in the militia. Finally, another interpretation is that the Amendment creates an individual right to keep and bear arms without any restriction relating to the militia.

Third Amendment (1791)

This amendment was a reaction to the British practice of quartering troops in persons' homes without their permission. It has never been interpreted by the Supreme Court and almost never has come up in practice.

Fourth Amendment (1791)

This amendment is particularly important in the investigation of crimes. It too is a reaction to British practice in the colonies where general warrants were used to search for customs violations. A major question is obviously: what is an "unreasonable" search? And should this be interpreted only to reject a search that would have been deemed unreasonable in 1791, or one that "we" would deem unreasonable today? If the National Security Agency intercepts all domestic cell phone traffic and then screens it by computer to find key words indicating terrorist intentions, is this a "search" within the meaning of the Fourth Amendment? These issues are usually dealt with in a course entitled Criminal Procedure rather than Constitutional Law.

Fifth Amendment (1791)

This amendment covers both criminal and non-criminal issues. It requires a grand jury indictment for what we generally today would call felonies. The grand jury at the time was considered a safeguard of citizens' rights, because the grand jury was made up of citizens. Thus, a person could not be charged with a major offense unless the person's peers believed he should be charged. This was a protection against government tyranny. Today, grand juries themselves are often thought to exert excessive government force, and while still made up of ordinary citizens, as a practical matter almost always do what the government attorney asks them to do.

This amendment also contains the Double Jeopardy Clause. Because the Bill of Rights was only intended to apply to the federal government, the double jeopardy prohibited is double jeopardy before federal courts. For example, a person could be tried and found not guilty by a state court, and the federal government could still prosecute the person for the same alleged act. And this does occur.

This amendment also contains the Self Incrimination Clause, which despite its language has been interpreted to protect a person from being forced by the government to incriminate himself with respect to a criminal offense as a witness in any proceeding.

Probably the most important part of the Fifth Amendment is the

Due Process Clause, prohibiting the federal government from depriving any person of life, liberty, or property without due process of law. Here the major question is: what is "due process of law," but there are also questions as to what constitutes protected liberty and property. Is liberty only freedom from bodily restraint, or does it also include the "liberty" to engage in a profession, to have consensual sexual relations with the person of one's choice, or to have an abortion?

Finally, the Fifth Amendment contains the Takings Clause or Just Compensation Clause. This clause is rife with ambiguities. What is private property? What does it mean to "take" it? For example, does government regulation of property that reduces the value of the property constitute a "taking"? What is a "public use"? For example, does it suffice that the property is taken for public purposes, even if the "public" does not get to use the property? Finally, what is "just compensation"? For example, is the fair market value of the property "just compensation," or should "just compensation" include reimbursing the property owner for the transaction costs necessarily imposed on him by the taking?

Sixth Amendment (1791)

This amendment is also dealt with in criminal procedure courses and provides federal criminal defendants with various rights designed to better assure a fair trial.

Seventh Amendment (1791)

This amendment preserves the right of a jury trial in federal civil cases "at common law" when the amount involved exceeds $20 and prohibits judges from second-guessing jury determinations except "according to the rules of the common law." As mentioned earlier, at the time of this amendment, cases in court could be either cases at common law or at equity. Cases at equity did not require juries, while common law cases did. This amendment prohibited the federal government from changing that in federal cases. Today, however, we no longer have separate "common law" and equity cases, having merged the two separate types of cases. Nevertheless, this constitutional requirement remains, so that courts have had to assess whether a given modern case would have been a "common law" case back in the day. If so, there must be an opportunity for a jury trial. This makes for some very technical legal history determinations.

Eighth Amendment (1791)

This ban on "cruel and unusual punishments" (or excessive bail and fines) has most recently been litigated with regard to the death penalty. Clearly, the death penalty was not cruel and unusual in 1791. Indeed, the Constitution mentions the possibility of the death penalty in two places in the Fifth Amendment—once in the requirement for a grand jury indictment in *capital* cases and second in the requirement for due process of law before one is deprived of *life*. But, did the Framers intend that only those punishments deemed cruel and unusual in their day would be prohibited? Or did they intend that whenever the punishment was being considered, if it was then deemed cruel and unusual, it would be prohibited? In other words, was the original meaning intended to vary with the morals of society? One member of Congress objected to this proposed amendment, declaring that if it were adopted, one day whipping would be prohibited. He was right, at least with respect to federal punishments. Again, despite the passive voice, this amendment only restricted the federal government.

Ninth Amendment (1791)

This amendment was designed to rebut an argument made against having any bill of rights, that a list of specific rights would suggest that these were all the rights that persons had. At the time, the dominant enlightenment philosophy was that persons enjoyed certain natural rights, even if the philosophers could not agree on exactly what those rights were. The Ninth Amendment was to make clear that the first eight amendments did not mean there were not other rights "retained by the people." Nevertheless, the Ninth Amendment poses two difficulties. First, we do not know what those other rights are or how to ascertain them. Second, even if we knew what they were, would they have any legal effect–would they be "constitutional" rights able to be enforced in courts against the government or only a recognition of rights that the government *should* respect? This difficulty has resulted in courts not affording the Ninth Amendment much substantive authority. Indeed, there is no Supreme Court decision finding a "Ninth Amendment right" that would prohibit federal government action.

Tenth Amendment (1791)

This amendment was to make explicit what was implicit in the Constitution itself–that the new national government only had those powers granted to it and that these powers were limited powers. The powers inherent in government that were not delegated to the new federal government were retained by the states (or the people). At the same time, it is not clear what the legal effect of the Tenth Amendment is, because if a power was not delegated to the new federal government, then it would necessarily have remained with the states, and if the power was delegated to the federal government, then the Tenth Amendment would not apply at all.

Eleventh Amendment (1798)

In *Chisholm v. Georgia*, 2 Dall. (2 U.S.) 419 (1793), the Supreme Court held that Article III authorized federal jurisdiction over a suit against a state by a citizen of another state despite the objections of the state of Georgia that it had sovereign immunity* from any lawsuit. In

* Sovereign immunity was a British legal doctrine that the monarch could not be sued in his courts without his consent, because he was the very source of their

response to that case, Congress immediately proposed and the states quickly ratified the Eleventh Amendment to overrule that case. Thus, the language of the amendment limits the judicial power of the United States, which had been set out in Article III, so that it does not extend to suits against a state by a citizen of another state or citizens of a foreign state. As will be seen later, however, this amendment has been interpreted to extend well beyond its language, in essence to constitutionalize both state and federal sovereign immunity.

Twelfth Amendment (1804)

In the election of 1800, the Federalists, who had controlled the presidency and the Congress since adoption of the Constitution, were swept from office by the Democratic–Republican party, which was led in the south by Thomas Jefferson and in the north by Aaron Burr, the governor of New York. Jefferson was slated by the party to be the candidate for President and Burr for Vice President, but one of the Republican electors who was supposed to vote for Jefferson and not for Burr, which would give Jefferson one more vote for President than Burr, messed up, and they both received the same number of votes, throwing the election to the House of Representatives for decision. Ironically, because the newly elected members of the House (overwhelmingly Republican) had not yet been seated, it was the Federalist controlled House that would choose the new President. After seven days and 35 ballots, Hamilton, as a Federalist leader, swung his influence in favor of Jefferson, and Jefferson was elected President with Burr as Vice President.*

The problems evidenced by this election led to the adoption of the Twelfth Amendment, which still governs how we conduct Presidential elections. The Electoral College and its method of selection remains unchanged from Article II, but now the electors cast one ballot for President and one for Vice President. If there is no majority for a choice for President, the House of Representatives, as it did under Article II, chooses the President from the top three finishers. Similarly, if there is no majority choice for Vice President, the Senate, as it did under Article II, chooses the Vice President from the two highest finishers. Since the election of 1800, however, no election has been decided in the House or Senate. But for the Supreme Court's decision in *Bush v. Gore*, 531 U.S. 98 (2000), that election might have been decided in the House and Senate if the electors from Florida had not been deemed to have been determined in time.

Thirteenth Amendment (1865)

The first of the three so-called Civil War Amendments, this amendment abolished slavery within the United States and any place subject

authority. The expression, "the king can do no wrong," reflects this notion of sovereign immunity. With the elimination of a monarch in the United States, sovereignty now resided in the people. Nevertheless, states continued to believe that sovereign immunity existed so that they could not be sued in any court.

* Four years later Burr would kill Hamilton in an illegal duel.

to its jurisdiction. It also provides authority to Congress to adopt legislation to enforce the prohibition. The scope of this enforcement power has been subject to some question. In 1866 Congress enacted the Civil Rights Act that guaranteed that:

> All persons within the jurisdiction of the United States shall have the same right in every State and Territory to make and enforce contracts, to sue, be parties, give evidence, and to the full and equal benefit of all laws and proceedings for the security of persons and property as is enjoyed by white citizens, and shall be subject to like punishment, pains, penalties, taxes, licenses, and exactions of every kind, and to no other.

In cases involving private discrimination in accommodations and in a theater, the Supreme Court held that, while "the power vested in congress to enforce the article by appropriate legislation, clothes congress with power to pass all laws necessary and proper for abolishing all badges and incidents of slavery in the United States," to regulate private discrimination was beyond Congress's enforcement powers, because such private discrimination did not inflict practically or legally either slavery or involuntary servitude on the victim. *The Civil Rights Cases*, 109 U.S. 3 (1883). This decision, however, was overruled on this point in 1968 (at the height of the modern civil rights era) by *Jones v. Alfred H. Mayer Co.*, 392 U.S. 409 (1968), in which the Supreme Court held that Congress could rationally find that private discrimination constituted the "badges and incidents of slavery" and thereby forbid it under its enforcement authority. Whether the Court today would reach the same result is another matter.

Fourteenth Amendment (1868)

The Fourteenth Amendment contains a number of provisions, some more important than others. Section 1 begins with a sentence designed to overrule the notorious pre-Civil War *Dred Scott* case, *Scott v. Sandford*, 19 How. (60 U.S.) 393 (1857), in which the Supreme Court held that a black person, even a free person, could not be a citizen of the United States. The first clause of the next sentence is known as the Privileges and Immunities Clause of the Fourteenth Amendment (to distinguish it from the Privileges and Immunities Clause of Article IV). The difficulty with this clause (which was also suffered by the Article IV Privileges and Immunities Clause) is determining what are the "privileges and immunities of citizens of the United States" that are protected from state abridgement. In a case decided only five years after the Amendment was ratified, *Slaughter–House Cases*, 16 Wall. (83 U.S.) 36 (1873), the Supreme Court by a narrow 5–4 margin held that the "privileges and immunities of citizens of the United States" were entirely different from the "privileges and immunities of citizens in the several states," the language of Article IV. The latter had been interpreted in prior cases to mean a person's "fundamental rights." These fundamental rights, the Court said, arise from *state* citizenship, rather than federal citizenship.

Only those rights a person enjoys by reason of federal citizenship would be protected by the Fourteenth Amendment. Otherwise, the Court said, the Amendment would work a radical change in the nature of American government by placing primary responsibility for the protection of fundamental rights in the federal government, rather than state governments. The Court then provided an illustrative list of the *federal* privileges and immunities:

> the right to come to the seat of government to assert any claim he may have upon that government, to transact any business he may have with it, to seek its protection, to share its offices, to engage in administering its functions[;] the right of free access to its seaports ..., to the subtreasuries, land offices, and courts of justice in the several States; to demand the care and protection of the Federal government over his life, liberty, and property when on the high seas or within the jurisdiction of a foreign government[;] to peaceably assemble and petition for redress of grievances, [to seek] the privilege of the writ of habeas corpus[;] to use the navigable waters of the United States.

The dissenting justices read the language entirely differently, believing that it was indeed the purpose of the Amendment to protect citizens of the United States (especially those who became citizens by reason of the first sentence of the Fourteenth Amendment) from deprivations of fundamental rights by the states. It is noteworthy that the Court split so evenly as to a basic understanding of the Amendment so shortly after it was proposed and ratified. While some other holdings of the *Slaughter House Cases* have been subsequently rejected by the Court, its decision regarding the Privileges and Immunities Clause remains the interpretation today.

The second clause of the second sentence is called the Due Process Clause of the Fourteenth Amendment. Its effect is to extend the same limitations to states that apply to the federal government under the Fifth Amendment's Due Process Clause before the government may deprive someone of life, liberty, or property.

The third clause of the second sentence is known as the Equal Protection Clause. Exactly what is meant by "equal protection of the laws" is not clear. Laws invariably make distinctions between persons. In order to be a lawyer, one must have graduated from law school and passed the bar exam. Those who have not cannot practice law. Thus, these two groups are treated differently. In one sense, we could say the Equal Protection Clause prohibits wrongful discrimination, but that still leaves the question: what is wrongful discrimination?

Section 2 eliminates the apportionment of representatives based upon three-fifths of non-free persons found in Article I. Of course, because the Thirteenth Amendment had eliminated slavery, all persons would be free persons. So, why was this sentence necessary? Recall that in Article I it is states that get to decide who votes for members of the House of Representatives, and the southern states were not allowing the freed slaves to vote. Thus, the southern states would now get more representatives in Congress, even though they would still not let black persons vote. Accordingly, the next sentence in Section 2 reduces the apportionment of representatives from any state that denies the vote to any male citizens having attained 21 years of age, reducing it by the proportion that those denied the vote have to all male citizens having attained 21 years of age. For example, if the population of male citizens 21 years old or older in South Carolina was 500,000, and half of them (former slaves) were denied the vote, then South Carolina's representation in the House would be cut in half.

Section 3 was to punish those who had supported the Confederacy in the Civil War in violation of their oath to support the Constitution (required by Article VI) by banning them from federal and state elected or appointed positions. This was to ensure that all the political leaders of the Confederacy could no longer wield any governmental power.

Section 4 reaffirmed the war debt of the United States but explicitly rejected any liability for debts contracted by the Confederacy. Those who supported it should not get their debts repaid. Moreover, it explicitly disavowed any requirement for compensation to be paid to those deprived of their slaves by the Emancipation Proclamation, state law, or the Thirteenth Amendment.

Finally, Section 5, like Section 2 of the Thirteenth Amendment, grants Congress authority to enforce this Amendment by appropriate legislation. The extent of this enforcement provision has also been subject to some question. First, the *Civil Rights Cases* established that Congress could not regulate private conduct under the Fourteenth Amendment. Because the Fourteenth Amendment only imposes restrictions on states, the enforcement of the Amendment cannot extend beyond protecting against state action. This element of the *Civil Rights Cases* is still "good" law. Second, even with respect to laws protecting against state action, it is not clear how far Congress can go beyond enforcing against action that is itself unconstitutional under the Fourteenth Amendment. For example, in the Age Discrimination in Employment Act Congress made it unlawful to discriminate in employment on the basis of age and provided that victims of unlawful discrimination could sue for money damages. The Supreme Court, however, held that Congress could not prohibit states from discriminating on the basis of age under Section 5 of the Fourteenth Amendment. Because state employment discrimination on the basis of age was unlikely to be unconstitutional under the Fourteenth Amendment, a blanket prohibition against it was not congruent and proportional to possible Fourteenth Amendment violations. *See Kimel v. Florida Bd. of Regents*, 528 U.S. 62 (2000). On the other hand, in *Nevada Dept. of Human Resources v. Hibbs*, 538 U.S. 721 (2003), the Court said Congress could require state employers to grant all employees limited, non-paid family and medical leave under Section

5, because it was an appropriate remedy for the identified constitutional violations by state employers discriminating on the basis of sex in granting family and medical leave.

Fifteenth Amendment (1870)

The inadequacy of the remedy in the Fourteenth Amendment for states denying newly freed slaves the ability to vote was quickly apparent, and the response was this amendment, prohibiting denial of the right to vote on the basis of race, color, or previous condition of servitude. This amendment as well gives Congress the power to enforce its provisions by law.

Sixteenth Amendment (1913)

This amendment was the direct result of the Supreme Court's decision in *Pollock v. Farmers' Loan & Trust Co.*, 158 U.S. 601 (1895), in which the Court held that an income tax was a direct tax and therefore prohibited unless apportioned among the states according to Article I. This case in effect prohibited federal income taxes. The purpose of this amendment was to overrule that case.

Seventeenth Amendment (1913)

The Progressive Era in American history lasted from about 1890 to 1920. One of its features was an attempt to further democratize American government. It was during this period that state constitutions were amended to enable citizens to make law directly through state initiatives and referenda. This amendment, providing for a popular vote for Senators, rather than their selection by the state legislature, was a product of that era and movement.

Eighteenth Amendment (1919)

Also a product of the Progressive Era with its propensity for reform, this amendment instituted Prohibition. This was the first proposed amendment with a time limitation on the period for ratification.

Nineteenth Amendment (1920)

The final amendment from the Progressive Era, this amendment prohibited denying the right to vote on account of sex.

Twentieth Amendment (1933)

Although the original Constitution did not specify a date for either the beginning of a new Congress or the inauguration of the President, the Continental Congress, having declared the new Constitution ratified on September 13, 1788, stated that the new government would begin on the following March 4. Thus, March 4 became the date upon which new Presidents and new Congresses would begin. While the long period from a November election to March might have been acceptable when methods of communication and transportation were still horse and buggy, by the Twentieth Century the long "lame duck" period was both unnecessary and problematical. First, the government was left in a form of partial paralysis for an extended period, and second, because before the days of air conditioners Congress had to adjourn for the summer, it left only a short period of time for legislative work. Finally, even after the Twelfth Amendment changed the method of electing the President, if the Electoral College did not cast a majority of votes for one person to be President and one person to be Vice President, the decision as to the President and Vice President would be made by the "old" House and Senate, not the newly elected one. The Twentieth Amendment solved these problems by advancing the date of the beginning of the new Congress to January 3 and the date of the inauguration to January 20.

Sections 3 and 4 provided answers to questions that had never arisen before and which have not arisen since–who is President, if on January 20 for some reason no living person has been elected President, and authorizing Congress to create a line of succession if both the President and Vice President die.

Twenty First Amendment (1933)

This amendment repealed Prohibition; it is the only amendment to rescind an earlier amendment. Section 2, like Prohibition itself, is one of the few provisions in the Constitution that acts directly on persons. That is, it prohibits anyone from transporting or importing alcoholic beverages into a state or into the United States or from using alcoholic beverages, if such transportation, importation, or use would violate the laws of the state or the United States. Thus, if you ever drank an alcoholic beverage when you were under-age, you actually violated the Constitution yourself, because you used an alcoholic beverage in violation of a state law. Normally, only a government can violate the Constitution. This prohibition was written into the Constitution to assure that states could forbid the sale and use of alcoholic beverages in their states if they wished, and the federal government would not be able to override such a state law.

Twenty Second Amendment (1951)

George Washington refused to run for a third term as President, stating that having escaped a monarchy, the American people should not in effect create a new one. This precedent was maintained, although there were few Presidents who realistically could have hoped to be elected to a third term, until Franklin Roosevelt, who was elected to a third term in 1940 and a fourth term in 1944. This amendment, proposed by a solidly Republican Congress, was to constitutionalize Washington's precedent.

Twenty Third Amendment (1961)

This amendment provided the means by which persons who live in the District of Columbia may vote in Presidential elections. Technically, it provided to the District the same number of electors in the Electoral College as it would have if it were a state. Because the District was predictably a solid Democratic stronghold, this amendment was a highly political amendment. A later proposed amendment that would give the District actual representation in the House and Senate, like a state, failed to achieve the necessary three-quarters states' ratifications. Again, this failure stemmed from the recognition that such representation would increase Democratic votes in the House and Senate.

Twenty Fourth Amendment (1964)

This amendment was proposed in the midst of the modern Civil Rights era. Poll taxes, among other things, had been used to discourage African–Americans from voting in the south. This amendment, while not prohibiting poll taxes, prohibited their non-payment from barring someone from voting *in federal elections*. Why did the amendment not also cover state and local elections? Probably for fear that it then would not pass three-fourths of the states. In any case, in 1966 the Supreme Court held that a poll tax in state elections was unconstitutional under the Fourteenth Amendment. *See Harper v. Virginia State Bd. of Elections*, 383 U.S. 663 (1966).

Twenty Fifth Amendment (1967)

The absence of a Vice President after Lyndon Johnson became President upon President Kennedy's assassination created an incentive for addressing the question of succession again and, imagining that President Kennedy had survived but been irreparably brain damaged, also the disability of the President. Section 1 clarified that upon the death, resignation, or removal of the President the Vice President becomes President; Article II had provided only that the "powers and duties" of the President would devolve upon the Vice President, not that he would become President. As a matter of practice, however, starting with the death of President William Henry Harrison in 1841 after 30 days in office, Vice Presidents maintained that they became President.

Section 2, recognizing that today a party's nominee for Vice President is usually hand picked as a running mate by the party's nominee for President, provides for the President to fill a vacancy in the Vice Presidency by nominating a person who must be confirmed by a majority of both houses. This change was fortuitous because in 1973 Vice President Agnew resigned, leaving the Vice Presidency vacant. President Nixon nominated Gerald Ford, a congressman from Michigan, who was confirmed as Vice President. Subsequently, Nixon himself resigned, thereby making Gerald Ford President, the only President never elected in any national election, and he nominated Nelson Rockefeller, the former governor of New York, who was confirmed by Congress.

Section 3 defines the procedure whereby a President may declare himself unable to discharge the duties of the office, so that the Vice President becomes Acting President for a period of time. In 1983, President Reagan sent a letter to the Speaker of the House and the President pro tem of the Senate informing them that Vice President George H.W. Bush would assume the duties and responsibilities of the President while he, President Reagan, was under anesthesia for cancer surgery.

Section 4 establishes the procedure for declaring the President unable to discharge his powers and duties, in which case the Vice President becomes Acting President. It has never been utilized, although there were occasions in American history before this amendment in which it might have been. For example, President Garfield lived for more than two months after he was shot, but he was in no condition to discharge his duties during that time. Under this section, if the President thereafter claims that he is able to discharge the powers and duties of his office, there is an involved procedure to determine whether the Vice President should continue as Acting President or whether the President regains control of the government. Inasmuch as this provision contains the potential for a coup d'etat, there is a difficult burden to be met to divest the President of his powers and duties when he claims that he is able to perform them. In essence, unless Congress by a two-thirds vote within three weeks of the dispute agrees that the President is unable to perform the functions of the office, the President resumes the powers and duties of the office. Note, however, that during the interim the Vice President acts as President.

Twenty Sixth Amendment (1971)

The Vietnam War, resulting in the draft of hundreds of thousands of young men under the age of 21, none of whom were entitled to vote under existing law, provided the impetus for this amendment. First, however, Congress tried to grant persons 18 years or older the right to vote by passing the Voting Rights Act of 1970. Because a person was subject to the draft at the age of 18, that was the age in this law by which one was entitled to vote. The Supreme Court in *Oregon v. Mitchell*, 400 U.S. 112 (1970), in a split decision held that, while Congress could set the age for voting in federal elections, it did not possess the authority under the Constitution to set the age for voting in state elections. With the upcoming elections in 1972, Congress quickly proposed this amendment, which was ratified within 107 days, the shortest period of ratification for any amendment.

Twenty Seventh Amendment (1992)

This amendment had the longest period of ratification of any amendment. It was in fact the second amendment proposed by Congress in 1789. [The first amendment proposed by Congress in 1789 still has not been ratified. It would cap at 50,000 the number of people a member of the House of Representatives could represent. Currently, a member of the House of Representatives represents approximately 600,000 persons. Were the "first amendment" ratified, instead of 435 members of the House of Representatives, there would be 5220. Probably not a good idea.] This amendment contains a simple idea: one Congress should not be able to raise its own salary; it should only be able to raise it for a subsequent Congress. Not quite the same level of importance as Freedom of Speech, Press, and Religion. By 1791 six states, not the then required ten, had ratified the amendment. Ohio ratified it in 1873 as a protest against a retroactive pay raise Congress had granted itself. Wyoming did the same in 1978. In 1982, a student at the University of Texas, Gregory Watson, discovered this unratified amendment and wrote a paper about it, suggesting that it could and should be ratified. He received a "C" on the paper. Nevertheless, Watson set out to have the amendment ratified. His crusade was picked up by conservative causes,* and in 1992 it had received ratification in thirty eight states, three-fourths of fifty, if you included the original six from 1791. The question then was whether this amendment had been validly ratified, inasmuch as there had passed over 200 years since its proposal. Congress called for hearings at which law professors opined that the amendment was not valid. However, before Congress did anything, the Archivist of the United States, who by statute has been entrusted with receiving and recording state ratifications of proposed amendments, announced that, the requisite ratifications having been received, the amendment was now in effect. Congress, faced with the option of overruling the Archivist, which would look like it wanted to vote itself pay raises, jumped on the bandwagon and passed resolutions agreeing with the Archivist. But who knows? Maybe the Twenty Seventh Amendment isn't an amendment at all.

B. BACKGROUND AND HISTORY

1. WHY STUDY HISTORY?

From the foregoing section and several of the questions, it is apparent that the text of the Constitution does not answer many of the most fundamental questions that can arise under it, much less more detailed questions that arise from its administration. How should the Constitution then be interpreted to answer those questions? It is a common, if not universal, approach to interpreting statutes passed by legislatures to look to the legislative intent behind the statute. What did the legislators intend when they adopted the statute? This would be one way of interpreting the Constitution. After all, it is a legal text and in that way is like a statute. What did the drafters in Philadelphia intend when they wrote the original Constitution, and what did members of Congress intend when they drafted constitutional amendments to be submitted to the states for ratification? Of course, unlike normal legislation, the adoption of the Constitution and its amendments involves more than just the drafters; the states had to ratify the Constitution and its amendments,

* Mr. Watson did not limit his historical interest to conservative causes, however. He also discovered that Mississippi had never ratified, and in fact had rejected, the Thirteenth Amendment banning slavery. He undertook a campaign to have Mississippi ratify the amendment, which was successful in 1995.

so perhaps we should also consider the intent of the ratifiers (the state constitutional conventions for the original Constitution and usually state legislatures for the amendments). Nevertheless, most commentators and judicial decisions interpreting the Constitution and its amendments generally only look to the intent of the framers, not the ratifiers.

How would one determine their intent? In the best case, as is the case with statutes, one could look to reports of congressional committees and statements made by legislators with regard to a proposed amendment. This is not an option with regard to the original Constitution, because it did not emanate from a congressional committee, and the actual proceedings in Philadelphia were not public. Indeed, there was a strict requirement of secrecy enforced on the delegates to the Constitutional Convention. Nevertheless, James Madison, one of the delegates from Virginia and today called "the father of the Constitution," kept a journal that has become the primary source of what little knowledge we have of what transpired in the Convention in Philadelphia. Partially because even Madison's journal is sketchy and also because it was not made public until after his death in 1836, probably the most important source for discerning the intent of the framers is the collection of essays published in New York newspapers prior to the ratification convention in New York and known today as The Federalist Papers. These 85 essays, authored pseudonymously by Madison, Alexander Hamilton (the only delegate from New York to vote for the Constitution), and John Jay (a prominent New York lawyer and former chief justice of the New York supreme court) were written as an attempt to convince the people of New York to support the adoption of the Constitution, and in so doing they explained its intents and purposes at some length. It is a fair criticism to note that The Federalist Papers were not written as a dispassionate exposition of the Constitution, but rather they present a one-sided view of the meaning of the Constitution. The "Anti–Federalists" had a different view that was expressed in essays printed in different New York newspapers, but history, they say, is written by the victors, and those supporting the adoption of the Constitution were the victors, so it is The Federalist Papers that today are relied upon to gauge the original intent.

The attempt to find the original intent of the Constitution as a means of interpreting the Constitution is often called "**Originalism**." However, there is another form of originalism that has been articulated by, among others, Justice Antonin Scalia. *See, e.g.*, A Matter of Interpretation: Federal Courts and the Law (1997). Justice Scalia, who does not believe in looking for legislative intent generally, argues in favor of finding the original *meaning*, rather than the original intent. In his theory, the text that was adopted is the law, not what the drafters may have intended it to mean. Only the text itself went through the necessary procedures to become law, not the unarticulated intent of the drafters. To discover the original meaning, Justice Scalia looks to then contemporary dictionaries to assess the meaning of words, but he can also look to contemporary documents, such as the Federalist Papers, to discern what was the context at the time for the law. His search is for how persons at the time would have reasonably read the constitutional or statutory text; his focus is on how the reader would have read the text, rather than on what the drafter intended.

There is a third form of "originalism" that differs markedly from the first two. This form of originalism has been articulated most recently by Professor Jack Balkin at the University of Texas. *See* Original Meaning and Constitutional Redemption, 24 Const. Comm. ___ (2007). While it pays lip service to the original text, it also stresses fidelity to the "principles that underlie the text." Where the text is unclear, one using this form of "originalism" would look to the underlying principles of the original Constitution to discern the correct meaning. But how does one find the "underlying principles" of the Constitution? Having read the Constitution, what do you think the Constitution's underlying principles are that bear on whether a state can criminalize abortion? Professor Balkin finds the underlying principles of the Fourteenth Amendment to create a constitutional right of women to obtain abortions. *See* Abortion and Original Meaning, 24 Const. Comm. ___ (2007). Critics of this form of "originalism" believe that it allows personal preferences to influence what one says are underlying principles of the Constitution. In other words, the determination of "constitutional law" would become subjective, rather than objective, allowing judges to "make up" constitutional law, rather than just apply constitutional law. Of course, critics of "original intent" and "original meaning" jurisprudence reply that these methodologies are equally prone to subjective manipulation, because history is rarely clear on the issue.

In any case, whether styled as original intent, original meaning, or original principles, this focus on the history and context underlying the adoption of constitutional provisions makes the history and background of the Constitution relevant to its interpretation and hence important to us.

2. HISTORY

a. *Pre-Constitution History*

As you know, the original 13 states began as colonies of Great Britain. Virginia was the first colony, followed closely by Massachusetts in the early 17th century, but Massachusetts differed greatly from Virginia in that Massachusetts was settled by religious dissenters (Pilgrims and Puritans) who came to America to be able to practice their religion freely, while Virginia was settled by fortune seekers, both rich and poor, rather than by religious dissenters. Several other colonies were founded by persons seeking a place to practice their particular religion—Rhode Island by followers of Roger Williams, Pennsylvania by Quakers, Maryland by Catholics. Others, like Virginia, had their origins more in economic considerations. New York and New Jersey had been Dutch colonies until

Great Britain seized them during the Second Dutch–Anglo War in 1664. Georgia, founded in 1732, was the last colony to be established. Substantial immigration followed the establishment of the colonies, so that, while in 1700 the population of the colonies barely reached a quarter million, by 1780 the population was more than 2.75 million. Moreover, the nature of the colonies had changed. Over 30% of the new white immigrants were from Germany, Scotland, and Ireland. The religious orientation of some of the colonies, such as Maryland, had ended. Only the New England colonies retained their homogenous English character. By far the largest state was Virginia, followed by Pennsylvania, Massachusetts, and North Carolina. Slavery was practiced in virtually all the colonies.

The colonies, although clearly subject to Great Britain, as a practical matter governed themselves on a day-to-day basis. Each colony had a lower house whose members were elected by free white property owners, as well as an upper house and a governor. While the upper house and governor were chosen by different means in different colonies, depending upon the manner in which they were created, the lower house or assembly had the power to make most laws governing daily life. These assemblies became in effect the training grounds for those who became the political leaders of the United States.

Prior to the French and Indian War between 1754 and 1760, Great Britain had not demanded much of the colonies, in part because trade with them was profitable to Great Britain. However, the French and Indian War, which despite the name was the American portion of the Seven Years War between Great Britain and France, and as a result of which Britain obtained all of Canada from France, resulted in a number of changes. First, as a way to avoid creating difficulties with the native Americans, the King placed restrictions on the settlement of western lands, but the expanding population of the colonies, plus the expectations of those who came to America in search of new property, created a great pressure for westward expansion. Second, the Quartering Act of 1765 required the colonies to provide housing and supplies to British troops. Third, because the war and administration of the colonies were expensive for Great Britain and the colonies were viewed as prosperous and a good source of revenue, Great Britain began a series of taxing measures, including the Sugar Tax, the Stamp Tax (which required all legal documents, newspapers, books, and playing cards to display a stamp purchased from the British government), and the Townshend Acts (placing import taxes on lead, glass, paint, paper, and tea). The Americans thought they were being taxed too much (Imagine that!) and, of course, had no opportunity to say anything in the matter. Taxation without representation! Accustomed to a benign neglect, the colonists viewed these numerous changes as threatening and the presence of British troops as an affront.

The Boston Massacre in 1770 in which British troops fired on an unarmed mob, killing five, elevated tensions. The colonies engaged in public protests, petitions, and a boycott of British goods, resulting in a repeal of most of these taxes, but the tea tax remained. This was widely evaded by American merchants, such as John Hancock, smuggling tea from Holland. Parliament retaliated in several ways. It increased British enforcement powers by bringing smuggling cases before admiralty courts, with judges appointed by the Crown and no juries, and by authorizing Writs of Assistance—general warrants allowing British customs officials to search for contraband anywhere they wished. In addition, parliament passed a law enabling the British East India Company, the British tea monopoly, to avoid the tax by selling direct to consumers. This, it was hoped, would bankrupt the smugglers. Americans, rather than viewing this as a way to obtain tea at a lower cost, correctly saw that this was an attempt to cut off and punish the American merchants, as well as increase British control over American affairs.

An attempt by the British East India Company to import tea to Boston in 1773 resulted in the famed Boston Tea Party, where the "Sons of Liberty," including noted revolutionary Samuel Adams, dumped tons of tea into Boston Harbor before a cheering crowd. The British Government responded by attempting to punish the Massachusetts Colony by closing the port of Boston until reimbursement was made for the tea destroyed, banning all town meetings without prior government permission, eliminating the elected council, and providing for trials of offenders to be held in England or other colonies rather than in Massachusetts. These laws, called the Coercive Acts by the British and the Intolerable Acts by the Americans, succeeded in uniting the colonies to provide assistance to Massachusetts and against Britain.

In 1774, representatives of all the colonies except Georgia met in Philadelphia in the First Continental Congress* to devise a unified strategy to deal with the British government. Some wished to compromise with Britain; others wanted full independence; the largest number, but short of a majority, sought a "Plan of Union" that would have a Grand Council elected by the colonies as the legislative arm of government and a President General appointed by the King. Unable to agree on any of these approaches, Congress adopted a Declaration and Resolves, which it sent to King George. The Declarations and Resolves as a forerunner to the Declaration of Independence bears inspection. It can be found at Appendix II. While professing loyalty to the Crown, it demanded the repeal of the Intolerable Acts and asserted various rights of the colonies and colonists. To put pressure on the Crown, the Congress agreed to boycott British goods and to invite Canada to join with the colonies. Finally, the Congress agreed to meet again the following year to consider what action to take in light of King George's response.

The British response was not to be conciliatory, and the British were

* Today, the word "Congress" to Americans suggests the national legislature in Washington, D.C., made up of the Senate and the House of Representatives, but in the 18th century the word meant simply a formal assembly of representatives, as of various nations, to discuss problems.

intent on putting down the incipient rebellion in Massachusetts, sending 12,000 troops to Boston. Meanwhile, the colonists were arming and training in militias, citizens organized and armed for military purposes. In April 1775, the British learned that the colonists were gathering weapons and ammunition in Concord, a town outside Boston, and troops were sent from Boston to find and seize that materiel. Paul Revere and two other patriots* rode out ahead to warn the militias. In Lexington, a town on the way to Concord, 77 militiamen gathered on the town common to meet the 700 British regulars. Neither the British nor the American commander wished to initiate hostilities, but from somewhere a shot was fired, and the American Revolution had begun. The British routed the militiamen and continued to Concord, from which most of the munitions had already been evacuated. Here the Concord Minutemen were supported by militia from other nearby towns, and more reinforcements continued to arrive, ultimately reaching more than 1000. An initial skirmish was won by the Americans, and the British began a retreat towards Boston. Repeatedly the Americans ambushed the retreating columns, inflicting serious damage, until British reinforcements from Boston joined the retreating troops. Word of the battles had spread, however, and more militia continued to arrive and join the fray until the British troops finally returned to Boston. The next day Boston was surrounded by some 20,000 militiamen.

Word of the hostilities quickly spread, and in May the already scheduled Second Continental Congress met in Philadelphia to determine a course of action. It quickly decided to create a unified Continental Army under the leadership of General George Washington, who was dispatched to take leadership of the various militias laying siege to Boston. Nevertheless, Congress still held hopes of achieving its previous goal of autonomy within the British empire, rather than actual independence. The Congress adopted a Declaration of the Causes and Necessity of Taking Up Arms, in which it declared that the colonies did not intend to dissolve its union with Great Britain and that it had not raised armies with the design of separating from Great Britain. This was quickly followed by a letter to the King expressing a desire to end hostilities and seeking a reconciliation. Moreover, the legislatures of Maryland, New Jersey, New York, North Carolina, and Pennsylvania voted against independence into late 1775. But the war was proceeding apace, with the Battle of Bunker Hill in Boston, the capture of Fort Ticonderoga in New York by Ethan Allen and the Green Mountain Boys, and most importantly the invasion of Canada in late 1775 led by General Benedict Arnold. Congress authorized this expedition in the hope that French–Canadians, only recently subject to British rule, would rise up and join the colonies in the fight. This was not to be, and Arnold's mission was a failure.

The British government, although itself split on the wisdom of a war

* The term "patriot" was a contemporary term to describe a supporter of the revolution. Those opposed to the revolution were called "tories" (or worse) by patriots and "loyalists" by others.

with the colonies, did not take the proffered olive branch letter seriously. Establishing sovereignty over the colonies became as much a matter of principle for them as autonomy from the government in London was for the Americans. And, in January 1776, Thomas Paine published his pamphlet *Common Sense* in which he rallied Americans to throw off the tyrannical rule of Britain and establish their own independent republic. This pamphlet, reflecting a natural rights philosophy also expressed in the later Declaration of Independence, is said to have been read by virtually every free American and had a dramatic effect on public and political opinion. Or maybe it just gave voice to what was rapidly becoming a foregone conclusion. In any case, on July 4, 1776, Congress adopted the Declaration of Independence, see Appendix III, irrevocably deciding on independence. Largely written by Thomas Jefferson with some assistance from Benjamin Franklin, the Declaration provided a justification for what had already taken place and an appeal to the international community for recognition of the thirteen states as new nations, united for purposes of securing their independence from Great Britain. The "United Colonies" in earlier declarations were now the "United States." At the same time, the Continental Congress began to act like a national government: appointing ambassadors, signing treaties, raising armies, appointing generals, obtaining loans from foreign states, issuing paper money (called "Continentals"), and disbursing funds. It did not, however, have the power to tax, and it had to rely on requests to the various colonies for support, which was often not forthcoming. At the same time, the states adopted their own constitutions, creating their own governments. These constitutions invariably began with a declaration or bill of rights, also reflecting the natural rights philosophy expressed in *Common Sense* and the Declaration of Independence. Thus, they prohibited cruel and inhuman punishment, general warrants, ex post facto laws, taking property without just compensation, and forced self incrimination, and they required freedom of the press, the availability of habeas corpus, the right to bear arms, and the right to a speedy and local trial by jury. These, of course, would later find their reiteration either in the Constitution or in its first ten amendments.

Immediately after the adoption of the Declaration of Independence, the first draft of the Articles of Confederation was presented to the Congress. The unanimity over establishing an army and finally declaring independence, however, did not extend to how the now united states should interact beyond the prosecution of war. It was not until a year later, in 1777, that a final draft of the Articles was completed and approved by the Congress for submission to each of the newly independent states for ratification. Delaware was the first state to ratify, but Maryland held out until 1781 due to land disputes with Virginia and New York. Nevertheless, as a practical matter, the Articles established the government of the United States from 1777 until the ratification of the Constitution in 1789. The Articles are truly the first American constitution and deserve close attention, because they contain the first legal framework governing the "United States," see Appendix IV.

The Articles have some similarities and some differences with the Constitution. Most fundamentally, the Articles did not unequivocally create one nation. Elements of the Articles look more like a league among nations, much like the European Union today. First, Article I styled the new entity a "confederacy," a term described at that time in international law as several sovereign and independent states uniting themselves together by a perpetual confederacy, without ceasing to be, each individually, a perfect state. In addition, Article III expressly provided that the states were entering "a firm league of friendship with each other, for their common defense, the security of their liberties, and their mutual and general welfare, binding themselves to assist each other, against all ... attacks...." Article II stated that each state "retain[ed] its sovereignty, freedom, and independence, and every power, jurisdiction, and right" not "expressly delegated to the United States, Congress assembled." Article V provided that each state would have one vote in Congress, just as each nation has one vote in the United Nations' General Assembly. Nowhere did the Articles provide the United States with the power to exercise sovereign authority over individuals within the several states. Again, just as the United Nations cannot make a law governing individuals but only laws governing nations, the Congress of the United States could only make laws binding the states within it. Finally, nowhere in the Articles is there a mention of citizenship in the United States; individuals were citizens of their states under such laws as those states might make.

On the other hand, there are elements in the Articles that reflect some sense of nationhood in the United States. For example, Article IV establishes a freedom of travel among the states and prohibits states from denying citizens of other states the same "privileges and immunities of free citizens" enjoyed by their own citizens. In addition, it provided that each state should give "full faith and credit ... to the records, acts, and judicial proceedings of the courts and magistrates" in other states. The Constitution largely repeats these provisions in its Article IV. Moreover, Article VI denies to states a number of powers that sovereign states would normally possess, such as the plenary power to send ambassadors to and receive ambassadors from foreign nations, to enter into treaties with other states or nations, to maintain a standing army or navy, to engage in war, and to grant letters of marque and reprisal. These restrictions, with little change, appear again in Article I, Section 10, of the Constitution. Finally, the Articles did expressly delegate certain traditional sovereign powers to the United States. For example, Congress is given the power to establish a national currency, a national standard of weights and measures, a national post office system, the power to borrow money, and the power to build and equip a navy. These and more are authorities later provided to Congress in the Constitution.

Whatever the legal status of the United States as a nation, as a practical matter, the United States was subordinate to the states. While Article XIII required every state to abide by determinations made by

Congress, there was no enforcement mechanism. There was neither a President of the United States* nor a federal court system. Congress could not itself levy taxes; it could only tell states what they should provide to the United States, but states ignored with impunity demands made by Congress to pay their required taxes to the United States. Congress could not even raise its own army but was limited to requisitioning land forces from the states, which they were required to supply, but for which there was also no enforcement mechanism. Again, much like the United Nations today, the United States was beholden to its member states, not as a practical matter sovereign over them. The weakness of Congress quickly became apparent, and fixing the problems was made nearly impossible by a requirement that any amendment to the Articles be unanimous among all the states.

After victory in Boston, forcing the British out, Washington and the Continental forces suffered a series of serious losses—the failed invasion of Quebec, the Battle of Long Island resulting in the British occupation of New York, and the New Jersey campaign resulting in the British occupation of Philadelphia, requiring the Continental Congress to flee—and the winter of 1776–77 spent at Valley Forge, lacking adequate supplies, nearly did the Continental Army in. Only Washington's surprise attack on the British base in Trenton, New Jersey, on a snowy Christmas night, capturing 1000 Hessian mercenaries, lifted the spirits of his troops enough that they extended their enlistments that otherwise would have expired six days later. Salvation came in the fall of 1777, when a British plan to lead an entire army south from Canada to New York City, effectively to sever the New England colonies from the rest, went awry. Under General Benedict Arnold the American forces surrounded the British army and forced it to surrender at the Battle of Saratoga. While a great triumph in itself, the real significance of the victory was that it convinced France to join the war on America's side. There is an irony in King Louis XVI supporting a revolution against a monarchy, a revolution that undoubtedly helped initiate the French Revolution twelve years later wherein he literally lost his head. One must remember, however, that the French and the British had been warring with one another for centuries and the adage that my enemy's enemy is my friend.

With more French money, French troops, and French ships, the tide turned dramatically. The *coup de grace* was dealt at Yorktown, Virginia, where the French fleet and American and French troops forced the surrender of a British army of 7000 under Lord Cornwallis in 1781. The peace negotiations dragged on and were finally concluded with the Peace of Paris in 1783. Great Britain accepted American independence, ceded lands east of the Mississippi and south of Canada, and granted American access to the Newfoundland fisheries. Congress was to recommend

* There was a President of Congress, but just as the Vice President under the Constitution is the President of the Senate, this kind of "president" is merely one who presides over the deliberations of the body; he is not an executive officer.

to the states that American loyalists be treated fairly and their confiscated property restored, and both parties agreed that creditors of neither country were to be impeded in the collection of their pre-war debts. This last requirement proved difficult to enforce under the Articles and again proved the weakness of the United States in attempting to control the states.

The one area in which the Articles proved sufficient was dealing with the western lands that were not within any state. Here the Congress could play the honest broker, and two laws were passed that helped shape the future of American westward expansion–the Land Ordinance of 1785, governing the disposition of public lands, and the Northwest Ordinance of 1787, providing territorial government of the western lands.

The inability of Congress under the Articles to deal with the economic depression following the War caused the greatest problem for the new governments. Farmers, who made up the bulk of the population of the states, purchased land, goods, and supplies on credit. The depression following the War, however, resulted in reduced income for farmers, and they were unable to pay their debts. States reacted in different ways depending upon their political makeup. States where the control of the government was in the hands of the debtor class either issued paper money and required creditors to accept it in payment of debts or simply passed laws delaying or excusing debts. This upset the merchant and professional classes, but there was nothing Congress could do. It had no power to make laws regarding commerce. States like Massachusetts, where the political establishment represented the merchant class, held fast and provided no breaks to the farmer/debtors. This led to the Shays Rebellion, in which farmers in the western part of the state took up arms against the state. While this rebellion was quickly put down by the local militia after Congress was unable to respond to an appeal for help from Massachusetts, it too demonstrated the weakness of Congress under the Articles. At the same time, there were several ongoing disputes between states regarding commerce in the waters adjoining them, and Congress was powerless to act. For example, Virginia, Maryland, Delaware, and Pennsylvania were all involved in a dispute over commerce in and around the Chesapeake Bay.

In 1786, Virginia invited all the states to send delegates to a meeting in Annapolis, Maryland, to consider possible amendments to the Articles. Only five states sent delegates, although these included Alexander Hamilton and James Madison, and the upshot of the Annapolis Convention was to request Congress to call for a convention of the states.

b. The Drafting and Ratification

Congress responded by inviting the states to send delegates to a convention in Philadelphia "for the sole and express purpose of revising the Articles of Confederation." Fifty five delegates from twelve states* arrived in May 1787. These delegates included most of the leading lights of the day, including Madison, Hamilton, Washington, and Franklin. Some, however, were notably absent, including Thomas Jefferson and John Adams, who were abroad on foreign missions, and Samuel Adams, Patrick Henry, and George Clinton (the Governor of New York), who were adamantly opposed to giving any greater powers to the national government. There was general agreement among those who attended that changes to the Articles were necessary, but there was no consensus yet on the nature of those changes.

A group of nationalists, who favored scrapping the Articles altogether and starting over, met together ahead of the convention to devise a plan to present at the beginning of the convention. This plan, dubbed the Virginia Plan, because the Virginia delegates were the primary instigators, provided for a national legislature with an upper and lower house, a national executive, and a national judiciary. While this sounds like what emerged as the Constitution, there were a number of fundamental differences. Both the upper and lower houses of the legislature would be apportioned according to population, so that large states would have greater representation in both houses. The legislature would have all the powers to legislate as under the Articles, as well as the additional powers to legislate "in all cases to which the separate states are incompetent" and to overrule any state law deemed by the legislature to be inconsistent with the constitution or any treaties. The national executive would be chosen by the national legislature. The national judiciary would consist of a Supreme Tribunal whose members would be appointed by the upper house of the legislature and such inferior tribunals as the legislature might appoint.

This plan was debated for the first two weeks of the Convention and had general support from the more populous states. Opposition to the plan arose from two different sources. First, New Jersey and Delaware opposed it because it deprived them of equal suffrage in the legislature, apportioning both houses on the basis of population and thus both seriously eroding their influence and striking at the principle of their equal sovereignty with the other states. New York and Connecticut (6th and 7th in population at the time) opposed alteration of the structure of the Articles and wished only to add some new legislative powers to Congress. Accordingly, together they presented a counter-proposal, known as the New Jersey Plan. The New Jersey Plan did not generally reject the Articles, although it did extend the authority of Congress beyond what was already in the Articles to also make laws to raise revenue and to regulate trade and commerce between the states and foreign nations. In addition, somewhat like the Virginia Plan, it also allowed Congress to create an Executive, but in this plan it would consist of several persons

* Rhode Island was not interested in any changes and boycotted the convention.

chosen by Congress who would execute federal acts, appoint inferior officers, and direct military operations. Also somewhat like the Virginia Plan, Congress could create a Supreme Tribunal, but whose judges would be appointed by the Executive. This Supreme Tribunal would hear in the first instance impeachments of federal officers, and it would have appellate jurisdiction over cases involving ambassadors, captures from an enemy, piracies and felonies on the high seas, foreigners, the construction of any treaty, and any of the acts for the regulation of trade or the collection of the federal revenue. All of these cases in the first instance, however, would be heard in state courts. Finally, and unlike the Virginia Plan, the New Jersey Plan contained a provision that is almost exactly the same as the Supremacy Clause in the Constitution.

The merits and demerits of the two plans were debated for several weeks, but neither side would give way on the basic issue of the makeup of Congress. A special committee was formed, which brought back a new plan, known as the Great Compromise, that provided for proportional representation in a House of Representatives, giving more power to the populous states, but equal representation in a Senate and a requirement that both would have to agree before a law could be made, thereby retaining an equality of power among the states. This broke the deadlock, and as a practical matter decided that the Articles would be jettisoned and that a national government would be created. Nevertheless, there were still many other issues to resolve. For example, while all were agreed that Congress needed the additional authority to make laws regulating commerce, the southern states, reflecting the Articles' requirement that all important laws must be agreed to by at least nine states, wanted to require a two-thirds majority to pass any law under this new authority. This was a sticking point for some time, but ultimately the southern states conceded on this point when the northern states agreed to prohibit Congress from passing export taxes (which would have fallen on the southern states' export of rice, tobacco, and cotton) and to prohibit any law regulating the importation of slaves until 1808. Another example was how to choose the President. There were supporters of a direct popular election, election by state representatives, election by state governors, and election by the Congress. The result, the electoral vote, was another grand compromise. Large states obtained generally proportional strength in the apportionment of electors, but the state legislatures retained the power to determine how the electors would be selected, and if the electors failed to choose a President by a majority vote, then the President would be chosen by a means in which each state would get one vote. As may be seen, much of what is in the Constitution is a product of political compromise rather than grand philosophy.

On September 17, 1787, the final text of the Constitution was adopted "by the unanimous consent of the States present." Of course, Rhode Island was not there. In addition, two of New York's delegates had left the convention because they were opposed to the direction it took in favor of creating a national government, leaving only supra-nationalist Hamilton to vote on behalf of New York. Indeed, of the 55 delegates who attended the convention, only 39 signed the Constitution. For example, George Mason, a delegate from Virginia and the author of Virginia's Declaration of Rights, refused to sign the Constitution because it did not contain a bill of rights, and the Governor of Virginia, Edmund Randolph, also a delegate, had left the convention when the Virginia Plan was not adopted.

Drafting the Constitution was hard enough, but it was only the first step. There still remained the need to have the states ratify it, and ratification was not a foregone conclusion. Today the Constitution may seem to have been inevitable, and in some states at the time ratification was simple. Delaware, again the first state to ratify, did so unanimously, as did Georgia and New Jersey. In Maryland and Connecticut the vote was over 75% in favor of ratification. Elsewhere, however, the Constitution was highly controversial. As noted, Rhode Island did not participate in the convention and did not recognize the call for state conventions to ratify the Constitution. In Massachusetts there was bitter debate, and ratification barely succeeded by a margin of 5%. In Pennsylvania, although the final margin was 17%, the struggle had been much closer than the numbers suggest. The outcome was the same in South Carolina. In North Carolina, the convention met but voted "neither to ratify nor reject the Constitution." When New Hampshire finally ratified the Constitution on June 21, 1788, by a narrow 5% margin, the requisite nine states had ratified the Constitution, but debates in Virginia, the largest state by far, and New York, a centrally important state, were ongoing. It was unthinkable that a new form of government could go into effect absent these states. In Virginia, several leading politicians, such as Patrick Henry and George Mason, were opposed to the Constitution. In New York, two thirds of the members of the convention were from the Anti–Federalist party, and ratification seemed doomed.

A major bone of contention in all the states where there was opposition to the Constitution was the absence of a bill of rights in the Constitution. The delegates in Philadelphia were not necessarily opposed to a bill of rights, but after the 16 weeks of daily work to finish the structural constitution to replace the Articles of Confederation, they were exhausted. Each of the states, however, already had their own bill of rights, and the absence of one in the Constitution for the new national government was viewed as gravely threatening to both individual and state rights. What finally enabled Massachusetts to garner enough votes to ratify the Constitution was the inclusion in its ratification of a recommendation to the new Congress that a bill of rights should be immediately proposed as amendments. This technique also worked in New Hampshire and Virginia to sway enough votes to ratify. Later, in New York, fearing that the new government might actually go forward without New York, the Anti-Federalists used such a letter to justify switching their support to ratification. Two days after New York ratified the

Constitution, the Congress sitting under the Articles of Confederation declared that there was a new government that would go into effect the following March. North Carolina held out until after the Bill of Rights had actually been proposed to the states by the new Congress of the United States. Rhode Island held out even longer, actually voting ratification down in its convention's first session. Later, after the United States imposed a tariff on goods from Rhode Island (treating it like a foreign nation), it ratified the Constitution by a vote of 34–32.

c. *Slavery*

No history of the United States prior to the Constitution, or after for that matter, would be sufficient without a discussion of slavery. Scholars are divided on the importance of slavery as an issue in the constitutional convention itself, but there can be no doubt that it was an important issue in 18th century America, and that it greatly affected the culture of at least the southern states, if not the entire country.

The first African slaves in British North America arrived in Jamestown in 1619. These and many others in the early years were treated in the European tradition of slavery—servitude for life or a term of years, more like a performance contract than standing in the position of property. As a result, many of these early slaves and their offspring became free persons with full citizenship rights. Indeed, some even became successful enough to have their own slaves. In the 1660s–70s, however, chattel slavery, perhaps imported from the British West Indies, became the virtually exclusive mode of slavery in the southern states and extended into the northern states as well. In chattel slavery, the slave is the property of the owner and the slaves' children likewise the property of the mother's owner. Slaves in the south were used largely on plantations, while slaves in the north tended to be domestics. South Carolina was the most notorious slave state, responsible for approximately 40% of all the slaves imported into the thirteen colonies, with a population of African slaves that by the early 18th century outnumbered whites by two-to-one, and the first colony to adopt a slave code. Slave codes were adopted by all the southern states in order to legalize not only the institution of slavery but also the repressive regime necessary to keep a majority or near-majority of the population in perpetual bondage and degradation. The southern economy, based on the production on large plantations of agricultural products largely for export, such as rice, cotton, tobacco, and indigo, relied upon large numbers of slaves to produce these goods at low cost. The mercantile and small farm economy of the north did not have the same needs.

In the mid–18th century, a movement for abolition began in the north, and the first laws providing for a gradual end to slavery began to be passed in 1780. Gradual abolition usually took the form of declaring that children of slaves would be born free, or setting a term of years by which time slaves would become free. Gradual abolition was a compromise between the principle of freedom and the economic concerns of the slave owners, who would be deprived of their property without compensation. Moreover, the northern states and even Virginia had banned further importation of slaves during the 1780s. Nevertheless, at the time of the Constitution there continued to be slaves in all of the states, and in the south the institution was thriving with no end in sight.

Several provisions of the Constitution relate to slavery. First, in Article I, Section 2, Clause 3, the apportionment among the states of representatives in the House of Representatives and of direct taxes is made according to the number of free persons (including indentured servants but not Indians not subject to taxation) and three-fifths of all other persons. "All other persons," of course, refers to African slaves. Thus, the southern states would have significantly more representation in the House of Representatives than if only free persons were counted. At the same time, the same states would be liable for a greater proportion of taxation of property than if only free persons were counted. Thus, the "three-fifths" formula was both a benefit and a detriment at the same time.

Second, Article II, Section 9, Clause 1, prohibited Congress until at least 1808 from restricting the importation of "such persons as any of the states now existing shall think proper to admit." "Such persons" are again slaves. Thus, this provision prohibited Congress from abolishing the importation of slaves under its new power to regulate commerce until 1808. This enabled the southern states to continue that importation for at least twenty more years. This provision was viewed as so important by the southern states that they insisted on the inclusion in Article VII, on amendments to the Constitution, a prohibition on amending this provision of the Constitution before 1808. Interestingly, however, South Carolina itself had banned the importation of slaves in 1787, although it reopened the trade in 1804. The ban on importation probably was not due to moral concerns but rather to the fact that additional supply from new importations would lower the value of the slaves owned and generated by South Carolina plantation owners.

Third, Article IV, Section 2, Clause 3, provides that if a "person held to service or labour" escapes to another state, that state was obliged to return the person to "the party to whom such serviced or labour may be due." Again, we see that the sensibilities of the Framers led them to avoid the use of the term slave. Nevertheless, this clause is known as the Fugitive Slave Clause.

C. CONSTITUTIONAL INTERPRETATION

The media often portrays judges and justices as "liberal," "conservative," or "activist." These terms, however, are often misused or misunderstood, or have no real meaning. For example, Justice Scalia is usually portrayed as a "conservative" justice. This is due to his appointment by a "conservative" President–Ronald Reagan–and opinions that are applauded by "conservative" politicians. At the same time, Justice Scalia is sometimes labeled an "activist" justice, because he has demonstrated a willingness to challenge accepted constitutional norms as well as a lack of reluctance to declare federal laws unconstitutional. Nevertheless, usually when persons call judges "activist," they use the term as a shorthand way of characterizing judges who are willing to find constitutional rights not expressly enumerated in the Constitution. Usually, these judges are also branded as "liberal" judges, because "liberal" political groups approve of their decisions. Historically, however, judges appointed by "liberal" Presidents and who were political "liberals" before donning the robe often were "conservative" jurists. That is, they viewed the role of the judiciary to be minimalist, and they were reluctant to interfere with majoritarian decisions. This is particularly true of Justices Black and Frankfurter, appointed by President Franklin Roosevelt.

The current political debates over appointments to the Supreme Court began with Republican President Richard Nixon, who promised to appoint only "strict constructionists" to the Court, by which he meant judges who would strictly construe, as opposed to liberally construe, the rights provisions of the Constitution. This was in reaction primarily to decisions rendered by the Court under Chief Justice Earl Warren, such as *Brown v. Board of Education* ending legalized school segregation, *Miranda v. Arizona*, *Gideon v. Wainwright*, and *Mapp v. Ohio* recognizing rights of the criminally accused, and *Reynolds v. Sims* imposing the requirement of one person/one vote. Virtually every Republican President since Nixon has reiterated the pledge to appoint "strict constructionists," and for twenty-five years, until President Bill Clinton, there was no opportunity for a Democratic President to appoint a Supreme Court justice. Nevertheless, sometimes persons expected to be "conservative" were not, such as Justice Souter, while others evolved from a relatively "conservative" position to a more "liberal" position, such as Justice Blackmun, who authored *Roe v. Wade*, Justice Stevens, now considered the most "liberal" member of the Court, and Justice Kennedy who has become the swing vote between two wings of the current Court. Today, pundits identify Chief Justice Roberts and Justice Alito, the two most recent appointments, as well as Justices Scalia and Thomas, as the "right" wing of the Court. On the "left" there is Justice Stevens, the longest serving current justice, and Justices Souter, Ginsburg, and Breyer, the latter two appointed by President Bill Clinton. As you progress through this book, see if you can discern why these justices are perceived in this way.

A more important question is why justices reach the decisions they do, and in particular why they so often disagree with one another. An idealized view of the Court might imagine that the justices would agree about what the Constitution requires, prohibits, or allows. After 200–plus years shouldn't we know what it says?

Cynics and some political scientists ascribe critical importance to the justices' political orientation, pointing out that there is some correspondence between how particular justices rule in cases and the political party that appointed them. That is, in the simplest sense, Justices Scalia, Thomas, Alito, and Chief Justice Roberts tend to decide cases in ways that would please the Presidents that appointed them. Similarly, Justices Breyer and Ginsburg tend to rule in ways that would please President Clinton, who appointed them. At the same time, this way of explaining how justices rule is highly imperfect. Not only do Justices Souter and Stevens rule in ways that would disappoint the Presidents that appointed them, but as mentioned earlier this is not a new phenomenon. Justice Blackmun did not follow the path Richard Nixon would have liked, and perhaps most dramatically Chief Justice Earl Warren, the former conservative Republican Attorney General and Governor of California, appointed Chief Justice by Republican President Dwight Eisenhower as a reward for Warren's political support of Eisenhower's nomination on the Republican ticket, became the symbol of the liberal, activist Court against which all subsequent Republican Presidents railed. In other words, explaining the split on the Court on the basis of political orientation is not descriptively accurate.

Nevertheless, it is not a coincidence that some justices appointed by a President from one party are likely to disagree with some justices appointed by a President from a different party. There are fundamental ideological differences between the current Republican and Democratic parties. One involves the relation between government and the marketplace; another involves the relation between government and morals. Finally, there is a basic disagreement between the parties regarding the role of the courts in deciding disputes in these areas.

President Ronald Reagan in his first inaugural address expressed the Republican view of the relation of government and the marketplace: "government is not the solution to our problem; government is the problem." Democrats, on the other hand, believe that "problems" in the marketplace, from health care and the environment to subprime mortgages and executive compensation, are problems appropriately dealt with by the government. Republicans, therefore, want the courts to be critical of government regulation of the marketplace, whereas Democrats want courts to be supportive of such regulation. With respect to the relation between morals and the government, here Republicans tend to be supportive of government regulation designed to preserve majoritarian senses of what is moral, while Democrats tend to believe that morals are a matter for the individual, not the government. Thus, Republicans tend to support laws against abortion, homosexuality, drug use, and pornography, whereas Democrats are more likely to view these issues as a matter reserved for individual choice. As a consequence, Republicans view as improper judicial intervention to overturn laws adopted through democratic processes dealing with these issues, while Democrats view courts as appropriate safeguards against majoritarian restrictions on individual choice in these areas.

There are philosophical underpinnings for the parties' different approaches to the relationships between government and the marketplace and government and morals, but the differences at the political level relating to the role of the courts appears to be more pragmatic. That is, Democrats want judges who will decide cases so that the outcomes favor the Democratic position, while Republicans want judges who will decide cases so that the outcomes favor their position. When they are in a position to affect who is appointed to the judiciary, the different parties attempt to bolster their positions by finding persons who they believe will rule in their favor. This is understandable, if not admirable. At the same time, the politicians cannot admit this in so many words, so they create labels or catchwords that supposedly reflect a judicial philosophy that is likely to result in decisions they favor. Hence the terms discussed above.

There are, however, real judicial philosophies relating to how one should interpret the Constitution. Earlier we discussed "originalism," which is one of them. Closely related is "textualism," meaning that one must interpret the text on its own basis. There are various interpretive canons on how to interpret texts, often with Latin names, such as *noscitur a sociis* (the meaning of a word can be determined by its association with other words in the same phrase or document). For instance, the Second Amendment's right to bear arms follows the phrase "a well regulated militia being necessary to the security of a free state." A textualist, therefore, would read the right to be somehow connected to the need for a militia, rather than, for example, the need to hunt or even for self-defense. Naturally, there are limits to textualism. The "well regulated militia" language does not tell us how the right to bear arms relates to the need for the militia, especially when state governments have abolished state militias as they all have.*

Both originalism and textualism anchor constitutional interpretation to a fixed idea. That is, the meaning of the Constitution does not change over time absent constitutional amendment. However, there is a tension between this concept and the judicial rule of *stare decisis*.** That rule provides that prior judicial interpretations should be followed except in extraordinary circumstances. Scholars argue whether the rule of *stare decisis* is constitutionally required, but it is largely an academic argument, because Congress has shown no interest in legislating on the subject. *Stare decisis* is in tension with concepts of a fixed constitution, because each decision of the Court in some way alters the prior meaning of the Constitution, if only by making it more specific by deciding a par-

* While the National Guard inherited some of mythology and tradition of state militias, the National Guard is not a "militia" within the meaning of the Constitution.

** *Stare decisis* has two forms–vertical and horizontal. Vertical *stare decisis* requires lower courts to follow the decisions of courts over them; horizontal *stare decisis* generally requires the same court to follow its own precedents. The difference is that the former is an absolute requirement, whereas the latter is a softer requirement that the later court can avoid by overruling its prior decision. When the Supreme Court interprets the Constitution or federal laws, its opinions are binding on all lower courts, state and federal, but the *stare decisis* effect on the Supreme Court in later cases is the horizontal, or softer, sort.

ticular case. As you will see, the repeated interpretation of particular parts of the Constitution has resulted in a significant change over time in what the Constitution "says." Thus, the Constitution becomes something of a moving target rather than a static instrument. Originalists and textualists have to deal with *stare decisis*, but for them it is a problem to be overcome in some way. Those who believe in a "living constitution," however, embrace the idea that the Constitution changes over time. This is not a problem; it is what keeps the Constitution alive and meaningful. Indeed, not to interpret the Constitution, and previous interpretations of it, in light of changes in the nation and the world would make the Constitution increasingly either counterproductive or irrelevant. At the same time, any interpretation must be faithful to the principles embedded in the Constitution in order for the interpretation to be deemed valid. Thus, any interpretation must explain how it is faithful to the Constitution, through its text, its history, prior interpretations of the Constitution, or Constitutional principles.

Take the death penalty and the Eighth Amendment. That amendment prohibits the infliction of "cruel and unusual punishments." We know for a fact that the death penalty was not considered cruel and unusual in 1791, so for an originalist that would decide the question. On the other hand, we also know that whipping was a common form of punishment in 1791, but it is generally accepted that it would be a cruel and unusual punishment today. A textualist not aligned with originalists could read the Eighth Amendment and interpret it to prohibit a punishment that is considered cruel and unusual at the time that it is administered, as opposed to what was considered cruel and unusual at the time of the amendment. Thus, the text itself could enable the Constitutional prohibition to change over time. Finally, in cases over the past two centuries, the Court has had to interpret how the amendment applies to a range of punishments, some of which were never considered in 1791. To decide these cases, the Court has adopted verbal formulations that attempt to capture the essence of the Eighth Amendment. For example, it has said that the amendment "must draw its meaning from the evolving standards of decency that mark the progress of a maturing society." *Trop v. Dulles*, 356 U.S. 86, 100–101 (1958)(plurality opinion). In addition, the Court has said that a punishment can be cruel and unusual because it is disproportionate to the offense involved. *See Weems v. United States*, 217 U.S. 349 (1910). In applying either of these two standards, the historical context in which the punishment is inflicted is important. Thus, to apply these standards necessarily means the Constitution is adapting to the circumstances.

Even if one accepts the idea that the Constitution must be interpreted in the context of its time, there can still be a dispute about how the underlying principles apply in the case, because many of the underlying principles of the Constitution are in tension with themselves. For example, the Constitution was a compromise between those who wished a strong central government and those who wished to protect the sovereignty of the states. The structure of the government was created to give effect to both of these principles, but to neither in an absolute sense. Thus, we will find that often there is a question about empowering the federal government at the expense of the states or vice versa, where the text of the Constitution is not clear and consequently how to mediate between these two principles is also not clear. A judge with a skeptical view of federal power is likely to give greater credence to the underlying principle of retained state sovereignty, whereas a judge skeptical of states rights is likely to give greater credence to the underlying principle of a strong central government.

Books and articles have been written about different approaches to constitutional interpretation, so here we have only scratched the surface by raising some of the issues. See if you discern yourself developing an interpretive philosophy as you go through this book.

D. WHAT COMES NEXT?

The above has been a general introduction to the text and background of the Constitution as a whole. However, as mentioned earlier, this book from here on will focus only on particular parts of the Constitution. We call them the structural aspects of the Constitution because they form the basis for how our governmental system works. We begin with an exploration of the powers of the different branches of the federal government: the legislative, executive, and judicial. In this exploration, we consider the extent of the power of each of these branches as well as how these powers can be both separated and overlapping, giving rise to the complementary concepts of **Separation of Powers** and **Checks and Balances.** In addition, we will be addressing the limits of federal power under the Constitution. It is often said that the United States is a government of limited powers, but to most people it is not clear how that is so. This focuses our attention on the concept of **Federalism**, or the vertical separation of powers–the assignment of powers between the states and the federal government. Then, having considered the extent of the powers of the federal government, we study how the Constitution limits the powers of the states in certain ways.

Chapter 2

THE JUDICIAL POWER

A. THE JUDICIARY

The Constitution begins with the legislative power, which it vests in Congress, and continues with the executive power, which it vests in the President, and only then addresses the judicial power of the United States,* which it vests in the Supreme Court and in such lower courts as Congress may create. There is, however, a reason why we begin this book with the judicial power. The reason is that from here on we will be studying the decisions of the Supreme Court interpreting and applying the Constitution in different situations. To help understand these decisions it may help to know something about how the Supreme Court operates and relates to other courts.

Today the Supreme Court consists of nine Justices—eight Associate Justices and one Chief Justice.** Originally, it consisted of six justices, then after about twenty years it was expanded to seven, and then after another twenty years to nine in 1837. Except for a five year period in the 1860s, when it was expanded to ten justices, it has remained at nine justices ever since. The first Jewish Justice was Justice Louis Brandeis, appointed with some controversy in 1916 by President Woodrow Wilson. The first African–American Justice was Justice Thurgood Marshall, appointed in 1967 by President Lyndon Johnson. Marshall had been the lead litigator for the NAACP Legal Defense Fund for years and had been the lead counsel in *Brown v. Bd. of Education*, the case that declared segregated public education unconstitutional. The first woman Justice was Justice Sandra Day O'Connor, appointed by President Ronald Reagan in 1981.

Originally, the Supreme Court justices not only sat on the Supreme Court, they also "rode circuit," meaning they sat as judges on a circuit court. The Judiciary Act of 1789, one of the first acts passed by Congress

* It bears repeating that when the Constitution refers to the "United States," it is referring to the federal government, not to the states. Thus, the "judicial power of the United States" refers to the judicial power of the federal courts, not the state courts. Just as there are legislatures and executives (governors) for states separate from the federal Congress and President, there are separate judicial systems as well.

** The title is Chief Justice of the United States, not Chief Justice of the Supreme Court.

and which first created federal courts, established a federal district court and a federal circuit court in every state. The district court had jurisdiction over the less important civil and criminal cases, while the circuit court had jurisdiction over the more important civil and criminal cases, as well as over appeals from the district court.* While a single district judge would preside over trials in district courts, a district judge and two Supreme Court justices,** called respectively a circuit judge and circuit justices, would preside over trials in the circuit court as well as hear appeals from district courts. Cases would be appealed to the Supreme Court from the circuit courts. This changed in 1891, when a new judiciary act eliminated circuit riding by justices and created circuit courts of appeals with their own judges to hear appeals from both district courts and circuit courts (which lost their appellate jurisdiction over district courts). In 1911 the trial level circuit courts were abolished, with their jurisdiction being placed in the district courts.

Today, all the federal trial courts of general jurisdiction*** are district courts. Each state has at least one district court, and many have more than one; California, New York, and Texas have four, each with jurisdiction over a portion of the state. Do you know what district you are in? While a case in a district court is presided over by one judge, there are usually a number of judges in a particular district court, all of whom may be hearing cases at the same time. For example, the Federal District Court for the Eastern District of New York, which is Long Island, has 14 judges in active service. The federal circuit courts are all courts of appeal. There are twelve circuit courts of appeal with jurisdiction over the district courts in their geographic region, and one circuit court with nationwide jurisdiction over the specialized courts. Do you know what circuit you are in? Three judges sit as a panel to hear a case in the court of appeals.

Before the Constitution, there were no federal courts, but of course each of the states had its own court system to apply its own state's law. Nothing in the Constitution changed that. Today, while state court systems differ somewhat from state to state, most mirror the federal system in having a trial level court, an intermediate court of appeals, and a supreme court. Recall that the Constitution left to Congress the decision whether to have federal courts below the Supreme Court. The reason was the expectation that state courts would hear cases within the "judicial power" of the United States, so it was unclear what need there would be for lower federal courts. Recall also that Article V requires that

* Many states continue to have both district and circuit state courts as trial courts with different jurisdiction based on the importance of the case.

** The Judiciary Act of 1802 reduced the number of circuit justices on a circuit court to one, and authorized the circuit justice and circuit judge to certify cases to the Supreme Court.

*** A court of general jurisdiction hears both civil and criminal cases, and the civil cases may be of any nature. There are federal courts of specialized jurisdiction, such as the Tax Court, that only hears federal tax cases, and the Court of Federal Claims, which generally hears cases in which people claim the federal government owes them money under a contract, from a tort, or for a "taking" under the Fifth Amendment.

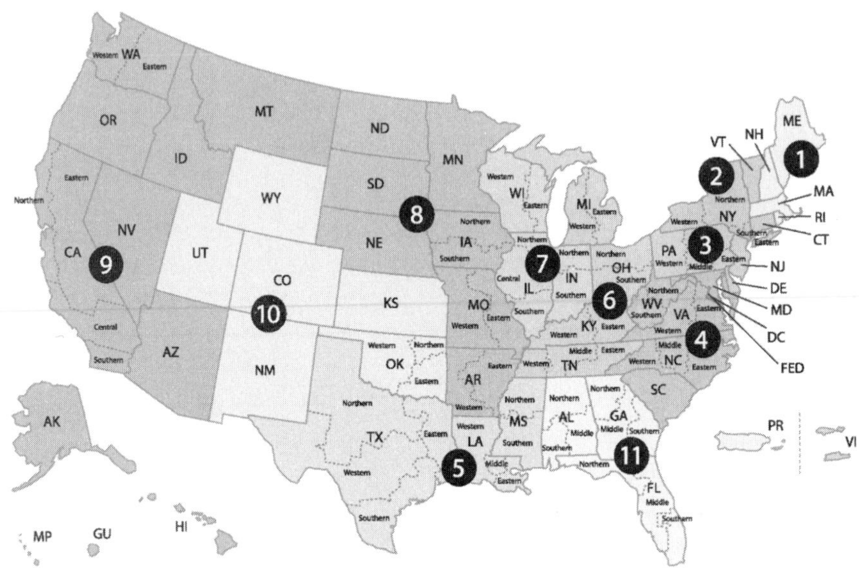

state judges are bound to accept the Constitution and federal laws as the "law of the land." The state court decisions that were within the "judicial power of the United States" could ultimately be appealed to the Supreme Court in order to assure a federal and uniform determination of cases. Lower federal courts have never in our history had jurisdiction over all the cases listed in Article III. Today, for example, diversity jurisdiction cases where the amount in controversy is not more than $75,000 may not be brought in lower federal courts. Moreover, in many areas "federal" cases may be brought in either state or federal courts. In addition, a purely state case may raise constitutional issues; for example, a state criminal prosecution might violate the defendant's constitutional rights, or a state punishment might be "cruel and unusual." Reviewing decisions from state courts remains a significant part of the Supreme Court's workload.

The Judiciary Act of 1891, besides creating the circuit courts of appeal, contained another important innovation. Under that Act certain decisions of the courts of appeals and certain final decisions from state courts could be "appealed" to the Supreme Court. However, for most types of cases, the Act instituted the writ of certiorari as the means of obtaining Supreme Court review of lower court decisions. Today, virtually all "appellate" cases come to the Court by way of certiorari. Certiorari is a Latin term meaning "to be informed of." It was a common-law writ in Britain before independence, and after independence, when all the states adopted British common law as American common law, it continued to be a writ here in both state and federal courts. The nature of the writ was an order to a lower court to provide the record of a case before it to the higher court for review. If this sounds like an "appeal," you are correct, except that an "appeal" to a higher court is required to be heard by the higher court, whereas whether to grant a writ of certiorari is discretionary with the higher court. A person petitions the Supreme Court for a writ of certiorari, and if the court grants the petition, then the Court hears the case. Notwithstanding the technical distinction between certiorari and appeal, you will often hear people (including lawyers and judges) refer to a case being appealed to the Supreme Court, when actually it was certiorari, rather than appeal.

In a non-public conference, the justices decide which cases will be heard. If four justices (less than a majority) vote to hear a case, then the Court grants the petition for a writ of certiorari. Interestingly, this "rule of four" is not written down anywhere—not in the Constitution, a statute, or even a court rule; it is just the time-honored practice that the Court could change tomorrow without telling anyone. If the Court "denies cert.," no legal status, such as precedent, attends the denial. It is the same as if the lower court decision had never been appealed at all. If the Court "grants cert.," it sets a schedule for briefs*—first, the petitioner; next, the respondent; and finally a reply brief from the petitioner. The Court may also seek an "amicus"** brief from the "United States"*** if it is not a party to the case, and the Court believes that the views of the "United States" are important to the case. In addition, often other interested persons or groups may "seek leave" (seek permission) to file an amicus brief in a case. Today, it is a rare case before the Supreme Court that does not have at least one amicus brief. Whether they ordinarily have any effect is doubtful, but the fact that on occasion they clearly have had a significant effect provides a sufficient incentive.

While cases in lower courts are titled with the plaintiff's name first, such as Jones v. Smith, where Jones is the plaintiff and Smith the defendant, in the Supreme Court the cases are titled with the petitioner's name first and the respondent's name second. For example, in *Brown v. Board of Education*, Brown was the loser in the court below and thus is the person petitioning the Supreme Court to hear its case and the Board of Education, which won in the court below, is the respondent. Consequently, it is possible that the defendant's name comes first and the plaintiff's name second in the Supreme Court title of the case, depending upon who prevailed in the court below.

Sometime after receiving written briefs in the case, the Court hears oral argument, where attorneys for the parties, and rarely for amici,

* A "brief" is the term for the written arguments made by a person to a court.

** "Amicus Curiae," or "friend of the court" in Latin, is a person a court allows to participate in a case by presenting briefs and/or oral argument but who is not a party to the case.

*** The "United States" is always represented by the office of the Solicitor General in the Department of Justice, whether the "United States" is the petitioner, respondent, or amicus in a case.

appear before the nine justices and plead their case and answer questions from the justices. On the Wednesday or Friday after oral argument, the members of the Court (and no one else) meet in the Supreme Court conference room to discuss the cases argued earlier that week. According to Supreme Court lore, because again this is not written down anywhere, the discussion of the case begins with the Chief Justice and then proceeds in order of seniority—that is, the length of service on the Court. If the Chief Justice is in the majority for how the case should be decided, he assigns the opinion to one of the justices in the majority or takes it on himself. If the Chief Justice is not in the majority, then the senior-most justice (the Associate Justice who has been on the Court the longest) in the majority assigns the opinion or writes it himself. When the justice has finished a draft, it is circulated among all the justices for comments. When the opinion for the Court is finished, and any concurring and/or dissenting opinions are finished, the decision of the Court is announced and the opinions released. Occasionally, either before or after oral argument, the Court may dismiss a case as improvidently granted ("DIG"), meaning that they have decided that they should not have taken the case after all. The legal effect is the same as if they had never granted certiorari.

If all the justices agree with the opinion written by the justice authoring the opinion, we say the Court's opinion is unanimous. One or more justices might write a "concurring opinion" even though they agree with the Court's opinion. The Court's opinion would still be unanimous. The purpose of the concurring opinion would be to express the justice's individual views that might expand on or express limits to the Court's opinion, even while not disagreeing with its reasoning. Sometimes a justice may write an "opinion concurring in the judgment of the Court." This means that the justice does *not* agree with the Court's opinion, but he does agree with the outcome of the case decided by the Court. For example, the Court might decide that the plaintiff loses for one reason, while one justice might disagree, believing the plaintiff should lose for a wholly different reason. Obviously, if the justice does not agree with the Court's opinion, the Court's opinion is not unanimous, even if all the justices agree on the same outcome. Often, one or more justices will dissent from the Court's opinion. This means they disagree with the opinion and outcome of the case. Sometimes a justice may concur in part and dissent in part. For example, the Court might find that the plaintiff has jurisdiction to bring the case but loses on the merits, while a justice may agree that the plaintiff has jurisdiction but also believe he should win on the merits. Here, the justice would concur in the opinion as to jurisdiction but dissent on the merits.

Sometimes there is no agreement by a majority of the Court on a particular opinion, but there is agreement by a majority on the outcome of the case. For example, three justices may think the plaintiff should win for one reason; two justices believe the plaintiff should win for another reason; and four justices think the plaintiff should lose. The opinion that commands the most votes and supports the outcome of the case is the "plurality opinion," in this example the three-vote opinion. A plurality opinion is not an opinion of the Court, so it does not have precedential effect. Instead, the precedential rule applicable to lower courts thereafter is that the opinion with the narrowest grounds supporting the outcome is the opinion that binds lower courts. *See Marks v. United States*, 430 U.S. 188 (1977). There are even circumstances where the Court splits 4–1–4–for example, four justices think the plaintiff should lose for one reason, one justice thinks the plaintiff should lose for another, narrower reason, and four justices think the plaintiff should win. In this circumstance, the opinion by the one justice—with whom no one else agreed—becomes binding precedent for lower courts. *See Grutter v. Bollinger*, 539 U.S. 306, 325 (2003)(discussing *Regents of the Univ. of Cal. v. Bakke*, 438 U.S. 265 (1978)).

All too often there are cases in which an opinion has several parts and some justices agree with some parts and some with others and some with none at all, and whether there is a majority opinion, or what it is, is difficult to determine. In the official reporters, however, the introduction to the case tells what parts are the opinion of the Court and what parts are only the opinion of certain justices.

If for some reason there are less than nine justices deciding a case, a "majority" is a majority of the justices deciding the case. Thus, if there were only seven justices deciding a case, an opinion joined by four justices would be a majority opinion and thus an opinion of the Court. If there are only an even number of justices deciding the case and they split evenly, for example, 4–4, then the case is "affirmed by an equally divided court." This Supreme Court affirmation, however, has no precedential effect. For purposes of precedent, it is as if the case had never been heard.

The Supreme Court still hears cases in its original jurisdiction, but it does not itself sit as a trial court. Instead, the Court appoints a "special master," perhaps a retired judge or even a law professor, who acts like the trial judge in the case and who renders a "report," which appears like a proposed opinion for the Court. Whichever parties are displeased with the report file a bill of exceptions, which looks like an appeal, with the Court. The Court receives briefs and oral argument like appellate cases and then renders a final decision.

The Supreme Court "sits" (hears oral arguments) from the first Monday in October each year, which begins the "October Term," until sometime in April. It renders its last opinions for the Term late in June.

B. JUDICIAL REVIEW

We now begin with the first of our Supreme Court opinions interpreting the Constitution, but one might ask why it is that we look to the Supreme Court for interpretations of the Constitution. Today, it may seem obvious that the Court is where we would look for interpretations of the Constitution, but it is not obvious from the text of the Constitution.

Recall that the President takes an oath to preserve, protect, and defend the Constitution. Perhaps it should be the President's interpretation that we should study. But then members of the House of Representatives and Senators also take an oath to support the Constitution. Perhaps the laws they pass, especially if signed by the President, should be taken as definitive interpretations of the Constitution. And what about state executive, legislative, and judicial officers? They too take an oath to support the Constitution. Why should the Supreme Court of the United States be able to overrule their considered interpretations of the Constitution? Moreover, to the extent that one believes that the United States is a democracy, is there not a problem with letting unelected judges overrule the laws passed by the representatives of the people simply because the judges disagree with the Congress and the President as to the constitutionality of the laws?

The case of *Marbury v. Madison* is generally considered the birth of constitutional law, inasmuch as it is the first case decided by the Supreme Court regarding the constitutionality of a federal statute. It is a difficult case, partly because of its language and partly because of the nature of the Court's analysis, but the following background may help to understand the context in which it occurred.

As long as George Washington, the national hero, had been President, the lingering differences between the Federalists and the Anti–Federalists remained relatively dormant. However, when Washington refused to serve a third term in 1796, the United States "enjoyed" its first contested Presidential election. The Federalists nominated the then Vice President, John Adams, and the anti-Federalists, having formed the Democratic–Republican party, nominated Thomas Jefferson. Under the system then in effect, Adams narrowly won the Presidency and his opponent, Jefferson, became Vice President with the next largest number of votes. At the time, revolutionary France and Great Britain were engaged in war, and while the United States remained neutral, the sympathies for the antagonists split along party lines. The Democratic–Republicans favored the radical democracy the French Revolution seemed to embody. The Federalists favored the moderate, socially conservative approach of British parliamentarianism and feared the spread of revolutionary attitudes in the United States. The Federalists responded by passing the Alien and Sedition Acts, which in essence made it a crime to publish "false, scandalous, and malicious writing" against the government or its officials, and enforcing it against their opponents.

The election of 1800 was viewed by the Federalists as a struggle to save the Constitution from the radicalism threatened by the Democratic–Republicans, while the Democratic–Republicans saw the election as the last opportunity to avoid tyranny. The vote was close but decisive. The Democratic–Republicans won control of the House, the

Senate, and the Presidency. To the Federalists, the future of the Constitution would depend upon the third branch, the Judiciary, whose judges were appointed for life. In their view, it would be the last bastion of a rule of law under the Constitution in opposition to the rule of the mob, so obvious in France. During the "lame duck" period, therefore, the then Federalist-controlled Congress passed the Judiciary Act of 1801, providing for broadened jurisdiction for federal courts and increasing the number of courts, which necessitated appointing new judges, which Adams quickly did. In addition, he appointed the then Acting Secretary of State, John Marshall, Chief Justice to fill a seat left vacant by resignation. Because the already sitting judges and the newly appointed ones had been appointed by Federalists, long-term Federalist control of the judiciary seemed assured. Moreover, the "lame-duck" Congress also passed an act for the government of the District of Columbia, which was just then first being used as the Nation's capital—both the Capitol and the White House were first occupied in November 1800. This included a provision for the appointment of justices of the peace, who were in effect the government administrators for the District, responsible for, among other things, maintaining public order. These too Adams appointed from among loyal Federalists. One was William Marbury.

Unfortunately for Marbury and several other of the justices of the peace, in the last minute rush, the then Acting Secretary of State, John Marshall, even as he was at the same time Chief Justice, failed to deliver all the commissions. A commission is the document that evidences an officer's authority, and without it Marbury could not exercise the powers and duties of a justice of the peace. When Marbury sought to obtain his commission from James Madison, the new Secretary of State in the Jefferson administration, Madison ignored him. Marbury accordingly sought to force its delivery by filing suit in the Supreme Court for mandamus. Mandamus, then and now, is a particular type of court order commanding a government officer to perform a particular legal duty. He filed in the Supreme Court because the Judiciary Act of 1789, passed by the first Congress of the United States, provided that: "the Supreme Court shall ... have power to issue ... writs of mandamus ... to any ... persons holding office, under the authority of the United States."

Before the Court could hear the case, however, Congress had taken dramatic action, repealing the Judiciary Act of 1801, which had broadened federal jurisdiction and created new courts. The Federalists argued that the removal of the already appointed judges would be unconstitutional, violating their required life tenure and inconsistent with the independence of the judiciary. Expecting these judges to sue, Congress also passed a law canceling the Supreme Court's term, delaying until 1803 the consideration of all the Supreme Court's cases, including Marbury's.

John Marshall

John Marshall is widely credited for modernizing a largely inchoate judicial branch, transforming it from a weak judicial body into an important, powerful mainstay of the American political system. Prior to Marshall's appointment, each justice wrote opinions in each case, and the law of the case had to be discerned from the numerous and often conflicting opinions. This process undermined the court's credibility and clout. Marshall instituted a one-opinion system to represent court decisions. This change, together with judicial review developed in *Marbury v. Madison*, cemented the Supreme Court's place in deciding constitutional matters. Marshall, a pragmatic federalist, bolstered federal supremacy by writing numerous decisions that supported the national government and broad constitutional interpretation during his lengthy tenure as Chief Justice, 1801-1835.

MARBURY v. MADISON

Supreme Court of the United States, 1803.
1 Cranch (5 U.S.) 137, 2 L.Ed. 60.

MARSHALL, C.J.

[T]he peculiar delicacy of this case, the novelty of some of its circumstances, and the real difficulty attending the points which occur in it, require a complete exposition of the principles, on which the opinion to be given by the court, is founded....

In the order in which the court has viewed this subject, the following questions have been considered and decided.

1st. Has the applicant a right to the commission he demands?

2dly. If he has a right, and that right has been violated, do the laws of his country afford him a remedy?

3dly. If they do afford him a remedy, is it a mandamus issuing from this court?

The first object of inquiry is,

1st. Has the applicant a right to the commission he demands?

[After a long discussion concerning how appointments are made under the Constitution and when they are final, the Court concluded:] It is therefore decidedly the opinion of the court, that when a commission has been signed by the President, the appointment is made; and that the commission is complete, when the seal of the United States has been affixed to it by the secretary of state....

Mr. Marbury, then, since his commission was signed by the President, and sealed by the secretary of state, was appointed; and as the law creating the office, gave the officer a right to hold for five years, independent of the executive, the appointment was not revocable; but vested in the officer legal rights, which are protected by the laws of this country.

To withhold his commission, therefore, is an act deemed by the court not warranted by law, but violative of a vested legal right.

This brings us to the second inquiry; which is,

2dly. If he has a right, and that right has been violated, do the laws of this country afford him a remedy?

The very essence of civil liberty certainly consists in the right of every individual to claim the protection of the laws, whenever he receives an injury. One of the first duties of government is to afford that protection. In Great Britain the king himself is sued in the respectful form of a petition, and he never fails to comply with the judgment of his court.

The government of the United States has been emphatically termed a government of laws, and not of men. It will certainly cease to deserve this high appellation, if the laws furnish no remedy for the violation of a vested legal right.

If this obloquy is to be cast on the jurisprudence of our country, it must arise from the peculiar character of the case.

It behooves us then to enquire whether there be in its composition any ingredient which shall exempt it from legal investigation, or exclude the injured party from legal redress....

Is it in the nature of the transaction? Is the act of delivering or withholding a commission to be considered as a mere political act, belonging to the executive department alone, for the performance of which, entire confidence is placed by our constitution in the supreme executive; and for any misconduct respecting which, the injured individual has no remedy?

That there may be such cases is not to be questioned; but that every act of duty, to be performed in any of the great departments of government, constitutes such a case, is not to be admitted.... Is it to be contended that where the law in precise terms, directs the performance of an act, in which an individual is interested, the law is incapable of securing obedience to its mandate? Is it on account of the character of the person against whom the complaint is made? Is it to be contended that the heads of departments are not amenable to the laws of their country?

Whatever the practice on particular occasions may be, the theory of this principle will certainly never be maintained. No act of the legislature confers so extraordinary a privilege, nor can it derive countenance from the doctrines of the common law....

It follows then that the question, whether the legality of an act of the head of a department be examinable in a court of justice or not, must always depend on the nature of that act.

If some acts be examinable, and others not, there must be some rule of law to guide the court in the exercise of its jurisdiction.

In some instances there may be difficulty in applying the rule to particular cases; but there cannot, it is believed, be much difficulty in laying down the rule.

By the constitution of the United States, the President is invested with certain important political powers, in the exercise of which he is to use his own discretion, and is accountable only to his country in his political character, and to his own conscience. To aid him in the performance of these duties, he is authorized to appoint certain officers, who act by his authority and in conformity with his orders.

In such cases, their acts are his acts; and whatever opinion may be entertained of the manner in which executive discretion may be used, still there exists, and can exist, no power to control that discretion. The subjects are political. They respect the nation, not individual rights, and being entrusted to the executive, the decision of the executive is conclusive. The application of this remark will be perceived by adverting to the act of congress for establishing the department of foreign affairs. This officer, as his duties were prescribed by that act, is to conform precisely to the will of the President. He is the mere organ by whom that will is communicated. The acts of such an officer, as an officer, can never be examinable by the courts.

But when the legislature proceeds to impose on that officer other duties; when he is directed peremptorily to perform certain acts; when the rights of individuals are dependent on the performance of those acts; he is so far the officer of the law; is amenable to the laws for his conduct; and cannot at his discretion sport away the vested rights of others.

The conclusion from this reasoning is, that where the heads of departments are the political or confidential agents of the executive, merely to execute the will of the President, or rather to act in cases in which the executive possesses a constitutional or legal discretion, nothing can be more perfectly clear than that their acts are only politically examinable. But where a specific duty is assigned by law, and individual rights depend upon the performance of that duty, it seems equally clear that the individual who considers himself injured, has a right to resort to the laws of his country for a remedy....

It is then the opinion of the court,

1st. That by signing the commission of Mr. Marbury, the president of the United States appointed him a justice of peace, for the county of Washington in the district of Columbia; and that the seal of the United States, affixed thereto by the secretary of state, is conclusive testimony of the verity of the signature, and of the completion of the appointment; and that the appointment conferred on him a legal right to the office for the space of five years.

2dly. That, having this legal title to the office, he has a consequent right to the commission; a refusal to deliver which, is a plain violation of that right, for which the laws of his country afford him a remedy.

It remains to be inquired whether,

3dly. He is entitled to the remedy for which he applies. This depends on,

1st. The nature of the writ applied for, and,

2dly. The power of this court.

1st. The nature of the writ.

[The Court held that mandamus would normally be the proper form of action.]

Still, to render the mandamus a proper remedy, the officer to whom it is to be directed, must be one to whom, on legal principles, such writ may be directed; and the person applying for it must be without any other specific and legal remedy.

1st. With respect to the officer to whom it would be directed. The intimate political relation, subsisting between the president of the United States and the heads of departments, necessarily renders any legal investigation of the acts of one of those high officers peculiarly irksome, as well as delicate; and excites some hesitation with respect to the propriety of entering into such investigation. Impressions are often received without much reflection or examination, and it is not wonderful that in such a case as this, the assertion, by an individual, of his legal claims in a court of justice; to which claims it is the duty of that court to attend; should at first view be considered by some, as an attempt to intrude into the cabinet, and to intermeddle with the prerogatives of the executive.

It is scarcely necessary for the court to disclaim all pretensions to such a jurisdiction. An extravagance, so absurd and excessive, could not have been entertained for a moment. The province of the court is, solely, to decide on the rights of individuals, not to enquire how the executive, or executive officers, perform duties in which they have a discretion. Questions, in their nature political, or which are, by the constitution and laws, submitted to the executive, can never be made in this court.

But, if this be not such a question; if so far from being an intrusion into the secrets of the cabinet, it respects a paper, which, according to law, is upon record, and to a copy of which the law gives a right, on the payment of ten cents; if it be no intermeddling with a subject, over which the executive can be considered as having exercised any control; what is there in the exalted station of the officer, which shall bar a citizen from asserting, in a court of justice, his legal rights, or shall forbid a court to listen to the claim; or to issue a mandamus, directing the performance of a duty, not depending on executive discretion, but on particular acts of congress and the general principles of law?

If one of the heads of departments commits any illegal act, under color of his office, by which an individual sustains an injury, it cannot be pretended that his office alone exempts him from being sued in the ordinary mode of proceeding, and being compelled to obey the judgment of the law....

It is not by the office of the person to whom the writ is directed, but the nature of the thing to be done that the propriety or impropriety of issuing a mandamus, is to be determined. Where the head of a department acts in a case, in which executive discretion is to be exercised; in which he is the mere organ of executive will; it is again repeated, that any application to a court to control, in any respect, his conduct, would be rejected without hesitation.

But where he is the head of a good department [and] is directed by law to do a certain act affecting the absolute rights of individuals, in the performance of which he is not placed under the particular direction of the President, and the performance of which, the President cannot lawfully forbid, and therefore is never presumed to have forbidden; as for example, to record a commission, or a patent for land, which has received all the legal solemnities; or to give a copy of such record; in such cases, it is not perceived on what ground the courts of the country are further excused from the duty of giving judgment, that right be done to an injured individual, than if the same services were to be performed by a person not the head of a department....

This, then, is a plain case for a mandamus, either to deliver the commission, or a copy of it from the record; and it only remains to be inquired,

Whether it can issue from this court.

The act to establish the judicial courts of the United States authorizes the supreme court "to issue writs of mandamus, in cases warranted by the principles and usages of law, to any courts appointed, or persons holding office, under the authority of the United States."

The secretary of state, being a person holding an office under the authority of the United States, is precisely within the letter of the description; and if this court is not authorized to issue a writ of mandamus to such an officer, it must be because the law is unconstitutional, and therefore absolutely incapable of conferring the authority, and assigning the duties which its words purport to confer and assign.

The constitution vests the whole judicial power of the United States in one supreme court, and such inferior courts as congress shall, from time to time, ordain and establish. This power is expressly extended to all cases arising under the laws of the United States; and consequently, in some form, may be exercised over the present case; because the right claimed is given by a law of the United States.

In the distribution of this power it is declared that "the supreme court shall have original jurisdiction in all cases affecting ambassadors, other public ministers and consuls, and those in which a state shall be a party. In all other cases, the supreme court shall have appellate jurisdiction."

It has been insisted, at the bar, that as the original grant of jurisdiction, to the supreme and inferior courts, is general, and the clause, assigning original jurisdiction to the supreme court, contains no negative or restrictive words; the power remains to the legislature, to assign original jurisdiction to that court in other cases than those specified in the article which has been recited; provided those cases belong to the judicial power of the United States.

If it had been intended to leave it in the discretion of the legislature to apportion the judicial power between the supreme and inferior courts according to the will of that body, it would certainly have been useless to have proceeded further than to have defined the judicial power, and the tribunals in which it should be vested. The subsequent part of the section is mere surplusage, is entirely without meaning, if such is to be the construction. If congress remains at liberty to give this court appellate jurisdiction, where the constitution has declared their jurisdiction shall be original; and original jurisdiction where the constitution has declared it shall be appellate; the distribution of jurisdiction, made in the constitution, is form without substance.

Affirmative words are often, in their operation, negative of other objects than those affirmed; and in this case, a negative or exclusive sense must be given to them or they have no operation at all.

It cannot be presumed that any clause in the constitution is intended to be without effect; and therefore such a construction is inadmissible, unless the words require it....

When an instrument organizing fundamentally a judicial system, divides it into one supreme, and so many inferior courts as the legislature may ordain and establish; then enumerates its powers, and proceeds so far to distribute them, as to define the jurisdiction of the supreme court by declaring the cases in which it shall take original jurisdiction, and that in others it shall take appellate jurisdiction; the plain import of the words seems to be, that in one class of cases its jurisdiction is original, and not appellate; in the other it is appellate, and not original. If any other construction would render the clause inoperative, that is an additional reason for rejecting such other construction, and for adhering to their obvious meaning.

To enable this court then to issue a mandamus, it must be shown to be an exercise of appellate jurisdiction, or to be necessary to enable them to exercise appellate jurisdiction....

It is the essential criterion of appellate jurisdiction, that it revises and corrects the proceedings in a cause already instituted, and does not create that cause. Although, therefore, a mandamus may be directed to courts, yet to issue such a writ to an officer for the delivery of a paper, is in effect the same as to sustain an original action for that paper, and therefore seems not to belong to appellate, but to original jurisdiction. Neither is it necessary in such a case as this, to enable the court to exercise its appellate jurisdiction.

The authority, therefore, given to the supreme court, by the act establishing the judicial courts of the United States, to issue writs of mandamus to public officers, appears not to be warranted by the constitution; and it becomes necessary to enquire whether a jurisdiction, so conferred, can be exercised.

The question, whether an act, repugnant to the constitution, can become the law of the land, is a question deeply interesting to the United States; but, happily, not of an intricacy proportioned to its interest. It seems only necessary to recognize certain principles, supposed to have been long and well established, to decide it.

That the people have an original right to establish, for their future government, such principles as, in their opinion, shall most conduce to their own happiness, is the basis, on which the whole American fabric has been erected. The exercise of this original right is a very great exertion; nor can it, nor ought it to be frequently repeated. The principles, therefore, so established, are deemed fundamental. And as the authority, from which they proceed, is supreme, and can seldom act, they are designed to be permanent.

This original and supreme will organizes the government, and assigns, to different departments, their respective powers. It may either stop here; or establish certain limits not to be transcended by those departments.

The government of the United States is of the latter description. The powers of the legislature are defined, and limited; and that those limits may not be mistaken, or forgotten, the constitution is written. To what purpose are powers limited, and to what purpose is that limitation committed to writing, if these limits may, at any time, be passed by those intended to be restrained? The distinction, between a government with limited and unlimited powers, is abolished, if those limits do not confine the persons on whom they are imposed, and if acts prohibited and acts allowed, are of equal obligation. It is a proposition too plain to be contested, that the constitution controls any legislative act repugnant to it; or, that the legislature may alter the constitution by an ordinary act.

Between these alternatives there is no middle ground. The constitution is either a superior, paramount law, unchangeable by ordinary means, or it is on a level with ordinary legislative acts, and like other acts, is alterable when the legislature shall please to alter it.

If the former part of the alternative be true, then a legislative act contrary to the constitution is not law: if the latter part be true, then written constitutions are absurd attempts, on the part of the people, to limit a power, in its own nature illimitable.

Certainly all those who have framed written constitutions contemplate them as forming the fundamental and paramount law of the nation, and consequently the theory of every such government must be, that an act of the legislature, repugnant to the constitution, is void.

This theory is essentially attached to a written constitution, and is consequently to be considered, by this court, as one of the fundamental principles of our society. It is not therefore to be lost sight of in the further consideration of this subject.

If an act of the legislature, repugnant to the constitution, is void, does it, notwithstanding its invalidity, bind the courts, and oblige them to give it effect? Or, in other words, though it be not law, does it constitute a rule as operative as if it was a law? This would be to overthrow in fact what was established in theory; and would seem, at first view, an absurdity too gross to be insisted on. It shall, however, receive a more attentive consideration.

It is emphatically the province and duty of the judicial department to say what the law is. Those who apply the rule to particular cases, must of necessity expound and interpret that rule. If two laws conflict with each other, the courts must decide on the operation of each.

So if a law be in opposition to the constitution; if both the law and the constitution apply to a particular case, so that the court must either decide that case conformably to the law, disregarding the constitution; or conformably to the constitution, disregarding the law; the court must determine which of these conflicting rules governs the case. This is of the very essence of judicial duty.

If then the courts are to regard the constitution; and the constitution is superior to any ordinary act of the legislature; the constitution, and not such ordinary act, must govern the case to which they both apply.

Those then who controvert the principle that the constitution is to be considered, in court, as a paramount law, are reduced to the necessity of maintaining that courts must close their eyes on the constitution, and see only the law.

This doctrine would subvert the very foundation of all written constitutions. It would declare that an act, which, according to the principles and theory of our government, is entirely void, is yet, in practice, completely obligatory. It would declare, that if the legislature shall do what is expressly forbidden, such act, notwithstanding the express prohibition, is in reality effectual. It would be giving to the legislature a practical and real omnipotence, with the same breath which professes to restrict their powers within narrow limits. It is prescribing limits, and declaring that those limits may be passed as pleasure.

That it thus reduces to nothing what we have deemed the greatest improvement on political institutions—a written constitution—would of itself be sufficient, in America, where written constitutions have been viewed with so much reverence, for rejecting the construction. But the peculiar expressions of the constitution of the United States furnish additional arguments in favor of its rejection.

The judicial power of the United States is extended to all cases arising under the constitution.

Could it be the intention of those who gave this power, to say that, in using it, the constitution should not be looked into? That a case arising under the constitution should be decided without examining the instrument under which it arises?

This is too extravagant to be maintained.

In some cases then, the constitution must be looked into by the judges. And if they can open it at all, what part of it are they forbidden to read, or to obey?

There are many other parts of the constitution which serve to illustrate this subject.

It is declared that "no tax or duty shall be laid on articles exported from any state." Suppose a duty on the export of cotton, of tobacco, or of flour; and a suit instituted to recover it. Ought judgment to be rendered in such a case? Ought the judges to close their eyes on the constitution, and only see the law?

The constitution declares that "no bill of attainder or ex post facto law shall be passed."

If, however, such a bill should be passed and a person should be prosecuted under it; must the court condemn to death those victims whom the constitution endeavors to preserve?

"No person," says the constitution, "shall be convicted of treason unless on the testimony of two witnesses to the same overt act, or on confession in open court."

Here the language of the constitution is addressed especially to the courts. It prescribes, directly for them, a rule of evidence not to be departed from. If the legislature should change that rule, and declare one witness, or a confession out of court, sufficient for conviction, must the constitutional principle yield to the legislative act?

From these, and many other selections which might be made, it is apparent, that the framers of the constitution contemplated that instrument, as a rule for the government of courts, as well as of the legislature.

Why otherwise does it direct the judges to take an oath to support it? This oath certainly applies, in an especial manner, to their conduct in their official character. How immoral to impose it on them, if they were to be used as the instruments, and the knowing instruments, for violating what they swear to support?

The oath of office, too, imposed by the legislature, is completely demonstrative of the legislative opinion on this subject. It is in these words, "I do solemnly swear that I will administer justice without respect to persons, and do equal right to the poor and to the rich; and that I will faithfully and impartially discharge all the duties incumbent on me as according to the best of my abilities and understanding, agreeably to the constitution, and laws of the United States."

Why does a judge swear to discharge his duties agreeably to the constitution of the United States, if that constitution forms no rule for his government? if it is closed upon him, and cannot be inspected by him?

If such be the real state of things, this is worse than solemn mockery. To prescribe, or to take this oath, becomes equally a crime.

It is also not entirely unworthy of observation, that in declaring what shall be the supreme law of the land, the constitution itself is first mentioned; and not the laws of the United States generally, but those only which shall be made in pursuance of the constitution, have that rank.

Thus, the particular phraseology of the constitution of the United States confirms and strengthens the principle, supposed to be essential to all written constitutions, that a law repugnant to the constitution is void; and that courts, as well as other departments, are bound by that instrument....

Comments and Questions

1. In trying to decipher this case, ask first: who wins. Marbury or Madison? The answer is Madison. Why does Madison win, or stated another way, why does Marbury lose?

2. *Marbury v. Madison* is widely recognized as the case that established the authority of the Court to hold federal statutes unconstitutional. What statute did the Court find unconstitutional and why?

3. The Federalist Papers explicitly address judicial review of laws for constitutionality. Why do you suppose the Court never mentions them?

4. *Marbury v. Madison* is less well known for its language regarding judicial review of executive action. As explained by the Court, when may executive action be reviewed and when not?

5. As you can see, in *Marbury* the Court announced that it could review not only the laws passed by the now Democratic–Republican Congress to assure they conformed to the dictates of the Constitution but also the acts of the Democratic–Republican President to assure they conformed to both the law and Constitution. This decision infuriated Jefferson and other Democratic–Republicans, even though they in essence won the case. In a further attempt to bring the judiciary under their thumb, Congress initiated impeachment proceedings against a Federalist judge from New Hampshire. Although a drunk and perhaps insane, no one seriously argued he had committed any "high crimes or misdemeanors," but he was impeached, convicted, and removed. Then

Congress took on a bigger fish, Supreme Court Justice Samuel Chase, a noted and outspoken Federalist. Again, there was no serious charge of any criminal behavior, although he had undoubtedly breached judicial decorum in statements from the bench attacking the Democratic–Republicans, but the House impeached him anyway. In the Senate, while a strict party-line vote would have convicted him, he narrowly avoided conviction. The vote may in fact have had more to do with politics than principle, but it established a precedent that Congress's disagreement with a judge's acts was not a sufficient basis for removal.

6. Although *Marbury* is *the* case establishing the power of courts to find laws unconstitutional, Marshall describes the issue in the marvelous language of the day as "deeply interesting to the United States; but, happily, not of an intricacy proportioned to its interest." In other words, this was not a difficult question. Indeed, not only had the Federalist papers opined that courts had this power, but it had been exercised by lower federal courts prior to *Marbury*, without any great perturbation. Moreover, as much as the Democratic–Republicans fulminated at *Marbury*, they had earlier called for the courts to declare the Alien and Sedition Acts unconstitutional under the prior administration. A more difficult issue, alluded to earlier in *Calder v. Bull*, 3 U.S. 386 (1798), is whether a court could declare a law invalid, not because it violated a constitutional provision, but because it violated principles of natural justice. In *Calder*, Justice Chase (the one later impeached but not convicted) suggested the power of courts to declare laws invalid on such a basis.

> There are certain vital principles in our free Republican governments, which will determine and over-rule an apparent and flagrant abuse of legislative power; as to authorize manifest injustice by positive law; or to take away that security for personal liberty, or private property, for the protection whereof the government was established. An ACT of the Legislature (for I cannot call it a law) contrary to the great first principles of the social compact, cannot be considered a rightful exercise of legislative authority.

3 U.S. at 388. Justice Iredell, however, disagreed, saying:

> If, then, a government, composed of Legislative, Executive and Judicial departments, were established, by a Constitution, which imposed no limits on the legislative power, the consequence would inevitably be, that whatever the legislative power chose to enact, would be lawfully enacted, and the judicial power could never interpose to pronounce it void. It is true, that some speculative jurists have held, that a legislative act against natural justice must, in itself, be void; but I cannot think that, under such a government, any Court of Justice would possess a power to declare it so.

3 U.S. at 398. Because all the justices agreed that the law in question in the case did not violate fundamental principles, it was not necessary to resolve the issue. Time, however, has effectively decided it. Today, virtually everyone agrees that a court can declare a law invalid only if it violates the Constitution, not if it only violates someone's notion of natural justice. Nevertheless, whether under the Due Process Clause, the Ninth Amendment, or the Fourteenth Amendment's Privileges and Immunities Clause, one arguably can find a constitutional provision that incorporates principles of natural justice.

Joseph Story
James Madison appointed Joseph Story to the Supreme Court in 1811. He remained on the court until his death in 1845. Like Chief Justice Marshall, Story supported a strong national government. Story wrote the opinion in *Martin v. Hunter's Lessee*, which enables the Supreme Court to review state judicial decisions involving federal issues and affirms the need for uniformity in federal decisions. Story's support for federal supremacy also shines in his *Swift v. Tyson* opinion that allowed federal courts under diversity jurisdiction to establish federal common law until *Erie v. Tompkins* overturned it nearly one hundred years later.

7. Another early case of great significance, although not nearly as well known as *Marbury*, is *Martin v. Hunter's Lessee*,* 14 U.S. (1 Wheat.) 304 (1816). In that case, there was a dispute over the ownership of land in Virginia due to the effect of the treaty of peace with Britain ending the Revolutionary War. The case arose in state court, and the Virginia Court of Appeals' interpretation of the treaty resulted in Hunter's lessee retaining possession. Martin appealed to the Supreme Court, and the Court interpreted the treaty differently, reversing the Virginia court and ordering that Martin be given possession. The Virginia court refused. Notwithstanding Article III's statement that the Supreme Court had appellate jurisdiction over cases "arising under [the] constitution, the laws of the United States, and treaties made ... under their authority," and Section 25 of the Judiciary Act of 1789 providing for such jurisdiction, Virginia argued that the Supreme Court had no jurisdiction over it, because Virginia was a separate sovereign, and therefore its courts were not subject to appeal to any higher authority. Just as the Supreme Court could not review a British court interpreting the treaty, the Supreme Court could not review the Virginia court. Martin again appealed to the Supreme Court, and Justice Story wrote the opinion declaring that state court judgments

* A lessee is a person who leases property from another, who is called the lessor.

involving questions of federal law, here the treaty with Britain, were subject to review by the Supreme Court, as provided in Article III and federal statute. The necessity of having one court able to maintain a national uniformity for federal law, so that the Constitution and laws of the United States would mean the same thing throughout the United States, has never been questioned since.

8. Does the decision in *Marbury* recognize a power of the Supreme Court to declare laws unconstitutional, or does it recognize a power of courts generally? Can a state trial court declare a federal law unconstitutional?

9. Despite the significance of *Marbury*, no federal law was declared unconstitutional thereafter until the decision in the *Dred Scott* case in 1857 declaring the Missouri Compromise's prohibition of slavery in certain northern territories unconstitutional. *Scott v. Sandford*, 60 U.S. (19 How.) 393 (1857). However, in the same period almost 30 state laws were declared unconstitutional. What does *Marbury* have to say about review of state laws?

10. Although today *Marbury* is settled law and its principle unquestioned, there continue to be disputes over the theory upon which it proceeds. Why does the Court believe that *its* determination of the constitutionality of the statutory provision is superior to Congress's? Or, that *its* determination of the lawfulness of the withholding of the commission is superior to the President's? Not long after *Marbury* was decided, President Jefferson wrote to Abigail Adams, the former President's wife: "the opinion which gives to the judges the right to decide what laws are constitutional and what not, not only for themselves in their own sphere of action but for the Legislature and Executive also in their spheres, would make the Judiciary a despotic branch." In *Marbury*, of course, the decision as to the constitutionality of the mandamus provision of the Judiciary Act of 1789 was a decision "in their own sphere of action."

Following the Supreme Court's decision in *Brown v. Board of Ed.*, 347 U.S. 483 (1954), declaring public schools segregated on the basis of race to be unconstitutional, there was widespread resistance in southern states. For example, the state of Arkansas amended its constitution to require the legislature to oppose "in every Constitutional manner the unconstitutional desegregation" decision in *Brown*. States maintained, as they had before the Civil War, that they could independently interpret the Constitution. A suit was brought in Little Rock, Arkansas, by nine school children (John Aaron was listed first alphabetically) against the school district (William Cooper was the president of the school district) to integrate the public schools. On the basis of *Brown*, the district court ordered the schools integrated, but the governor, Orville Faubus, and the state legislature argued that they were not bound by *Brown*, because they had not been parties to that suit, which involved school districts in other states. The governor called out the National Guard to prevent integration of the Little Rock Central High School by the nine Negro students. The district court ordered the governor to cease his interference, and he did, but it took troops from the 82d Airborne Division dispatched to Little Rock by President Eisenhower to maintain sufficient order to enable the students to enter the school. Because of the riots and public disorder, the school district asked for a delay of two and one half years in its requirement to integrate the schools. While the district court granted that delay, it was reversed by the Eighth Circuit, and the Supreme Court affirmed. In rendering its decision, the Court did something it had never done before and has never done since—all nine justices announced the opinion.* It clearly meant to send a message to the resisting states that there was no hidden reluctance on the Court to enforcing integration; that all the justices were fully committed to this path.

In affirming the Eighth Circuit, the Court agreed that there was no legal reason to delay integration and that concerted official resistance was no basis for not enforcing the Constitution. However, the Court went further.

COOPER v. AARON

Supreme Court of the United States, 1958.
358 U.S. 1, 78 S.Ct. 1401, 3 L.Ed.2d 5.

Opinion of the Court by The CHIEF JUSTICE, Mr. Justice BLACK, Mr. Justice FRANKFURTER, Mr. Justice DOUGLAS, Mr. Justice BURTON, Mr. Justice CLARK, Mr. Justice HARLAN, Mr. Justice BRENNAN, and Mr. Justice WHITTAKER.

As this case reaches us it raises questions of the highest importance to the maintenance of our federal system of government. It necessarily involves a claim by the Governor and Legislature of a State that there is no duty on state officials to obey federal court orders resting on this Court's considered interpretation of the United States Constitution. Specifically it involves actions by the Governor and Legislature of Arkansas upon the premise that they are not bound by our holding in *Brown v. Board of Education*. That holding was that the Fourteenth Amendment forbids States to use their governmental powers to bar children on racial grounds from attending schools where there is state participation through any arrangement, management, funds or property. We are urged to uphold a suspension of the Little Rock School Board's plan to do away with segregated public schools in Little Rock until state laws and efforts to upset and nullify our holding in *Brown v. Board of Education* have been further challenged and tested in the courts. We reject these contentions.

* There are many unanimous decisions by the Supreme Court. Indeed, *Marbury* was such a decision, but the opinion for the Court in *Marbury* was rendered by Chief Justice Marshall, with which all members agreed. In *Cooper v. Aaron*, it was not an opinion by one justice with which all the others agreed, it was *the* opinion of *all* the justices jointly.

[The Court then explained why it would not delay the integration plan.]

What has been said, in the light of the facts developed, is enough to dispose of the case. However, we should answer the premise of the actions of the Governor and Legislature that they are not bound by our holding in the *Brown* case. It is necessary only to recall some basic constitutional propositions which are settled doctrine.

Article VI of the Constitution makes the Constitution the "supreme Law of the Land." In 1803, Chief Justice Marshall, speaking for a unanimous Court, referring to the Constitution as "the fundamental and paramount law of the nation," declared in the notable case of *Marbury v. Madison* that "It is emphatically the province and duty of the judicial department to say what the law is." This decision declared the basic principle that the federal judiciary is supreme in the exposition of the law of the Constitution, and that principle has ever since been respected by this Court and the Country as a permanent and indispensable feature of our constitutional system. It follows that the interpretation of the Fourteenth Amendment enunciated by this Court in the *Brown* case is the supreme law of the land, and Art. VI of the Constitution makes it of binding effect on the States "any Thing in the Constitution or Laws of any State to the Contrary notwithstanding." Every state legislator and executive and judicial officer is solemnly committed by oath taken pursuant to Art. VI, ¶ 3 "to support this Constitution." ...

No state legislator or executive or judicial officer can war against the Constitution without violating his undertaking to support it. Chief Justice Marshall spoke for a unanimous Court in saying that: "If the legislatures of the several states may, at will, annul the judgments of the courts of the United States, and destroy the rights acquired under those judgments, the constitution itself becomes a solemn mockery * * *." *United States v. Peters*, 5 Cranch 115, 136, 3 L.Ed. 53. A Governor who asserts a power to nullify a federal court order is similarly restrained....

The basic decision in *Brown* was unanimously reached by this Court only after the case had been briefed and twice argued and the issues had been given the most serious consideration. Since the first *Brown* opinion three new Justices have come to the Court. They are at one with the Justices still on the Court who participated in that basic decision as to its correctness, and that decision is now unanimously reaffirmed. The principles announced in that decision and the obedience of the States to them, according to the command of the Constitution, are indispensable for the protection of the freedoms guaranteed by our fundamental charter for all of us....

Comments and Questions

1. The actual decision in *Cooper* that the integration plan should not be delayed because of official resistance, the part of the opinion that has been edited out, is undoubtedly correct. Moreover, the Court's statement that persons must comply with federal court orders—here the

order to integrate the schools issued by the district court and affirmed by the Eighth Circuit, and which was not appealed to the Supreme Court—is generally unobjectionable.* However, the Court's statement that the Court's interpretation of the Constitution itself becomes the Constitution, which all state and federal officers have sworn to uphold, has engendered substantial debate. *Compare* Larry Alexander and Frederick Schauer, *On Extrajudicial Constitutional Interpretation*, 110 Harv. L. Rev. 1359 (1997), and Daniel A. Farber, *The Supreme Court and the Rule of Law:* Cooper v. Aaron *Revisited*, 1982 U. Ill. L. Rev. 387 (defending the statement) *with* Mark V. Tushnet, *The Hardest Question in Constitutional Law*, 81 Minn. L. Rev. 1, 25–28 (1996) and Edwin Meese III, *The Law of the Constitution*, 61 Tul. L. Rev. 979, 983–86 (1987)(challenging the statement). Would a congressman violate his oath of office if he introduced a bill making it a crime to burn the United States flag in public, inasmuch as the Supreme Court has twice declared flag-burning to be constitutionally protected expression? Would the President violate his oath of office if he vetoed a bill because he believed it would be unconstitutional, even though the Supreme Court had upheld an identical law?

2. Whatever the academic debates, for most practical purposes, what the Supreme Court says the Constitution means is the last word. If a decision is sufficiently objectionable, the amendment process has been used to overturn it. However, again for most practical purposes, this is not a realistic option. Accordingly, courts hold tremendous power, and as Lord Acton said, "power tends to corrupt, and absolute power corrupts absolutely."** Under a Constitution that uses checks and balances to keep any one branch from excessive power, the question becomes, what is the check on this judicial power?

C. CHECKS ON JUDICIAL POWER

1. LEGISLATIVE CHECKS

Already, prior to *Marbury,* we saw one legislative attempt at checking the judiciary when Congress canceled the Supreme Court's scheduled August term. Can you see why this type of check might not be very effective?

The following case involved a more targeted form of trying to deny Supreme Court review.

* In *United States v. Nixon*, 418 U.S. 683 (1974), the Supreme Court affirmed a lower court order requiring President Nixon to turn over tapes made of conversations in the White House Oval Office over his objection that they were constitutionally protected from disclosure. Inasmuch as those tapes revealed the so-called "smoking gun" of his participation in the cover-up of criminal activity, which sealed his fate as President, if ever there were a case where a President might refuse to comply with a court order, this would seem to be it. Nevertheless, he did comply.

** John Emerich Edward Dalberg–Acton, commonly known as Lord Acton, was a 19th century English historian, most famous for this dictum.

EX PARTE McCARDLE

Supreme Court of the United States, 1869.
74 U.S. (7 Wall.) 506, 19 L.Ed. 264.

[In 1867, William McCardle, a former Confederate soldier and newspaper publisher, was arrested by the federal military authorities for publishing inflammatory articles opposing Reconstruction.* He was held in military custody awaiting trial by a military commission for four alleged offenses under the Military Reconstruction Act: disturbing the peace, inciting to insurrection and disorder, libel, and impeding reconstruction. McCardle, claiming that the Act was unconstitutional, filed a petition for habeas corpus in federal circuit court pursuant to a new habeas statute that broadened the grounds for federal habeas relief. The court denied the petition, and McCardle appealed to the Supreme Court. The Supreme Court heard oral argument in early March, 1868, but members of Congress were concerned that the Court might declare the Military Reconstruction Act, the foundation for all reconstruction, unconstitutional, so they attached to an otherwise uncontroversial bill a rider** that would deny the Supreme Court jurisdiction over any appeal under the new habeas statute. The bill with its rider passed Congress, was vetoed by President Johnson (five days before his impeachment hearings began), and then repassed over his veto.]

The CHIEF JUSTICE delivered the opinion of the court.

The first question necessarily is that of jurisdiction; for, if the act of March, 1868 [the bill that contained the rider], takes away the jurisdiction defined by the act of February, 1867 [the new habeas statute that broadened the scope of habeas], it is useless, if not improper, to enter into any discussion of other questions.

It is quite true, as was argued by the counsel for the petitioner, that the appellate jurisdiction of this court is not derived from acts of Congress. It is, strictly speaking, conferred by the Constitution. But it is conferred "with such exceptions and under such regulations as Congress shall make."

It is unnecessary to consider whether, if Congress had made no exceptions and no regulations, this court might not have exercised general appellate jurisdiction under rules prescribed by itself. For among the earliest acts of the first Congress, at its first session, was the act of September 24th, 1789, to establish the judicial courts of the United States. That act provided for the organization of this court, and prescribed regulations for the exercise of its jurisdiction.

* Reconstruction is the term used to describe the period after the Civil War when Congress placed the former Confederate states under federal military occupation in order to protect the newly freed slaves and to attempt to enforce their newly acquired rights under the Civil War Amendments and the Civil Rights Acts. The state and local governments operated under military supervision.

** A "rider" is a provision attached to a legislative bill to which it has no substantial relationship, usually for the purposes of hiding it from scrutiny, thereby increasing its chances of passage.

The source of that jurisdiction, and the limitations of it by the Constitution and by statute, have been on several occasions subjects of consideration here. In the case of *Durousseau v. The United States*, 10 U.S. 307 (1810), particularly, the whole matter was carefully examined, and the court held, that while "the appellate powers of this court are not given by the judicial act, but are given by the Constitution," they are, nevertheless, "limited and regulated by that act, and by such other acts as have been passed on the subject." The court said, further, that the judicial act was an exercise of the power given by the Constitution to Congress "of making exceptions to the appellate jurisdiction of the Supreme Court." "They have described affirmatively," said the court, "its jurisdiction, and this affirmative description has been understood to imply a negation of the exercise of such appellate power as is not comprehended within it."

The principle that the affirmation of appellate jurisdiction implies the negation of all such jurisdiction not affirmed having been thus established, it was an almost necessary consequence that acts of Congress, providing for the exercise of jurisdiction, should come to be spoken of as acts granting jurisdiction, and not as acts making exceptions to the constitutional grant of it.

The exception to appellate jurisdiction in the case before us, however, is not an inference from the affirmation of other appellate jurisdiction. It is made in terms. The provision of the act of 1867, affirming the appellate jurisdiction of this court in cases of habeas corpus is expressly repealed. It is hardly possible to imagine a plainer instance of positive exception.

We are not at liberty to inquire into the motives of the legislature. We can only examine into its power under the Constitution; and the power to make exceptions to the appellate jurisdiction of this court is given by express words.

What, then, is the effect of the repealing act upon the case before us? We cannot doubt as to this. Without jurisdiction the court cannot proceed at all in any cause. Jurisdiction is power to declare the law, and when it ceases to exist, the only function remaining to the court is that of announcing the fact and dismissing the cause. And this is not less clear upon authority than upon principle.

Several cases were cited by the counsel for the petitioner in support of the position that jurisdiction of this case is not affected by the repealing act. But none of them, in our judgment, afford any support to it. They are all cases of the exercise of judicial power by the legislature, or of legislative interference with courts in the exercising of continuing jurisdiction.

On the other hand, the general rule, supported by the best elementary writers, is, that "when an act of the legislature is repealed, it must be considered, except as to transactions past and closed, as if it never existed." And the effect of repealing acts upon suits under acts repealed, has been determined by the adjudications of this court ... [in which] it was held that no judgment could be rendered in a suit after the repeal of the act under which it was brought and prosecuted.

It is quite clear, therefore, that this court cannot proceed to pronounce judgment in this case, for it has no longer jurisdiction of the appeal; and judicial duty is not less fitly performed by declining ungranted jurisdiction than in exercising firmly that which the Constitution and the laws confer.

Comments and Questions

1. Again, who wins and who loses this case?

2. In light of this ruling, would it be constitutional for Congress to pass a law creating an "exception" to the Supreme Court's appellate jurisdiction over any case dealing with the constitutionality of a law regulating abortion? How would such a law be different from or the same as *McCardle*? Would the difference compel a different conclusion from that in *McCardle*?

3. What if Congress passed a law stating that the Supreme Court would have no appellate jurisdiction over any case brought by a person of color? Would such a law be constitutional? How would it be different from *McCardle*?

4. The Court notes the "general rule" that until a case is finished—that is, there is a final, unappealable judgment—changes in the law are given effect even in on-going cases. Thus, in *McCardle*, the fact that the case was still on-going did not stop Congress from eliminating the Court's jurisdiction over it. At the same time, the Court distinguished earlier cases, which it described as "the exercise of judicial power by the legislature, or of legislative interference with courts in the exercising of continuing jurisdiction." These, it suggested, would not be permissible. What might be examples of such impermissible legislative actions? Consider the following case.

UNITED STATES v. KLEIN

Supreme Court of the United States, 1871.
80 U.S. 128, 20 L.Ed. 519.

[This is another post-Civil War case in which Congress did not like what it perceived to be the direction of the Court, and so it created a statute to try to foreclose the Court from reaching a decision the Congress did not like. Here, there had been a law during the Civil War authorizing the confiscation of all property of persons who participated in the rebellion. However, as an inducement to people to abandon support of the Confederacy, there was another law to the effect that, if the President pardoned someone, subject to the condition that the person would swear thereafter to uphold the Constitution and support the Union, the proceeds from the property that had been confiscated would be returned upon a claim filed in the Court of Claims. The Radical Republicans after the war wished to punish those who had actually taken up arms against the United States, so they enacted a law requiring persons who wished to obtain the return of confiscated property to prove affirmatively that they had not supported the Confederacy during the war. The Supreme Court, however, in *United States v. Padelford*, 76 U.S. 531 (1869), held that the Presidential pardon in effect eliminated any disability related to participation in the rebellion, so that the person could obtain their property without having to make the affirmative proof. Klein was the executor of the estate of someone whose property had been seized, but who had taken the requisite oath and received a presidential pardon, and Klein filed suit in the Court of Claims for the proceeds from that property. The Court of Claims ruled in his favor, and the government appealed to the Supreme Court. Congress, however, upset with the decision in *Padelford*, enacted a proviso to an appropriation law saying that acceptance of such a pardon "shall be taken and deemed in such suit in the said Court of Claims, and on appeal therefrom, conclusive evidence that such person did take part in, and give aid and comfort to, the late rebellion, and did not maintain true allegiance or consistently adhere to the United States; and on proof of such pardon and acceptance ..., the jurisdiction of the court in the case shall cease, and the court shall forthwith dismiss the suit of such claimant."]

The CHIEF JUSTICE delivered the opinion of the court.

This proviso declares in substance that no pardon, acceptance, oath, or other act performed in pursuance, or as a condition of pardon, shall be admissible in evidence in support of any claim against the United States in the Court of Claims, or to establish the right of any claimant to bring suit in that court; nor, if already put in evidence, shall be used or considered on behalf of the claimant, by said court, or by the appellate court on appeal. Proof of loyalty is required to be made according to the provisions of certain statutes, irrespective of the effect of any executive proclamation, pardon, or amnesty, or act of oblivion; and when judgment has been already rendered on other proof of loyalty, the Supreme Court, on appeal, shall have no further jurisdiction of the cause, and shall dismiss the same for want of jurisdiction....

The substance of this enactment is that an acceptance of a pardon ... shall be conclusive evidence of the acts pardoned, but shall be null and void as evidence of the rights conferred by it, both in the Court of Claims and in this court on appeal....

Undoubtedly the legislature has complete control over the organization and existence of [the Court of Claims] and may confer or withhold the right of appeal from its decisions. And if this act did nothing more, it would be our duty to give it effect. If it simply denied the right of appeal in a particular class of cases, there could be no doubt that it must be regarded as an exercise of the power of Congress to make "such exceptions from the appellate jurisdiction" as should seem to it expedient.

But the language of the proviso shows plainly that it does not intend to withhold appellate jurisdiction except as a means to an end. Its great and controlling purpose is to deny to pardons granted by the President the effect which this court had adjudged them to have. The proviso declares that pardons shall not be considered by this court on appeal. We had already decided that it was our duty to consider them and give them effect, in cases like the present, as equivalent to proof of loyalty. It provides that whenever it shall appear that any judgment of the Court of Claims shall have been founded on such pardons, without other proof of loyalty, the Supreme Court shall have no further jurisdiction of the case and shall dismiss the same for want of jurisdiction....

It is evident from this statement that the denial of jurisdiction to this court, as well as to the Court of Claims, is founded solely on the application of a rule of decision, in causes pending, prescribed by Congress. The court has jurisdiction of the cause to a given point; but when it ascertains that a certain state of things exists, its jurisdiction is to cease and it is required to dismiss the cause for want of jurisdiction.

It seems to us that this is not an exercise of the acknowledged power of Congress to make exceptions and prescribe regulations to the appellate power.

The court is required to ascertain the existence of certain facts and thereupon to declare that its jurisdiction on appeal has ceased, by dismissing the bill. What is this but to prescribe a rule for the decision of a cause in a particular way? In the case before us, the Court of Claims has rendered judgment for the claimant and an appeal has been taken to this court. We are directed to dismiss the appeal, if we find that the judgment must be affirmed, because of a pardon granted to the intestate of the claimants. Can we do so without allowing one party to the controversy to decide it in its own favor? Can we do so without allowing that the legislature may prescribe rules of decision to the Judicial Department of the government in cases pending before it?

We think not; and thus thinking, we do not at all question what was decided in the case of *Pennsylvania v. Wheeling Bridge Company*, 59 U.S. 421 (1855). In that case, after a decree in this court that the bridge, in the then state of the law, was a nuisance and must be abated as such, Congress passed an act legalizing the structure and making it a post-road; and the court, on a motion for process to enforce the decree, held that the bridge had ceased to be a nuisance by the exercise of the constitutional powers of Congress, and denied the motion. No arbitrary rule of decision was prescribed in that case, but the court was left to apply its ordinary rules to the new circumstances created by the act. In the case before us no new circumstances have been created by legislation. But the court is forbidden to give the effect to evidence which, in its own judgment, such evidence should have, and is directed to give it an effect precisely contrary.

We must think that Congress has inadvertently passed the limit which separates the legislative from the judicial power.

It is of vital importance that these powers be kept distinct. The Constitution provides that the judicial power of the United States shall be vested in one Supreme Court and such inferior courts as the Congress shall from time to time ordain and establish. The same instrument, in the last clause of the same article, provides that in all cases other than those of original jurisdiction, "the Supreme Court shall have appellate jurisdiction both as to law and fact, with such exceptions and under such regulations as the Congress shall make."

Congress has already provided that the Supreme Court shall have jurisdiction of the judgments of the Court of Claims on appeal. Can it prescribe a rule in conformity with which the court must deny to itself the jurisdiction thus conferred, because and only because its decision, in accordance with settled law, must be adverse to the government and favorable to the suitor? This question seems to us to answer itself.

Mr. Justice MILLER (with whom concurred Mr. Justice BRADLEY), dissent[ed].

Comments and Questions

1. The Court holds that the proviso is unconstitutional. On what basis? How is this case like or unlike *McCardle*?

2. Who raised the *Pennsylvania v. Wheeling Bridge Company* case and why? How did the Court distinguish that case from *Klein*?

3. In 1990, upset with some lower federal court decisions enjoining timber sales on federal lands because the courts found the federal agencies had not complied with the requirements of various environmental laws, Congress enacted a proviso to an appropriations bill. That proviso stated that "Congress hereby determines and directs that management of areas according to subsections (b)(3) and (b)(5) of this section on the thirteen national forests in Oregon and Washington and Bureau of Land Management lands in western Oregon known to contain northern spotted owls is adequate consideration for the purpose of meeting the statutory requirements that are the basis for the consolidated cases captioned *Seattle Audubon Society v. Robertson*, Civil No. 89–160, and *Washington Contract Loggers Assoc. v. Robertson*, Civil No. 89–99 (order granting preliminary injunction) and the case *Portland Audubon Society v. Lujan*, Civil No. 87–1160–FR." The environmental groups appealed in the Ninth Circuit, arguing that this proviso was unconstitutional pursuant to *United States v. Klein*, and the Ninth Circuit agreed. The government appealed to the Supreme Court, which unanimously reversed the Ninth Circuit, finding this case to be a *Pennsylvania v. Wheeling Bridge Company* case, not a *United States v. Klein* case. Can you see why? Could Congress have achieved its end in *Klein* (to keep the Supreme Court from ruling in favor of Klein) if it had written its proviso differently?

4. Another case in which the Court said Congress went too far was *Plaut v. Spendthrift Farm, Inc.* 514 U.S. 211 (1995). Earlier, the Supreme Court had interpreted the Securities Exchange Act of 1934 as

requiring a suit alleging fraud in the sale of securities to be brought within one year of the discovery of the alleged fraud and within three years of the date of the alleged fraud. As a result, a number of securities fraud cases were dismissed as barred by the statute of limitations.* Congress, upset with these decisions, amended the Securities Exchange Act to provide specifically that the statute of limitations under the Act would be the limitations period applicable under state law (which normally would be longer than what the Supreme Court had interpreted the Act to require). That did not create any problem. Congress can change the limitations periods for suits under its statutes, but the new law went further. It also said that anyone who had had their case dismissed because of the prior statute of limitations (but who would not have had their case dismissed if the new law had then been in existence) could have their case reinstated by filing a motion with the court that had dismissed their case. This the Supreme Court said unconstitutionally intruded on the judicial function. Once a case has been finally decided by the courts, Congress cannot change the law applicable to that case.

5. *McCardle* upheld the power of Congress to restrict the appellate jurisdiction of the Supreme Court, relying upon the language in Article III, that says the Court's appellate jurisdiction is subject to "such exceptions ... as the Congress shall make." What would be the constitutional basis for Congress to limit the jurisdiction of lower federal courts? Could it provide that lower courts will only have jurisdiction over cases based on diversity of citizenship if the amount in dispute is over $100,000? How about if the law limited diversity jurisdiction to cases in which the plaintiff is a male? How about a law providing that no federal court shall have jurisdiction to hear any case challenging the constitutionality of a law regulating abortion, would such a law be constitutional? If it were, might there be other reasons Congress might not want to pass it, even if Congress did not like federal courts ruling on this subject?

6. If any (or all) of these laws were constitutional, would this deprive the plaintiffs of the ability to have their cases heard somewhere? Could Congress pass a law prohibiting state courts from hearing any case challenging the constitutionality of a law regulating abortion?

2. SELF-IMPOSED CHECKS

As may be seen, Congress actually has a fair amount of power to "check" the judicial power of the United States, although you may perceive some practical problems involved in using this checking power. At the same time, however, throughout our history the Supreme Court has been sensitive to the role of courts in American government. In a sense, it has imposed checks on itself (and lower courts) through its interpretation of the Constitution. It begins even before *Marbury*.

* A "statute of limitations" is a law that specifies the period within which a person must bring a lawsuit to avoid being time-barred, as well as a law that specifies the period within which the government must prosecute a person for a crime.

a. Advisory Opinions

In 1793, on behalf of President Washington, Secretary of State Thomas Jefferson wrote a letter to the Supreme Court justices asking for their opinion concerning certain legal matters relating to the United States' neutrality in the then ongoing war between France and Great Britain.

> Gentlemen:
>
> The war which has taken place among the powers of Europe produces frequent transactions within our ports and limits, on which questions arise of considerable difficulty, and of greater importance to the peace of the United States. Their questions depend for their solution on the construction of our treaties, on the laws of nature and nations, and on the laws of the land, and are often presented under circumstances which do not give a cognisance of them to the tribunals of the country. Yet their decision is so little analogous to the ordinary functions of the executive, as to occasion much embarrassment and difficulty to them. The President therefore would be much relieved if he found himself free to refer questions of this description to the opinions of the judges of the Supreme Court of the United States, whose knowledge of the subject would secure us against errors dangerous to the peace of the United States, and their authority insure the respect of all parties. He has therefore asked the attendance of such of the judges as could be collected in time for the occasion, to know, in the first place, their opinion, whether the public may, with propriety, be availed of their advice on these questions? And if they may, to present, for their advice, the abstract questions which have already occurred, or may soon occur, from which they will themselves strike out such as any circumstances might, in their opinion, forbid them to pronounce on.

Attached to the letter was a list of 29 questions. Ultimately, the Court responded:

> We have considered the previous question stated in a letter written by your direction to us by the Secretary of State on the 18th of last month, [regarding] the lines of separation drawn by the Constitution between the three departments of the government. These being in certain respects checks upon each other, and our being judges of a court of the last resort, are considerations which afford strong arguments against the propriety of our extra-judicially deciding the questions alluded to, especially as the power given by the Constitution to the President, of calling on the heads of departments for opinions, seems to have been purposely as well as expressly united to the executive departments. We exceedingly regret every event that may cause embarrassment to your administration, but we derive consola-

> tion from the reflection that your judgment will discern what is right, and that your usual prudence, decision, and firmness will surmount every obstacle to the preservation of the rights, peace, and dignity of the United States.

Thus, Washington as President wished to know what the Supreme Court thought the law was, so that he could follow their advice. The Court, however, refused his invitation. Notice the basis for their refusal. The Court refers to the Constitution's separation of powers and checks of one branch on another. Then it characterizes what it is being asked to do as extra-judicial and therefore presumably inappropriate. Rather, the Court says, the Constitution's explicit authority for the President to ask heads of departments for opinions suggests that it is those officers, rather than the Court, that the Constitution expects to render advice to the President.

The refusal of the Court to provide "advisory opinions," first expressed in this letter, has been followed ever since. *See, e.g., Massachusetts v. EPA*, 127 S.Ct. 1438, 1452 (2007). But why was the Court so reluctant to render an advisory opinion? What harm would it have caused? Canada provides for them; the constitution of the state of Massachusetts requires its Supreme Judicial Court to answer questions posed to it by the governor or either branch of the legislature.

Perhaps the answer lies in what transpired the year before. In 1792 a case was brought before the Supreme Court seeking it to order lower federal circuit courts to administer a law providing for pensions to disabled soldiers of the Revolutionary War. *See Hayburn's Case*, 2 U.S. 408 (1892). Three circuit courts had refused to comply with that law because they believed it unconstitutionally required them to perform non-judicial functions. The law required the courts to determine whether a person qualified for a pension. The courts' decisions were subject to review and reversal by the Secretary of War, and, if not reversed by the Secretary of War, to review and possible revision by Congress. Each of the circuits expressed a similar analysis: that each branch of government is separate and distinct with only the powers granted to it by the Constitution; that the judicial branch is only authorized to exercise judicial power; that to perform acts not in their nature judicial would be beyond its delegated judicial power; and that acts subject to revision by either the executive or the legislative branches would be acts not in their nature judicial. While the Supreme Court did not decide the issue, because Congress changed the law before the Court could render its decision, this case made the Court aware of lurking issues regarding the use of the judiciary for non-traditional, non-judicial functions and perhaps heightened its sensitivity to a request for an advisory opinion.

b. Standing

Imagine two law students who, having read the Constitution, discover that a congressman from Indiana's fourth congressional district, is a Lieutenant Colonel in the Army Reserve. They recall that Article I, Section 6, Clause 2, which is known as the Incompatibility Clause, states that "no person holding any office under the United States, shall be a Member of either House during his continuance in office." One student believes the congressman is in violation of the Constitution; the other does not. They argue but cannot convince one another. May they sue each other in federal court? After all, is this not a dispute arising under the Constitution? The answer, of course, is that they cannot sue one another to resolve this dispute. Could one of them sue the Secretary of Defense or the Secretary of the Army to have the person removed from office? In *Schlesinger v. Reservists Committee to Stop the War*, 418 U.S. 208 (1974), the Supreme Court dismissed a case challenging the constitutionality of members of Congress being reserve officers in the military, saying that the persons bringing the suit, whether as taxpayers or citizens, lacked a sufficient particularized adverse interest for them to have **standing**.

Earl Warren
President Eisenhower appointed Earl Warren, the former Republican governor of California, to be Chief Justice in 1953. It was widely believed that Eisenhower was rewarding Warren for his support during the 1952 presidential campaign. Although Warren had been the Attorney General of California at the beginning of World War II, when he was a strong supporter of the Japanese internment, and an active Republican politician his whole life, as Chief Justice he moved the Court in a distinctly liberal and activist direction. This led Eisenhower allegedly to have remarked that appointing Warren was "the biggest damned-fool mistake I ever made." Appointed to the Court after the case of *Brown v. Bd. of Education* had been first argued but before it was decided, Warren managed to deliver a unanimous opinion declaring segregated schools unconstitutional.

What it takes to establish standing and even what its basis in the law is has varied over the years. The case of *Flast v. Cohen*, 392 U.S. 83 (1968), reflected an activist stance by the Court, as it allowed a person to challenge a federal government expenditure on Establishment Clause grounds merely because the person was a taxpayer. The Court, in an opinion written by Chief Justice Earl Warren, said:

> The fundamental aspect of standing is that it focuses on the party seeking to get his complaint before a federal court and not on the issues he wishes to have adjudicated. The "gist of the question of standing" is whether the party seeking relief has "alleged such a personal stake in the outcome of the controversy as to assure that concrete adverseness which sharpens the presentation of issues upon which the court so largely depends for illumination of difficult constitutional questions." In other words,

> when standing is placed in issue in a case, the question is whether the person whose standing is challenged is a proper party to request an adjudication of a particular issue and not whether the issue itself is justiciable.... A proper party is demanded so that federal courts will not be asked to decide "ill defined controversies over constitutional issues," or a case which is of "a hypothetical or abstract character." ...
>
> [T]he question whether a particular person is a proper party to maintain the action does not, by its own force, raise separation of powers problems related to improper judicial interference in areas committed to other branches of the Federal Government. Such problems arise, if at all, only from the substantive issues the individual seeks to have adjudicated. Thus, in terms of Article III limitations on federal court jurisdiction, the question of standing is related only to whether the dispute sought to be adjudicated will be presented in an adversary context and in a form historically viewed as capable of judicial resolution.... Therefore, we find no absolute bar in Article III to suits by federal taxpayers challenging allegedly unconstitutional federal taxing and spending programs. There remains, however, the problem of determining the circumstances under which a federal taxpayer will be deemed to have the personal stake and interest that impart the necessary concrete adverseness to such litigation so that standing can be conferred on the taxpayer qua taxpayer consistent with the constitutional limitations of Article III.

392 U.S. at 99–100.

That was the last time the Supreme Court allowed a federal taxpayer to have standing to challenge a federal program,* and subsequent cases, if they did not overrule *Flast*, limited it strictly to its facts. *See Valley Forge Christian College v. Americans United for Separation of Church and State, Inc.*, 454 U.S. 464 (1982)(finding no standing for taxpayers to challenge the federal donation of land to a religious institution on Establishment Clause grounds); *Hein v. Freedom From Religion Foundation, Inc.*, 127 S.Ct. 2553 (2007)(finding no standing for taxpayers to bring Establishment Clause challenge against federal agency's use of federal money to fund conferences to promote President's "faith-based initiatives"). Moreover, later cases seem to have a different conception of the Article III nature of standing from that described in the *Flast* opinion, which focused not on separation of powers concerns but on assuring sufficient adverseness between the parties to ensure the case is well presented to the court. The following case is probably the current leading case on standing.

* It would, of course, be different if the taxpayer were challenging the lawfulness or constitutionality of a tax imposed on the taxpayer. A person clearly would have standing to challenge a tax the person was required to pay.

LUJAN v. DEFENDERS OF WILDLIFE

Supreme Court of the United States, 1992.
504 U.S. 555, 112 S.Ct. 2130, 119 L.Ed.2d 351.

Justice SCALIA delivered the opinion of the Court with respect to Parts I, II, III–A, and IV, and an opinion with respect to Part III–B, in which THE CHIEF JUSTICE, Justice WHITE, and Justice THOMAS join.

This case involves a challenge to a rule promulgated by the Secretary of the Interior [Manuel Lujan] interpreting § 7 of the Endangered Species Act of 1973 (ESA) in such fashion as to render it applicable only to actions within the United States or on the high seas. The preliminary issue, and the only one we reach, is whether respondents here, plaintiffs below, have standing to seek judicial review of the rule.

Antonin Scalia
Ronald Reagan appointed Antonin Scalia to the Supreme Court in 1986. A proponent of originalism, Scalia often consults old dictionaries to determine the then meaning of words in the Constitution or statutes. He also is "conservative" in the sense that he believes judges should decide cases only when necessary. Scalia writes well-crafted opinions replete with colorful phrases, and occasionally uses harsh language directed toward his fellow Justices. His wit, intelligence, and influence make him personally popular but a controversial member of the Court, gaining him both fans and opponents. Scalia has been one of the most recognized and influential members of the Rehnquist and Roberts Courts due to his strong personality, combative charm, and poignant written opinions.

I

The ESA seeks to protect species of animals against threats to their continuing existence caused by man.... Section 7(a)(2) of the Act then provides, in pertinent part: "Each Federal agency shall, in consultation with and with the assistance of the Secretary [of the Interior], insure that any action authorized, funded, or carried out by such agency ... is not likely to jeopardize the continued existence of any endangered species or threatened species...."

In 1978, the Fish and Wildlife Service (FWS) and the National Marine Fisheries Service (NMFS), on behalf of the Secretary of the Interior and the Secretary of Commerce respectively, promulgated a joint regulation stating that the obligations imposed by § 7(a)(2) extend to actions taken in foreign nations. The next year, however, the Interior Department began to reexamine its position. A revised joint regulation, reinterpreting § 7(a)(2) to require consultation only for actions taken in the United States or on the high seas, was proposed in 1983 and promulgated in 1986.

Shortly thereafter, respondents, organizations dedicated to wildlife conservation and other environmental causes, filed this action against the Secretary of the Interior, seeking a declaratory judgment that the new regulation is in error as to the geographic scope of § 7(a)(2) and an injunction requiring the Secretary to promulgate a new regulation restoring the initial interpretation. The District Court granted the Secretary's motion to dismiss for lack of standing. The Court of Appeals for the Eighth Circuit reversed by a divided vote.... We granted certiorari.

II

While the Constitution of the United States divides all power conferred upon the Federal Government into "legislative Powers," Art. I, § 1, "[t]he executive Power," Art. II, § 1, and "[t]he judicial Power," Art. III, § 1, it does not attempt to define those terms. To be sure, it limits the jurisdiction of federal courts to "Cases" and "Controversies," but an executive inquiry can bear the name "case" (the Hoffa case) and a legislative dispute can bear the name "controversy" (the Smoot–Hawley controversy). Obviously, then, the Constitution's central mechanism of separation of powers depends largely upon common understanding of what activities are appropriate to legislatures, to executives, and to courts. In The Federalist No. 48, Madison expressed the view that "[i]t is not infrequently a question of real nicety in legislative bodies whether the operation of a particular measure will, or will not, extend beyond the legislative sphere," whereas "the executive power [is] restrained within a narrower compass and ... more simple in its nature," and "the judiciary [is] described by landmarks still less uncertain." One of those landmarks, setting apart the "Cases" and "Controversies" that are of the justiciable sort referred to in Article III–"serv[ing] to identify those disputes which are appropriately resolved through the judicial process,"—is the doctrine of standing. Though some of its elements express merely prudential considerations that are part of judicial self-government, the core component of standing is an essential and unchanging part of the case-or-controversy requirement of Article III.

Over the years, our cases have established that the irreducible constitutional minimum of standing contains three elements. First, the plaintiff must have suffered an "injury in fact"—an invasion of a legally protected interest which is (a) concrete and particularized[1] and (b) "actual or imminent, not 'conjectural' or 'hypothetical.' " Second, there must be a causal connection between the injury and the conduct complained of—the injury has to be "fairly ... trace[able] to the challenged action of the defendant, and not ... th[e] result [of] the independent action of some third party not before the court." Third, it must be "likely," as opposed to merely "speculative," that the injury will be "redressed by a favorable decision."

1. By particularized, we mean that the injury must affect the plaintiff in a personal and individual way.

The party invoking federal jurisdiction bears the burden of establishing these elements. Since they are not mere pleading requirements but rather an indispensable part of the plaintiff's case, each element must be supported in the same way as any other matter on which the plaintiff bears the burden of proof, i.e., with the manner and degree of evidence required at the successive stages of the litigation. At the pleading stage, general factual allegations of injury resulting from the defendant's conduct may suffice, for on a motion to dismiss we "presum[e] that general allegations embrace those specific facts that are necessary to support the claim." In response to a summary judgment motion, however, the plaintiff can no longer rest on such "mere allegations," but must "set forth" by affidavit or other evidence "specific facts," which for purposes of the summary judgment motion will be taken to be true. And at the final stage, those facts (if controverted) must be "supported adequately by the evidence adduced at trial."

When the suit is one challenging the legality of government action or inaction, the nature and extent of facts that must be averred (at the summary judgment stage) or proved (at the trial stage) in order to establish standing depends considerably upon whether the plaintiff is himself an object of the action (or forgone action) at issue. If he is, there is ordinarily little question that the action or inaction has caused him injury, and that a judgment preventing or requiring the action will redress it. When, however, as in this case, a plaintiff's asserted injury arises from the government's allegedly unlawful regulation (or lack of regulation) of someone else, much more is needed. In that circumstance, causation and redressability ordinarily hinge on the response of the regulated (or regulable) third party to the government action or inaction—and perhaps on the response of others as well. The existence of one or more of the essential elements of standing "depends on the unfettered choices made by independent actors not before the courts and whose exercise of broad and legitimate discretion the courts cannot presume either to control or to predict," and it becomes the burden of the plaintiff to adduce facts showing that those choices have been or will be made in such manner as to produce causation and permit redressability of injury. Thus, when the plaintiff is not himself the object of the government action or inaction he challenges, standing is not precluded, but it is ordinarily "substantially more difficult" to establish.

III

We think the Court of Appeals failed to apply the foregoing principles in denying the Secretary's motion for summary judgment. Respondents had not made the requisite demonstration of (at least) injury and redressability.

A

Respondents' claim to injury is that the lack of consultation with respect to certain funded activities abroad "increas[es] the rate of extinction of endangered and threatened species." Of course, the desire to use or observe an animal species, even for purely esthetic purposes, is undeniably a cognizable interest for purpose of standing. *See, e.g., Sierra Club v. Morton*, 405 U.S. 727, at 734 (1972). "But the 'injury in fact' test requires more than an injury to a cognizable interest. It requires that the party seeking review be himself among the injured." To survive the Secretary's summary judgment motion, respondents had to submit affidavits or other evidence showing, through specific facts, not only that listed species were in fact being threatened by funded activities abroad, but also that one or more of respondents' members would thereby be "directly" affected apart from their " 'special interest' in th[e] subject."

With respect to this aspect of the case, the Court of Appeals focused on the affidavits of two Defenders' members—Joyce Kelly and Amy Skilbred. Ms. Kelly stated that she traveled to Egypt in 1986 and "observed the traditional habitat of the endangered Nile crocodile there and intend[s] to do so again, and hope[s] to observe the crocodile directly," and that she "will suffer harm in fact as the result of [the] American ... role ... in overseeing the rehabilitation of the Aswan High Dam on the Nile ... and [in] develop [ing] ... Egypt's ... Master Water Plan." Ms. Skilbred averred that she traveled to Sri Lanka in 1981 and "observed th[e] habitat" of "endangered species such as the Asian elephant and the leopard" at what is now the site of the Mahaweli project funded by the Agency for International Development (AID), although she "was unable to see any of the endangered species"; "this development project," she continued, "will seriously reduce endangered, threatened, and endemic species habitat including areas that I visited ... [, which] may severely shorten the future of these species"; that threat, she concluded, harmed her because she "intend[s] to return to Sri Lanka in the future and hope[s] to be more fortunate in spotting at least the endangered elephant and leopard." When Ms. Skilbred was asked at a subsequent deposition if and when she had any plans to return to Sri Lanka, she reiterated that "I intend to go back to Sri Lanka," but confessed that she had no current plans: "I don't know [when]. There is a civil war going on right now. I don't know. Not next year, I will say. In the future."

We shall assume for the sake of argument that these affidavits contain facts showing that certain agency-funded projects threaten listed species—though that is questionable. They plainly contain no facts, however, showing how damage to the species will produce "imminent" injury to Mses. Kelly and Skilbred. That the women "had visited" the areas of the projects before the projects commenced proves nothing. As we have said in a related context, " 'Past exposure to illegal conduct does not in itself show a present case or controversy regarding injunctive relief ... if unaccompanied by any continuing, present adverse effects.' " And the affiants' profession of an "inten[t]" to return to the places they had visited before—where they will presumably, this time, be deprived of the opportunity to observe animals of the endangered species—is simply not enough. Such "some day" intentions—without any description of concrete plans, or indeed even any specification of when the some day will be—do not support a finding of the "actual or imminent" injury that our cases require.[2]

Besides relying upon the Kelly and Skilbred affidavits, respondents propose a series of novel standing theories. The first, inelegantly styled "ecosystem nexus," proposes that any person who uses any part of a "contiguous ecosystem" adversely affected by a funded activity has standing even if the activity is located a great distance away. This approach, as the Court of Appeals correctly observed, is inconsistent with our opinion in *National Wildlife Federation*, which held that a plaintiff claiming injury from environmental damage must use the area affected by the challenged activity and not an area roughly "in the vicinity" of it....

Respondents' other theories are called, alas, the "animal nexus" approach, whereby anyone who has an interest in studying or seeing the endangered animals anywhere on the globe has standing; and the "vocational nexus" approach, under which anyone with a professional interest in such animals can sue. Under these theories, anyone who goes to see Asian elephants in the Bronx Zoo, and anyone who is a keeper of Asian elephants in the Bronx Zoo, has standing to sue because the Director of the Agency for International Development (AID) did not consult with the Secretary regarding the AID-funded project in Sri Lanka. This is beyond all reason. Standing is not "an ingenious academic exercise in the conceivable," but as we have said requires, at the summary judgment stage, a factual showing of perceptible harm. It is clear that the person who observes or works with a particular animal threatened by a federal decision is facing perceptible harm, since the very subject of his interest will no longer exist. It is even plausible—though it goes to the outermost limit of plausibility—to think that a person who observes or works with animals of a particular species in the very area of the world where that species is threatened by a federal decision is facing such harm, since some animals that might have been the subject of his interest will no longer exist. It goes beyond the limit, however, and into pure speculation

2. The dissent acknowledges the settled requirement that the injury complained of be, if not actual, then at least imminent, but it contends that respondents could get past summary judgment because "a reasonable finder of fact could conclude ... that ... Kelly or Skilbred will soon return to the project sites." This analysis suffers either from a factual or from a legal defect, depending on what the "soon" is supposed to mean. If "soon" refers to the standard mandated by our precedents—that the injury be "imminent"—we are at a loss to see how, as a factual matter, the standard can be met by respondents' mere profession of an intent, some day, to return. But if, as we suspect, "soon" means nothing more than "in this lifetime," then the dissent has undertaken quite a departure from our precedents. Although "imminence" is concededly a somewhat elastic concept, it cannot be stretched beyond its purpose, which is to ensure that the alleged injury is not too speculative for Article III purposes-that the injury is " 'certainly impending,' " It has been stretched beyond the breaking point when, as here, the plaintiff alleges only an injury at some indefinite future time, and the acts necessary to make the injury happen are at least partly within the plaintiff's own control. In such circumstances we have insisted that the injury proceed with a high degree of immediacy, so as to reduce the possibility of deciding a case in which no injury would have occurred at all....

and fantasy, to say that anyone who observes or works with an endangered species, anywhere in the world, is appreciably harmed by a single project affecting some portion of that species with which he has no more specific connection.

B

Besides failing to show injury, respondents failed to demonstrate redressability. Instead of attacking the separate decisions to fund particular projects allegedly causing them harm, respondents chose to challenge a more generalized level of Government action (rules regarding consultation), the invalidation of which would affect all overseas projects. This programmatic approach has obvious practical advantages, but also obvious difficulties insofar as proof of causation or redressability is concerned....

The most obvious problem in the present case is redressability. Since the agencies funding the projects were not parties to the case, the District Court could accord relief only against the Secretary: He could be ordered to revise his regulation to require consultation for foreign projects. But this would not remedy respondents' alleged injury unless the funding agencies were bound by the Secretary's regulation, which is very much an open question.... When the Secretary promulgated the regulation at issue here, he thought it was binding on the agencies. The Solicitor General, however, has repudiated that position here, and the agencies themselves apparently deny the Secretary's authority. (During the period when the Secretary took the view that § 7(a)(2) did apply abroad, AID and FWS engaged in a running controversy over whether consultation was required with respect to the Mahaweli project, AID insisting that consultation applied only to domestic actions.)

[T]he short of the matter is that redress of the only injury in fact respondents complain of requires action (termination of funding until consultation) by the individual funding agencies; and any relief the District Court could have provided in this suit against the Secretary was not likely to produce that action.

A further impediment to redressability is the fact that the agencies generally supply only a fraction of the funding for a foreign project. AID, for example, has provided less than 10% of the funding for the Mahaweli project. Respondents have produced nothing to indicate that the projects they have named will either be suspended, or do less harm to listed species, if that fraction is eliminated. [I]t is entirely conjectural whether the nonagency activity that affects respondents will be altered or affected by the agency activity they seek to achieve. There is no standing.

IV

The Court of Appeals found that respondents had standing for an additional reason: because they had suffered a "procedural injury." The so-called "citizen-suit" provision of the ESA provides, in pertinent part, that "any person may commence a civil suit on his own behalf (A) to enjoin any person, including the United States and any other governmental instrumentality or agency ... who is alleged to be in violation of any provision of this chapter." The court held that, because § 7(a)(2) requires interagency consultation, the citizen-suit provision creates a "procedural righ[t]" to consultation in all "persons"—so that anyone can file suit in federal court to challenge the Secretary's (or presumably any other official's) failure to follow the assertedly correct consultative procedure, notwithstanding his or her inability to allege any discrete injury flowing from that failure. To understand the remarkable nature of this holding one must be clear about what it does not rest upon: This is not a case where plaintiffs are seeking to enforce a procedural requirement the disregard of which could impair a separate concrete interest of theirs (e.g., the procedural requirement for a hearing prior to denial of their license application, or the procedural requirement for an environmental impact statement before a federal facility is constructed next door to them).[7] Nor is it simply a case where concrete injury has been suffered by many persons, as in mass fraud or mass tort situations. Nor, finally, is it the unusual case in which Congress has created a concrete private interest in the outcome of a suit against a private party for the government's benefit, by providing a cash bounty for the victorious plaintiff. Rather, the court held that the injury-in-fact requirement had been satisfied by congressional conferral upon all persons of an abstract, self-contained, noninstrumental "right" to have the Executive observe the procedures required by law. We reject this view.[8]

We have consistently held that a plaintiff raising only a generally available grievance about government—claiming only harm to his and

7. There is this much truth to the assertion that "procedural rights" are special: The person who has been accorded a procedural right to protect his concrete interests can assert that right without meeting all the normal standards for redressability and immediacy. Thus, under our case law, one living adjacent to the site for proposed construction of a federally licensed dam has standing to challenge the licensing agency's failure to prepare an environmental impact statement, even though he cannot establish with any certainty that the statement will cause the license to be withheld or altered, and even though the dam will not be completed for many years. (That is why we do not rely, in the present case, upon the Government's argument that, even if the other agencies were obliged to consult with the Secretary, they might not have followed his advice.) What respondents' "procedural rights" argument seeks, however, is quite different from this: standing for persons who have no concrete interests affected-persons who live (and propose to live) at the other end of the country from the dam.

8. The dissent's discussion of this aspect of the case distorts our opinion. We do not hold that an individual cannot enforce procedural rights; he assuredly can, so long as the procedures in question are designed to protect some threatened concrete interest of his that is the ultimate basis of his standing. The dissent, however, asserts that there exist "classes of procedural duties ... so enmeshed with the prevention of a substantive, concrete harm that an individual plaintiff may be able to demonstrate a sufficient likelihood of injury just through the breach of that procedural duty." If we understand this correctly, it means that the Government's violation of a certain (undescribed) class of procedural duty satisfies the concrete-injury requirement by itself, without any showing that the procedural violation endangers a concrete interest of the plaintiff (apart from his interest in having the procedure observed). We cannot agree. The dissent is unable to cite a single case in which we actually found standing solely on the basis of a "procedural right" unconnected to the plaintiff's own concrete harm....

every citizen's interest in proper application of the Constitution and laws, and seeking relief that no more directly and tangibly benefits him than it does the public at large—does not state an Article III case or controversy. For example, in *Fairchild v. Hughes*, 258 U.S. 126, 129–130 (1922), we dismissed a suit challenging the propriety of the process by which the Nineteenth Amendment was ratified. Justice Brandeis wrote for the Court: "[This is] not a case within the meaning of ... Article III.... Plaintiff has [asserted] only the right, possessed by every citizen, to require that the Government be administered according to law and that the public moneys be not wasted. Obviously this general right does not entitle a private citizen to institute in the federal courts a suit...."

In *Massachusetts v. Mellon*, 262 U.S. 447 (1923), we dismissed for lack of Article III standing a taxpayer suit challenging the propriety of certain federal expenditures. We said: "The party who invokes the power [of judicial review] must be able to show not only that the statute is invalid but that he has sustained or is immediately in danger of sustaining some direct injury as the result of its enforcement, and not merely that he suffers in some indefinite way in common with people generally.... Here the parties plaintiff have no such case.... [T]heir complaint ... is merely that officials of the executive department of the government are executing and will execute an act of Congress asserted to be unconstitutional; and this we are asked to prevent. To do so would be not to decide a judicial controversy, but to assume a position of authority over the governmental acts of another and co-equal department, an authority which plainly we do not possess."

In *Ex parte Levitt*, 302 U.S. 633 (1937), we dismissed a suit contending that Justice Black's appointment to this Court violated the Ineligibility Clause, Art. I, § 6, cl. 2. "It is an established principle," we said, "that to entitle a private individual to invoke the judicial power to determine the validity of executive or legislative action he must show that he has sustained or is immediately in danger of sustaining a direct injury as the result of that action and it is not sufficient that he has merely a general interest common to all members of the public."

More recent cases are to the same effect. In *United States v. Richardson*, 418 U.S. 166 (1974), we dismissed for lack of standing a taxpayer suit challenging the Government's failure to disclose the expenditures of the Central Intelligence Agency, in alleged violation of the constitutional requirement, Art. I, § 9, cl. 7, that "a regular Statement and Account of the Receipts and Expenditures of all public Money shall be published from time to time." We held that such a suit rested upon an impermissible "generalized grievance," and was inconsistent with "the framework of Article III" because "the impact on [plaintiff] is plainly undifferentiated and 'common to all members of the public.'" And in *Schlesinger v. Reservists Comm. to Stop the War*, we dismissed for the same reasons a citizen-taxpayer suit contending that it was a violation of the Incompatibility Clause, Art. I, § 6, cl. 2, for Members of Congress to hold commissions in the military Reserves. We said that the challenged action, "standing alone, would adversely affect only the generalized interest of all citizens in constitutional governance...." Since *Schlesinger* we have on two occasions held that an injury amounting only to the alleged violation of a right to have the Government act in accordance with law was not judicially cognizable because " 'assertion of a right to a particular kind of Government conduct, which the Government has violated by acting differently, cannot alone satisfy the requirements of Art. III without draining those requirements of meaning.' " And only two Terms ago, we rejected the notion that Article III permits a citizen suit to prevent a condemned criminal's execution on the basis of " 'the public interest protections of the Eighth Amendment' "; once again, "[t]his allegation raise [d] only the 'generalized interest of all citizens in constitutional governance' ... and [was] an inadequate basis on which to grant ... standing."

To be sure, our generalized-grievance cases have typically involved Government violation of procedures assertedly ordained by the Constitution rather than the Congress. But there is absolutely no basis for making the Article III inquiry turn on the source of the asserted right. Whether the courts were to act on their own, or at the invitation of Congress, in ignoring the concrete injury requirement described in our cases, they would be discarding a principle fundamental to the separate and distinct constitutional role of the Third Branch—one of the essential elements that identifies those "Cases" and "Controversies" that are the business of the courts rather than of the political branches. "The province of the court," as Chief Justice Marshall said in *Marbury v. Madison*, "is, solely, to decide on the rights of individuals." Vindicating the public interest (including the public interest in Government observance of the Constitution and laws) is the function of Congress and the Chief Executive. The question presented here is whether the public interest in proper administration of the laws (specifically, in agencies' observance of a particular, statutorily prescribed procedure) can be converted into an individual right by a statute that denominates it as such, and that permits all citizens (or, for that matter, a subclass of citizens who suffer no distinctive concrete harm) to sue. If the concrete injury requirement has the separation-of-powers significance we have always said, the answer must be obvious: To permit Congress to convert the undifferentiated public interest in executive officers' compliance with the law into an "individual right" vindicable in the courts is to permit Congress to transfer from the President to the courts the Chief Executive's most important constitutional duty, to "take Care that the Laws be faithfully executed," Art. II, § 3. It would enable the courts, with the permission of Congress, "to assume a position of authority over the governmental acts of another and co-equal department," and to become " 'virtually continuing monitors of the wisdom and soundness of Executive action.' " We have always rejected that vision of our role:

> When Congress passes an Act empowering administrative agencies to carry on governmental activities, the power of those

> agencies is circumscribed by the authority granted. This permits the courts to participate in law enforcement entrusted to administrative bodies only to the extent necessary to protect justiciable individual rights against administrative action fairly beyond the granted powers.... This is very far from assuming that the courts are charged more than administrators or legislators with the protection of the rights of the people. Congress and the Executive supervise the acts of administrative agents.... But under Article III, Congress established courts to adjudicate cases and controversies as to claims of infringement of individual rights whether by unlawful action of private persons or by the exertion of unauthorized administrative power.

"Individual rights," within the meaning of this passage, do not mean public rights that have been legislatively pronounced to belong to each individual who forms part of the public.

Nothing in this contradicts the principle that "[t]he ... injury required by Art. III may exist solely by virtue of 'statutes creating legal rights, the invasion of which creates standing.' " ... As we said in *Sierra Club*, "[Statutory] broadening [of] the categories of injury that may be alleged in support of standing is a different matter from abandoning the requirement that the party seeking review must himself have suffered an injury." ...

We hold that respondents lack standing to bring this action and that the Court of Appeals erred in denying the summary judgment motion filed by the United States. The opinion of the Court of Appeals is hereby reversed, and the cause is remanded for proceedings consistent with this opinion.

Justice KENNEDY, with whom Justice SOUTER joins, concurring in part and concurring in the judgment.

Although I agree with the essential parts of the Court's analysis, I write separately to make several observations.

I agree with the Court's conclusion in Part III–A that, on the record before us, respondents have failed to demonstrate that they themselves are "among the injured." This component of the standing inquiry is not satisfied unless

> [p]laintiffs ... demonstrate a 'personal stake in the outcome.' ... Abstract injury is not enough. The plaintiff must show that he 'has sustained or is immediately in danger of sustaining some direct injury' as the result of the challenged official conduct and the injury or threat of injury must be both 'real and immediate,' not 'conjectural' or 'hypothetical.'

While it may seem trivial to require that Mses. Kelly and Skilbred acquire airline tickets to the project sites or announce a date certain upon which they will return, this is not a case where it is reasonable to assume that the affiants will be using the sites on a regular basis nor do the affiants claim to have visited the sites since the projects commenced. With respect to the Court's discussion of respondents' "ecosystem nexus," "animal nexus," and "vocational nexus" theories, I agree that on this record respondents' showing is insufficient to establish standing on any of these bases. I am not willing to foreclose the possibility, however, that in different circumstances a nexus theory similar to those proffered here might support a claim to standing.

In light of the conclusion that respondents have not demonstrated a concrete injury here sufficient to support standing under our precedents, I would not reach the issue of redressability that is discussed by the plurality in Part III–B.

I also join Part IV of the Court's opinion with the following observations. As Government programs and policies become more complex and farreaching, we must be sensitive to the articulation of new rights of action that do not have clear analogs in our common-law tradition. Modern litigation has progressed far from the paradigm of Marbury suing Madison to get his commission.... In my view, Congress has the power to define injuries and articulate chains of causation that will give rise to a case or controversy where none existed before, and I do not read the Court's opinion to suggest a contrary view. In exercising this power, however, Congress must at the very least identify the injury it seeks to vindicate and relate the injury to the class of persons entitled to bring suit. The citizen-suit provision of the Endangered Species Act does not meet these minimal requirements, because while the statute purports to confer a right on "any person ... to enjoin ... the United States and any other governmental instrumentality or agency ... who is alleged to be in violation of any provision of this chapter," it does not of its own force establish that there is an injury in "any person" by virtue of any "violation."

The Court's holding that there is an outer limit to the power of Congress to confer rights of action is a direct and necessary consequence of the case and controversy limitations found in Article III. I agree that it would exceed those limitations if, at the behest of Congress and in the absence of any showing of concrete injury, we were to entertain citizen suits to vindicate the public's nonconcrete interest in the proper administration of the laws. While it does not matter how many persons have been injured by the challenged action, the party bringing suit must show that the action injures him in a concrete and personal way. This requirement is not just an empty formality. It preserves the vitality of the adversarial process by assuring both that the parties before the court have an actual, as opposed to professed, stake in the outcome, and that "the legal questions presented ... will be resolved, not in the rarified atmosphere of a debating society, but in a concrete factual context conducive to a realistic appreciation of the consequences of judicial action." In addition, the requirement of concrete injury confines the Judicial Branch to its proper, limited role in the constitutional framework of Government.

An independent judiciary is held to account through its open proceedings and its reasoned judgments. In this process it is essential for the public to know what persons or groups are invoking the judicial power, the reasons that they have brought suit, and whether their claims are vindicated or denied. The concrete injury requirement helps assure that there can be an answer to these questions; and, as the Court's opinion is careful to show, that is part of the constitutional design.

With these observations, I concur in Parts I, II, III–A, and IV of the Court's opinion and in the judgment of the Court.

Justice STEVENS, concurring in the judgment.

Because I am not persuaded that Congress intended the consultation requirement in § 7(a)(2) of the Endangered Species Act of 1973 (ESA) to apply to activities in foreign countries, I concur in the judgment of reversal. I do not, however, agree with the Court's conclusion that respondents lack standing because the threatened injury to their interest in protecting the environment and studying endangered species is not "imminent." Nor do I agree with the plurality's additional conclusion that respondents' injury is not "redressable" in this litigation.

I

In my opinion a person who has visited the critical habitat of an endangered species has a professional interest in preserving the species and its habitat, and intends to revisit them in the future has standing to challenge agency action that threatens their destruction. Congress has found that a wide variety of endangered species of fish, wildlife, and plants are of "aesthetic, ecological, educational, historical, recreational, and scientific value to the Nation and its people." Given that finding, we have no license to demean the importance of the interest that particular individuals may have in observing any species or its habitat, whether those individuals are motivated by esthetic enjoyment, an interest in professional research, or an economic interest in preservation of the species. Indeed, this Court has often held that injuries to such interests are sufficient to confer standing and the Court reiterates that holding today.

The Court nevertheless concludes that respondents have not suffered "injury in fact" because they have not shown that the harm to the endangered species will produce "imminent" injury to them. I disagree. An injury to an individual's interest in studying or enjoying a species and its natural habitat occurs when someone (whether it be the Government or a private party) takes action that harms that species and habitat. In my judgment, therefore, the "imminence" of such an injury should be measured by the timing and likelihood of the threatened environmental harm, rather than—as the Court seems to suggest—by the time that might elapse between the present and the time when the individuals would visit the area if no such injury should occur.

To understand why this approach is correct and consistent with our precedent, it is necessary to consider the purpose of the standing doctrine. Concerned about "the proper—and properly limited—role of the courts in a democratic society," we have long held that "Art. III judicial power exists only to redress or otherwise to protect against injury to the complaining party." The plaintiff must have a "personal stake in the outcome" sufficient to "assure that concrete adverseness which sharpens the presentation of issues upon which the court so largely depends for illumination of difficult ... questions." For that reason, "[a]bstract injury is not enough. It must be alleged that the plaintiff 'has sustained or is immediately in danger of sustaining some direct injury' as the result of the challenged statute or official conduct.... The injury or threat of injury must be both 'real and immediate,' not 'conjectural,' or 'hypothetical.' "

Consequently, we have denied standing to plaintiffs whose likelihood of suffering any concrete adverse effect from the challenged action was speculative. In this case, however, the likelihood that respondents will be injured by the destruction of the endangered species is not speculative. If respondents are genuinely interested in the preservation of the endangered species and intend to study or observe these animals in the future, their injury will occur as soon as the animals are destroyed. Thus the only potential source of "speculation" in this case is whether respondents' intent to study or observe the animals is genuine.[2] In my view, Joyce Kelly and Amy Skilbred have introduced sufficient evidence to negate petitioner's contention that their claims of injury are "speculative" or "conjectural." As Justice BLACKMUN explains, a reasonable finder of fact could conclude, from their past visits, their professional backgrounds, and their affidavits and deposition testimony, that Ms. Kelly and Ms. Skilbred will return to the project sites and, consequently, will be injured by the destruction of the endangered species and critical habitat.

The plurality also concludes that respondents' injuries are not redressable in this litigation for two reasons. First, respondents have sought only a declaratory judgment that the Secretary of the Interior's regulation interpreting § 7(a)(2) to require consultation only for agency actions in the United States or on the high seas is invalid and an injunc-

2. As we recognized in *Sierra Club v. Morton*, the impact of changes in the esthetics or ecology of a particular area does "not fall indiscriminately upon every citizen. The alleged injury will be felt directly only by those who use [the area,] and for whom the aesthetic and recreational values of the area will be lessened...." Thus, respondents would not be injured by the challenged projects if they had not visited the sites or studied the threatened species and habitat. But, as discussed above, respondents did visit the sites; moreover, they have expressed an intent to do so again. This intent to revisit the area is significant evidence tending to confirm the genuine character of respondents' interest, but I am not at all sure that an intent to revisit would be indispensable in every case. The interest that confers standing in a case of this kind is comparable, though by no means equivalent, to the interest in a relationship among family members that can be immediately harmed by the death of an absent member, regardless of when, if ever, a family reunion is planned to occur. Thus, if the facts of this case had shown repeated and regular visits by the respondents, proof of an intent to revisit might well be superfluous.

tion requiring him to promulgate a new regulation requiring consultation for agency actions abroad as well. But, the plurality opines, even if respondents succeed and a new regulation is promulgated, there is no guarantee that federal agencies that are not parties to this case will actually consult with the Secretary. Furthermore, the plurality continues, respondents have not demonstrated that federal agencies can influence the behavior of the foreign governments where the affected projects are located. Thus, even if the agencies consult with the Secretary and terminate funding for foreign projects, the foreign governments might nonetheless pursue the projects and jeopardize the endangered species. Neither of these reasons is persuasive.

We must presume that if this Court holds that § 7(a)(2) requires consultation, all affected agencies would abide by that interpretation and engage in the requisite consultations. Certainly the Executive Branch cannot be heard to argue that an authoritative construction of the governing statute by this Court may simply be ignored by any agency head. Moreover, if Congress has required consultation between agencies, we must presume that such consultation will have a serious purpose that is likely to produce tangible results. As Justice BLACKMUN explains, it is not mere speculation to think that foreign governments, when faced with the threatened withdrawal of United States assistance, will modify their projects to mitigate the harm to endangered species.

II

Although I believe that respondents have standing, I nevertheless concur in the judgment of reversal because I am persuaded that the Government is correct in its submission that § 7(a)(2) does not apply to activities in foreign countries....

In short, a reading of the entire statute persuades me that Congress did not intend the consultation requirement in § 7(a)(2) to apply to activities in foreign countries. Accordingly, notwithstanding my disagreement with the Court's disposition of the standing question, I concur in its judgment.

Justice BLACKMUN, with whom Justice O'CONNOR joins, dissenting.

I part company with the Court in this case in two respects. First, I believe that respondents have raised genuine issues of fact—sufficient to survive summary judgment—both as to injury and as to redressability. Second, I question the Court's breadth of language in rejecting standing for "procedural" injuries. I fear the Court seeks to impose fresh limitations on the constitutional authority of Congress to allow citizen suits in the federal courts for injuries deemed "procedural" in nature. I dissent.

I

Article III of the Constitution confines the federal courts to adjudication of actual "Cases" and "Controversies." To ensure the presence of a "case" or "controversy," this Court has held that Article III requires, as an irreducible minimum, that a plaintiff allege (1) an injury that is (2) "fairly traceable to the defendant's allegedly unlawful conduct" and that is (3) "likely to be redressed by the requested relief."

A

* * *

The Court also concludes that injury is lacking, because respondents' allegations of "ecosystem nexus" failed to demonstrate sufficient proximity to the site of the environmental harm.... Many environmental injuries, however, cause harm distant from the area immediately affected by the challenged action. Environmental destruction may affect animals traveling over vast geographical ranges, *see, e.g.*, *Japan Whaling Assn. v. American Cetacean Society*, 478 U.S. 221 (1986) (harm to American whale watchers from Japanese whaling activities), or rivers running long geographical courses, see, e.g., *Arkansas v. Oklahoma*, 503 U.S. 91 (1992) (harm to Oklahoma residents from wastewater treatment plant 39 miles from border). It cannot seriously be contended that a litigant's failure to use the precise or exact site where animals are slaughtered or where toxic waste is dumped into a river means he or she cannot show injury.

The Court also rejects respondents' claim of vocational or professional injury. The Court says that it is "beyond all reason" that a zoo "keeper" of Asian elephants would have standing to contest his Government's participation in the eradication of all the Asian elephants in another part of the world. I am unable to see how the distant location of the destruction necessarily (for purposes of ruling at summary judgment) mitigates the harm to the elephant keeper. If there is no more access to a future supply of the animal that sustains a keeper's livelihood, surely there is harm....

II

The Court concludes that any "procedural injury" suffered by respondents is insufficient to confer standing. It rejects the view that the "injury-in-fact requirement [is] satisfied by congressional conferral upon all persons of an abstract, self-contained, noninstrumental 'right' to have the Executive observe the procedures required by law." Whatever the Court might mean with that very broad language, it cannot be saying that "procedural injuries" as a class are necessarily insufficient for purposes of Article III standing.

Most governmental conduct can be classified as "procedural." Many injuries caused by governmental conduct, therefore, are categorizable at some level of generality as "procedural" injuries. Yet, these injuries are not categorically beyond the pale of redress by the federal courts. When the Government, for example, "procedurally" issues a pollution permit, those affected by the permittee's pollutants are not without standing to sue. Only later cases will tell just what the Court means by its intimation that "procedural" injuries are not constitutionally cognizable injuries. In the meantime, I have the greatest of sympathy for the courts across the country that will struggle to understand the Court's standardless exposition of this concept today.

The Court expresses concern that allowing judicial enforcement of "agencies' observance of a particular, statutorily prescribed procedure" would "transfer from the President to the courts the Chief Executive's most important constitutional duty, to 'take Care that the Laws be faithfully executed,' Art. II, § 3." In fact, the principal effect of foreclosing judicial enforcement of such procedures is to transfer power into the hands of the Executive at the expense—not of the courts—but of Congress, from which that power originates and emanates....

III

In conclusion, I cannot join the Court on what amounts to a slash-and-burn expedition through the law of environmental standing. In my view, "[t]he very essence of civil liberty certainly consists in the right of every individual to claim the protection of the laws, whenever he receives an injury." *Marbury v. Madison.*

I dissent.

Comments and Questions

1. In this opinion the Court identifies the three requirements for standing: Injury, Causation, and Redressability. Try to identify the different bases upon which the plaintiffs tried to establish injury and the basis upon which the Court rejected those bases. What is the issue with respect to redressability? Which justices find a problem with redressability here?

2. "Redress," it is worth noting, can be of two different types: after-the-fact redress in the form of damages for the injury and before-the-fact avoidance of the injury about to occur. It is the latter that is usually involved in standing cases, as it is here.

3. Note that Justice Scalia's opinion regarding redressability does not command agreement from a majority of the Court. Justices Kennedy and Souter agree with the rest of his opinion for the Court, but not with respect to redressability, and Justices Stevens, Blackmun, and O'Connor disagree with all of Scalia's opinion. So, what does the Court decide regarding redressability?

4. What point is Justice Kennedy making in his concurrence?

5. Does Justice Scalia's description of the purpose of the standing requirement seem consistent with the description in *Flast* or with Justice Stevens' description?

6. Note that the plaintiff in the case is the organization Defenders of the Wildlife, but it is the failure of two of its members to establish standing that results in the case being lost. Groups like Defenders can

establish standing in their own right if the group itself is injured by an allegedly unlawful action that can be redressed by a court. For example, a law denying a tax exemption to all non-profit organizations that try to protect the environment would directly injure the organization itself. However, in *Defenders* that is not the case. Instead, Defenders tries to establish standing based upon the doctrine of "associational standing," or sometimes called "organizational standing." In order to establish "associational standing," an organization needs to show three things: first, that one or more of its members would themselves have standing [hence the concern in *Defenders* with whether the two members can establish standing]; second, that the purpose of the organization relates to the subject matter of the lawsuit [here, Defenders, an organization with the specific purpose of protecting endangered species, easily qualified]; and third, that the member of the group with standing does not need to be a named party. This third requirement is a little confusing, but what it means in effect is that the action is either for an injunction or for a declaratory judgment.

John Paul Stevens

President Gerald Ford appointed Stevens to the Court in 1975, and he is currently the oldest and longest serving member of the Court. After law school he clerked for Supreme Court Justice Wiley Rutledge and then undertook a 20+ year career in a private law firm in Chicago, specializing in antitrust law. His work as General Counsel for a special commission appointed by the Illinois Supreme Court to investigate corruption brought him some prominence and probably led to President Richard Nixon appointing him to the Seventh Circuit. There he had a reputation as a moderate conservative, which he maintained in his first years on the Supreme Court. Thereafter, however, he has gravitated to the liberal wing of the Court, where he is now considered the most liberal.

MASSACHUSETTS v. ENVIRONMENTAL PROTECTION AGENCY

Supreme Court of the United States, 2007.
127 S.Ct. 1438, 167 L.Ed.2d 248.

Justice STEVENS delivered the opinion of the Court.

[C]alling global warming "the most pressing environmental challenge of our time," a group of States, local governments, and private organizations, alleged in a petition for certiorari that the Environmental Protection Agency (EPA) has abdicated its responsibility under the Clean Air Act [by failing] to regulate the emissions of four greenhouse gases, including carbon dioxide [emitted by automobiles]....

In response, EPA, supported by 10 intervening States and six trade associations, correctly argued that we may not address [the merits of the case] unless at least one petitioner has standing to invoke our jurisdiction under Article III of the Constitution....

IV

Article III of the Constitution limits federal-court jurisdiction to "Cases" and "Controversies." Those two words confine "the business of federal courts to questions presented in an adversary context and in a form historically viewed as capable of resolution through the judicial process." *Flast v. Cohen,* 392 U.S. 83 (1968)....

The parties' dispute turns on the proper construction of a congressional statute, a question eminently suitable to resolution in federal court. Congress has moreover authorized this type of challenge to EPA action. See 42 U.S.C. § 7607(b)(1). That authorization is of critical importance to the standing inquiry: "Congress has the power to define injuries and articulate chains of causation that will give rise to a case or controversy where none existed before." *Lujan v. Defenders of Wildlife,* 504 U.S. 555, 580 (KENNEDY, J., concurring in part and concurring in judgment). "In exercising this power, however, Congress must at the very least identify the injury it seeks to vindicate and relate the injury to the class of persons entitled to bring suit." *Ibid.* We will not, therefore, "entertain citizen suits to vindicate the public's nonconcrete interest in the proper administration of the laws." *Id.,* at 581.

EPA maintains that because greenhouse gas emissions inflict widespread harm, the doctrine of standing presents an insuperable jurisdictional obstacle. We do not agree. At bottom, "the gist of the question of standing" is whether petitioners have "such a personal stake in the outcome of the controversy as to assure that concrete adverseness which sharpens the presentation of issues upon which the court so largely depends for illumination." *Baker v. Carr,* 369 U.S. 186, 204 (1962). As Justice KENNEDY explained in his *Lujan* concurrence:

> "While it does not matter how many persons have been injured by the challenged action, the party bringing suit must show that the action injures him in a concrete and personal way. This requirement is not just an empty formality. It preserves the vitality of the adversarial process by assuring both that the parties before the court have an actual, as opposed to professed, stake in the outcome, and that the legal questions presented ... will be resolved, not in the rarified atmosphere of a debating society, but in a concrete factual context conducive to a realistic appreciation of the consequences of judicial action." 504 U.S., at 581 (internal quotation marks omitted).

To ensure the proper adversarial presentation, *Lujan* holds that a litigant must demonstrate that it has suffered a concrete and particularized injury that is either actual or imminent, that the injury is fairly traceable to the defendant, and that it is likely that a favorable decision will redress that injury. However, a litigant to whom Congress has "accorded a procedural right to protect his concrete interests," *id.,* at 572, n. 7—here, the right to challenge agency action unlawfully withheld, § 7607(b)(1)—"can assert that right without meeting all the normal standards for redressability and immediacy," *ibid.* When a litigant is vested with a procedural right, that litigant has standing if there is some possibility that the requested relief will prompt the injury-causing party to reconsider the decision that allegedly harmed the litigant. *Ibid.*

Only one of the petitioners needs to have standing to permit us to consider the petition for review. We stress here, as did Judge Tatel below, the special position and interest of Massachusetts. It is of considerable relevance that the party seeking review here is a sovereign State and not, as it was in *Lujan,* a private individual.

Well before the creation of the modern administrative state, we recognized that States are not normal litigants for the purposes of invoking federal jurisdiction. As Justice Holmes explained in *Georgia v. Tennessee Copper Co.,* 206 U.S. 230, 237 (1907), a case in which Georgia sought to protect its citizens from air pollution originating outside its borders:

> "The case has been argued largely as if it were one between two private parties; but it is not. The very elements that would be relied upon in a suit between fellow-citizens as a ground for equitable relief are wanting here. The State owns very little of the territory alleged to be affected, and the damage to it capable of estimate in money, possibly, at least, is small. This is a suit by a State for an injury to it in its capacity of *quasi*-sovereign. In that capacity the State has an interest independent of and behind the titles of its citizens, in all the earth and air within its domain. It has the last word as to whether its mountains shall be stripped of their forests and its inhabitants shall breathe pure air."

Just as Georgia's "independent interest ... in all the earth and air within its domain" supported federal jurisdiction a century ago, so too does Massachusetts' well-founded desire to preserve its sovereign territory today. That Massachusetts does in fact own a great deal of the "territory alleged to be affected" only reinforces the conclusion that its stake in the outcome of this case is sufficiently concrete to warrant the exercise of federal judicial power.

When a State enters the Union, it surrenders certain sovereign prerogatives. Massachusetts cannot invade Rhode Island to force reductions in greenhouse gas emissions, it cannot negotiate an emissions treaty with China or India, and in some circumstances the exercise of its police powers to reduce in-state motor-vehicle emissions might well be preempted.

These sovereign prerogatives are now lodged in the Federal Government, and Congress has ordered EPA to protect Massachusetts (among others) by prescribing standards applicable to the "emission of any air pollutant from any class or classes of new motor vehicle engines, which in [the Administrator's] judgment cause, or contribute to, air pollution which may reasonably be anticipated to endanger public health or welfare." 42 U.S.C. § 7521(a)(1). Congress has moreover recognized a concomitant procedural right to challenge the rejection of its rulemaking petition as arbitrary and capricious. § 7607(b)(1). Given that procedural right and Massachusetts' stake in protecting its quasi-sovereign interests, the Commonwealth is entitled to special solicitude in our standing analysis.

With that in mind, it is clear that petitioners' submissions as they pertain to Massachusetts have satisfied the most demanding standards of the adversarial process. EPA's steadfast refusal to regulate greenhouse gas emissions presents a risk of harm to Massachusetts that is both "actual" and "imminent." *Lujan,* 504 U.S., at 560 (internal quotation marks omitted). There is, moreover, a "substantial likelihood that the judicial relief requested" will prompt EPA to take steps to reduce that risk. *Duke Power Co. v. Carolina Environmental Study Group, Inc.,* 438 U.S. 59, 79 (1978).

The Injury

The harms associated with climate change are serious and well recognized. Indeed, the National Research Council Report itself—which EPA regards as an "objective and independent assessment of the relevant science,"—identifies a number of environmental changes that have already inflicted significant harms, including "the global retreat of mountain glaciers, reduction in snow-cover extent, the earlier spring melting of rivers and lakes, [and] the accelerated rate of rise of sea levels during the 20th century relative to the past few thousand years...."

Petitioners allege that this only hints at the environmental damage yet to come. According to the climate scientist Michael MacCracken, "qualified scientific experts involved in climate change research" have reached a "strong consensus" that global warming threatens (among other things) a precipitate rise in sea levels by the end of the century, "severe and irreversible changes to natural ecosystems," a "significant reduction in water storage in winter snowpack in mountainous regions with direct and important economic consequences," and an increase in the spread of disease. He also observes that rising ocean temperatures may contribute to the ferocity of hurricanes.

That these climate-change risks are "widely shared" does not minimize Massachusetts' interest in the outcome of this litigation. See *Federal Election Comm'n v. Akins,* 524 U.S. 11, 24 (1998) ("[W]here a harm is concrete, though widely shared, the Court has found 'injury in fact' "). According to petitioners' unchallenged affidavits, global sea levels rose somewhere between 10 and 20 centimeters over the 20th century as a result of global warming. These rising seas have already begun to swallow Massachusetts' coastal land. Because the Commonwealth "owns a substantial portion of the state's coastal property," it has alleged a particularized injury in its capacity as a landowner. The severity of that injury will only increase over the course of the next century: If sea levels continue to rise as predicted, one Massachusetts official believes that a significant fraction of coastal property will be "either permanently lost through inundation or temporarily lost through periodic storm surge and flooding events." Remediation costs alone, petitioners allege, could run well into the hundreds of millions of dollars.

Causation

EPA does not dispute the existence of a causal connection between man-made greenhouse gas emissions and global warming. At a minimum, therefore, EPA's refusal to regulate such emissions "contributes" to Massachusetts' injuries.

EPA nevertheless maintains that its decision not to regulate greenhouse gas emissions from new motor vehicles contributes so insignificantly to petitioners' injuries that the agency cannot be haled into federal court to answer for them. For the same reason, EPA does not believe that any realistic possibility exists that the relief petitioners seek would mitigate global climate change and remedy their injuries. That is especially so because predicted increases in greenhouse gas emissions from developing nations, particularly China and India, are likely to offset any marginal domestic decrease.

But EPA overstates its case. Its argument rests on the erroneous assumption that a small incremental step, because it is incremental, can never be attacked in a federal judicial forum. Yet accepting that premise would doom most challenges to regulatory action. Agencies, like legislatures, do not generally resolve massive problems in one fell regulatory swoop. They instead whittle away at them over time, refining their preferred approach as circumstances change and as they develop a more-nuanced understanding of how best to proceed. That a first step might be tentative does not by itself support the notion that federal courts lack jurisdiction to determine whether that step conforms to law.

And reducing domestic automobile emissions is hardly a tentative step. Even leaving aside the other greenhouse gases, the United States transportation sector emits an enormous quantity of carbon dioxide into the atmosphere—according to the MacCracken affidavit, more than 1.7 billion metric tons in 1999 alone. That accounts for more than 6% of worldwide carbon dioxide emissions. To put this in perspective: Considering just emissions from the transportation sector, which represent less than one-third of this country's total carbon dioxide emissions, the United States would still rank as the third-largest emitter of carbon dioxide in the world, outpaced only by the European Union and China. Judged by any standard, U.S. motor-vehicle emissions make a meaningful contribution to greenhouse gas concentrations and hence, according to petitioners, to global warming.

The Remedy

While it may be true that regulating motor-vehicle emissions will not by itself *reverse* global warming, it by no means follows that we lack jurisdiction to decide whether EPA has a duty to take steps to *slow* or *reduce* it. See also *Larson v. Valente,* 456 U.S. 228, 244, n. 15 (1982) ("[A] plaintiff satisfies the redressability requirement when he shows that a favorable decision will relieve a discrete injury to himself. He need not show that a favorable decision will relieve his *every* injury"). Because of the enormity of the potential consequences associated with man-made climate change, the fact that the effectiveness of a remedy might be delayed during the (relatively short) time it takes for a new motor-vehicle fleet to replace an older one is essentially irrelevant.[23] Nor is it dispositive that developing countries such as China and India are poised to increase greenhouse gas emissions substantially over the next century: A reduction in domestic emissions would slow the pace of global emissions increases, no matter what happens elsewhere.

We moreover attach considerable significance to EPA's "agree[ment] with the President that 'we must address the issue of global climate change,' " and to EPA's ardent support for various voluntary emission-reduction programs. As Judge Tatel observed in dissent below, "EPA would presumably not bother with such efforts if it thought emissions reductions would have no discernable impact on future global warming."

In sum—at least according to petitioners' uncontested affidavits—the rise in sea levels associated with global warming has already harmed and will continue to harm Massachusetts. The risk of catastrophic harm, though remote, is nevertheless real. That risk would be reduced to some extent if petitioners received the relief they seek. We therefore hold that petitioners have standing to challenge the EPA's denial of their rulemaking petition. [The Court then went on to rule on the merits in plaintiffs' favor.]

Chief Justice ROBERTS, with whom Justice SCALIA, Justice THOMAS, and Justice ALITO join, dissenting.

Global warming may be a "crisis," even "the most pressing environmental problem of our time." Indeed, it may ultimately affect nearly everyone on the planet in some potentially adverse way, and it may be that governments have done too little to address it. It is not a problem, however, that has escaped the attention of policymakers in the Executive and Legislative Branches of our Government, who continue to consider regulatory, legislative, and treaty-based means of addressing global climate change.

Apparently dissatisfied with the pace of progress on this issue in the elected branches, petitioners have come to the courts claiming broad-ranging injury, and attempting to tie that injury to the Government's

23. See also *Mountain States Legal Foundation v. Glickman,* 92 F.3d 1228, 1234 (C.A.D.C.1996) ("The more drastic the injury that government action makes more likely, the lesser the increment in probability to establish standing"); *Village of Elk Grove Village v. Evans,* 997 F.2d 328, 329 (C.A.7 1993) ("[E]ven a small probability of injury is sufficient to create a case or controversy-to take a suit out of the category of the hypothetical-provided of course that the relief sought would, if granted, reduce the probability").

alleged failure to comply with a rather narrow statutory provision. I would reject these challenges as nonjusticiable. Such a conclusion involves no judgment on whether global warming exists, what causes it, or the extent of the problem. Nor does it render petitioners without recourse. This Court's standing jurisprudence simply recognizes that redress of grievances of the sort at issue here "is the function of Congress and the Chief Executive," not the federal courts. *Lujan v. Defenders of Wildlife,* 504 U.S. 555, 576 (1992). I would vacate the judgment below and remand for dismissal of the petitions for review.

John Roberts

President George W. Bush appointed Roberts Chief Justice in 2005. Previously Roberts had been a judge on the D.C. Circuit Court of Appeals to which he had been appointed in 2003. As a young attorney, Roberts clerked for Justice William Rehnquist and then worked in the Reagan administration in both the Justice Department and White House. He then went to private practice in Washington, DC, for three years where he focused on appellate litigation. This prepared him for a four-year stint in the Solicitor General's office in the Department of Justice, where he argued 39 cases before the Supreme Court. He then returned to private practice until his appointment to the DC Circuit. In his confirmation hearings, Roberts indicated a desire to bring the Court together, to avoid major split decisions. In that he has not been successful, but he has established himself as a solid vote on the conservative wing of the Court.

I

Article III, § 2, of the Constitution limits the federal judicial power to the adjudication of "Cases" and "Controversies." "If a dispute is not a proper case or controversy, the courts have no business deciding it, or expounding the law in the course of doing so." *DaimlerChrysler Corp. v. Cuno,* 126 S.Ct. 1854, 1860–1861 (2006). "Standing to sue is part of the common understanding of what it takes to make a justiciable case," *Steel Co. v. Citizens for Better Environment,* 523 U.S. 83, 102 (1998), and has been described as "an essential and unchanging part of the case-or-controversy requirement of Article III," *Defenders of Wildlife, supra,* at 560.

Our modern framework for addressing standing is familiar: "A plaintiff must allege personal injury fairly traceable to the defendant's allegedly unlawful conduct and likely to be redressed by the requested relief." *DaimlerChrysler, supra,* at 1861. Applying that standard here, petitioners bear the burden of alleging an injury that is fairly traceable to the Environmental Protection Agency's failure to promulgate new motor vehicle greenhouse gas emission standards, and that is likely to be redressed by the prospective issuance of such standards.

Before determining whether petitioners can meet this familiar test, however, the Court changes the rules. It asserts that

"States are not normal litigants for the purposes of invoking federal jurisdiction," and that given "Massachusetts' stake in protecting its quasi-sovereign interests, the Commonwealth is entitled to *special solicitude* in our standing analysis."

Relaxing Article III standing requirements because asserted injuries are pressed by a State, however, has no basis in our jurisprudence, and support for any such "special solicitude" is conspicuously absent from the Court's opinion. The general judicial review provision cited by the Court, 42 U.S.C. § 7607(b)(1), affords States no special rights or status.... Under the law on which petitioners rely, Congress treated public and private litigants exactly the same.

Nor does the case law cited by the Court provide any support for the notion that Article III somehow implicitly treats public and private litigants differently. The Court has to go back a full century in an attempt to justify its novel standing rule, but even there it comes up short. The Court's analysis hinges on *Georgia v. Tennessee Copper Co.,* 206 U.S. 230 (1907)–a case that did indeed draw a distinction between a State and private litigants, but solely with respect to available remedies. The case had nothing to do with Article III standing....

In contrast to the present case, there was no question in *Tennessee Copper* about Article III injury. There was certainly no suggestion that the State could show standing where the private parties could not; there was no dispute, after all, that the private landowners had "an action at law." *Tennessee Copper* has since stood for nothing more than a State's right, in an original jurisdiction action, to sue in a representative capacity as *parens patriae*. Nothing about a State's ability to sue in that capacity dilutes the bedrock requirement of showing injury, causation, and redressability to satisfy Article III....

A claim of *parens patriae* standing is distinct from an allegation of direct injury. Far from being a substitute for Article III injury, *parens patriae* actions raise an additional hurdle for a state litigant: the articulation of a "quasi-sovereign interest" "*apart* from the interests of particular private parties." Just as an association suing on behalf of its members must show not only that it represents the members but that at least one satisfies Article III requirements, so too a State asserting quasi-sovereign interests as *parens patriae* must still show that its citizens satisfy Article III. Focusing on Massachusetts's interests as quasi-sovereign makes the required showing here harder, not easier. The Court, in effect, takes what has always been regarded as a *necessary* condition for *parens patriae* standing—a quasi-sovereign interest—and converts it into a *sufficient* showing for purposes of Article III....

All of this presumably explains why petitioners never cited *Tennessee Copper* in their briefs before this Court or the D.C. Circuit. It presumably explains why not one of the legion of *amici* supporting petitioners ever cited the case. And it presumably explains why not one of the three judges writing below ever cited the case either.

II

It is not at all clear how the Court's "special solicitude" for Massachusetts plays out in the standing analysis, except as an implicit concession that petitioners cannot establish standing on traditional terms. But the status of Massachusetts as a State cannot compensate for petitioners' failure to demonstrate injury in fact, causation, and redressability.

When the Court actually applies the three-part test, it focuses ... on the State's asserted loss of coastal land as the injury in fact. If petitioners rely on loss of land as the Article III injury, however, they must ground the rest of the standing analysis in that specific injury. That alleged injury must be "concrete and particularized," and "distinct and palpable." Central to this concept of "particularized" injury is the requirement that a plaintiff be affected in a "personal and individual way" and seek relief that "directly and tangibly benefits him" in a manner distinct from its impact on "the public at large." Without "particularized injury, there can be no confidence of 'a real need to exercise the power of judicial review' or that relief can be framed 'no broader than required by the precise facts to which the court's ruling would be applied.' "

The very concept of global warming seems inconsistent with this particularization requirement. Global warming is a phenomenon "harmful to humanity at large," and the redress petitioners seek is focused no more on them than on the public generally—it is literally to change the atmosphere around the world.

If petitioners' particularized injury is loss of coastal land, it is also that injury that must be "actual or imminent, not conjectural or hypothetical," "real and immediate," and "certainly impending."

As to "actual" injury, the Court observes that "global sea levels rose somewhere between 10 and 20 centimeters over the 20th century as a result of global warming" and that "[t]hese rising seas have already begun to swallow Massachusetts' coastal land." But none of petitioners' declarations supports that connection....

The Court's attempts to identify "imminent" or "certainly impending" loss of Massachusetts coastal land fares no better. One of petitioners' declarants predicts global warming will cause sea level to rise by 20 to 70 centimeters *by the year 2100*. [A]ccepting a century-long time horizon and a series of compounded estimates renders requirements of imminence and immediacy utterly toothless. "Allegations of possible future injury do not satisfy the requirements of Art. III. A threatened injury must be *certainly impending* to constitute injury in fact."

III

Petitioners' reliance on Massachusetts's loss of coastal land as their injury in fact for standing purposes creates insurmountable problems for them with respect to causation and redressability. To establish standing, petitioners must show a causal connection between that specific injury and the lack of new motor vehicle greenhouse gas emission standards, and that the promulgation of such standards would likely redress that injury. As is often the case, the questions of causation and redressability overlap. And importantly, when a party is challenging the Government's allegedly unlawful regulation, or lack of regulation, of a third party, satisfying the causation and redressability requirements becomes "substantially more difficult."

Petitioners view the relationship between their injuries and EPA's failure to promulgate new motor vehicle greenhouse gas emission standards as simple and direct: Domestic motor vehicles emit carbon dioxide and other greenhouse gases. Worldwide emissions of greenhouse gases contribute to global warming and therefore also to petitioners' alleged injuries. Without the new vehicle standards, greenhouse gas emissions—and therefore global warming and its attendant harms—have been higher than they otherwise would have been; once EPA changes course, the trend will be reversed.

The Court ignores the complexities of global warming, and does so by now disregarding the "particularized" injury it relied on in step one, and using the dire nature of global warming itself as a bootstrap for finding causation and redressability. First, it is important to recognize the extent of the emissions at issue here. Because local greenhouse gas emissions disperse throughout the atmosphere and remain there for anywhere from 50 to 200 years, it is global emissions data that are relevant. According to one of petitioners' declarations, domestic motor vehicles contribute about 6 percent of global carbon dioxide emissions and 4 percent of global greenhouse gas emissions. The amount of global emissions at issue here is smaller still; § 202(a)(1) of the Clean Air Act covers only *new* motor vehicles and *new* motor vehicle engines, so petitioners' desired emission standards might reduce only a fraction of 4 percent of global emissions.

This gets us only to the relevant greenhouse gas emissions; linking them to global warming and ultimately to petitioners' alleged injuries next requires consideration of further complexities. As EPA explained in its denial of petitioners' request for rulemaking,

> "predicting future climate change necessarily involves a complex web of economic and physical factors including: our ability to predict future global anthropogenic emissions of [greenhouse gases] and aerosols; the fate of these emissions once they enter the atmosphere (e.g., what percentage are absorbed by vegetation or are taken up by the oceans); the impact of those emissions that remain in the atmosphere on the radiative properties of the atmosphere; changes in critically important climate feedbacks (e.g., changes in cloud cover and ocean circulation); changes in temperature characteristics (e.g., average temperatures, shifts in daytime and evening temperatures); changes in other climatic parameters (e.g., shifts in precipitation, storms);

and ultimately the impact of such changes on human health and welfare (e.g., increases or decreases in agricultural productivity, human health impacts)."

Petitioners are never able to trace their alleged injuries back through this complex web to the fractional amount of global emissions that might have been limited with EPA standards. In light of the bit-part domestic new motor vehicle greenhouse gas emissions have played in what petitioners describe as a 150–year global phenomenon, and the myriad additional factors bearing on petitioners' alleged injury—the loss of Massachusetts coastal land—the connection is far too speculative to establish causation.

IV

Redressability is even more problematic. To the tenuous link between petitioners' alleged injury and the indeterminate fractional domestic emissions at issue here, add the fact that petitioners cannot meaningfully predict what will come of the 80 percent of global greenhouse gas emissions that originate outside the United States. As the Court acknowledges, "developing countries such as China and India are poised to increase greenhouse gas emissions substantially over the next century," so the domestic emissions at issue here may become an increasingly marginal portion of global emissions, and any decreases produced by petitioners' desired standards are likely to be overwhelmed many times over by emissions increases elsewhere in the world....

No matter, the Court reasons, because *any* decrease in domestic emissions will "slow the pace of global emissions increases, no matter what happens elsewhere." Every little bit helps, so Massachusetts can sue over any little bit.

The Court's sleight-of-hand is in failing to link up the different elements of the three-part standing test. What must be *likely* to be redressed is the particular injury in fact. The injury the Court looks to is the asserted loss of land. The Court contends that regulating domestic motor vehicle emissions will reduce carbon dioxide in the atmosphere, *and therefore* redress Massachusetts's injury. But even if regulation *does* reduce emissions—to some indeterminate degree, given events elsewhere in the world—the Court never explains why that makes it *likely* that the injury in fact—the loss of land—will be redressed. Schoolchildren know that a kingdom might be lost "all for the want of a horseshoe nail," but "likely" redressability is a different matter. The realities make it pure conjecture to suppose that EPA regulation of new automobile emissions will *likely* prevent the loss of Massachusetts coastal land....

[Justice SCALIA authored a dissent on the merits which Chief Justice ROBERTS and Justices ALITO and THOMAS joined.]

Comments and Questions

1. Compare the justices involved in *Defenders* and *Massachusetts*, how has the membership changed? How does that affect the different outcomes in these cases?

2. It seems clear that Massachusetts will be injured by global warming. It also seems clear that global warming is due at least in part from human activities, including automobile emissions. Why is it then that Chief Justice Roberts believes that Massachusetts lacks standing here?

3. Justice Stevens' opinion begins by stressing, first, that the Clean Air Act has a provision granting judicial review for final agency actions under that Act (here the denial of the petition for rulemaking), *see* 42 U.S.C. 7607(b), and second, that this was a case brought by a state, rather than a private litigant. How were these important to the conclusion that Massachusetts had standing? Didn't Justice Stevens demonstrate (at least to the majority's satisfaction) that Massachusetts was suffering an immediate, particularlized harm caused by EPA's failure to act and that its action would at least remedy that harm—the normal standard for assessing standing?

4. Are *Defenders* and *Massachusetts* consistent? What would Justice Stevens say? What would Justice Scalia say? Beginning in 1998, the Supreme Court seemed to become a little more relaxed with regard to standing. In *Federal Election Commission v. Akins*, 524 U.S. 11 (1998), the Court held (6–3) that a group that monitored political action committees had standing to challenge the failure of the FEC to require a particular PAC to submit reports, which would have been publicly available if made. Justice Scalia in dissent argued that this was a generalized grievance, complaining about executive failure to comply with the law, not a particularized injury. Justice Breyer for the Court said that the group's inability to obtain the reports was a particularized injury as to that group. In *Friends of the Earth v. Laidlaw Environmental Services*, 528 U.S. 167 (2000), the Court held (7–2) that an environmental group had standing to sue a wastewater treatment plant illegally discharging pollutants into a river, even though there was no evidence of any harm to the environment from the pollution, because members of the group had a "reasonable fear" that kept them from using the river for recreational purposes.

5. Congressmen have from time-to-time thought that they should have standing to challenge the constitutionality of laws which they thought violated the Constitution with respect to the procedures or prerogatives of Congress. In *Raines v. Byrd*, 521 U.S. 811 (1997), the Court denied standing to congressmen challenging the Line Item Veto Act (which will be considered later in this book). The Act allowed the President to cancel specific line item appropriations after they became law, and the congressmen argued that this authority diluted their votes for the appropriations, because they could be canceled thereafter. This was not a sufficient injury for them to have standing. If Congress passed a law prohibiting certain members from voting on certain types of bills, that would be different.

6. As of this writing, there is a congressman, Steve Buyer, who is at the same time a Lieutenant Colonel in the U.S. Army, and he is not

the only congressman who currently is a reserve officer. Is this constitutional? Who can decide that issue?

Problems

1. Congress passes a law prohibiting any person from practicing before federal courts unless they finished in the top half of their law school class. If the American Bar Association wished to challenge this law as unconstitutional, what would it have to demonstrate in order to avoid having the case dismissed as not presenting a case or controversy?

2. A city adopts a contracting rule that the city will not employ contractors unless they have at least 10 years of experience in the field. However, the rule creates an exception for any contractor owned by an underrepresented minority, in which case the contractor need only have two years experience in the field. A contractor not owned by an underrepresented minority sues, seeking an injunction against the rule's exception, on the grounds that it violates his right to equal protection of the laws. What must the contractor show in order to establish standing to bring this suit?

c. Political Questions

In *Marbury*, Chief Justice Marshall writes that, while executive acts may be reviewed if they are subject to law, "by the constitution of the United States, the President is invested with certain important political powers, in the exercise of which he is to use his own discretion, and is accountable only to his country in his political character, and to his own conscience." Thus, from the beginning, so to speak, the Court has recognized that certain matters are committed to the political arena, not the judicial arena, and the political arena is not limited to the Presidency. The difficulty is to determine which matters go where.

The case that is always referred to as best describing the taxonomy of political questions is *Baker v. Carr*.

BAKER v. CARR

United States Supreme Court, 1962.
369 U.S. 186, 82 S.Ct. 691, 7 L.Ed.2d 663.

[In this case, Baker was a voter living in an urban area of Tennessee, and Carr was the Secretary of State of Tennessee, one of whose responsibilities was administering elections in Tennessee. Baker complained that the 99 representatives in the state House of Representatives and the 33 Senators were apportioned to districts in the state based upon a 1901 law. He argued that, as a result of changes in the population in the intervening 60 years, he and persons like him in urban areas were systematically discriminated against in terms of their representation in violation of the Equal Protection Clause of the Fourteenth Amendment. The initial question, however, was whether this was a case able to be heard by federal courts. In other words, was it "justiciable"? The Court first determined that Baker had standing to bring the case. Then, the Court addressed the defendant's argument that the apportionment of representatives was a political question left to state legislatures and was not a justiciable issue for judicial resolution.]

William Brennan
President Eisenhower appointed Brennan to the Supreme Court in 1956. At the time Brennan was serving on the New Jersey Supreme Court, and political advisors to Eisenhower believed appointing a Catholic Democrat from the Northeast would help in Eisenhower's reelection campaign. Brennan was an eager ally for Chief Justice Warren's activist view of the judiciary to protect individual rights, and he served as its prime mover after Warren left the Court and until 1990 when he retired for reasons of ill health.

Mr. Justice BRENNAN delivered the opinion of the Court.

[W]e hold that this challenge to an apportionment presents no nonjusticiable "political question." Of course the mere fact that the suit seeks protection of a political right does not mean it presents a political question.... Rather, [Tennessee argues] that apportionment cases, whatever the actual wording of the complaint, can involve no federal constitutional right except one resting on the guaranty of a republican form of government,[30] and that complaints based on that clause have been held to present political questions which are nonjusticiable.

We hold that the claim pleaded here neither rests upon nor implicates the Guaranty Clause and that its justiciability is therefore not foreclosed by our decisions of cases involving that clause.... To show why we reject the argument based on the Guaranty Clause, we must examine the authorities under it. But because there appears to be some uncertainty as to why those cases did present political questions, and specifically as to whether this apportionment case is like those cases, we deem it necessary first to consider the contours of the "political question" doctrine.

Our discussion, even at the price of extending this opinion, requires review of a number of political question cases, in order to expose the attributes of the doctrine—attributes which, in various settings, diverge, combine, appear, and disappear in seeming disorderliness. Since that review is undertaken solely to demonstrate that neither singly nor collectively do these cases support a conclusion that this apportionment case is nonjusti-

30. "The United States shall guarantee to every State in this Union a Republican Form of Government, and shall protect each of them against Invasion; and on Application of the Legislature, or of the Executive (when the Legislature cannot be convened) against domestic Violence." U.S.Const. Art. IV, § 4.

ciable, we of course do not explore their implications in other contexts. That review reveals that in the Guaranty Clause cases and in the other "political question" cases, it is the relationship between the judiciary and the coordinate branches of the Federal Government, and not the federal judiciary's relationship to the States, which gives rise to the "political question."

We have said that "In determining whether a question falls within (the political question) category, the appropriateness under our system of government of attributing finality to the action of the political departments and also the lack of satisfactory criteria for a judicial determination are dominant considerations." The nonjusticiability of a political question is primarily a function of the separation of powers. Much confusion results from the capacity of the "political question" label to obscure the need for case-by-case inquiry. Deciding whether a matter has in any measure been committed by the Constitution to another branch of government, or whether the action of that branch exceeds whatever authority has been committed, is itself a delicate exercise in constitutional interpretation, and is a responsibility of this Court as ultimate interpreter of the Constitution. To demonstrate this requires no less than to analyze representative cases and to infer from them the analytical threads that make up the political question doctrine. We shall then show that none of those threads catches this case.

Foreign relations: There are sweeping statements to the effect that all questions touching foreign relations are political questions. Not only does resolution of such issues frequently turn on standards that defy judicial application, or involve the exercise of a discretion demonstrably committed to the executive or legislature; but many such questions uniquely demand single-voiced statement of the Government's views. Yet it is error to suppose that every case or controversy which touches foreign relations lies beyond judicial cognizance. Our cases in this field seem invariably to show a discriminating analysis of the particular question posed, in terms of the history of its management by the political branches, of its susceptibility to judicial handling in the light of its nature and posture in the specific case, and of the possible consequences of judicial action. For example, though a court will not ordinarily inquire whether a treaty has been terminated, since on that question "governmental action * * * must be regarded as of controlling importance," if there has been no conclusive "governmental action" then a court can construe a treaty and may find it provides the answer....

Dates of duration of hostilities: Though it has been stated broadly that "the power which declared the necessity is the power to declare its cessation, and what the cessation requires," here too analysis reveals isolable reasons for the presence of political questions, underlying this Court's refusal to review the political departments' determination of when or whether a war has ended....

Validity of enactments: In *Coleman v. Miller*, [307 U.S. 433 (1939)], this Court held that the questions of how long a proposed amendment to the Federal Constitution remained open to ratification, and what effect a prior rejection had on a subsequent ratification, were committed to congressional resolution and involved criteria of decision that necessarily escaped the judicial grasp. Similar considerations apply to the enacting process: "The respect due to coequal and independent departments," and the need for finality and certainty about the status of a statute contribute to judicial reluctance to inquire whether, as passed, it complied with all requisite formalities. But it is not true that courts will never delve into a legislature's records upon such a quest: If the enrolled statute lacks an effective date, a court will not hesitate to seek it in the legislative journals in order to preserve the enactment. The political question doctrine, a tool for maintenance of governmental order, will not be so applied as to promote only disorder.

The status of Indian tribes: This Court's deference to the political departments in determining whether Indians are recognized as a tribe, while it reflects familiar attributes of political questions, also has a unique element in that "the relation of the Indians to the United States is marked by peculiar and cardinal distinctions which exist no where else. * * * (The Indians are) domestic dependent nations * * * in a state of pupilage. Their relation to the United States resembles that of a ward to his guardian." Yet, here too, there is no blanket rule....

It is apparent that several formulations which vary slightly according to the settings in which the questions arise may describe a political question, although each has one or more elements which identify it as essentially a function of the separation of powers. Prominent on the surface of any case held to involve a political question is found a textually demonstrable constitutional commitment of the issue to a coordinate political department; or a lack of judicially discoverable and manageable standards for resolving it; or the impossibility of deciding without an initial policy determination of a kind clearly for nonjudicial discretion; or the impossibility of a court's undertaking independent resolution without expressing lack of the respect due coordinate branches of government; or an unusual need for unquestioning adherence to a political decision already made; or the potentiality of embarrassment from multifarious pronouncements by various departments on one question.

Unless one of these formulations is inextricable from the case at bar, there should be no dismissal for non-justiciability on the ground of a political question's presence. The doctrine of which we treat is one of "political questions," not one of "political cases." The courts cannot reject as "no law suit" a bona fide controversy as to whether some action denominated "political" exceeds constitutional authority. The cases we have reviewed show the necessity for discriminating inquiry into the precise facts and posture of the particular case, and the impossibility of resolution by any semantic cataloguing.

But it is argued that this case shares the characteristics of decisions that constitute a category not yet considered, cases concerning the Constitution's guaranty, in Art. IV, § 4, of a republican form of government.

A conclusion as to whether the case at bar does present a political question cannot be confidently reached until we have considered those cases with special care. We shall discover that Guaranty Clause claims involve those elements which define a "political question," and for that reason and no other, they are nonjusticiable. In particular, we shall discover that the nonjusticiability of such claims has nothing to do with their touching upon matters of state governmental organization.

Republican form of government: *Luther v. Borden*, 7 How. 1, 12 L.Ed. 581 [1849], though in form simply an action for damages for trespass was, as Daniel Webster said in opening the argument for the defense, "an unusual case." The defendants, admitting an otherwise tortious breaking and entering, sought to justify their action on the ground that they were agents of the established lawful government of Rhode Island, which State was then under martial law to defend itself from active insurrection; that the plaintiff was engaged in that insurrection; and that they entered under orders to arrest the plaintiff. The case arose "out of the unfortunate political differences which agitated the people of Rhode Island in 1841 and 1842," and which had resulted in a situation wherein two groups laid competing claims to recognition as the lawful government....

[N]o provision of the Constitution could be or had been invoked for this purpose except Art. IV, § 4, the Guaranty Clause. Having already noted the absence of standards whereby the choice between governments could be made by a court acting independently, Chief Justice Taney now found further textual and practical reasons for concluding that, if any department of the United States was empowered by the Guaranty Clause to resolve the issue, it was not the judiciary: "Under this article of the Constitution it rests with Congress to decide what government is the established one in a State. For as the United States guarantee to each State a republican government, Congress must necessarily decide what government is established in the State before it can determine whether it is republican or not. And when the senators and representatives of a State are admitted into the councils of the Union, the authority of the government under which they are appointed, as well as its republican character, is recognized by the proper constitutional authority. And its decision is binding on every other department of the government, and could not be questioned in a judicial tribunal. It is true that the contest in this case did not last long enough to bring the matter to this issue; and * * * Congress was not called upon to decide the controversy. Yet the right to decide is placed there, and not in the courts....

Clearly, several factors were thought by the Court in Luther to make the question there "political": the commitment to the other branches of the decision as to which is the lawful state government; the unambiguous action by the President, in recognizing the charter government as the lawful authority; the need for finality in the executive's decision; and the lack of criteria by which a court could determine which form of government was republican.

But the only significance that Luther could have for our immediate purposes is in its holding that the Guaranty Clause is not a repository of judicially manageable standards which a court could utilize independently in order to identify a State's lawful government. The Court has since refused to resort to the Guaranty Clause—which alone had been invoked for the purpose—as the source of a constitutional standard for invalidating state action....

We come, finally, to the ultimate inquiry whether our precedents as to what constitutes a nonjusticiable "political question" bring the case before us under the umbrella of that doctrine. A natural beginning is to note whether any of the common characteristics which we have been able to identify and label descriptively are present. We find none: The question here is the consistency of state action with the Federal Constitution. We have no question decided, or to be decided, by a political branch of government coequal with this Court. Nor do we risk embarrassment of our government abroad, or grave disturbance at home if we take issue with Tennessee as to the constitutionality of her action here challenged. Nor need the appellants, in order to succeed in this action, ask the Court to enter upon policy determinations for which judicially manageable standards are lacking. Judicial standards under the Equal Protection Clause are well developed and familiar, and it has been open to courts since the enactment of the Fourteenth Amendment to determine, if on the particular facts they must, that a discrimination reflects no policy, but simply arbitrary and capricious action....

The judgment of the District Court is reversed and the cause is remanded for further proceedings consistent with this opinion.

Reversed and remanded.

[Mr. Justice FRANKFURTER, whom Mr. Justice HARLAN joined, dissented, believing the case was a political question.]

Comments and Questions

1. This decision occurs in the midst of an "activist" period in the Court's history. Justice Brennan, the author of the opinion, was a noted liberal and activist judge. Justice Frankfurter, one of the dissenters, was a political liberal, appointed by President Franklin Roosevelt, but a judicial conservative—meaning that he conceived of the courts as a last shield, not as an active sword, in protecting individuals. Here, he believed the Court would be engaging in an essentially political function in second-guessing the apportionment decisions of states, notwithstanding that a rural voter had more than 10 times the representation in the Tennessee legislature as an urban voter. *Baker v. Carr* remanded the case to the district court to decide the merits, the Supreme Court having found only that the case was justiciable. While Baker prevailed on the merits, Tennessee did not appeal that decision, so that the Supreme Court finally decided the one person/one vote requirement (meaning that states had to apportion their state representatives and federal represen-

tatives in proportion to the population as derived from the decennial census) in a different, but factually similar case from Alabama, *Reynolds v. Sims*, 377 U.S. 533 (1964). The effects of that case were felt nationwide, because the misapportionment in Tennessee and Alabama was reproduced in almost every state.

2. *Baker v. Carr* runs for some 90 pages in the United States Reports, so it has been radically edited here. Nonetheless, there is one paragraph in the opinion that states the doctrine that has been applied subsequently. Can you find it?

3. Knowing the doctrine still leaves a lot to judgment in individual cases. The following two cases provide a sample of its application.

POWELL v. McCORMACK

United States Supreme Court, 1969.
395 U.S. 486, 89 S.Ct. 1944, 23 L.Ed.2d 491.

[Adam Clayton Powell was an African–American congressman elected from the district in New York City that included Harlem. Prior to being elected to Congress, Powell had been a charismatic pastor of a local church and a prominent civil rights leader, who went on to be the first Black person elected to the New York City Council. Later, in 1944, Powell was elected to the U.S. House of Representatives—the first Black congressman from New York. In 1961, on the basis of seniority, he became the Chair of the House Education and Labor Committee. There he championed a number of progressive bills that became law. However, by the mid–60s, his dedication to the cause, if not his popularity in his district, seemed to flag. He spent increasing amounts of time at his private villa on Bimini in the Bahamas, living a luxurious life style with various female friends, apparently sustained by funds taken from his committee's budget, even while his wife was on the committee payroll but not performing any functions. Moreover, because he was perpetually absent, his committee no longer met. Between those members who disliked him for the progressive things he had done and those who were upset with his present abandonment of his duties and misuse of committee funds, in 1967 the 90th Congress voted to exclude him from his seat despite his reelection. He sued to reclaim his seat.]

Mr. Chief Justice WARREN delivered the opinion of the Court.

In November 1966, petitioner Adam Clayton Powell, Jr., was duly elected from the 18th Congressional District of New York to serve in the United States House of Representatives for the 90th Congress. However, pursuant to a House resolution, he was not permitted to take his seat. Powell (and some of the voters of his district) then filed suit in Federal District Court, claiming that the House could exclude him only if it found he failed to meet the standing requirements of age, citizenship, and residence contained in Art. I, § 2, of the Constitution—requirements the House specifically found Powell met—and thus had excluded him unconstitutionally....

VI.

Justiciability.

[W]e turn to the question whether the case is justiciable. [W]e must determine whether the structure of the Federal Government renders the issue presented a "political question"—that is, a question which is not justiciable in federal court because of the separation of powers provided by the Constitution.

B. Political Question Doctrine.

1. Textually Demonstrable Constitutional Commitment.

Respondents maintain that even if this case is otherwise justiciable, it presents only a political question. It is well established that the federal courts will not adjudicate political questions. In *Baker v. Carr* we noted that political questions are not justiciable primarily because of the separation of powers within the Federal Government. After reviewing our decisions in this area, we concluded that on the surface of any case held to involve a political question was at least one of the following formulations:

> a textually demonstrable constitutional commitment of the issue to a co-ordinate political department; or a lack of judicially discoverable and manageable standards for resolving it; or the impossibility of deciding without an initial policy determination of a kind clearly for nonjudicial discretion; or the impossibility of a court's undertaking independent resolution without expressing lack of the respect due co-ordinate branches of government; or an unusual need for unquestioning adherence to a political decision already made; or the potentiality of embarrassment from multifarious pronouncements by various departments on one question.

Respondents' first contention is that this case presents a political question because under Art. I, § 5, there has been a "textually demonstrable constitutional commitment" to the House of the "adjudicatory power" to determine Powell's qualifications. Thus it is argued that the House, and the House alone, has power to determine who is qualified to be a member.

In order to determine whether there has been a textual commitment to a coordinate department of the Government, we must interpret the Constitution. In other words, we must first determine what power the Constitution confers upon the House through Art. I, § 5, before we can determine to what extent, if any, the exercise of that power is subject to judicial review. Respondents maintain that the House has broad power under § 5, and, they argue, the House may determine which are the qualifications necessary for membership. On the other hand, petitioners allege that the Constitution provides that an elected representative may be denied his seat only if the House finds he does not meet one of the standing qualifications expressly prescribed by the Constitution.

If examination of § 5 disclosed that the Constitution gives the House judicially unreviewable power to set qualifications for membership and to judge whether prospective members meet those qualifications, further review of the House determination might well be barred by the political question doctrine. On the other hand, if the Constitution gives the House power to judge only whether elected members possess the three standing qualifications set forth in the Constitution, further consideration would be necessary to determine whether any of the other formulations of the political question doctrine are "inextricable from the case at bar."[41]

In other words, whether there is a "textually demonstrable constitutional commitment of the issue to a coordinate political department" of government and what is the scope of such commitment are questions we must resolve for the first time in this case. For, as we pointed out in *Baker v. Carr*, "(d)eciding whether a matter has in any measure been committed by the Constitution to another branch of government, or whether the action of that branch exceeds whatever authority has been committed, is itself a delicate exercise in constitutional interpretation, and is a responsibility of this Court as ultimate interpreter of the Constitution."

In order to determine the scope of any "textual commitment" under Art. I, § 5, we necessarily must determine the meaning of the phrase to "be the Judge of the Qualifications of its own Members." Petitioners argue that the records of the debates during the Constitutional Convention; available commentary from the post-Convention, pre-ratification period; and early congressional applications of Art. I, § 5, support their construction of the section. Respondents insist, however, that a careful examination of the pre-Convention practices of the English Parliament and American colonial assemblies demonstrates that by 1787, a legislature's power to judge the qualifications of its members was generally understood to encompass exclusion or expulsion on the ground that an individual's character or past conduct rendered him unfit to serve. When the Constitution and the debates over its adoption are thus viewed in historical perspective, argue respondents, it becomes clear that the "qualifications" expressly set forth in the Constitution were not meant to

41. In addition to the three qualifications set forth in Art. I, § 2, Art. I, § 3, cl. 7, authorizes the disqualification of any person convicted in an impeachment proceeding from "any Office of honor, Trust or Profit under the United States"; Art. I, § 6, cl. 2, provides that "no Person holding any Office under the United States, shall be a Member of either House during his Continuance in Office"; and § 3 of the 14th Amendment disqualifies any person "who, having previously taken an oath * * * to support the Constitution of the United States, shall have engaged in insurrection or rebellion against the same, or given aid or comfort to the enemies thereof." It has been argued that each of these provisions, as well as the Guarantee Clause of Article IV and the oath requirement of Art. VI, cl. 3, is no less a "qualification" within the meaning of Art. I, § 5, than those set forth in Art. I, § 2. We need not reach this question, however, since both sides agree that Powell was not ineligible under any of these provisions.

limit the long-recognized legislative power to exclude or expel at will, but merely to establish "standing incapacities," which could be altered only by a constitutional amendment. Our examination of the relevant historical materials leads us to the conclusion that petitioners are correct and that the Constitution leaves the House without authority to exclude any person, duly elected by his constituents, who meets all the requirements for membership expressly prescribed in the Constitution.

[The Court considered the practice in England before independence and found that, while earlier parliament had excluded members who otherwise met the qualifications for office, there had been a strong reaction against that so that by the time of independence such exclusion was discredited. The Court then considered the ratification debates and found that they solidly, if not explicitly, supported the notion that exclusion could only be based on failure to meet the specified qualifications in the Constitution.]

c. Post–Ratification.

[Respondents] suggest that far more relevant is Congress' own understanding of its power to judge qualifications as manifested in post-ratification exclusion cases. Unquestionably, both the House and the Senate have excluded members-elect for reasons other than their failure to meet the Constitution's standing qualifications. For almost the first 100 years of its existence, however, Congress strictly limited its power to judge the qualifications of its members to those enumerated in the Constitution....

Had these congressional exclusion precedents been more consistent, their precedential value still would be quite limited. That an unconstitutional action has been taken before surely does not render that same action any less unconstitutional at a later date. Particularly in view of the Congress' own doubts in those few cases where it did exclude members-elect, we are not inclined to give its precedents controlling weight. The relevancy of prior exclusion cases is limited largely to the insight they afford in correctly ascertaining the draftsmen's intent. Obviously, therefore, the precedential value of these cases tends to increase in proportion to their proximity to the Convention in 1787. And, what evidence we have of Congress' early understanding confirms our conclusion that the House is without power to exclude any member-elect who meets the Constitution's requirements for membership.

d. Conclusion.

Had the intent of the Framers emerged from these materials with less clarity, we would nevertheless have been compelled to resolve any ambiguity in favor of a narrow construction of the scope of Congress' power to exclude members-elect. A fundamental principle of our representative democracy is, in Hamilton's words, "that the people should choose whom they please to govern them." As Madison pointed out at the Convention, this principle is undermined as much by limiting whom the people can select as by limiting the franchise itself. In apparent agreement with this basic philosophy, the Convention adopted his suggestion limiting the power to expel.... Moreover, it would effectively nullify the Convention's decision to require a two-thirds vote for expulsion. Unquestionably, Congress has an interest in preserving its institutional integrity, but in most cases that interest can be sufficiently safeguarded by the exercise of its power to punish its members for disorderly behavior and, in extreme cases, to expel a member with the concurrence of two-thirds. In short, both the intention of the Framers, to the extent it can be determined, and an examination of the basic principles of our democratic system persuade us that the Constitution does not vest in the Congress a discretionary power to deny membership by a majority vote.

For these reasons, we have concluded that Art. I, § 5, is at most a "textually demonstrable commitment" to Congress to judge only the qualifications expressly set forth in the Constitution. Therefore, the "textual commitment" formulation of the political question doctrine does not bar federal courts from adjudicating petitioners' claims....

Mr. Justice DOUGLAS [issued a concurring opinion].

Mr. Justice STEWART, dissent[ed on the grounds that the case was moot, because the session of Congress from which Powell was excluded had expired; he had been reelected and had been seated in the current Congress.]

William Rehnquist
Richard Nixon appointed Rehnquist an Associate Justice in 1971. In 1986, Chief Justice Burger resigned, and President Ronald Reagan appointed Rehnquist Chief Justice. Preferring to interpret the Constitution narrowly, Rehnquist penned several opinions that endorsed conservative ideals. In particular, he protected state interests relative to federal interests, authoring opinions finding federal statutes beyond Congress's power and upholding state sovereign immunity. Rehnquist also reflected conservative values by denying the existence of constitutional rights, like the right to privacy, that did not have a clear textual basis in the Constitution.

NIXON v. UNITED STATES

United States Supreme Court, 1993.
506 U.S. 224, 113 S.Ct. 732, 122 L.Ed.2d 1.

Chief Justice REHNQUIST delivered the opinion of the Court.

Petitioner Walter L. Nixon, Jr., asks this Court to decide whether Senate Rule XI, which allows a committee of Senators to hear evidence against an individual who has been impeached and to report that evidence to the full Senate, violates the Impeachment Trial Clause, Art. I, § 3, cl. 6. That Clause provides that the "Senate shall have the sole Power to try all Impeachments." But before we reach the merits of such a claim, we must decide whether it is "justiciable," that is, whether it is a claim that may be resolved by the courts. We conclude that it is not.

Nixon, a former Chief Judge of the United States District Court for the Southern District of Mississippi, was convicted by a jury of two counts of making false statements before a federal grand jury and sentenced to prison. The grand jury investigation stemmed from reports that Nixon had accepted a gratuity from a Mississippi businessman in exchange for asking a local district attorney to halt the prosecution of the businessman's son. Because Nixon refused to resign from his office as a United States District Judge, he continued to collect his judicial salary while serving out his prison sentence.

On May 10, 1989, the House of Representatives adopted three articles of impeachment for high crimes and misdemeanors. The first two articles charged Nixon with giving false testimony before the grand jury and the third article charged him with bringing disrepute on the Federal Judiciary.

After the House presented the articles to the Senate, the Senate voted to invoke its own Impeachment Rule XI, under which the presiding officer appoints a committee of Senators to "receive evidence and take testimony." The Senate committee held four days of hearings, during which 10 witnesses, including Nixon, testified. Pursuant to Rule XI, the committee presented the full Senate with a complete transcript of the proceeding and a Report stating the uncontested facts and summarizing the evidence on the contested facts. Nixon and the House impeachment managers submitted extensive final briefs to the full Senate and delivered arguments from the Senate floor during the three hours set aside for oral argument in front of that body. Nixon himself gave a personal appeal, and several Senators posed questions directly to both parties. The Senate voted by more than the constitutionally required two-thirds majority to convict Nixon on the first two articles. The presiding officer then entered judgment removing Nixon from his office as United States District Judge.

Nixon thereafter commenced the present suit, arguing that Senate Rule XI violates the constitutional grant of authority to the Senate to "try" all impeachments because it prohibits the whole Senate from taking part in the evidentiary hearings. Nixon sought a declaratory judgment that his impeachment conviction was void and that his judicial salary and privileges should be reinstated. The District Court held that his claim was nonjusticiable, and the Court of Appeals for the District of Columbia Circuit agreed. We granted certiorari.

A controversy is nonjusticiable—*i.e.,* involves a political question—where there is "a textually demonstrable constitutional commitment of the issue to a coordinate political department; or a lack of judicially discoverable and manageable standards for resolving it...." *Baker v. Carr.* But the courts must, in the first instance, interpret the text in question and determine whether and to what extent the issue is textually committed. See *ibid.; Powell v. McCormack.* As the discussion that follows makes clear, the concept of a textual commitment to a coordinate political department is not completely separate from the concept of a lack of judicially discoverable and manageable standards for resolving it; the lack of judicially manageable standards may strengthen the conclusion that there is a textually demonstrable commitment to a coordinate branch.

In this case, we must examine Art. I, § 3, cl. 6, to determine the scope of authority conferred upon the Senate by the Framers regarding impeachment. It provides:

> "The Senate shall have the sole Power to try all Impeachments. When sitting for that Purpose, they shall be on Oath or Affirmation. When the President of the United States is tried, the Chief Justice shall preside: And no Person shall be convicted without the Concurrence of two thirds of the Members present."

The language and structure of this Clause are revealing. The first sentence is a grant of authority to the Senate, and the word "sole" indicates that this authority is reposed in the Senate and nowhere else. The next two sentences specify requirements to which the Senate proceedings shall conform: The Senate shall be on oath or affirmation, a two-thirds vote is required to convict, and when the President is tried the Chief Justice shall preside.

Petitioner argues that the word "try" in the first sentence imposes by implication an additional requirement on the Senate in that the proceedings must be in the nature of a judicial trial. From there petitioner goes on to argue that this limitation precludes the Senate from delegating to a select committee the task of hearing the testimony of witnesses, as was done pursuant to Senate Rule XI. "[T]ry" means more than simply "vote on" or "review" or "judge." In 1787 and today, trying a case means hearing the evidence, not scanning a cold record. Brief for Petitioner 25. Petitioner concludes from this that courts may review whether or not the Senate "tried" him before convicting him.

There are several difficulties with this position which lead us ultimately to reject it. The word "try," both in 1787 and later, has considerably broader meanings than those to which petitioner would limit it. Older dictionaries define try as "[t]o examine" or "[t]o examine as a judge." *See* 2 S. Johnson, A Dictionary of the English Language (1785). In more modern usage the term has various meanings. For example, try can mean "to examine or investigate judicially," "to conduct the trial of," or "to put to the test by experiment, investigation, or trial." Webster's Third New International Dictionary 2457 (1971). Petitioner submits that "try," as contained in T. Sheridan, Dictionary of the English Language (1796), means "to examine as a judge; to bring before a judicial tribunal."

Based on the variety of definitions, however, we cannot say that the Framers used the word "try" as an implied limitation on the method by which the Senate might proceed in trying impeachments. "As a rule the Constitution speaks in general terms, leaving Congress to deal with subsidiary matters of detail as the public interests and changing conditions may require...."

The conclusion that the use of the word "try" in the first sentence of the Impeachment Trial Clause lacks sufficient precision to afford any judicially manageable standard of review of the Senate's actions is fortified by the existence of the three very specific requirements that the Constitution does impose on the Senate when trying impeachments: The Members must be under oath, a two-thirds vote is required to convict, and the Chief Justice presides when the President is tried. These limitations are quite precise, and their nature suggests that the Framers did not intend to impose additional limitations on the form of the Senate proceedings by the use of the word "try" in the first sentence.

Petitioner devotes only two pages in his brief to negating the significance of the word "sole" in the first sentence of Clause 6. As noted above, that sentence provides that "[t]he Senate shall have the sole Power to try all Impeachments." We think that the word "sole" is of considerable significance. Indeed, the word "sole" appears only one other time in the Constitution—with respect to the House of Representatives' "*sole* Power of Impeachment." Art. I, § 2, cl. 5 (emphasis added). The commonsense meaning of the word "sole" is that the Senate alone shall have authority to determine whether an individual should be acquitted or convicted. The dictionary definition bears this out. "Sole" is defined as "having no companion," "solitary," "being the only one," and "functioning ... independently and without assistance or interference." Webster's Third New International Dictionary 2168 (1971). If the courts may review the actions of the Senate in order to determine whether that body "tried" an impeached official, it is difficult to see how the Senate would be "functioning ... independently and without assistance or interference." ...

Petitioner finally argues that even if significance be attributed to the word "sole" in the first sentence of the Clause, the authority granted is to the Senate, and this means that "the Senate—not the courts, not a lay jury, not a Senate Committee—shall try impeachments." It would be possible to read the first sentence of the Clause this way, but it is not a natural reading. Petitioner's interpretation would bring into judicial purview not merely the sort of claim made by petitioner, but other similar claims based on the conclusion that the word "Senate" has imposed by implication limitations on procedures which the Senate might adopt. Such limitations would be inconsistent with the construction of the Clause as a whole, which, as we have noted, sets out three express limitations in separate sentences.

The history and contemporary understanding of the impeachment provisions support our reading of the constitutional language. The parties do not offer evidence of a single word in the history of the Constitutional Convention or in contemporary commentary that even alludes to the possibility of judicial review in the context of the impeachment powers. This silence is quite meaningful in light of the several explicit references to the availability of judicial review as a check on the Legislature's power with respect to bills of attainder, *ex post facto* laws, and statutes.

The Framers labored over the question of where the impeachment power should lie. Significantly, in at least two considered scenarios the power was placed with the Federal Judiciary. Indeed, James Madison and the Committee of Detail proposed that the Supreme Court should have the power to determine impeachments. Despite these proposals, the Convention ultimately decided that the Senate would have "the sole Power to try all Impeachments." Art. I, § 3, cl. 6. According to Alexander Hamilton, the Senate was the "most fit depositary of this important trust" because its Members are representatives of the people. The Supreme Court was not the proper body because the Framers "doubted whether the members of that tribunal would, at all times, be endowed with so eminent a portion of fortitude as would be called for in the execution of so difficult a task" or whether the Court "would possess the degree of credit and authority" to carry out its judgment if it conflicted with the accusation brought by the Legislature—the people's representative. In addition, the Framers believed the Court was too small in number: "The awful discretion, which a court of impeachments must necessarily have, to doom to honor or to infamy the most confidential and the most distinguished characters of the community, forbids the commitment of the trust to a small number of persons."

There are two additional reasons why the Judiciary, and the Supreme Court in particular, were not chosen to have any role in impeachments. First, the Framers recognized that most likely there would be two sets of proceedings for individuals who commit impeachable offenses—the impeachment trial and a separate criminal trial. In fact, the Constitution explicitly provides for two separate proceedings. *See* Art. I, § 3, cl. 7. The Framers deliberately separated the two forums to avoid raising the specter of bias and to ensure independent judgments:

> "Would it be proper that the persons, who had disposed of his fame and his most valuable rights as a citizen in one trial, should in another trial, for the same offence, be also the disposers of his life and his fortune? Would there not be the greatest reason to apprehend, that error in the first sentence would be the parent of error in the second sentence? That the strong bias of one decision would be apt to overrule the influence of any new lights, which might be brought to vary the complexion of another decision?" The Federalist No. 65, p. 442 (J. Cooke ed. 1961).

Certainly judicial review of the Senate's "trial" would introduce the same risk of bias as would participation in the trial itself.

Second, judicial review would be inconsistent with the Framers' insistence that our system be one of checks and balances. In our constitutional system, impeachment was designed to be the *only* check on the Judicial Branch by the Legislature. On the topic of judicial accountability, Hamilton wrote:

> "The precautions for their responsibility are comprised in the article respecting impeachments. They are liable to be impeached for mal-conduct by the house of representatives, and tried by the senate, and if convicted, may be dismissed from office and disqualified for holding any other. *This is the only provision on the point, which is consistent with the necessary independence of the judicial character, and is the only one which we find in our own constitution in respect to our own judges."* *Id.*, No. 79, at 532–533 (emphasis added).

Judicial involvement in impeachment proceedings, even if only for purposes of judicial review, is counterintuitive because it would eviscerate the "important constitutional check" placed on the Judiciary by the Framers. Nixon's argument would place final reviewing authority with respect to impeachments in the hands of the same body that the impeachment process is meant to regulate.

Nevertheless, Nixon argues that judicial review is necessary in order to place a check on the Legislature. Nixon fears that if the Senate is given unreviewable authority to interpret the Impeachment Trial Clause, there is a grave risk that the Senate will usurp judicial power. The Framers anticipated this objection and created two constitutional safeguards to keep the Senate in check. The first safeguard is that the whole of the impeachment power is divided between the two legislative bodies, with the House given the right to accuse and the Senate given the right to judge. This split of authority "avoids the inconvenience of making the same persons both accusers and judges; and guards against the danger of persecution from the prevalency of a factious spirit in either of those branches." The second safeguard is the two-thirds supermajority vote requirement. Hamilton explained that "[a]s the concurrence of two-thirds of the senate will be requisite to a condemnation, the security to innocence, from this additional circumstance, will be as complete as itself can desire."

In addition to the textual commitment argument, we are persuaded that the lack of finality and the difficulty of fashioning relief counsel against justiciability. We agree with the Court of Appeals that opening the door of judicial review to the procedures used by the Senate in trying impeachments would "expose the political life of the country to months, or perhaps years, of chaos." This lack of finality would manifest itself most dramatically if the President were impeached. The legitimacy of any successor, and hence his effectiveness, would be impaired severely, not merely while the judicial process was running its course, but during any retrial that a differently constituted Senate might conduct if its first judgment of conviction were invalidated. Equally uncertain is the question of what relief a court may give other than simply setting aside the judgment of conviction. Could it order the reinstatement of a convicted federal judge, or order Congress to create an additional judgeship if the seat had been filled in the interim?

Petitioner finally contends that a holding of nonjusticiability cannot be reconciled with our opinion in *Powell v. McCormack*. The relevant issue in *Powell* was whether courts could review the House of Representatives' conclusion that Powell was "unqualified" to sit as a Member because he had been accused of misappropriating public funds and abusing the process of the New York courts. We stated that the question of justiciability turned on whether the Constitution committed authority to the House to judge its Members' qualifications, and if so, the extent of that commitment. Article I, § 5, provides that "Each House shall be the Judge of the Elections, Returns and Qualifications of its own Members." In turn, Art. I, § 2, specifies three requirements for membership in the House: The candidate must be at least 25 years of age, a citizen of the United States for no less than seven years, and an inhabitant of the State he is chosen to represent. We held that, in light of the three requirements specified in the Constitution, the word "qualifications"—of which the House was to be the Judge—was of a precise, limited nature.

Our conclusion in *Powell* was based on the fixed meaning of "[q]ualifications" set forth in Art. I, § 2. The claim by the House that its power to "be the Judge of the Elections, Returns and Qualifications of its own Members" was a textual commitment of unreviewable authority was defeated by the existence of this separate provision specifying the only qualifications which might be imposed for House membership. The decision as to whether a Member satisfied these qualifications *was* placed with the House, but the decision as to what these qualifications consisted of was not.

In the case before us, there is no separate provision of the Constitution that could be defeated by allowing the Senate final authority to determine the meaning of the word "try" in the Impeachment Trial Clause. We agree with Nixon that courts possess power to review either legislative or executive action that transgresses identifiable textual limits. As we have made clear, "whether the action of [either the Legislative or Executive Branch] exceeds whatever authority has been committed, is itself a delicate exercise in constitutional interpretation, and is a responsibility of this Court as ultimate interpreter of the Constitution." But we conclude, after exercising that delicate responsibility, that the word "try" in the Impeachment Trial Clause does not provide an identifiable textual limit on the authority which is committed to the Senate.

For the foregoing reasons, the judgment of the Court of Appeals is

Affirmed.

Justice STEVENS, [wrote a concurring opinion.]

Justice WHITE, with whom Justice BLACKMUN joins, concurring in the judgment.

Petitioner contends that the method by which the Senate convicted him on two articles of impeachment violates Art. I, § 3, cl. 6, of the Constitution, which mandates that the Senate "try" impeachments. The Court is of the view that the Constitution forbids us even to consider his contention. I find no such prohibition and would therefore reach the merits of the claim. I concur in the judgment because the Senate fulfilled its constitutional obligation to "try" petitioner.

I

It should be said at the outset that, as a practical matter, it will likely make little difference whether the Court's or my view controls this case. This is so because the Senate has very wide discretion in specifying impeachment trial procedures and because it is extremely unlikely that the Senate would abuse its discretion and insist on a procedure that could not be deemed a trial by reasonable judges. Even taking a wholly practical approach, I would prefer not to announce an unreviewable discretion in the Senate to ignore completely the constitutional direction to "try" impeachment cases. When asked at oral argument whether that direction would be satisfied if, after a House vote to impeach, the Senate, without any procedure whatsoever, unanimously found the accused guilty of being "a bad guy," counsel for the United States answered that the Government's theory "leads me to answer that question yes." Especially in light of this advice from the Solicitor General, I would not issue an invitation to the Senate to find an excuse, in the name of other pressing business, to be dismissive of its critical role in the impeachment process.

Practicalities aside, however, since the meaning of a constitutional provision is at issue, my disagreement with the Court should be stated.

II

The majority states that the question raised in this case meets two of the criteria for political questions set out in *Baker v. Carr*. It concludes first that there is "a textually demonstrable constitutional commitment of the issue to a coordinate political department." It also finds that the question cannot be resolved for "a lack of judicially discoverable and manageable standards."

Of course the issue in the political question doctrine is *not* whether the constitutional text commits exclusive responsibility for a particular governmental function to one of the political branches. There are numerous instances of this sort of textual commitment, *e.g.*, Art. I, § 8, and it is not thought that disputes implicating these provisions are nonjusticiable. Rather, the issue is whether the Constitution has given one of the political branches final responsibility for interpreting the scope and nature of such a power.

Although *Baker* directs the Court to search for "a textually demonstrable constitutional commitment" of such responsibility, there are few, if any, explicit and unequivocal instances in the Constitution of this sort of textual commitment.... The courts therefore are usually left to infer the presence of a political question from the text and structure of the Constitution. In drawing the inference that the Constitution has committed final interpretive authority to one of the political branches, courts are sometimes aided by textual evidence that the Judiciary was not meant to exercise judicial review—a coordinate inquiry expressed in *Baker's* "lack of judicially discoverable and manageable standards" criterion. See, *e.g., Coleman v. Miller,* where the Court refused to determine the life span of a proposed constitutional amendment given Art. V's placement of the amendment process with Congress and the lack of any judicial standard for resolving the question.

A

The majority finds a clear textual commitment in the Constitution's use of the word "sole" in the phrase "[t]he Senate shall have the sole Power to try all Impeachments." It attributes "considerable significance" to the fact that this term appears in only one other passage in the Constitution. The Framers' sparing use of "sole" is thought to indicate that its employment in the Impeachment Trial Clause demonstrates a concern to give the Senate exclusive interpretive authority over the Clause.

In disagreeing with the Court, I note that the Solicitor General stated at oral argument that "[w]e don't rest our submission on sole power to try." The Government was well advised in this respect. The significance of the Constitution's use of the term "sole" lies not in the infrequency with which the term appears, but in the fact that it appears exactly twice, in parallel provisions concerning impeachment. That the word "sole" is found only in the House and Senate Impeachment Clauses demonstrates that its purpose is to emphasize the distinct role of each in the impeachment process. As the majority notes, the Framers, following English practice, were very much concerned to separate the prosecutorial from the adjudicative aspects of impeachment. Giving each House "sole" power with respect to its role in impeachments effected this division of labor. While the majority is thus right to interpret the term "sole" to indicate that the Senate ought to "functio[n] independently and without assistance or interference," it wrongly identifies the Judiciary, rather than the House, as the source of potential interference with which the Framers were concerned when they employed the term "sole."

Even if the Impeachment Trial Clause is read without regard to its Companion clause, the Court's willingness to abandon its obligation to review the constitutionality of legislative acts merely on the strength of the word "sole" is perplexing. Consider, by comparison, the treatment of Art. I, § 1, which grants "All legislative powers" to the House and Senate. As used in that context "all" is nearly synonymous with "sole"—both connote entire and exclusive authority. Yet the Court has never thought it would unduly interfere with the operation of the Legislative Branch to entertain difficult and important questions as to the extent of the legislative power. Quite the opposite, we have stated that the proper interpretation of the Clause falls within the province of the Judiciary....

The majority also claims support in the history and early interpretations of the Impeachment Clauses.... In light of these materials there can be little doubt that the Framers came to the view at the Convention that the trial of officials' public misdeeds should be conducted by representatives of the people; that the fledgling Judiciary lacked the wherewithal to adjudicate political intrigues; that the Judiciary ought not to try both impeachments and subsequent criminal cases emanating from them; and that the impeachment power must reside in the Legislative Branch to provide a check on the largely unaccountable Judiciary.

The majority's review of the historical record thus explains why the power to try impeachments properly resides with the Senate. It does not explain, however, the sweeping statement that the Judiciary was "not chosen to have any role in impeachments." Not a single word in the historical materials cited by the majority addresses judicial review of the Impeachment Trial Clause. And a glance at the arguments surrounding the Impeachment Clauses negates the majority's attempt to infer nonjusticiability from the Framers' arguments in support of the Senate's power to try impeachments.

What the relevant history mainly reveals is deep ambivalence among many of the Framers over the very institution of impeachment, which, by its nature, is not easily reconciled with our system of checks and balances. As they clearly recognized, the branch of the Federal Government which is possessed of the authority to try impeachments, by having final say over the membership of each branch, holds a potentially unanswerable power over the others. In addition, that branch, insofar as it is called upon to try not only members of other branches, but also its own, will have the advantage of being the judge of its own members' causes....

In essence, the majority suggests that the Framers' conferred upon Congress a potential tool of legislative dominance yet at the same time rendered Congress' exercise of that power one of the very few areas of legislative authority immune from any judicial review. While the majority rejects petitioner's justiciability argument as espousing a view "inconsistent with the Framers' insistence that our system be one of checks and balances," it is the Court's finding of nonjusticiability that truly upsets the Framers' careful design. In a truly balanced system, impeachments tried by the Senate would serve as a means of controlling the largely unaccountable Judiciary, even as judicial review would ensure that the Senate adhered to a minimal set of procedural standards in conducting impeachment trials.

B

The majority also contends that the term "try" does not present a judicially manageable standard. It notes that in 1787, as today, the word "try" may refer to an inquiry in the nature of a judicial proceeding, or, more generally, to experimentation or investigation. In light of the term's multiple senses, the Court finds itself unable to conclude that the Framers used the word "try" as "an implied limitation on the method by which the Senate might proceed in trying impeachments." Also according to the majority, comparison to the other more specific requirements listed in the Impeachment Trial Clause—that the senators must proceed under oath and vote by two-thirds to convict, and that the Chief Justice must preside over an impeachment trial of the President—indicates that the word "try" was not meant by the Framers to constitute a limitation on the Senate's conduct and further reveals the term's unmanageability.

It is apparently on this basis that the majority distinguishes *Powell v. McCormack*.... The majority finds this case different from *Powell* only on the grounds that, whereas the qualifications of Art. I, § 2, are readily susceptible to judicial interpretation, the term "try" does not provide an "identifiable textual limit on the authority which is committed to the Senate."

This argument comes in two variants. The first, which asserts that one simply cannot ascertain the sense of "try" which the Framers employed and hence cannot undertake judicial review, is clearly untenable. To begin with, one would intuitively expect that, in defining the power of a political body to conduct an inquiry into official wrongdoing, the Framers used "try" in its legal sense. That intuition is borne out by reflection on the alternatives. The third Clause of Art. I, § 3, cannot seriously be read to mean that the Senate shall "attempt" or "experiment with" impeachments. It is equally implausible to say that the Senate is charged with "investigating" impeachments given that this description would substantially overlap with the House of Representatives' "sole" power to draw up articles of impeachment. That these alternatives are not realistic possibilities is finally evidenced by the use of "tried" in the third sentence of the Impeachment Trial Clause ("[w]hen the President of the United States is tried ..."), and by Art. III, § 2, cl. 3 ("[t]he Trial of all Crimes, except in Cases of Impeachment ...").

The other variant of the majority position focuses not on which sense of "try" is employed in the Impeachment Trial Clause, but on whether the legal sense of that term creates a judicially manageable standard. The majority concludes that the term provides no "identifiable textual limit." Yet, as the Government itself conceded at oral argument, the term "try" is hardly so elusive as the majority would have it. Were the Senate, for example, to adopt the practice of automatically entering a judgment of conviction whenever articles of impeachment were delivered from the House, it is quite clear that the Senate will have failed to "try" impeachments. Indeed in this respect, "try" presents no greater, and perhaps fewer, interpretive difficulties than some other constitutional standards that have been found amenable to familiar techniques of judicial construction, including, for example, "Commerce ... among the several States," Art. I, § 8, cl. 3, and "due process of law," Amdt. 5.[3]

III

The majority's conclusion that "try" is incapable of meaningful judicial construction is not without irony. One might think that if any class of concepts would fall within the definitional abilities of the Judiciary, it would be that class having to do with procedural justice. Examination of the remaining question—whether proceedings in accordance with Senate Rule XI are compatible with the Impeachment Trial Clause—confirms this intuition.

Petitioner bears the rather substantial burden of demonstrating that, simply by employing the word "try," the Constitution prohibits the Senate from relying on a fact-finding committee. It is clear that the Framers were familiar with English impeachment practice and with that of the States employing a variant of the English model at the time of the Constitutional Convention. Hence there is little doubt that the term "try" as used in Art. I, § 3, cl. 6, meant that the Senate should conduct its proceedings in a manner somewhat resembling a judicial proceeding. Indeed, it is safe to assume that Senate trials were to follow the practice in England and the States, which contemplated a formal hearing on the charges, at which the accused would be represented by counsel, evidence would be presented, and the accused would have the opportunity to be heard.

Petitioner argues, however, that because committees were not used in state impeachment trials prior to the Convention, the word "try" cannot be interpreted to permit their use. It is, however, a substantial leap to infer from the absence of a particular device of parliamentary procedure that its use has been forever barred by the Constitution. And there is textual and historical evidence that undermines the inference sought to be drawn in this case.

[Justice White then analyses the historical practice of impeachment and the text of the Constitution.] In short, textual and historical evidence reveals that the Impeachment Trial Clause was not meant to bind the hands of the Senate beyond establishing a set of minimal procedures. Without identifying the exact contours of these procedures, it is suffi-

3. The majority's in terrorem argument against justiciability—that judicial review of impeachments might cause national disruption and that the courts would be unable to fashion effective relief—merits only brief attention. In the typical instance, court review of impeachments would no more render the political system dysfunctional than has this litigation. Moreover, the same capacity for disruption was noted and rejected as a basis for not hearing *Powell*. The relief granted for unconstitutional impeachment trials would presumably be similar to the relief granted to other unfairly tried public employee-litigants. Finally, as applied to the special case of the President, the majority's argument merely points out that, were the Senate to convict the President without any kind of a trial, a constitutional crisis might well result. It hardly follows that the Court ought to refrain from upholding the Constitution in all impeachment cases. Nor does it follow that, in cases of Presidential impeachment, the Justices ought to abandon their constitutional responsibilities because the Senate has precipitated a crisis.

cient to say that the Senate's use of a factfinding committee under Rule XI is entirely compatible with the Constitution's command that the Senate "try all impeachments." Petitioner's challenge to his conviction must therefore fail.

IV

Petitioner has not asked the Court to conduct his impeachment trial; he has asked instead that it determine whether his impeachment was tried by the Senate. The majority refuses to reach this determination out of a laudable desire to respect the authority of the Legislature. Regrettably, this concern is manifested in a manner that does needless violence to the Constitution.[4] The deference that is owed can be found in the Constitution itself, which provides the Senate ample discretion to determine how best to try impeachments.

Justice SOUTER, concurring in the judgment.

I agree with the Court that this case presents a nonjusticiable political question. Because my analysis differs somewhat from the Court's, however, I concur in its judgment by this separate opinion.

As we cautioned in *Baker v. Carr*, "the 'political question' label" tends "to obscure the need for case-by-case inquiry." The need for such close examination is nevertheless clear from our precedents, which demonstrate that the functional nature of the political question doctrine requires analysis of "the precise facts and posture of the particular case," and precludes "resolution by any semantic cataloguing." ...

Whatever considerations feature most prominently in a particular case, the political question doctrine is "essentially a function of the separation of powers," existing to restrain courts "from inappropriate interference in the business of the other branches of Government," and deriving in large part from prudential concerns about the respect we owe the political departments. Not all interference is inappropriate or disrespectful, however, and application of the doctrine ultimately turns, as Learned Hand put it, on "how importunately the occasion demands an answer."

4. Although our views might well produce identical results in most cases, the same objection may be raised against the prudential version of political question doctrine presented by Justice SOUTER. According to the prudential view, judicial determination of whether the Senate has conducted an impeachment trial would interfere unacceptably with the Senate's work and should be avoided except where necessitated by the threat of grave harm to the constitutional order. As articulated, this position is missing its premise: No explanation is offered as to why it would show disrespect or cause disruption or embarrassment to review the action of the Senate in this case as opposed to, say, the enactment of legislation under the Commerce Clause. The Constitution requires the courts to determine the validity of statutes passed by Congress when they are challenged, even though such laws are passed with the firm belief that they are constitutional. The exercise of judicial review of this kind, with all of its attendant risk of interference and disrespect, is not conditioned upon a showing in each case that without it the Republic would be at risk. Some account is therefore needed as to why prudence does not counsel against judicial review in the typical case, yet does so in this case....

This occasion does not demand an answer.... It seems fair to conclude that the Clause contemplates that the Senate may determine, within broad boundaries, such subsidiary issues as the procedures for receipt and consideration of evidence necessary to satisfy its duty to "try" impeachments....

One can, nevertheless, envision different and unusual circumstances that might justify a more searching review of impeachment proceedings. If the Senate were to act in a manner seriously threatening the integrity of its results, convicting, say, upon a coin toss, or upon a summary determination that an officer of the United States was simply " 'a bad guy,' "judicial interference might well be appropriate. In such circumstances, the Senate's action might be so far beyond the scope of its constitutional authority, and the consequent impact on the Republic so great, as to merit a judicial response despite the prudential concerns that would ordinarily counsel silence....

Comments and Questions

1. Are these two cases compatible? Why is the question whether the judge was "tried" by the Senate a political question, but whether Powell met the "qualifications" to be a congressman was not?

2. What is the significance of the word "sole" in the Impeachment Clause? Is not the House the "sole" judge of the qualifications of its members?

3. In what way does Justice White disagree with Chief Justice Rehnquist? Note that Justice White concurs in the "judgment" of the Court, not in its opinion. This means that he agrees with the outcome of the case—Walter Nixon loses—but he does not agree with the Court's rationale. He has his own. What is it?

4. What point is Justice Souter making? He also concurs in the judgment but not in the opinion. How does he disagree with the Chief Justice?

5. Which opinions are "activist" and which are "conservative"?

6. Both these opinions turn on an assessment whether the Constitution has placed the decision in question in a place other than the judiciary. This is the essence of what a "political question" is. Often, however, unlike both *Powell* and *Nixon*, there is no constitutional language suggesting the commitment of the question in another branch. The Court in *Baker v. Carr* gives several examples. In those cases, the commitment to another branch must be inferred from the circumstances, rather than from any textual commitment. Even in *Nixon* we see Chief Justice Rehnquist bolster his textual argument by reference to other factors that suggest courts should not be involved. One of these other factors is when there is no legal standard to apply. If there is no legal standard to apply, that would suggest the decision is inappropriate for courts, because courts apply legal standards. However, to say there is no legal standard, such as whether there is a time limit for proposed

amendments to be ratified, *see Coleman v. Miller* (finding the issue a political question because the Constitution provided no legal standard to apply), is different from saying the legal standard is unclear. Which do you think was the case in *Nixon*?

7. Nevertheless, there are a number of cases we will come across where the Constitution is totally silent on an issue, but the Court demonstrates no reluctance to decide the case. For example, the Constitution says absolutely nothing about the removal of officers within the executive branch, other than by impeachment, and no one ever imagined that that was the sole manner of removing such officers; it is just the sole means by which *Congress* can remove such officers. The Court, however, has decided a number of cases dealing with the means by which executive officers may be removed.

8. It is well to state explicitly that a "political question" that keeps a court from reaching the merits does not mean it is a question involving politics. There are many questions involving politics that are justiciable—*Bush v. Gore*, 531 U.S. 98 (2000), for example, that effectively decided the 2000 Presidential election.

9. Another political question case involved President Jimmy Carter's termination of a mutual defense treaty with Taiwan. Several senators sued, alleging that treaties could only be terminated in the same manner in which they were made—by the President with the concurrence of two-thirds of the Senate. Because this termination had not been submitted to the Senate for concurrence, they argued it was invalid. The Court held that the case was not justiciable, but there was no majority opinion. A plurality joined Justice Rehnquist's opinion that the case involved a "political question." The opinion relied principally upon the fact that this involved foreign relations and the President's authority. The opinion noted that this was really a dispute between co-equal branches of government, both of which had ample resources to press its points. In other words, those branches could settle the issue politically. Moreover, the Constitution says nothing about the termination of treaties, only their creation. Justice Powell, who concurred in the judgment, found no basis for a "political question," because there was no textual basis for a commitment of the question to another branch of government; instead, he found the decision not "ripe" for decision. Justice Brennan likewise did not believe the case raised a "political question," and he would have decided the case on the merits, albeit upholding the President's power to terminate treaties without Senate approval. *See Goldwater v. Carter*, 444 U.S. 996 (1979).

Problems

1. A congressional election in an Ohio district is extremely close. According to the tally by the Ohio electoral districts, certified by the Ohio Secretary of State, the Republican candidate won by 21 votes out of over 100,000 cast. The closeness of the election required an automatic recount under Ohio law, and the recount resulted in the Democratic can-

didate winning by 7 votes. Because of allegations of irregularities in the recount, another state recount was held, resulting this time in the Republican winning by 37 votes. By a straight party line vote, the U.S. House of Representatives decided to institute a proceeding to determine the winner of the election. After reviewing the various records of the count and recount, the House again by a straight party line vote voted to seat the Democratic candidate. If the Republican candidate sues in federal court to overturn that decision, how should the federal court rule on a motion to dismiss on the grounds that the suit raises only a "political question"?

2. The United States participates in a United Nations Peacekeeping Operation. Pursuant to an authorization by Congress, the President orders a battalion of the 101st Airborne Division to report to Darfur, to don United Nations blue helmets and UN insignia, and to be subject to the local command of the UN commander, who is a French military officer. A soldier in the battalion seeks a declaratory judgment in federal court that the order is unconstitutional because war has not been declared and because having to report to a French officer violates the constitutional statement that the President is the Commander in Chief. How should a court rule on a motion to dismiss on the grounds that the suit raises a "political question"?

d. Mootness

Mootness is still another basis upon which the Court has refused to consider cases. Mootness refers to the situation where, although there may have been a valid case or controversy when the suit was brought, subsequent events have eliminated the complained of effects, or, stated differently, have rendered the case moot. In *Powell v. McCormack*, Justice Stewart dissented, because he believed the case was moot. By the time the case was before the Supreme Court, the session of Congress from which Adam Clayton Powell, Jr., was excluded had expired. Powell had been re-elected to the next Congress, and he had been seated (i.e., not excluded). As a result, his exclusion was totally in the past. Justice Stewart thought that this was no longer a live controversy, requiring a judicial decision. The Court, however, noted that Congress had withheld his salary for the two years of the session of Congress from which he was excluded, so that his claim to that salary certainly made this a live controversy.

A recurring issue with regard to mootness is whether a case is mooted if, in an action for an injunction or declaratory judgment, the defendant simply stops engaging in the challenged conduct. Is there still a live controversy? For example, imagine that the President directs the National Security Agency to monitor all the international communications of persons in the United States of the Muslim faith. Members of that faith bring suit against the NSA, alleging that such monitoring would be unconstitutional and seeking an injunction ordering NSA to stop. After the suit is brought, but before the court has any opportunity to rule on it, the President withdraws the order, and the NSA stops monitoring. Should the case be dismissed as moot? Assume for a moment that it is. Then, the President revives his order, and NSA starts monitoring again; and again the Muslims bring suit; and again the President then tells NSA to stop. You can see the problem. As a result, the Court has established the rule that the voluntary cessation of the allegedly unlawful conduct will not necessarily moot a case. The burden is on the defendant to show by a preponderance of the evidence that the allegedly unlawful activity will not recur. Unless the defendant can satisfy that burden, which is not easy to do, the case will not be moot, but the court will go on to decide it. Note, however, that this is an "activist" approach, because it is asserting that, even though there is in fact no live controversy at the moment, courts can still decide the matter.

Another circumstance where the Court has allowed cases to go forward in the absence of an actual, continuing live controversy is where the facts giving rise to the plaintiff's case have passed, but they are likely to recur. For example, in *Roe v. Wade*, 410 U.S. 113 (1973), the case was brought by a pregnant woman challenging the law criminalizing abortion. By the time the case was before the Supreme Court, however, she was no longer pregnant. The defendants argued that the case was moot, but the Court held that there was an exception to mootness when a case was "capable of repetition yet evading review." In other words, any challenge to a law premised on the plaintiff being pregnant would never be able to reach the Supreme Court while the person was still pregnant, and thus the issue would always evade review, if mootness was applied strictly. Again, note that this is "activist" in the sense that the Court is deciding in favor of hearing the case, rather than not hearing the case, in order that the issue can be decided by a court.

e. Other Grounds for Avoiding Decision

The above rules for avoiding review are from the Court's perspective all commanded by the Constitution's requirement that the judicial power of the United States is limited to "case and controversies." Thus, Congress by statute cannot change those rules. As in *Defenders of Wildlife*, Congress cannot grant standing to persons who are not injured or about to be injured. There are, however, a number of "prudential" grounds for avoiding review. They are called "prudential" because the Court has invented them in the exercise of its "good judgment," not because the Constitution, as interpreted, commands them. Unfortunately, the Court is often not explicit as to whether its justiciability decisions are constitutionally or prudentially based. Indeed, occasionally a determination that a case is a "political question" seems more based upon a prudential judgment than a constitutional judgment. That is, the Court seems to say that it believes it would be better not to have the Court decide the issue, rather than say it is interpreting the Constitution to forbid the Court from deciding the issue. "Ripeness" is another example. In *Goldwater v. Carter*, Justice Powell's opinion concurring in the judgment, rejected the political question determination of the plurality and instead found that the case was not "ripe" for decision.

> Prudential considerations persuade me that a dispute between Congress and the President is not ready for judicial review unless and until each branch has taken action asserting its constitutional authority. Differences between the President and the Congress are commonplace under our system. The differences should, and almost invariably do, turn on political rather than legal considerations. The Judicial Branch should not decide issues affecting the allocation of power between the President and Congress until the political branches reach a constitutional impasse. Otherwise, we would encourage small groups or even individual Members of Congress to seek judicial resolution of issues before the normal political process has the opportunity to resolve the conflict.

444 U.S. at 996. This explanation seems to turn on the timing of the bringing of the case. If the political branches cannot work it out, and they have reached an impasse, then Justice Powell believes the case would be justiciable, but until that time the case would not be "ripe."

The main difference between a constitutionally based justiciability requirement and a prudentially based justiciability requirement is that Congress can overrule or create exceptions to the latter, while it cannot with respect to the former. Many of these prudential bases for avoiding review are covered either in courses on administrative law or on federal courts.

3. ELEVENTH AMENDMENT

Above we have addressed legislative checks on the judicial power and checks on judicial power the Court has found embedded in Article III's "case" and "controversy" language, as well as in general prudential considerations. The Eleventh Amendment provides yet another check on a particular application of judicial power.

During the Revolutionary War, Robert Farquhar, a citizen of South Carolina, supplied some goods to the state of Georgia on credit. When Georgia did not pay, Alexander Chisholm, as executor of Farquhar's estate, in 1792 sued Georgia in the Supreme Court for the money due, invoking the Supreme Court's original jurisdiction. At first Georgia did not appear in court to answer the suit, so the case was put over until the next term. At the next term, lawyers for Georgia filed a formal protest against the Supreme Court exercising jurisdiction over the state of Georgia upon a suit filed by a citizen of another state. Their argument was that Georgia, as a sovereign state, was immune from private suit under the long-standing British tradition that one cannot sue the sovereign.

Four justices of the Supreme Court, however, read the Constitution literally.[17] Article III specifically provides that the judicial power of the United States extends "to controversies ... between a state and citizens of another state," and that the Supreme Court has original jurisdiction over such cases. The Judiciary Act of 1789 also contained an explicit provision providing for the Supreme Court to exercise original jurisdiction over controversies between a state and citizens of another state. Consequently, the four justices read these provisions to override any state sovereign immunity that might exist in the absence of the Constitution. One justice, Justice Iredell, agreed with Georgia. Consequently, the Court issued an order that unless Georgia appeared at the term of court the following year, a default judgment would be entered against Georgia. Georgia did not appear the next year, and a default judgment was entered against it.

The Court's decision issued in 1793 raised such a firestorm of protest in the states that Congress proposed an amendment to overrule the decision in early 1794, which was ratified by the requisite number of states in less than a year. The amendment, the Eleventh Amendment, provides:

> The Judicial power of the United States shall not be construed to extend to any suit in law or equity, commenced or prosecuted against one of the United States by Citizens of another State, or by Citizens or Subjects of any Foreign State.

This amendment thus eliminated some of the judicial power granted to the Court in Article III.

But, what about a suit against a state by a citizen of that state in a case "arising under th[e] Constitution [or] laws of the United States"? Article III says that the judicial power of the United States extends to "all cases" "arising under th[e] Constitution [or] laws of the United States," with no exception where the defendant is a state, and the Eleventh Amendment says nothing about a suit against a state brought by one of its own citizens.

HANS v. LOUISIANA

United States Supreme Court, 1890.
134 U.S. 1, 10 S.Ct. 504, 33 L.Ed. 842.

BRADLEY, J.

This is an action brought in the circuit court of the United States, in December, 1884, against the state of Louisiana, by Hans, a citizen of that state, to recover the amount [due him under certain bonds of the state issued in 1874. In 1879, Louisiana amended its constitution to provide that the state would not pay the monies due on these bonds. Hans argued that this state constitutional amendment was in violation of

17. As a case decided before John Marshall became Chief Justice, the practice was for each Justice to write his own opinion without regard to the others, with the opinions printed one after another in the opposite order of seniority.

Article I, Section 10, Clause 1, the Contracts Clause, because it impaired the obligation of a lawful contract. The state of Louisiana filed an exception in circuit court, arguing that the court did not have jurisdiction.] Plaintiff cannot sue the state without its permission; the constitution and laws do not give this honorable court jurisdiction of a suit against the state; and its jurisdiction is respectfully declined. Wherefore respondent prays to be hence dismissed, with costs, and for general relief. [The circuit court agreed with Louisiana and dismissed the case. Hans, however, appealed to the Supreme Court.] [T]he question is presented whether a state can be sued in a circuit court of the United States by one of its own citizens upon a suggestion that the case is one that arises under the constitution or laws of the United States.

The ground taken is that under the constitution, as well as under the act of congress passed to carry it into effect, a case is within the jurisdiction of the federal courts, without regard to the character of the parties, if it arises under the constitution or laws of the United States, or, which is the same thing, if it necessarily involves a question under said constitution or laws. The language relied on is that clause of the third article of the constitution, which declares that "the judicial power of the United States shall extend to all cases in law and equity arising under this constitution, the laws of the United States, and treaties made, or which shall be made, under their authority;" and the corresponding clause of the act conferring jurisdiction upon the circuit court. It is said that these jurisdictional clauses make no exception arising from the character of the parties, and therefore that a state can claim no exemption from suit, if the case is really one arising under the constitution, laws, or treaties of the United States. It is conceded that, where the jurisdiction depends alone upon the character of the parties, a controversy between a state and its own citizens is not embraced within it; but it is contended that, though jurisdiction does not exist on that ground, it nevertheless does exist if the case itself is one which necessarily involves a federal question; and, with regard to ordinary parties, this is undoubtedly true. The question now to be decided is whether it is true where one of the parties is a state, and is sued as a defendant by one of its own citizens.

That a state cannot be sued by a citizen of another state, or of a foreign state, on the mere ground that the case is one arising under the constitution or laws of the United States, is clearly established by the decisions of this court in several recent cases. Those were cases arising under the constitution of the United States, upon laws complained of as impairing the obligation of contracts, one of which was the constitutional amendment of Louisiana, complained of in the present case. Relief was sought against state officers who professed to act in obedience to those laws. This court held that the suits were virtually against the states themselves, and were consequently violative of the eleventh amendment of the constitution, and could not be maintained. It was not denied that they presented cases arising under the constitution; but, notwithstanding that, they were held to be prohibited by the amendment referred to.

In the present case the plaintiff in error* contends that he, being a citizen of Louisiana, is not embarrassed by the obstacle of the eleventh amendment, inasmuch as that amendment only prohibits suits against a state which are brought by the citizens of another state, or by citizens or subjects of a foreign state. It is true the amendment does so read, and, if there were no other reason or ground for abating his suit, it might be maintainable; and then we should have this anomalous result, that, in cases arising under the constitution or laws of the United States, a state may be sued in the federal courts by its own citizens, though it cannot be sued for a like cause of action by the citizens of other states, or of a foreign state; and may be thus sued in the federal courts, although not allowing itself to be sued in its own courts. If this is the necessary consequence of the language of the constitution and the law, the result is no less startling and unexpected than was the original decision of this court, that, under the language of the constitution and of the judiciary act of 1789, a state was liable to be sued by a citizen of another state or of a foreign country. That decision was made in the case of *Chisholm v. Georgia* and created such a shock of surprise throughout the country that, at the first meeting of congress thereafter, the eleventh amendment to the constitution was almost unanimously proposed, and was in due course adopted by the legislatures of the states. This amendment, expressing the will of the ultimate sovereignty of the whole country, superior to all legislatures and all courts, actually reversed the decision of the supreme court. It did not in terms prohibit suits by individuals against the states, but declared that the constitution should not be construed to import any power to authorize the bringing of such suits. The language of the amendment is that "the judicial power of the United States shall not be construed to extend to any suit, in law or equity, commenced or prosecuted against one of the United States by citizens of another state, or by citizens or subjects of any foreign state." The supreme court had construed the judicial power as extending to such a suit, and its decision was thus overruled. The court itself so understood the effect of the amendment.

This view of the force and meaning of the amendment is important. It shows that, on this question of the suability of the states by individuals, the highest authority of this country** was in accord rather with the minority than with the majority of the court in the decision of the case of *Chisholm v. Georgia*; and this fact lends additional interest to the able opinion of Mr. Justice IREDELL*** on that occasion. The other justices were more swayed by a close observance of the letter of the constitu-

* The term "plaintiff in error" means the person who is appealing the lower court case, or stated otherwise, the plaintiff in the appellate court. Here it refers to Hans. [author's note]

** "[T]he highest authority of this country" the Court is referring to is the people of the United States who amended the Constitution to overrule *Chisholm*.[author's note]

*** Justice Iredell was the one justice who agreed with Georgia in *Chisholm v. Georgia*. [author's note]

tion*, without regard to former experience and usage; and because the letter said that the judicial power shall extend to controversies "between a state and citizens of another state;" and "between a state and foreign states, citizens or subjects," they felt constrained to see in this language a power to enable the individual citizens of one state, or of a foreign state, to sue another state of the Union in the federal courts. Justice IREDELL, on the contrary, contended that it was not the intention to create new and unheard of remedies, by subjecting sovereign states to actions at the suit of individuals, (which he conclusively showed was never done before,) but only, by proper legislation, to invest the federal courts with jurisdiction to hear and determine controversies and cases, between the parties designated, that were properly susceptible of litigation in courts. Looking back from our present stand-point at the decision in *Chisholm v. Georgia*, we do not greatly wonder at the effect which it had upon the country. Any such power as that of authorizing the federal judiciary to entertain suits by individuals against the states had been expressly disclaimed, and even resented, by the great defenders of the constitution while it was on its trial before the American people. As some of their utterances are directly pertinent to the question now under consideration, we deem it proper to quote them.

The eighty-first number of the Federalist, written by Hamilton, has the following profound remarks:

> [I]t is inherent in the nature of sovereignty not to be amenable to the suit of an individual without its consent. This is the general sense and the general practice of mankind; and the exemption, as one of the attributes of sovereignty, is now enjoyed by the government of every state in the Union. Unless, therefore, there is a surrender of this immunity in the plan of the convention, it will remain with the states, and the danger intimated must be merely ideal. [T]here is no color to pretend that the state governments would, by the adoption of that plan, be divested of the privilege of paying their own debts in their own way, free from every constraint but that which flows from the obligations of good faith. The contracts between a nation and individuals are only binding on the conscience of the sovereign, and have no pretension to a compulsive force. They confer no right of action independent of the sovereign will....

The obnoxious clause to which Hamilton's argument was directed, and which was the ground of the objections which he so forcibly met, was that which declared that "the judicial power shall extend to all * * * controversies between a state and citizens of another state, * * * and between a state and foreign states, citizens, or subjects." It was argued by the opponents of the constitution that this clause would authorize jurisdiction to be given to the federal courts to entertain suits against a

* The term, the "letter of the Constitution," shortened to just "the letter" subsequently in the opinion, means the literal words of the Constitution, as in the term "letter of the law." [author's note]

state brought by the citizens of another state or of a foreign state. Adhering to the mere letter, it might be so, and so, in fact, the supreme court held in *Chisholm v. Georgia*; but looking at the subject as Hamilton did, and as Mr. Justice IREDELL did, in the light of history and experience and the established order of things, the views of the latter were clearly right, as the people of the United States in their sovereign capacity subsequently decided....

It seems to us that these views of those great advocates and defenders of the constitution were most sensible and just, and they apply equally to the present case as to that then under discussion. The letter is appealed to now, as it was then, as a ground for sustaining a suit brought by an individual against a state. The reason against it is as strong in this case as it was in that. It is an attempt to strain the constitution and the law to a construction never imagined or dreamed of. Can we suppose that, when the eleventh amendment was adopted, it was understood to be left open for citizens of a state to sue their own state in the federal courts, while the idea of suits by citizens of other states, or of foreign states, was indignantly repelled? Suppose that congress, when proposing the eleventh amendment, had appended to it a proviso that nothing therein contained should prevent a state from being sued by its own citizens in cases arising under the constitution or laws of the United Shates, can we imagine that it would have been adopted by the states? The supposition that it would is almost an absurdity on its face.

The truth is that the cognizance of suits and actions unknown to the law, and forbidden by the law, was not contemplated by the constitution when establishing the judicial power of the United States. Some things, undoubtedly, were made justi[c]iable which were not known as such at the common law; such, for example, as controversies between states as to boundary lines, and other questions admitting of judicial solution.... The establishment of this new branch of jurisdiction seemed to be necessary from the extinguishment of diplomatic relations between the states....

The suability of a state, without its consent, was a thing unknown to the law. This has been so often laid down and acknowledged by courts and jurists that it is hardly necessary to be formally asserted. It was fully shown by an exhaustive examination of the old law by Mr. Justice IREDELL in his opinion in *Chisholm v. Georgia*; and it has been conceded in every case since, where the question has, in any way, been presented....

HARLAN, J.

I concur with the court in holding that a suit directly against a state by one of its own citizens is not one to which the judicial power of the United States extends, unless the state itself consents to be sued. Upon this ground alone I assent to the judgment. But I cannot give my assent to many things said in the opinion. The comments made upon the decision in *Chisholm v. Georgia* do not meet my approval. They are not necessary to the determination of the present case. Besides, I am of opinion that the decision in that case was based upon a sound interpretation of the constitution as that instrument then was.

Comments and Questions

1. Although it does not use the term, the Court in *Hans* relates the rule of "sovereign immunity." The sovereign is immune from suit absent its consent. Moreover, as implied in *Hans*, and as was even recognized in *Chisholm*, the federal government also has sovereign immunity. A person cannot sue the federal government without its consent. After *Hans*, what is the rule—that a person may not sue either a state or the federal government for violating the person's constitutional rights? If so, what sort of protection is there for a person's constitutional rights?

2. First, the state and federal government can consent to suit. Given the strength of opposition to being sued that one sees states reflecting in adopting the Eleventh Amendment, one might wonder when, if ever, a state would consent to suit. In fact, states and the federal government have consented to being sued in numerous circumstances. For example, the federal government and all the states allow persons to sue them for various torts committed by agents of the government. In addition, they generally allow suits based on contracts with the government. They all allow suits based upon claims that government has unconstitutionally taken property without just compensation.

3. Second, in *Ex parte Young*, 209 U.S. 123 (1908), the Supreme Court allowed a suit against a state officer that alleged he was acting unconstitutionally. This was not a suit against the state, the Court reasoned, but against the officer in his personal capacity, because if he were violating the constitution, he could not be acting officially. This is called a "legal fiction," because if he were not acting officially, he could not violate the Constitution, inasmuch as the Constitution (generally) only restricts governments, not individuals. For example, if a suit alleged a state officer was depriving a person of equal protection of the laws, the officer would have to be acting in his capacity as an officer of the state to violate the Equal Protection Clause, because it prohibits only "states" from denying equal protection. Nevertheless, the doctrine of *Ex parte Young* enables persons to sue state officers to enjoin them from violating the Constitution or laws of the United States. The same theory should hold true for federal officers, but it is not necessary, because the federal Administrative Procedure Act generally waives sovereign immunity for suits against federal agencies alleging they have violated federal laws or the Constitution.

4. Third, as will be addressed in more detail later in this book, if Congress acts pursuant to its legislative authority under the Fourteenth Amendment, it may override state sovereign immunity and provide a federal judicial forum for enforcement of rights under the Fourteenth Amendment or laws passed pursuant thereto. *See Fitzpatrick v. Bitzer*,

427 U.S. 445 (1976). The Court flirted with the idea that Congress could override a state's sovereign immunity and create judicially enforceable federal rights pursuant to Congress's authorities under Article I, *see Pennsylvania v. Union Gas Co.*, 491 U.S. 1 (1989), but in *Seminole Tribe of Florida v. Florida*, 517 U.S. 44 (1996), the Court by a 5–4 vote held that Congress had no such power, relying on *Hans*.

5. Fourth, states do not have sovereign immunity from suits brought by the federal government, so the federal government could bring suit to enforce its laws or the Constitution.

6. Local governments, such as cities and counties, although subdivisions of the state, do not enjoy sovereign immunity in federal courts. On the other hand, state "agencies" do have sovereign immunity in federal courts. A state university, for example, is a state "agency."

7. In *Hans*, consider the interpretive methodology the Court uses. Is it textual? Originalist? Does it try to determine original intent? Is it an activist decision or is it judicially conservative? Is the Court enforcing the Constitution or its view of what the law should be?

8. The Eleventh Amendment is a constitutional check on the judicial power of the United States, but unlike most of the other types of checks we have considered, which were checks and balances within and among the three branches of the federal government, it reflects federalism concerns. It is a check on the federal government vis a vis states, as opposed to a check on judicial power vis a vis the legislative and executive branches.

Chapter 3

THE LEGISLATIVE POWER

In the last chapter, on the judicial power of the United States, we learned that the judicial power is the power to decide cases, and in the process, as necessary to decide those cases, to review laws passed by Congress and acts performed by the executive branch, as well as to review the similar laws and executive acts of states, in order to determine their lawfulness under the Constitution and laws of the United States. In this chapter we will explore the extent and limitations on the power of Congress to make laws—the legislative power of the United States.

The power of Congress to make laws is largely contained in Article I, Section 8. We will begin with the canonical case of *McCulloch v. Maryland*, dealing with the Necessary and Proper Clause in that Section, and then we will explore in some depth the case law regarding the Commerce Clause, which has received more judicial attention than any of the other powers of Congress to make laws. We will then consider the Taxing and Spending Clause and the power to implement treaties. After a consideration of certain limitations on the exercise of the powers of Congress under the Tenth Amendment, the chapter concludes with a section on the powers of Congress under the Fourteenth Amendment.

Much of what we read regarding the checks on the judicial power involved checks in favor of one of the political branches of the federal government—the legislative and executive branches. This reflects the horizontal separation of powers, but the genius (or flaw depending upon your perspective) of the Constitution is that it separates powers not only horizontally, but also vertically—between the federal government and state governments. In this chapter regarding the legislative powers, the focus is on this vertical separation, or what is also called "federalism."

A. THE NECESSARY AND PROPER CLAUSE

The following case involves a challenge to the constitutionality of the Bank of the United States, a bank chartered pursuant to an act of Congress. The state of Maryland required any bank not chartered by the state to pay an annual tax of $15,000. The Bank of the United States was the only bank not chartered by the state, and it did not pay the required tax. James McCulloch was the "cashier" of the Baltimore branch of the Bank; today we would call him the branch manager or president. Maryland fined him $100 for circulating a bank note from a bank that was neither a Maryland chartered bank nor a bank that had paid the required tax. He refused to pay, and Maryland brought an action in state court to collect the fine. Of course, from the beginning this case was not about the $100 or even the $15,000; it was about the power of Congress to charter this bank.

McCulloch defended on the grounds that the state law imposing the fee on the Bank of the United States was unconstitutional, and Maryland argued that because chartering a bank was beyond the enumerated powers of Congress, its law was not unconstitutional, and even if the bank was constitutional, Maryland could still enact this tax. The trial court found against McCulloch, and he appealed to the Maryland Court of Appeals, the highest state court, which affirmed the lower court, finding the Bank unconstitutional. McCulloch then appealed to the United States Supreme Court.

This Bank of the United States is often called the Second Bank of the United States, although it might as well be called the third bank of the United States. In 1781, during the Revolutionary War and under the Articles of Confederation, Finance Minister Robert Morris proposed to the Continental Congress that it charter a Bank of North America pursuant to a plan devised by the then 23-year old Alexander Hamilton. Questions were raised as to the authority of the Continental Congress to charter the bank, but James Wilson, a member of Congress, argued in support of it, and the bank was chartered and handled the financing of the rest of the Revolutionary War.

In the Constitutional Convention, there was consideration given to authorizing Congress to charter canal corporations—canals being probably the most important means of transportation across land—there already having been agreement to authorize Congress to make post roads.* Some delegates suggested expanding the authority to any corporations, but the first motion to authorize canal corporations was defeated, so the broader authorization was never again raised. Robert Morris and James Wilson, as well as Hamilton, were among the framers in Philadelphia.

Nevertheless, in 1791, as part of his financial plan, Secretary of the Treasury Alexander Hamilton proposed that Congress charter a Bank of the United States to serve as a central bank for the country. Congress debated the creation of a Bank of the United States. Madison argued strongly against it, saying that the Constitution did not authorize it, but Congress passed the measure and sent it to the President for signature. Washington then asked both Hamilton and Jefferson, the Secretary of

* A "post road" was essentially a toll road that would charge its users a fee in order to pay for the cost of creating and maintaining the road, and potentially as a source of profit.

State, for their views on the constitutionality of the Bank. Jefferson opposed the Bank on the grounds that the Constitution did not specifically give Congress such a power, and that under a limited government, Congress had no powers other than those explicitly given to it. Hamilton responded by arguing that Congress had all powers except those specifically denied to it in the Constitution, and that moreover, the "necessary and proper" clause of Article I required a broad reading of the specified powers. President Washington backed Hamilton, and the bank was given a twenty-year charter. The charter expired in 1811, and Madison, now President, and his party of Democratic–Republicans, did not renew it.

Financial difficulties arising out of the War of 1812, however, led members of his own party to propose a second Bank of the United States, and while Madison vetoed a bill to create one in 1815, later the same year even he became convinced of its desirability and asked Congress to create one, which it did in 1816. The bank quickly established branches throughout the Union. If there was agreement at the federal level for a Bank of the United States, however, there was not necessarily agreement at the state level, and a number of states adopted anti-Bank legislation, of which the Maryland $15,000 annual fee was an example.

Today, it may not be clear why first the Democratic–Republicans and later the states would oppose a Bank of the United States. What was the big deal? First, one has to appreciate the political and cultural divide between the merchants and the farmers. Merchants tended to be Federalists, nationalists, and supportive of financial institutions that would support a strong economy. Farmers tended to be Democratic–Republicans, states-rightists, and suspicious of financial institutions generally and centralized financial institutions especially. States whose economies were predominately merchant oriented, such as Massachusetts, New York, and Pennsylvania, for example, were in the nationalist camp. States whose economies were predominately farmer oriented tended in the other direction. In addition, state chartered banks saw the Bank of the United States as a competitor generally and a monopolist with respect to federal funds. That is, the federal government would utilize only the Bank of the United States, at the expense of the state banks, and the state banks looked to their state for protection. Finally, as a matter of principle, states regarded the chartering of a federal corporation, potentially immune from its laws, as a serious imposition on their sovereignty. This latter point is not just an historical issue; in 2007 states objected to national banks' immunity from state banking laws designed to protect consumers, but the Supreme Court upheld the immunity of the national banks from state regulation. *See Watters v. Wachovia Bank*, 127 S.Ct. 1559 (2007).

What does it mean for a bank to be chartered by the United States, as opposed to by a state? In both cases, the bank is a private, for-profit institution whose investors hope to make a profit. In the former case, the legal existence of the bank depends upon federal law, while in the latter case the legal existence of the bank depends upon state law. That is, for the bank, as a entity, to be able to make contracts, sue, make loans, etc., it must be recognized as a legal entity. In order to have rights and responsibilities under the law, one must be a legal entity. Natural persons are by nature legal entities, but organizations, in order to be a legal entity, must be recognized as such by the government.* The government that charters the corporation, whether bank or otherwise, also establishes the rules under which it must operate. Private persons owned 80% of the stock in the Bank of the United States at issue in the following case. The federal government owned the remainder.

McCULLOCH v. MARYLAND

United States Supreme Court, 1819.
4 Wheat. (17 U.S.) 316, 4 L.Ed. 579.

MARSHALL, Ch. J., delivered the opinion of the court.

In the case now to be determined, the defendant, a sovereign state, denies the obligation of a law enacted by the legislature of the Union, and the plaintiff, on his part, contests the validity of an act which has been passed by the legislature of that state. The constitution of our country, in its most interesting and vital parts, is to be considered; the conflicting powers of the government of the Union and of its members, as marked in that constitution, are to be discussed; and an opinion given, which may essentially influence the great operations of the government. No tribunal can approach such a question without a deep sense of its importance, and of the awful responsibility involved in its decision. But it must be decided peacefully, or remain a source of hostile legislation, perhaps, of hostility of a still more serious nature; and if it is to be so decided, by this tribunal alone can the decision be made. On the supreme court of the United States has the constitution of our country devolved this important duty.

The first question made in the cause is—has congress power to incorporate a bank? It has been truly said, that this can scarcely be considered as an open question, entirely unprejudiced by the former proceedings of the nation respecting it. The principle now contested was introduced at a very early period of our history, has been recognized by many successive legislatures, and has been acted upon by the judicial department, in cases of peculiar delicacy, as a law of undoubted obligation.

* Today, virtually all corporations are created under state law, rather than federal law. Even the biggest, multi-national corporations, like General Motors and Exxon, are creatures of state, rather than federal, law. They are, of course, regulated by federal law in various ways, but their existence derives from state law. For reasons you will learn when you take a course in Business Associations or Corporations, most big American corporations are creatures of Delaware law. For years, Ralph Nader has lobbied to have corporations that do business nationally or internationally be incorporated (or in other words chartered) by the federal government, rather than by state governments.

It will not be denied, that a bold and daring usurpation might be resisted, after an acquiescence still longer and more complete than this. But it is conceived, that a doubtful question, one on which human reason may pause, and the human judgment be suspended, in the decision of which the great principles of liberty are not concerned, but the respective powers of those who are equally the representatives of the people, are to be adjusted; if not put at rest by the practice of the government, ought to receive a considerable impression from that practice. An exposition of the constitution, deliberately established by legislative acts, on the faith of which an immense property has been advanced, ought not to be lightly disregarded.

The power now contested was exercised by the first congress elected under the present constitution. The bill for incorporating the Bank of the United States did not steal upon an unsuspecting legislature, and pass unobserved. Its principle was completely understood, and was opposed with equal zeal and ability. After being resisted, first, in the fair and open field of debate, and afterwards, in the executive cabinet, with as much persevering talent as any measure has ever experienced, and being supported by arguments which convinced minds as pure and as intelligent as this country can boast, it became a law. The original act was permitted to expire; but a short experience of the embarrassments to which the refusal to revive it exposed the government, convinced those who were most prejudiced against the measure of its necessity, and induced the passage of the present law. It would require no ordinary share of intrepidity, to assert that a measure adopted under these circumstances, was a bold and plain usurpation, to which the constitution gave no countenance. These observations belong to the cause; but they are not made under the impression, that, were the question entirely new, the law would be found irreconcilable with the constitution.

In discussing this question, the counsel for the state of Maryland have deemed it of some importance, in the construction of the constitution, to consider that instrument, not as emanating from the people, but as the act of sovereign and independent states. The powers of the general government, it has been said, are delegated by the states, who alone are truly sovereign; and must be exercised in subordination to the states, who alone possess supreme dominion. It would be difficult to sustain this proposition. The convention which framed the constitution was indeed elected by the state legislatures. But the instrument, when it came from their hands, was a mere proposal, without obligation, or pretensions to it. It was reported to the then existing congress of the United States, with a request that it might "be submitted to a convention of delegates, chosen in each state by the people thereof, under the recommendation of its legislature, for their assent and ratification." This mode of proceeding was adopted; and by the convention, by congress, and by the state legislatures, the instrument was submitted to the people. They acted upon it in the only manner in which they can act safely, effectively and wisely, on such a subject, by assembling in convention. It is true, they assembled in their several states—and where else should they have assembled? No political dreamer was ever wild enough to think of breaking down the lines which separate the states, and of compounding the American people into one common mass. Of consequence, when they act, they act in their states. But the measures they adopt do not, on that account, cease to be the measures of the people themselves, or become the measures of the state governments.

From these conventions, the constitution derives its whole authority. The government proceeds directly from the people; is "ordained and established," in the name of the people; and is declared to be ordained, "in order to form a more perfect union, establish justice, insure domestic tranquillity, and secure the blessings of liberty to themselves and to their posterity." The assent of the states, in their sovereign capacity, is implied, in calling a convention, and thus submitting that instrument to the people. But the people were at perfect liberty to accept or reject it; and their act was final. It required not the affirmance, and could not be negatived, by the state governments. The constitution, when thus adopted, was of complete obligation, and bound the state sovereignties ..... The government of the Union, then (whatever may be the influence of this fact on the case), is, emphatically and truly, a government of the people. In form, and in substance, it emanates from them. Its powers are granted by them, and are to be exercised directly on them, and for their benefit.

This government is acknowledged by all, to be one of enumerated powers. The principle, that it can exercise only the powers granted to it, would seem too apparent, to have required to be enforced by all those arguments, which its enlightened friends, while it was depending before the people, found it necessary to urge; that principle is now universally admitted. But the question respecting the extent of the powers actually granted, is perpetually arising, and will probably continue to arise, so long as our system shall exist. In discussing these questions, the conflicting powers of the general and state governments must be brought into view, and the supremacy of their respective laws, when they are in opposition, must be settled.

If any one proposition could command the universal assent of mankind, we might expect it would be this—that the government of the Union, though limited in its powers, is supreme within its sphere of action. This would seem to result, necessarily, from its nature. It is the government of all; its powers are delegated by all; it represents all, and acts for all. Though any one state may be willing to control its operations, no state is willing to allow others to control them. The nation, on those subjects on which it can act, must necessarily bind its component parts. But this question is not left to mere reason: the people have, in express terms, decided it, by saying, "this constitution, and the laws of the United States, which shall be made in pursuance thereof," "shall be the supreme law of the land," and by requiring that the members of the state legislatures, and the officers of the executive and judicial departments of the states, shall take the oath of fidelity to it. The government of the United States, then, though limited in its powers, is supreme; and its laws, when made in pursuance of the constitution, form the supreme law of the land, "anything in the constitution or laws of any state to the contrary notwithstanding."

Among the enumerated powers, we do not find that of establishing a bank or creating a corporation. But there is no phrase in the instrument which, like the articles of confederation, excludes incidental or implied powers; and which requires that everything granted shall be expressly and minutely described. Even the 10th amendment, which was framed for the purpose of quieting the excessive jealousies which had been excited, omits the word "expressly," and declares only, that the powers "not delegated to the United States, nor prohibited to the states, are reserved to the states or to the people;" thus leaving the question, whether the particular power which may become the subject of contest, has been delegated to the one government, or prohibited to the other, to depend on a fair construction of the whole instrument. The men who drew and adopted this amendment had experienced the embarrassments resulting from the insertion of this word ["expressly"] in the articles of confederation, and probably omitted it, to avoid those embarrassments. A constitution, to contain an accurate detail of all the subdivisions of which its great powers will admit, and of all the means by which they may be carried into execution, would partake of the prolixity of a legal code, and could scarcely be embraced by the human mind. It would, probably, never be understood by the public. Its nature, therefore, requires, that only its great outlines should be marked, its important objects designated, and the minor ingredients which compose those objects, be deduced from the nature of the objects themselves. That this idea was entertained by the framers of the American constitution, is not only to be inferred from the nature of the instrument, but from the language. Why else were some of the limitations, found in the 9th section of the 1st article, introduced? It is also, in some degree, warranted, by their having omitted to use any restrictive term which might prevent its receiving a fair and just interpretation. In considering this question, then, we must never forget that it is a constitution we are expounding.

Although, among the enumerated powers of government, we do not find the word "bank" or "incorporation," we find the great powers, to lay and collect taxes; to borrow money; to regulate commerce; to declare and conduct a war; and to raise and support armies and navies. The sword and the purse, all the external relations, and no inconsiderable portion of the industry of the nation, are intrusted to its government. It can never be pretended, that these vast powers draw after them others of inferior importance, merely because they are inferior. Such an idea can never be advanced. But it may with great reason be contended, that a government, intrusted with such ample powers, on the due execution of which the happiness and prosperity of the nation so vitally depends, must also be intrusted with ample means for their execution. The power being given, it is the interest of the nation to facilitate its execution. It can never be their interest, and cannot be presumed to have been their intention, to clog and embarrass its execution, by withholding the most appropriate means. Throughout this vast republic, from the St. Croix to the Gulf of Mexico, from the Atlantic to the Pacific, revenue is to be collected and expended, armies are to be marched and supported. The exigencies of the nation may require, that the treasure raised in the north should be transported to the south, that raised in the east, conveyed to the west, or that this order should be reversed. Is that construction of the constitution to be preferred, which would render these operations difficult, hazardous and expensive? Can we adopt that construction (unless the words imperiously require it), which would impute to the framers of that instrument, when granting these powers for the public good, the intention of impeding their exercise, by withholding a choice of means? If, indeed, such be the mandate of the constitution, we have only to obey; but that instrument does not profess to enumerate the means by which the powers it confers may be executed; nor does it prohibit the creation of a corporation, if the existence of such a being be essential, to the beneficial exercise of those powers. It is, then, the subject of fair inquiry, how far such means may be employed.

It is not denied, that the powers given to the government imply the ordinary means of execution. That, for example, of raising revenue, and applying it to national purposes, is admitted to imply the power of conveying money from place to place, as the exigencies of the nation may require, and of employing the usual means of conveyance. But it is denied, that the government has its choice of means; or, that it may employ the most convenient means, if, to employ them, it be necessary to erect a corporation. On what foundation does this argument rest? On this alone: the power of creating a corporation, is one appertaining to sovereignty, and is not expressly conferred on congress. This is true. But all legislative powers appertain to sovereignty. The original power of giving the law on any subject whatever, is a sovereign power; and if the government of the Union is restrained from creating a corporation, as a means for performing its functions, on the single reason that the creation of a corporation is an act of sovereignty; if the sufficiency of this reason be acknowledged, there would be some difficulty in sustaining the authority of congress to pass other laws for the accomplishment of the same objects. The government which has a right to do an act, and has imposed on it, the duty of performing that act, must, according to the dictates of reason, be allowed to select the means; and those who contend that it may not select any appropriate means, that one particular mode of effecting the object is excepted, take upon themselves the burden of establishing that exception.

The creation of a corporation, it is said, appertains to sovereignty. This is admitted. But to what portion of sovereignty does it appertain? Does it belong to one more than to another? In America, the powers of sovereignty are divided between the government of the Union, and those of the states. They are each sovereign, with respect to the objects committed to it, and neither sovereign, with respect to the objects committed to the other.... The power of creating a corporation, though appertaining to sovereignty, is not, like the power of making war, or levying taxes, or of regulating commerce, a great substantive and independent power, which cannot be implied as incidental to other powers, or used as a means of executing them. It is never the end for which other powers are exercised, but a means by which other objects are accomplished.... The power of creating a corporation is never used for its own sake, but for the purpose of effecting something else. No sufficient reason is, therefore, perceived, why it may not pass as incidental to those powers which are expressly given, if it be a direct mode of executing them.

But the constitution of the United States has not left the right of congress to employ the necessary means, for the execution of the powers conferred on the government, to general reasoning. To its enumeration of powers is added, that of making "all laws which shall be necessary and proper, for carrying into execution the foregoing powers, and all other powers vested by this constitution, in the government of the United States, or in any department thereof." The counsel for the state of Maryland have urged various arguments, to prove that this clause, though, in terms, a grant of power, is not so, in effect; but is really restrictive of the general right, which might otherwise be implied, of selecting means for executing the enumerated powers....

[T]he argument on which most reliance is placed, is drawn from that peculiar language of this clause. Congress is not empowered by it to make all laws, which may have relation to the powers conferred on the government, but such only as may be "necessary and proper" for carrying them into execution. The word "necessary" is considered as controlling the whole sentence, and as limiting the right to pass laws for the execution of the granted powers, to such as are indispensable, and without which the power would be nugatory. That it excludes the choice of means, and leaves to congress, in each case, that only which is most direct and simple.

Is it true, that this is the sense in which the word "necessary" is always used? Does it always import an absolute physical necessity, so strong, that one thing to which another may be termed necessary, cannot exist without that other? We think it does not. If reference be had to its use, in the common affairs of the world, or in approved authors, we find that it frequently imports no more than that one thing is convenient, or useful, or essential to another. To employ the means necessary to an end, is generally understood as employing any means calculated to produce the end, and not as being confined to those single means, without which the end would be entirely unattainable. Such is the character of human language, that no word conveys to the mind, in all situations, one single definite idea; and nothing is more common than to use words in a figurative sense.... The word "necessary" is of this description. It has not a fixed character, peculiar to itself. It admits of all degrees of comparison; and is often connected with other words, which increase or diminish the impression the mind receives of the urgency it imports. A thing may be necessary, very necessary, absolutely or indispensably necessary. To no mind would the same idea be conveyed by these several phrases. The comment on the word is well illustrated by the ... 10th section of the 1st article of the constitution. It is, we think, impossible to compare the sentence which prohibits a state from laying "imposts, or duties on imports or exports, except what may be absolutely necessary for executing its inspection laws," with that which authorizes congress "to make all laws which shall be necessary and proper for carrying into execution" the powers of the general government, without feeling a conviction, that the convention understood itself to change materially the meaning of the word "necessary," by prefixing the word "absolutely." This word, then, like others, is used in various senses; and, in its construction, the subject, the context, the intention of the person using them, are all to be taken into view.

Let this be done in the case under consideration. The subject is the execution of those great powers on which the welfare of a nation essentially depends. It must have been the intention of those who gave these powers, to insure, so far as human prudence could insure, their beneficial execution. This could not be done, by confiding the choice of means to such narrow limits as not to leave it in the power of congress to adopt any which might be appropriate, and which were conducive to the end. This provision is made in a constitution, intended to endure for ages to come, and consequently, to be adapted to the various crises of human affairs. To have prescribed the means by which government should, in all future time, execute its powers, would have been to change, entirely, the character of the instrument, and give it the properties of a legal code. It would have been an unwise attempt to provide, by immutable rules, for exigencies which, if foreseen at all, must have been seen dimly, and which can be best provided for as they occur. To have declared, that the best means shall not be used, but those alone, without which the power given would be nugatory, would have been to deprive the legislature of the capacity to avail itself of experience, to exercise its reason, and to accommodate its legislation to circumstances....

Take, for example, the power "to establish post-offices and post-roads." This power is executed, by the single act of making the establishment. But, from this has been inferred the power and duty of carrying the mail along the post-road, from one post-office to another. And from this implied power, has again been inferred the right to punish those who steal letters from the post-office, or rob the mail. It may be said, with some plausibility, that the right to carry the mail, and to punish those who rob it, is not indispensably necessary to the establishment of a post-office and post-road....

If this limited construction of the word "necessary" must be abandoned, in order to punish, whence is derived the rule which would reinstate it, when the government would carry its powers into execution, by means not vindictive in their nature? If the word "necessary" means "needful," "requisite," "essential," "conducive to," in order to let in the power of punishment for the infraction of law; why is it not equally comprehensive, when required to authorize the use of means which facilitate the execution of the powers of government, without the infliction of punishment?

In ascertaining the sense in which the word "necessary" is used in this clause of the constitution, we may derive some aid from that with which it is associated. Congress shall have power "to make all laws which shall be necessary and *proper* to carry into execution" the powers of the government. If the word "necessary" was used in that strict and rigorous sense for which the counsel for the state of Maryland contend, it would be an extraordinary departure from the usual course of the human mind, as exhibited in composition, to add a word ["proper"], the only possible effect of which is, to qualify that strict and rigorous meaning; to present to the mind the idea of some choice of means of legislation, not strained and compressed within the narrow limits for which gentlemen contend.

But the argument which most conclusively demonstrates the error of the construction contended for by the counsel for the state of Maryland, is founded on the intention of the convention, as manifested in the whole clause. To waste time and argument in proving that, without it, congress might carry its powers into execution, would be not much less idle, than to hold a lighted taper to the sun. As little can it be required to prove, that in the absence of this clause, congress would have some choice of means. That it might employ those which, in its judgment, would most advantageously effect the object to be accomplished. That any means adapted to the end, any means which tended directly to the execution of the constitutional powers of the government, were in themselves constitutional. This clause, as construed by the state of Maryland, would abridge, and almost annihilate, this useful and necessary right of the legislature to select its means. That this could not be intended, is, we should think, had it not been already controverted, too apparent for controversy.

We think so for the following reasons: 1st. The clause is placed among the powers of congress, not among the limitations on those powers. 2d. Its terms purport to enlarge, not to diminish the powers vested in the government. It purports to be an additional power, not a restriction on those already granted. No reason has been, or can be assigned, for thus concealing an intention to narrow the discretion of the national legislature, under words which purport to enlarge it....

The result of the most careful and attentive consideration bestowed upon this clause is, that if it does not enlarge, it cannot be construed to restrain the powers of congress, or to impair the right of the legislature to exercise its best judgment in the selection of measures to carry into execution the constitutional powers of the government. If no other motive for its insertion can be suggested, a sufficient one is found in the desire to remove all doubts respecting the right to legislate on that vast mass of incidental powers which must be involved in the constitution, if that instrument be not a splendid bauble.

We admit, as all must admit, that the powers of the government are limited, and that its limits are not to be transcended. But we think the sound construction of the constitution must allow to the national legislature that discretion, with respect to the means by which the powers it confers are to be carried into execution, which will enable that body to perform the high duties assigned to it, in the manner most beneficial to the people. Let the end be legitimate, let it be within the scope of the constitution, and all means which are appropriate, which are plainly adapted to that end, which are not prohibited, but consist with the letter and spirit of the constitution, are constitutional.

That a corporation must be considered as a means not less usual, not of higher dignity, not more requiring a particular specification than other means, has been sufficiently proved. If we look to the origin of corporations, to the manner in which they have been framed in that government from which we have derived most of our legal principles and ideas, or to the uses to which they have been applied, we find no reason to suppose, that a constitution, omitting, and wisely omitting, to enumerate all the means for carrying into execution the great powers vested in government, ought to have specified this. Had it been intended to grant this power, as one which should be distinct and independent, to be exercised in any case whatever, it would have found a place among the enumerated powers of the government. But being considered merely as a means, to be employed only for the purpose of carrying into execution the given powers, there could be no motive for particularly mentioning it....

If a corporation may be employed, indiscriminately with other means, to carry into execution the powers of the government, no particular reason can be assigned for excluding the use of a bank, if required for its fiscal operations. To use one must be within the discretion of congress, if it be an appropriate mode of executing the powers of government. That it is a convenient, a useful, and essential instrument in the prosecution of its fiscal operations, is not now a subject of controversy. All those who have been concerned in the administration of our finances, have concurred in representing its importance and necessity; and so strongly have they been felt, that statesmen of the first class, whose previous opinions against it had been confirmed by every circumstance which can fix the human judgment, have yielded those opinions to the exigencies of the nation....

But were its necessity less apparent, none can deny its being an appropriate measure; and if it is, the decree of its necessity, as has been very justly observed, is to be discussed in another place. Should congress, in the execution of its powers, adopt measures which are prohibited by the constitution; or should congress, under the pretext of executing its powers, pass laws for the accomplishment of objects not intrusted to the government; it would become the painful duty of this tribunal, should a case requiring such a decision come before it, to say, that such an act was not the law of the land. But where the law is not prohibited, and is really calculated to effect any of the objects intrusted to the government, to undertake here to inquire into the decree of its necessity, would be to pass the line which circumscribes the judicial department, and to tread on legislative ground. This court disclaims all pretensions to such a power.

After this declaration, it can scarcely be necessary to say, that the existence of state banks can have no possible influence on the question. No trace is to be found in the constitution, of an intention to create a dependence of the government of the Union on those of the states, for the execution of the great powers assigned to it. Its means are adequate to its ends; and on those means alone was it expected to rely for the accomplishment of its ends. To impose on it the necessity of resorting to means which it cannot control, which another government may furnish or withhold, would render its course precarious, the result of its measures uncertain, and create a dependence on other governments, which might disappoint its most important designs, and is incompatible with the language of the constitution. But were it otherwise, the choice of means implies a right to choose a national bank in preference to state banks, and congress alone can make the election.

After the most deliberate consideration, it is the unanimous and decided opinion of this court, that the act to incorporate the Bank of the United States is a law made in pursuance of the constitution, and is a part of the supreme law of the land....

It being the opinion of the court, that the act incorporating the bank is constitutional; and that the power of establishing a branch in the state of Maryland might be properly exercised by the bank itself, we proceed to inquire—2. Whether the state of Maryland may, without violating the constitution, tax that branch?

[T]hat the power to tax involves the power to destroy; that the power to destroy may defeat and render useless the power to create; that there is a plain repugnance in conferring on one government a power to control the constitutional measures of another, which other, with respect to those very measures, is declared to be supreme over that which exerts the control, are propositions not to be denied.... This was not intended by the American people. They did not design to make their government dependent on the states.

Comments and Questions

1. In many ways Marshall's opinion for the Court is a response to the original objections by Madison and Jefferson, and in that response established an expansive rather than restricted view of the Constitution's grants of authority to Congress.

2. Recognize how the interests and arguments align. That is, Maryland argues for a narrow interpretation of the federal constitu-

tional powers in order to preserve its own powers and prerogatives. The federal government argues for a broad interpretation to advance its own powers and prerogatives. Thus, this case is all about federalism.

3. How does Marshall justify that "necessary" does not really mean "necessary"?

4. How is it that a Bank of the United States facilitates the carrying into execution any of the specified power of the United States?

5. Marshall's statement that "we must never forget that it is a constitution we are expounding" has often been cited. What did he mean? How would this concept apply to Article III's description of the Supreme Court's original jurisdiction, or to the First Amendment?

6. Clearly, Marshall's formulation of congressional power is expansive. What limitations does he find in the Constitution on when the "necessary and proper" clause would authorize congressional action?

7. It is really not relevant to anything, but for constitutional trivia you may be interested to learn that McCulloch was later convicted for embezzling money from the Bank.

B. THE COMMERCE CLAUSE

As indicated earlier, the bulk of this chapter involves a close examination of the Court's jurisprudence under the Commerce Clause. It is presented in a chronological fashion from the earliest to the latest Court cases. Think of it as a journey through time. Like a journey, it reflects twists and turns, not a straight line. There are "good" cases and "bad" cases as viewed through our eyes today. The last cases in this section reflect "current law," but this is a journey that is not finished, and to perceive where we may be going, it is well to see where we have been.

1. THE FOUNDATIONS

Recall that the absence of the power to regulate commerce under the Articles of Confederation was one of the primary motivations for the Philadelphia Convention, and that under the Articles states engaged in trade wars. The mere ratification of the Constitution did not end those problems. The case that follows, the first Commerce Clause case, reflects the situation. The state of New York granted a monopoly to Robert Fulton (who invented the steamboat according to American history) and Robert Livingston, his financial backer, to operate steamboats within the state. They in turn had assigned this right to Aaron Ogden, presumably for a handsome sum. Granting monopoly rights to an entrepreneur to encourage investment in an enterprise is something that was frequently done at the time and still is done in certain situations. Thus, no one could operate a steamboat in New York without a license from Ogden. Operation without such a license could lead to forfeiture of the boat.

At the same time, Connecticut, interested in supporting its own steamboat fleet, prohibited anyone possessing a license from Fulton and Livingston from operating a steamboat in its waters. New Jersey had a law creating treble damages for any New Jersey citizen against any person who restrained the New Jersey citizen from operating a steamboat in New York.

Thomas Gibbons, who had a federal license to engage in "the coasting trade," began operating a steamboat between New York City and New Jersey. Ogden sought an injunction from the New York state courts prohibiting Gibbons from operating his steamboats in New York state. The New York courts granted the injunction, and Gibbons appealed to the United States Supreme Court.

GIBBONS v. OGDEN

United States States Supreme Court, 1824.
9 Wheat. (22 U.S.) 1, 6 L.Ed. 23.

Mr. Chief Justice MARSHALL delivered the opinion of the Court, and, after stating the case, proceeded as follows:

The appellant contends that this decree is erroneous, because the laws which purport to give the exclusive privilege it sustains, are repugnant to the constitution and laws of the United States....

The words are, "Congress shall have power to regulate commerce with foreign nations, and among the several States, and with the Indian tribes."

The subject to be regulated is commerce; and our constitution being, as was aptly said at the bar, one of enumeration, and not of definition, to ascertain the extent of the power, it becomes necessary to settle the meaning of the word. The counsel for the appellee would limit it to traffic, to buying and selling, or the interchange of commodities, and do not admit that it comprehends navigation....

If commerce does not include navigation, the government of the Union has no direct power over that subject, and can make no law prescribing what shall constitute American vessels, or requiring that they shall be navigated by American seamen. Yet this power has been exercised from the commencement of the government, has been exercised with the consent of all, and has been understood by all to be a commercial regulation. All America understands, and has uniformly understood, the word "commerce," to comprehend navigation. It was so understood, and must have been so understood, when the constitution was framed. The power over commerce, including navigation, was one of the primary objects for which the people of America adopted their government, and must have been contemplated in forming it. The convention must have used the word in that sense, because all have understood it in that sense; and the attempt to restrict it comes too late....

The word used in the constitution, then, comprehends, and has been always understood to comprehend, navigation within its meaning; and a power to regulate navigation, is as expressly granted, as if that term had been added to the word "commerce."

To what commerce does this power extend? The constitution informs us, to commerce "with foreign nations, and among the several States, and with the Indian tribes."

It has, we believe, been universally admitted, that these words comprehend every species of commercial intercourse between the United States and foreign nations. No sort of trade can be carried on between this country and any other, to which this power does not extend. It has been truly said, that commerce, as the word is used in the constitution, is a unit, every part of which is indicated by the term.

If this be the admitted meaning of the word, in its application to foreign nations, it must carry the same meaning throughout the sentence, and remain a unit, unless there be some plain intelligible cause which alters it.

The subject to which the power is next applied, is to commerce "among the several States." The word "among" means intermingled with. A thing which is among others, is intermingled with them. Commerce among the States, cannot stop at the external boundary line of each State, but may be introduced into the interior.

It is not intended to say that these words comprehend that commerce, which is completely internal, which is carried on between man and man in a State, or between different parts of the same State, and which does not extend to or affect other States. Such a power would be inconvenient, and is certainly unnecessary.

Comprehensive as the word "among" is, it may very properly be restricted to that commerce which concerns more States than one. The phrase is not one which would probably have been selected to indicate the completely interior traffic of a State, because it is not an apt phrase for that purpose; and the enumeration of the particular classes of commerce, to which the power was to be extended, would not have been made, had the intention been to extend the power to every description. The enumeration presupposes something not enumerated; and that something, if we regard the language or the subject of the sentence, must be the exclusively internal commerce of a State. The genius and character of the whole government seem to be, that its action is to be applied to all the external concerns of the nation, and to those internal concerns which affect the States generally; but not to those which are completely within a particular State, which do not affect other States, and with which it is not necessary to interfere, for the purpose of executing some of the general powers of the government. The completely internal commerce of a State, then, may be considered as reserved for the State itself.

But, in regulating commerce with foreign nations, the power of Congress does not stop at the jurisdictional lines of the several States. It would be a very useless power, if it could not pass those lines. The commerce of the United States with foreign nations, is that of the whole United States. Every district has a right to participate in it. The deep streams which penetrate our country in every direction, pass through the interior of almost every State in the Union, and furnish the means of exercising this right. If Congress has the power to regulate it, that power must be exercised whenever the subject exists. If it exists within the States, if a foreign voyage may commence or terminate at a port within a State, then the power of Congress may be exercised within a State.

This principle is, if possible, still more clear, when applied to commerce "among the several States." They either join each other, in which case they are separated by a mathematical line, or they are remote from each other, in which case other States lie between them.... Commerce among the States must, of necessity, be commerce with the States.... The power of Congress, then, whatever it may be, must be exercised within the territorial jurisdiction of the several States....

We are now arrived at the inquiry—What is this power?

It is the power to regulate; that is, to prescribe the rule by which commerce is to be governed. This power, like all others vested in Congress, is complete in itself, may be exercised to its utmost extent, and acknowledges no limitations, other than are prescribed in the constitution.... If, as has always been understood, the sovereignty of Congress, though limited to specified objects, is plenary as to those objects, the power over commerce with foreign nations, and among the several States, is vested in Congress as absolutely as it would be in a single government, having in its constitution the same restrictions on the exercise of the power as are found in the constitution of the United States. The wisdom and the discretion of Congress, their identity with the people, and the influence which their constituents possess at elections, are, in this, as in many other instances, as that, for example, of declaring war, the sole restraints on which they have relied, to secure them from its abuse. They are the restraints on which the people must often they solely, in all representative governments.

The power of Congress, then, comprehends navigation, within the limits of every State in the Union; so far as that navigation may be, in any manner, connected with "commerce with foreign nations, or among the several States, or with the Indian tribes." It may, of consequence, pass the jurisdictional line of New York, and act upon the very waters to which the prohibition now under consideration applies.

But it has been urged with great earnestness, that, although the power of Congress to regulate commerce with foreign nations, and among the several States, be co-extensive with the subject itself, and have no other limits than are prescribed in the constitution, yet the States may severally exercise the same power, within their respective jurisdictions. In support of this argument, it is said, that they possessed it as an inseparable attribute of sovereignty, before the formation of the constitution, and still retain it, except so far as they have surrendered it by that instrument; that this principle results from the nature of the government, and is secured by the tenth amendment; that an affirmative grant of power is not exclusive, unless in its own nature it be such that the continued exercise of it by the former possessor is inconsistent with the grant, and that this is not of that description....

In discussing the question, whether this power is still in the States, in the case under consideration, we may dismiss from it the inquiry, whether it is surrendered by the mere grant to Congress, or is retained until Congress shall exercise the power. We may dismiss that inquiry, because it has been exercised, and the regulations which Congress deemed it proper to make, are now in full operation....

Since, however, in exercising the power of regulating their own purely internal affairs, whether of trading or police, the States may sometimes enact laws, the validity of which depends on their interfering with, and being contrary to, an act of Congress passed in pursuance of the constitution, the Court will enter upon the inquiry, whether the laws of New York, as expounded by the highest tribunal of that State, have, in their application to this case, come into collision with an act of Congress, and deprived a citizen of a right to which that act entitles him. Should this collision exist, it will be immaterial whether those laws were passed in virtue of a concurrent power "to regulate commerce with foreign nations and among the several States," or, in virtue of a power to regulate their domestic trade and police. In one case and the other, the acts of New York must yield to the law of Congress; and the decision sustaining the privilege they confer, against a right given by a law of the Union, must be erroneous.

This opinion has been frequently expressed in this Court, and is founded, as well on the nature of the government as on the words of the constitution. In argument, however, it has been contended, that if a law passed by a State, in the exercise of its acknowledged sovereignty, comes into conflict with a law passed by Congress in pursuance of the constitution, they affect the subject, and each other, like equal opposing powers.

But the framers of our constitution foresaw this state of things, and provided for it, by declaring the supremacy not only of itself, but of the laws made in pursuance of it. The nullity of any act, inconsistent with the constitution, is produced by the declaration, that the constitution is the supreme law.... In every such case, the act of Congress, or the treaty, is supreme; and the law of the State, though enacted in the exercise of powers not controverted, must yield to it....

[T]he State of New York cannot prevent an enrolled and licensed vessel, proceeding from Elizabethtown, in New Jersey, to New York, from enjoying, in her course, and on her entrance into port, all the privileges conferred by the act of Congress.... To the Court it seems very clear, that the whole act on the subject of the coasting trade, according to those principles which govern the construction of statutes, implies, unequivocally, an authority to licensed vessels to carry on the coasting trade....

Comments and Questions

1. While Chief Justice Marshall's language may sometimes be difficult to decipher, the case seems hardly a difficult one. If Congress could not regulate the interstate transportation of passengers by steamboat, the Commerce Clause would have accomplished little. It does not take a nationalist like Marshall to see the necessity of this outcome. Nevertheless, the effect of the case is to seriously diminish the sovereignty of New York state. It no longer can further its domestic industries by establishing monopolies with respect to industries engaged in interstate commerce, at least if Congress does not agree. Imagine that today Congress enacted a law authorizing persons to import toys from China. Would a state be able to ban the importation of toys from China if the state found they contained lead paint?

2. Note that Ogden argued that the New York law and the federal law were of equal power. Again, this was not a hard case even in 1824, but we see the Court articulate the notion of what we call "preemption," the preemption of state law as a result of a conflict with federal law.

3. In a portion of *Gibbons v. Ogden* that has been edited out here, Marshall discusses what had been a major point of argument before the Court, that the New York law was unconstitutional even if Gibbons had not had a license to engage in the coastal trade. Indeed, one justice concurred with the Court on the basis of that argument. We will address that issue later in this book, when we deal with something called the "dormant Commerce Clause."

THE DANIEL BALL*

United States Supreme Court, 1870.
77 U.S. 557, 19 L.Ed. 999.

[This is another steamboat case. Steamboats were, of course, an important invention, providing the first mechanical means of propulsion, significantly reducing the time required to transport people and goods by ship. Steamboats work by using steam under pressure to drive pistons, which then drive the propellor or paddle wheel. Steam under pressure, however, can be very dangerous, and in the early days boiler explosions occurred all too often, and the effects were disastrous, rapidly sinking the boats and killing large numbers of passengers and crew. As a result, beginning in 1833, the federal government passed laws regulating boilers used on steamboats and requiring their regular inspection. Failure to comply with this law would subject the owners to substantial penalties.

* Note that this case is not entitled *someone v. someone*. It is what is known as an *in rem* action, in which the plaintiff, here the United States, proceeds directly against an object alleged to be in violation of the law, here the good ship Daniel Ball.

In March, 1868, the Daniel Ball, a one hundred and twenty-three ton steamboat, was engaged in the transportation of merchandise and passengers on the Grand River, in the State of Michigan, between the cities of Grand Rapids and Grand Haven, without having been inspected or licensed under the laws of the United States. The United States filed suit to impose a penalty. The answer of the owners, who appeared in the case, admitted the employment of the steamer as alleged, but set up as a defense that the Grand River was not a navigable water of the United States, and that the steamer was engaged solely in domestic trade and commerce, and was not engaged in trade or commerce between two or more States, or in any trade by reason of which she was subject to the navigation laws of the United States, or was required to be inspected and licensed. It was conceded that the Daniel Ball only operated between the two cities in Michigan and never left the state. It was also conceded that some of the goods that she loaded at Grand Rapids and carried to Grand Haven were destined and marked for places in other states than Michigan, and that some of the goods which she loaded at Grand Haven came from other states and were destined for places within Michigan. Finally, it was also conceded that the Grand River connected to other waters (in particular Lake Michigan), which enabled vessels to travel interstate. The district court dismissed the suit on the basis that the federal law, as applied to the Daniel Ball, was beyond the powers of Congress under the Commerce Clause. The circuit court reversed, and appeal was taken to the Supreme Court.]

Stephen Johnson Field

Abraham Lincoln appointed Field, then a California Supreme Court Justice, to the newly created tenth seat on the Supreme Court in 1863. As a westerner and a Democrat, Field brought geographic and political balance to the Court. Over his thirty-three years on the Court – the longest period of any justice to that point, exceeding John Marshall's tenure by a few months – Field, perhaps reflecting his pioneer background, generally was antagonistic to government regulation, despite his opinion in *The Daniel Ball,* authoring opinions restricting the antitrust laws, limiting the power of the Interstate Commerce Commission, and championing substantive due process protections of property and commercial liberty. In 1889, a former California Supreme Court Justice, David Terry, apparently tried to kill Field while he was eating lunch at a train station near Stockton, California, but was instead himself killed by a U.S. Marshall guarding Field. It was still the wild west.

Mr. Justice FIELD, after stating the case, delivered the opinion of the court, as follows:

Two questions are presented in this case for our determination.

First: Whether the steamer was at the time ... engaged in transporting merchandise and passengers on a navigable water of the

United States within the meaning of the acts of Congress; and,

Second: Whether those acts are applicable to a steamer engaged as a common carrier between places in the same State, when a portion of the merchandise transported by her is destined to places in other States, or comes from places without the State, she not running in connection with or in continuation of any line of steamers or other vessels, or any railway line leading to or from another State.

Upon the first of these questions we entertain no doubt.... A ... test must ... be applied to determine the navigability of our rivers, and that is found in their navigable capacity. Those rivers must be regarded as public navigable rivers in law which are navigable in fact. And they are navigable in fact when they are used, or are susceptible of being used, in their ordinary condition, as highways for commerce, over which trade and travel are or may be conducted in the customary modes of trade and travel on water. And they constitute navigable waters of the United States within the meaning of the acts of Congress, in contradistinction from the navigable waters of the States, when they form in their ordinary condition by themselves, or by uniting with other waters, a continued highway over which commerce is or may be carried on with other States or foreign countries in the customary modes in which such commerce is conducted by water.

If we apply this test to Grand River, the conclusion follows that it must be regarded as a navigable water of the United States. From the conceded facts in the case the stream is capable of bearing a steamer of one hundred and twenty-three tons burden, laden with merchandise and passengers, as far as Grand Rapids, a distance of forty miles from its mouth in Lake Michigan. And by its junction with the lake it forms a continued highway for commerce, both with other States and with foreign countries, and is thus brought under the direct control of Congress in the exercise of its commercial power.

That power authorizes all appropriate legislation for the protection or advancement of either interstate or foreign commerce, and for that purpose such legislation as will insure the convenient and safe navigation of all the navigable waters of the United States, whether that legislation consists in requiring the removal of obstructions to their use, in prescribing the form and size of the vessels employed upon them, or in subjecting the vessels to inspection and license, in order to insure their proper construction and equipment. "The power to regulate commerce," this court said in *Gilman v. Philadelphia*, "comprehends the control for that purpose, and to the extent necessary, of all navigable waters of the United States which are accessible from a State other than those in which they lie. For this purpose they are the public property of the nation, and subject to all the requisite legislation of Congress."

But it is contended that the steamer Daniel Ball was only engaged in the internal commerce of the State of Michigan, and was not, therefore, required to be inspected or licensed, even if it be conceded that

Grand River is a navigable water of the United States; and this brings us to the consideration of the second question presented.

There is undoubtedly an internal commerce which is subject to the control of the States. The power delegated to Congress is limited to commerce "among the several States," with foreign nations, and with the Indian tribes. This limitation necessarily excludes from Federal control all commerce not thus designated, and of course that commerce which is carried on entirely within the limits of a State, and does not extend to or affect other States.[7] In this case it is admitted that the steamer was engaged in shipping and transporting down Grand River, goods destined and marked for other States than Michigan, and in receiving and transporting up the river goods brought within the State from without its limits; but inasmuch as her agency in the transportation was entirely within the limits of the State, and she did not run in connection with, or in continuation of, any line of vessels or railway leading to other States, it is contended that she was engaged entirely in domestic commerce. But this conclusion does not follow. So far as she was employed in transporting goods destined for other States, or goods brought from without the limits of Michigan and destined to places within that State, she was engaged in commerce between the States, and however limited that commerce may have been, she was, so far as it went, subject to the legislation of Congress. She was employed as an instrument of that commerce; for whenever a commodity has begun to move as an article of trade from one State to another, commerce in that commodity between the States has commenced. The fact that several different and independent agencies are employed in transporting the commodity, some acting entirely in one State, and some acting through two or more States, does in no respect affect the character of the transaction. To the extent in which each agency acts in that transportation, it is subject to the regulation of Congress.

It is said that if the position here asserted be sustained, there is no such thing as the domestic trade of a State; that Congress may take the entire control of the commerce of the country, and extend its regulations to the railroads within a State on which grain or fruit is transported to a distant market.

We answer that the present case relates to transportation on the navigable waters of the United States, and we are not called upon to express an opinion upon the power of Congress over interstate commerce when carried on by land transportation. And we answer further, that we are unable to draw any clear and distinct line between the authority of Congress to regulate an agency employed in commerce between the States, when that agency extends through two or more States, and when it is confined in its action entirely within the limits of a single State. If its authority does not extend to an agency in such commerce, when that agency is confined within the limits of a State, its entire authority over

7. *Gibbons v. Ogden*, 9 Wheat. (22 U.S.) 1, 194 (1824).

interstate commerce may be defeated. Several agencies combining, each taking up the commodity transported at the boundary line at one end of a State, and leaving it at the boundary line at the other end, the Federal jurisdiction would be entirely ousted, and the constitutional provision would become a dead letter.

Comments and Questions

1. The Court begins by posing two questions. When it concludes that the Grand River is a "navigable water of the United States," what is the consequence of that decision in terms of the powers of Congress over that water?

2. With respect to the second question, how is it that regulating the Daniel Ball is regulating commerce among the states, when the Daniel Ball never leaves Michigan? Is it even necessary that the Daniel Ball was on "navigable waters of the United States"?

3. Even if the Daniel Ball were traveling between states, how is regulating a boiler on the ship and requiring its inspection regulating "commerce among the states"? Would it be more accurate to say that regulating the boiler and requiring its inspection are necessary and proper to regulating commerce?

4. The owners of the Daniel Ball argue that, if Congress can regulate things that occur totally within a state simply because they involve in some way goods traveling in interstate commerce, there would be no limit on Congress's power. What do you think? Could Congress set the standards for the safety equipment on your bicycle because you sometimes carry items that came from out-of-state? And if it could, it could preclude the state from setting a different standard.

2. THE PROGRESSIVE ERA

The Progressive Era in American history spans roughly 1890–1920. Progressives supported women's suffrage, the temperance movement (banning alcohol), government regulation of business, legislation to restrict labor exploitation generally, but particularly of women and children, and increasing citizen participation in government through the enactment of initiative and referendum provisions in state constitutions. The judicial response to Progressive measures depended upon the orientation of the Court.

UNITED STATES v. E. C. KNIGHT CO.

United States Supreme Court, 1895.
156 U.S. 1, 15 S.Ct. 249, 39 L.Ed. 325.

[The E.C. Knight Company purchased the stock of several other sugar refineries with the result that Knight acquired nearly complete control of the manufacture of refined sugar within the United States. The United States charged that the contracts under which these purchases were made constituted combinations in restraint of trade, and that in entering into them the defendants combined and conspired to restrain the trade and commerce in refined sugar among the several states and with foreign nations contrary to the Sherman Antitrust Act of 1890.]

Mr. Chief Justice FULLER, after stating the facts in the foregoing language, delivered the opinion of the court.

[T]he fundamental question is whether, conceding that the existence of a monopoly in manufacture is established by the evidence, that monopoly can be directly suppressed under the act of congress in the mode attempted by this bill.

It cannot be denied that the power of a state to protect the lives, health, and property of its citizens, and to preserve good order and the public morals, "the power to govern men and things within the limits of its dominion," is a power originally and always belonging to the states, not surrendered by them to the general government, nor directly restrained by the constitution of the United States, and essentially exclusive. The relief of the citizens of each state from the burden of monopoly and the evils resulting from the restraint of trade among such citizens was left with the states to deal with.... On the other hand, the power of congress to regulate commerce among the several states is also exclusive. "Commerce undoubtedly is traffic," said Chief Justice Marshall, "but it is something more; it is intercourse. It describes the commercial intercourse between nations and parts of nations in all its branches, and is regulated by prescribing rules for carrying on that intercourse." That which belongs to commerce is within the jurisdiction of the United States, but that which does not belong to commerce is within the jurisdiction of the police power of the state. *Gibbons v. Ogden*, 9 Wheat. 1.

The argument is that the power to control the manufacture of refined sugar is a monopoly over a necessary of life, to the enjoyment of which by a large part of the population of the United States interstate commerce is indispensable, and that, therefore, the general government, in the exercise of the power to regulate commerce, may repress such monopoly directly, and set aside the instruments which have created it. But this argument cannot be confined to necessaries of life merely, and must include all articles of general consumption. Doubtless the power to control the manufacture of a given thing involves, in a certain sense, the control of its disposition, but this is a secondary, and not the primary, sense; and, although the exercise of that power may result in bringing the operation of commerce into play, it does not control it, and affects it only incidentally and indirectly. Commerce succeeds to manufacture, and is not a part of it. The power to regulate commerce is the power to prescribe the rule by which commerce shall be governed, and is a power independent of the power to suppress monopoly. But it may operate in repression of monopoly whenever that comes within the rules by which commerce is governed, or whenever the transaction is itself a monopoly of commerce.

It is vital that the independence of the commercial power and of the police power, and the delimitation between them, however sometimes perplexing, should always be recognized and observed, for, while the one furnishes the strongest bond of union, the other is essential to the preservation of the autonomy of the states as required by our dual form of government; and acknowledged evils, however grave and urgent they may appear to be, had better be borne, than the risk be run, in the effort to suppress them, of more serious consequences by resort to expedients of even doubtful constitutionality.

It will be perceived how far-reaching the proposition is that the power of dealing with a monopoly directly may be exercised by the general government whenever interstate or international commerce may be ultimately affected. The regulation of commerce applies to the subjects of commerce, and not to matters of internal police. Contracts to buy, sell, or exchange goods to be transported among the several states, the transportation and its instrumentalities, and articles bought, sold, or exchanged for the purposes of such transit among the states, or put in the way of transit, may be regulated; but this is because they form part of interstate trade or commerce. The fact that an article is manufactured for export to another state does not of itself make it an article of interstate commerce, and the intent of the manufacturer does not determine the time when the article or product passes from the control of the state and belongs to commerce.... There must be a point of time when they cease to be governed exclusively by the domestic law, and begin to be governed and protected by the national law of commercial regulation; and that moment seems to us to be a legitimate one for this purpose in which they commence their final movement from the state of their origin to that of their destination.

"[N]o distinction is more popular to the common mind, or more clearly expressed in economic and political literature, than that between manufacture and commerce. Manufacture is transformation,—the fashioning of raw materials into a change of form for use. The functions of commerce are different. The buying and selling, and the transportation incidental thereto, constitute commerce; and the regulation of commerce in the constitutional sense embraces the regulation at least of such transportation. * * * If it be held that the term includes the regulation of all such manufactures as are intended to be the subject of commercial transactions in the future, it is impossible to deny that it would also include all productive industries that contemplate the same thing. The result would be that congress would be invested, to the exclusion of the states, with the power to regulate, not only manufactures, but also agriculture, horticulture, stock-raising, domestic fisheries, mining; in short, every branch of human industry. For is there one of them that does not contemplate, more or less clearly, an interstate or foreign market? Does not the wheat grower of the Northwest, and the cotton planter of the South, plant, cultivate, and harvest his crop with an eye on the prices at Liverpool, New York, and Chicago? The power being vested in congress and denied to the states, it would follow as an inevitable result that the duty would devolve on congress to regulate all of these delicate, multiform, and vital interests,—interests which in their nature are, and must be, local in all the details of their successful management...."

Contracts, combinations, or conspiracies to control domestic enterprise in manufacture, agriculture, mining, production in all its forms, or to raise or lower prices or wages, might unquestionably tend to restrain external as well as domestic trade, but the restraint would be an indirect result, however inevitable.... Slight reflection will show that, if the national power extends to all contracts and combinations in manufacture, agriculture, mining, and other productive industries, whose ultimate result may affect external commerce, comparatively little of business operations and affairs would be left for state control....

John Marshall Harlan
President Rutherford B. Hayes appointed Harlan to the Supreme Court in 1877. From Kentucky, Harlan had been a slave owner and a defender of slavery prior to the Civil War, but he supported maintaining the Union and became an officer in the Union Army. After the war, he became a Republican and repudiated his earlier support of slavery. He is known as the "Great Dissenter" because of his dissents in *Plessy v. Ferguson*, which established the doctrine of "separate but equal" to support segregation, the *Civil Rights Cases*, which narrowly construed the Fourteenth Amendment, and *Lochner v. New York*, which limited the ability of government to regulate labor conditions.

Mr. Justice HARLAN, dissenting.

In its consideration of the important constitutional question presented this court assumes on the record before us that the result of the transactions disclosed by the pleadings and proof was the creation of a monopoly in the manufacture of a necessary of life. If this combination, so far as its operations necessarily or directly affect interstate commerce, cannot be restrained or suppressed under some power granted to congress, it will be cause for regret that the patriotic statesmen who framed the constitution did not foresee the necessity of investing the national government with power to deal with gigantic monopolies holding in their grasp, and injuriously controlling in their own interest, the entire trade among the states in food products that are essential to the comfort of every household in the land.

The court holds it to be vital in our system of government to recognize and give effect to both the commercial power of the nation and the police powers of the states, to the end that the Union be strengthened, and the autonomy of the states preserved. In this view I entirely concur. Undoubtedly, the preservation of the just authority of the states is an object of deep concern to every lover of his country.... But it is equally true that the preservation of the just authority of the general government is essential as well to the safety of the states as to the attainment of the important ends for which that government was ordained by the people of the United States; and the destruction of that authority would be fatal to the peace and well-being of the American people. The constitution, which enumerates the powers committed to the nation for objects of interest to the people of all the states, should not, therefore, be subjected to an interpretation so rigid, technical, and narrow that those objects cannot be accomplished....

Comments and Questions

1. Why was the United States unable to regulate the monopolization of the manufacture of sugar?

2. Do you think *E.C. Knight* and *The Daniel Ball* are consistent in their approaches to the Commerce Clause?

3. Note that in *The Daniel Ball* the Court rejects the argument that if the United States could regulate the Daniel Ball, it could regulate anything, but in *E.C. Knight* the Court accepts the argument that if Congress could regulate manufacture because it might end up in interstate commerce, it could regulate anything. Why is it concerned about whether Congress can regulate anything or everything? Is it a concern for regulation, or is it a concern about who can regulate?

CHAMPION v. AMES (LOTTERY CASE)

United States Supreme Court, 1903.
188 U.S. 321, 23 S.Ct. 321, 47 L.Ed. 492.

Mr. Justice HARLAN delivered the opinion of the court:

The general question arising upon this appeal involves the constitutionality of the 1st section of the act of Congress ... entitled An Act for the Suppression of Lottery Traffic through National and Interstate Commerce and the Postal Service, Subject to the Jurisdiction and Laws of the United States....

The 1st section of the act 1895 ... is as follows:

> § 1. That any person who shall cause to be brought within the United States from abroad, for the purpose of disposing of the same, or deposited in or carried by the mails of the United States, or carried from one state to another in the United States, any paper, certificate, or instrument purporting to be or represent a ticket, chance, share, or interest in or dependent upon the event of a lottery, ... or similar enterprise, offering prizes dependent upon lot or chance ... shall be punishable [for] the first offense by imprisonment for not more than two years, or by a fine of not more than $1,000, or both, and in the second and after offenses by such imprisonment only.

[Charles Champion was arrested for conspiracy to commit this offense by shipping] from Dallas, in the state of Texas, to Fresno, in the state of California, certain papers, certificates, and instruments purporting to be and representing tickets, as [he] then and there well knew, chances, shares, and interests in and dependent upon the event of a lottery, offering prizes dependent upon lot and chance.... [He sued for a writ of habeas corpus, arguing that the law was beyond the power of Congress.]

The appellant insists that the carrying of lottery tickets from one state to another state by an express company engaged in carrying freight and packages from state to state, although such tickets may be contained in a box or package, does not constitute, and cannot by any act of Congress be legally made to constitute, commerce among the states within the meaning of the clause of the Constitution of the United States providing that Congress shall have power "to regulate commerce with foreign nations, and among the several states, and with the Indian tribes;" consequently, that Congress cannot make it an offense to cause such tickets to be carried from one state to another.

The government insists that express companies, when engaged, for hire, in the business of transportation from one state to another, are instrumentalities of commerce among the states; that the carrying of lottery tickets from one state to another is commerce which Congress may regulate; and that as a means of executing the power to regulate interstate commerce Congress may make it an offense against the United States to cause lottery tickets to be carried from one state to another....

What is the import of the word "commerce" as used in the Constitution? It is not defined by that instrument. Undoubtedly, the carrying from one state to another by independent carriers of things or commodities that are ordinary subjects of traffic, and which have in themselves a recognized value in money, constitutes interstate commerce. But does not commerce among the several states include something more? Does not the carrying from one state to another, by independent carriers, of lottery tickets that entitle the holder to the payment of a certain amount of money therein specified, also constitute commerce among the states?

[The Court reviewed its past decisions interpreting the Commerce Clause, concluding that the transporting lottery tickets would be commerce within the meaning of the Clause.]

This reference to prior adjudications could be extended if it were necessary to do so. The cases cited, however, sufficiently indicate the grounds upon which this court has proceeded when determining the meaning and scope of the commerce clause. They show that commerce among the states embraces navigation, intercourse, communication, traffic, the transit of persons, and the transmission of messages by telegraph. They also show that the power to regulate commerce among the several states is vested in Congress as absolutely as it would be in a single government, having in its constitution the same restrictions on the exercise of the power as are found in the Constitution of the United States; that such power is plenary, complete in itself, and may be exerted by Congress to its utmost extent, subject only to such limitations as the Constitution imposes upon the exercise of the powers granted by it; and that in determining the character of the regulations to be adopted Congress has a large discretion which is not to be controlled by the courts, simply because, in their opinion, such regulations may not be the best or most effective that could be employed.

We come, then, to inquire whether there is any solid foundation upon which to rest the contention that Congress may not regulate the carrying of lottery tickets from one state to another, at least by corporations or companies whose business it is, for hire, to carry tangible property from one state to another....

But it is said that the statute in question does not regulate the carrying of lottery tickets from state to state, but by punishing those who cause them to be so carried Congress in effect prohibits such carrying; that in respect of the carrying from one state to another of articles or things that are, in fact, or according to usage in business, the subjects of commerce, the authority given Congress was not to prohibit, but only to regulate. This view was earnestly pressed at the bar by learned counsel, and must be examined.

It is to be remarked that the Constitution does not define what is to be deemed a legitimate regulation of interstate commerce. In *Gibbons v. Ogden* it was said that the power to regulate such commerce is the power to prescribe the rule by which it is to be governed. But this general observation leaves it to be determined, when the question comes before the court, whether Congress, in prescribing a particular rule, has exceeded its power under the Constitution....

We have said that the carrying from state to state of lottery tickets constitutes interstate commerce, and that the regulation of such commerce is within the power of Congress under the Constitution. Are we prepared to say that a provision which is, in effect, a prohibition of the carriage of such articles from state to state is not a fit or appropriate mode for the regulation of that particular kind of commerce? If lottery traffic, carried on through interstate commerce, is a matter of which Congress may take cognizance and over which its power may be exerted, can it be possible that it must tolerate the traffic, and simply regulate the manner in which it may be carried on? Or may not Congress, for the protection of the people of all the states, and under the power to regulate interstate commerce, devise such means, within the scope of the Constitution, and not prohibited by it, as will drive that traffic out of commerce among the states?

In determining whether regulation may not under some circumstances properly take the form or have the effect of prohibition, the nature of the interstate traffic which it was sought by the act of May 2d,

1895, to suppress cannot be overlooked. When enacting that statute Congress no doubt shared the views upon the subject of lotteries heretofore expressed by this court. [A]fter observing that the suppression of nuisances injurious to public health or morality is among the most important duties of government, this court said: "Experience has shown that the common forms of gambling are comparatively innocuous when placed in contrast with the widespread pestilence of lotteries. The former are confined to a few persons and places, but the latter infests the whole community; it enters every dwelling; it reaches every class; it preys upon the hard earnings of the poor; it plunders the ignorant and simple."....

If a state, when considering legislation for the suppression of lotteries within its own limits, may properly take into view the evils that inhere in the raising of money, in that mode, why may not Congress, invested with the power to regulate commerce among the several states, provide that such commerce shall not be polluted by the carrying of lottery tickets from one state to another? In this connection it must not be forgotten that the power of Congress to regulate commerce among the states is plenary, is complete in itself, and is subject to no limitations except such as may be found in the Constitution. What provision in that instrument can be regarded as limiting the exercise of the power granted? What clause can be cited which, in any degree, countenances the suggestion that one may, of right, carry or cause to be carried from one state to another that which will harm the public morals? ...

If it be said that the act of 1894 is inconsistent with the 10th Amendment, reserving to the states respectively, or to the people, the powers not delegated to the United States, the answer is that the power to regulate commerce among the states has been expressly delegated to Congress.

Besides, Congress, by that act, does not assume to interfere with traffic or commerce in lottery tickets carried on exclusively within the limits of any state, but has in view only commerce of that kind among the several states. It has not assumed to interfere with the completely internal affairs of any state, and has only legislated in respect of a matter which concerns the people of the United States. As a state may, for the purpose of guarding the morals of its own people, forbid all sales of lottery tickets within its limits, so Congress, for the purpose of guarding the people of the United States against the "widespread pestilence of lotteries" and to protect the commerce which concerns all the states, may prohibit the carrying of lottery tickets from one state to another. In legislating upon the subject of the traffic in lottery tickets, as carried on through interstate commerce, Congress only supplemented the action of those states—perhaps all of them—which, for the protection of the public morals, prohibit the drawing of lotteries, as well as the sale or circulation of lottery tickets, within their respective limits. It said, in effect, that it would not permit the declared policy of the states, which sought to protect their people against the mischiefs of the lottery business, to be overthrown or disregarded by the agency of interstate commerce. We should hesitate long before adjudging that an evil of such appalling character, carried on through interstate commerce, cannot be met and crushed by the only power competent to that end. We say competent to that end, because Congress alone has the power to occupy, by legislation, the whole field of interstate commerce.... If the carrying of lottery tickets from one state to another be interstate commerce, and if Congress is of opinion that an effective regulation for the suppression of lotteries, carried on through such commerce, is to make it a criminal offense to cause lottery tickets to be carried from one state to another, we know of no authority in the courts to hold that the means thus devised are not appropriate and necessary to protect the country at large against a species of interstate commerce which, although in general use and somewhat favored in both national and state legislation in the early history of the country, has grown into disrepute, and has become offensive to the entire people of the nation. It is a kind of traffic which no one can be entitled to pursue as of right.

That regulation may sometimes appropriately assume the form of prohibition is also illustrated by the case of diseased cattle, transported from one state to another. Such cattle may have, notwithstanding their condition, a value in money for some purposes, and yet it cannot be doubted that Congress, under its power to regulate commerce, may either provide for their being inspected before transportation begins, or, in its discretion, may prohibit their being transported from one state to another....

It is said, however, that if, in order to suppress lotteries carried on through interstate commerce, Congress may exclude lottery tickets from such commerce, that principle leads necessarily to the conclusion that Congress may arbitrarily exclude from commerce among the states any article, commodity, or thing, of whatever kind or nature, or however useful or valuable, which it may choose, no matter with what motive, to declare shall not be carried from one state to another. It will be time enough to consider the constitutionality of such legislation when we must do so. The present case does not require the court to declare the full extent of the power that Congress may exercise in the regulation of commerce among the states. We may, however, repeat, in this connection, what the court has heretofore said, that the power of Congress to regulate commerce among the states, although plenary, cannot be deemed arbitrary, since it is subject to such limitations or restrictions as are prescribed by the Constitution. This power, therefore, may not be exercised so as to infringe rights secured or protected by that instrument. It would not be difficult to imagine legislation that would be justly liable to such an objection as that stated, and be hostile to the objects for the accomplishment of which Congress was invested with the general power to regulate commerce among the several states. But, as often said, the possible abuse of a power is not an argument against its existence. There is probably no governmental power that may not be exerted to the injury of the public. If what is done by Congress is manifestly in excess of the powers granted to it, then upon the courts will rest the duty of adjudging that its action is neither legal nor binding upon the people. But if what Congress does is within the limits of its power, and is simply unwise or injurious, the remedy is that suggested by Chief Justice Marshall in *Gibbons v. Ogden*, when he said: "The wisdom and the discretion of Congress, their identity with the people, and the influence which their constituents possess at elections, are, in this, as in many other instances, as that, for example, of declaring war, the sole restraints on which they have relied, to secure them from its abuse. They are the restraints on which the people must often rely solely, in all representative governments." ...

Mr. Chief Justice FULLER, with whom concur Mr. Justice BREWER, Mr. Justice SHIRAS, and Mr. Justice PECKHAM, dissenting:

[T]he naked question is whether the prohibition by Congress of the carriage of lottery tickets from one state to another by means other than the mails is within the powers vested in that body by the Constitution of the United States. That the purpose of Congress in this enactment was the suppression of lotteries cannot reasonably be denied. That purpose is avowed in the title of the act, and is its natural and reasonable effect, and by that its validity must be tested.

The power of the state to impose restraints and burdens on persons and property in conservation and promotion of the public health, good order, and prosperity is a power originally and always belonging to the states, not surrendered by them to the general government, nor directly restrained by the Constitution of the United States, and essentially exclusive, and the suppression of lotteries as a harmful business falls within this power, commonly called, of police.*

It is urged, however, that because Congress is empowered to regulate commerce between the several states, it, therefore, may suppress lotteries by prohibiting the carriage of lottery matter. Congress may, indeed, make all laws necessary and proper for carrying the powers granted to it into execution, and doubtless an act prohibiting the carriage of lottery matter would be necessary and proper to the execution of a power to suppress lotteries; but that power belongs to the states and not to Congress. To hold that Congress has general police power would be to hold that it may accomplish objects not intrusted to the general government, and to defeat the operation of the 10th Amendment, declaring that "the powers not delegated to the United States by the Constitution, nor prohibited by it to the states, are reserved to the states respectively, or to the people." ...

But apart from the question of bona fides, this act cannot be brought

* The "police power" is the power to place restraints on the personal freedom and property rights of persons for the protection of the public safety, health, welfare, and morals of the community. It is an inherent power of the state that arises out of sovereignty. It does not refer to the officers of the law that we today call "the police." [author's note]

within the power to regulate commerce among the several states, unless lottery tickets are articles of commerce, and, therefore, when carried across state lines, of interstate commerce; or unless the power to regulate interstate commerce includes the absolute and exclusive power to prohibit the transportation of anything or anybody from one state to another.... [The opinion then argues that lottery tickets are not articles of commerce.]

If a lottery ticket is not an article of commerce, how can it become so when placed in an envelope or box or other covering, and transported by an express company? To say that the mere carrying of an article which is not an article of commerce in and of itself nevertheless becomes such the moment it is to be transported from one state to another, is to transform a non-commercial article into a commercial one simply because it is transported. I cannot conceive that any such result can properly follow.

It would be to say that everything is an article of commerce the moment it is taken to be transported from place to place, and of interstate commerce if from state to state.

An invitation to dine, or to take a drive, or a note of introduction, all become articles of commerce under the ruling in this case, by being deposited with an express company for transportation. This in effect breaks down all the differences between that which is, and that which is not, an article of commerce, and the necessary consequence is to take from the states all jurisdiction over the subject so far as interstate communication is concerned. It is a long step in the direction of wiping out all traces of state lines, and the creation of a centralized government.

Does the grant to Congress of the power to regulate interstate commerce import the absolute power to prohibit it? ...

It will not do to say—a suggestion which has heretofore been made in this case—that state laws have been found to be ineffective for the suppression of lotteries, and therefore Congress should interfere. The scope of the commerce clause of the Constitution cannot be enlarged because of present views of public interest....

Comments and Questions

1. This is a close case, 5–4, but why is it a close case? What is it that leads four justices to say that the law is beyond the power of Congress under the Commerce Clause?

2. Prior to the Constitution, the "police power" resided in the states, not the United States. The dissent maintains that the Constitution did not alter the placement of the police power and that only the states have the police power—nothing in Article I, Section 8 grants Congress any police power. What do you think?

3. What do you think of the majority's argument that Congress needed to pass this law in order to protect those states that wished to

ban lotteries, because absent this law it would be difficult to suppress lotteries in states? What do you think of the dissent's response?

4. Is the dissent correct that if Congress can regulate the carriage of lottery tickets across state lines, it can regulate the carriage of anything across state lines, and if that is so, the notion of a federal government of limited powers would be destroyed?

5. Two years later the Court decided another case that broadened the scope of the Commerce Clause. In *Swift & Co. v. United States*, 196 U.S. 375 (1905), the Court upheld the constitutionality of an application of the Sherman Antitrust Act against meat dealers. Recall that in *E.C. Knight Co.*, ten years before, the Court had found the application of the Sherman Antitrust Act against sugar manufacturers was beyond Congress's power. The Court in an opinion by Justice Oliver Wendell Holmes distinguished *E.C. Knight* as involving something occurring wholly within a state—manufacture—but here the combination was between sellers of meat. While sales of meat might occur only within a state,

> [w]hen cattle are sent for sale from a place in one state, with the expectation that they will end their transit, after purchase, in another, and when in effect they do so, with only the interruption necessary to find a purchaser at the stock yards, and when this is a typical, constantly recurring course, the current thus existing is a current of commerce among the states, and the purchase of the cattle is a part and incident of such commerce.

196 U.S. at 398–99. This "current of commerce" became a "stream of commerce" in a later case, *Stafford v. Wallace*, 258 U.S. 495 (1922). There the Court said:

> The application of the commerce clause of the Constitution in the *Swift Case* was the result of the natural development of interstate commerce under modern conditions. It was the inevitable recognition of the great central fact that such streams of commerce from one part of the country to another, which are ever flowing, are in their very essence the commerce among the states and with foreign nations, which historically it was one of the chief purposes of the Constitution to bring under national protection and control. This court declined to defeat this purpose in respect of such a stream and take it out of complete national regulation by a nice and technical inquiry into the non-interstate character of some of its necessary incidents and facilities, when considered alone and without reference to their association with the movement of which they were an essential but subordinate part.

258 U.S. at 518–19. Thus, if something occurred in the "stream of commerce," it was subject to national regulation under the Commerce Clause even if the actual matter regulated only occurred within a state. Does this remind you at all of *Gibbons v. Ogden*? *The Daniel Ball?*

HAMMER v. DAGENHART (CHILD LABOR CASE)

Supreme Court of the United States, 1918.
247 U.S. 251, 38 S.Ct. 529, 62 L.Ed. 1101.

Mr. Justice DAY delivered the opinion of the Court.

A bill was filed in the United States District Court for the Western District of North Carolina by a father in his own behalf and as next friend of his two minor sons, one under the age of fourteen years and the other between the ages of fourteen and sixteen years, employees in a cotton mill at Charlotte, North Carolina, to enjoin the enforcement of the act of Congress intended to prevent interstate commerce in the products of child labor.

The District Court held the act unconstitutional and entered a decree enjoining its enforcement. This appeal brings the case here....

The controlling question for decision is: Is it within the authority of Congress in regulating commerce among the states to prohibit the transportation in interstate commerce of manufactured goods, the product of a factory in which, within thirty days prior to their removal therefrom, children under the age of fourteen have been employed or permitted to work, or children between the ages of fourteen and sixteen years have been employed or permitted to work more than eight hours in any day, or more than six days in any week, or after the hour of 7 o'clock p. m., or before the hour of 6 o'clock a. m.?

The power essential to the passage of this act, the government contends, is found in the commerce clause of the Constitution which authorizes Congress to regulate commerce with foreign nations and among the states.

In *Gibbons v. Ogdon*, Chief Justice Marshall, speaking for this court, and defining the extent and nature of the commerce power, said, "It is the power to regulate; that is, to prescribe the rule by which commerce is to be governed." In other words, the power is one to control the means by which commerce is carried on, which is directly the contrary of the assumed right to forbid commerce from moving and thus destroying it as to particular commodities. But it is insisted that adjudged cases in this court establish the doctrine that the power to regulate given to Congress incidentally includes the authority to prohibit the movement of ordinary commodities and therefore that the subject is not open for discussion. The cases demonstrate the contrary. They rest upon the character of the particular subjects dealt with and the fact that the scope of governmental authority, state or national, possessed over them is such that the authority to prohibit is as to them but the exertion of the power to regulate.

The first of these cases is *Champion v. Ames*, the so-called *Lottery Case*, in which it was held that Congress might pass a law having the effect to keep the channels of commerce free from use in the transportation of tickets used in the promotion of lottery schemes. In *Hipolite Egg*

Co. v. United States, 220 U. S. 45, this court sustained the power of Congress to pass the Pure Food and Drug Act, which prohibited the introduction into the states by means of interstate commerce of impure foods and drugs. In *Hoke v. United States*, 227 U. S. 308, this court sustained the constitutionality of the so-called "White Slave Traffic Act," whereby the transportation of a woman in interstate commerce for the purpose of prostitution was forbidden.... In *Caminetti v. United States*, 242 U. S. 470, we held that Congress might prohibit the transportation of women in interstate commerce for the purposes of debauchery and kindred purposes. In *Clark Distilling Co. v. Western Maryland Railway Co.*, 242 U. S. 311, the power of Congress over the transportation of intoxicating liquors was sustained.... And concluding the discussion which sustained the authority of the Government to prohibit the transportation of liquor in interstate commerce, the court said : " * * * The exceptional nature of the subject here regulated is the basis upon which the exceptional power exerted must rest and affords no ground for any fear that such power may be constitutionally extended to things which it may not, consistently with the guaranties of the Constitution embrace."

In each of these instances the use of interstate transportation was necessary to the accomplishment of harmful results. In other words, although the power over interstate transportation was to regulate, that could only be accomplished by prohibiting the use of the facilities of interstate commerce to effect the evil intended.

This element is wanting in the present case. The thing intended to be accomplished by this statute is the denial of the facilities of interstate commerce to those manufacturers in the states who employ children within the prohibited ages. The act in its effect does not regulate transportation among the states, but aims to standardize the ages at which children may be employed in mining and manufacturing within the states. The goods shipped are of themselves harmless. The act permits them to be freely shipped after thirty days from the time of their removal from the factory. When offered for shipment, and before transportation begins, the labor of their production is over, and the mere fact that they were intended for interstate commerce transportation does not make their production subject to federal control under the commerce power.

Commerce "consists of intercourse and traffic * * * and includes the transportation of persons and property, as well as the purchase, sale and exchange of commodities." The making of goods and the mining of coal are not commerce, nor does the fact that these things are to be afterwards shipped, or used in interstate commerce, make their production a part thereof.

Over interstate transportation, or its incidents, the regulatory power of Congress is ample, but the production of articles, intended for interstate commerce, is a matter of local regulation.... If it were otherwise, all manufacture intended for interstate shipment would be brought under federal control to the practical exclusion of the authority of the states, a result certainly not contemplated by the framers of the Constitution when they vested in Congress the authority to regulate commerce among the States.

It is further contended that the authority of Congress may be exerted to control interstate commerce in the shipment of childmade goods because of the effect of the circulation of such goods in other states where the evil of this class of labor has been recognized by local legislation, and the right to thus employ child labor has been more rigorously restrained than in the state of production. In other words, that the unfair competition, thus engendered, may be controlled by closing the channels of interstate commerce to manufacturers in those states where the local laws do not meet what Congress deems to be the more just standard of other states.

There is no power vested in Congress to require the states to exercise their police power so as to prevent possible unfair competition. Many causes may co-operate to give one state, by reason of local laws or conditions, an economic advantage over others. The commerce clause was not intended to give to Congress a general authority to equalize such conditions. In some of the states laws have been passed fixing minimum wages for women, in others the local law regulates the hours of labor of women in various employments. Business done in such states may be at an economic disadvantage when compared with states which have no such regulations; surely, this fact does not give Congress the power to deny transportation in interstate commerce to those who carry on business where the hours of labor and the rate of compensation for women have not been fixed by a standard in use in other states and approved by Congress.

The grant of power of Congress over the subject of interstate commerce was to enable it to regulate such commerce, and not to give it authority to control the states in their exercise of the police power over local trade and manufacture.

The grant of authority over a purely federal matter was not intended to destroy the local power always existing and carefully reserved to the states in the Tenth Amendment to the Constitution....

That there should be limitations upon the right to employ children in mines and factories in the interest of their own and the public welfare, all will admit. That such employment is generally deemed to require regulation is shown by the fact that the brief of counsel states that every state in the Union has a law upon the subject, limiting the right to thus employ children. In North Carolina, the state wherein is located the factory in which the employment was had in the present case, no child under twelve years of age is permitted to work.

It may be desirable that such laws be uniform, but our federal government is one of enumerated powers; "this principle," declared Chief Justice Marshall in *McCulloch v. Maryland*, "is universally admitted."

A statute must be judged by its natural and reasonable effect. The control by Congress over interstate commerce cannot authorize the exercise of authority not entrusted to it by the Constitution. The maintenance of the authority of the states over matters purely local is as essential to the preservation of our institutions as is the conservation of the supremacy of the federal power in all matters entrusted to the nation by the federal Constitution.

In interpreting the Constitution it must never be forgotten that the nation is made up of states to which are entrusted the powers of local government. And to them and to the people the powers not expressly delegated to the national government are reserved. The power of the states to regulate their purely internal affairs by such laws as seem wise to the local authority is inherent and has never been surrendered to the general government. To sustain this statute would not be in our judgment a recognition of the lawful exertion of congressional authority over interstate commerce, but would sanction an invasion by the federal power of the control of a matter purely local in its character, and over which no authority has been delegated to Congress in conferring the power to regulate commerce among the states.

We have neither authority nor disposition to question the motives of Congress in enacting this legislation. The purposes intended must be attained consistently with constitutional limitations and not by an invasion of the powers of the states. This court has no more important function than that which devolves upon it the obligation to preserve inviolate the constitutional limitations upon the exercise of authority federal and state to the end that each may continue to discharge, harmoniously with the other, the duties entrusted to it by the Constitution.

In our view the necessary effect of this act is, by means of a prohibition against the movement in interstate commerce of ordinary commercial commodities to regulate the hours of labor of children in factories and mines within the states, a purely state authority. Thus the act in a two-fold sense is repugnant to the Constitution. It not only transcends the authority delegated to Congress over commerce but also exerts a power as to a purely local matter to which the federal authority does not extend. The far reaching result of upholding the act cannot be more plainly indicated than by pointing out that if Congress can thus regulate matters entrusted to local authority by prohibition of the movement of commodities in interstate commerce, all freedom of commerce will be at an end, and the power of the states over local matters may be eliminated, and thus our system of government be practically destroyed.

For these reasons we hold that this law exceeds the constitutional authority of Congress.

Mr. Justice HOLMES, dissenting.

The single question in this case is whether Congress has power to prohibit the shipment in interstate or foreign commerce of any product of a cotton mill situated in the United States, in which within thirty days before the removal of the product children under fourteen have been employed, or children between fourteen and sixteen have been employed more than eight hours in a day, or more than six days in any week, or between seven in the evening and six in the morning. The objection urged against the power is that the States have exclusive control over their methods of production and that Congress cannot meddle with them, and taking the proposition in the sense of direct intermeddling I agree to it and suppose that no one denies it. But if an act is within the powers specifically conferred upon Congress, it seems to me that it is not made any less constitutional because of the indirect effects that it may have, however obvious it may be that it will have those effects, and that we are not at liberty upon such grounds to hold it void.

Oliver Wendell Holmes, Jr.
Theodore Roosevelt appointed Holmes to the Supreme Court in 1902 when he was 61 years old and on which he served until 1932, when he was 91. An uncommonly strong writer, Holmes is notable both for a number of his dissents and his decisions for the Court. He expressed a view of judicial restraint in construing the legislative powers of Congress and the states during the Progressive era, while believing in an active judiciary to protect rights enumerated in the Bill of Rights. His dissents in particular have virtually all been vindicated by later decisions of the Court. Later, during the New Deal, however, he joined the majority in finding various New Deal laws unconstitutional.

The first step in my argument is to make plain what no one is likely to dispute—that the statute in question is within the power expressly given to Congress if considered only as to its immediate effects and that if invalid it is so only upon some collateral ground. The statute confines itself to prohibiting the carriage of certain goods in interstate or foreign commerce. Congress is given power to regulate such commerce in unqualified terms. It would not be argued today that the power to regulate does not include the power to prohibit. Regulation means the prohibition of something, and when interstate commerce is the matter to be regulated I cannot doubt that the regulation may prohibit any part of such commerce that Congress sees fit to forbid. At all events it is established by the *Lottery Case* and others that have followed it that a law is not beyond the regulative power of Congress merely because it prohibits certain transportation out and out. So I repeat that this statute in its immediate operation is clearly within the Congress's constitutional power.

The question then is narrowed to whether the exercise of its otherwise constitutional power by Congress can be pronounced unconstitutional because of its possible reaction upon the conduct of the States in a matter upon which I have admitted that they are free from direct control. I should have thought that that matter had been disposed of so fully as to leave no room for doubt....

The notion that prohibition is any less prohibition when applied to things now thought evil I do not understand. But if there is any matter upon which civilized countries have agreed—far more unanimously than they have with regard to intoxicants and some other matters over which this country is now emotionally aroused—it is the evil of premature and excessive child labor. I should have thought that if we were to introduce our own moral conceptions where is my opinion they do not belong, this was preeminently a case for upholding the exercise of all its powers by the United States.

But I had thought that the propriety of the exercise of a power admitted to exist in some cases was for the consideration of Congress alone and that this Court always had disavowed the right to intrude its judgment upon questions of policy or morals. It is not for this Court to pronounce when prohibition is necessary to regulation if it ever may be necessary—to say that it is permissible as against strong drink but not as against the product of ruined lives.

The Act does not meddle with anything belonging to the States. They may regulate their internal affairs and their domestic commerce as they like. But when they seek to send their products across the State line they are no longer within their rights. If there were no Constitution and no Congress their power to cross the line would depend upon their neighbors. Under the Constitution such commerce belongs not to the States but to Congress to regulate. It may carry out its views of public policy whatever indirect effect they may have upon the activities of the States. Instead of being encountered by a prohibitive tariff at her boundaries the State encounters the public policy of the United States which it is for Congress to express. The public policy of the United States is shaped with a view to the benefit of the nation as a whole. If, as has been the case within the memory of men still living, a State should take a different view of the propriety of sustaining a lottery from that which generally prevails, I cannot believe that the fact would require a different decision from that reached in *Champion v. Ames*. Yet in that case it would be said with quite as much force as in this that Congress was attempting to intermeddle with the State's domestic affairs. The national welfare as understood by Congress may require a different attitude within its sphere from that of some self-seeking State. It seems to me entirely constitutional for Congress to enforce its understanding by all the means at its command.

Mr. Justice McKENNA, Mr. Justice BRANDEIS, and Mr. Justice CLARKE concur in this opinion.

Comments and Questions

1. Between the *Lottery Case* and the *Child Labor Case*, eight justices had been replaced. Nevertheless, the closeness of the case

remained, but this time with the majority finding the law beyond Congress's powers. Is this case consistent with the *Lottery Case*?

2. How does the majority in the *Child Labor Case* distinguish the *Lottery Case*?

3. Do you agree with the majority that if Congress could regulate the shipment across state lines of goods from factories employing child labor, it could regulate anything, destroying the notion of limited federal powers?

4. What limit on Congress's power does Holmes envision?

5. Do you think Congress's power to "regulate" includes the power to "prohibit"?

6. Should Congress be able in effect to override a state's considered judgment with respect to the working conditions in a state? Should Congress be able to override some states' views in order to eliminate their competitive advantage over other states that have chosen a different view on the appropriate working conditions?

3. THE NEW DEAL

The Progressive era stalled in the tumultuous period of the Twenties, with its celebration of the modern and the exuberance of an expansive post-war economy. A succession of Republican presidents and congresses took a hands-off approach to business and social issues while engaged in a concerted repression of socialists and communists at both national and state levels. The Great Depression, initiated by the stock market crash in 1929, resulted in a political upheaval. Democrats controlled Congress and Franklin Roosevelt was elected President in 1932 with the promise of a New Deal. The Court, however, reflected the past, with seven of the nine justices appointed by a Republican president, and it demonstrated its hostility to New Deal legislation by its consistent rulings against the constitutionality of the various acts designed to ameliorate or overcome the Great Depression. The Court's conservative approach to the Commerce Clause reflected in the *Child Labor Case* continued into the New Deal. In 1935 the Court invalidated two New Deal laws on Commerce Clause grounds. In *Railroad Retirement Bd. v. Alton RR. Co.*, 295 U.S. 330 (1935) the Court found the Railroad Retirement Act, which established a mandatory retirement and pension program for railroads, beyond Congress's Commerce Clause authority. In *A.L.A. Schechter Poulty Corp. v. United States*, 295 U.S. 495 (1935), the Court found the National Industrial Recovery Act unconstitutional, in part as beyond Congress's Commerce Clause authority. The next year it held the Bituminous Coal Conservation Act, which regulated the price at which coal could be sold and set minimum wages and maximum hours for coal workers, beyond the Commerce Clause as well. *See Carter v. Carter Coal Co.*, 298 U.S. 238 (1936). Nevertheless, most of the cases were decided by slender 5–4 majorities.

The obstacles the Court placed in the way of legislative and executive attempts to deal with the depression resulted in the President Roosevelt's so-called Court-packing plan. In 1937, following an overwhelming Democratic victory in the 1936 election, Roosevelt proposed that Congress enact a law to add a new seat to the Supreme Court for every member of the Court who was over 70½ years old, which at that time was six members. Billed as a measure to relieve the burden on elderly justices, it was transparently a means by which Roosevelt would be able to add six new justices. Despite the substantial Democratic majority in both houses, the plan was not generally supported. There was a widespread feeling that, notwithstanding the errors of the Court in the view of Congress, playing politics with the Court to overturn its decisions was inappropriate. Moreover, the narrow majority against the New Deal legislation seemed to crumble in a case in which one justice switched sides. This led to the expression—the switch in time that saved the nine.*

Shortly thereafter, the Court upheld by a 5–4 vote the constitutionality of the National Labor Relations Act, the basic federal law permitting unions to exist. *See NLRB v. Jones & Laughlin Steel Corp.*, 301 U.S. 1 (1937). This case involved an order by the National Labor Relations Board to the steel company, prohibiting it from discriminating against employees because of union activity. The company argued that the law was beyond Congress's Commerce Clause authority, because it regulated labor relations wholly within one state. The Court, however, noted that the company was a vertically integrated firm, owning iron ore mines in Minnesota, steamships that carried the ore on the Great Lakes, coal mines in Pennsylvania, two railroads, steel mills in Pennsylvania, and fabricating plants in New York and Louisiana. The Court found that a labor disruption in one place would affect the entire chain of commerce from mining to ultimate sale of finished steel products. Building on the "stream of commerce" theory from earlier cases, the Court said that Congress could regulate labor relations at one plant in one state, because of its affect on the entire stream of commerce.

While Congress did not adopt the Roosevelt plan, it did adopt a generous retirement plan—full pay for judges who retired over the age of 70—with the result that one of the "four horsemen,"** the conservative core of the Court, retired, allowing Roosevelt to appoint Justice Hugo Black, a New Deal Democratic Senator, in 1937. This assured a "liberal" majority on the Court, and the cases reflected the new orientation.

* This is a play on the adage, "a stitch in time saves nine," meaning preventive maintenance can eliminate the need for major repairs later.

** This is a reference to the four horsemen of the apocalypse described in the Book of Revelations.

Harlan Fiske Stone
President Calvin Coolidge appointed Stone to the Supreme Court in 1925. Stone had been a partner in a New York law firm, a professor, and then dean of Columbia Law School. When the Attorney General was forced to resign in a scandal, Coolidge needed a person above reproach for the position, and he reached out to Stone. As a reward, when a vacancy on the Court arose, Coolidge appointed Stone. Although appointed by a Republican, Stone was one of the "Three Musketeers" (opposed to the "Four Horsemen") who dissented from the Court's invalidation of most of the New Deal legislation. Consequently, when the Chief Justice retired, Franklin Roosevelt appointed Stone Chief Justice.

UNITED STATES v. DARBY

United States Supreme Court, 1941.
312 U.S. 100, 61 S.Ct. 451, 85 L.Ed. 609.

Mr. Justice STONE delivered the opinion of the Court.

The two principal questions raised by the record in this case are, first, whether Congress has constitutional power to prohibit the shipment in interstate commerce of lumber manufactured by employees whose wages are less than a prescribed minimum or whose weekly hours of labor at that wage are greater than a prescribed maximum, and, second, whether it has power to prohibit the employment of workmen in the production of goods "for interstate commerce" at other than prescribed wages and hours....

[Darby, a Georgia lumber manufacturer, was indicted for violating the Fair Labor Standards Act, which imposed these requirements in § 15(a)(1) & (2). The district court quashed the indictment on the grounds that the Act was unconstitutional, and the case came directly to the Supreme Court pursuant to a statute at the time that authorized the direct appeal to the Court when the district court judgment "is based upon the invalidity, or construction of the statute upon which the indictment is founded."]

The Fair Labor Standards Act set up a comprehensive legislative scheme for preventing the shipment in interstate commerce of certain products and commodities produced in the United States under labor conditions as respects wages and hours which fail to conform to standards set up by the Act. Its purpose [as reflected in its findings and declaration of policy[1]] is to exclude from interstate commerce goods produced for the commerce and to prevent their production for interstate commerce, under conditions detrimental to the maintenance of the minimum standards of living necessary for health and general well-being; and to prevent the use of interstate commerce as the means of competition in the distribution of goods so produced, and as the means of

1. The Congress hereby finds that the existence, in industries engaged in commerce or in the production of goods for commerce, of labor conditions detrimental to

spreading and perpetuating such substandard labor conditions among the workers of the several states....

The district court quashed the indictment in its entirety upon the broad grounds that the Act, which it interpreted as a regulation of manufacture within the states, is unconstitutional. It declared that manufacture is not interstate commerce and that the regulation by the Fair Labor Standards Act of wages and hours of employment of those engaged in the manufacture of goods which it is intended at the time of production "may or will be" after production "sold in interstate commerce in part or in whole" is not within the congressional power to regulate interstate commerce.

The effect of the court's decision and judgment are thus to deny the power of Congress to prohibit shipment in interstate commerce of lumber produced for interstate commerce under the proscribed substandard labor conditions of wages and hours [and] its power to penalize the employer for his failure to conform to the wage and hour provisions in the case of employees engaged in the production of lumber which he intends thereafter to ship in interstate commerce in part or in whole according to the normal course of his business....

The prohibition of shipment of the proscribed goods in interstate commerce. [§ 15(a)(1)]

[W]hile manufacture is not of itself interstate commerce, the shipment of manufactured goods interstate is such commerce and the prohibition of such shipment by Congress is indubitably a regulation of the commerce. The power to regulate commerce is the power "to prescribe the rule by which commerce is to be governed." *Gibbons v. Ogden*. It extends not only to those regulations which aid, foster and protect the commerce, but embraces those which prohibit it. *Lottery Case (Champion v. Ames)*....

But it is said that the present prohibition falls within the scope of none of these categories; that while the prohibition is nominally a regulation of the commerce its motive or purpose is regulation of wages and hours of persons engaged in manufacture, the control of which has been reserved to the states and upon which Georgia and some of the states of destination have placed no restriction; that the effect of the present statute is not to exclude the prescribed articles from interstate commerce in aid of state regulation ... but instead, under the guise of a regulation of interstate commerce, it undertakes to regulate wages and hours within the state contrary to the policy of the state which has elected to leave them unregulated.

the maintenance of the minimum standard of living necessary for health, efficiency, and general well-being of workers (1) causes commerce and the channels and instrumentalities of commerce to be used to spread and perpetuate such labor conditions among the workers of the several States; (2) burdens commerce and the free flow of goods in commerce; (3) constitutes an unfair method of competition in commerce; (4) leads to labor disputes burdening and obstructing commerce and the free flow of goods in commerce; and (5) interferes with the orderly and fair marketing of goods in commerce.

The power of Congress over interstate commerce "is complete in itself, may be exercised to its utmost extent, and acknowledges no limitations, other than are prescribed by the constitution." *Gibbons v. Ogden*.... Congress, following its own conception of public policy concerning the restrictions which may appropriately be imposed on interstate commerce, is free to exclude from the commerce articles whose use in the states for which they are destined it may conceive to be injurious to the public health, morals or welfare, even though the state has not sought to regulate their use.

Such regulation is not a forbidden invasion of state power merely because either its motive or its consequence is to restrict the use of articles of commerce within the states of destination and is not prohibited unless by other Constitutional provisions. It is no objection to the assertion of the power to regulate interstate commerce that its exercise is attended by the same incidents which attend the exercise of the police power of the states.

The motive and purpose of the present regulation are plainly to make effective the Congressional conception of public policy that interstate commerce should not be made the instrument of competition in the distribution of goods produced under substandard labor conditions, which competition is injurious to the commerce and to the states from and to which the commerce flows. The motive and purpose of a regulation of interstate commerce are matters for the legislative judgment upon the exercise of which the Constitution places no restriction and over which the courts are given no control.... Whatever their motive and purpose, regulations of commerce which do not infringe some constitutional prohibition are within the plenary power conferred on Congress by the Commerce Clause. Subject only to that limitation, presently to be considered, we conclude that the prohibition of the shipment interstate of goods produced under the forbidden substandard labor conditions is within the constitutional authority of Congress.

In the more than a century which has elapsed since the decision of *Gibbons v. Ogden*, these principles of constitutional interpretation have been so long and repeatedly recognized by this Court as applicable to the Commerce Clause, that there would be little occasion for repeating them now were it not for the decision of this Court twenty-two years ago in *Hammer v. Dagenhart*. In that case it was held by a bare majority of the Court over the powerful and now classic dissent of Mr. Justice Holmes setting forth the fundamental issues involved, that Congress was without power to exclude the products of child labor from interstate commerce. The reasoning and conclusion of the Court's opinion there cannot be reconciled with the conclusion which we have reached, that the power of Congress under the Commerce Clause is plenary to exclude any article from interstate commerce subject only to the specific prohibitions of the Constitution.

Hammer v. Dagenhart has not been followed. The distinction on which the decision was rested that Congressional power to prohibit interstate commerce is limited to articles which in themselves have some harmful or deleterious property—a distinction which was novel when made and unsupported by any provision of the Constitution—has long since been abandoned. The thesis of the opinion that the motive of the prohibition or its effect to control in some measure the use or production within the states of the article thus excluded from the commerce can operate to deprive the regulation of its constitutional authority has long since ceased to have force. And finally we have declared "The authority of the Federal Government over interstate commerce does not differ in extent or character from that retained by the states over intrastate commerce." *United States v. Rock Royal Co–Operative, Inc.*, 307 U.S. 533 (1939).

The conclusion is inescapable that *Hammer v. Dagenhart*, was a departure from the principles which have prevailed in the interpretation of the commerce clause both before and since the decision and that such vitality, as a precedent, as it then had has long since been exhausted. It should be and now is overruled.

Validity of the wage and hour requirements—[§ 15(a)(2)]

[T]he validity of the prohibition turns on the question whether the employment, under other than the prescribed labor standards, of employees engaged in the production of goods for interstate commerce is so related to the commerce and so affects it as to be within the reach of the power of Congress to regulate it....

[T]he power of Congress over interstate commerce is not confined to the regulation of commerce among the states. It extends to those activities intrastate which so affect interstate commerce or the exercise of the power of Congress over it as to make regulation of them appropriate means to the attainment of a legitimate end, the exercise of the granted power of Congress to regulate interstate commerce. *See McCulloch v. Maryland.*

[I]n the absence of Congressional legislation on the subject state laws which are not regulations of the commerce itself or its instrumentalities are not forbidden even though they affect interstate commerce.

But it does not follow that Congress may not by appropriate legislation regulate intrastate activities where they have a substantial effect on interstate commerce. A recent example is the National Labor Relations Act for the regulation of employer and employee relations in industries in which strikes, induced by unfair labor practices named in the Act, tend to disturb or obstruct interstate commerce. *See National Labor Relations Board v. Jones & Laughlin Steel Corp.* But long before the adoption of the National Labor Relations Act, this Court had many times held that the power of Congress to regulate interstate commerce extends to the regulation through legislative action of activities intrastate which have a substantial effect on the commerce or the exercise of the Congressional power over it.

[C]ongress, having by the present Act adopted the policy of excluding from interstate commerce all goods produced for the commerce which do not conform to the specified labor standards, it may choose the means reasonably adapted to the attainment of the permitted end, even though they involve control of intrastate activities. Such legislation has often been sustained with respect to powers, other than the commerce power granted to the national government, when the means chosen, although not themselves within the granted power, were nevertheless deemed appropriate aids to the accomplishment of some purpose within an admitted power of the national government.

[W]e think also that § 15(a)(2), now under consideration, is sustainable independently of § 15(a)(1), which prohibits shipment or transportation of the proscribed goods. As we have said the evils aimed at by the Act are the spread of substandard labor conditions through the use of the facilities of interstate commerce for competition by the goods so produced with those produced under the prescribed or better labor conditions; and the consequent dislocation of the commerce itself caused by the impairment or destruction of local businesses by competition made effective through interstate commerce. The Act is thus directed at the suppression of a method or kind of competition in interstate commerce which it has in effect condemned as "unfair." ...

The means adopted by § 15(a)(2) for the protection of interstate commerce by the suppression of the production of the condemned goods for interstate commerce is so related to the commerce and so affects it as to be within the reach of the commerce power....

Comments and Questions

1. This is our first "modern" Commerce Clause case, modern in the sense that its doctrine is still good law. Note, by the way, that it is unanimous. In essence, it has three separate parts: the power of Congress to regulate commerce that crosses state lines, the power of Congress under the Necessary and Proper Clause to take measures to implement that power, and the power of Congress to regulate intrastate matters that have a substantial effect on interstate commerce. Can you see where the Court addresses these three separate issues?

2. Note that the opinion restates the conclusion of *E.C. Knight* that "manufacture is not of itself interstate commerce." That so, how is it that the Court upholds the regulation of hours and wages by manufacturing employees?

3. What are the last two paragraphs of the opinion saying?

4. If the federal government can regulate anything that crosses a state line, anything that substantially affects something that crosses a state line, or anything that happens in one state that would substantially affect competition in goods or services between states, what is beyond Congress's power to regulate?

WICKARD v. FILBURN

United States Supreme Court, 1942.
317 U.S. 111, 63 S.Ct. 82, 87 L.Ed. 122.

Mr. Justice JACKSON delivered the opinion of the Court.

The appellee [Roscoe Filburn] filed his complaint against the Secretary of Agriculture of the United States [Claude Wickard].... He sought to enjoin enforcement against himself of the marketing penalty imposed by ... the Agricultural Adjustment Act of 1938 upon that part of his 1941 wheat crop which was available for marketing in excess of the marketing quota established for his farm. He also sought a declaratory judgment that the wheat marketing quota provisions of the Act as amended and applicable to him were unconstitutional because not sustainable under the Commerce Clause....

Robert Jackson
President Franklin Roosevelt appointed Jackson to the Supreme Court in 1941. Previously he was serving as Roosevelt's Attorney General, where he earned the President's trust through a number of legal opinions supporting the President's actions in supporting Great Britain and preparing for our seemingly inevitable entry into World War II. As a Justice, Jackson was known for his writing style, as well as his opinions in several famous cases. In 1945 he took a leave from the Court to be the Chief Prosecutor at the Nuremburg War Crimes trial. Thereafter he returned to the Court until his death in 1954, shortly after the Court's decision in *Brown v. Bd. of Ed.*

The appellee for many years past has owned and operated a small farm in Montgomery County, Ohio, maintaining a herd of dairy cattle, selling milk, raising poultry, and selling poultry and eggs. It has been his practice to raise a small acreage of winter wheat, sown in the Fall and harvested in the following July; to sell a portion of the crop; to feed part to poultry and livestock on the farm, some of which is sold; to use some in making flour for home consumption; and to keep the rest for the following seeding. The intended disposition of the crop here involved has not been expressly stated.

In July of 1940, pursuant to the Agricultural Adjustment Act of 1938 ..., there were established for the appellee's 1941 crop a wheat acreage allotment of 11.1 acres and a normal yield of 20.1 bushels of wheat an acre.... He sowed, however, 23 acres, and harvested from his 11.9 acres of excess acreage 239 bushels, which under the terms of the Act as amended on May 26, 1941, constituted farm marketing excess, subject to a penalty of 49 cents a bushel, or $117.11 in all....

The general scheme of the Agricultural Adjustment Act of 1938 as related to wheat is to control the volume moving in interstate and foreign commerce in order to avoid surpluses and shortages and the consequent abnormally low or high wheat prices and obstructions to commerce.* Within prescribed limits and by prescribed standards the Secretary of Agriculture is directed to ascertain and proclaim each year a national acreage allotment for the next crop of wheat, which is then apportioned to the states and their counties, and is eventually broken up into allotments for individual farms....

It is urged that under the Commerce Clause of the Constitution, Article I, § 8, clause 3, Congress does not possess the power it has in this instance sought to exercise. The question would merit little consideration since our decision in *United States v. Darby*, sustaining the federal power to regulate production of goods for commerce except for the fact that this Act extends federal regulation to production not intended in any part for commerce but wholly for consumption on the farm. The Act includes a definition of "market" and its derivatives so that as related to wheat in addition to its conventional meaning it also means to dispose of "by feeding (in any form) to poultry or livestock which, or the products of which, are sold, bartered, or exchanged, or to be so disposed of." Hence, marketing quotas not only embrace all that may be sold without penalty but also what may be consumed on the premises.... The sum of this is that the Federal Government fixes a quota including all that the farmer may harvest for sale or for his own farm needs, and declares that wheat produced on excess acreage may neither be disposed of nor used except upon payment of the penalty or except it is stored as required by the Act or delivered to the Secretary of Agriculture.

Appellee says that this is a regulation of production and consumption of wheat. Such activities are, he urges, beyond the reach of Congressional power under the Commerce Clause, since they are local in character, and their effects upon interstate commerce are at most "indirect." In answer the Government argues that the statute regulates neither production nor consumption, but only marketing; and, in the alternative, that if the Act does go beyond the regulation of marketing it is sustainable as a "necessary and proper" implementation of the power of Congress over interstate commerce.

The Government's concern lest the Act be held to be a regulation of production or consumption rather than of marketing is attributable to a few dicta and decisions of this Court which might be understood to lay it down that activities such as "production," "manufacturing," and "mining" are strictly "local" and, except in special circumstances which are not present here, cannot be regulated under the commerce power

* As you may recall, one of the features of the Great Depression was a surplus of goods relative to the demand for them. The demand was low because people did not have enough money to buy very much. Just as inflation results when there is more money relative to the supply of goods and services, thereby bidding up the price of those goods and services, deflation results when there are not enough bidders to maintain the previous prices. The Agricultural Adjustment Act was intended to restrict the supply of commodity crops, so that the price would naturally rise. This type of regulatory system to maintain prices at a certain level, rather than at the level the "free market" would set, continues to exist today with respect to certain commodities, for example, milk and hazelnuts. [author's note]

because their effects upon interstate commerce are, as matter of law, only "indirect." Even today, when this power has been held to have great latitude, there is no decision of this Court that such activities may be regulated where no part of the product is intended for interstate commerce or intermingled with the subjects thereof. We believe that a review of the course of decision under the Commerce Clause will make plain, however, that questions of the power of Congress are not to be decided by reference to any formula which would give controlling force to nomenclature such as "production" and "indirect" and foreclose consideration of the actual effects of the activity in question upon interstate commerce.

At the beginning Chief Justice Marshall described the Federal commerce power with a breadth never yet exceeded. *Gibbons v. Ogden*. He made emphatic the embracing and penetrating nature of this power by warning that effective restraints on its exercise must proceed from political rather than from judicial processes.

For nearly a century [thereafter], however, decisions of this Court under the Commerce Clause dealt rarely with questions of what Congress might do in the exercise of its granted power under the Clause....

It was not until 1887 with the enactment of the Interstate Commerce Act that the interstate commerce power began to exert positive influence in American law and life. This first important federal resort to the commerce power was followed in 1890 by the Sherman Anti–Trust Act and, thereafter, mainly after 1903, by many others. These statutes ushered in new phases of adjudication, which required the Court to approach the interpretation of the Commerce Clause in the light of an actual exercise by Congress of its power thereunder.

When it first dealt with this new legislation, the Court ... allowed but little scope to the power of Congress. *United States v. E. C. Knight Co.* ...

Even while important opinions in this line of restrictive authority were being written, however, other cases called forth broader interpretations of the Commerce Clause destined to supersede the earlier ones, and to bring about a return to the principles first enunciated by Chief Justice Marshall in *Gibbons v. Ogden*.

Not long after the decision of *United States v. E. C. Knight Co.*, Mr. Justice Holmes, in sustaining the exercise of national power over intrastate activity, stated for the Court that "commerce among the states is not a technical legal conception, but a practical one, drawn from the course of business." *Swift & Co. v. United States*....

The Court's recognition of the relevance of the economic effects in the application of the Commerce Clause exemplified by this statement has made the mechanical application of legal formulas no longer feasible. Once an economic measure of the reach of the power granted to Congress in the Commerce Clause is accepted, questions of federal power cannot be decided simply by finding the activity in question to be "production" nor can consideration of its economic effects be foreclosed by calling them "indirect." ...

Whether the subject of the regulation in question was "production," "consumption," or "marketing" is, therefore, not material for purposes of deciding the question of federal power before us. That an activity is of local character may help in a doubtful case to determine whether Congress intended to reach it.... But even if appellee's activity be local and though it may not be regarded as commerce, it may still, whatever its nature, be reached by Congress if it exerts a substantial economic effect on interstate commerce and this irrespective of whether such effect is what might at some earlier time have been defined as "direct" or "indirect."

The parties have stipulated a summary of the economics of the wheat industry. Commerce among the states in wheat is large and important. Although wheat is raised in every state but one, production in most states is not equal to consumption. Sixteen states on average have had a surplus of wheat above their own requirements for feed, seed, and food. Thirty-two states and the District of Columbia, where production has been below consumption, have looked to these surplus-producing states for their supply as well as for wheat for export and carryover.

The wheat industry has been a problem industry for some years. Largely as a result of increased foreign production and import restrictions, annual exports of wheat and flour from the United States during the ten-year period ending in 1940 averaged less than 10 per cent of total production, while during the 1920's they averaged more than 25 per cent. The decline in the export trade has left a large surplus in production....

The effect of consumption of homegrown wheat on interstate commerce is due to the fact that it constitutes the most variable factor in the disappearance of the wheat crop. Consumption on the farm where grown appears to vary in an amount greater than 20 per cent of average production. The total amount of wheat consumed as food varies but relatively little, and use as seed is relatively constant.

The maintenance by government regulation of a price for wheat undoubtedly can be accomplished as effectively by sustaining or increasing the demand as by limiting the supply. The effect of the statute before us is to restrict the amount which may be produced for market and the extent as well to which one may forestall resort to the market by producing to meet his own needs. That appellee's own contribution to the demand for wheat may be trivial by itself is not enough to remove him from the scope of federal regulation where, as here, his contribution, taken together with that of many others similarly situated, is far from trivial.

It is well established by decisions of this Court that the power to regulate commerce includes the power to regulate the prices at which commodities in that commerce are dealt in and practices affecting such prices. One of the primary purposes of the Act in question was to increase the market price of wheat and to that end to limit the volume thereof that could affect the market. It can hardly be denied that a factor of such volume and variability as home-consumed wheat would have a substantial influence on price and market conditions. This may arise because being in marketable condition such wheat overhangs the market and if induced by rising prices tends to flow into the market and check price increases. But if we assume that it is never marketed, it supplies a need of the man who grew it which would otherwise be reflected by purchases in the open market. Home-grown wheat in this sense competes with wheat in commerce. The stimulation of commerce is a use of the regulatory function quite as definitely as prohibitions or restrictions thereon. This record leaves us in no doubt that Congress may properly have considered that wheat consumed on the farm where grown if wholly outside the scheme of regulation would have a substantial effect in defeating and obstructing its purpose to stimulate trade therein at increased prices.

It is said, however, that this Act, forcing some farmers into the market to buy what they could provide for themselves, is an unfair promotion of the markets and prices of specializing wheat growers. It is of the essence of regulation that it lays a restraining hand on the self interest of the regulated and that advantages from the regulation commonly fall to others. The conflicts of economic interest between the regulated and those who advantage by it are wisely left under our system to resolution by the Congress under its more flexible and responsible legislative process. Such conflicts rarely lend themselves to judicial determination. And with the wisdom, workability, or fairness, of the plan of regulation we have nothing to do....

Comments and Questions

1. *Wickard* makes two notable expansions of Congress's Commerce Clause power. First, even though the actual case does not involve commerce (no buying or selling, merely consumption on the farm of wheat grown on the farm), it affects commerce because otherwise the farmer would have to engage in commerce (by buying wheat to feed to his animals). Second, the aggregation doctrine says that, even though a small amount may be involved in an individual case, if it is aggregated with all the cases like it, there would be a substantial effect on interstate commerce and that is sufficient. Thus, while Filburn did not himself engage in any relevant commerce at all, and his measly 239 bushels of wheat would have no effect on interstate commerce, if all farmers were able to do what he did, in aggregate they would have had a substantial effect on interstate commerce. Or stated another way, if Congress could *not* regulate the small amount, then all the small amounts together could escape regulation even though together they would have a substantial effect on interstate commerce.

2. In light of this justification, is there anything left that the federal government cannot regulate? And if so, so what?

3. Does *Wickard* really change the law from what Justice Field suggested it was in the *Daniel Ball*? From what Marshall suggested it was in *Gibbons*? Or, has the economy itself changed from one that was basically local with some interstate characteristics to one that is almost totally interstate and international with almost no totally local characteristics?

4. THE MODERN AND POST-MODERN PERIOD

Darby and *Wickard* seemed to settle the Commerce Clause question for a number of years. The Supreme Court only granted certiorari in a few cases in which lower courts had found something beyond the Commerce Clause, and the Supreme Court reversed. For example, in *United States v. Sullivan*, 332 U.S. 689 (1948), a druggist in Columbus, Georgia, had purchased a bottle of pills from a wholesaler in Atlanta, which had bought a large number of such bottles from a company in Chicago that manufactured the pills. While the bottle was properly labeled, the druggist took twelve pills out of the bottle, put them in a pill box that was not properly labeled, and sold them to a customer. He was prosecuted for violation of the Food, Drug and Cosmetic Act's provision that prohibits "misbranding" of drugs "held for sale after shipment in interstate commerce." The court of appeals reversed his conviction, refusing to apply the law literally, because to do so would raise grave doubts about its constitutionality under the Commerce Clause. The Supreme Court reversed the court of appeals, finding no constitutional problem with application of the law to the facts involved.

The civil rights era of the 1960s, however, raised some new questions. The Civil Rights Act of 1964 prohibited discrimination on the basis of race in any "place of public accommodation." A "place of public accommodation" was defined to include, among other things, motels and restaurants if their "operations affect commerce." The statute provided that any motel that offered lodging to transient guests, other than an owner-occupied structure with less than five rooms, was *per se* an operation affecting commerce. It also provided that any restaurant that either served interstate travelers or served food that had moved in interstate commerce was also an operation affecting commerce. In *Heart of Atlanta Motel, Inc. v. United States*, 379 U.S. 241 (1964), the Court considered whether the law was constitutional as applied to the Heart of Atlanta Motel, a motel that had 216 rooms and 75% of whose customers were from out-of-state, but which refused to rent rooms to Negroes. The Court noted that Congress had found that racial discrimination in the hotel industry had obstructed interstate commerce by making it difficult for Negro travelers to find accommodations and thereby created a disincentive for Negroes to travel. The fact that the motive for the law might be moral, rather than economic, was held to be irrelevant.

A companion case, *Katzenbach v. McClung*, 379 U.S. 294 (1964), involved Ollie's Barbecue, a family-owned restaurant in Birmingham, Alabama. There was no evidence that interstate travelers used the restaurant, but 46% of the meat sold (worth $69,000) came from out-of-state. Negro customers could not be seated in the restaurant, although they could purchase food for takeout from a takeout window dedicated to Negro customers. Again, Congress had found that discrimination against Negroes in restaurants resulted in lower per capita expenditures, corrected for income differentials. Thus, but for the discrimination, there would be more spent in restaurants obtaining food from interstate commerce, thereby increasing the amount traveling in interstate commerce. Even though Ollie's effect on interstate commerce would not be significant, the Court cited to *Wickard* as a basis to reach Ollie's actions. Moreover, the Court held it was not necessary to determine whether Ollie's discrimination affected the amount of out-of-state food it bought. Because Congress's determination was reasonable that racial discrimination in restaurants would generally affect the amount of out-of-state food bought, that was sufficient. So long as the defined class was within the power of Congress, and Ollie's was within the defined class, there was no basis for courts to excise individual instances. *See also Perez v. United States*, 402 U.S. 146 (1971)(federal law criminalizing loan sharking was within the Commerce Clause power).

In addition, the environmental movement raised new questions. In *Hodel v. Virginia Surface Mining and Reclamation Assn.*, 452 U.S. 264 (1981), and *Hodel v. Indiana*, 452 U.S. 314 (1981), the Court considered the constitutionality of the Surface Mining Control and Reclamation Act. That act required companies engaged in surface mining of coal to meet certain standards in the mining and to reclaim the land when done. Congress made findings that surface mining had various negative environmental effects. The Court cited three separate reasons for upholding the law under the Commerce Clause. First, Congress can regulate local conditions that have an adverse effect on interstate commerce, suggesting that the environmental effects would have such an effect on interstate commerce. Second, citing *Darby*, the Court said Congress can regulate local activities in order to protect fair competition between the states, suggesting that allowing some states to avoid surface mining controls would be unfair competition with those states that would regulate surface mining. Third, the Court said it agreed with the lower courts that had held the Commerce Clause authority was broad enough to regulate "activities causing air or water pollution, or other environmental hazards that may have effects in more than one State."

At this point, many observers believed that the Supreme Court had given up trying to police any restrictions on Congress's Commerce Clause authority, leaving that to the political processes. Then the Court decided the following case.

UNITED STATES v. LOPEZ

United States Supreme Court, 1995.
514 U.S. 549, 115 S.Ct. 1624, 131 L.Ed.2d 626.

Chief Justice REHNQUIST delivered the opinion of the Court.

In the Gun–Free School Zones Act of 1990, Congress made it a federal offense for any individual knowingly to possess a firearm at a place that the individual knows, or has reasonable cause to believe, is a school zone. 18 U.S.C. § 922(q). The Act neither regulates a commercial activity nor contains a requirement that the possession be connected in any way to interstate commerce. We hold that the Act exceeds the authority of Congress [t]o regulate Commerce ... among the several States....

On March 10, 1992, respondent, who was then a 12th-grade student, arrived at Edison High School in San Antonio, Texas, carrying a concealed .38–caliber handgun and five bullets. Acting upon an anonymous tip, school authorities confronted respondent, who admitted that he was carrying the weapon. He was arrested and charged under Texas law with firearm possession on school premises. The next day, the state charges were dismissed after federal agents charged respondent by complaint with violating the Gun–Free School Zones Act of 1990.[1]

[He was convicted, and o]n appeal respondent challenged his conviction based on his claim that § 922(q) exceeded Congress' power to legislate under the Commerce Clause. The Court of Appeals for the Fifth Circuit agreed and reversed respondent's conviction.... Because of the importance of the issue, we granted certiorari, and we now affirm.

We start with first principles. The Constitution creates a Federal Government of enumerated powers. As James Madison wrote: The powers delegated by the proposed Constitution to the federal government are few and defined. Those which are to remain in the State governments are numerous and indefinite. The Federalist No. 45. This constitutionally mandated division of authority was adopted by the Framers to ensure protection of our fundamental liberties. Just as the separation and independence of the coordinate branches of the Federal Government serve to prevent the accumulation of excessive power in any one branch, a healthy balance of power between the States and the Federal Government will reduce the risk of tyranny and abuse from either front.

The Constitution delegates to Congress the power [t]o regulate Commerce with foreign Nations, and among the several States, and with the Indian Tribes. The Court, through Chief Justice Marshall, first defined the nature of Congress' commerce power in *Gibbons v. Ogden*.... The *Gibbons* Court, however, acknowledged that limitations on the commerce power are inherent in the very language of the Commerce Clause.[C]omprehensive as the word among is, it may very properly be restricted to

1. The term school zone is defined as in, or on the grounds of, a public, parochial or private school or within a distance of 1,000 feet from the grounds of a public, parochial or private school.

that commerce which concerns more States than one.... The enumeration presupposes something not enumerated; and that something, if we regard the language, or the subject of the sentence, must be the exclusively internal commerce of a State....

Jones & Laughlin Steel, *Darby*, and *Wickard* ushered in an era of Commerce Clause jurisprudence that greatly expanded the previously defined authority of Congress under that Clause. In part, this was a recognition of the great changes that had occurred in the way business was carried on in this country. Enterprises that had once been local or at most regional in nature had become national in scope. But the doctrinal change also reflected a view that earlier Commerce Clause cases artificially had constrained the authority of Congress to regulate interstate commerce.

But even these modern-era precedents which have expanded congressional power under the Commerce Clause confirm that this power is subject to outer limits.... In *Jones & Laughlin Steel*, the Court warned that the scope of the interstate commerce power must be considered in the light of our dual system of government and may not be extended so as to embrace effects upon interstate commerce so indirect and remote that to embrace them, in view of our complex society, would effectually obliterate the distinction between what is national and what is local and create a completely centralized government. Since that time, the Court has heeded that warning and undertaken to decide whether a rational basis existed for concluding that a regulated activity sufficiently affected interstate commerce. See, e.g., *Hodel v. Virginia Surface Mining & Reclamation Assn., Inc.*; *Perez v. United States*; *Katzenbach v. McClung*; *Heart of Atlanta Motel, Inc. v. United States*....

Consistent with this structure, we have identified three broad categories of activity that Congress may regulate under its commerce power. First, Congress may regulate the use of the channels of interstate commerce. Second, Congress is empowered to regulate and protect the instrumentalities of interstate commerce, or persons or things in interstate commerce, even though the threat may come only from intrastate activities. Finally, Congress' commerce authority includes the power to regulate those activities having a substantial relation to interstate commerce, *i.e.*, those activities that substantially affect interstate commerce.

Within this final category, admittedly, our case law has not been clear whether an activity must affect or substantially affect interstate commerce in order to be within Congress' power to regulate it under the Commerce Clause. We conclude, consistent with the great weight of our case law, that the proper test requires an analysis of whether the regulated activity substantially affects interstate commerce.

We now turn to consider the power of Congress, in the light of this framework, to enact § 922(q). The first two categories of authority may be quickly disposed of: § 922(q) is not a regulation of the use of the channels of interstate commerce, nor is it an attempt to prohibit the interstate transportation of a commodity through the channels of commerce; nor can § 922(q) be justified as a regulation by which Congress has sought to protect an instrumentality of interstate commerce or a thing in interstate commerce. Thus, if § 922(q) is to be sustained, it must be under the third category as a regulation of an activity that substantially affects interstate commerce.

First, we have upheld a wide variety of congressional Acts regulating intrastate economic activity where we have concluded that the activity substantially affected interstate commerce. Examples include the regulation of intrastate coal mining; *Hodel*, intrastate extortionate credit transactions, *Perez*, restaurants utilizing substantial interstate supplies, *McClung*, inns and hotels catering to interstate guests, *Heart of Atlanta Motel*, and production and consumption of homegrown wheat, *Wickard v. Filburn*. These examples are by no means exhaustive, but the pattern is clear. Where economic activity substantially affects interstate commerce, legislation regulating that activity will be sustained.

Even *Wickard*, which is perhaps the most far reaching example of Commerce Clause authority over intrastate activity, involved economic activity in a way that the possession of a gun in a school zone does not....

Section 922(q) is a criminal statute that by its terms has nothing to do with commerce or any sort of economic enterprise, however broadly one might define those terms.[3] Section 922(q) is not an essential part of a larger regulation of economic activity, in which the regulatory scheme could be undercut unless the intrastate activity were regulated. It cannot, therefore, be sustained under our cases upholding regulations of activities that arise out of or are connected with a commercial transaction, which viewed in the aggregate, substantially affects interstate commerce.

Second, § 922(q) contains no jurisdictional element which would ensure, through case-by-case inquiry, that the firearm possession in question affects interstate commerce.... [Section] 922(q) has no express jurisdictional element which might limit its reach to a discrete set of firearm possessions that additionally have an explicit connection with or effect on interstate commerce.

Although as part of our independent evaluation of constitutionality under the Commerce Clause we of course consider legislative findings, and indeed even congressional committee findings, regarding effect on

3. Under our federal system, the "States possess primary authority for defining and enforcing the criminal law." When Congress criminalizes conduct already denounced as criminal by the States, it effects a change in the sensitive relation between federal and state criminal jurisdiction. The Government acknowledges that § 922(q) displace[s] state policy choices in ... that its prohibitions apply even in States that have chosen not to outlaw the conduct in question. *See also* Statement of President George Bush on Signing the Crime Control Act of 1990, 26 Weekly Comp. of Pres. Doc. 1944, 1945 (Nov. 29, 1990) (Most egregiously, section [922(q)] inappropriately overrides legitimate State firearms laws with a new and unnecessary Federal law. The policies reflected in these provisions could legitimately be adopted by the States, but they should not be imposed upon the States by the Congress).

interstate commerce, the Government concedes that [n]either the statute nor its legislative history contain[s] express congressional findings regarding the effects upon interstate commerce of gun possession in a school zone. We agree with the Government that Congress normally is not required to make formal findings as to the substantial burdens that an activity has on interstate commerce. But to the extent that congressional findings would enable us to evaluate the legislative judgment that the activity in question substantially affected interstate commerce, even though no such substantial effect was visible to the naked eye, they are lacking here....

The Government's essential contention, in fine, is that we may determine here that § 922(q) is valid because possession of a firearm in a local school zone does indeed substantially affect interstate commerce. The Government argues that possession of a firearm in a school zone may result in violent crime and that violent crime can be expected to affect the functioning of the national economy in two ways. First, the costs of violent crime are substantial, and, through the mechanism of insurance, those costs are spread throughout the population. Second, violent crime reduces the willingness of individuals to travel to areas within the country that are perceived to be unsafe. The Government also argues that the presence of guns in schools poses a substantial threat to the educational process by threatening the learning environment. A handicapped educational process, in turn, will result in a less productive citizenry. That, in turn, would have an adverse effect on the Nation's economic well-being. As a result, the Government argues that Congress could rationally have concluded that § 922(q) substantially affects interstate commerce.

We pause to consider the implications of the Government's arguments. The Government admits, under its costs of crime reasoning, that Congress could regulate not only all violent crime, but all activities that might lead to violent crime, regardless of how tenuously they relate to interstate commerce. Similarly, under the Government's national productivity reasoning, Congress could regulate any activity that it found was related to the economic productivity of individual citizens: family law (including marriage, divorce, and child custody), for example. Under the theories that the Government presents in support of § 922(q), it is difficult to perceive any limitation on federal power, even in areas such as criminal law enforcement or education where States historically have been sovereign. Thus, if we were to accept the Government's arguments, we are hard pressed to posit any activity by an individual that Congress is without power to regulate.

Although Justice BREYER argues that acceptance of the Government's rationales would not authorize a general federal police power, he is unable to identify any activity that the States may regulate but Congress may not. Justice BREYER posits that there might be some limitations on Congress' commerce power, such as family law or certain aspects of education. These suggested limitations, when viewed in light of the dissent's expansive analysis, are devoid of substance.

Justice BREYER focuses, for the most part, on the threat that firearm possession in and near schools poses to the educational process and the potential economic consequences flowing from that threat. Specifically, the dissent reasons that (1) gun-related violence is a serious problem; (2) that problem, in turn, has an adverse effect on classroom learning; and (3) that adverse effect on classroom learning, in turn, represents a substantial threat to trade and commerce. This analysis would be equally applicable, if not more so, to subjects such as family law and direct regulation of education.

For instance, if Congress can, pursuant to its Commerce Clause power, regulate activities that adversely affect the learning environment, then, a fortiori, it also can regulate the educational process directly. Congress could determine that a school's curriculum has a significant effect on the extent of classroom learning. As a result, Congress could mandate a federal curriculum for local elementary and secondary schools because what is taught in local schools has a significant effect on classroom learning, and that, in turn, has a substantial effect on interstate commerce.

Justice BREYER rejects our reading of precedent and argues that Congress ... could rationally conclude that schools fall on the commercial side of the line. Again, Justice BREYER's rationale lacks any real limits because, depending on the level of generality, any activity can be looked upon as commercial. Under the dissent's rationale, Congress could just as easily look at child rearing as fall[ing] on the commercial side of the line because it provides a valuable service—namely, to equip [children] with the skills they need to survive in life and, more specifically, in the workplace. We do not doubt that Congress has authority under the Commerce Clause to regulate numerous commercial activities that substantially affect interstate commerce and also affect the educational process. That authority, though broad, does not include the authority to regulate each and every aspect of local schools.

Admittedly, a determination whether an intrastate activity is commercial or noncommercial may in some cases result in legal uncertainty. But, so long as Congress' authority is limited to those powers enumerated in the Constitution, and so long as those enumerated powers are interpreted as having judicially enforceable outer limits, congressional legislation under the Commerce Clause always will engender legal uncertainty. Chief Justice Marshall stated in *McCulloch v. Maryland*:

> Th[e] [federal] government is acknowledged by all to be one of enumerated powers. The principle, that it can exercise only the powers granted to it ... is now universally admitted. But the question respecting the extent of the powers actually granted, is perpetually arising, and will probably continue to arise, as long as our system shall exist....

These are not precise formulations, and in the nature of things they cannot be. But we think they point the way to a correct decision of this case. The possession of a gun in a local school zone is in no sense an economic activity that might, through repetition elsewhere, substantially affect any sort of interstate commerce. Respondent was a local student at a local school; there is no indication that he had recently moved in interstate commerce, and there is no requirement that his possession of the firearm have any concrete tie to interstate commerce.

To uphold the Government's contentions here, we would have to pile inference upon inference in a manner that would bid fair to convert congressional authority under the Commerce Clause to a general police power of the sort retained by the States. Admittedly, some of our prior cases have taken long steps down that road, giving great deference to congressional action. The broad language in these opinions has suggested the possibility of additional expansion, but we decline here to proceed any further. To do so would require us to conclude that the Constitution's enumeration of powers does not presuppose something not enumerated, and that there never will be a distinction between what is truly national and what is truly local. This we are unwilling to do.

For the foregoing reasons the judgment of the Court of Appeals is Affirmed.

Justice KENNEDY, with whom Justice O'CONNOR joins, concurring.

The history of the judicial struggle to interpret the Commerce Clause during the transition from the economic system the Founders knew to the single, national market still emergent in our own era counsels great restraint before the Court determines that the Clause is insufficient to support an exercise of the national power. That history gives me some pause about today's decision, but I join the Court's opinion with these observations on what I conceive to be its necessary though limited holding....

The history of our Commerce Clause decisions contains at least two lessons of relevance to this case. The first ... is the imprecision of content-based boundaries used without more to define the limits of the Commerce Clause. The second, related to the first but of even greater consequence, is that the Court as an institution and the legal system as a whole have an immense stake in the stability of our Commerce Clause jurisprudence as it has evolved to this point. *Stare decisis* operates with great force in counseling us not to call in question the essential principles now in place respecting the congressional power to regulate transactions of a commercial nature. That fundamental restraint on our power forecloses us from reverting to an understanding of commerce that would serve only an 18th-century economy, dependent then upon production and trading practices that had changed but little over the preceding centuries; it also mandates against returning to the time when congressional authority to regulate undoubted commercial activities was limited by a judicial determination that those matters had an insufficient connection to an interstate system. Congress can regulate in the commercial sphere on the assumption that we have a single market and a unified purpose to build a stable national economy....

Of the various structural elements in the Constitution, separation of powers, checks and balances, judicial review, and federalism, only concerning the last does there seem to be much uncertainty respecting the existence, and the content, of standards that allow the Judiciary to play a significant role in maintaining the design contemplated by the Framers....

There is irony in this, because of the four structural elements in the Constitution just mentioned, federalism was the unique contribution of the Framers to political science and political theory. Though on the surface the idea may seem counterintuitive, it was the insight of the Framers that freedom was enhanced by the creation of two governments, not one. In the compound republic of America, the power surrendered by the people is first divided between two distinct governments, and then the portion allotted to each subdivided among distinct and separate departments. Hence a double security arises to the rights of the people. The different governments will control each other, at the same time that each will be controlled by itself. The Federalist No. 51 (J. Madison).

[W]ere the Federal Government to take over the regulation of entire areas of traditional state concern, areas having nothing to do with the regulation of commercial activities, the boundaries between the spheres of federal and state authority would blur and political responsibility would become illusory. The resultant inability to hold either branch of the government answerable to the citizens is more dangerous even than devolving too much authority to the remote central power....

The statute before us upsets the federal balance to a degree that renders it an unconstitutional assertion of the commerce power, and our intervention is required. As THE CHIEF JUSTICE explains, unlike the earlier cases to come before the Court here neither the actors nor their conduct has a commercial character, and neither the purposes nor the design of the statute has an evident commercial nexus.... If Congress attempts that extension, then at the least we must inquire whether the exercise of national power seeks to intrude upon an area of traditional state concern.

An interference of these dimensions occurs here, for it is well established that education is a traditional concern of the States. The proximity to schools, including of course schools owned and operated by the States or their subdivisions, is the very premise for making the conduct criminal. In these circumstances, we have a particular duty to ensure that the federal-state balance is not destroyed....

The statute now before us forecloses the States from experimenting and exercising their own judgment in an area to which States lay claim by right of history and expertise, and it does so by regulating an activity beyond the realm of commerce in the ordinary and usual sense of that term.

Justice THOMAS, concurring.

The Court today properly concludes that the Commerce Clause does not grant Congress the authority to prohibit gun possession within 1,000 feet of a school, as it attempted to do in the Gun-Free School Zones Act of 1990. Although I join the majority, I write separately to observe that our case law has drifted far from the original understanding of the Commerce Clause. In a future case, we ought to temper our Commerce Clause jurisprudence in a manner that both makes sense of our more recent case law and is more faithful to the original understanding of that Clause.

We have said that Congress may regulate not only Commerce ... among the several States, but also anything that has a substantial effect on such commerce. This test, if taken to its logical extreme, would give Congress a police power over all aspects of American life....

In an appropriate case, I believe that we must further reconsider our substantial effects test with an eye toward constructing a standard that reflects the text and history of the Commerce Clause without totally rejecting our more recent Commerce Clause jurisprudence....

Justice STEVENS, dissenting.

[G]uns are both articles of commerce and articles that can be used to restrain commerce. Their possession is the consequence, either directly or indirectly, of commercial activity. In my judgment, Congress' power to regulate commerce in firearms includes the power to prohibit possession of guns at any location because of their potentially harmful use; it necessarily follows that Congress may also prohibit their possession in particular markets. The market for the possession of handguns by school-age children is, distressingly, substantial. Whether or not the national interest in eliminating that market would have justified federal legislation in 1789, it surely does today.

Justice SOUTER, dissenting.

In reviewing congressional legislation under the Commerce Clause, we defer to what is often a merely implicit congressional judgment that its regulation addresses a subject substantially affecting interstate commerce if there is any rational basis for such a finding. *Hodel v. Virginia Surface Mining & Reclamation Assn., Inc.* ...

The practice of deferring to rationally based legislative judgments is a paradigm of judicial restraint. In judicial review under the Commerce Clause, it reflects our respect for the institutional competence of the Congress on a subject expressly assigned to it by the Constitution and our appreciation of the legitimacy that comes from Congress's political accountability in dealing with matters open to a wide range of possible choices.

It was not ever thus, however, as even a brief overview of Commerce Clause history during the past century reminds us. The modern respect for the competence and primacy of Congress in matters affecting commerce developed only after one of this Court's most chastening experiences, when it perforce repudiated an earlier and untenably expansive conception of judicial review in derogation of congressional commerce power. A look at history's sequence will serve to show how today's decision tugs the Court off course, leading it to suggest opportunities for further developments that would be at odds with the rule of restraint to which the Court still wisely states adherence....

II

There is today, however, a backward glance at both the old pitfalls, as the Court treats deference under the rationality rule as subject to gradation according to the commercial or noncommercial nature of the immediate subject of the challenged regulation. The distinction between what is patently commercial and what is not looks much like the old distinction between what directly affects commerce and what touches it only indirectly....

Justice BREYER, with whom Justice STEVENS, Justice SOUTER, and Justice GINSBURG join, dissenting.

The issue in this case is whether the Commerce Clause authorizes Congress to enact a statute that makes it a crime to possess a gun in, or near, a school. In my view, the statute falls well within the scope of the commerce power as this Court has understood that power over the last half century.

I

In reaching this conclusion, I apply three basic principles of Commerce Clause interpretation. First, the power to regulate Commerce ... among the several States encompasses the power to regulate local activities insofar as they significantly affect interstate commerce. *See, e.g., Gibbons v. Ogden*; *Wickard v. Filburn*. As the majority points out, the Court, in describing how much of an effect the Clause requires, sometimes has used the word substantial and sometimes has not.... But to speak of substantial effect rather than significant effect would make no difference in this case.

Second, in determining whether a local activity will likely have a significant effect upon interstate commerce, a court must consider, not the effect of an individual act (a single instance of gun possession), but rather the cumulative effect of all similar instances (i.e., the effect of all guns possessed in or near schools). *See, e.g., Wickard*....

Third, the Constitution requires us to judge the connection between a regulated activity and interstate commerce, not directly, but at one remove. Courts must give Congress a degree of leeway in determining the existence of a significant factual connection between the regulated activity and interstate commerce—both because the Constitution delegates the commerce power directly to Congress and because the determination requires an empirical judgment of a kind that a legislature is more likely than a court to make with accuracy. The traditional words rational basis capture this leeway. Thus, the specific question before us, as the Court recognizes, is not whether the regulated activity sufficiently affected interstate commerce, but, rather, whether Congress could have had a rational basis for so concluding.

I recognize that we must judge this matter independently.... And, I also recognize that Congress did not write specific interstate commerce findings into the law under which Lopez was convicted. Nonetheless, as I have already noted, the matter that we review independently (i.e., whether there is a rational basis) already has considerable leeway built into it. And, the absence of findings, at most, deprives a statute of the benefit of some extra leeway....

II

Applying these principles to the case at hand, we must ask whether Congress could have had a rational basis for finding a significant (or substantial) connection between gun-related school violence and interstate commerce. As long as one views the commerce connection, not as a technical legal conception, but as a practical one, *Swift & Co. v. United States* (Holmes, J.), the answer to this question must be yes. Numerous reports and studies—generated both inside and outside government—make clear that Congress could reasonably have found the empirical connection that its law, implicitly or explicitly, asserts.

For one thing, reports, hearings, and other readily available literature make clear that the problem of guns in and around schools is widespread and extremely serious. These materials report, for example, that four percent of American high school students (and six percent of inner-city high school students) carry a gun to school at least occasionally; that 12 percent of urban high school students have had guns fired at them; that 20 percent of those students have been threatened with guns; and that, in any 6–month period, several hundred thousand schoolchildren are victims of violent crimes in or near their schools. And, they report that this widespread violence in schools throughout the Nation significantly interferes with the quality of education in those schools. Based on reports such as these, Congress obviously could have thought that guns and learning are mutually exclusive. Congress could therefore have found a substantial educational problem—teachers unable to teach, students unable to learn—and concluded that guns near schools contribute substantially to the size and scope of that problem.

Having found that guns in schools significantly undermine the quality of education in our Nation's classrooms, Congress could also have found, given the effect of education upon interstate and foreign commerce, that gun-related violence in and around schools is a commercial, as well as a human, problem. Education, although far more than a matter of economics, has long been inextricably intertwined with the Nation's economy. When this Nation began, most workers received their education in the workplace, typically (like Benjamin Franklin) as apprentices. As late as the 1920's, many workers still received general education directly from their employers—from large corporations, such as General Electric, Ford, and Goodyear, which created schools within their firms to help both the worker and the firm. (Throughout most of the 19th century fewer than one percent of all Americans received secondary education through attending a high school.) As public school enrollment grew in the early 20th century, the need for industry to teach basic educational skills diminished. But, the direct economic link between basic education and industrial productivity remained. Scholars estimate that nearly a quarter of America's economic growth in the early years of this century is traceable directly to increased schooling; that investment in human capital (through spending on education) exceeded investment in physical capital by a ratio of almost two to one; and that the economic returns to this investment in education exceeded the returns to conventional capital investment.

In recent years the link between secondary education and business has strengthened, becoming both more direct and more important. Scholars on the subject report that technological changes and innovations in management techniques have altered the nature of the workplace so that more jobs now demand greater educational skills. There is evidence that service, manufacturing or construction jobs are being displaced by technology that requires a better-educated worker or, more likely, are being exported overseas; that workers with truly few skills by the year 2000 will find that only one job out of ten will remain; and that

> [o]ver the long haul the best way to encourage the growth of high-wage jobs is to upgrade the skills of the work force.... [B]etter-trained workers become more productive workers, enabling a company to become more competitive and expand.

[T]he economic links I have just sketched seem fairly obvious. Why then is it not equally obvious, in light of those links, that a widespread, serious, and substantial physical threat to teaching and learning also substantially threatens the commerce to which that teaching and learning is inextricably tied? That is to say, guns in the hands of six percent of inner-city high school students and gun-related violence throughout a city's schools must threaten the trade and commerce that those schools support. The only question, then, is whether the latter threat is (to use the majority's terminology) substantial. The evidence of (1) the extent of the gun-related violence problem, (2) the extent of the resulting negative effect on classroom learning, and (3) the extent of the consequent negative commercial effects, when taken together, indicate a threat to trade and commerce that is substantial. At the very least, Congress could rationally have concluded that the links are substantial....

To hold this statute constitutional is not to obliterate the distinction between what is national and what is local; nor is it to hold that the Commerce Clause permits the Federal Government to regulate any activity that it found was related to the economic productivity of individual citizens, to regulate marriage, divorce, and child custody, or to regulate any and all aspects of education. First, this statute is aimed at curbing a particularly acute threat to the educational process—the possession (and use) of life-threatening firearms in, or near, the classroom. The empirical evidence that I have discussed above unmistakably documents the special way in which guns and education are incompatible.... Second, the immediacy of the connection between education and the national economic well-being is documented by scholars and accepted by society at large in a way and to a degree that may not hold true for other social institutions. It must surely be the rare case, then, that a statute strikes at conduct that (when considered in the abstract) seems so removed from commerce, but which (practically speaking) has so significant an impact upon commerce.

In sum, a holding that the particular statute before us falls within the commerce power would not expand the scope of that Clause. Rather, it simply would apply preexisting law to changing economic circumstances. It would recognize that, in today's economic world, gun-related violence near the classroom makes a significant difference to our economic, as well as our social, well-being. In accordance with well-accepted precedent, such a holding would permit Congress to act in terms of economic ... realities, would interpret the commerce power as an affirmative power commensurate with the national needs, and would acknowledge that the commerce clause does not operate so as to render the nation powerless to defend itself against economic forces that Congress decrees inimical or destructive of the national economy.

III

The majority's holding ... creates three serious legal problems. First, the majority's holding runs contrary to modern Supreme Court cases that have upheld congressional actions despite connections to interstate or foreign commerce that are less significant than the effect of school violence....

The second legal problem the Court creates comes from its apparent belief that it can reconcile its holding with earlier cases by making a critical distinction between commercial and noncommercial transaction[s]. That is to say, the Court believes the Constitution would distinguish between two local activities, each of which has an identical effect upon interstate commerce, if one, but not the other, is commercial in nature.... Moreover, the majority's test is not consistent with what the Court saw as the point of the cases that the majority now characterizes. Although the majority today attempts to categorize *Perez*, *McClung*, and *Wickard* as involving intrastate economic activity, the Courts that decided each of those cases did not focus upon the economic nature of the activity regulated. Rather, they focused upon whether that activity affected interstate or foreign commerce. In fact, the *Wickard* Court expressly held that Filburn's consumption of home-grown wheat, though it may not be regarded as commerce, could nevertheless be regulated—whatever its nature—so long as it exerts a substantial economic effect on interstate commerce.

[R]egardless, if there is a principled distinction that could work both here and in future cases, Congress (even in the absence of vocational classes, industry involvement, and private management) could rationally conclude that schools fall on the commercial side of the line. In 1990, the year Congress enacted the statute before us, primary and secondary schools spent $230 billion—that is, nearly a quarter of a trillion dollars—which accounts for a significant portion of our $5.5 trillion gross domestic product for that year. The business of schooling requires expenditure of these funds on student transportation, food and custodial services, books, and teachers' salaries....

The third legal problem created by the Court's holding is that it threatens legal uncertainty in an area of law that, until this case, seemed reasonably well settled. Congress has enacted many statutes (more than 100 sections of the United States Code), including criminal statutes (at least 25 sections), that use the words affecting commerce to define their scope and other statutes that contain no jurisdictional language at all. Do these, or similar, statutes regulate noncommercial activities? If so, would that alter the meaning of affecting commerce in a jurisdictional element? More importantly, in the absence of a jurisdictional element, are the courts nevertheless to take *Wickard* (and later similar cases) as inapplicable, and to judge the effect of a single noncommercial activity on interstate commerce without considering similar instances of the forbidden conduct? However these questions are eventually resolved, the legal uncertainty now created will restrict Congress' ability to enact criminal laws aimed at criminal behavior that, considered problem by problem rather than instance by instance, seriously threatens the economic, as well as social, well-being of Americans....

Comments and Questions

1. *Lopez* was a shock to the legal community. It was the first case in over a half-century to find a limit to Congress's power under the Commerce Clause. That it was not a flash in the pan was shown by the Court's decision five years later in *United States v. Morrison*, 529 U.S. 598 (2000). In that case the statute in question was the civil damages portion of the Violence Against Women Act (VAWA), which despite the title, provided for damages against any person who "commits a crime of violence motivated by gender." Christy Brzonkala alleged that she had been raped by two football players, and she sued them in federal court under VAWA. In passing VAWA, informed by the Court's decision in *Lopez*, Congress made extensive findings that gender-motivated violence affects interstate commerce "by deterring potential victims from traveling interstate, from engaging in employment in interstate business, and from transacting with business, and in places involved in interstate commerce; ... by diminishing national productivity, increasing medical and other costs, and decreasing the supply or and the demand for interstate products." Nevertheless, the Court, by the same 5–4 split, found the damages provision unconstitutional under the rationale of *Lopez*. If

these listed impacts on interstate commerce were sufficient to authorize federal regulation, the Court said, Congress would be able to regulate any criminal activity. Gender-motivated violence, the Court found, was not any part of economic or commercial activity.

2. *Lopez* was decided before Columbine and other school shooting incidents. Do you think the lack of federal regulation had any causal relationship to those incidents? If some of those incidents had predated *Lopez*, do you think the Court (or at least one member of the majority) might have reached a different conclusion as to the constitutionality of the law?

3. Justice Thomas in both *Lopez* and *Morrison* called for abolition of the "substantial effects" test, arguing that the Constitution only authorizes regulation *of* commerce, not regulation of things that affect commerce. This is typical of Justice Thomas to suggest radical revisions of existing doctrine on the basis of his perceived understanding of the original meaning of the Constitution. In this regard, he goes further than Justice Scalia, who despite his originalist rhetoric seems more willing to accept long-standing precedent.

4. What is the point of Justice Kennedy's concurrence? Recall Justice Kennedy's concurrence in *Lujan v. Defenders of Wildlife*.

5. A year after *Lopez*, Congress amended § 922(q) to read: "It shall be unlawful for any individual knowingly to possess a firearm that has moved in or that otherwise affects interstate or foreign commerce at a place that the individual knows, or has reasonable cause to believe, is a school zone." The amendment has been upheld by every circuit court of appeals to have considered it. Similarly, the criminal provision of VAWA provides: "A person who travels across a State line or enters or leaves Indian country with the intent to injure, harass, or intimidate that person's spouse or intimate partner, and who, in the course of or as a result of such travel, intentionally commits a crime of violence and thereby causes bodily injury to such spouse or intimate partner, shall be punished...." The Court in *Morrison* noted without criticism that this law had been upheld by all the circuits that had considered it.

6. Assuming that Alfonso Lopez's gun was not manufactured in Texas, and the amended law had been in place at the time of his arrest, would his prosecution under this law be constitutional? If so, what is the point of the Court's parade of horribles as to what would happen if Congress could prohibit such behavior?

7. How would a law prohibiting persons from having guns within 500 feet of a federal building be different from the law in *Lopez*? Would it be constitutional? How about a law prohibiting guns within commercial establishments? How about a law prohibiting the possession of marijuana anywhere?

GONZALES v. RAICH

United States Supreme Court, 2005.
545 U.S. 1, 125 S.Ct. 2195, 162 L.Ed.2d 1.

Justice STEVENS delivered the opinion of the Court.

California is one of at least nine States that authorize the use of marijuana for medicinal purposes. The question presented in this case is whether the power vested in Congress by Article I, § 8, of the Constitution [t]o make all Laws which shall be necessary and proper for carrying into Execution its authority to regulate Commerce with foreign Nations, and among the several States includes the power to prohibit the local cultivation and use of marijuana in compliance with California law.

California has been a pioneer in the regulation of marijuana. In 1913, California was one of the first States to prohibit the sale and possession of marijuana, and at the end of the century, California became the first State to authorize limited use of the drug for medicinal purposes. In 1996, California voters passed Proposition 215, [known as the Compassionate Use Act].... The proposition was designed to ensure that seriously ill residents of the State have access to marijuana for medical purposes, and to encourage Federal and State Governments to take steps towards ensuring the safe and affordable distribution of the drug to patients in need.

Respondents Angel Raich and Diane Monson are California residents who suffer from a variety of serious medical conditions and have sought to avail themselves of medical marijuana pursuant to the terms of the Compassionate Use Act.

Respondent Monson cultivates her own marijuana, and ingests the drug in a variety of ways including smoking and using a vaporizer. Respondent Raich, by contrast, is unable to cultivate her own, and thus relies on two caregivers, litigating as John Does, to provide her with locally grown marijuana at no charge. These caregivers also process the cannabis into hashish or keif, and Raich herself processes some of the marijuana into oils, balms, and foods for consumption.

On August 15, 2002, county deputy sheriffs and agents from the federal Drug Enforcement Administration (DEA) came to Monson's home. After a thorough investigation, the county officials concluded that her use of marijuana was entirely lawful as a matter of California law. Nevertheless, after a 3–hour standoff, the federal agents seized and destroyed all six of her cannabis plants.

Respondents thereafter brought this action against the Attorney General of the United States and the head of the DEA seeking injunctive and declaratory relief prohibiting the enforcement of the federal Controlled Substances Act (CSA), to the extent it prevents them from possessing, obtaining, or manufacturing cannabis for their personal medical use.... Respondents claimed that enforcing the CSA against them would violate the Commerce Clause ... of the Constitution....

The District Court denied respondents' motion for a preliminary injunction....

A divided panel of the Court of Appeals for the Ninth Circuit reversed and ordered the District Court to enter a preliminary injunction....

The majority placed heavy reliance on our decisions in *United States v. Lopez* and *United States v. Morrison*, ... to hold that this separate class of purely local activities was beyond the reach of federal power....

The obvious importance of the case prompted our grant of certiorari. The case is made difficult by respondents' strong arguments that they will suffer irreparable harm because, despite a congressional finding to the contrary, marijuana does have valid therapeutic purposes. The question before us, however, is not whether it is wise to enforce the statute in these circumstances; rather, it is whether Congress' power to regulate interstate markets for medicinal substances encompasses the portions of those markets that are supplied with drugs produced and consumed locally. Well-settled law controls our answer. The CSA is a valid exercise of federal power, even as applied to the troubling facts of this case. We accordingly vacate the judgment of the Court of Appeals....

Respondents in this case do not dispute that passage of the CSA, as part of the Comprehensive Drug Abuse Prevention and Control Act, was well within Congress' commerce power. Nor do they contend that any provision or section of the CSA amounts to an unconstitutional exercise of congressional authority. Rather, respondents' challenge is actually quite limited; they argue that the CSA's categorical prohibition of the manufacture and possession of marijuana as applied to the intrastate manufacture and possession of marijuana for medical purposes pursuant to California law exceeds Congress' authority under the Commerce Clause.

In assessing the validity of congressional regulation, none of our Commerce Clause cases can be viewed in isolation. As charted in considerable detail in *United States v. Lopez*, our understanding of the reach of the Commerce Clause, as well as Congress' assertion of authority thereunder, has evolved over time....

Cases [now] identif[y] three general categories of regulation in which Congress is authorized to engage under its commerce power. First, Congress can regulate the channels of interstate commerce. Second, Congress has authority to regulate and protect the instrumentalities of interstate commerce, and persons or things in interstate commerce. Third, Congress has the power to regulate activities that substantially affect interstate commerce. Only the third category is implicated in the case at hand.

Our case law firmly establishes Congress' power to regulate purely local activities that are part of an economic class of activities that have a substantial effect on interstate commerce. *See, e.g.*, *Wickard v. Filburn*.

As we stated in *Wickard*, even if appellee's activity be local and though it may not be regarded as commerce, it may still, whatever its nature, be reached by Congress if it exerts a substantial economic effect on interstate commerce. We have never required Congress to legislate with scientific exactitude. When Congress decides that the total incidence of a practice poses a threat to a national market, it may regulate the entire class. In this vein, we have reiterated that when a general regulatory statute bears a substantial relation to commerce, the de minimis character of individual instances arising under that statute is of no consequence.

Our decision in *Wickard* is of particular relevance....

Wickard thus establishes that Congress can regulate purely intrastate activity that is not itself commercial, in that it is not produced for sale, if it concludes that failure to regulate that class of activity would undercut the regulation of the interstate market in that commodity.

The similarities between this case and *Wickard* are striking. Like the farmer in *Wickard*, respondents are cultivating, for home consumption, a fungible commodity for which there is an established, albeit illegal, interstate market.[28] Just as the Agricultural Adjustment Act was designed to control the volume [of wheat] moving in interstate and foreign commerce in order to avoid surpluses ... and consequently control the market price, a primary purpose of the CSA is to control the supply and demand of controlled substances in both lawful and unlawful drug markets. In *Wickard*, we had no difficulty concluding that Congress had a rational basis for believing that, when viewed in the aggregate, leaving home-consumed wheat outside the regulatory scheme would have a substantial influence on price and market conditions. Here too, Congress had a rational basis for concluding that leaving home-consumed marijuana outside federal control would similarly affect price and market conditions.

More concretely, one concern prompting inclusion of wheat grown for home consumption in the 1938 Act was that rising market prices could draw such wheat into the interstate market, resulting in lower market prices. The parallel concern making it appropriate to include marijuana grown for home consumption in the CSA is the likelihood that the high demand in the interstate market will draw such marijuana into that market. While the diversion of homegrown wheat tended to frustrate the federal interest in stabilizing prices by regulating the volume of commercial transactions in the interstate market, the diversion of homegrown marijuana tends to frustrate the federal interest in eliminating commercial transactions in the interstate market in their entirety. In both cases, the regulation is squarely within Congress' commerce power because production of the commodity meant for home consumption, be it wheat

28. Even respondents acknowledge the existence of an illicit market in marijuana; indeed, Raich has personally participated in that market, and Monson expresses a willingness to do so in the future.

or marijuana, has a substantial effect on supply and demand in the national market for that commodity.[29]

Nonetheless, respondents suggest that *Wickard* differs from this case in three respects: (1) the Agricultural Adjustment Act, unlike the CSA, exempted small farming operations; (2) *Wickard* involved a quintessential economic activity—a commercial farm—whereas respondents do not sell marijuana; and (3) the *Wickard* record made it clear that the aggregate production of wheat for use on farms had a significant impact on market prices. Those differences, though factually accurate, do not diminish the precedential force of this Court's reasoning.

The fact that Filburn's own impact on the market was trivial by itself was not a sufficient reason for removing him from the scope of federal regulation. That the Secretary of Agriculture elected to exempt even smaller farms from regulation does not speak to his power to regulate all those whose aggregated production was significant, nor did that fact play any role in the Court's analysis. Moreover, even though Filburn was indeed a commercial farmer, the activity he was engaged in—the cultivation of wheat for home consumption—was not treated by the Court as part of his commercial farming operation. And while it is true that the record in the *Wickard* case itself established the causal connection between the production for local use and the national market, we have before us findings by Congress to the same effect....

In assessing the scope of Congress' authority under the Commerce Clause, we stress that the task before us is a modest one. We need not determine whether respondents' activities, taken in the aggregate, substantially affect interstate commerce in fact, but only whether a rational basis exists for so concluding. Given the enforcement difficulties that attend distinguishing between marijuana cultivated locally and marijuana grown elsewhere, and concerns about diversion into illicit channels, we have no difficulty concluding that Congress had a rational basis for believing that failure to regulate the intrastate manufacture and possession of marijuana would leave a gaping hole in the CSA. Thus, as in *Wickard*, when it enacted comprehensive legislation to regulate the interstate market in a fungible commodity, Congress was acting well within its authority to make all Laws which shall be necessary and proper to regulate Commerce ... among the several States. That the regulation ensnares some purely intrastate activity is of no moment. As we have done many times before, we refuse to excise individual components of that larger scheme.

To support their contrary submission, respondents rely heavily on two of our more recent Commerce Clause cases. In their myopic focus, they overlook the larger context of modern-era Commerce Clause juris-

29. To be sure, the wheat market is a lawful market that Congress sought to protect and stabilize, whereas the marijuana market is an unlawful market that Congress sought to eradicate. This difference, however, is of no constitutional import. It has long been settled that Congress' power to regulate commerce includes the power to prohibit commerce in a particular commodity.

prudence preserved by those cases. Moreover, even in the narrow prism of respondents' creation, they read those cases far too broadly. Those two cases, of course, are *Lopez* and *Morrison*....

At issue in *Lopez* was the validity of the Gun–Free School Zones Act of 1990, which was a brief, single-subject statute making it a crime for an individual to possess a gun in a school zone. The Act did not regulate any economic activity and did not contain any requirement that the possession of a gun have any connection to past interstate activity or a predictable impact on future commercial activity. Distinguishing our earlier cases holding that comprehensive regulatory statutes may be validly applied to local conduct that does not, when viewed in isolation, have a significant impact on interstate commerce, we held the statute invalid. We explained: Section 922(q) is a criminal statute that by its terms has nothing to do with commerce or any sort of economic enterprise, however broadly one might define those terms. Section 922(q) is not an essential part of a larger regulation of economic activity, in which the regulatory scheme could be undercut unless the intrastate activity were regulated. It cannot, therefore, be sustained under our cases upholding regulations of activities that arise out of or are connected with a commercial transaction, which viewed in the aggregate, substantially affects interstate commerce.

The statutory scheme that the Government is defending in this litigation is at the opposite end of the regulatory spectrum. [T]he CSA, enacted in 1970 as part of the Comprehensive Drug Abuse Prevention and Control Act was a lengthy and detailed statute creating a comprehensive framework for regulating the production, distribution, and possession of five classes of controlled substances. Most of those substances—those listed in Schedules II through V—have a useful and legitimate medical purpose and are necessary to maintain the health and general welfare of the American people. The regulatory scheme is designed to foster the beneficial use of those medications, to prevent their misuse, and to prohibit entirely the possession or use of substances listed in Schedule I, except as a part of a strictly controlled research project.

[O]ur opinion in Lopez casts no doubt on the validity of such a program.

Nor does this Court's holding in *Morrison*. The Violence Against Women Act of 1994 ..., like the statute in *Lopez*, ... did not regulate economic activity. We concluded that the noneconomic, criminal nature of the conduct at issue was central to our decision in *Lopez*, and that our prior cases had identified a clear pattern of analysis: Where economic activity substantially affects interstate commerce, legislation regulating that activity will be sustained.

Unlike those at issue in *Lopez* and *Morrison*, the activities regulated by the CSA are quintessentially economic. Economics refers to the production, distribution, and consumption of commodities. Webster's Third

New International Dictionary 720 (1966). The CSA is a statute that regulates the production, distribution, and consumption of commodities for which there is an established, and lucrative, interstate market. Prohibiting the intrastate possession or manufacture of an article of commerce is a rational (and commonly utilized) means of regulating commerce in that product.... Because the CSA is a statute that directly regulates economic, commercial activity, our opinion in *Morrison* casts no doubt on its constitutionality....

Justice SCALIA, concurring in the judgment.

I agree with the Court's holding that the Controlled Substances Act (CSA) may validly be applied to respondents' cultivation, distribution, and possession of marijuana for personal, medicinal use. I write separately because my understanding of the doctrinal foundation on which that holding rests is, if not inconsistent with that of the Court, at least more nuanced.

Since [1971], our cases have mechanically recited that the Commerce Clause permits congressional regulation of three categories: (1) the channels of interstate commerce; (2) the instrumentalities of interstate commerce, and persons or things in interstate commerce; and (3) activities that substantially affect interstate commerce. The first two categories are self-evident, since they are the ingredients of interstate commerce itself. The third category, however, is different in kind, and its recitation without explanation is misleading and incomplete.

It is misleading because, unlike the channels, instrumentalities, and agents of interstate commerce, activities that substantially affect interstate commerce are not themselves part of interstate commerce, and thus the power to regulate them cannot come from the Commerce Clause alone. Rather, as this Court has acknowledged ..., Congress's regulatory authority over intrastate activities that are not themselves part of interstate commerce (including activities that have a substantial effect on interstate commerce) derives from the Necessary and Proper Clause. And the category of activities that substantially affect interstate commerce is incomplete because the authority to enact laws necessary and proper for the regulation of interstate commerce is not limited to laws governing intrastate activities that substantially affect interstate commerce. Where necessary to make a regulation of interstate commerce effective, Congress may regulate even those intrastate activities that do not themselves substantially affect interstate commerce.

[A]lthough th[e] power to make ... regulation effective commonly overlaps with the authority to regulate economic activities that substantially affect interstate commerce, and may in some cases have been confused with that authority, the two are distinct. The regulation of an intrastate activity may be essential to a comprehensive regulation of interstate commerce even though the intrastate activity does not itself substantially affect interstate commerce. Moreover, ... Congress may regulate even noneconomic local activity if that regulation is a necessary part of a more general regulation of interstate commerce. The relevant question is simply whether the means chosen are reasonably adapted to the attainment of a legitimate end under the commerce power....

The application of these principles to the case before us is straightforward. In the CSA, Congress has undertaken to extinguish the interstate market in Schedule I controlled substances, including marijuana. The Commerce Clause unquestionably permits this. To effectuate its objective, Congress has prohibited almost all intrastate activities related to Schedule I substances—both economic activities (manufacture, distribution, possession with the intent to distribute) and noneconomic activities (simple possession). That simple possession is a noneconomic activity is immaterial to whether it can be prohibited as a necessary part of a larger regulation. Rather, Congress's authority to enact all of these prohibitions of intrastate controlled-substance activities depends only upon whether they are appropriate means of achieving the legitimate end of eradicating Schedule I substances from interstate commerce....

Justice O'CONNOR, with whom THE CHIEF JUSTICE and Justice THOMAS join as to all but Part III, dissenting.

We enforce the outer limits of Congress' Commerce Clause authority not for their own sake, but to protect historic spheres of state sovereignty from excessive federal encroachment and thereby to maintain the distribution of power fundamental to our federalist system of government. One of federalism's chief virtues, of course, is that it promotes innovation by allowing for the possibility that a single courageous State may, if its citizens choose, serve as a laboratory; and try novel social and economic experiments without risk to the rest of the country.

This case exemplifies the role of States as laboratories. The States' core police powers have always included authority to define criminal law and to protect the health, safety, and welfare of their citizens. Exercising those powers, California (by ballot initiative and then by legislative codification) has come to its own conclusion about the difficult and sensitive question of whether marijuana should be available to relieve severe pain and suffering. Today the Court sanctions an application of the federal Controlled Substances Act that extinguishes that experiment, without any proof that the personal cultivation, possession, and use of marijuana for medicinal purposes, if economic activity in the first place, has a substantial effect on interstate commerce and is therefore an appropriate subject of federal regulation....

Justice THOMAS, dissenting.

Respondents Diane Monson and Angel Raich use marijuana that has never been bought or sold, that has never crossed state lines, and that has had no demonstrable effect on the national market for marijuana. If Congress can regulate this under the Commerce Clause, then it can regulate virtually anything—and the Federal Government is no longer one of limited and enumerated powers.

Respondents' local cultivation and consumption of marijuana is not

Commerce ... among the several States. By holding that Congress may regulate activity that is neither interstate nor commerce under the Interstate Commerce Clause, the Court abandons any attempt to enforce the Constitution's limits on federal power. The majority supports this conclusion by invoking, without explanation, the Necessary and Proper Clause. Regulating respondents' conduct, however, is not necessary and proper for carrying into Execution Congress' restrictions on the interstate drug trade. Thus, neither the Commerce Clause nor the Necessary and Proper Clause grants Congress the power to regulate respondents' conduct....

More difficult, however, is whether the CSA is a valid exercise of Congress' power to enact laws that are necessary and proper for carrying into Execution its power to regulate interstate commerce. The Necessary and Proper Clause is not a warrant to Congress to enact any law that bears some conceivable connection to the exercise of an enumerated power. Nor is it, however, a command to Congress to enact only laws that are absolutely indispensable to the exercise of an enumerated power.

In *McCulloch v. Maryland*, this Court, speaking through Chief Justice Marshall, set forth a test for determining when an Act of Congress is permissible under the Necessary and Proper Clause: Let the end be legitimate, let it be within the scope of the constitution, and all means which are appropriate, which are plainly adapted to that end, which are not prohibited, but consist with the letter and spirit of the constitution, are constitutional.

[T]he CSA, as applied to respondents' conduct, is not a valid exercise of Congress' power under the Necessary and Proper Clause.

[O]n its face, a ban on the intrastate cultivation, possession and distribution of marijuana may be plainly adapted to stopping the interstate flow of marijuana. Unregulated local growers and users could swell both the supply and the demand sides of the interstate marijuana market, making the market more difficult to regulate. But respondents do not challenge the CSA on its face. Instead, they challenge it as applied to their conduct. The question is thus whether the intrastate ban is necessary and proper as applied to medical marijuana users like respondents.

Respondents are not regulable simply because they belong to a large class (local growers and users of marijuana) that Congress might need to reach, if they also belong to a distinct and separable subclass (local growers and users of state-authorized, medical marijuana) that does not undermine the CSA's interstate ban....

In sum, neither in enacting the CSA nor in defending its application to respondents has the Government offered any obvious reason why banning medical marijuana use is necessary to stem the tide of interstate drug trafficking. Congress' goal of curtailing the interstate drug trade would not plainly be thwarted if it could not apply the CSA to patients like Monson and Raich. That is, unless Congress' aim is really to exercise police power of the sort reserved to the States in order to eliminate even the intrastate possession and use of marijuana.

Comments and Questions

1. The membership of the Court did not change between *Lopez* and *Raich*, but *Raich* upholds the constitutionality of the law by a 6–3 vote. What happened? Justice Scalia provides an opinion to explain his position. Do you see the distinction he sees between *Raich* and *Lopez*? And what should we make of Justice Kennedy's silent vote with the majority here? Since *Raich*, Chief Justice Rehnquist and Justice O'Connor have been replaced by Chief Justice Roberts and Justice Alito. Do you think that will change anything? Why or why not?

2. The majority says their decision is consistent with *Lopez* and *Morrison*; the dissent says that it is not. With whom do you agree?

3. Presumably, the dissenters are not favorably disposed toward marijuana users, and perhaps those in the majority (Justice Scalia excepted) might be more forgiving, but neither group is moved by its views toward marijuana use to change its attitude toward the federal government's ability to regulate local matters.

4. Subsequent to *Lopez*, there were a number of challenges to the authority of Congress to enact the Endangered Species Act (ESA) to protect species for which there is no commercial market and which have no known value for any purpose. One involved the Arroyo Southwestern Toad which lives in southern California; one involved the Delhi Sands Flower–Loving Fly, which lives in two counties in California; and one involved four spiders and two beetles that only live underground in two counties in Texas. While each of the courts upheld the ESA, the nine judges involved authored seven different opinions. One judge thought the ESA unconstitutional as beyond Congress's power under the Commerce Clause in light of *Lopez*. One justification for it being within Congress's authority was that, even if the species itself had no effect on interstate commerce, the activity that was prohibited (in order to protect the endangered species) was closely related to interstate commerce—*e.g.*, building an on-ramp to an interstate highway or building a new subdivision. Another justification was that the destruction of biodiversity generally would have a substantial effect on interstate commerce, so it is necessary for Congress to be able to protect each aspect of biodiversity, or else all of biodiversity could be destroyed one species at a time. Still another justification was that it is necessary for Congress to be able to protect endangered species in order to protect against unfair competition between states that might occur if some states protected such species and others did not. The Supreme Court denied certiorari in all three cases. What do you think?

Problems

1. Congress passes a law creating a federal crime for anyone who uses any drug that traveled in interstate commerce for the purposes of facilitating suicide. Is this law constitutional?

2. Congress passes a law creating a federal crime for anyone who possesses a loaded firearm within the firearm's range of any runway of any airport. Is this law constitutional?

3. Congress makes findings that arson of owner-occupied residential housing affects commerce by raising the price of fire insurance for residential housing, by raising the price of housing generally by decreasing the supply, by destroying the collateral for mortgages, by interfering with the delivery of electricity and gas or oil used by the residence, and by increasing the cost of fire protection. These findings are then included in a federal law creating a crime for anyone who commits arson of an owner-occupied residence. Max travels from California to Arizona to firebomb the home of a businessman who had not paid the gambling debts he incurred in Nevada. Max is caught and prosecuted under the federal law. He defends on the basis that the law is unconstitutional. How should the court rule?

C. TAXING AND SPENDING CLAUSE

The so-called Taxing and Spending Clause is Article I, Section 8, Clause 1: The Congress shall have the power to lay and collect taxes, duties, imposts, and excises, to pay the debts and provide for the common defense and general welfare of the United States.... Compared to the Commerce Clause, the Taxing and Spending Clause has not engendered as many disputes. An early dispute was whether Congress could only tax and spend for the purposes enumerated in the subsequent clauses of Section 8, or whether it could tax and spend for anything that paid the Nation's debts, involved defense, or furthered the general welfare. Obviously, if it was only the former, many of the same issues we have seen with regard to the Commerce Clause would come into play, whereas if it was the latter, there would seem to be little if any substantive limit on what Congress could tax or spend for—what is not for the general welfare? Hamilton was emphatic that the latter was the right interpretation, while Madison espoused the former. The Court did not definitively decide this issue until 1936 in *United States v. Butler*, 297 U.S. 1 (1936), holding that Hamilton's position was correct.

Nevertheless, despite that determination, the Court in *Butler* found the Agricultural Adjustment Act of 1933 unconstitutional as a violation of the Taxing and Spending Clause. In reaching this conclusion, it relied on an earlier case, *Bailey v. Drexel Furniture Co.* (*Child Labor Tax Case*), 259 U.S. 20 (1922). Recall that the Court had found federal regulation of child labor beyond Congress's authority under the Commerce Clause in *Hammer v. Dagenhart*, 247 U.S. 251 (1918). Congress responded by enacting a tax of 10% on the net profits of any company employing children under the age of fourteen. In *Bailey*, the Court correctly discerned that the purpose of the tax was not to raise revenue but to regulate child labor in the states, something the Court had denied it the power to do under the Commerce Clause. The Court viewed this as an attempt to avoid its decision in *Hammer* and struck the tax down. Similarly, in *Butler*, the Court interpreted the tax not to raise revenue to be spent for the general welfare but to regulate the volume of production of agricultural commodities.* As such, the Court found it beyond Congress's power because Congress had no power, the Court believed, to regulate agricultural production. Today, of course, we recognize that Congress does have the power to regulate child labor and agricultural production to the extent that they substantially affect interstate commerce, so this element of *Butler* and *Bailey* is no longer good law. What is worth remembering, however, is that, denied the authority to act under one of its Article I, Section 8 powers, Congress responded by trying to use one of its other authorities, and the question became whether it could achieve that regulatory end through another means. This type of issue continues to arise.

SOUTH DAKOTA v. DOLE

United States Supreme Court, 1987.
483 U.S. 203, 107 S.Ct. 2793, 97 L.Ed.2d 171.

Chief Justice REHNQUIST delivered the opinion of the Court.

Petitioner South Dakota permits persons 19 years of age or older to purchase beer containing up to 3.2% alcohol. In 1984 Congress enacted 23 U.S.C. § 158 (1982 ed., Supp. III), which directs the Secretary of Transportation to withhold a percentage of federal highway funds otherwise allocable from States in which the purchase or public possession ... of any alcoholic beverage by a person who is less than twenty-one years of age is lawful. The State sued in United States District Court seeking a declaratory judgment that § 158 violates the constitutional limitations on congressional exercise of the spending power.... The District Court rejected the State's claims, and the Court of Appeals for the Eighth Circuit affirmed....

The Constitution empowers Congress to lay and collect Taxes, Duties, Imposts, and Excises, to pay the Debts and provide for the common Defence and general Welfare of the United States. Incident to this power, Congress may attach conditions on the receipt of federal funds, and has repeatedly employed the power to further broad policy objectives by conditioning receipt of federal moneys upon compliance by the recipient with federal statutory and administrative directives. The breadth of this power was made clear in *United States v. Butler*, where the Court, resolving a longstanding debate over the scope of the Spending Clause, determined that the power of Congress to authorize expenditure of public moneys for public purposes is not limited by the direct grants of legislative power found in the Constitution. Thus, objectives not thought to be within Article I's enumerated legislative fields may

* Recall *Wickard v. Filburn*, in which the Court upheld an amended version of this act years later.

nevertheless be attained through the use of the spending power and the conditional grant of federal funds.

The spending power is of course not unlimited, but is instead subject to several general restrictions articulated in our cases. The first of these limitations is derived from the language of the Constitution itself: the exercise of the spending power must be in pursuit of the general welfare. In considering whether a particular expenditure is intended to serve general public purposes, courts should defer substantially to the judgment of Congress.[1] Second, we have required that if Congress desires to condition the States' receipt of federal funds, it must do so unambiguously ..., enabl[ing] the States to exercise their choice knowingly, cognizant of the consequences of their participation. Third, our cases have suggested (without significant elaboration) that conditions on federal grants might be illegitimate if they are unrelated to the federal interest in particular national projects or programs. Finally, we have noted that other constitutional provisions may provide an independent bar to the conditional grant of federal funds.

South Dakota does not seriously claim that § 158 is inconsistent with any of the first three restrictions mentioned above. We can readily conclude that the provision is designed to serve the general welfare, especially in light of the fact that the concept of welfare or the opposite is shaped by Congress.... Congress found that the differing drinking ages in the States created particular incentives for young persons to combine their desire to drink with their ability to drive, and that this interstate problem required a national solution. The means it chose to address this dangerous situation were reasonably calculated to advance the general welfare. The conditions upon which States receive the funds, moreover, could not be more clearly stated by Congress. And the State itself, rather than challenging the germaneness of the condition to federal purposes, admits that it has never contended that the congressional action was ... unrelated to a national concern.... Indeed, the condition imposed by Congress is directly related to one of the main purposes for which highway funds are expended—safe interstate travel.[2] This goal of the interstate highway system had been frustrated by varying drinking ages among the States.... By enacting § 158, Congress conditioned the receipt of federal funds in a way reasonably calculated to address this particular impediment to a purpose for which the funds are expended.

The remaining question about the validity of § 158 ... is whether

1. The level of deference to the congressional decision is such that the Court has more recently questioned whether general welfare is a judicially enforceable restriction at all.

2. Our cases have not required that we define the outer bounds of the germaneness or relatedness limitation on the imposition of conditions under the spending power. Amici urge that we take this occasion to establish that a condition on federal funds is legitimate only if it relates directly to the purpose of the expenditure to which it is attached. Because petitioner has not sought such a restriction, and because we find any such limitation on conditional federal grants satisfied in this case in any event, we do not address whether conditions less directly related to the particular purpose of the expenditure might be outside the bounds of the spending power.

the Twenty-first Amendment constitutes an independent constitutional bar to the conditional grant of federal funds. Petitioner, relying on its view that the Twenty-first Amendment prohibits direct regulation of drinking ages by Congress, asserts that Congress may not use the spending power to regulate that which it is prohibited from regulating directly under the Twenty-first Amendment. But our cases show that this independent constitutional bar limitation on the spending power is not of the kind petitioner suggests....

These cases establish that the independent constitutional bar limitation on the spending power is not, as petitioner suggests, a prohibition on the indirect achievement of objectives which Congress is not empowered to achieve directly. Instead, we think that the language in our earlier opinions stands for the unexceptionable proposition that the power may not be used to induce the States to engage in activities that would themselves be unconstitutional. Thus, for example, a grant of federal funds conditioned on invidiously discriminatory state action or the infliction of cruel and unusual punishment would be an illegitimate exercise of the Congress' broad spending power. But no such claim can be or is made here. Were South Dakota to succumb to the blandishments offered by Congress and raise its drinking age to 21, the State's action in so doing would not violate the constitutional rights of anyone.

Our decisions have recognized that in some circumstances the financial inducement offered by Congress might be so coercive as to pass the point at which pressure turns into compulsion. Here, however, Congress has directed only that a State desiring to establish a minimum drinking age lower than 21 lose a relatively small percentage of certain federal highway funds. Petitioner contends that the coercive nature of this program is evident from the degree of success it has achieved. We cannot conclude, however, that a conditional grant of federal money of this sort is unconstitutional simply by reason of its success in achieving the congressional objective.

When we consider, for a moment, that all South Dakota would lose if she adheres to her chosen course as to a suitable minimum drinking age is 5% of the funds otherwise obtainable under specified highway grant programs, the argument as to coercion is shown to be more rhetoric than fact....

Here Congress has offered relatively mild encouragement to the States to enact higher minimum drinking ages than they would otherwise choose. But the enactment of such laws remains the prerogative of the States not merely in theory but in fact. Even if Congress might lack the power to impose a national minimum drinking age directly, we conclude that encouragement to state action found in § 158 is a valid use of the spending power. Accordingly, the judgment of the Court of Appeals is

Affirmed.

Justice BRENNAN, dissenting.

I agree with Justice O'CONNOR that regulation of the minimum age of purchasers of liquor falls squarely within the ambit of those powers reserved to the States by the Twenty-first Amendment. Since States possess this constitutional power, Congress cannot condition a federal grant in a manner that abridges this right. The Amendment, itself, strikes the proper balance between federal and state authority. I therefore dissent.

Sandra Day O'Connor
President Reagan appointed O'Connor to the Supreme Court in 1981, the first woman to serve on the Court. She was known for her support of women's rights and states' rights. After dissenting from several decisions upholding *Roe v. Wade*, she provided a necessary fifth vote in the crucial final case of *Planned Parenthood v. Casey* to continue a woman's right to an abortion. Her jurisprudence was characterized by an attempt to decide only the particular case before her, rather than to make broad, sweeping rules on the basis of the particular case. She retired from the Court in 2006 and was replaced by Samuel Alito.

Justice O'CONNOR, dissenting.

The Court today upholds the National Minimum Drinking Age Amendment as a valid exercise of the spending power conferred by Article I, § 8. But § 158 is not a condition on spending reasonably related to the expenditure of federal funds and cannot be justified on that ground. Rather, it is an attempt to regulate the sale of liquor, an attempt that lies outside Congress' power to regulate commerce because it falls within the ambit of § 2 of the Twenty-first Amendment.

My disagreement with the Court is relatively narrow on the spending power issue: it is a disagreement about the application of a principle rather than a disagreement on the principle itself. I agree with the Court that Congress may attach conditions on the receipt of federal funds to further the federal interest in particular national projects or programs. I also subscribe to the established proposition that the reach of the spending power is not limited by the direct grants of legislative power found in the Constitution. Finally, I agree that there are four separate types of limitations on the spending power: the expenditure must be for the general welfare, the conditions imposed must be unambiguous, they must be reasonably related to the purpose of the expenditure, and the legislation may not violate any independent constitutional prohibition. Insofar as two of those limitations are concerned, the Court is clearly correct that § 158 is wholly unobjectionable. Establishment of a national minimum drinking age certainly fits within the broad concept of the general welfare and the statute is entirely unambiguous. I am also willing to assume, arguendo, that the Twenty-first Amendment does not constitute an independent constitutional bar to a spending condition.

But the Court's application of the requirement that the condition imposed be reasonably related to the purpose for which the funds are expended is cursory and unconvincing.... In my view, establishment of a minimum drinking age of 21 is not sufficiently related to interstate highway construction to justify so conditioning funds appropriated for that purpose....

[T]he Court asserts the reasonableness of the relationship between the supposed purpose of the expenditure—safe interstate travel—and the drinking age condition. The Court reasons that Congress wishes that the roads it builds may be used safely, that drunken drivers threaten highway safety, and that young people are more likely to drive while under the influence of alcohol under existing law than would be the case if there were a uniform national drinking age of 21. It hardly needs saying, however, that if the purpose of § 158 is to deter drunken driving, it is far too over and under-inclusive. It is over-inclusive because it stops teenagers from drinking even when they are not about to drive on interstate highways. It is under-inclusive because teenagers pose only a small part of the drunken driving problem in this Nation. *See, e.g.*,130 Cong.Rec. 18648 (1984) (remarks of Sen. Humphrey) (Eighty-four percent of all highway fatalities involving alcohol occur among those whose ages exceed 21).

When Congress appropriates money to build a highway, it is entitled to insist that the highway be a safe one. But it is not entitled to insist as a condition of the use of highway funds that the State impose or change regulations in other areas of the State's social and economic life because of an attenuated or tangential relationship to highway use or safety. Indeed, if the rule were otherwise, the Congress could effectively regulate almost any area of a State's social, political, or economic life on the theory that use of the interstate transportation system is somehow enhanced. If, for example, the United States were to condition highway moneys upon moving the state capital, I suppose it might argue that interstate transportation is facilitated by locating local governments in places easily accessible to interstate highways—or, conversely, that highways might become overburdened if they had to carry traffic to and from the state capital. In my mind, such a relationship is hardly more attenuated than the one which the Court finds supports § 158.

There is a clear place at which the Court can draw the line between permissible and impermissible conditions on federal grants. It is the line identified in the Brief for the National Conference of State Legislatures et al. as Amici Curiae:

> Congress has the power to spend for the general welfare, it has the power to legislate only for delegated purposes.... The appropriate inquiry, then, is whether the spending requirement or prohibition is a condition on a grant or whether it is regulation. The difference turns on whether the requirement specifies in some way how the money should be spent, so that Congress' intent in making the grant will be effectuated. Congress has no

> power under the Spending Clause to impose requirements on a grant that go beyond specifying how the money should be spent. A requirement that is not such a specification is not a condition, but a regulation, which is valid only if it falls within one of Congress' delegated regulatory powers.

This approach harks back to *United States v. Butler*, the last case in which this Court struck down an Act of Congress as beyond the authority granted by the Spending Clause. There the Court wrote that [t]here is an obvious difference between a statute stating the conditions upon which moneys shall be expended and one effective only upon assumption of a contractual obligation to submit to a regulation which otherwise could not be enforced. The *Butler* Court saw the Agricultural Adjustment Act for what it was—an exercise of regulatory, not spending, power. The error in *Butler* was not the Court's conclusion that the Act was essentially regulatory, but rather its crabbed view of the extent of Congress' regulatory power under the Commerce Clause. The Agricultural Adjustment Act was regulatory but it was regulation that today would likely be considered within Congress' commerce power.

While *Butler*'s authority is questionable insofar as it assumes that Congress has no regulatory power over farm production, its discussion of the spending power and its description of both the power's breadth and its limitations remain sound. The Court's decision in *Butler* also properly recognizes the gravity of the task of appropriately limiting the spending power. If the spending power is to be limited only by Congress' notion of the general welfare, the reality, given the vast financial resources of the Federal Government, is that the Spending Clause gives power to the Congress to tear down the barriers, to invade the states' jurisdiction, and to become a parliament of the whole people, subject to no restrictions save such as are self-imposed. This, of course, as *Butler* held, was not the Framers' plan and it is not the meaning of the Spending Clause....

Comments and Questions

1. As Justice Brennan and O'Connor make clear, lurking in this case is the Twenty First Amendment, repealing Prohibition. In addition to eliminating Prohibition, however, that amendment states that:

> The transportation or importation into any state ... for delivery or use therein of intoxicating liquors, in violation of the laws thereof, is hereby prohibited.

Justices Brennan and O'Connor suggest that this language precludes the federal government from regulating liquor consumption contrary to what a state provides. Is that what the language of the amendment says? Presumably, if a state prohibited someone under 21 from drinking alcohol, Congress could not pass a law authorizing people under 21 to drink alcohol. That would be contrary to the language of the amendment, because Congress would be authorizing what the amendment says is prohibited. On the other hand, if a state allowed persons between 18 and 21 to drink alcohol—the situation in South Dakota in this case—and Congress passed a law prohibiting anyone under 21 from drinking alcohol, that would not run afoul of the language in the amendment, because the federal law would not be authorizing anything that would be in violation of state law. Nevertheless, some have read the amendment's language to reserve to the states exclusive regulatory authority over commerce in liquor. That has not, however, been the majority position of the Court.

2. What does Justice O'Connor say is the effect of the Twenty First Amendment on the federal statute here? Compare the third sentence in her opinion with her last five paragraphs.

3. Does Chief Justice Rehnquist answer the arguments?

4. Chief Justice Rehnquist is known for his movement of the Court towards state rights versus federal regulation. Recall his opinion in *United States v. Lopez*. How do you view his opinion here? Clearly, it comes down on the side of federal power against state power, but do you think the opinion is broadly written or narrowly written? In answering that question, ask what limits does the opinion place on Congress in creating conditions on federal expenditures to states. Could Congress condition federal funds to states for K–12 education on states enacting laws criminalizing the possession of guns within 500 feet of a school?

D. IMPLEMENTING TREATIES

The Necessary and Proper Clause states that Congress may make all laws necessary and proper, not only "for carrying into execution the foregoing powers" [the powers in the earlier enumerated powers provisions], but also "for carrying into execution ... all other powers vested by this Constitution in the Government of the United States...." Another power vested by the Constitution in the federal government is the power to make treaties with foreign nations. The following case is an example of the use of the Necessary and Proper Clause to carry into execution the power to make treaties.

MISSOURI v. HOLLAND

Supreme Court of the United States, 1920.
252 U.S. 416, 40 S.Ct. 382, 64 L.Ed. 641.

Mr. Justice HOLMES delivered the opinion of the Court.

This is a bill in equity brought by the State of Missouri to prevent a game warden of the United States from attempting to enforce the Migratory Bird Treaty Act of July 3, 1918, and the regulations made by the Secretary of Agriculture in pursuance of the same. The ground of the bill is that the statute is an unconstitutional interference with the rights reserved to the States by the Tenth Amendment, and that the acts of the defendant done and threatened under that authority invade the sovereign right of the State and contravene its will manifested in statutes. The State also alleges a pecuniary interest, as owner of the wild birds within its borders and otherwise, admitted by the Government to be sufficient, but it is enough that the bill is a reasonable and proper means to assert the alleged quasi sovereign rights of a State. A motion to dismiss was sustained by the District Court on the ground that the Act of Congress is constitutional. The State appeals.

On December 8, 1916, a treaty between the United States and Great Britain* was proclaimed by the President. It recited that many species of birds in their annual migrations traversed many parts of the United States and of Canada, that they were of great value as a source of food and in destroying insects injurious to vegetation, but were in danger of extermination through lack of adequate protection. It therefore provided for specified closed seasons and protection in other forms, and agreed that the two powers would take or propose to their lawmaking bodies the necessary measures for carrying the treaty out. The above mentioned act of July 3, 1918, entitled an act to give effect to the convention, prohibited the killing, capturing or selling any of the migratory birds included in the terms of the treaty except as permitted by regulations compatible with those terms, to be made by the Secretary of Agriculture. Regulations were proclaimed on July 31, and October 25, 1918. It is unnecessary to go into any details, because, as we have said, the question raised is the general one whether the treaty and statute are void as an interference with the rights reserved to the States.

To answer this question it is not enough to refer to the Tenth Amendment, reserving the powers not delegated to the United States, because by Article 2, Section 2, the power to make treaties is delegated expressly, and by Article 6 treaties made under the authority of the United States, along with the Constitution and laws of the United States made in pursuance thereof, are declared the supreme law of the land. If the treaty is valid there can be no dispute about the validity of the statute under Article 1, Section 8, as a necessary and proper means to execute the powers of the Government. The language of the Constitution as to the supremacy of treaties being general, the question before us is narrowed to an inquiry into the ground upon which the present supposed exception is placed.

It is said that a treaty cannot be valid if it infringes the Constitution, that there are limits, therefore, to the treaty-making power, and that one such limit is that what an act of Congress could not do unaided, in derogation of the powers reserved to the States, a treaty cannot do. An earlier act of Congress that attempted by itself and not in pursuance of a treaty to regulate the killing of migratory birds within the States had

* At this time, Great Britain still exercised the foreign affairs powers for Canada, so the treaty, although relating to Canada, was contracted with Great Britain. [author's note]

been held bad in the District Court.* Those decisions were supported by arguments that migratory birds were owned by the States in their sovereign capacity for the benefit of their people, and that ... this control was one that Congress had no power to displace. The same argument is supposed to apply now with equal force.

Whether the [district court cases] were decided rightly or not they cannot be accepted as a test of the treaty power. Acts of Congress are the supreme law of the land only when made in pursuance of the Constitution, while treaties are declared to be so when made under the authority of the United States.... It is obvious that there may be matters of the sharpest exigency for the national well being that an act of Congress could not deal with but that a treaty followed by such an act could.... The treaty in question does not contravene any prohibitory words to be found in the Constitution. The only question is whether it is forbidden by some invisible radiation from the general terms of the Tenth Amendment. We must consider what this country has become in deciding what that amendment has reserved.

The State as we have intimated founds its claim of exclusive authority upon an assertion of title to migratory birds, an assertion that is embodied in statute. No doubt it is true that as between a State and its inhabitants the State may regulate the killing and sale of such birds, but it does not follow that its authority is exclusive of paramount powers. To put the claim of the State upon title is to lean upon a slender reed. Wild birds are not in the possession of anyone; and possession is the beginning of ownership. The whole foundation of the State's rights is the presence within their jurisdiction of birds that yesterday had not arrived, tomorrow may be in another State and in a week a thousand miles away. If we are to be accurate we cannot put the case of the State upon higher ground than that the treaty deals with creatures that for the moment are within the state borders, that it must be carried out by officers of the United States within the same territory, and that but for the treaty the State would be free to regulate this subject itself.

As most of the laws of the United States are carried out within the States and as many of them deal with matters which in the silence of such laws the State might regulate, such general grounds are not enough to support Missouri's claim....

Here a national interest of very nearly the first magnitude is involved. It can be protected only by national action in concert with that of another power. The subject matter is only transitorily within the State and has no permanent habitat therein. But for the treaty and the statute there soon might be no birds for any powers to deal with. We see nothing in the Constitution that compels the Government to sit by while a food supply is cut off and the protectors of our forests and our crops are

* Actually, two separate district court decisions, one in Arkansas and one in Kansas, had held that the earlier act was unconstitutional as not authorized by any provision of the Constitution. [author's note]

destroyed. It is not sufficient to rely upon the States. The reliance is vain, and were it otherwise, the question is whether the United States is forbidden to act. We are of opinion that the treaty and statute must be upheld.

Mr. Justice VAN DEVANTER and Mr. Justice PITNEY dissent.

Comments and Questions

1. Here we see again a situation in which a law passed by Congress, the 1913 Act, was deemed unconstitutional, and thereafter the federal government (here the President and the Senate by treaty, followed by Congress in passing the law) attempt to achieve the same end by a different means—using the Necessary and Proper Clause to implement the treaty. The Court upholds this action.

2. If Congress can implement any treaty adopted by the United States, is there any limitation what Congress can regulate? Imagine that the United States enters into a multilateral United Nations convention [another name for a treaty] pledging to protect women from violence. Can Congress then constitutionally adopt the damage provisions in the Violence Against Women Act that the Court found unconstitutional in *United States v. Morrison*? Is there any hint in Holmes' opinion for where a limit might be found?

E. THE TENTH AMENDMENT

So far in this chapter, we have been exploring the extent of Congress's powers under various grants of power in Article I, in particular, the Necessary and Proper Clause, the Commerce Clause, and the Taxing and Spending Clause. If a law is beyond Congress's powers, as in *Lopez*, that law is unconstitutional. Of course, something may be within Congress's positive authority, such as regulating the channels of commerce, but unconstitutional because of an express limitation of the Constitution. For example, Congress could not deny the use of the interstate highways to anyone who criticized the President of the United States. That would clearly violate the First Amendment's Free Speech Clause. A question we have already seen adverted to is whether the Tenth Amendment is a limitation on Congress's authority in the same manner as, for example, the First Amendment.

The text of the Tenth Amendment is relatively clear as constitutional provisions go:

> The powers not delegated to the United States by the Constitution, nor prohibited by it to the States, are reserved to the states respectively, or to the people.

Thus, if the power *is* delegated to the United States, the Tenth Amendment simply does not apply. That was the Court's conclusion in *Missouri v. Holland*. Of course, if the power is *not* delegated to the United States, then its exercise is unconstitutional separate from the Tenth Amendment; it is beyond Congress's authority. This textual construction led the Court in a number of cases to refer to the amendment as a truism. *See, e.g., United States v. Darby*, 312 U.S. 100, 124 (1941). This construction, however, was interrupted by *National League of Cities v. Usery*, 426 U.S. 833 (1976). That case challenged the application of a federal minimum wage, maximum hours law to almost all state employees. It was conceded that the wages and hours paid to state employees had a substantial effect on interstate commerce, but the Court, in a 5–4 decision written by then Justice Rehnquist, held that the Tenth Amendment in effect prohibited the application of the law to these state employees, overruling a case decided eight years before, *Maryland v. Wirtz*, 392 U.S. 183 (1968), that had upheld a challenge to federal minimum wages and maximum hours laws applied to state workers. Nine years later, however, the Court changed its mind again.

GARCIA v. SAN ANTONIO METROPOLITAN TRANSIT AUTHORITY

United States Supreme Court, 1985.
469 U.S. 528, 105 S.Ct. 1005, 83 L.Ed.2d 1016.

Justice BLACKMUN delivered the opinion of the Court.

We revisit in these cases an issue raised in *National League of Cities v. Usery*. In that litigation, this Court, by a sharply divided vote, ruled that the Commerce Clause does not empower Congress to enforce the minimum-wage and overtime provisions of the Fair Labor Standards Act (FLSA) against the States in areas of traditional governmental functions. Although *National League of Cities* supplied some examples of traditional governmental functions, it did not offer a general explanation of how a traditional function is to be distinguished from a nontraditional one. Since then, federal and state courts have struggled with the task, thus imposed, of identifying a traditional function for purposes of state immunity under the Commerce Clause.

In the present cases, a Federal District Court concluded that municipal ownership and operation of a mass-transit system is a traditional governmental function and thus, under *National League of Cities*, is exempt from the obligations imposed by the FLSA. Faced with the identical question, three Federal Courts of Appeals and one state appellate court have reached the opposite conclusion.

Our examination of this function standard applied in these and other cases over the last eight years now persuades us that the attempt to draw the boundaries of state regulatory immunity in terms of traditional governmental function is not only unworkable but is also inconsistent with established principles of federalism and, indeed, with those very federalism principles on which *National League of Cities* purported to rest. That case, accordingly, is overruled.

[The San Antonio Metropolitan Transit Authority (SAMTA) sued the Secretary of Labor, seeking a declaratory judgment that FLSA was unconstitutional in light of *National League of Cities*. At the same time, a SAMTA worker, Joe Garcia, sued SAMTA seeking overtime pay as mandated by FLSA. The latter case was stayed, but Garcia was allowed to intervene in the other case. The district court found for SAMTA, and the Secretary and Garcia appealed directly to the Supreme Court.]

Appellees have not argued that SAMTA is immune from regulation under the FLSA on the ground that it is a local transit system engaged in intrastate commercial activity. In a practical sense, SAMTA's operations might well be characterized as local. Nonetheless, it long has been settled that Congress' authority under the Commerce Clause extends to intrastate economic activities that affect interstate commerce. Were SAMTA a privately owned and operated enterprise, it could not credibly argue that Congress exceeded the bounds of its Commerce Clause powers in prescribing minimum wages and overtime rates for SAMTA's employees. Any constitutional exemption from the requirements of the FLSA therefore must rest on SAMTA's status as a governmental entity rather than on the local nature of its operations.

The prerequisites for governmental immunity under *National League of Cities* [have been] summarized by this Court.... Under that summary, four conditions must be satisfied before a state activity may be deemed immune from a particular federal regulation under the Commerce Clause. First, it is said that the federal statute at issue must regulate the States as States. Second, the statute must address matters that are indisputably attribute[s] of state sovereignty. Third, state compliance with the federal obligation must directly impair [the States'] ability to structure integral operations in areas of traditional governmental functions. Finally, the relation of state and federal interests must not be such that the nature of the federal interest ... justifies state submission.

The controversy in the present cases has focused on the third ... requirement—that the challenged federal statute trench on traditional governmental functions. The District Court voiced a common concern: Despite the abundance of adjectives, identifying which particular state functions are immune remains difficult. Just how troublesome the task has been is revealed by the results reached in other federal cases. Thus, courts have held that regulating ambulance services; licensing automobile drivers; operating a municipal airport; performing solid waste disposal; and operating a highway authority are functions protected under *National League of Cities*. At the same time, courts have held that issuance of industrial development bonds; regulation of intrastate natural gas sales; regulation of traffic on public roads; regulation of air transportation; operation of a telephone system; leasing and sale of natural gas; operation of a mental health facility; and provision of in-house domestic services for the aged and handicapped are not entitled to immunity. We find it difficult, if not impossible, to identify an organizing principle that places each of the cases in the first group on one side of a line and each of the cases in the second group on the other side....

The most obvious defect of a historical approach to state immunity is that it prevents a court from accommodating changes in the historical functions of States, changes that have resulted in a number of once-private functions like education being assumed by the States and their subdivisions.[9] At the same time, the only apparent virtue of a rigorous historical standard, namely, its promise of a reasonably objective measure for state immunity, is illusory....

A nonhistorical standard for selecting immune governmental functions is likely to be just as unworkable as is a historical standard. The goal of identifying uniquely governmental functions, for example, has been rejected by the Court in the field of governmental tort liability in part because the notion of a uniquely governmental function is unmanageable....

We believe, however, that there is a more fundamental problem at work here.... The problem is that neither the governmental/proprietary distinction nor any other that purports to separate out important governmental functions can be faithful to the role of federalism in a democratic society. The essence of our federal system is that within the realm of authority left open to them under the Constitution, the States must be equally free to engage in any activity that their citizens choose for the common weal, no matter how unorthodox or unnecessary anyone else—including the judiciary—deems state involvement to be. Any rule of state immunity that looks to the traditional, integral, or necessary nature of governmental functions inevitably invites an unelected federal judiciary to make decisions about which state policies it favors and which ones it dislikes....

We therefore now reject, as unsound in principle and unworkable in practice, a rule of state immunity from federal regulation that turns on a judicial appraisal of whether a particular governmental function is integral or traditional. Any such rule leads to inconsistent results at the same time that it disserves principles of democratic self-governance, and it breeds inconsistency precisely because it is divorced from those principles. If there are to be limits on the Federal Government's power to interfere with state functions—as undoubtedly there are—we must look elsewhere to find them. We accordingly return to the underlying issue that confronted this Court in *National League of Cities*—the manner in which the Constitution insulates States from the reach of Congress' power under the Commerce Clause.

9. Indeed, the traditional nature of a particular governmental function can be a matter of historical nearsightedness; today's self-evidently traditional function is often yesterday's suspect innovation. Thus, *National League of Cities* offered the provision of public parks and recreation as an example of a traditional governmental function. A scant 80 years earlier, however, the Court pointed out that city commons originally had been provided not for recreation but for grazing domestic animals in common, and that [i]n the memory of men now living, a proposition to take private property [by eminent domain] for a public park ... would have been regarded as a novel exercise of legislative power.

The central theme of *National League of Cities* was that the States occupy a special position in our constitutional system and that the scope of Congress' authority under the Commerce Clause must reflect that position. Of course, the Commerce Clause by its specific language does not provide any special limitation on Congress' actions with respect to the States.... *National League of Cities* reflected the general conviction that the Constitution precludes the National Government [from] devour[ing] the essentials of state sovereignty....

The States unquestionably do retai[n] a significant measure of sovereign authority. They do so, however, only to the extent that the Constitution has not divested them of their original powers and transferred those powers to the Federal Government....

When we look for the States' residuary and inviolable sovereignty, in the shape of the constitutional scheme rather than in predetermined notions of sovereign power, a different measure of state sovereignty emerges. Apart from the limitation on federal authority inherent in the delegated nature of Congress' Article I powers, the principal means chosen by the Framers to ensure the role of the States in the federal system lies in the structure of the Federal Government itself. It is no novelty to observe that the composition of the Federal Government was designed in large part to protect the States from overreaching by Congress. The Framers thus gave the States a role in the selection both of the Executive and the Legislative Branches of the Federal Government. The States were vested with indirect influence over the House of Representatives and the Presidency by their control of electoral qualifications and their role in Presidential elections. They were given more direct influence in the Senate, where each State received equal representation and each Senator was to be selected by the legislature of his State....

The extent to which the structure of the Federal Government itself was relied on to insulate the interests of the States is evident in the views of the Framers.... In short, the Framers chose to rely on a federal system in which special restraints on federal power over the States inhered principally in the workings of the National Government itself, rather than in discrete limitations on the objects of federal authority. State sovereign interests, then, are more properly protected by procedural safeguards inherent in the structure of the federal system than by judicially created limitations on federal power.

The effectiveness of the federal political process in preserving the States' interests is apparent even today in the course of federal legislation. On the one hand, the States have been able to direct a substantial proportion of federal revenues into their own treasuries in the form of general and program-specific grants in aid.... Moreover, at the same time that the States have exercised their influence to obtain federal support, they have been able to exempt themselves from a wide variety of obligations imposed by Congress under the Commerce Clause.... The fact that some federal statutes such as the FLSA extend general obligations to the States cannot obscure the extent to which the political position of the States in the federal system has served to minimize the burdens that the States bear under the Commerce Clause.

[A]gainst this background, we are convinced that the fundamental limitation that the constitutional scheme imposes on the Commerce Clause to protect the States as States is one of process rather than one of result. Any substantive restraint on the exercise of Commerce Clause powers must find its justification in the procedural nature of this basic limitation, and it must be tailored to compensate for possible failings in the national political process rather than to dictate a sacred province of state autonomy.

Insofar as the present cases are concerned, then, we need go no further than to state that we perceive nothing in the overtime and minimum-wage requirements of the FLSA, as applied to SAMTA, that is destructive of state sovereignty or violative of any constitutional provision. SAMTA faces nothing more than the same minimum-wage and overtime obligations that hundreds of thousands of other employers, public as well as private, have to meet.

This analysis makes clear that Congress' action in affording SAMTA employees the protections of the wage and hour provisions of the FLSA contravened no affirmative limit on Congress' power under the Commerce Clause. The judgment of the District Court therefore must be reversed.

Of course, we continue to recognize that the States occupy a special and specific position in our constitutional system and that the scope of Congress' authority under the Commerce Clause must reflect that position. But the principal and basic limit on the federal commerce power is that inherent in all congressional action—the built-in restraints that our system provides through state participation in federal governmental action. The political process ensures that laws that unduly burden the States will not be promulgated. In the factual setting of these cases the internal safeguards of the political process have performed as intended.

These cases do not require us to identify or define what affirmative limits the constitutional structure might impose on federal action affecting the States under the Commerce Clause....

Justice POWELL, with whom THE CHIEF JUSTICE, Justice REHNQUIST, and Justice O'CONNOR join, dissenting.

The Court today, in its 5–4 decision, overrules *National League of Cities v. Usery*, a case in which we held that Congress lacked authority to impose the requirements of the Fair Labor Standards Act on state and local governments. Because I believe this decision substantially alters the federal system embodied in the Constitution, I dissent.

There are, of course, numerous examples over the history of this Court in which prior decisions have been reconsidered and overruled. There have been few cases, however, in which the principle of stare decisis and the rationale of recent decisions were ignored as abruptly as we now witness.[1] ...

Whatever effect the Court's decision may have in weakening the application of stare decisis, it is likely to be less important than what the Court has done to the Constitution itself. A unique feature of the United States is the federal system of government guaranteed by the Constitution and implicit in the very name of our country. Despite some genuflecting in the Court's opinion to the concept of federalism, today's decision effectively reduces the Tenth Amendment to meaningless rhetoric when Congress acts pursuant to the Commerce Clause....

To leave no doubt about its intention, the Court renounces its decision in *National League of Cities* because it inevitably invites an unelected federal judiciary to make decisions about which state policies it favors and which ones it dislikes. In other words, the extent to which the States may exercise their authority, when Congress purports to act under the Commerce Clause, henceforth is to be determined from time to time by political decisions made by members of the Federal Government, decisions the Court says will not be subject to judicial review. I note that it does not seem to have occurred to the Court that it—an unelected majority of five Justices—today rejects almost 200 years of the understanding of the constitutional status of federalism. In doing so, there is only a single passing reference to the Tenth Amendment. Nor is so much as a dictum of any court cited in support of the view that the role of the States in the federal system may depend upon the grace of elected federal officials, rather than on the Constitution as interpreted by this Court....

[M]ore troubling than the logical infirmities in the Court's reasoning is the result of its holding, i.e., that federal political officials, invoking the Commerce Clause, are the sole judges of the limits of their own power. This result is inconsistent with the fundamental principles of our constitutional system. At least since *Marbury v. Madison*, it has been the settled province of the federal judiciary to say what the law is with respect to the constitutionality of Acts of Congress....

In our federal system, the States have a major role that cannot be pre-empted by the National Government. As contemporaneous writings and the debates at the ratifying conventions make clear, the States' ratification of the Constitution was predicated on this understanding of federalism. Indeed, the Tenth Amendment was adopted specifically to ensure that the important role promised the States by the proponents of the Constitution was realized.

Much of the initial opposition to the Constitution was rooted in the fear that the National Government would be too powerful and eventually would eliminate the States as viable political entities. This concern

1. *National League of Cities*, following some changes in the composition of the Court, had overruled *Maryland v. Wirtz*. Unlike *National League of Cities*, the rationale of *Wirtz* had not been repeatedly accepted by our subsequent decisions.

was voiced repeatedly until proponents of the Constitution made assurances that a Bill of Rights, including a provision explicitly reserving powers in the States, would be among the first business of the new Congress....

This history, which the Court simply ignores, documents the integral role of the Tenth Amendment in our constitutional theory. It exposes as well, I believe, the fundamental character of the Court's error today. Far from being unsound in principle, judicial enforcement of the Tenth Amendment is essential to maintaining the federal system so carefully designed by the Framers and adopted in the Constitution.

The Framers had definite ideas about the nature of the Constitution's division of authority between the Federal and State Governments....

The Framers believed that the separate sphere of sovereignty reserved to the States would ensure that the States would serve as an effective counterpoise to the power of the Federal Government. The States would serve this essential role because they would attract and retain the loyalty of their citizens. The roots of such loyalty, the Founders thought, were found in the objects peculiar to state government....

Thus, the harm to the States that results from federal overreaching under the Commerce Clause is not simply a matter of dollars and cents.... Rather, by usurping functions traditionally performed by the States, federal overreaching under the Commerce Clause undermines the constitutionally mandated balance of power between the States and the Federal Government, a balance designed to protect our fundamental liberties.

The emasculation of the powers of the States that can result from the Court's decision is predicated on the Commerce Clause as a power delegated to the United States by the Constitution....

To be sure, this Court has construed the Commerce Clause to accommodate unanticipated changes over the past two centuries. As these changes have occurred, the Court has had to decide whether the Federal Government has exceeded its authority by regulating activities beyond the capability of a single State to regulate or beyond legitimate federal interests that outweighed the authority and interests of the States. In so doing, however, the Court properly has been mindful of the essential role of the States in our federal system....

This Court has recognized repeatedly that state sovereignty is a fundamental component of our system of government.

In contrast, the Court today propounds a view of federalism that pays only lipservice to the role of the States. Although it says that the States unquestionably do retai[n] a significant measure of sovereign authority, it fails to recognize the broad, yet specific areas of sovereignty that the Framers intended the States to retain. Indeed, the Court barely acknowledges that the Tenth Amendment exists....

As I view the Court's decision today as rejecting the basic precepts of our federal system and limiting the constitutional role of judicial review, I dissent.

Justice REHNQUIST, dissenting.

I join both Justice POWELL's and Justice O'CONNOR's thoughtful dissents.... But ... I do not think it incumbent on those of us in dissent to spell out further the fine points of a principle that will, I am confident, in time again command the support of a majority of this Court.

Justice O'CONNOR, with whom Justice POWELL and Justice REHNQUIST join, dissenting.

The Court today surveys the battle scene of federalism and sounds a retreat. Like Justice POWELL, I would prefer to hold the field and, at the very least, render a little aid to the wounded. I join Justice POWELL's opinion. I also write separately to note my fundamental disagreement with the majority's views of federalism and the duty of this Court....

In my view, federalism cannot be reduced to the weak essence distilled by the majority today....

Due to the emergence of an integrated and industrialized national economy, this Court has been required to examine and review a breathtaking expansion of the powers of Congress. In doing so the Court correctly perceived that the Framers of our Constitution intended Congress to have sufficient power to address national problems.... Just as surely as the Framers envisioned a National Government capable of solving national problems, they also envisioned a republic whose vitality was assured by the diffusion of power not only among the branches of the Federal Government, but also between the Federal Government and the States. In the 18th century these intentions did not conflict because technology had not yet converted every local problem into a national one. A conflict has now emerged, and the Court today retreats rather than reconcile the Constitution's dual concerns for federalism and an effective commerce power....

The operative language of [our] cases varies, but the underlying principle is consistent: state autonomy is a relevant factor in assessing the means by which Congress exercises its powers.

This principle requires the Court to enforce affirmative limits on federal regulation of the States to complement the judicially crafted expansion of the interstate commerce power. *National League of Cities v. Usery* represented an attempt to define such limits. The Court today rejects *National League of Cities* and washes its hands of all efforts to protect the States. In the process, the Court opines that unwarranted federal encroachments on state authority are and will remain horrible possibilities that never happen in the real world. There is ample reason to believe to the contrary....

The problems of federalism in an integrated national economy are capable of more responsible resolution than holding that the States as States retain no status apart from that which Congress chooses to let them retain. The proper resolution, I suggest, lies in weighing state autonomy as a factor in the balance when interpreting the means by which Congress can exercise its authority on the States as States. It is insufficient, in assessing the validity of congressional regulation of a State pursuant to the commerce power, to ask only whether the same regulation would be valid if enforced against a private party. That reasoning, embodied in the majority opinion, is inconsistent with the spirit of our Constitution. It remains relevant that a State is being regulated.... I share Justice REHNQUIST's belief that this Court will in time again assume its constitutional responsibility.

I respectfully dissent.

Comments and Questions

1. The dissent complains that *SAMTA* overrules *National League of Cities* a mere nine years after it was decided. However, the dissent does not mention the irony that *National League of Cities* overruled *Maryland v. Wirtz*, only eight years after it was decided; that *National League of Cities* was decided by a split Court 5–4; and that *National League of Cities* had rejected over a century of jurisprudence that the Tenth Amendment did not have substantive effect.

2. There was no change in the membership of the Court between *National League of Cities* and *SAMTA*. Instead, Justice Blackmun, who had concurred in *National League of Cities*, saying that he was "not untroubled by certain possible implications of the Court's opinion," switched sides and wrote the new majority opinion. The other members of the Court making up the majority had dissented in *National League of Cities* on the basis that the Tenth Amendment simply was not a restriction on Congress's Commerce Clause authority. Is this what Justice Blackmun's opinion for the Court says, or does he adopt a different theory to uphold the law?

3. The Court's opinion faithfully describes the *National League of Cities*' test for whether a law would transgress the Tenth Amendment. The Court focuses on the difficulty of determining whether a particular activity is a traditional state function, but another of the criteria is whether the federal statute regulates "states as states." Does the FLSA regulate states as states? Does it not just regulate employers whoever they are, making no exceptions for states? Should this make a difference? Consider that in light of the next case.

4. The Court concludes that the role of states in our federal system can be adequately protected through the political process. How does the political process protect the role of states? Is this conclusion in tension with *Marbury v. Madison*? How would you feel about a decision that left protection of First Amendment rights to the political process? Is that a fair analogy?

5. The dissenters in *SAMTA* confidently predict that in time *SAMTA* will be overruled and *National League of Cities* reinstated. Is that what the next case does?

NEW YORK v. UNITED STATES

United States Supreme Court, 1992.
505 U.S. 144, 112 S.Ct. 2408, 120 L.Ed.2d 120.

Justice O'CONNOR delivered the opinion of the Court.

These cases implicate one of our Nation's newest problems of public policy and perhaps our oldest question of constitutional law. The public policy issue involves the disposal of radioactive waste: In these cases, we address the constitutionality of three provisions of the Low–Level Radioactive Waste Policy Amendments Act of 1985. The constitutional question is as old as the Constitution: It consists of discerning the proper division of authority between the Federal Government and the States. We conclude that while Congress has substantial power under the Constitution to encourage the States to provide for the disposal of the radioactive waste generated within their borders, the Constitution does not confer upon Congress the ability simply to compel the States to do so. We therefore find that only two of the Act's three provisions at issue are consistent with the Constitution's allocation of power to the Federal Government.

We live in a world full of low level radioactive waste. Radioactive material is present in luminous watch dials, smoke alarms, measurement devices, medical fluids, research materials, and the protective gear and construction materials used by workers at nuclear power plants.... Millions of cubic feet of low level radioactive waste must be disposed of each year.

[S]ince 1979 only three disposal sites—those in Nevada, Washington, and South Carolina—have been in operation. Waste generated in the rest of the country must be shipped to one of these three sites for disposal.... The Governors of Washington and Nevada announced plans to shut their sites permanently.

Faced with the possibility that the Nation would be left with no disposal sites for low level radioactive waste, Congress responded by enacting the Low–Level Radioactive Waste Policy Act.... The ... Act was ... based largely on a proposal submitted by the National Governors' Association. In broad outline, the Act embodies a compromise among the sited and unsited States....

The mechanics of this compromise are intricate. [It requires each state to be responsible for providing for the disposal of low-level radioactive waste generated within the State, either by itself or in cooperation with other States through adoption of an interstate compact.]

The Act provides three types of incentives to encourage the States to comply with their statutory obligation to provide for the disposal of waste generated within their borders.

1. *Monetary incentives.* [The Secretary of Energy makes payments to each state that complies with the Act.]

2. *Access incentives.* The second type of incentive involves the denial of access to disposal sites. States that fail to meet the [requirements] may be denied access to disposal facilities thereafter [by those states that have disposal facilities.]

3. *The take title provision.* The third type of incentive is the most severe. The Act provides [that if a State in which low-level radioactive waste is generated is unable to provide for the disposal of all such waste generated within such State or compact region by January 1, 1996, each State in which such waste is generated, upon the request of the generator or owner of the waste, shall take title to the waste, be obligated to take possession of the waste, and shall be liable for all damages directly or indirectly incurred by such generator or owner as a consequence of the failure of the State to take possession of the waste.]

These three incentives are the focus of petitioners' constitutional challenge.

[P]etitioners—the State of New York and ... two counties—filed this suit against the United States in 1990. They sought a declaratory judgment that the Act is inconsistent with the Tenth ... Amendment[] to the Constitution ... and with the Guarantee Clause of Article IV of the Constitution....

At least as far back as [1816], the Court has resolved questions of great importance and delicacy in determining whether particular sovereign powers have been granted by the Constitution to the Federal Government or have been retained by the States. These questions can be viewed in either of two ways. In some cases the Court has inquired whether an Act of Congress is authorized by one of the powers delegated to Congress in Article I of the Constitution. *See, e.g., Perez v. United States*; *McCulloch v. Maryland*. In other cases the Court has sought to determine whether an Act of Congress invades the province of state sovereignty reserved by the Tenth Amendment. *See, e.g., Garcia v. San Antonio Metropolitan Transit Authority*. In a case like these, involving the division of authority between federal and state governments, the two inquiries are mirror images of each other. If a power is delegated to Congress in the Constitution, the Tenth Amendment expressly disclaims any reservation of that power to the States; if a power is an attribute of state sovereignty reserved by the Tenth Amendment, it is necessarily a power the Constitution has not conferred on Congress. It is in this sense that the Tenth Amendment states but a truism that all is retained which has not been surrendered. *United States v. Darby*....

Congress exercises its conferred powers subject to the limitations contained in the Constitution. Thus, for example, under the Commerce

Clause Congress may regulate publishers engaged in interstate commerce, but Congress is constrained in the exercise of that power by the First Amendment. The Tenth Amendment likewise restrains the power of Congress, but this limit is not derived from the text of the Tenth Amendment itself, which, as we have discussed, is essentially a tautology. Instead, the Tenth Amendment confirms that the power of the Federal Government is subject to limits that may, in a given instance, reserve power to the States. The Tenth Amendment thus directs us to determine, as in this case, whether an incident of state sovereignty is protected by a limitation on an Article I power....

Petitioners do not contend that Congress lacks the power to regulate the disposal of low level radioactive waste. Space in radioactive waste disposal sites is frequently sold by residents of one State to residents of another. Regulation of the resulting interstate market in waste disposal is therefore well within Congress' authority under the Commerce Clause. Petitioners likewise do not dispute that under the Supremacy Clause Congress could, if it wished, pre-empt state radioactive waste regulation. Petitioners contend only that the Tenth Amendment limits the power of Congress to regulate in the way it has chosen. Rather than addressing the problem of waste disposal by directly regulating the generators and disposers of waste, petitioners argue, Congress has impermissibly directed the States to regulate in this field.

Most of our recent cases interpreting the Tenth Amendment have concerned the authority of Congress to subject state governments to generally applicable laws. The Court's jurisprudence in this area has traveled an unsteady path. *See Maryland v. Wirtz*; *National League of Cities v. Usery*; *Garcia v. San Antonio Metropolitan Transit Authority*. This litigation presents no occasion to apply or revisit the holdings of any of these cases, as this is not a case in which Congress has subjected a State to the same legislation applicable to private parties.

This litigation instead concerns the circumstances under which Congress may use the States as implements of regulation; that is, whether Congress may direct or otherwise motivate the States to regulate in a particular field or a particular way. Our cases have established a few principles that guide our resolution of the issue.

As an initial matter, Congress may not simply commandee[r] the legislative processes of the States by directly compelling them to enact and enforce a federal regulatory program.... While Congress has substantial powers to govern the Nation directly, including in areas of intimate concern to the States, the Constitution has never been understood to confer upon Congress the ability to require the States to govern according to Congress' instructions.... Indeed, the question whether the Constitution should permit Congress to employ state governments as regulatory agencies was a topic of lively debate among the Framers. Under the Articles of Confederation, Congress lacked the authority in most respects to govern the people directly....

The [Constitutional] Convention generated a great number of proposals for the structure of the new Government, but two quickly took center stage. Under the Virginia Plan, ... Congress would exercise legislative authority directly upon individuals, without employing the States as intermediaries. Under the New Jersey Plan, ... Congress would continue to require the approval of the States before legislating, as it had under the Articles of Confederation.... In the end, the Convention opted for a Constitution in which Congress would exercise its legislative authority directly over individuals rather than over States; for a variety of reasons, it rejected the New Jersey Plan in favor of the Virginia Plan.... In providing for a stronger central government, therefore, the Framers explicitly chose a Constitution that confers upon Congress the power to regulate individuals, not States. The allocation of power contained in the Commerce Clause, for example, authorizes Congress to regulate interstate commerce directly; it does not authorize Congress to regulate state governments' regulation of interstate commerce.

This is not to say that Congress lacks the ability to encourage a State to regulate in a particular way, or that Congress may not hold out incentives to the States as a method of influencing a State's policy choices. Our cases have identified a variety of methods, short of outright coercion, by which Congress may urge a State to adopt a legislative program consistent with federal interests. Two of these methods are of particular relevance here.

First, under Congress' spending power, Congress may attach conditions on the receipt of federal funds. *South Dakota v. Dole*.... Where the recipient of federal funds is a State, ... the conditions attached to the funds by Congress may influence a State's legislative choices....

Second, where Congress has the authority to regulate private activity under the Commerce Clause, we have recognized Congress' power to offer States the choice of regulating that activity according to federal standards or having state law pre-empted by federal regulation. This arrangement, which has been termed a program of cooperative federalism, is replicated in numerous federal statutory schemes. These include the Clean Water Act; the Occupational Safety and Health Act of 1970; the Resource Conservation and Recovery Act of 1976; and the Alaska National Interest Lands Conservation Act.

By either of these methods, as by any other permissible method of encouraging a State to conform to federal policy choices, the residents of the State retain the ultimate decision as to whether or not the State will comply. If a State's citizens view federal policy as sufficiently contrary to local interests, they may elect to decline a federal grant. If state residents would prefer their government to devote its attention and resources to problems other than those deemed important by Congress, they may choose to have the Federal Government rather than the State bear the expense of a federally mandated regulatory program, and they may continue to supplement that program to the extent state law is not pre-empted. Where Congress encourages state regulation rather than compelling it, state governments remain responsive to the local electorate's preferences; state officials remain accountable to the people.

By contrast, where the Federal Government compels States to regulate, the accountability of both state and federal officials is diminished. If the citizens of New York, for example, do not consider that making provision for the disposal of radioactive waste is in their best interest, they may elect state officials who share their view. That view can always be pre-empted under the Supremacy Clause if it is contrary to the national view, but in such a case it is the Federal Government that makes the decision in full view of the public, and it will be federal officials that suffer the consequences if the decision turns out to be detrimental or unpopular. But where the Federal Government directs the States to regulate, it may be state officials who will bear the brunt of public disapproval, while the federal officials who devised the regulatory program may remain insulated from the electoral ramifications of their decision. Accountability is thus diminished when, due to federal coercion, elected state officials cannot regulate in accordance with the views of the local electorate in matters not pre-empted by federal regulation.

With these principles in mind, we turn to the three challenged provisions of the [Act].

III

A

The first set of incentives [essentially provides funds to states as they achieve a series of milestones toward disposing of the waste.] [This] is a conditional exercise of Congress' authority under the Spending Clause: Congress has placed conditions—the achievement of the milestones—on the receipt of federal funds. Petitioners do not contend that Congress has exceeded its [Spending Clause] authority in any of the ... respects our cases have identified.... The Act's first set of incentives, in which Congress has conditioned grants to the States upon the States' attainment of a series of milestones, is thus well within the authority of Congress under the Commerce and Spending Clauses. Because the first set of incentives is supported by affirmative constitutional grants of power to Congress, it is not inconsistent with the Tenth Amendment.

B

In the second set of incentives, Congress has authorized States and regional compacts with disposal sites ... to deny access altogether to radioactive waste generated in States that do not meet federal deadlines.... [In other words,] States may either regulate the disposal of radioactive waste according to federal standards by attaining local or regional self-sufficiency, or their residents who produce radioactive waste will be subject to federal regulation authorizing sited States and regions to deny access to their disposal sites. The affected States are not compelled by Congress to regulate, because any burden caused by a State's refusal to regulate will fall on those who generate waste and find no outlet for its disposal, rather than on the State as a sovereign.... The Act's second set of incentives thus represents a conditional exercise of Congress' commerce power, along the lines of those we have held to be within Congress' authority. As a result, the second set of incentives does not intrude on the sovereignty reserved to the States by the Tenth Amendment.

C

The take title provision is of a different character. This third so-called incentive offers States, as an alternative to regulating pursuant to Congress' direction, the option of taking title to and possession of the low level radioactive waste generated within their borders and becoming liable for all damages waste generators suffer as a result of the States' failure to do so promptly. In this provision, Congress has crossed the line distinguishing encouragement from coercion.

[T]he take title provision offers state governments a choice of either accepting ownership of waste or regulating according to the instructions of Congress.... Because an instruction to state governments to take title to waste, standing alone, would be beyond the authority of Congress, and because a direct order to regulate, standing alone, would also be beyond the authority of Congress, it follows that Congress lacks the power to offer the States a choice between the two. Unlike the first two sets of incentives, the take title incentive does not represent the conditional exercise of any congressional power enumerated in the Constitution. In this provision, Congress has not held out the threat of exercising its spending power or its commerce power; it has instead held out the threat, should the States not regulate according to one federal instruction, of simply forcing the States to submit to another federal instruction. A choice between two unconstitutionally coercive regulatory techniques is no choice at all. Either way, the Act commandeers the legislative processes of the States by directly compelling them to enact and enforce a federal regulatory program, an outcome that has never been understood to lie within the authority conferred upon Congress by the Constitution....

V

Petitioners also contend that the Act is inconsistent with the Constitution's Guarantee Clause, which directs the United States to guarantee to every State in this Union a Republican Form of Government. Because we have found the take title provision of the Act irreconcilable with the powers delegated to Congress by the Constitution and hence with the Tenth Amendment's reservation to the States of those powers not delegated to the Federal Government, we need only address the applicability of the Guarantee Clause to the Act's other two challenged provisions.

We approach the issue with some trepidation, because the Guarantee Clause has been an infrequent basis for litigation throughout our history. In most of the cases in which the Court has been asked to apply the Clause, the Court has found the claims presented to be nonjusticiable under the political question doctrine....

More recently, the Court has suggested that perhaps not all claims under the Guarantee Clause present nonjusticiable political questions. Contemporary commentators have likewise suggested that courts should address the merits of such claims, at least in some circumstances.

We need not resolve this difficult question today. Even if we assume that petitioners' claim is justiciable, neither the monetary incentives provided by the Act nor the possibility that a State's waste producers may find themselves excluded from the disposal sites of another State can reasonably be said to deny any State a republican form of government....

VII

[S]tates are not mere political subdivisions of the United States. State governments are neither regional offices nor administrative agencies of the Federal Government. The positions occupied by state officials appear nowhere on the Federal Government's most detailed organizational chart. The Constitution instead leaves to the several States a residuary and inviolable sovereignty, reserved explicitly to the States by the Tenth Amendment.

Whatever the outer limits of that sovereignty may be, one thing is clear: The Federal Government may not compel the States to enact or administer a federal regulatory program. The Constitution permits both the Federal Government and the States to enact legislation regarding the disposal of low level radioactive waste. The Constitution enables the Federal Government to pre-empt state regulation contrary to federal interests, and it permits the Federal Government to hold out incentives to the States as a means of encouraging them to adopt suggested regulatory schemes. It does not, however, authorize Congress simply to direct the States to provide for the disposal of the radioactive waste generated within their borders. While there may be many constitutional methods of achieving regional self-sufficiency in radioactive waste disposal, the method Congress has chosen is not one of them.

Justice WHITE, with whom Justice BLACKMUN and Justice STEVENS join, concurring in part and dissenting in part.

[T]he Court strikes down and severs [the] third component of the 1985 Act, the take title provision, which requires a noncomplying State to take title to or to assume liability for its low-level radioactive waste if it fails to provide for the disposal of such waste by January 1, 1996. The Court deems this last provision unconstitutional under principles of federalism. Because I believe the Court has mischaracterized the essential inquiry, misanalyzed the inquiry it has chosen to undertake, and undervalued the effect the seriousness of this public policy problem should have on the constitutionality of the take title provision, I can only join Parts III–A and III–B, and I respectfully dissent from the rest of its opinion and the judgment reversing in part the judgment of the Court of Appeals....

To justify its holding that the take title provision contravenes the Constitution, the Court posits that [i]n this provision, Congress has crossed the line distinguishing encouragement from coercion....

Curiously absent from the Court's analysis is any effort to place the take title provision within the overall context of the legislation.... Congress could have pre-empted the field by directly regulating the disposal of this waste pursuant to its powers under the Commerce and Spending Clauses, but instead it unanimously assented to the States' request for congressional ratification of agreements to which they had acceded. As the floor statements of Members of Congress reveal, the States wished to take the lead in achieving a solution to this problem and agreed among themselves to the various incentives and penalties implemented by Congress to ensure adherence to the various deadlines and goals. The chief executives of the States proposed this approach, and I am unmoved by the Court's vehemence in taking away Congress' authority to sanction a recalcitrant unsited State now that New York has reaped the benefits of the sited States' concessions....

Finally, to say, as the Court does, that the incursion on state sovereignty cannot be ratified by the consent of state officials, is flatly wrong. In a case involving a congressional ratification statute to an interstate compact, ... the Court determined that a State may be found to have waived a fundamental aspect of its sovereignty—the right to be immune from suit—in the formation of an interstate compact. I fail to understand the reasoning behind the Court's selective distinctions among the various aspects of sovereignty that may and may not be waived and do not believe these distinctions will survive close analysis in future cases....

The Court's distinction between a federal statute's regulation of States and private parties for general purposes, as opposed to a regulation solely on the activities of States, is unsupported by our recent Tenth Amendment cases. In no case has the Court rested its holding on such a distinction.... Certainly one would be hard-pressed to read the spirited exchanges between the Court and dissenting Justices in *National League of Cities* and in *Garcia v. San Antonio Metropolitan Transit Authority* as having been based on the distinction now drawn by the Court. An incursion on state sovereignty hardly seems more constitutionally acceptable if the federal statute that commands specific action also applies to private parties. The alleged diminution in state authority over its own affairs is not any less because the federal mandate restricts the activities of private parties....

The ultimate irony of the decision today is that in its formalistically rigid obeisance to federalism, the Court gives Congress fewer incentives to defer to the wishes of state officials in achieving local solutions to local problems. This legislation was a classic example of Congress acting as arbiter among the States in their attempts to accept responsibility for managing a problem of grave import. The States urged the National Legislature not to impose from Washington a solution to the country's low-level radioactive waste management problems. Instead, they sought a reasonable level of local and regional autonomy consistent with Art. I, § 10, cl. 3, of the Constitution....

Justice STEVENS, concurring in part and dissenting in part.

Under the Articles of Confederation, the Federal Government had the power to issue commands to the States. See Arts. VIII, IX. Because that indirect exercise of federal power proved ineffective, the Framers of the Constitution empowered the Federal Government to exercise legislative authority directly over individuals within the States, even though that direct authority constituted a greater intrusion on state sovereignty. Nothing in that history suggests that the Federal Government may not also impose its will upon the several States as it did under the Articles. The Constitution enhanced, rather than diminished, the power of the Federal Government.

The notion that Congress does not have the power to issue a simple command to state governments to implement legislation enacted by Congress is incorrect and unsound. There is no such limitation in the Constitution. The Tenth Amendment surely does not impose any limit on Congress' exercise of the powers delegated to it by Article I. Nor does the structure of the constitutional order or the values of federalism mandate such a formal rule. To the contrary, the Federal Government directs state governments in many realms. The Government regulates state-operated railroads, state school systems, state prisons, state elections, and a host of other state functions. Similarly, there can be no doubt that, in time of war, Congress could either draft soldiers itself or command the States to supply their quotas of troops. I see no reason why Congress may not also command the States to enforce federal water and air quality standards or federal standards for the disposition of low-level radioactive wastes.

Comments and Questions

1. What is the status of *Garcia v. SAMTA* after *New York v. United States*?

2. How is *New York v. United States* a Tenth Amendment case?

3. The Court says that the Constitution rejected the plan of the Articles of Confederation, in which the laws of the United States directed the states to take action, in favor of laws of the United States that would act directly on people. Justice Stevens argues that the Constitution *added* the power for Congress to make laws that would act directly on people without taking away the power to direct states to take action. What do you think? Does it make any difference that the Articles provided that "[e]ach state retains its sovereignty, freedom, and independence, and every power, jurisdiction, and right, which is not by this Confederation expressly delegated to the United States ...," and the Tenth

Amendment provides that "[t]he powers not delegated to the United States by the Constitution ... are reserved to the states respectively, or the people"?

4. There is an irony, noted by the dissent, that the law suggested to Congress by the National Governors Association is held unconstitutional as improperly interfering with states' rights. Moreover, persons normally can waive their rights under the Bill of Rights. For example, you can waive your right to a trial; you can consent to a search without a warrant. Why can states not waive their rights under the Tenth Amendment?

5. What is the difference between the first two parts of the Act and the third part that makes only the latter unconstitutional?

6. Five years later, the Court applied the anti-commandeering principle of *New York v. United States* to a provision of the Brady Handgun Violence Prevention Act, which required state and local law enforcement officers to conduct background checks on prospective handgun purchasers pending the development of a national instant background check. *Printz v. United States*, 521 U.S. 898 (1997). While *New York v. United States* had involved "commandeering" of state legislature, *Printz* involved "commandeering" of state officers. While this made a difference to Justice Souter, who had joined the Court's opinion in *New York v. United States*, but dissented in *Printz*, the other members of the Court essentially saw them as indistinguishable.

7. Three years after *Printz*, South Carolina challenged the Driver's Privacy Protection Act (DPPA), which restricted the ability of any person to sell or disclose to private parties the personal information contained on drivers' licenses without the consent of the driver involved. States routinely sold this information to businesses that then used it for marketing purposes. The state argued that this law was like *Printz* and *New York* in that it directed what the state could and could not do, essentially requiring it to carry out the federal law. The Court disagreed. In a unanimous opinion for the Court, Chief Justice Rehnquist distinguished those two cases. In those cases states were required to regulate citizens on behalf of the federal government, but here the states themselves were subject to the regulation. Moreover, this information was clearly an article in commerce and therefore clearly something subject to federal regulation. The statute did not single out states as the only entity subject to the law; indeed, the law applied to anyone who sold this information. *See Reno v. Condon*, 528 U.S. 141 (2000). It is not surprising, perhaps, that Chief Justice Rehnquist did not cite *Garcia v. SAMTA* in support of his position. Nevertheless, does not this case suggest the continued vitality of that case?

F. THE CIVIL WAR AMENDMENTS

Up to this point, we have been dealing with the congressional legislative powers contained in the original Constitution. Each of the Civil

War Amendments (the Thirteenth, Fourteenth, and Fifteenth Amendments), however, also contains a provision stating that Congress shall have the power to enforce the provisions of the amendment. The Thirteenth Amendment, adopted in 1865, prohibits slavery, and in 1866 Congress enacted the Civil Rights Act of 1866 to implement that amendment. That act, however, went well beyond merely prohibiting slavery. Intending to overturn the "black codes"* by which southern states were attempting to maintain the newly freed slaves in a subjugated state, Congress provided that all persons "of every race and color" born in the United States were citizens of the United States and entitled to a list of specified rights, including the same right to contract and to own property "as is enjoyed by white citizens." The act made violations of those rights federal crimes. The Fourteenth Amendment was adopted in 1868. The Fifteenth Amendment was adopted in 1870, and Congress passed the 1870 Civil Rights Act to protect against state denials of voting rights. Congress passed new Civil Rights Acts in 1871 and 1875. The 1871 Act, known as the Ku Klux Klan Act, among other things, created a private cause of action against persons who, under color of state law, deprive a person of rights established by the Constitution or federal law. This provision, codified today as 42 U.S.C. § 1983, is a frequent basis for suits alleging a violation of federal or constitutional rights by state officers. The 1875 Act prohibited discrimination on the basis of race in public accommodations, such as common carriers (*e.g.*, railroads), inns, and theaters. The constitutionality of this Act was challenged in the so-called *Civil Rights Cases*, which follows.

This period is known as Reconstruction. Under military occupation, Confederate leaders were barred from politics, and a combination of Freedmen, migrants from the North (known as "Carpetbaggers" after the luggage they typically brought), and southern whites (known as "Scalawags" by those opposed to Reconstruction) controlled the state legislatures under the banner of the Republican party.

1. WHAT RIGHTS CAN CONGRESS PROTECT?

THE CIVIL RIGHTS CASES

United States Supreme Court, 1883.
109 U.S. 3, 3 S.Ct. 18, 27 L.Ed. 835.

BRADLEY, J.

These cases are all founded on the first and second sections of the

* The so-called "Black Codes" were enacted by every southern state after the Thirteenth Amendment. Although they differed in detail, in essence they required all freedmen to be employed upon pain of being arrested as a vagrant, for which there was a large fine that would be paid off by leasing the "vagrant" at a public cry out (think: auction) and using all the wages so earned to pay the fine. Employment contracts provided that the freedman could not quit, and if he did, he could be arrested and returned to his employer. The employment contracts typically provided that the freedman would work from sun-up to sun-down six days a week. Freedmen employees were termed "servants" and their employers "masters." Freed children were to be apprenticed. Freedmen could not possess firearms, knives, or alcoholic beverages.

act of congress known as the "Civil Rights Act," passed March 1, 1875, entitled "An act to protect all citizens in their civil and legal rights." Two of the cases ... are indictments for denying to persons of color the accommodations and privileges of an inn or hotel; two of them ... are for denying to individuals the privileges and accommodations of a theater, [one is] for refusing a colored person a seat in the dress circle of Maguire's theater in San Francisco....

It is obvious that the primary and important question in all the cases is the constitutionality of the law; for if the law is unconstitutional none of the prosecutions can stand.

The sections of the law referred to provide as follows:

> Section 1. That all persons within the jurisdiction of the United States shall be entitled to the full and equal enjoyment of the accommodations, advantages, facilities, and privileges of inns, public conveyances on land or water, theaters, and other places of public amusement; subject only to the conditions and limitations established by law, and applicable alike to citizens of every race and color, regardless of any previous condition of servitude.
>
> Sec. 2. That any person who shall violate the foregoing section ... shall, for every such offense, forfeit and pay the sum of $500 to the person aggrieved thereby ... ; and shall, also, for every such offense, be deemed guilty of a misdemeanor, and upon conviction thereof shall be fined not less than $500 nor more than $1,000, or shall be imprisoned not less than 30 days nor more than one year....

Has congress constitutional power to make such a law? Of course, no one will contend that the power to pass it was contained in the constitution before the adoption of the last three amendments. The power is sought, first, in the fourteenth amendment, and the views and arguments of distinguished senators, advanced while the law was under consideration, claiming authority to pass it by virtue of that amendment, are the principal arguments adduced in favor of the power....

The first section of the fourteenth amendment—which is the one relied on—after declaring who shall be citizens of the United States, and of the several states, is prohibitory in its character, and prohibitory upon the states.... It is state action of a particular character that is prohibited. Individual invasion of individual rights is not the subject-matter of the amendment. It has a deeper and broader scope. It nullifies and makes void all state legislation, and state action of every kind, which impairs the privileges and immunities of citizens of the United States, or which injures them in life, liberty, or property without due process of law, or which denies to any of them the equal protection of the laws. It not only does this, but ... the last section of the amendment invests congress with power to enforce it by appropriate legislation. To enforce what? To enforce the prohibition. To adopt appropriate legislation for correcting the effects of such prohibited state law and state acts, and thus to render them effectually null, void, and innocuous. This is the legislative power conferred upon congress, and this is the whole of it. It does not invest congress with power to legislate upon subjects which are within the domain of state legislation; but to provide modes of relief against state legislation, or state action, of the kind referred to. It does not authorize congress to create a code of municipal law for the regulation of private rights....

If the principles of interpretation which we have laid down are correct, as we deem them to be, ... it is clear that the law in question cannot be sustained by any grant of legislative power made to congress by the fourteenth amendment.... The law in question, without any reference to adverse state legislation on the subject, declares that all persons shall be entitled to equal accommodation and privileges of inns, public conveyances, and places of public amusement, and imposes a penalty upon any individual who shall deny to any citizen such equal accommodations and privileges. This is not corrective legislation; it is primary and direct; it takes immediate and absolute possession of the subject of the right of admission to inns, public conveyances, and places of amusement. It supersedes and displaces state legislation on the same subject, or only allows it permissive force. It ignores such legislation, and assumes that the matter is one that belongs to the domain of national regulation. Whether it would not have been a more effective protection of the rights of citizens to have clothed congress with plenary power over the whole subject, is not now the question. What we have to decide is, whether such plenary power has been conferred upon congress by the fourteenth amendment, and, in our judgment, it has not....

But the power of congress to adopt direct and primary, as distinguished from corrective, legislation on the subject in hand, is sought, in the second place, from the thirteenth amendment, which abolishes slavery....

This amendment, as well as the fourteenth, is undoubtedly self-executing without any ancillary legislation, so far as its terms are applicable to any existing state of circumstances. By its own unaided force it abolished slavery, and established universal freedom. Still, legislation may be necessary and proper to meet all the various cases and circumstances to be affected by it, and to prescribe proper modes of redress for its violation in letter or spirit. And such legislation may be primary and direct in its character; for the amendment is not a mere prohibition of state laws establishing or upholding slavery, but an absolute declaration that slavery or involuntary servitude shall not exist in any part of the United States.

[I]t is assumed that the power vested in congress to enforce the article by appropriate legislation, clothes congress with power to pass all laws necessary and proper for abolishing all badges and incidents of slavery in the United Stated; and upon this assumption it is claimed that this is sufficient authority for declaring by law that all persons shall have equal accommodations and privileges in all inns, public conveyances, and places of public amusement; the argument being that the denial of such equal accommodations and privileges is in itself a subjection to a species of servitude within the meaning of the amendment. Conceding the major proposition to be true, that congress has a right to enact all necessary and proper laws for the obliteration and prevention of slavery, with all its badges and incidents, is the minor proposition also true, that the denial to any person of admission to the accommodations and privileges of an inn, a public conveyance, or a theater, does subject that person to any form of servitude, or tend to fasten upon him any badge of slavery? If it does not, then power to pass the law is not found in the thirteenth amendment....

Can the act of a mere individual, the owner of the inn, the public conveyance, or place of amusement, refusing the accommodation, be justly regarded as imposing any badge of slavery or servitude upon the applicant, or only as inflicting an ordinary civil injury, properly cognizable by the laws of the state, and presumably subject to redress by those laws until the contrary appears?

After giving to these questions all the consideration which their importance demands, we are forced to the conclusion that such an act of refusal has nothing to do with slavery or involuntary servitude, and that if it is violative of any right of the party, his redress is to be sought under the laws of the state; or, if those laws are adverse to his rights and do not protect him, his remedy will be found in the corrective legislation which congress has adopted, or may adopt, for counteracting the effect of state laws, or state action, prohibited by the fourteenth amendment. It would be running the slavery argument into the ground to make it apply to every act of discrimination which a person may see fit to make as to the guests he will entertain, or as to the people he will take into his coach or cab or car, or admit to his concert or theater, or deal with in other matters of intercourse or business....

When a man has emerged from slavery, and by the aid of beneficent legislation has shaken off the inseparable concomitants of that state, there must be some stage in the progress of his elevation when he takes the rank of a mere citizen, and ceases to be the special favorite of the laws, and when his rights as a citizen, or a man, are to be protected in the ordinary modes by which other men's rights are protected. There were thousands of free colored people in this country before the abolition of slavery, enjoying all the essential rights of life, liberty, and property the same as white citizens; yet no one, at that time, thought that it was any invasion of their personal *status* as freemen because they were not admitted to all the privileges enjoyed by white citizens, or because they were subjected to discriminations in the enjoyment of accommodations in inns, public conveyances, and places of amusement. Mere discriminations on account of race or color were not regarded as badges of slavery. If, since that time, the enjoyment of equal rights in all these respects has become established by constitutional enactment, it is not by force of the thirteenth amendment, (which merely abolishes slavery) but by force of the fourteenth and fifteenth amendments.

On the whole, we are of opinion that no countenance of authority for the passage of the law in question can be found in either the thirteenth or fourteenth amendment of the constitution; and no other ground of authority for its passage being suggested, it must necessarily be declared void, at least so far as its operation in the several states is concerned....

HARLAN, J., *dissenting.*

The opinion in these cases proceeds, as it seems to me, upon grounds entirely too narrow and artificial. The substance and spirit of the recent amendments of the constitution have been sacrificed by a subtle and ingenious verbal criticism.... Constitutional provisions, adopted in the interest of liberty, and for the purpose of securing, through national legislation, if need be, rights inhering in a state of freedom, and belonging to American citizenship, have been so construed as to defeat the ends the people desired to accomplish, which they attempted to accomplish, and which they supposed they had accomplished by changes in their fundamental law. By this I do not mean that the determination of these cases should have been materially controlled by considerations of mere expediency or policy. I mean only, in this form, to express an earnest conviction that the court has departed from the familiar rule requiring, in the interpretation of constitutional provisions, that full effect be given to the intent with which they were adopted.

The purpose of the first section of the act of congress of March 1, 1875, was to prevent *race* discrimination. It does not assume to define the general conditions and limitations under which inns, public conveyances, and places of public amusement may be conducted, but only declares that such conditions and limitations, whatever they may be, shall not be applied, by way of discrimination, *on account of race, color, or previous condition of servitude....*

The court adjudges that congress is without power, under either the thirteenth or fourteenth amendment, to establish such regulations, and that the first and second sections of the statute are, in all their parts, unconstitutional and void....

The thirteenth amendment, my brethren concede, did something more than to prohibit slavery as an *institution*, resting upon distinctions of race, and upheld by positive law. They admit that it established and decreed universal civil freedom throughout the United States. But did the freedom thus established involve nothing more than exemption from actual slavery? ...

That there are burdens and disabilities which constitute badges of slavery and servitude, and that the express power delegated to congress to enforce, by appropriate legislation, the thirteenth amendment, may be exerted by legislation of a direct and primary character, for the eradication, not simply of the institution, but of its badges and incidents, are propositions which ought to be deemed indisputable....

I do not contend that the thirteenth amendment invests congress with authority, by legislation, to regulate the entire body of the civil rights which citizens enjoy, or may enjoy, in the several states. But I do hold that since slavery, as the court has repeatedly declared, was the moving or principal cause of the adoption of that amendment, and since that institution rested wholly upon the inferiority, as a race, of those held in bondage, their freedom necessarily involved immunity from, and protection against, all discrimination against them, because of their race, in respect of such civil rights as belong to freemen of other races. Congress, therefore, under its express power to enforce that amendment, by appropriate legislation, may enact laws to protect that people against the deprivation, *on account of their race*, of any civil rights enjoyed by other freemen in the same state; and such legislation may be of a direct and primary character, operating upon states, their officers and agents, and also upon, at least, such individuals and corporations as exercise public functions and wield power and authority under the state.

What has been said is sufficient to show that the power of congress under the thirteenth amendment is not necessarily restricted to legislation against slavery as an institution upheld by positive law, but may be exerted to the extent at least of protecting the race, so liberated, against discrimination, in respect of legal rights belonging to freemen, where such discrimination is based upon race.

It remains now to inquire what are the legal rights of colored persons in respect of the accommodations, privileges, and facilities of public conveyances, inns, and places of public amusement. [Harlan then maintained that common carriers, inns, and places of public amusement (the latter because they held licenses to operate) all exercised public functions, not merely private functions.]

I am of the opinion that such discrimination practiced by corporations and individuals in the exercise of their public or quasi-public functions is a badge of servitude, the imposition of which congress may prevent under its power. By appropriate legislation, to enforce the thirteenth amendment; and consequently, without reference to its enlarged power under the fourteenth amendment, the act of March 1, 1875, is not, in my judgment, repugnant to the constitution.

It remains now to consider these cases with reference to the power congress has possessed since the adoption of the fourteenth amendment....

This court has always given a broad and liberal construction to the constitution, so as to enable congress, by legislation, to enforce rights secured by that instrument. The legislation congress may enact, in execution of its power to enforce the provisions of this amendment, is that which is appropriate to protect the right granted. Under given circumstances, that which the court characterizes as corrective legislation might be sufficient. Under other circumstances primary direct legislation may be required. But it is for congress, not the judiciary, to say which is best adapted to the end to be attained.... *McCulloch* v. *Maryland*....

The opinion of the court, as I have said, proceeds upon the ground that the power of congress to legislate for the protection of the rights and privileges secured by the fourteenth amendment cannot be brought into activity except with the view, and as it may become necessary, to correct and annul state laws and state proceedings in hostility to such rights and privileges. In the absence of state laws or state action, adverse to such rights and privileges, the nation may not actively interfere for their protection and security. Such I understand to be the position of my brethren. If the grant to colored citizens of the United States of citizenship in their respective states imports exemption from race discrimination, in their states, in respect of the civil rights belonging to citizenship, then, to hold that the amendment remits that right to the states for their protection, primarily, and stays the hands of the nation, until it is assailed by state laws or state proceedings, is to adjudge that the amendment, so far from enlarging the powers of congress—as we have heretofore said it did—not only curtails them, but reverses the policy which the general government has pursued from its very organization. Such an interpretation of the amendment is a denial to congress of the power, by appropriate legislation, to enforce one of its provisions....

My brethren say that when a man has emerged from slavery, and by the aid of beneficient legislation has shaken off the inseparable concomitants of that state, there must be some stage in the progress of his elevation when he takes the rank of a mere citizen, and ceases to be the special favorite of the laws, and when his rights as a citizen, or a man, are to be protected in the ordinary modes by which other men's rights are protected. It is, I submit, scarcely just to say that the colored race has been the special favorite of the laws. What the nation, through congress, has sought to accomplish in reference to that race is, what had already been done in every state in the Union for the white race, to secure and protect rights belonging to them as freemen and citizens; nothing more. The one underlying purpose of congressional legislation has been to enable the black race to take the rank of mere citizens. The difficulty has been to compel a recognition of their legal right to take that rank, and to secure the enjoyment of privileges belonging, under the law, to them as a component part of the people for whose welfare and happiness government is ordained.

For the reasons stated I feel constrained to withhold my assent to the opinion of the court.

Comments and Questions

1. This case illustrates why Congress in the 1964 Civil Rights Act relied on the Commerce Clause as a basis for the constitutionality of Title II, prohibiting discrimination on the basis of race in certain places of public accommodation, which the Supreme Court upheld in *Heart of*

Atlanta Motel v. United States and *Katzenbach v. McClung*. In this case in 1883, however, the Commerce Clause was not invoked. Instead, Congress relied upon the enforcement provisions of both the Thirteenth and Fourteenth Amendments, and the Court found neither provision a sufficient basis for the law.

2. The Court notes that the Fourteenth Amendment prohibits the states from doing various things, such as denying equal protection, and so it concludes that enforcing the Fourteenth Amendment is limited to prohibiting states, not private persons, from engaging in the prohibited acts. Moreover, the Court suggests that, because the Fourteenth Amendment requires states to provide persons of color with equal protection of the law, if persons are discriminated against because of their race, they will have recourse to state law and courts to protect them, and if the state law and courts do not, then Congress may act under Section 5 of the Fourteenth Amendment to force the states to do so. What is Justice Harlan's argument to the contrary? Recall from the *E.C. Knight* case that Justice Harlan is known as the "Great Dissenter" in part for his dissent in the *Civil Rights Cases*. Who do you think is right?

3. The Court acknowledges that Congress under the Thirteenth Amendment can act directly against individuals and that Congress can act to eliminate the "badges and incidents of slavery." Nevertheless, the Court concludes that the Thirteenth Amendment does not authorize this law. Why not? What is Justice Harlan's response? Who do you think is right?

4. Prior to the Civil Rights Cases, the Court had addressed a provision of the 1870 Civil Rights Act in the case of *United States v. Cruikshank*, 92 U.S. 542 (1875). There a group of white men had lynched two men of color, and the white men were prosecuted for "prevent[ing the colored persons'] free exercise and enjoyment of any right or privilege granted or secured to [them] by the constitution or laws of the United States." The specific "right or privilege" the persons of color were prevented from exercising was the "right and privilege peaceably to assemble." The Court held that this "right or privilege" was not a right or privilege granted or secured to them by the Constitution or laws of the United States.

> The right of the people peaceably to assemble for lawful purposes existed long before the adoption of the Constitution of the United States. In fact, it is, and always has been, one of the attributes of citizenship under a free government.... It was not, therefore, a right granted to the people by the Constitution. The government of the United States when established found it in existence, with the obligation on the part of the States to afford it protection. As no direct power over it was granted to Congress, it remains ... subject to State jurisdiction.

The Court allowed, however, that if the charge instead had been that the white men interfered with a persons' right to assemble "for the purpose of petitioning Congress for the redress of grievances," the prosecution then would have been constitutional. Why? Because the former "right" was a general civil right and could be protected by state law, whereas the latter was a "right" emanating specifically from the U.S. Constitution and, therefore, could appropriately be protected by Congress. Thus, the Court did not foreclose Congress from acting against individuals under its enforcement authority of Section 5 of the Fourteenth Amendment, if what the individuals did was interfere with a right granted by the Constitution rather than by natural law or general civil law. This allowance, however, is not repeated in the *Civil Rights Cases*. Of course, there the "right" involved—equal treatment by common carriers, inns, and places of public amusement—would have come from natural or general civil law, not the Constitution. Nevertheless, there remained a question whether enforcement against individuals pursuant to the Fourteenth Amendment was always barred or whether it could pass muster when the right being protected came from the Constitution.

5. The decision in the *Civil Rights Cases* coincided with a change in the national climate concerning civil rights and their enforcement. The active lawmaking and vigorous enforcement that characterized Reconstruction were abandoned by the Republican party and, together with the end of military occupation, resulted in a recapture of southern state politics by traditional forces, known as Redeemers then but later as southern Democrats. These new state governments then passed the Jim Crow laws* that mandated segregated public and private facilities. These laws remained in effect until the Civil Rights Movement in the 1950s and 1960s. We have already been exposed to the Civil Rights Act of 1964, which in essence reinstituted the 1875 Civil Rights Act under the authority of the Commerce Clause, but there remained discriminatory private activities not covered by the 1964 law.

JONES v. ALFRED H. MAYER CO.

United States Supreme Court, 1968.
392 U.S. 409, 88 S.Ct. 2186, 20 L.Ed.2d 1189.

Mr. Justice STEWART delivered the opinion of the Court.

In this case we are called upon to determine the scope and constitutionality of an Act of Congress, the Civil Rights Act of 1866, [codified today at] 42 U.S.C. § 1982, which provides that: "All citizens of the United States shall have the same right, in every State and Territory, as is enjoyed by white citizens thereof to inherit, purchase, lease, sell, hold, and convey real and personal property."

On September 2, 1965, the petitioners filed a complaint in the District Court for the Eastern District of Missouri, alleging that the respondents had refused to sell them a home ... for the sole reason that peti-

* Jim Crow laws derived their name from a minstrel character named Jim Crow, depicting a poor, rural freedman.

tioner Joseph Lee Jones is a Negro. Relying ... upon § 1982, the petitioners sought injunctive and other relief. The District Court sustained the respondents' motion to dismiss the complaint, and the Court of Appeals for the Eighth Circuit affirmed, concluding that § 1982 applies only to state action and does not reach private refusals to sell. We granted certiorari to consider the questions thus presented. For the reasons that follow, we reverse the judgment of the Court of Appeals. We hold that § 1982 bars all racial discrimination, private as well as public, in the sale or rental of property, and that the statute, thus construed, is a valid exercise of the power of Congress to enforce the Thirteenth Amendment.[5]

[T]he statute in this case deals only with racial discrimination and does not address itself to discrimination on grounds of religion or national origin....

[The Court then engaged in a lengthy interpretation of the meaning of the statute, specifically whether it protected against private discrimination or only public action, as in a state law that would deny persons of color from the ability to inherit, purchase, lease, sell, hold, and convey real and personal property. The Court concluded that the statute did reach private discrimination.]

The remaining question is whether Congress has power under the Constitution to do what § 1982 purports to do: to prohibit all racial discrimination, private and public, in the sale and rental of property. Our starting point is the Thirteenth Amendment, for it was pursuant to that constitutional provision that Congress originally enacted what is now § 1982.... As its text reveals, the Thirteenth Amendment "is not a mere prohibition of state laws establishing or upholding slavery, but an absolute declaration that slavery or involuntary servitude shall not exist in any part of the United States." *Civil Rights Cases*. It has never been doubted, therefore, "that the power vested in Congress to enforce the article by appropriate legislation," includes the power to enact laws "direct and primary, operating upon the acts of individuals, whether sanctioned by state legislation or not."

Thus, the fact that § 1982 operates upon the unofficial acts of private individuals, whether or not sanctioned by state law, presents no constitutional problem.... The constitutional question in this case, therefore, comes to this: Does the authority of Congress to enforce the Thirteenth Amendment "by appropriate legislation" include the power to eliminate all racial barriers to the acquisition of real and personal property? We think the answer to that question is plainly yes.

"By its own unaided force and effect," the Thirteenth Amendment "abolished slavery, and established universal freedom." *Civil Rights*

5. Because we have concluded that the discrimination alleged in the petitioners' complaint violated a federal statute that Congress had the power to enact under the Thirteenth Amendment, we find it unnecessary to decide whether that discrimination also violated the Equal Protection Clause of the Fourteenth Amendment.

Cases. Whether or not the Amendment itself did any more than that—a question not involved in this case—it is at least clear that the Enabling Clause of that Amendment empowered Congress to do much more. For that clause clothed "Congress with power to pass all laws necessary and proper for abolishing all badges and incidents of slavery in the United States."*Ibid.*

Those who opposed passage of the Civil Rights Act of 1866 argued in effect that the Thirteenth Amendment merely authorized Congress to dissolve the legal bond by which the Negro slave was held to his master. Yet many had earlier opposed the Thirteenth Amendment on the very ground that it would give Congress virtually unlimited power to enact laws for the protection of Negroes in every State. And the majority leaders in Congress—who were, after all, the authors of the Thirteenth Amendment—had no doubt that its Enabling Clause contemplated the sort of positive legislation that was embodied in the 1866 Civil Rights Act. Their chief spokesman, Senator Trumbull of Illinois, the Chairman of the Judiciary Committee, had brought the Thirteenth Amendment to the floor of the Senate in 1864. In defending the constitutionality of the 1866 Act, he argued that, if the narrower construction of the Enabling Clause were correct, then

> the trumpet of freedom that we have been blowing throughout the land has given an uncertain sound, and the promised freedom is a delusion. Such was not the intention of Congress, which proposed the constitutional amendment, nor is such the fair meaning of the amendment itself. * * * I have no doubt that under this provision * * * we may destroy all these discriminations in civil rights against the black man; and if we cannot, our constitutional amendment amounts to nothing. It was for that purpose that the second clause of that amendment was adopted, which says that Congress shall have authority, by appropriate legislation, to carry into effect the article prohibiting slavery. Who is to decide what that appropriate legislation is to be? The Congress of the United States; and it is for Congress to adopt such appropriate legislation as it may think proper, so that it be a means to accomplish the end.

Surely Senator Trumbull was right. Surely Congress has the power under the Thirteenth Amendment rationally to determine what are the badges and the incidents of slavery, and the authority to translate that determination into effective legislation. Nor can we say that the determination Congress has made is an irrational one. For this Court recognized long ago that, whatever else they may have encompassed, the badges and incidents of slavery—its "burdens and disabilities"—included restraints upon "those fundamental rights which are the essence of civil freedom, namely, the same right * * * to inherit, purchase, lease, sell and convey property, as is enjoyed by white citizens."

Civil Rights Cases.[78] Just as the Black Codes, enacted after the Civil War to restrict the free exercise of those rights, were substitutes for the slave system, so the exclusion of Negroes from white communities became a substitute for the Black Codes. And when racial discrimination herds men into ghettos and makes their ability to buy property turn on the color of their skin, then it too is a relic of slavery.

Negro citizens, North and South, who saw in the Thirteenth Amendment a promise of freedom—freedom to "go and come at pleasure" and to "buy and sell when they please"—would be left with "a mere paper guarantee" if Congress were powerless to assure that a dollar in the hands of a Negro will purchase the same thing as a dollar in the hands of a white man. At the very least, the freedom that Congress is empowered to secure under the Thirteenth Amendment includes the freedom to buy whatever a white man can buy, the right to live wherever a white man can live. If Congress cannot say that being a free man means at least this much, then the Thirteenth Amendment made a promise the Nation cannot keep....

Mr. Justice DOUGLAS, concurring.

The true curse of slavery is not what it did to the black man, but what it has done to the white man. For the existence of the institution produced the notion that the white man was of superior character, intelligence, and morality. The blacks were little more than livestock—to be fed and fattened for the economic benefits they could bestow through their labors, and to be subjected to authority, often with cruelty, to make clear who was master and who slave.

Some badges of slavery remain today. While the institution has been outlawed, it has remained in the minds and hearts of many white men. Cases which have come to this Court depict a spectacle of slavery unwilling to die. We have seen contrivances by States designed to thwart Negro voting. Negroes have been excluded over and again from juries solely on account of their race, or have been forced to sit in segregated seats in courtrooms. They have been made to attend segregated and inferior schools, or been denied entrance to colleges or graduate schools

78. The Court did conclude in the *Civil Rights Cases* that "the act of * * * the owner of the inn, the public conveyance or place of amusement, refusing * * * accommodation" cannot be "justly regarded as imposing any badge of slavery or servitude upon the applicant." "It would be running the slavery argument into the ground," the Court thought, "to make it apply to every act of discrimination which a person may see fit to make as to the guests he will entertain, or as to the people he will take into his coach or cab or car, or admit to his concert or theatre, or deal with in other matters of intercourse or business." ... Whatever the present validity of the position taken by the majority on that issue—a question rendered largely academic by Title II of the Civil Rights Act of 1964 (*see Heart of Atlanta Motel v. United States; Katzenbach v. McClung*)—we note that the entire Court agreed upon at least one proposition: The Thirteenth Amendment authorizes Congress not only to outlaw all forms of slavery and involuntary servitude but also to eradicate the last vestiges and incidents of a society half slave and half free, by securing to all citizens, of every race and color, "the same right to make and enforce contracts, to sue, be parties, give evidence, and to inherit, purchase, lease, sell and convey property, as is enjoyed by white citizens." *Civil Rights Cases* (dissenting opinion).

because of their color. Negroes have been prosecuted for marrying whites. They have been forced to live in segregated residential districts and residents of white neighborhoods have denied them entrance. Negroes have been forced to use segregated facilities in going about their daily lives, having been excluded from railway coaches, public parks, restaurants, public beaches, municipal golf courses, amusement parks, buses, public libraries....

Today the black is protected by a host of civil rights laws. But the forces of discrimination are still strong.

A member of his race, duly elected by the people to a state legislature, is barred from that assembly because of his views on the Vietnam.

Real estate agents use artifice to avoid selling "white property" to the blacks. The blacks who travel the country, though entitled by law to the facilities for sleeping and dining that are offered all tourists may well learn that the "vacancy" sign does not mean what it says, especially if the motel has a swimming pool.

On entering a half-empty restaurant they may find "reserved" signs on all unoccupied tables. The black is often barred from a labor union because of his race.

He learns that the order directing admission of his children into white schools has not been obeyed "with all deliberate speed," but has been delayed by numerous stratagems and devices. State laws, at times, have encouraged discrimination in housing.

This recital is enough to show how prejudices, once part and parcel of slavery, still persist. The men who sat in Congress in 1866 were trying to remove some of the badges or "customs" of slavery when they enacted § 1982.

Mr. Justice HARLAN, whom Mr. Justice WHITE joins, dissenting.

The decision in this case appears to me to be most ill-considered and ill-advised.

[The dissent disagrees with the majority's interpretation of the statute as applying to private conduct unrelated to state action, citing legislative history from its enactment.]

[I]n holding that the Thirteenth Amendment is sufficient constitutional authority for § 1982 as interpreted, the Court also decides a question of great importance. Even contemporary supporters of the aims of the 1866 Civil Rights Act doubted that those goals could constitutionally be achieved under the Thirteenth Amendment, and this Court has twice expressed similar doubts. [Believing that the 1968 Civil Rights Act banning discrimination in housing, enacted after this case began and which therefore would not provide relief to plaintiffs here, eliminated prospectively whatever was prohibited by the § 1982, the dissent believed the difficult constitutional question should be avoided.]

For these reasons, I would dismiss the writ of certiorari as improvidently granted.

Comments and Questions

1. Which opinion do you find more persuasive, the Court's or Justice Douglas's? And, whatever your answer to that question, why?

2. Do you agree with Justice Douglas that "the existence of the institution [of slavery] produced the notion that the white man was of superior character, intelligence, and morality"? Or was it that "the notion that the white man was of superior character, intelligence, and morality" produced the institution of slavery? If the former, then it might well be accurate to call subsequent racial discrimination as a product or "badge or incident of slavery." If, however, the latter is more accurate, then subsequent racial discrimination might not be the product of slavery but a product of the same prejudice that produced slavery.

3. After quoting from the *Civil Rights Cases* several times, the Court recognizes in a footnote that the *Civil Rights Cases* actually held that the Thirteenth Amendment did not authorize a statute banning discrimination on the basis of race in common carriers, inns, and places of public amusement. How does the Court rationalize that outcome with the decision in this case? What was different about the rights involved there compared with the right to buy or lease real estate? Or stated another way, if "the act of ... the owner of the inn, the public conveyance or place of amusement, refusing ... accommodation" cannot be "justly regarded as imposing any badge of slavery or servitude" on a person of color, how can the act of a home owner refusing to sell the home to a person of color be regarded as imposing any badge of slavery or servitude?

4. In that same footnote, the Court quotes from the dissent in the *Civil Rights Cases* for the proposition that "the entire Court agreed upon at least one proposition: The Thirteenth Amendment authorizes Congress ... to eradicate the last vestiges and incidents of a society half slave and half free, by securing to all citizens, of every race and color, 'the same right to make and enforce contracts, to sue, be parties, give evidence, and to inherit, purchase, lease, sell and convey property, as is enjoyed by white citizens.'" Did you find it odd that the Court cited to the dissent for what supposedly the "entire Court agreed upon"? And if the Court agreed on that, how could it find in the *Civil Rights Cases* that the 1875 Act was unconstitutional, inasmuch as that Act protected the right to contract for carriage on railroads, rooms in inns, and seats in a theater?

5. The answer is a little complicated. First, the majority in the *Civil Rights Cases* agreed (in a portion of the opinion edited from the version here) that either the Thirteenth or Fourteenth Amendment authorized the Civil Rights Act of 1866 (§ 1982 today). However, unlike the Court in *Jones*, the majority in the *Civil Rights Cases* interpreted § 1982 only to prohibit government discrimination, not private acts of discrimination (the argument of the dissent in *Jones*). The majority in the *Civil Rights Cases* only mentioned § 1982 to distinguish why it was

constitutional—because it only applied to public acts—and the Civil Rights Act of 1875 was not constitutional—because it applied to private acts of discrimination. In short, the citation by the Court in *Jones* suggesting that the *Civil Rights Act* supported the decision in *Jones* is either disingenuous (a euphemism for dishonest) or in error. But so what? *Jones* is the later case. What should we make of the *Civil Rights Cases* now? Consider the next case.

UNITED STATES v. MORRISON

United States Supreme Court, 2000.
529 U.S. 598, 120 S.Ct. 1740, 146 L.Ed.2d 658.

[This case was discussed in a note under the Commerce Clause. It involves a private action brought under the Violence Against Women Act (VAWA) by a female student against several football players who allegedly raped her. Following *United States v. Lopez*, this case held that this private right of action could not be authorized by Congress under the Commerce Clause. The plaintiff and the intervening United States also argued that Congress could pass this law under the authority of the Fourteenth Amendment.]

Chief Justice REHNQUIST delivered the opinion of the Court.

In these cases we consider the constitutionality of 42 U.S.C. § 13981, which provides a federal civil remedy for the victims of gender-motivated violence.... Believing that these cases are controlled by our decisions in *United States v. Lopez* and the *In re Civil Rights Cases*, we affirm....

III

Because we conclude that the Commerce Clause does not provide Congress with authority to enact § 13981, we address petitioners' alternative argument that the section's civil remedy should be upheld as an exercise of Congress' remedial power under § 5 of the Fourteenth Amendment....

The principles governing an analysis of congressional legislation under § 5 are well settled. Section 5 states that Congress may " 'enforce' by 'appropriate legislation' the constitutional guarantee that no State shall deprive any person of 'life, liberty, or property, without due process of law,' nor deny any person 'equal protection of the laws.' " Section 5 is "a positive grant of legislative power," that includes authority to "prohibit conduct which is not itself unconstitutional and [to] intrud[e] into 'legislative spheres of autonomy previously reserved to the States.' " However, "[a]s broad as the congressional enforcement power is, it is not unlimited." In fact, as we discuss in detail below, several limitations inherent in § 5's text and constitutional context have been recognized since the Fourteenth Amendment was adopted.

Petitioners' § 5 argument is founded on an assertion that there is pervasive bias in various state justice systems against victims of gender-motivated violence. This assertion is supported by a voluminous congressional record. Specifically, Congress received evidence that many participants in state justice systems are perpetuating an array of erroneous stereotypes and assumptions. Congress concluded that these discriminatory stereotypes often result in insufficient investigation and prosecution of gender-motivated crime, inappropriate focus on the behavior and credibility of the victims of that crime, and unacceptably lenient punishments for those who are actually convicted of gender-motivated violence. Petitioners contend that this bias denies victims of gender-motivated violence the equal protection of the laws and that Congress therefore acted appropriately in enacting a private civil remedy against the perpetrators of gender-motivated violence to both remedy the States' bias and deter future instances of discrimination in the state courts.

As our cases have established, state-sponsored gender discrimination violates equal protection unless it " 'serves' important governmental objectives and ... the discriminatory means employed" are "substantially related to the achievement of those objectives." However, the language and purpose of the Fourteenth Amendment place certain limitations on the manner in which Congress may attack discriminatory conduct. These limitations are necessary to prevent the Fourteenth Amendment from obliterating the Framers' carefully crafted balance of power between the States and the National Government. Foremost among these limitations is the time-honored principle that the Fourteenth Amendment, by its very terms, prohibits only state action. "[T]he principle has become firmly embedded in our constitutional law that the action inhibited by the first section of the Fourteenth Amendment is only such action as may fairly be said to be that of the States. That Amendment erects no shield against merely private conduct, however discriminatory or wrongful."

Shortly after the Fourteenth Amendment was adopted, we decided two cases interpreting the Amendment's provisions, *United States v. Harris,* 106 U.S. 629 (1883), and the *Civil Rights Cases*. In *Harris,* the Court considered a challenge to § 2 of the Civil Rights Act of 1871. That section sought to punish "private persons" for "conspiring to deprive any one of the equal protection of the laws enacted by the State." We concluded that this law exceeded Congress' § 5 power because the law was "directed exclusively against the action of private persons, without reference to the laws of the State, or their administration by her officers." ...

We reached a similar conclusion in the *Civil Rights Cases.* In those consolidated cases, we held that the public accommodation provisions of the Civil Rights Act of 1875, which applied to purely private conduct, were beyond the scope of the § 5 enforcement power.

The force of the doctrine of *stare decisis* behind these decisions stems not only from the length of time they have been on the books, but also from the insight attributable to the Members of the Court at that time. Every Member had been appointed by President Lincoln, Grant,

Hayes, Garfield, or Arthur—and each of their judicial appointees obviously had intimate knowledge and familiarity with the events surrounding the adoption of the Fourteenth Amendment.

Petitioners contend that [a] more recent decision[has] in effect overruled this longstanding limitation on Congress' § 5 authority. They rely on *United States v. Guest,* 383 U.S. 745 (1966), for the proposition that the rule laid down in the *Civil Rights Cases* is no longer good law. In *Guest,* the Court reversed the construction of an indictment under 18 U.S.C. § 241, saying in the course of its opinion that "we deal here with issues of statutory construction, not with issues of constitutional power." Three Members of the Court, in a separate opinion by Justice Brennan, expressed the view that the *Civil Rights Cases* were wrongly decided, and that Congress could under § 5 prohibit actions by private individuals. Three other Members of the Court, who joined the opinion of the Court, joined a separate opinion by Justice Clark which in two or three sentences stated the conclusion that Congress could "punis[h] all conspiracies—with or without state action—that interfere with Fourteenth Amendment rights....

Though these three Justices saw fit to opine on matters not before the Court in *Guest,* the Court had no occasion to revisit the *Civil Rights Cases* and *Harris,* having determined "the indictment [charging private individuals with conspiring to deprive blacks of equal access to state facilities] in fact contain[ed] an express allegation of state involvement." The Court concluded that the implicit allegation of "active connivance by agents of the State" eliminated any need to decide "the threshold level that state action must attain in order to create rights under the Equal Protection Clause." ...

To accept petitioners' argument, moreover, one must add to the three Justices joining Justice Brennan's reasoned explanation for his belief that the *Civil Rights Cases* were wrongly decided, the three Justices joining Justice Clark's opinion who gave no explanation whatever for their similar view. This is simply not the way that reasoned constitutional adjudication proceeds. We accordingly have no hesitation in saying that it would take more than the naked dicta contained in Justice Clark's opinion, when added to Justice Brennan's opinion, to cast any doubt upon the enduring vitality of the *Civil Rights Cases* and *Harris*....

We believe that the description of the § 5 power contained in the *Civil Rights Cases* is correct:

> But where a subject is not submitted to the general legislative power of Congress, but is only submitted thereto for the purpose of rendering effective some prohibition against particular [s]tate legislation or [s]tate action in reference to that subject, the power given is limited by its object, and any legislation by Congress in the matter must necessarily be corrective in its character, adapted to counteract and redress the operation of such prohibited state laws or proceedings of [s]tate officers.

Petitioners alternatively argue that, unlike the situation in the *Civil Rights Cases,* here there has been gender-based disparate treatment by state authorities, whereas in those cases there was no indication of such state action. There is abundant evidence, however, to show that the Congresses that enacted the Civil Rights Acts of 1871 and 1875 had a purpose similar to that of Congress in enacting § 13981: There were state laws on the books bespeaking equality of treatment, but in the administration of these laws there was discrimination against newly freed slaves....

But even if that distinction were valid, we do not believe it would save § 13981's civil remedy. For the remedy is simply not "corrective in its character, adapted to counteract and redress the operation of such prohibited [s]tate laws or proceedings of [s]tate officers." *Civil Rights Cases*.... Section 13981 is not aimed at proscribing discrimination by officials which the Fourteenth Amendment might not itself proscribe; it is directed not at any State or state actor, but at individuals who have committed criminal acts motivated by gender bias....

For these reasons, we conclude that Congress' power under § 5 does not extend to the enactment of § 13981....

Justice THOMAS, concurring.

[Justice Thomas only addressed the Commerce Clause issue.]

Justice SOUTER, with whom Justice STEVENS, Justice GINSBURG, and Justice BREYER join, dissenting.

[Justice Souter only addressed the Commerce Clause issue.]

Justice BREYER, with whom Justice STEVENS joins, and with whom Justice SOUTER and Justice GINSBURG join as to Part I–A, dissenting.

I

[Justice Breyer begins by disagreeing with the majority regarding the Commerce Clause issue.]

II

Given my conclusion on the Commerce Clause question, I need not consider Congress' authority under § 5 of the Fourteenth Amendment. Nonetheless, I doubt the Court's reasoning rejecting that source of authority. The Court points out that in *United States v. Harris* and the *Civil Rights Cases*, the Court held that § 5 does not authorize Congress to use the Fourteenth Amendment as a source of power to remedy the conduct of *private persons.* That is certainly so. The Federal Government's argument, however, is that Congress used § 5 to remedy the actions of *state actors,* namely, those States which, through discriminatory design or the discriminatory conduct of their officials, failed to provide adequate (or any) state remedies for women injured by gender-motivated violence—a failure that the States, and Congress, documented in depth.

Neither *Harris* nor the *Civil Rights Cases* considered this kind of claim....

But why can Congress not provide a remedy against private actors? Those private actors, of course, did not themselves violate the Constitution. But this Court has held that Congress at least sometimes can enact remedial "[l]egislation ... [that] prohibits conduct which is not itself unconstitutional." The statutory remedy does not in any sense purport to "determine what constitutes a constitutional violation." It intrudes little upon either States or private parties. It may lead state actors to improve their own remedial systems, primarily through example. It restricts private actors only by imposing liability for private conduct that is, in the main, already forbidden by state law....

Despite my doubts about the majority's § 5 reasoning, I need not, and do not, answer the § 5 question, which I would leave for more thorough analysis if necessary on another occasion. Rather, in my view, the Commerce Clause provides an adequate basis for the statute before us. And I would uphold its constitutionality as the "necessary and proper" exercise of legislative power granted to Congress by that Clause.

Comments and Questions

1. *Morrison* seems to answer the question what we are to make of the *Civil Rights Cases* now. Despite the questioning of those cases in modern decisions, the *Morrison* Court reaffirms the principle that the Fourteenth Amendment cannot provide a basis for federal laws regulating private discriminatory conduct. On the other hand, the decision in *Jones* would seem to continue to be good law for the proposition that private discriminatory conduct can constitute the "badges and incidents of slavery" that Congress can act to eliminate under the Thirteenth Amendment, notwithstanding the *Civil Rights Cases* contrary conclusion. However, even liberally construed, the Thirteenth Amendment limits Congress to dealing with racial discrimination, whereas the Equal Protection Clause of the Fourteenth Amendment would authorize Congress to deal with any unconstitutional discrimination, not just racial discrimination, at least with respect to state actors.

2. TO WHAT EXTENT CAN CONGRESS PROTECT THOSE RIGHTS?

In the Voting Rights Act of 1965, Congress took a more aggressive approach to protecting the voting rights of persons of color under the Fifteenth Amendment than it had previously. Laws like the 1870 Civil Rights Act had merely criminalized interference with voting rights on the basis of race, color, or previous condition of servitude. The 1965 Act, among other things, prohibited the use of literacy tests as a qualification for voting in those places where less than 50% of the voting age residents were registered to vote. Not only did this Act by its terms not address a voting requirement based on race, color, or previous condition of servitude, but six years before the Supreme Court had held that literacy tests by themselves were not unconstitutional. South Carolina challenged the Act, but the Supreme Court upheld the Act as an appropriate exercise of Congress's powers under the enforcement provision of the Fifteenth Amendment. *See South Carolina v. Katzenbach*, 383 U.S. 301 (1966). The Court noted that the Justice Department and the Civil Rights Commission had amassed overwhelming evidence that literacy tests were being used as a means to deny the vote to persons of color and that a low registration rate was a signal for discriminatory infringement of the right to vote. Five years later Congress made the ban on literacy tests nationwide. Again the Court upheld the law, *Oregon v. Mitchell*, 400 U.S. 112 (1970), saying that Congress had evidence "that literacy tests reduce voter participation in a discriminatory manner not only in the South but throughout the Nation."

Another provision of the Voting Rights Act of 1965 provided that "no person who has successfully completed the sixth primary grade in [an accredited school in] Puerto Rico in which the language of instruction was other than English shall be denied the right to vote in any election because of his inability to read or write English."* In enacting this provision, Congress referred to its authority to enforce the Equal Protection Clause pursuant to Section 5 of the Fourteenth Amendment rather than the enforcement provision of the Fifteenth Amendment, presumably because discrimination against Spanish-speaking persons from Puerto Rico was not deemed racial discrimination. In a challenge brought by New York state, the Court upheld the provision without itself deciding whether the New York English literacy requirement was a violation of equal protection. The Court said: "it is enough that we perceive a basis upon which Congress might predicate a judgment that the application of New York's [requirement] constituted an invidious discrimination in violation of the Equal Protection Clause." In other words, the Court seemed to say that, in exercising its authority under Section 5 of the Fourteenth Amendment, Congress itself could determine whether there was a constitutional violation, and the Court would defer to that determination. The Court then asked whether the means employed in the Act were appropriate to address the problem Congress identified. Citing to *McCulloch v. Maryland*, the Court deferred to Congress's decision on that point as well. *See Katzenbach v. Morgan*, 384 U.S. 641 (1966).

The suggestion in *Katzenbach* that Congress itself could determine whether there was a constitutional violation requiring enforcement under Section 5 arose again in a challenge to another provision of the Voting Rights Act of 1970. This provision prohibited states from denying

* Persons born in Puerto Rico are citizens of the United States and are free to change their residence to anywhere else in the United States, like any citizen. Once they reside in a state, they are citizens of the state pursuant to the Fourteenth Amendment. Nevertheless, it was alleged that New York adopted an English literacy requirement in order to keep immigrant Puerto Ricans from being able to vote in New York.

the right to vote in any election to any person on the basis of age, if the person was 18 years or older. The argument was that Congress had determined that denying the right to vote to persons between the ages of 18 and 21 served no legitimate governmental interest and therefore violated the Equal Protection Clause. In a highly split opinion, four justices held that the law was constitutional as applied to both federal and state elections; four justices held that the law was unconstitutional as applied to both federal and state elections; and one justice held that the law was constitutional as applied to federal elections but not as to state elections.* The four justices who would have upheld the law altogether reiterated the suggestion in *Katzenbach* that the only question was "whether Congress could rationally have concluded that denial of the franchise to citizens between the ages of 18 and 21 was [a violation of the Equal Protection Clause]," and they believed Congress could have so concluded. None of the other justices were willing to go so far. Four believed that the flexibility given Congress in *Katzenbach* turned on the case involving invidious discrimination, and here difference in age was not such invidious discrimination as discrimination on the basis of race or national origin. One justice believed that the Equal Protection Clause simply did not apply to discrimination in voting rights, inasmuch as, if it did, the Fifteenth Amendment would have been unnecessary. *See Oregon v. Mitchell*, 400 U.S. 112 (1970). In short, whether the suggestion in *Katzenbach* survived *Mitchell* was unclear.

In *Employment Division v. Smith*, 494 U.S. 872 (1990), the Court in a 5–4 decision held that a law of general applicability (such as a law banning the possession of peyote), that merely happened to substantially burden a person's free exercise of religion, did not violate the Free Exercise Clause of the First Amendment. In so ruling, the Court rejected what some had thought the rule—that such a law would be unconstitutional unless the law served a compelling government interest that could not be achieved by a law that did not so burden a person's free exercise of a religion. Unhappy with this decision, Congress passed the Religious Freedom Restoration Act (RFRA) to require that before any federal, state, or local government agency could apply any law that substantially burdened the exercise of a religion, that agency would have to determine that there was a compelling government interest in so applying the law that could not be satisfied in a manner that would be less burdensome on the exercise of the religion. In passing RFRA, Congress relied on Section 5 of the Fourteenth Amendment in order to apply it to state and local government. Its theory was that the Free Exercise Clause of the First Amendment had been incorporated against the states by the Fourteenth Amendment, so Section 5's enforcement provision could be used to enforce the Free Exercise Clause, just as it had been used to enforce the Equal Protection Clause of the Fourteenth Amendment itself. In the case below, the Court responded to what it viewed as an attempt by Congress

* The failure of the law with respect to state and local elections led to the proposal and adoption of the Twenty Sixth Amendment in 1971.

to overrule its *Employment Division* decision.

Anthony Kennedy

Anthony Kennedy was appointed to the Supreme Court by President Reagan in 1988 after the failed nominations of Robert Bork and Douglas Ginsburg. Born in 1936, he is the third oldest member of the Court. Prior to his appointment to the Supreme Court, Kennedy had been a judge on the Ninth Circuit since 1975. Kennedy has become the swing vote on the Court, sometimes siding with the liberals, such as in the case of *Lawrence v. Texas*, in which he wrote the Court's opinion finding state sodomy laws unconstitutional, and sometimes siding with the conservatives, such as in *Gonzales v. Carhart*, in which he wrote the opinion upholding the federal ban on partial-birth abortions. Indeed, in the 2006 Term, Justice Kennedy was the fifth vote in each of the 24 cases decided by a 5-4 vote.

CITY OF BOERNE v. FLORES

United States Supreme Court, 1997.
521 U.S. 507, 117 S.Ct. 2157, 138 L.Ed.2d 624.

Justice KENNEDY delivered the opinion of the Court.

A decision by local zoning authorities to deny a church a building permit was challenged under the Religious Freedom Restoration Act of 1993 (RFRA or Act). The case calls into question the authority of Congress to enact RFRA. We conclude the statute exceeds Congress' power.

Situated on a hill in the city of Boerne, Texas, ... is St. Peter Catholic Church. Built in 1923, the church's structure replicates the mission style of the region's earlier history. The church seats about 230 worshippers, a number too small for its growing parish.... In order to meet the needs of the congregation the Archbishop of San Antonio gave permission to the parish to plan alterations to enlarge the building.

A few months later, the Boerne City Council passed an ordinance authorizing the city's Historic Landmark Commission to prepare a preservation plan with proposed historic landmarks and districts. Under the ordinance, the commission must preapprove construction affecting historic landmarks or buildings in a historic district.

Soon afterwards, the Archbishop applied for a building permit so construction to enlarge the church could proceed. City authorities, relying on the ordinance and the designation of a historic district (which, they argued, included the church), denied the application. The Archbishop brought this suit challenging the permit denial....

The complaint contained various claims, but to this point the litigation has centered on RFRA and the question of its constitutionality. The Archbishop relied upon RFRA as one basis for relief from the refusal to issue the permit. The District Court concluded that by enacting RFRA Congress exceeded the scope of its enforcement power under § 5 of the Fourteenth Amendment. The court certified its order for interlocutory appeal and the Fifth Circuit reversed, finding RFRA to be constitutional. We granted certiorari and now reverse.

Congress enacted RFRA in direct response to the Court's decision in *Employment Div. v. Smith.* There we considered a Free Exercise Clause claim brought by members of the Native American Church who were denied unemployment benefits when they lost their jobs because they had used peyote. Their practice was to ingest peyote for sacramental purposes, and they challenged an Oregon statute of general applicability which made use of the drug criminal. In evaluating the claim, we declined to apply the balancing test set forth in *Sherbert v. Verner,* 374 U.S. 398 (1963), under which we would have asked whether Oregon's prohibition substantially burdened a religious practice and, if it did, whether the burden was justified by a compelling government interest.... By contrast, where a general prohibition, such as Oregon's, is at issue, "the sounder approach, and the approach in accord with the vast majority of our precedents, is to hold the test inapplicable to [free exercise] challenges." *Smith* held that neutral, generally applicable laws may be applied to religious practices even when not supported by a compelling governmental interest....

These points of constitutional interpretation were debated by Members of Congress in hearings and floor debates. Many criticized the Court's reasoning, and this disagreement resulted in the passage of RFRA....

The Act's stated purposes are:"(1) to restore the compelling interest test as set forth in *Sherbert v. Verner* and to guarantee its application in all cases where free exercise of religion is substantially burdened;" and "(2) to provide a claim or defense to persons whose religious exercise is substantially burdened by government."

RFRA prohibits "[g]overnment" from "substantially burden[ing]" a person's exercise of religion even if the burden results from a rule of general applicability unless the government can demonstrate the burden "(1) is in furtherance of a compelling governmental interest; and (2) is the least restrictive means of furthering that compelling governmental interest." The Act's mandate applies to any "branch, department, agency, instrumentality, and official (or other person acting under color of law) of the United States," as well as to any "State, or ... subdivision of a State." ...

[C]ongress relied on its Fourteenth Amendment enforcement power in enacting the most far-reaching and substantial of RFRA's provisions, those which impose its requirements on the States....

The parties disagree over whether RFRA is a proper exercise of Congress' § 5 power "to enforce" by "appropriate legislation" the constitutional guarantee that no State shall deprive any person of "life, liberty, or property, without due process of law" nor deny any person "equal protection of the laws."

In defense of the Act, respondent the Archbishop contends, with support from the United States, that RFRA is permissible enforcement legislation. Congress, it is said, is only protecting by legislation one of the liberties guaranteed by the Fourteenth Amendment's Due Process Clause, the free exercise of religion, beyond what is necessary under *Smith*. It is said the congressional decision to dispense with proof of deliberate or overt discrimination and instead concentrate on a law's effects accords with the settled understanding that § 5 includes the power to enact legislation designed to prevent, as well as remedy, constitutional violations. It is further contended that Congress' § 5 power is not limited to remedial or preventive legislation....

[I]n assessing the breadth of § 5's enforcement power, we begin with its text. Congress has been given the power "to enforce" the "provisions of this article." We agree with respondent, of course, that Congress can enact legislation under § 5 enforcing the constitutional right to the free exercise of religion. The "provisions of this article," to which § 5 refers, include the Due Process Clause of the Fourteenth Amendment. Congress' power to enforce the Free Exercise Clause follows from our holding ... that the "fundamental concept of liberty embodied in [the Fourteenth Amendment's Due Process Clause] embraces the liberties guaranteed by the First Amendment."

Congress' power under § 5, however, extends only to "enforc[ing]" the provisions of the Fourteenth Amendment. The Court has described this power as "remedial." The design of the Amendment and the text of § 5 are inconsistent with the suggestion that Congress has the power to decree the substance of the Fourteenth Amendment's restrictions on the States. Legislation which alters the meaning of the Free Exercise Clause cannot be said to be enforcing the Clause. Congress does not enforce a constitutional right by changing what the right is. It has been given the power "to enforce," not the power to determine what constitutes a constitutional violation. Were it not so, what Congress would be enforcing would no longer be, in any meaningful sense, the "provisions of [the Fourteenth Amendment]."

While the line between measures that remedy or prevent unconstitutional actions and measures that make a substantive change in the governing law is not easy to discern, and Congress must have wide latitude in determining where it lies, the distinction exists and must be observed. There must be a congruence and proportionality between the injury to be prevented or remedied and the means adopted to that end. Lacking such a connection, legislation may become substantive in operation and effect. History and our case law support drawing the distinction, one apparent from the text of the Amendment....

The remedial and preventive nature of Congress' enforcement

power, and the limitation inherent in the power, were confirmed in our earliest cases on the Fourteenth Amendment....

Any suggestion that Congress has a substantive, non-remedial power under the Fourteenth Amendment is not supported by our case law. In *Oregon v. Mitchell,* a majority of the Court concluded Congress had exceeded its enforcement powers by enacting legislation lowering the minimum age of voters from 21 to 18 in state and local elections. The five Members of the Court who reached this conclusion explained that the legislation intruded into an area reserved by the Constitution to the States. Four of these five were explicit in rejecting the position that § 5 endowed Congress with the power to establish the meaning of constitutional provisions....

There is language in our opinion in *Katzenbach v. Morgan,* which could be interpreted as acknowledging a power in Congress to enact legislation that expands the rights contained in § 1 of the Fourteenth Amendment. This is not a necessary interpretation, however, or even the best one.... The Court provided two related rationales for its conclusion that § 4(e) could "be viewed as a measure to secure for the Puerto Rican community residing in New York nondiscriminatory treatment by government." ... Both rationales for upholding § 4(e) rested on unconstitutional discrimination by New York and Congress' reasonable attempt to combat it....

If Congress could define its own powers by altering the Fourteenth Amendment's meaning, no longer would the Constitution be "superior paramount law, unchangeable by ordinary means." It would be "on a level with ordinary legislative acts, and, like other acts, ... alterable when the legislature shall please to alter it." ... Shifting legislative majorities could change the Constitution and effectively circumvent the difficult and detailed amendment process contained in Article V.

We now turn to consider whether RFRA can be considered enforcement legislation under § 5 of the Fourteenth Amendment.

Respondent contends that RFRA is a proper exercise of Congress' remedial or preventive power. The Act, it is said, is a reasonable means of protecting the free exercise of religion as defined by *Smith.* It prevents and remedies laws which are enacted with the unconstitutional object of targeting religious beliefs and practices. To avoid the difficulty of proving such violations, it is said, Congress can simply invalidate any law which imposes a substantial burden on a religious practice unless it is justified by a compelling interest and is the least restrictive means of accomplishing that interest....

While preventive rules are sometimes appropriate remedial measures, there must be a congruence between the means used and the ends to be achieved. The appropriateness of remedial measures must be considered in light of the evil presented. Strong measures appropriate to address one harm may be an unwarranted response to another, lesser one.

A comparison between RFRA and the Voting Rights Act is instructive. In contrast to the record which confronted Congress and the Judiciary in the voting rights cases, RFRA's legislative record lacks examples of modern instances of generally applicable laws passed because of religious bigotry. The history of persecution in this country detailed in the hearings mentions no episodes occurring in the past 40 years.... Rather, the emphasis of the hearings was on laws of general applicability which place incidental burdens on religion.... This lack of support in the legislative record, however, is not RFRA's most serious shortcoming. Judicial deference, in most cases, is based not on the state of the legislative record Congress compiles but "on due regard for the decision of the body constitutionally appointed to decide." As a general matter, it is for Congress to determine the method by which it will reach a decision.

Regardless of the state of the legislative record, RFRA cannot be considered remedial, preventive legislation, if those terms are to have any meaning. RFRA is so out of proportion to a supposed remedial or preventive object that it cannot be understood as responsive to, or designed to prevent, unconstitutional behavior. It appears, instead, to attempt a substantive change in constitutional protections. Preventive measures prohibiting certain types of laws may be appropriate when there is reason to believe that many of the laws affected by the congressional enactment have a significant likelihood of being unconstitutional. Remedial legislation under § 5 "should be adapted to the mischief and wrong which the [Fourteenth] [A]mendment was intended to provide against."

RFRA is not so confined. Sweeping coverage ensures its intrusion at every level of government, displacing laws and prohibiting official actions of almost every description and regardless of subject matter.... RFRA applies to all federal and state law, statutory or otherwise, whether adopted before or after its enactment. RFRA has no termination date or termination mechanism. Any law is subject to challenge at any time by any individual who alleges a substantial burden on his or her free exercise of religion.

The reach and scope of RFRA distinguish it from other measures passed under Congress' enforcement power, even in the area of voting rights. In *South Carolina v. Katzenbach,* the challenged provisions were confined to those regions of the country where voting discrimination had been most flagrant and affected a discrete class of state laws, *i.e.,* state voting laws.... The provisions restricting and banning literacy tests, upheld in *Katzenbach v. Morgan* and *Oregon v. Mitchell,* attacked a particular type of voting qualification, one with a long history as a "notorious means to deny and abridge voting rights on racial grounds." ... This is not to say, of course, that § 5 legislation requires termination dates, geographic restrictions, or egregious predicates. Where, however, a congressional enactment pervasively prohibits constitutional state action in an effort to remedy or to prevent unconstitutional state action, limitations of this kind tend to ensure Congress' means are proportionate to ends legitimate under § 5.

The stringent test RFRA demands of state laws reflects a lack of proportionality or congruence between the means adopted and the legitimate end to be achieved. If an objector can show a substantial burden on his free exercise, the State must demonstrate a compelling governmental interest and show that the law is the least restrictive means of furthering its interest. Claims that a law substantially burdens someone's exercise of religion will often be difficult to contest.... Laws valid under *Smith* would fall under RFRA without regard to whether they had the object of stifling or punishing free exercise. We make these observations not to reargue the position of the majority in *Smith* but to illustrate the substantive alteration of its holding attempted by RFRA....

The substantial costs RFRA exacts, both in practical terms of imposing a heavy litigation burden on the States and in terms of curtailing their traditional general regulatory power, far exceed any pattern or practice of unconstitutional conduct under the Free Exercise Clause as interpreted in *Smith.* Simply put, RFRA is not designed to identify and counteract state laws likely to be unconstitutional because of their treatment of religion. In most cases, the state laws to which RFRA applies are not ones which will have been motivated by religious bigotry. If a state law disproportionately burdened a particular class of religious observers, this circumstance might be evidence of an impermissible legislative motive. RFRA's substantial-burden test, however, is not even a discriminatory effects or disparate-impact test. It is a reality of the modern regulatory state that numerous state laws, such as the zoning regulations at issue here, impose a substantial burden on a large class of individuals. When the exercise of religion has been burdened in an incidental way by a law of general application, it does not follow that the persons affected have been burdened any more than other citizens, let alone burdened because of their religious beliefs....

Our national experience teaches that the Constitution is preserved best when each part of the Government respects both the Constitution and the proper actions and determinations of the other branches. When the Court has interpreted the Constitution, it has acted within the province of the Judicial Branch, which embraces the duty to say what the law is. When the political branches of the Government act against the background of a judicial interpretation of the Constitution already issued, it must be understood that in later cases and controversies the Court will treat its precedents with the respect due them under settled principles, including *stare decisis,* and contrary expectations must be disappointed. RFRA was designed to control cases and controversies, such as the one before us; but as the provisions of the federal statute here invoked are beyond congressional authority, it is this Court's precedent, not RFRA, which must control....

Justice STEVENS, concurring.

In my opinion, the Religious Freedom Restoration Act of 1993

(RFRA) is a "law respecting an establishment of religion" that violates the First Amendment to the Constitution....

Justice SCALIA, with whom Justice STEVENS joins, concurring in part. [omitted]

Justice O'CONNOR, with whom Justice BREYER joins except as to the first paragraph of Part I, dissenting.

I dissent from the Court's disposition of this case. I agree with the Court that the issue before us is whether the Religious Freedom Restoration Act of 1993 (RFRA) is a proper exercise of Congress' power to enforce § 5 of the Fourteenth Amendment. But as a yardstick for measuring the constitutionality of RFRA, the Court uses its holding in *Employment Div., Dept. of Human Resources of Oregon v. Smith,* the decision that prompted Congress to enact RFRA as a means of more rigorously enforcing the Free Exercise Clause. I remain of the view that *Smith* was wrongly decided, and I would use this case to reexamine the Court's holding there....

I

I agree with much of the reasoning set forth in ... the Court's opinion. Indeed, if I agreed with the Court's standard in *Smith,* I would join the opinion. As the Court's careful and thorough historical analysis shows, Congress lacks the "power to decree the *substance* of the Fourteenth Amendment's restrictions on the States." Rather, its power under § 5 of the Fourteenth Amendment extends only to *enforcing* the Amendment's provisions. In short, Congress lacks the ability independently to define or expand the scope of constitutional rights by statute. Accordingly, whether Congress has exceeded its § 5 powers turns on whether there is a "congruence and proportionality between the injury to be prevented or remedied and the means adopted to that end." This recognition does not, of course, in any way diminish Congress' obligation to draw its own conclusions regarding the Constitution's meaning. Congress, no less than this Court, is called upon to consider the requirements of the Constitution and to act in accordance with its dictates. But when it enacts legislation in furtherance of its delegated powers, Congress must make its judgments consistent with this Court's exposition of the Constitution and with the limits placed on its legislative authority by provisions such as the Fourteenth Amendment....

Justice SOUTER, dissenting.

To decide whether the Fourteenth Amendment gives Congress sufficient power to enact the Religious Freedom Restoration Act of 1993, the Court measures the legislation against the free-exercise standard of *Employment Div., Dept. of Human Resources of Oregon v. Smith*.... I have serious doubts about the precedential value of the *Smith* rule and its entitlement to adherence....

Justice BREYER, dissenting.

I agree with Justice O'CONNOR that the Court should direct the parties to brief the question whether *Employment Div., Dept. of Human Resources of Oregon v. Smith* was correctly decided, and set this case for reargument.

Comments and Questions

1. *Boerne* (pronounced "bernie") makes several things clear. First, it makes clear that Congress can indeed enforce Free Exercise rights with respect to the states pursuant to Section 5 of the Fourteenth Amendment, but it also makes clear that it is the Court, not Congress, that gets to define what those rights are. The suggestion in *Katzenbach* that Congress might be able to define the contours of constitutional rights subject to its enforcement powers is rejected. Second, *Boerne* makes clear that Congress in enforcing constitutional rights is not limited merely to prohibiting or punishing violations of those rights; it can engage in preventative and remedial measures. Third, the Court is clear that, if Congress engages in preventative or remedial measures under its Section 5 enforcement powers, those measures must be congruent and proportional to actual violations that do or are about to exist.

2. What specifically was wrong with RFRA? Was it that Congress had defined the right, not the Court? Was it that Congress had no preventative or remedial measure in mind? Was it that any preventative or remedial measure was not congruent and proportional?

BOARD OF TRUSTEES OF THE UNIVERSITY OF ALABAMA v. GARRETT

United States Supreme Court, 2001.
531 U.S. 356, 121 S.Ct. 955, 148 L.Ed.2d 866.

Chief Justice REHNQUIST delivered the opinion of the Court.

We decide here whether employees of the State of Alabama may recover money damages by reason of the State's failure to comply with the provisions of Title I of the Americans with Disabilities Act of 1990 (ADA or Act). We hold that such suits are barred by the Eleventh Amendment.

The ADA prohibits certain employers, including the States, from "discriminat [ing] against a qualified individual with a disability because of the disability of such individual in regard to job application procedures, the hiring, advancement, or discharge of employees, employee compensation, job training, and other terms, conditions, and privileges of employment." ...

Respondent Patricia Garrett, a registered nurse, was employed as the Director of Nursing, OB/Gyn/Neonatal Services, for the University of Alabama in Birmingham Hospital. In 1994, Garrett was diagnosed with breast cancer and subsequently underwent a lumpectomy, radiation treatment, and chemotherapy. Garrett's treatments required her to take substantial leave from work. Upon returning to work in July 1995, Garrett's supervisor informed Garrett that she would have to give up her Director position. Garrett then applied for and received a transfer to another, lower paying position as a nurse manager....

Garrett ... filed [a lawsuit] in the District Court, both seeking money damages under the ADA. Petitioners moved for summary judgment, claiming that the ADA exceeds Congress' authority to abrogate the State's Eleventh Amendment immunity. [T]he District Court agreed with petitioner['s] position and granted [her motion] for summary judgment.... The Court of Appeals reversed.... We granted certiorari to resolve a split among the Courts of Appeals on the question whether an individual may sue a State for money damages in federal court under the ADA....

Although by its terms the Amendment applies only to suits against a State by citizens of another State, our cases have extended the Amendment's applicability to suits by citizens against their own States. The ultimate guarantee of the Eleventh Amendment is that nonconsenting States may not be sued by private individuals in federal court.

We have recognized, however, that Congress may abrogate the States' Eleventh Amendment immunity when it both unequivocally intends to do so and "act[s] pursuant to a valid grant of constitutional authority." The first of these requirements is not in dispute here. The question, then, is whether Congress acted within its constitutional authority by subjecting the States to suits in federal court for money damages under the ADA.

Congress may not, of course, base its abrogation of the States' Eleventh Amendment immunity upon the powers enumerated in Article I. In *Fitzpatrick v. Bitzer,* 427 U.S. 445 (1976), however, we held that "the Eleventh Amendment, and the principle of state sovereignty which it embodies, are necessarily limited by the enforcement provisions of § 5 of the Fourteenth Amendment." As a result, we concluded, Congress may subject nonconsenting States to suit in federal court when it does so pursuant to a valid exercise of its § 5 power.... Accordingly, the ADA can apply to the States only to the extent that the statute is appropriate § 5 legislation....

Section 5 of the Fourteenth Amendment grants Congress the power to enforce the substantive guarantees contained in Section 1 of [the Fourteenth Amendment] by enacting "appropriate legislation." *See City of Boerne v. Flores*. Congress is not limited to mere legislative repetition of this Court's constitutional jurisprudence. "Rather, Congress' power 'to enforce' the Amendment includes the authority both to remedy and to deter violation of rights guaranteed thereunder by prohibiting a somewhat broader swath of conduct, including that which is not itself forbidden by the Amendment's text."

City of Boerne also confirmed, however, the long-settled principle that it is the responsibility of this Court, not Congress, to define the substance of constitutional guarantees. Accordingly, § 5 legislation reaching beyond the scope of § 1's actual guarantees must exhibit "congruence and proportionality between the injury to be prevented or remedied and the means adopted to that end."

The first step in applying these now familiar principles is to identify with some precision the scope of the constitutional right at issue. Here, that inquiry requires us to examine the limitations § 1 of the Fourteenth Amendment places upon States' treatment of the disabled....

[The Court assessed how it had in the past analyzed Equal Protection claims regarding the disabled and concluded that it only required a "rational-basis review." This contrasts with "strict scrutiny" applicable to racial discrimination and "quasi-suspect scrutiny" applicable to sex discrimination.]

Under rational-basis review, where a group possesses "distinguishing characteristics relevant to interests the State has the authority to implement," a State's decision to act on the basis of those differences does not give rise to a constitutional violation. "Such a classification cannot run afoul of the Equal Protection Clause if there is a rational relationship between the disparity of treatment and some legitimate governmental purpose." Moreover, the State need not articulate its reasoning at the moment a particular decision is made. Rather, the burden is upon the challenging party to negative " 'any reasonably conceivable state of facts that could provide a rational basis for the classification.' " ...

Thus, the result of [our past cases] is that States are not required by the Fourteenth Amendment to make special accommodations for the disabled, so long as their actions toward such individuals are rational. They could quite hardheadedly—and perhaps hardheartedly—hold to job-qualification requirements which do not make allowance for the disabled. If special accommodations for the disabled are to be required, they have to come from positive law and not through the Equal Protection Clause.

Once we have determined the metes and bounds of the constitutional right in question, we examine whether Congress identified a history and pattern of unconstitutional employment discrimination by the States against the disabled. Just as § 1 of the Fourteenth Amendment applies only to actions committed "under color of state law," Congress' § 5 authority is appropriately exercised only in response to state transgressions. The legislative record of the ADA, however, simply fails to show that Congress did in fact identify a pattern of irrational state discrimination in employment against the disabled.

Respondents contend that the inquiry as to unconstitutional discrimination should extend not only to States themselves, but to units of local governments, such as cities and counties. All of these, they say, are "state actors" for purposes of the Fourteenth Amendment. This is quite true, but the Eleventh Amendment does not extend its immunity to units of local government. These entities are subject to private claims for damages under the ADA without Congress' ever having to rely on § 5 of the Fourteenth Amendment to render them so. It would make no sense to consider constitutional violations on their part, as well as by the States themselves, when only the States are the beneficiaries of the Eleventh Amendment....

Respondents in their brief cite half a dozen examples from the record that did involve States.... Several of these incidents undoubtedly evidence an unwillingness on the part of state officials to make the sort of accommodations for the disabled required by the ADA. Whether they were irrational under our decision[s] is more debatable, particularly when the incident is described out of context. But even if it were to be determined that each incident upon fuller examination showed unconstitutional action on the part of the State, these incidents taken together fall far short of even suggesting the pattern of unconstitutional discrimination on which § 5 legislation must be based....

Even were it possible to squeeze out of these examples a pattern of unconstitutional discrimination by the States, the rights and remedies created by the ADA against the States would raise the same sort of concerns as to congruence and proportionality as were found in *City of Boerne.* For example, whereas it would be entirely rational (and therefore constitutional) for a state employer to conserve scarce financial resources by hiring employees who are able to use existing facilities, the ADA requires employers to "mak[e] existing facilities used by employees readily accessible to and usable by individuals with disabilities." The ADA does except employers from the "reasonable accommodatio[n]" requirement where the employer "can demonstrate that the accommodation would impose an undue hardship on the operation of the business of such covered entity." However, even with this exception, the accommodation duty far exceeds what is constitutionally required in that it makes unlawful a range of alternative responses that would be reasonable but would fall short of imposing an "undue burden" upon the employer. The Act also makes it the employer's duty to prove that it would suffer such a burden, instead of requiring (as the Constitution does) that the complaining party negate reasonable bases for the employer's decision....

The ADA's constitutional shortcomings are apparent when the Act is compared to Congress' efforts in the Voting Rights Act of 1965 to respond to a serious pattern of constitutional violations. In *South Carolina v. Katzenbach,* we considered whether the Voting Rights Act was "appropriate" legislation to enforce the Fifteenth Amendment's protection against racial discrimination in voting. Concluding that it was a valid exercise of Congress' enforcement power under § 2 of the Fifteenth Amendment, we noted that "[b]efore enacting the measure, Congress explored with great care the problem of racial discrimination in voting." In that Act, Congress documented a marked pattern of unconstitutional action by the States. State officials, Congress found, routinely applied voting tests in order to exclude African–American citizens from registering to vote. Congress also determined that litigation had proved ineffective and that there persisted an otherwise inexplicable 50–percentage-point gap in the registration of white and African–American voters in some States. Congress' response was to promulgate in the Voting Rights Act a detailed but limited remedial scheme designed to guarantee meaningful enforcement of the Fifteenth Amendment in those areas of the Nation where abundant evidence of States' systematic denial of those rights was identified.

The contrast between this kind of evidence, and the evidence that Congress considered in the present case, is stark. Congressional enactment of the ADA represents its judgment that there should be a "comprehensive national mandate for the elimination of discrimination against individuals with disabilities." Congress is the final authority as to desirable public policy, but in order to authorize private individuals to recover money damages against the States, there must be a pattern of discrimination by the States which violates the Fourteenth Amendment, and the remedy imposed by Congress must be congruent and proportional to the targeted violation. Those requirements are not met here, and to uphold the Act's application to the States would allow Congress to rewrite the Fourteenth Amendment law laid down by this Court.[9] …

Justice KENNEDY, with whom Justice O'CONNOR joins, concurring.

[F]or the reasons explained by the Court, an equal protection violation has not been shown with respect to the several States in this case….

It must be noted, moreover, that what is in question is not whether the Congress, acting pursuant to a power granted to it by the Constitution, can compel the States to act. What is involved is only the question whether the States can be subjected to liability in suits brought not by the Federal Government (to which the States have consented …), but by private persons seeking to collect moneys from the state treasury without the consent of the State. The predicate for money damages against an unconsenting State in suits brought by private persons must be a federal statute enacted upon the documentation of patterns of constitutional violations committed by the State in its official capacity. That predicate, for reasons discussed here and in the decision of the Court, has not been established. With these observations, I join the Court's opinion.

Justice BREYER, with whom Justice STEVENS, Justice SOUTER, and Justice GINSBURG join, dissenting.

Reviewing the congressional record as if it were an administrative agency record, the Court holds the statutory provision before us uncon-

9. Our holding here that Congress did not validly abrogate the States' sovereign immunity from suit by private individuals for money damages under Title I does not mean that persons with disabilities have no federal recourse against discrimination. Title I of the ADA still prescribes standards applicable to the States. Those standards can be enforced by the United States in actions for money damages, as well as by private individuals in actions for injunctive relief under *Ex parte Young*. In addition, state laws protecting the rights of persons with disabilities in employment and other aspects of life provide independent avenues of redress.

stitutional. The Court concludes that Congress assembled insufficient evidence of unconstitutional discrimination, that Congress improperly attempted to "rewrite" the law we established in [our past cases], and that the law is not sufficiently tailored to address unconstitutional discrimination.

Section 5, however, grants Congress the "power to enforce, by appropriate legislation," the Fourteenth Amendment's equal protection guarantee. As the Court recognizes, state discrimination in employment against persons with disabilities might " 'run afoul of the Equal Protection Clause' "where there is no " 'rational relationship between the disparity of treatment and some legitimate governmental purpose.' " In my view, Congress reasonably could have concluded that the remedy before us constitutes an "appropriate" way to enforce this basic equal protection requirement. And that is all the Constitution requires.

Comments and Questions

1. *Garrett* is a more common type of case raising Congress's Section 5 powers than is *Boerne*. That is, in *Garrett*, everyone agrees that Congress can enact the Americans with Disabilities Act (ADA) under its Commerce Clause powers, and that under those powers Congress can bind the states like other employers. Recall *Garcia v. SAMTA*. The problem is the Eleventh Amendment. As we discovered in Chapter 2, the Eleventh Amendment as interpreted by the Supreme Court generally precludes private damage actions against states (including state agencies). The notes at the end of the Eleventh Amendment section listed the exceptions to this general rule. One of those exceptions is when Congress authorizes the suit pursuant to its enforcement powers under the Fourteenth Amendment. In *Garrett*, because the suit is one for damages against a state agency, the Court must determine whether the ADA is authorized by Section 5 of the Fourteenth Amendment.

2. *Garrett* gives us some feel for how to apply the "congruent and proportional" test, especially where Congress is purportedly enforcing the Equal Protection Clause. First, what is the constitutional test for determining whether there has been an Equal Protection Clause violation with respect to this kind of discrimination? While the ins and outs of the Equal Protection Clause are the subject of other Constitutional Law courses and casebooks, it is sufficient to know here that some types of discrimination are subject to stricter judicial scrutiny than other types. As you might imagine, racial discrimination is subject to strict judicial scrutiny, whereas many other forms of discrimination (such as disability, age, obesity, drug addiction, poverty) are subject to a very lax form of scrutiny—rational basis review. These latter forms of discrimination are presumed to be rational and therefore lawful. Second, what is the extent of demonstrated equal protection violations? The greater the extent of the violations, the greater the appropriate remedial or preventative power. Normally, where the judicial scrutiny is stricter, there will be a greater extent of violations, and where the judicial scrutiny is lax,

there are unlikely to be many violations.

3. Prior to *Garrett*, the Court decided *Kimel v. Florida Board of Regents*, 528 U.S. 62 (2000), involving a private damages action by employees of Florida State University under the Age Discrimination in Employment Act (ADEA), which prohibits employers from discriminating against employees because of age. There too the Court by a 5–4 vote held that the law was not authorized under Section 5 of the Fourteenth Amendment and therefore could not provide a basis for a private damages action. The Court noted that its past cases had upheld discrimination based upon age in cases alleging a violation of the Equal Protection Clause, so a broad prohibition against such discrimination was not congruent or proportional to any unconstitutional conduct shown to exist.

NEVADA DEPARTMENT OF HUMAN RESOURCES v. HIBBS

United States Supreme Court, 2003.
538 U.S. 721, 123 S.Ct. 1972, 155 L.Ed.2d 953.

Chief Justice REHNQUIST delivered the opinion of the Court.

The Family and Medical Leave Act of 1993 (FMLA or Act) entitles eligible employees to take up to 12 work weeks of unpaid leave annually for any of several reasons, including the onset of a "serious health condition" in an employee's spouse, child, or parent. The Act creates a private right of action to seek both equitable relief and money damages "against any employer (including a public agency) in any Federal or State court of competent jurisdiction," should that employer "interfere with, restrain, or deny the exercise of" FMLA rights. We hold that employees of the State of Nevada may recover money damages in the event of the State's failure to comply with the family-care provision of the Act.

Petitioners include the Nevada Department of Human Resources (Department).... Respondent William Hibbs (hereinafter respondent) worked for the Department's Welfare Division. In April and May 1997, he sought leave under the FMLA to care for his ailing wife, who was recovering from a car accident and neck surgery....

Respondent sued petitioners in the United States District Court seeking damages and injunctive and declaratory relief for violations of [FMLA]. The District Court awarded petitioners summary judgment on the grounds that the FMLA claim was barred by the Eleventh Amendment and that respondent's Fourteenth Amendment rights had not been violated. Respondent appealed, and the United States intervened ... to defend the validity of the FMLA's application to the States. The Ninth Circuit reversed.

We granted certiorari to resolve a split among the Courts of Appeals on the question whether an individual may sue a State for money damages in federal court for violation of [FMLA].

For over a century now, we have made clear that the Constitution does not provide for federal jurisdiction over suits against nonconsenting States. Congress may, however, abrogate such immunity in federal court if it makes its intention to abrogate unmistakably clear in the language of the statute and acts pursuant to a valid exercise of its power under § 5 of the Fourteenth Amendment. The clarity of Congress' intent here is not fairly debatable.... This case turns, then, on whether Congress acted within its constitutional authority when it sought to abrogate the States' immunity for purposes of the FMLA's family-leave provision.

In enacting the FMLA, Congress relied on two of the powers vested in it by the Constitution: its Article I commerce power and its power under § 5 of the Fourteenth Amendment to enforce that Amendment's guarantees. Congress may not abrogate the States' sovereign immunity pursuant to its Article I power over commerce. Congress may, however, abrogate States' sovereign immunity through a valid exercise of its § 5 power, for "the Eleventh Amendment, and the principle of state sovereignty which it embodies, are necessarily limited by the enforcement provisions of § 5 of the Fourteenth Amendment."

Two provisions of the Fourteenth Amendment are relevant here: Section 5 grants Congress the power "to enforce" the substantive guarantees of § 1—among them, equal protection of the laws—by enacting "appropriate legislation." Congress may, in the exercise of its § 5 power, do more than simply proscribe conduct that we have held unconstitutional. " 'Congress' power "to enforce" the Amendment includes the authority both to remedy and to deter violation of rights guaranteed thereunder by prohibiting a somewhat broader swath of conduct, including that which is not itself forbidden by the Amendment's text." In other words, Congress may enact so-called prophylactic legislation that proscribes facially constitutional conduct, in order to prevent and deter unconstitutional conduct.

City of Boerne also confirmed, however, that it falls to this Court, not Congress, to define the substance of constitutional guarantees.... Section 5 legislation reaching beyond the scope of § 1's actual guarantees must be an appropriate remedy for identified constitutional violations, not "an attempt to substantively redefine the States' legal obligations." We distinguish appropriate prophylactic legislation from "substantive redefinition of the Fourteenth Amendment right at issue," by applying the test set forth in *City of Boerne:* Valid § 5 legislation must exhibit "congruence and proportionality between the injury to be prevented or remedied and the means adopted to that end."

The FMLA aims to protect the right to be free from gender-based discrimination in the workplace. We have held that statutory classifications that distinguish between males and females are subject to heightened scrutiny. For a gender-based classification to withstand such scrutiny, it must "serv[e] important governmental objectives," and "the discriminatory means employed [must be] substantially related to the achievement of those objectives." ... We now inquire whether Congress had evidence of a pattern of constitutional violations on the part of the States in this area.

The history of the many state laws limiting women's employment opportunities is chronicled in—and, until relatively recently, was sanctioned by—this Court's own opinions. For example, ... the Court upheld state laws prohibiting women from practicing law and tending bar, respectively. State laws frequently subjected women to distinctive restrictions, terms, conditions, and benefits for those jobs they could take. [F]or example, this Court approved a state law limiting the hours that women could work for wages, and observed that 19 States had such laws at the time. Such laws were based on the related beliefs that (1) a woman is, and should remain, "the center of home and family life," and (2) "a proper discharge of [a woman's] maternal functions—having in view not merely her own health, but the well-being of the race—justif[ies] legislation to protect her from the greed as well as the passion of man." Until our decision in *Reed v. Reed,* 404 U.S. 71 (1971), "it remained the prevailing doctrine that government, both federal and state, could withhold from women opportunities accorded men so long as any 'basis in reason' "—such as the above beliefs—"could be conceived for the discrimination."

Congress responded to this history of discrimination by abrogating States' sovereign immunity in Title VII of the Civil Rights Act of 1964 and we sustained this abrogation in *Fitzpatrick.* But state gender discrimination did not cease.... According to evidence that was before Congress when it enacted the FMLA, States continue to rely on invalid gender stereotypes in the employment context, specifically in the administration of leave benefits. Reliance on such stereotypes cannot justify the States' gender discrimination in this area. The long and extensive history of sex discrimination prompted us to hold that measures that differentiate on the basis of gender warrant heightened scrutiny; here, as in *Fitzpatrick,* the persistence of such unconstitutional discrimination by the States justifies Congress' passage of prophylactic § 5 legislation.

As the FMLA's legislative record reflects, a 1990 Bureau of Labor Statistics (BLS) survey stated that 37 percent of surveyed private-sector employees were covered by maternity leave policies, while only 18 percent were covered by paternity leave policies.... Thus, stereotype-based beliefs about the allocation of family duties remained firmly rooted, and employers' reliance on them in establishing discriminatory leave policies remained widespread.[3]

Congress also heard testimony that "[p]arental leave for fathers ... is rare. Even ... [w]here child-care leave policies do exist, men, *both in the public and private sectors,* receive notoriously discriminatory treat-

3. While this and other material described leave policies in the private sector, a 50-state survey also before Congress demonstrated that "[t]he proportion and construction of leave policies available to public sector employees differs little from those offered private sector employees." ...

ment in their requests for such leave." ... This and other differential leave policies were not attributable to any differential physical needs of men and women, but rather to the pervasive sex-role stereotype that caring for family members is women's work....

In sum, the States' record of unconstitutional participation in, and fostering of, gender-based discrimination in the administration of leave benefits is weighty enough to justify the enactment of prophylactic § 5 legislation.

We reached the opposite conclusion in *Garrett* and *Kimel*. In those cases, the § 5 legislation under review responded to a purported tendency of state officials to make age- or disability-based distinctions. Under our equal protection case law, discrimination on the basis of such characteristics is not judged under a heightened review standard, and passes muster if there is "a rational basis for doing so at a class-based level, even if it 'is probably not true' that those reasons are valid in the majority of cases." Thus, in order to impugn the constitutionality of state discrimination against the disabled or the elderly, Congress must identify, not just the existence of age- or disability-based state decisions, but a "widespread pattern" of irrational reliance on such criteria. We found no such showing with respect to the ADEA and Title I of the Americans with Disabilities Act of 1990(ADA).

Here, however, Congress directed its attention to state gender discrimination, which triggers a heightened level of scrutiny. Because the standard for demonstrating the constitutionality of a gender-based classification is more difficult to meet than our rational-basis test—it must "serv[e] important governmental objectives" and be "substantially related to the achievement of those objectives,"—it was easier for Congress to show a pattern of state constitutional violations. Congress was similarly successful in *South Carolina v. Katzenbach*, where we upheld the Voting Rights Act of 1965: Because racial classifications are presumptively invalid, most of the States' acts of race discrimination violated the Fourteenth Amendment.

The impact of the discrimination targeted by the FMLA is significant. Congress determined:

> "Historically, denial or curtailment of women's employment opportunities has been traceable directly to the pervasive presumption that women are mothers first, and workers second. This prevailing ideology about women's roles has in turn justified discrimination against women when they are mothers or mothers-to-be."

Stereotypes about women's domestic roles are reinforced by parallel stereotypes presuming a lack of domestic responsibilities for men. Because employers continued to regard the family as the woman's domain, they often denied men similar accommodations or discouraged them from taking leave. These mutually reinforcing stereotypes created a self-fulfilling cycle of discrimination that forced women to continue to assume the role of primary family caregiver, and fostered employers' stereotypical views about women's commitment to work and their value as employees. Those perceptions, in turn, Congress reasoned, lead to subtle discrimination that may be difficult to detect on a case-by-case basis.

We believe that Congress' chosen remedy, the family-care leave provision of the FMLA, is "congruent and proportional to the targeted violation." Congress had already tried unsuccessfully to address this problem through Title VII and the amendment of Title VII by the Pregnancy Discrimination Act. Here, as in *Katzenbach*, Congress again confronted a "difficult and intractable proble[m], where previous legislative attempts had failed. Such problems may justify added prophylactic measures in response.

By creating an across-the-board, routine employment benefit for all eligible employees, Congress sought to ensure that family-care leave would no longer be stigmatized as an inordinate drain on the workplace caused by female employees, and that employers could not evade leave obligations simply by hiring men. By setting a minimum standard of family leave for *all* eligible employees, irrespective of gender, the FMLA attacks the formerly state-sanctioned stereotype that only women are responsible for family caregiving, thereby reducing employers' incentives to engage in discrimination by basing hiring and promotion decisions on stereotypes....

Unlike the statutes at issue in *City of Boerne, Kimel*, and *Garrett,* which applied broadly to every aspect of state employers' operations, the FMLA is narrowly targeted at the faultline between work and family—precisely where sex-based overgeneralization has been and remains strongest—and affects only one aspect of the employment relationship.

We also find significant the many other limitations that Congress placed on the scope of this measure. The FMLA requires only unpaid leave and applies only to employees who have worked for the employer for at least one year and provided 1,250 hours of service within the last 12 months Employees in high-ranking or sensitive positions are simply ineligible for FMLA leave; of particular importance to the States, the FMLA expressly excludes from coverage state elected officials, their staffs, and appointed policymakers. Employees must give advance notice of foreseeable leave, and employers may require certification by a health care provider of the need for leave. In choosing 12 weeks as the appropriate leave floor, Congress chose "a middle ground, a period long enough to serve 'the needs of families' but not so long that it would upset 'the legitimate interests of employers.' " Moreover, the cause of action under the FMLA is a restricted one: The damages recoverable are strictly defined and measured by actual monetary losses, and the accrual period for backpay is limited by the Act's 2–year statute of limitations (extended to three years only for willful violations).

For the above reasons, we conclude that § 2612(a)(1)(C) is congruent and proportional to its remedial object, and can "be understood as responsive to, or designed to prevent, unconstitutional behavior."

Justice SOUTER, with whom Justice GINSBURG and Justice BREYER join, concurring.

Even on this Court's view of the scope of congressional power under § 5 of the Fourteenth Amendment, the Family and Medical Leave Act of 1993 is undoubtedly valid legislation, and application of the Act to the States is constitutional; the same conclusions follow *a fortiori* from my own understanding of § 5. I join the Court's opinion here without conceding [my former] dissenting positions....

Justice STEVENS, concurring in the judgment.

Because I have never been convinced that an Act of Congress can amend the Constitution and because I am uncertain whether the congressional enactment before us was truly " 'needed to secure the guarantees of the Fourteenth Amendment,' " I write separately to explain why I join the Court's judgment. [Justice Stevens goes on to explain why he believes Congress under the Commerce Clause can override states' Eleventh Amendment sovereign immunity in a case brought by a citizen of the state.]

Justice SCALIA, dissenting.

I join Justice KENNEDY's dissent, and add one further observation: The constitutional violation that is a prerequisite to "prophylactic" congressional action to "enforce" the Fourteenth Amendment is a violation *by the State against which the enforcement action is taken.* There is no guilt by association, enabling the sovereignty of one State to be abridged under § 5 of the Fourteenth Amendment because of violations by another State, or by most other States, or even by 49 other States....

Justice KENNEDY, with whom Justice SCALIA and Justice THOMAS join, dissenting.

[T]he Court is unable to show that States have engaged in a pattern of unlawful conduct which warrants the remedy of opening state treasuries to private suits. The inability to adduce evidence of alleged discrimination, coupled with the inescapable fact that the federal scheme is not a remedy but a benefit program, demonstrates the lack of the requisite link between any problem Congress has identified and the program it mandated.

In examining whether Congress was addressing a demonstrated "pattern of unconstitutional employment discrimination by the States," the Court gives superficial treatment to the requirement that we "identify with some precision the scope of the constitutional right at issue." The Court suggests the issue is "the right to be free from gender-based discrimination in the workplace," and then it embarks on a survey of our precedents speaking to "[t]he history of the many state laws limiting women's employment opportunities." All would agree that women historically have been subjected to conditions in which their employment opportunities are more limited than those available to men. As the Court acknowledges, however, Congress responded to this problem by abrogating States' sovereign immunity in Title VII of the Civil Rights Act of 1964 The provision now before us has a different aim than Title VII. It seeks to ensure that eligible employees, irrespective of gender, can take a minimum amount of leave time to care for an ill relative.

The relevant question, as the Court seems to acknowledge, is whether, notwithstanding the passage of Title VII and similar state legislation, the States continued to engage in widespread discrimination on the basis of gender in the provision of family leave benefits. If such a pattern were shown, the Eleventh Amendment would not bar Congress from devising a congruent and proportional remedy. The evidence to substantiate this charge must be far more specific, however, than a simple recitation of a general history of employment discrimination against women. When the federal statute seeks to abrogate state sovereign immunity, the Court should be more careful to insist on adherence to the analytic requirements set forth in its own precedents. Persisting overall effects of gender-based discrimination at the workplace must not be ignored; but simply noting the problem is not a substitute for evidence which identifies some real discrimination the family leave rules are designed to prevent....

Respondents fail to make the requisite showing.

As the Court seems to recognize, the evidence considered by Congress concerned discriminatory practices of the private sector, not those of state employers.... The Court seeks to connect the evidence of private discrimination to an alleged pattern of unconstitutional behavior by States through inferences drawn from two sources [both of which related to parenting leave, not family medical leave, in 1986....]

Even if this isolated testimony could support an inference that private sector's gender-based discrimination in the provision of parenting leave was parallel to the behavior by state actors in 1986, the evidence would not be probative of the States' conduct some seven years later with respect to a statutory provision conferring a different benefit....

The Court's reliance on evidence suggesting States provided men and women with the parenting leave of different length suffers from the same flaw. This evidence concerns the Act's grant of parenting leave and is too attenuated to justify the family leave provision.... The charge that a State has engaged in a pattern of unconstitutional discrimination against its citizens is a most serious one. It must be supported by more than conjecture.

The Court maintains the evidence pertaining to the parenting leave is relevant because both parenting and family leave provisions respond to "the same gender stereotype: that women's family duties trump those of the workplace." This sets the contours of the inquiry at too high a level of abstraction. The question is not whether the family leave provision is a congruent and proportional response to general gender-based stereotypes in employment which "ha[ve] historically produced discrimination in the hiring and promotion of women," the question is whether it is a proper remedy to an alleged pattern of unconstitutional discrimination by States in the grant of family leave. The evidence of gender-based stereotypes is too remote to support the required showing....

Considered in its entirety, the evidence fails to document a pattern of unconstitutional conduct sufficient to justify the abrogation of States' sovereign immunity. The few incidents identified by the Court "fall far short of even suggesting the pattern of unconstitutional discrimination on which § 5 legislation must be based." ...

Our concern with gender discrimination, which is subjected to heightened scrutiny, as opposed to age- or disability-based distinctions, which are reviewed under rational standard does not alter this conclusion. The application of heightened scrutiny is designed to ensure gender-based classifications are not based on the entrenched and pervasive stereotypes which inhibit women's progress in the workplace. This consideration does not divest respondents of their burden to show that "Congress identified a history and pattern of unconstitutional employment discrimination by the States." The Court seems to reaffirm this requirement. In my submission, however, the Court does not follow it. Given the insufficiency of the evidence that States discriminated in the provision of family leave, the unfortunate fact that stereotypes about women continue to be a serious and pervasive social problem would not alone support the charge that a State has engaged in a practice designed to deny its citizens the equal protection of the laws.

The paucity of evidence to support the case the Court tries to make demonstrates that Congress was not responding with a congruent and proportional remedy to a perceived course of unconstitutional conduct. Instead, it enacted a substantive entitlement program of its own. If Congress had been concerned about different treatment of men and women with respect to family leave, a congruent remedy would have sought to ensure the benefits of any leave program enacted by a State are available to men and women on an equal basis. Instead, the Act imposes, across the board, a requirement that States grant a minimum of 12 weeks of leave per year....

It bears emphasis that, even were the Court to bar unconsented federal suits by private individuals for money damages from a State, individuals whose rights under the Act were violated would not be without recourse. The Act is likely a valid exercise of Congress' power under the Commerce Clause, and so the standards it prescribes will be binding upon the States. The United States may enforce these standards in actions for money damages; and private individuals may bring actions against state officials for injunctive relief under *Ex parte Young*. What is at issue is only whether the States can be subjected, without consent, to suits brought by private persons seeking to collect moneys from the state treasury. Their immunity cannot be abrogated without documentation of a pattern of unconstitutional acts by the States, and only then by a congruent and proportional remedy. There has been a complete failure by respondents to carry their burden to establish each of these necessary propositions. I would hold that the Act is not a valid abrogation of state sovereign immunity and dissent with respect from the Court's conclusion to the contrary.

Comments and Questions

1. *Hibbs* is another case involving a private damages suit against a state agency, and again the issue is whether the federal statute authorizing the suit can be an exercise of Congress's Section 5 enforcement authority under the Fourteenth Amendment, which would override the state's Eleventh Amendment sovereign immunity. *Hibbs*, however, comes out differently from *Garrett*. Chief Justice Rehnquist and Justice O'Connor have switched sides. What are the factors that lead them (and the other four justices who would have found the ADA within Congress's Section 5 powers) to find that the FMLA is within Congress's Section 5 powers? Does the dissent disagree on the test to be applied?

2. What are the equal protection violations the majority says states have engaged in, justifying the FMLA's preventative and remedial measures? And, then, why are FMLA's preventative and remedial measures "congruent and proportional" to those violations?

3. What is the relevance of the fact that discrimination based on sex is subject to a higher level of scrutiny than age and disability?

4. Subsequent to *Hibbs*, the Court decided *Tennessee v. Lane*, 541 U.S. 509 (2004), still another private damages suit against a state, this time under Title II of the ADA. Title II of the ADA, unlike the employment portion—Title I—involved in *Garrett*, provides that: "no qualified individual with a disability shall, by reason of such disability, be excluded from participation or denied the benefits of the services, programs or activities of a public entity." Lane was a paraplegic who was a defendant in a state criminal case, whose case was to be heard on the second floor of a courthouse that had no elevator. At his first appearance, Lane crawled up two flights of stairs in order to reach his courtroom. At his second appearance, he refused to crawl or be carried by officers and was arrested for failing to appear. He sued for damages under Title II of the ADA. The Court in a 5–4 vote held that Congress could enact Title II of the ADA under the authority of Section 5 of the Fourteenth Amendment to the extent that it prohibited discrimination against disabled persons in access to essential government functions, such as access to the courts. The Court did not rely on evidence of equal protection violations, but rather looked to evidence of state violations of due process, which of course are also prohibited by the Fourteenth Amendment. The Court noted its past cases finding a due process right of access to courts and the fact that state laws that limited access to courts were subject to heightened judicial scrutiny. This made *Lane* like *Hibbs* in that Congress was acting in an area that the Court had found laws presumptively unconstitutional, rather than presumptively constitutional. The dissent argued that the evidence of state constitutional violations was inad-

equate to justify this wide-ranging remedy, and in particular that the wide ranging prohibition in Title II involved many situations other than courthouses and other state functions to which persons have a due process right of access. For example, Title II would apply to state-owned theaters and hockey stadiums, to which there is no due process right of access. The Court, however, said that the fact that there might be instances under which Title II's prohibitions might not be authorized under Section 5 did not mean that there could not be other instances in which it would be so authorized—such as the instance in *Lane*.

5. The majority in *Lane* was made up of the four dissenting justices in *Garrett*, who would have found Title I of the ADA authorized by Section 5 of the Fourteenth Amendment, and Justice O'Connor. Justice O'Connor, of course, has been replaced on the Court by Justice Alito. When a judge on the Court of Appeals for the Third Circuit, Judge Alito wrote an opinion for that court holding that a provision of the FMLA was not authorized by Congress's powers under Section 5 of the Fourteenth Amendment. Although that case did not go to the Supreme Court, in *Hibbs* the Supreme Court held that a parallel provision in the FMLA was a valid exercise of Congress's powers under Section 5. Does this suggest how Justice Alito might rule on the next Section 5 case?

G. PREEMPTION

The term "preemption" refers to the effect on a state or local law that under the Supremacy Clause, Article VI, Clause 2, is rendered invalid because it conflicts with a federal law. We say that the federal law preempts the state law, or that the state law is preempted. We have run into preemption before. In *Gibbons v. Ogden*, for example, the New York law granting the monopoly to Ogden conflicted with the federal law granting Gibbons a license to engage in the coastal trade, and as a result the New York law was rendered invalid, and Gibbons could carry passengers between New Jersey and New York.

Whether state law is preempted by federal law depends on the particulars of the federal law. The federal law may explicitly preempt state law. This is called express preemption. For example, imagine that Congress passes a law under its Commerce Clause powers stating that no person may practice law in the United States unless they have graduated from an American Bar Association accredited law school. The law further provides that no state may impose any other requirement on the ability to practice law in the state. This federal law expressly preempts any state law providing different or additional requirements, so that existing state requirements that a person must, in addition to graduating from an ABA accredited law school, pass the state bar exam in order to practice law in the state would be preempted by the federal law.

Often, however, the language of the federal statute may not be entirely clear, so there may be a question to what extent it preempts state law. For example, a recurring issue today is whether a federal statute expressly preempting any state "requirement or prohibition" preempts state common law tort law or only preempts state statutory or regulatory requirements or prohibitions. *See Cipollone v. Liggett Group, Inc.*, 505 U.S. 504 (1992) (federal prohibition of other state requirements held to include state tort law). Thus, often a court must interpret an unclear federal statutory preemption provision to determine what Congress intended.

Frequently, if not usually, there is no express preemption language, and a court must interpret the federal statute to determine whether Congress intended to preempt state law. This is called "implied preemption." For example, imagine that Congress had passed the same law establishing graduation from an ABA-accredited law school as the federal requirement for the practice of law in the United States, but that it left off the provision that no state could impose any other requirement on the ability to practice law in the state. The question then might arise whether there was a conflict between the federal law and existing state laws. Congress might have intended the federal requirement to be a floor, not a ceiling, on the requirements to practice law, so that an additional state requirement that a person must also pass a state bar exam would not conflict with the federal law. On the other hand, Congress might have intended that the federal requirement be the only requirement for a person to practice law in the United States, in which case any additional requirement imposed by a state, such as a requirement to pass a state bar exam, would conflict with the intent of the federal law. In this case, the additional state requirement would be preempted by the federal law.

There are actually three forms of implied preemption: field preemption, direct conflict preemption, and obstacle preemption. Field preemption refers to the situation where the federal government so fully regulates the field that any state regulation, whether or not it actually conflicts with the federal regulation, is seen as incompatible with exclusive federal regulation. For example, in *United States v. Locke*, 529 U.S. 89 (2000), the Court found that the federal Ports and Waterways Safety Act, governing the design, construction, alteration, repair, maintenance, operation, equipping, personnel qualification, and manning of oil tankers occupied the entire field, so that Congress left no room for state regulation of these matters. Direct conflict preemption occurs when a person cannot comply with both the state and the federal laws at the same time, such as in *Gibbons v. Ogden*. Obstacle preemption is when the state law does not actually conflict with a federal law, but it "stands as an obstacle to the accomplishment and execution of the full purposes and objectives of Congress." This is perhaps the hardest of the preemption categories to apply.

GEIER v. AMERICAN HONDA MOTOR CO.

United States Supreme Court, 2000.
529 U.S. 861, 120 S.Ct. 1913, 146 L.Ed.2d 914.

Stephen Breyer
President Bill Clinton appointed Breyer to the Supreme Court in 1994, after he had served for fourteen years on the United States Court of Appeals for the First Circuit. Prior to that Breyer had been a professor at Harvard Law School since 1967, although he took time off to serve as special counsel and then as chief counsel to the Senate Committee on the Judiciary. Breyer is generally considered to be part of the liberal wing of the current Court, but his background in administrative law has led him to place a high value on the views and actions of government agencies, often deferring to them because of their perceived expertise.

Justice BREYER delivered the opinion of the Court.

This case focuses on the 1984 version of a Federal Motor Vehicle Safety Standard promulgated by the Department of Transportation under the authority of the National Traffic and Motor Vehicle Safety Act of 1966. The standard, FMVSS 208, required auto manufacturers to equip some but not all of their 1987 vehicles with passive restraints. We ask whether the Act pre-empts a state common-law tort action in which the plaintiff claims that the defendant auto manufacturer, who was in compliance with the standard, should nonetheless have equipped a 1987 automobile with airbags. We conclude that the Act, taken together with FMVSS 208, pre-empts the lawsuit.

In 1992, petitioner Alexis Geier, driving a 1987 Honda Accord, collided with a tree and was seriously injured. The car was equipped with manual shoulder and lap belts which Geier had buckled up at the time. The car was not equipped with airbags or other passive restraint devices.

Geier and her parents, also petitioners, sued the car's manufacturer, American Honda Motor Company, Inc., and its affiliates (hereinafter American Honda), under District of Columbia tort law. They claimed, among other things, that American Honda had designed its car negligently and defectively because it lacked a driver's side airbag. The District Court dismissed the lawsuit....

The Court of Appeals [affirmed].... We granted certiorari.... We now hold that this kind of "no airbag" lawsuit conflicts with the objectives of FMVSS 208, a standard authorized by the Act, and is therefore pre-empted by the Act....

In petitioners' and the dissent's view, FMVSS 208 sets a minimum airbag standard. As far as FMVSS 208 is concerned, the more airbags, and the sooner, the better. But that was not the Secretary's view. The Department of Transportation's (DOT's) comments, which accompanied the promulgation of FMVSS 208, make clear that the standard deliberately provided the manufacturer with a range of choices among different passive restraint devices. Those choices would bring about a mix of different devices introduced gradually over time; and FMVSS 208 would thereby lower costs, overcome technical safety problems, encourage technological development, and win widespread consumer acceptance—all of which would promote FMVSS 208's safety objectives.

The history of FMVSS 208 helps explain why and how DOT sought these objectives. [The Court then describes the tortured history of federal attempts to regulate the use of manual seat belts, passive restraints such as automatic seat belts, interlock systems, continuous warning signals, and air bags, with changes resulting from new administrations with different attitudes toward government regulation, from congressional overrides of federal regulations because of popular objection, and from industry objections.]

Read in light of this history, DOT's own contemporaneous explanation of FMVSS 208 makes clear that the 1984 version of FMVSS 208 reflected the following significant considerations. First, buckled up seatbelts are a vital ingredient of automobile safety. Second, despite the enormous and unnecessary risks that a passenger runs by not buckling up manual lap and shoulder belts, more than 80% of front seat passengers would leave their manual seatbelts unbuckled. Third, airbags could make up for the dangers caused by unbuckled manual belts, but they could not make up for them entirely. Fourth, passive restraint systems had their own disadvantages, for example, the dangers associated with, intrusiveness of, and corresponding public dislike for, nondetachable automatic belts. Fifth, airbags brought with them their own special risks to safety, such as the risk of danger to out-of-position occupants (usually children) in small cars. Sixth, airbags were expected to be significantly more expensive than other passive restraint devices, raising the average cost of a vehicle price $320 for full frontal airbags over the cost of a car with manual lap and shoulder seatbelts (and potentially much more if production volumes were low). And the agency worried that the high replacement cost—estimated to be $800—could lead car owners to refuse to replace them after deployment. Seventh, the public, for reasons of cost, fear, or physical intrusiveness, might resist installation or use of any of the then-available passive restraint devices—a particular concern with respect to airbags.

FMVSS 208 reflected these considerations in several ways. Most importantly, that standard deliberately sought variety—a mix of several different passive restraint systems. It did so by setting a performance requirement for passive restraint devices and allowing manufacturers to choose among different passive restraint mechanisms, such as airbags, automatic belts, or other passive restraint technologies to satisfy that requirement. And DOT explained why FMVSS 208 sought the mix of devices that it expected its performance standard to produce. DOT wrote that it had *rejected* a proposed FMVSS 208 "all airbag" standard because of safety concerns (perceived or real) associated with airbags, which concerns threatened a "backlash" more easily overcome "if airbags" were "not the only way of complying." It added that a mix of devices would help develop data on comparative effectiveness, would allow the industry time to overcome the safety problems and the high production costs associated with airbags, and would facilitate the development of alternative, cheaper, and safer passive restraint systems. And it would thereby build public confidence....

The 1984 FMVSS 208 standard also deliberately sought a *gradual* phase-in of passive restraints. It required the manufacturers to equip only 10% of their car fleet manufactured after September 1, 1986, with passive restraints. It then increased the percentage in three annual stages, up to 100% of the new car fleet for cars manufactured after September 1, 1989. And it explained that the phased-in requirement would allow more time for manufacturers to develop airbags or other, better, safer passive restraint systems. It would help develop information about the comparative effectiveness of different systems, would lead to a mix in which airbags and other nonseatbelt passive restraint systems played a more prominent role than would otherwise result, and would promote public acceptance....

In sum, as DOT now tells us through the Solicitor General, the 1984 version of FMVSS 208 "embodies the Secretary's policy judgment that safety would best be promoted if manufacturers installed *alternative* protection systems in their fleets rather than one particular system in every car." Petitioners' tort suit claims that the manufacturers of the 1987 Honda Accord "had a duty to design, manufacture, distribute and sell a motor vehicle with an effective and safe passive restraint system, including, but not limited to, airbags."

In effect, petitioners' tort action depends upon its claim that manufacturers had a duty to install an airbag when they manufactured the 1987 Honda Accord. Such a state law—*i.e.,* a rule of state tort law imposing such a duty—by its terms would have required manufacturers of all similar cars to install airbags rather than other passive restraint systems, such as automatic belts or passive interiors. It thereby would have presented an obstacle to the variety and mix of devices that the federal regulation sought. It would have required all manufacturers to have installed airbags ..., even though FMVSS 208 at that time required only that 10% of a manufacturer's nationwide fleet be equipped with any passive restraint device at all. It thereby also would have stood as an obstacle to the gradual passive restraint phase-in that the federal regulation deliberately imposed. In addition, it could have made less likely the adoption of a state mandatory buckle-up law. Because the rule of law for which petitioners contend would have stood "as an obstacle to the accomplishment and execution of" the important means-related federal objectives that we have just discussed, it is pre-empted....

Justice STEVENS, with whom Justice SOUTER, Justice THOMAS, and Justice GINSBURG join, dissenting.

Airbag technology has been available to automobile manufacturers for over 30 years. There is now general agreement on the proposition "that, to be safe, a car must have an airbag." Indeed, current federal law imposes that requirement on all automobile manufacturers. The question raised by petitioners' common-law tort action is whether that proposition was sufficiently obvious when Honda's 1987 Accord was manufactured to make the failure to install such a safety feature actionable under theories of negligence or defective design. The Court holds that an interim regulation motivated by the Secretary of Transportation's desire to foster gradual development of a variety of passive restraint devices deprives state courts of jurisdiction to answer that question. I respectfully dissent from that holding, and especially from the Court's unprecedented extension of the doctrine of pre-emption....

"This is a case about federalism," that is, about respect for "the constitutional role of the States as sovereign entities." It raises important questions concerning the way in which the Federal Government may exercise its undoubted power to oust state courts of their traditional jurisdiction over common-law tort actions. The rule the Court enforces today was not enacted by Congress and is not to be found in the text of any Executive Order or regulation. It has a unique origin: It is the product of the Court's interpretation of the final commentary accompanying an interim administrative regulation and the history of airbag regulation generally. Like many other judge-made rules, its contours are not precisely defined....

It is ... clear to me that the objectives that the Secretary intended to achieve through the adoption of Federal Motor Vehicle Safety Standard 208 would not be frustrated one whit by allowing state courts to determine whether in 1987 the lifesaving advantages of airbags had become sufficiently obvious that their omission might constitute a design defect in some new cars....

When a state statute, administrative rule, or common-law cause of action conflicts with a federal statute, it is axiomatic that the state law is without effect. On the other hand, it is equally clear that the Supremacy Clause does not give unelected federal judges *carte blanche* to use federal law as a means of imposing their own ideas of tort reform on the States. Because of the role of States as separate sovereigns in our federal system, we have long presumed that state laws—particularly those, such as the provision of tort remedies to compensate for personal injuries, that are within the scope of the States' historic police powers—are not to be pre-empted by a federal statute unless it is the clear and manifest purpose of Congress to do so....

When a federal statute contains an express pre-emption provision, "the task of statutory construction must in the first instance focus on the plain wording of [that provision], which necessarily contains the best evidence of Congress' pre-emptive intent." ...

Even though the Safety Act does not expressly pre-empt common-law claims, Honda contends that Standard 208—of its own force—implicitly pre-empts the claims in this case.

> We have recognized that a federal statute implicitly overrides state law either when the scope of a statute indicates that Congress intended federal law to occupy a field exclusively, or when state law is in actual conflict with federal law. We have found implied conflict pre-emption where it is "impossible for a private party to comply with both state and federal requirements or where state law 'stands as an obstacle' to the accomplishment and execution of the full purposes and objectives of Congress."

[I]n this case, Honda relies on the last of the implied pre-emption principles ..., arguing that the imposition of common-law liability for failure to install an airbag would frustrate the purposes and objectives of Standard 208.

Both the text of the statute and the text of the standard provide persuasive reasons for rejecting this argument....

Honda argues, and the Court now agrees, that the risk of liability presented by common-law claims that vehicles without airbags are negligently and defectively designed would frustrate the policy decision that the Secretary made in promulgating Standard 208. This decision, in their view, was that safety—including a desire to encourage "public acceptance of the airbag technology and experimentation with better passive restraint systems"—would best be promoted through gradual implementation of a passive restraint requirement making airbags only one of a variety of systems that a manufacturer could install in order to comply, rather than through a requirement mandating the use of one particular system in every vehicle. In its brief supporting Honda, the United States agreed with this submission. It argued that if the manufacturers had known in 1984 that they might later be held liable for failure to install airbags, that risk "would likely have led them to install airbags in all cars," thereby frustrating the Secretary's safety goals and interfering with the methods designed to achieve them.

There are at least three flaws in this argument that provide sufficient grounds for rejecting it. First, the entire argument is based on an unrealistic factual predicate. Whatever the risk of liability on a no-airbag claim may have been prior to the promulgation of the 1984 version of Standard 208, that risk did not lead any manufacturer to install airbags in even a substantial portion of its cars. If there had been a realistic likelihood that the risk of tort liability would have that consequence, there would have been no need for Standard 208....

Second, even if the manufacturers' assessment of their risk of liability ultimately proved to be wrong, the purposes of Standard 208 would not be frustrated. In light of the inevitable time interval between the eventual filing of a tort action alleging that the failure to install an airbag is a design defect and the possible resolution of such a claim against a manufacturer, as well as the additional interval between such a resolution (if any) and manufacturers' "compliance with the state-law duty in question," by modifying their designs to avoid such liability in the future, it is obvious that the phase-in period would have ended long before its purposes could have been frustrated by the specter of tort liability. Thus, even without pre-emption, the public would have been given the time that the Secretary deemed necessary to gradually adjust to the increasing use of airbag technology and allay their unfounded concerns about it....

Third, the Court completely ignores the important fact that by definition all of the standards established under the Safety Act—like the British regulations that governed the number and capacity of lifeboats aboard the Titanic—impose minimum, rather than fixed or maximum, requirements. The phase-in program authorized by Standard 208 thus set minimum percentage requirements for the installation of passive restraints, increasing in annual stages of 10, 25, 40, and 100%. Those requirements were not ceilings, and it is obvious that the Secretary favored a more rapid increase. The possibility that exposure to potential tort liability might accelerate the rate of increase would actually further the only goal explicitly mentioned in the standard itself: reducing the number of deaths and severity of injuries of vehicle occupants. Had gradualism been independently important as a method of achieving the Secretary's safety goals, presumably the Secretary would have put a ceiling as well as a floor on each annual increase in the required percentage of new passive restraint installations....

For these reasons, it is evident that Honda has not crossed the high threshold established by our decisions regarding pre-emption of state laws that allegedly frustrate federal purposes: it has not demonstrated that allowing a common-law no-airbag claim to go forward would impose an obligation on manufacturers that directly and irreconcilably contradicts any primary objective that the Secretary set forth with clarity in Standard 208. Furthermore, it is important to note that the text of Standard 208 (which the Court does not even bother to quote in its opinion), ... does not contain any expression of an intent to displace state law. Given our repeated emphasis on the importance of the presumption against pre-emption, this silence lends additional support to the conclusion that the continuation of whatever common-law liability may exist in a case like this poses no danger of frustrating any of the Secretary's primary purposes in promulgating Standard 208.

The Court apparently views the question of pre-emption in this case as a close one. Under "ordinary experience-proved principles of conflict pre-emption," therefore, the presumption against pre-emption should control. Instead, the Court simply ignores the presumption, preferring instead to put the burden on petitioners to show that their tort claim would not frustrate the Secretary's purposes....

Our presumption against pre-emption is rooted in the concept of federalism. It recognizes that when Congress legislates "in a field which the States have traditionally occupied ... [,] we start with the assumption that the historic police powers of the States were not to be superseded by the Federal Act unless that was the clear and manifest purpose of Congress." The signal virtues of this presumption are its placement of the power of pre-emption squarely in the hands of Congress, which is far more suited than the Judiciary to strike the appropriate state/federal balance (particularly in areas of traditional state regulation), and its requirement that Congress speak clearly when exercising that power. In this way, the structural safeguards inherent in the normal operation of the legislative process operate to defend state interests from undue infringement. *Garcia v. San Antonio Metropolitan Transit Authority*. In addition, the presumption serves as a limiting principle that prevents federal judges from running amok with our potentially boundless (and perhaps inadequately considered) doctrine of implied conflict preemption based on frustration of purposes—*i.e.,* that state law is preempted if it "stands as an obstacle to the accomplishment and execution of the full purposes and objectives of Congress." ...

Comments and Questions

1. The majority and the dissent both focus on how and to what extent a state tort claim for negligent design would frustrate the purposes of the federal regulation phasing in passive restraints and airbags. Obviously, the majority and dissent disagree as to the extent of that frustration. The dissent, however, also discusses concerns of federalism. That is, the dissent notes that the Court has stated that there is a presumption against preemption, at least where the state law relates to health and safety considerations, because historically states have had the primary responsibility for the health and safety of its citizens. Thus, unless Congress by some affirmative sign demonstrates an intent that the federal law preempt the state's health and safety regulation, the presumption should be that the state law would not be preempted. And the dissent is correct that there is significant precedent for this type of analysis. The majority, however, largely ignores this framework for analysis and simply attempts to discern the most likely intent of Congress without any thumb on the scale. And there are cases consistent with this approach as well.

2. In addition, the dissent notes the indeterminancy of the obstacle preemption analysis. At least when not cabined by a presumption against preemption, this indeterminancy, in the eyes of the dissent, provides judges with such flexibility or discretion or judgment that their decisions are likely to be more a product of their personal predilections than the law. This is another reason to give effect to a presumption, the dissent argues.

3. Ultimately, the case is close, decided by a 5–4 margin. But look at the line up. Justice Breyer, writes the Court's opinion, joined by Chief Justice Rehnquist and Justices Scalia, Kennedy, and O'Connor. Rehnquist and O'Connor are generally considered to be solicitous of states interests, but here they come out on the side of federal preemption of state law in a close case. Justice Breyer tends to favor exercises of administrative expertise, so it is perhaps not surprising that he comes down on the side of the position of the Department of Transportation. One of Justice Scalia's pet peeves is rules of law that enable judges to have so much discretion that they can indulge their policy preferences, yet he also comes out on the side of a broad concept of obstacle preemption, which provides judges with wide ranging discretion. However, there is another theme in play here—the use of tort law to affect behavior. Chief Justice Rehnquist in particular reflected in his rulings a deep distrust of tort law, so ruling in favor of preemption here is consistent with that aspect of his jurisprudence. Moreover, to find preemption in this case has the effect of lessening government burdens on private enterprise, a value shared by Chief Justice Rehnquist and Justices Scalia and O'Connor. The dissent is equally schizophrenic. The author of the opinion, Justice Stevens, is not a frequent defender of federalism. Recall his votes in the Commerce Clause cases. On the other hand, as a "liberal" he tends to support laws that regulate business for health and safety reasons. Recall his opinion for the Court in *Massachusetts v. EPA* regarding federal regulation of greenhouse gases. Here by opposing preemption, he is supporting the more aggressive state tort law to promote safer automobiles. Justices Souter and Ginsburg may be said to share the same views. But then there is Justice Thomas, who generally does not like government regulation of business, but who consistently supports federalism and prefers to rely on statutory and constitutional text. Here, the dissent is supporting federalism and decrying the majority's finding of preemption without any textual basis in the statute or regulation, so that is in accord with his views. Earlier, we suggested that the labels of "conservative" and "liberal" were not very helpful. Here too we see that in a given case there may be several different and even contradictory values that a particular decision might further, so that justices with quite different jurisprudential views may find common ground.

Chapter 4

OTHER FEDERALISM LIMITATIONS IN THE CONSTITUTION

In the previous chapter, the recurring issue was one of federalism—the respective roles of the Federal and state governments. The issue was always whether Congress could enact the laws in question (and what the effect of those laws would be) under our constitutional structure. In the face of uncertain constitutional text, the Court attempted to define the appropriate roles of the state and federal governments. This chapter addresses two additional aspects of the Constitution that help define the appropriate roles the federal and state governments.

A. THE DORMANT COMMERCE CLAUSE

1. THE ORIGINS

We return to the Commerce Clause. Previously we considered the extent of Congress's authority to enact legislation under the Commerce Clause. Recall the first Commerce Clause case, *Gibbons v. Ogden*. There the Court concluded that the New York state law granting a monopoly to Ogden conflicted with the federal law granting a license to Gibbons to engage in the coastal trade, and because the federal law was constitutional under the Commerce Clause, the federal law governed. In a portion of the opinion that was edited out of the version we read earlier, Chief Justice Marshall discussed the possibility that even in the absence of the federal law the New York state law might be invalid under the Commerce Clause itself. And Justice Johnson, who concurred in the judgment, wrote an opinion finding New York's law unconstitutional on precisely that ground. The idea that the Commerce Clause by itself, without any action by Congress, can preclude some state action is what is known today as the "Dormant Commerce Clause" or sometimes as the "Negative Commerce Clause."

GIBBONS v. OGDEN

United States Supreme Court, 1824.
9 Wheat. (22 U.S.) 1, 6 L.Ed. 23.

Mr. Chief Justice MARSHALL delivered the opinion of the Court:

[After its analysis, the Court concluded:] The power of Congress, then, comprehends navigation, within the limits of every State in the Union; so far as that navigation may be, in any manner, connected with "commerce with foreign nations, or among the several States, or with the Indian tribes." It may, of consequence, pass the jurisdictional line of New York, and act upon the very waters to which the prohibition now under consideration applies.

But it has been urged with great earnestness, that, although the power of Congress to regulate commerce with foreign nations, and among the several States, be co-extensive with the subject itself, and have no other limits than are prescribed in the constitution, yet the States may severally exercise the same power, within their respective jurisdictions. In support of this argument, it is said, that they possessed it as an inseparable attribute of sovereignty, before the formation of the constitution, and still retain it, except so far as they have surrendered it by that instrument; that this principle results from the nature of the government, and is secured by the tenth amendment; that an affirmative grant of power is not exclusive, unless in its own nature it be such that the continued exercise of it by the former possessor is inconsistent with the grant, and that this is not of that description.

The appellant, conceding these postulates, except the last, contends, that full power to regulate a particular subject, implies the whole power, and leaves no residuum; that a grant of the whole is incompatible with the existence of a right in another to any part of it....

The grant of the power to lay and collect taxes is, like the power to regulate commerce, made in general terms, and has never been understood to interfere with the exercise of the same power by the State; and hence has been drawn an argument which has been applied to the question under consideration. But the two grants are not, it is conceived, similar in their terms or their nature. Although many of the powers formerly exercised by the States, are transferred to the government of the Union, yet the State governments remain, and constitute a most important part of our system. The power of taxation is indispensable to their existence, and is a power which, in its own nature, is capable of residing in, and being exercised by, different authorities at the same time. We are accustomed to see it placed, for different purposes, in different hands. Taxation is the simple operation of taking small portions from a perpetually accumulating mass, susceptible of almost infinite division; and a power in one to take what is necessary for certain purposes, is not, in its nature, incompatible with a power in another to take what is necessary for other purposes. Congress is authorized to lay and collect taxes, &c. to pay the debts, and provide for the common defence and general welfare of the United States. This does not interfere with the power of the States to tax for the support of their own governments; nor is the exercise of that power by the States, an exercise of any portion of the power that is granted to the United States. In imposing taxes for State purposes, they are not doing what Congress is empowered to do. Congress is not empowered to tax for those purposes which are within the exclusive province of the States. When, then, each government exercises the power of taxation, neither is exercising the power of the other. But, when a State proceeds to regulate commerce with foreign nations, or among the several States, it is exercising the very power that is granted to Congress, and is doing the very thing which Congress is authorized to do. There is no analogy, then, between the power of taxation and the power of regulating commerce. ...

It has been contended by the counsel for the appellant, that, as the word "to regulate' " implies in its nature, full power over the thing to be regulated, it excludes, necessarily, the action of all others that would perform the same operation on the same thing. That regulation is designed for the entire result, applying to those parts which remain as they were, as well as to those which are altered. It produces a uniform whole, which is as much disturbed and deranged by changing what the regulating power designs to leave untouched, as that on which it has operated.

There is great force in this argument, and the Court is not satisfied that it has been refuted.

Since, however, in exercising the power of regulating their own purely internal affairs, whether of trading or police, the States may sometimes enact laws, the validity of which depends on their interfering with, and being contrary to, an act of Congress passed in pursuance of the constitution, the Court will enter upon the inquiry, whether the laws of New York, as expounded by the highest tribunal of that State, have, in their application to this case, come into collision with an act of Congress, and deprived a citizen of a right to which that act entitles him. Should this collision exist, it will be immaterial whether those laws were passed in virtue of a concurrent power "to regulate commerce with foreign nations and among the several States," or, in virtue of a power to regulate their domestic trade and police. In one case and the other, the acts of New York must yield to the law of Congress; and the decision sustaining the privilege they confer, against a right given by a law of the Union, must be erroneous. [The Court concluded that here the New York law did conflict with the federal law that authorized Gibbons to engage in the coastal trade.]

Mr. Justice JOHNSON.

The judgment entered by the Court in this cause, has my entire approbation; but having adopted my conclusions on views of the subject materially different from those of my brethren, I feel it incumbent on me to exhibit those views. I have, also, another inducement: in questions of great importance and great delicacy, I feel my duty to the public best discharged, by an effort to maintain my opinions in my own way....

The words of the constitution are, "Congress shall have power to regulate commerce with foreign nations, and among the several States, and with the Indian tribes." ...

The "power to regulate commerce," here meant to be granted, was that power to regulate commerce which previously existed in the States. But what was that power? The States were, unquestionably, supreme; and each possessed that power over commerce, which is acknowledged to reside in every sovereign State.... The power of a sovereign state over commerce ... amounts to nothing more than a power to limit and restrain it at pleasure. And since the power to prescribe the limits to its freedom, necessarily implies the power to determine what shall remain unrestrained, it follows, that the power must be exclusive; it can reside but in one potentate; and hence, the grant of this power carries with it the whole subject, leaving nothing for the State to act upon.

And such has been the practical construction of the act. Were every law on the subject of commerce repealed tomorrow, all commerce would be lawful; and, in practice, merchants never inquire what is permitted, but what is forbidden commerce. Of all the endless variety of branches of foreign commerce, now carried on to every quarter of the world, I know of no one that is permitted by act of Congress, any otherwise than by not being forbidden. No statute of the United States, that I know of, was ever passed to permit a commerce, unless in consequence of its having been prohibited by some previous statute....

The grant to Livingston and Fulton, interferes with the freedom of intercourse and on this principle its constitutionality is contested....

Commerce, in its simplest signification, means an exchange of goods; but in the advancement of society, labour, transportation, intelligence, care, and various mediums of exchange, become commodities, and enter into commerce; the subject, the vehicle, the agent, and their various operations, become the objects of commercial regulation. Ship building, the carrying trade, and propagation of seamen, are such vital agents of commercial prosperity, that the nation which could not legislate over these subjects, would not possess power to regulate commerce....

It is impossible, with the views which I entertain of the principle on which the commercial privileges of the people of the United States, among themselves, rests, to concur in the view which this Court takes of the effect of the coasting license in this cause. I do not regard it as the foundation of the right set up in behalf of the appellant. If there was any one object riding over every other in the adoption of the constitution, it was to keep the commercial intercourse among the States free from all invidious and partial restraints. And I cannot overcome the conviction, that if the licensing act was repealed tomorrow, the rights of the appellant to a reversal of the decision complained of, would be as strong as it is under this license....

Comments and Questions

1. Recall that Chief Justice Marshall instituted the tradition of there being an opinion of the Court, rather than separate opinions by each justice. Justice Johnson's opening paragraph suggests he was not fully supportive of that change.

2. Chief Justice Marshall's discussion and Justice Johnson's opinion would read the positive grant of authority to Congress to regulate commerce among the states as a prohibition on the ability of states to regulate commerce among the states. Unlike the taxing power, which Chief Justice Marshall suggested could be exercised by both sovereigns, he believed that the power of regulation could only be held by one sovereign. If the matter were one subject to federal regulation, it could not be regulated by the states. Clearly, that theory was not the basis for *Gibbons*, which ultimately relied on the fact that Congress had exercised its authority and the federal law conflicted with New York's law. Nevertheless, the notion persisted that, if something was within Congress's power under the Commerce Clause, then it was no longer subject to state power. This perhaps explains some of the reluctance of the Court to extend the federal commerce power at various points in history—not just concern about the federal government having the power, but the implication that perhaps the mere possession of the power would disable the states from regulating in that field *even when the federal government did not exercise its power.*

3. While the original notion suggested by Marshall and Johnson—that federal authority under the Commerce Clause would preempt the entire field—never commanded a Court majority, the Court did overturn some state actions solely on the grounds that it interfered with interstate commerce in a particular way, even in the absence of any federal legislation. For example, in *Pennsylvania v. Wheeling & Belmont Bridge Co.*, 54 U.S. 518 (1851), the state of Virginia authorized the construction of a bridge over the Ohio River at a height that would not allow steamships to go under it. Pennsylvania brought a suit alleging that the bridge obstructed navigation and therefore was a violation of the negative implications of the Commerce Clause. While the Court's decision finding the bridge unlawful is particularly opaque, many have read it to be based upon the Dormant Commerce Clause.

4. Attempts to discern the dividing line between what states could regulate and what was forbidden by the Dormant Commerce Clause were not very successful. Early on there were attempts to distinguish between exercises of the state police power (which would be authorized) and exercises of commercial regulation (which would be precluded), *see, e.g.*, *Mayor of the City of New York v. Miln*, 36 U.S. 102 (1837); between regulation of things local (which would be authorized) and things national (which would be precluded), *see, e.g.*, *Cooley v. Board of Wardens*, 53 U.S. 299 (1851); and between state regulation that only indirectly affected interstate commerce (which would be authorized) and state regulation that directly regulated interstate commerce (which would be precluded), *see, e.g., Di Santo v. Pennsylvania*, 273 U.S. 34 (1927). Some would say that this lack of success in providing a bright line continues today.

2. THE MODERN APPROACH

One could say that modern (since the 1930s) Dormant Commerce

Clause Doctrine comes in two flavors—discriminatory state laws and non-discriminatory state laws. Each has its own particular test for whether the law is unconstitutional under the Dormant Commerce Clause. We begin with the easier of the two strands.

a. Discriminatory State Laws

PHILADELPHIA v. NEW JERSEY

United States Supreme Court, 1978.
437 U.S. 617, 98 S.Ct. 2531, 57 L.Ed.2d 475.

Mr. Justice STEWART delivered the opinion of the Court.

A New Jersey law prohibits the importation of most "solid or liquid waste which originated or was collected outside the territorial limits of the State...." In this case we are required to decide whether this statutory prohibition violates the Commerce Clause of the United States Constitution.

Immediately affected by th[is law] were the operators of private landfills in New Jersey, and several cities in other States that had agreements with these operators for waste disposal. They brought suit against New Jersey and its Department of Environmental Protection in state court, attacking the statute and regulations on a number of state and federal grounds. In an oral opinion granting the plaintiffs' motion for summary judgment, the trial court declared the law unconstitutional because it discriminated against interstate commerce. The New Jersey Supreme Court ... found that [the law] advanced vital health and environmental objectives with no economic discrimination against, and with little burden upon, interstate commerce, and that the law was therefore permissible under the Commerce Clause of the Constitution.

The plaintiffs then appealed to this Court.... The dispositive question ... is whether the law is constitutionally permissible in light of the Commerce Clause of the Constitution....

Although the Constitution gives Congress the power to regulate commerce among the States, many subjects of potential federal regulation under that power inevitably escape congressional attention "because of their local character and their number and diversity." In the absence of federal legislation, these subjects are open to control by the States so long as they act within the restraints imposed by the Commerce Clause itself. The bounds of these restraints appear nowhere in the words of the Commerce Clause, but have emerged gradually in the decisions of this Court giving effect to its basic purpose....

The opinions of the Court through the years have reflected an alertness to the evils of "economic isolation" and protectionism, while at the same time recognizing that incidental burdens on interstate commerce may be unavoidable when a State legislates to safeguard the health and safety of its people. Thus, where simple economic protectionism is effected by state legislation, a virtually *per se* rule of invalidity has been erected. The clearest example of such legislation is a law that overtly blocks the flow of interstate commerce at a State's borders. But where other legislative objectives are credibly advanced and there is no patent discrimination against interstate trade, the Court has adopted a much more flexible approach, the general contours of which were outlined in *Pike v. Bruce Church, Inc.*, 397 U.S. 137, 142:

> "Where the statute regulates evenhandedly to effectuate a legitimate local public interest, and its effects on interstate commerce are only incidental, it will be upheld unless the burden imposed on such commerce is clearly excessive in relation to the putative local benefits.... If a legitimate local purpose is found, then the question becomes one of degree. And the extent of the burden that will be tolerated will of course depend on the nature of the local interest involved, and on whether it could be promoted as well with a lesser impact on interstate activities."

The crucial inquiry, therefore, must be directed to determining whether [the New Jersey law] is basically a protectionist measure, or whether it can fairly be viewed as a law directed to legitimate local concerns, with effects upon interstate commerce that are only incidental.

The purpose of [the law] is set out in the statute itself as follows:

> "The Legislature finds and determines that ... the volume of solid and liquid waste continues to rapidly increase, that the treatment and disposal of these wastes continues to pose an even greater threat to the quality of the environment of New Jersey, that the available and appropriate land fill sites within the State are being diminished, that the environment continues to be threatened by the treatment and disposal of waste which originated or was collected outside the State, and that the public health, safety and welfare require that the treatment and disposal within this State of all wastes generated outside of the State be prohibited."

The New Jersey Supreme Court accepted this statement of the state legislature's purpose. The state court additionally found that New Jersey's existing landfill sites will be exhausted within a few years; that to go on using these sites or to develop new ones will take a heavy environmental toll, both from pollution and from loss of scarce open lands; that new techniques to divert waste from landfills to other methods of disposal and resource recovery processes are under development, but that these changes will require time; and finally, that "the extension of the lifespan of existing landfills, resulting from the exclusion of out-of-state waste, may be of crucial importance in preventing further virgin wetlands or other undeveloped lands from being devoted to landfill purposes." Based on these findings, the court concluded that [the law] was designed to protect, not the State's economy, but its environment, and that its substantial benefits outweigh its "slight" burden on interstate commerce.

The appellants strenuously contend that [the law], "while outwardly cloaked 'in the currently fashionable garb of environmental protection,' ... is actually no more than a legislative effort to suppress competition and stabilize the cost of solid waste disposal for New Jersey residents...." They cite passages of legislative history suggesting that the problem addressed by [the law] is primarily financial: Stemming the flow of out-of-state waste into certain landfill sites will extend their lives, thus delaying the day when New Jersey cities must transport their waste to more distant and expensive sites.

The appellees, on the other hand, deny that [the law] was motivated by financial concerns or economic protectionism. In the words of their brief, "[n]o New Jersey commercial interests stand to gain advantage over competitors from outside the state as a result of the ban on dumping out-of-state waste." Noting that New Jersey landfill operators are among the plaintiffs, the appellee's brief argues that "[t]he complaint is not that New Jersey has forged an economic preference for its own commercial interests, but rather that it has denied a small group of its entrepreneurs an economic opportunity to traffic in waste in order to protect the health, safety and welfare of the citizenry at large."

This dispute about ultimate legislative purpose need not be resolved, because its resolution would not be relevant to the constitutional issue to be decided in this case. Contrary to the evident assumption of the state court and the parties, the evil of protectionism can reside in legislative means as well as legislative ends. Thus, it does not matter whether the ultimate aim of [the law] is to reduce the waste disposal costs of New Jersey residents or to save remaining open lands from pollution, for we assume New Jersey has every right to protect its residents' pocketbooks as well as their environment. And it may be assumed as well that New Jersey may pursue those ends by slowing the flow of *all* waste into the State's remaining landfills, even though interstate commerce may incidentally be affected. But whatever New Jersey's ultimate purpose, it may not be accomplished by discriminating against articles of commerce coming from outside the State unless there is some reason, apart from their origin, to treat them differently. Both on its face and in its plain effect, [the law] violates this principle of nondiscrimination.

The Court has consistently found parochial legislation of this kind to be constitutionally invalid, whether the ultimate aim of the legislation was to assure a steady supply of milk by erecting barriers to allegedly ruinous outside competition, or to create jobs by keeping industry within the State, or to preserve the State's financial resources from depletion by fencing out indigent immigrants. In each of these cases, a presumably legitimate goal was sought to be achieved by the illegitimate means of isolating the State from the national economy.

Also relevant here are the Court's decisions holding that a State may not accord its own inhabitants a preferred right of access over consumers in other States to natural resources located within its borders.

These cases stand for the basic principle that a "State is without power to prevent privately owned articles of trade from being shipped and sold in interstate commerce on the ground that they are required to satisfy local demands or because they are needed by the people of the State."[6]

The New Jersey law at issue in this case falls squarely within the area that the Commerce Clause puts off limits to state regulation. On its face, it imposes on out-of-state commercial interests the full burden of conserving the State's remaining landfill space. It is true that in our previous cases the scarce natural resource was itself the article of commerce, whereas here the scarce resource and the article of commerce are distinct. But that difference is without consequence. In both instances, the State has overtly moved to slow or freeze the flow of commerce for protectionist reasons. It does not matter that the State has shut the article of commerce inside the State in one case and outside the State in the other. What is crucial is the attempt by one State to isolate itself from a problem common to many by erecting a barrier against the movement of interstate trade.

The appellees argue that not all laws which facially discriminate against out-of-state commerce are forbidden protectionist regulations. In particular, they point to quarantine laws, which this Court has repeatedly upheld even though they appear to single out interstate commerce for special treatment. In the appellees' view, [the New Jersey law] is analogous to such health-protective measures, since it reduces the exposure of New Jersey residents to the allegedly harmful effects of landfill sites.

It is true that certain quarantine laws have not been considered forbidden protectionist measures, even though they were directed against out-of-state commerce. But those quarantine laws banned the importation of articles such as diseased livestock that required destruction as soon as possible because their very movement risked contagion and other evils. Those laws thus did not discriminate against interstate commerce as such, but simply prevented traffic in noxious articles, whatever their origin.

The New Jersey statute is not such a quarantine law. There has been no claim here that the very movement of waste into or through New Jersey endangers health, or that waste must be disposed of as soon and as close to its point of generation as possible. The harms caused by waste are said to arise after its disposal in landfill sites, and at that point, as New Jersey concedes, there is no basis to distinguish out-of-state waste from domestic waste. If one is inherently harmful, so is the other. Yet New Jersey has banned the former while leaving its landfill sites open to the latter. The New Jersey law blocks the importation of waste in an obvious effort to saddle those outside the State with the

6. We express no opinion about New Jersey's power, consistent with the Commerce Clause, to restrict to state residents access to state-owned resources, or New Jersey's power to spend state funds solely on behalf of state residents and businesses.

entire burden of slowing the flow of refuse into New Jersey's remaining landfill sites. That legislative effort is clearly impermissible under the Commerce Clause of the Constitution.

Today, cities in Pennsylvania and New York find it expedient or necessary to send their waste into New Jersey for disposal, and New Jersey claims the right to close its borders to such traffic. Tomorrow, cities in New Jersey may find it expedient or necessary to send their waste into Pennsylvania or New York for disposal, and those States might then claim the right to close their borders. The Commerce Clause will protect New Jersey in the future, just as it protects her neighbors now, from efforts by one State to isolate itself in the stream of interstate commerce from a problem shared by all.

Mr. Justice REHNQUIST, with whom THE CHIEF JUSTICE joins, dissenting.

A growing problem in our Nation is the sanitary treatment and disposal of solid waste.... In [the New Jersey law], the State of New Jersey legislatively recognized the unfortunate fact that landfills also present extremely serious health and safety problems. First, in New Jersey, "virtually all sanitary landfills can be expected to produce leachate, a noxious and highly polluted liquid which is seldom visible and frequently pollutes ... ground and surface waters." The natural decomposition process which occurs in landfills also produces large quantities of methane and thereby presents a significant explosion hazard. Landfills can also generate "health hazards caused by rodents, fires and scavenger birds" and, "needless to say, do not help New Jersey's aesthetic appearance nor New Jersey's noise or water or air pollution problems."

The health and safety hazards associated with landfills present appellees with a currently unsolvable dilemma. Other, hopefully safer, methods of disposing of solid wastes are still in the development stage and cannot presently be used. But appellees obviously cannot completely stop the tide of solid waste that its citizens will produce in the interim. For the moment, therefore, appellees must continue to use sanitary landfills to dispose of New Jersey's own solid waste despite the critical environmental problems thereby created.

The question presented in this case is whether New Jersey must also continue to receive and dispose of solid waste from neighboring States, even though these will inexorably increase the health problems discussed above. The Court answers this question in the affirmative. New Jersey must either prohibit *all* landfill operations, leaving itself to cast about for a presently nonexistent solution to the serious problem of disposing of the waste generated within its own borders, or it must accept waste from every portion of the United States, thereby multiplying the health and safety problems which would result if it dealt only with such wastes generated within the State. Because past precedents establish that the Commerce Clause does not present appellees with such a Hobson's choice, I dissent....

The Supreme Court of New Jersey expressly found that [the law] was passed "to preserve the health of New Jersey residents by keeping their exposure to solid waste and landfill areas to a minimum." The Court points to absolutely no evidence that would contradict this finding by the New Jersey Supreme Court. Because I find no basis for distinguishing the laws under challenge here from our past cases upholding state laws that prohibit the importation of items that could endanger the population of the State, I dissent.

Comments and Questions

1. *Philadelphia* is a good example of a case involving facial discrimination against interstate commerce. That is, the law itself on its face discriminates against commerce from out-of-state. The state argues that trash is not commerce, because it has no value, but that is clearly wrong when there is an active trade in its treatment and disposal and when there is active commerce in its transportation. *Philadelphia* is also a good case for demonstrating how the evil of this discrimination is "protectionism." Protectionism is when a state (or locality) enacts a law to benefit or protect a state or local business or economic interest at the expense of out-of-state businesses or interests. The Court asserts that the Dormant Commerce Clause maintains a national common market, so that goods and services can flow freely within the United States, benefitting all through free trade.

2. Free trade across international boundaries is today a debated political issue, but economically it is difficult to fault the logic and history of free trade as a powerful tool for growing economies—whether it was the common market that the Constitution originally established among the thirteen states or the common market that was established in western Europe after World War II.

DEAN MILK CO. v. MADISON

United States Supreme Court, 1951.
340 U.S. 349, 71 S.Ct. 295, 95 L.Ed. 329.

Mr. Justice CLARK delivered the opinion of the Court.

This appeal challenges the constitutional validity … of an ordinance of the City of Madison, Wisconsin, regulating the sale of milk and milk products within the municipality's jurisdiction. [The ordinance] makes it unlawful to sell any milk as pasteurized unless it has been processed and bottled at an approved pasteurization plant within a radius of five miles from the central square of Madison….

Appellant is an Illinois corporation engaged in distributing milk and milk products in Illinois and Wisconsin. It contended below, as it does here, that … the five-mile limit on pasteurization plants … violate[s] the Commerce Clause…. The Supreme Court of Wisconsin upheld the five-mile limit on pasteurization….

The City of Madison is the county seat of Dane County. Within the county are some 5,600 dairy farms with total raw milk production in excess of 600,000,000 pounds annually and more than ten times the requirements of Madison. Aside from the milk supplied to Madison, fluid milk produced in the county moves in large quantities to Chicago and more distant consuming areas, and the remainder is used in making cheese, butter and other products. At the time of trial the Madison milk-shed was not of "Grade A" quality by the standards recommended by the United States Public Health Service, and no milk labeled "Grade A" was distributed in Madison.

The area defined by the ordinance with respect to milk sources encompasses practically all of Dane County and includes some 500 farms which supply milk for Madison. Within the five-mile area for pasteurization are plants of five processors, only three of which are engaged in the general wholesale and retail trade in Madison. Inspection of these farms and plants is scheduled once every thirty days and is performed by two municipal inspectors, one of whom is full-time. The courts below found that the ordinance in question promotes convenient, economical and efficient plant inspection.

Appellant purchases and gathers milk from approximately 950 farms in northern Illinois and southern Wisconsin, none being within twenty-five miles of Madison. Its pasteurization plants are located at Chemung and Huntley, Illinois, about 65 and 85 miles respectively from Madison. Appellant was denied a license to sell its products within Madison solely because its pasteurization plants were more than five miles away.

It is conceded that the milk which appellant seeks to sell in Madison is supplied from farms and processed in plants licensed and inspected by public health authorities of Chicago, and is labeled "Grade A" under the Chicago ordinance which adopts the rating standards recommended by the United States Public Health Service.... Madison contends and we assume that in some particulars its ordinance is more rigorous than that of Chicago.

Upon these facts we find it necessary to determine only the issue raised under the Commerce Clause, for we agree with appellant that the ordinance imposes an undue burden on interstate commerce....

[There can be no] objection to the avowed purpose of this enactment. We assume that difficulties in sanitary regulation of milk and milk products originating in remote areas may present a situation in which "upon a consideration of all the relevant facts and circumstances it appears that the matter is one which may appropriately be regulated in the interest of the safety, health and well-being of local communities * * *."

...

But this regulation ... in practical effect excludes from distribution in Madison wholesome milk produced and pasteurized in Illinois.... In thus erecting an economic barrier protecting a major local industry against competition from without the State, Madison plainly discriminates against interstate commerce.[4] This it cannot do, even in the exercise of its unquestioned power to protect the health and safety of its people, if reasonable nondiscriminatory alternatives, adequate to conserve legitimate local interests, are available. A different view, that the ordinance is valid simply because it professes to be a health measure, would mean that the Commerce Clause of itself imposes no limitations on state action other than those laid down by the Due Process Clause, save for the rare instance where a state artlessly discloses an avowed purpose to discriminate against interstate goods. Our issue then is whether the discrimination inherent in the Madison ordinance can be justified in view of the character of the local interests and the available methods of protecting them.

It appears that reasonable and adequate alternatives are available. If the City of Madison prefers to rely upon its own officials for inspection of distant milk sources, such inspection is readily open to it without hardship for it could charge the actual and reasonable cost of such inspection to the importing producers and processors. Moreover, appellee Health Commissioner of Madison testified that as proponent of the local milk ordinance he had submitted the provisions here in controversy and an alternative proposal based on § 11 of the Model Milk Ordinance recommended by the United States Public Health Service. The model provision imposes no geographical limitation on location of milk sources and processing plants but excludes from the municipality milk not produced and pasteurized conformably to standards as high as those enforced by the receiving city. In implementing such an ordinance, the importing city obtains milk ratings based on uniform standards and established by health authorities in the jurisdiction where production and processing occur. The receiving city may determine the extent of enforcement of sanitary standards in the exporting area by verifying the accuracy of safety ratings of specific plants or of the milkshed in the distant jurisdiction through the United States Public Health Service, which routinely and on request spot checks the local ratings. The Commissioner testified that Madison consumers "would be safeguarded adequately" under either proposal and that he had expressed no preference. The milk sanitarian of the Wisconsin State Board of Health testified that the State Health Department recommends the adoption of a provision based on the Model Ordinance. Both officials agreed that a local health officer would be justified in relying upon the evaluation by the Public Health Service of enforcement conditions in remote producing areas.

To permit Madison to adopt a regulation not essential for the protection of local health interests and placing a discriminatory burden on interstate commerce would invite a multiplication of preferential trade areas destructive of the very purpose of the Commerce Clause....

For these reasons we conclude that the judgment below sustaining

4. It is immaterial that Wisconsin milk from outside the Madison area is subjected to the same proscription as that moving in interstate commerce.

the five-mile provision as to pasteurization must be reversed....

Mr. Justice BLACK, with whom Mr. Justice DOUGLAS and Mr. Justice MINTON concur, dissenting.

Today's holding invalidates § 7.21 of the Madison, Wisconsin, ordinance on the following reasoning: (1) the section excludes wholesome milk coming from Illinois; (2) this imposes a discriminatory burden on interstate commerce; (3) such a burden cannot be imposed where, as here, there are reasonable, nondiscriminatory and adequate alternatives available. I disagree with the Court's premises, reasoning, and judgment.

(1) This ordinance does not exclude wholesome milk coming from Illinois or anywhere else. It does require that all milk sold in Madison must be pasteurized within five miles of the center of the city. But there was no finding in the state courts, nor evidence to justify a finding there or here, that appellant, Dean Milk Company, is unable to have its milk pasteurized within the defined geographical area. As a practical matter, so far as the record shows, Dean can easily comply with the ordinance whenever it wants to. Therefore, Dean's personal preference to pasteurize in Illinois, not the ordinance, keeps Dean's milk out of Madison.

(2) Characterization of § 7.21 as a "discriminatory burden" on interstate commerce is merely a statement of the Court's result, which I think incorrect. The section does prohibit the sale of milk in Madison by interstate and intrastate producers who prefer to pasteurize over five miles distant from the city. But both state courts below found that § 7.21 represents a good-faith attempt to safeguard public health by making adequate sanitation inspection possible. While we are not bound by these findings, I do not understand the Court to overturn them. Therefore, the fact that § 7.21, like all health regulations, imposes some burden on trade, does not mean that it "discriminates" against interstate commerce.

(3) This health regulation should not be invalidated merely because the Court believes that alternative milk-inspection methods might insure the cleanliness and healthfulness of Dean's Illinois milk.... Since the days of Chief Justice Marshall, federal courts have left states and municipalities free to pass bona fide health regulations subject only "to the paramount authority of Congress if it decides to assume control * * *." This established judicial policy of refusing to invalidate genuine local health laws under the Commerce Clause has been approvingly noted even in our recent opinions measuring state regulation by stringent standards. No case is cited, and I have found none, in which a bona fide health law was struck down on the ground that some other method of safeguarding health would be as good as, or better than, the one the Court was called on to review. In my view, to use this ground now elevates the right to traffic in commerce for profit above the power of the people to guard the purity of their daily diet of milk....

C & A CARBONE, INC. v. CLARKSTOWN

United States Supreme Court, 1994.
511 U.S. 383, 114 S.Ct. 1677, 128 L.Ed.2d 399.

Justice KENNEDY delivered the opinion of the Court.

As solid waste output continues apace and landfill capacity becomes more costly and scarce, state and local governments are expending significant resources to develop trash control systems that are efficient, lawful, and protective of the environment. The difficulty of their task is evident from the number of recent cases that we have heard involving waste transfer and treatment. The case decided today, while perhaps a small new chapter in that course of decisions, rests nevertheless upon well-settled principles of our Commerce Clause jurisprudence.

We consider a so-called flow control ordinance, which requires all solid waste to be processed at a designated transfer station before leaving the municipality. The avowed purpose of the ordinance is to retain the processing fees charged at the transfer station to amortize the cost of the facility. Because it attains this goal by depriving competitors, including out-of-state firms, of access to a local market, we hold that the flow control ordinance violates the Commerce Clause.

[I]n August 1989, Clarkstown entered into a consent decree with the New York State Department of Environmental Conservation. The town agreed to close its landfill located on Route 303 in West Nyack and build a new solid waste transfer station on the same site. The station would receive bulk solid waste and separate recyclable from nonrecyclable items. Recyclable waste would be baled for shipment to a recycling facility; nonrecyclable waste, to a suitable landfill or incinerator.

The cost of building the transfer station was estimated at $1.4 million. A local private contractor agreed to construct the facility and operate it for five years, after which the town would buy it for $1. During those five years, the town guaranteed a minimum waste flow of 120,000 tons per year, for which the contractor could charge the hauler a so-called tipping fee of $81 per ton. If the station received less than 120,000 tons in a year, the town promised to make up the tipping fee deficit. The object of this arrangement was to amortize the cost of the transfer station: The town would finance its new facility with the income generated by the tipping fees.

The problem, of course, was how to meet the yearly guarantee. This difficulty was compounded by the fact that the tipping fee of $81 per ton exceeded the disposal cost of unsorted solid waste on the private market. The solution the town adopted was the flow control ordinance here in question. The ordinance requires all nonhazardous solid waste within the town to be deposited at the Route 303 transfer station....

The petitioners in this case are C & A Carbone, Inc., a company engaged in the processing of solid waste.... Carbone operates a recycling center in Clarkstown, where it receives bulk solid waste, sorts and bales it, and then ships it to other processing facilities—much as occurs at the town's new transfer station. While the flow control ordinance permits recyclers like Carbone to continue receiving solid waste, it requires them to bring the nonrecyclable residue from that waste to the Route 303 station. It thus forbids Carbone to ship the nonrecyclable waste itself, and it requires Carbone to pay a tipping fee on trash that Carbone has already sorted....

[Carbone was found to be violating the ordinance, so Clarkstown sued in state court seeking an injunction requiring Carbone to comply with the ordinance.] [T]he New York court granted summary judgment to [Clarkstown]. The court declared the flow control ordinance constitutional and enjoined Carbone to comply with it....

The Appellate Division affirmed. The court found that the ordinance did not discriminate against interstate commerce because it "applies evenhandedly to all solid waste processed within the Town, regardless of point of origin." The New York Court of Appeals denied Carbone's motion for leave to appeal. We granted certiorari and now reverse.

At the outset we confirm that the flow control ordinance does regulate interstate commerce, despite the town's position to the contrary. The town says that its ordinance reaches only waste within its jurisdiction and is in practical effect a quarantine: It prevents garbage from entering the stream of interstate commerce until it is made safe. This reasoning is premised, however, on an outdated and mistaken concept of what constitutes interstate commerce.

While the immediate effect of the ordinance is to direct local transport of solid waste to a designated site within the local jurisdiction, its economic effects are interstate in reach. The Carbone facility in Clarkstown receives and processes waste from places other than Clarkstown, including from out of State. By requiring Carbone to send the nonrecyclable portion of this waste to the Route 303 transfer station at an additional cost, the flow control ordinance drives up the cost for out-of-state interests to dispose of their solid waste. Furthermore, even as to waste originating in Clarkstown, the ordinance prevents everyone except the favored local operator from performing the initial processing step. The ordinance thus deprives out-of-state businesses of access to a local market. These economic effects are more than enough to bring the Clarkstown ordinance within the purview of the Commerce Clause. It is well settled that actions are within the domain of the Commerce Clause if they burden interstate commerce or impede its free flow.

The real question is whether the flow control ordinance is valid despite its undoubted effect on interstate commerce. For this inquiry, our case law yields two lines of analysis: first, whether the ordinance discriminates against interstate commerce, *Philadelphia v. New Jersey*; and second, whether the ordinance imposes a burden on interstate commerce that is "clearly excessive in relation to the putative local benefits," *Pike v. Bruce Church, Inc.*, 397 U.S. 137 (1970). As we find that the ordinance discriminates against interstate commerce, we need not resort to the *Pike* test.

The central rationale for the rule against discrimination is to prohibit state or municipal laws whose object is local economic protectionism, laws that would excite those jealousies and retaliatory measures the Constitution was designed to prevent. We have interpreted the Commerce Clause to invalidate local laws that impose commercial barriers or discriminate against an article of commerce by reason of its origin or destination out of State. *See, e.g., Philadelphia, supra* (striking down New Jersey statute that prohibited the import of solid waste); *Hughes v. Oklahoma,* 441 U.S. 322 (1979) (striking down Oklahoma law that prohibited the export of natural minnows).

Clarkstown protests that its ordinance does not discriminate because it does not differentiate solid waste on the basis of its geographic origin. All solid waste, regardless of origin, must be processed at the designated transfer station before it leaves the town. Unlike the statute in *Philadelphia,* says the town, the ordinance erects no barrier to the import or export of any solid waste but requires only that the waste be channeled through the designated facility.

Our initial discussion of the effects of the ordinance on interstate commerce goes far toward refuting the town's contention that there is no discrimination in its regulatory scheme. The town's own arguments go the rest of the way. As the town itself points out, what makes garbage a profitable business is not its own worth but the fact that its possessor must pay to get rid of it. In other words, the article of commerce is not so much the solid waste itself, but rather the service of processing and disposing of it.

With respect to this stream of commerce, the flow control ordinance discriminates, for it allows only the favored operator to process waste that is within the limits of the town. The ordinance is no less discriminatory because in-state or in-town processors are also covered by the prohibition. In *Dean Milk Co. v. Madison,* we struck down a city ordinance that required all milk sold in the city to be pasteurized within five miles of the city lines. We found it "immaterial that Wisconsin milk from outside the Madison area is subjected to the same proscription as that moving in interstate commerce."

In this light, the flow control ordinance is just one more instance of local processing requirements that we long have held invalid. See *Minnesota v. Barber,* 136 U.S. 313 (1890) (striking down a Minnesota statute that required any meat sold within the State, whether originating within or without the State, to be examined by an inspector within the State); *Foster-Fountain Packing Co. v. Haydel,* 278 U.S. 1 (1928) (striking down a Louisiana statute that forbade shrimp to be exported unless the heads and hulls had first been removed within the State); *Johnson v. Haydel,* 278 U.S. 16 (1928) (striking down analogous Louisiana statute for oysters); *Toomer v. Witsell,* 334 U.S. 385 (1948) (striking down

South Carolina statute that required shrimp fishermen to unload, pack, and stamp their catch before shipping it to another State); *Pike v. Bruce Church, Inc., supra* (striking down Arizona statute that required all Arizona-grown cantaloupes to be packaged within the State prior to export); *South-Central Timber Development, Inc. v. Wunnicke,* 467 U.S. 82 (1984) (striking down an Alaska regulation that required all Alaska timber to be processed within the State prior to export). The essential vice in laws of this sort is that they bar the import of the processing service. Out-of-state meat inspectors, or shrimp hullers, or milk pasteurizers, are deprived of access to local demand for their services. Put another way, the offending local laws hoard a local resource—be it meat, shrimp, or milk—for the benefit of local businesses that treat it.

The flow control ordinance has the same design and effect. It hoards solid waste, and the demand to get rid of it, for the benefit of the preferred processing facility. The only conceivable distinction from the cases cited above is that the flow control ordinance favors a single local proprietor. But this difference just makes the protectionist effect of the ordinance more acute. In *Dean Milk,* the local processing requirement at least permitted pasteurizers within five miles of the city to compete. An out-of-state pasteurizer who wanted access to that market might have built a pasteurizing facility within the radius. The flow control ordinance at issue here squelches competition in the waste-processing service altogether, leaving no room for investment from outside.

Discrimination against interstate commerce in favor of local business or investment is *per se* invalid, save in a narrow class of cases in which the municipality can demonstrate, under rigorous scrutiny, that it has no other means to advance a legitimate local interest. *Maine v. Taylor,* 477 U.S. 131 (1986) (upholding Maine's ban on the import of baitfish because Maine had no other way to prevent the spread of parasites and the adulteration of its native fish species). A number of *amici* contend that the flow control ordinance fits into this narrow class. They suggest that as landfill space diminishes and environmental cleanup costs escalate, measures like flow control become necessary to ensure the safe handling and proper treatment of solid waste.

The teaching of our cases is that these arguments must be rejected absent the clearest showing that the unobstructed flow of interstate commerce itself is unable to solve the local problem. The Commerce Clause presumes a national market free from local legislation that discriminates in favor of local interests. Here Clarkstown has any number of nondiscriminatory alternatives for addressing the health and environmental problems alleged to justify the ordinance in question. The most obvious would be uniform safety regulations enacted without the object to discriminate. These regulations would ensure that competitors like Carbone do not underprice the market by cutting corners on environmental safety.

Nor may Clarkstown justify the flow control ordinance as a way to steer solid waste away from out-of-town disposal sites that it might deem harmful to the environment. To do so would extend the town's police power beyond its jurisdictional bounds. States and localities may not attach restrictions to exports or imports in order to control commerce in other States.

The flow control ordinance does serve a central purpose that a non-protectionist regulation would not: It ensures that the town-sponsored facility will be profitable, so that the local contractor can build it and Clarkstown can buy it back at nominal cost in five years. In other words, as the most candid of *amici* and even Clarkstown admit, the flow control ordinance is a financing measure. By itself, of course, revenue generation is not a local interest that can justify discrimination against interstate commerce. Otherwise States could impose discriminatory taxes against solid waste originating outside the State. See *Chemical Waste Management, Inc. v. Hunt,* 504 U.S. 334 (1992) (striking down Alabama statute that imposed additional fee on all hazardous waste generated outside the State and disposed of within the State); *Oregon Waste Systems, Inc. v. Department of Environmental Quality of Ore.,* 511 U.S. 93 (1994) (striking down Oregon statute that imposed additional fee on solid waste generated outside the State and disposed of within the State).

Clarkstown maintains that special financing is necessary to ensure the long-term survival of the designated facility. If so, the town may subsidize the facility through general taxes or municipal bonds. But having elected to use the open market to earn revenues for its project, the town may not employ discriminatory regulation to give that project an advantage over rival businesses from out of State....

State and local governments may not use their regulatory power to favor local enterprise by prohibiting patronage of out-of-state competitors or their facilities. We reverse the judgment and remand the case for proceedings not inconsistent with this decision.

Justice O'CONNOR, concurring in the judgment.

The town of Clarkstown's flow control ordinance requires all "acceptable waste" generated or collected in the town to be disposed of only at the town's solid waste facility. The Court holds today that this ordinance violates the Commerce Clause because it discriminates against interstate commerce. I agree with the majority's ultimate conclusion that the ordinance violates the dormant Commerce Clause. In my view, however, the town's ordinance is unconstitutional not because of facial or effective discrimination against interstate commerce, but rather because it imposes an excessive burden on interstate commerce....

The scope of the dormant Commerce Clause is a judicial creation. On its face, the Clause provides only that "[t]he Congress shall have Power ... To regulate Commerce ... among the several States...." This Court long ago concluded, however, that the Clause not only empowers Congress to regulate interstate commerce, but also imposes limitations on the States in the absence of congressional action:

> "This principle that our economic unit is the Nation, which alone has the gamut of powers necessary to control of the economy, including the vital power of erecting customs barriers against foreign competition, has as its corollary that the states are not separable economic units.... [W]hat is ultimate is the principle that one state in its dealings with another may not place itself in a position of economic isolation."

Our decisions therefore hold that the dormant Commerce Clause forbids States and their subdivisions to regulate interstate commerce.

We have generally distinguished between two types of impermissible regulations. A facially nondiscriminatory regulation supported by a legitimate state interest which incidentally burdens interstate commerce is constitutional unless the burden on interstate trade is clearly excessive in relation to the local benefits. Where, however, a regulation "affirmatively" or "clearly" discriminates against interstate commerce on its face or in practical effect, it violates the Constitution unless the discrimination is demonstrably justified by a valid factor unrelated to protectionism. Of course, there is no clear line separating these categories....

Local Law 9 prohibits anyone except the town-authorized transfer station operator from processing discarded waste and shipping it out of town. In effect, the town has given a waste processing monopoly to the transfer station. The majority concludes that this processing monopoly facially discriminates against interstate commerce. In support of this conclusion, the majority cites previous decisions of this Court striking down regulatory enactments requiring that a particular economic activity be performed within the jurisdiction.

Local Law 9, however, lacks an important feature common to the regulations at issue in these cases—namely, discrimination on the basis of geographic origin. In each of the cited cases, the challenged enactment gave a competitive advantage to local business *as a group* vis-à-vis their out-of-state or nonlocal competitors *as a group.* In effect, the regulating jurisdiction—be it a State, a county, or a city—drew a line around itself and treated those inside the line more favorably than those outside the line. Thus, in *Pike,* the Court held that an Arizona law requiring that Arizona cantaloupes be packaged in Arizona before being shipped out of state facially discriminated against interstate commerce: The benefits of the discriminatory scheme benefited the Arizona packaging industry, at the expense of its competition in California. Similarly, in *Dean Milk,* on which the majority heavily relies, the city of Madison drew a line around its perimeter and required that all milk sold in the city be pasteurized only by dairies located inside the line. This type of geographic distinction, which confers an economic advantage on local interests in general, is common to all the local processing cases cited by the majority. And the Court has, I believe, correctly concluded that these arrangements are protectionist either in purpose or practical effect, and thus amount to virtually *per se* discrimination.

In my view, the majority fails to come to terms with a significant distinction between the laws in the local processing cases discussed above and Local Law 9. Unlike the regulations we have previously struck down, Local Law 9 does not give more favorable treatment to local interests as a group as compared to out-of-state or out-of-town economic interests. Rather, the garbage sorting monopoly is achieved at the expense of all competitors, be they local or nonlocal. That the ordinance does not discriminate on the basis of geographic origin is vividly illustrated by the identity of the plaintiffs in this very action: Petitioners are a *local* recyclers, physically located *in Clarkstown,* that desire to process waste themselves, and thus bypass the town's designated transfer facility. Because in-town processors—like petitioners—and out-of-town processors are treated equally, I cannot agree that Local Law 9 "discriminates" against interstate commerce. Rather, Local Law 9 "discriminates" evenhandedly against all potential participants in the waste processing business, while benefiting only the chosen operator of the transfer facility.

I believe this distinction has more doctrinal significance than the majority acknowledges. In considering state health and safety regulations such as Local Law 9, we have consistently recognized that the fact that interests within the regulating jurisdiction are equally affected by the challenged enactment counsels against a finding of discrimination. And for good reason. The existence of substantial in-state interests harmed by a regulation is "a powerful safeguard" against legislative discrimination. The Court generally defers to health and safety regulations because "their burden usually falls on local economic interests as well as other States' economic interests, thus insuring that a State's own political processes will serve as a check against unduly burdensome regulations." Thus, while there is no bright line separating those enactments which are virtually *per se* invalid and those which are not, the fact that in-town competitors of the transfer facility are equally burdened by Local Law 9 leads me to conclude that Local Law 9 does not discriminate against interstate commerce.

[Justice O'Connor then concluded that, while the ordinance did not discriminate against interstate commerce, it did impose an excessive burden on interstate trade when considered in relation to the local benefits conferred. Therefore, it violated the Dormant Commerce Clause.]

Justice SOUTER, with whom THE CHIEF JUSTICE and Justice BLACKMUN join, dissenting.

The majority may invoke "well-settled principles of our Commerce Clause jurisprudence," but it does so to strike down an ordinance unlike anything this Court has ever invalidated. Previous cases have held that the "negative" or "dormant" aspect of the Commerce Clause renders state or local legislation unconstitutional when it discriminates against out-of-state or out-of-town businesses such as those that pasteurize milk, hull shrimp, or mill lumber, and the majority relies on these cases because of what they have in common with this one: out-of-state processors are excluded from the local market (here, from the market for trash processing services). What the majority ignores, however, are the differences between our local processing cases and this one: the exclusion worked by Clarkstown's Local Law 9 bestows no benefit on a class of local private actors, but instead directly aids the government in satisfying a traditional governmental responsibility. The law does not differentiate between all local and all out-of-town providers of a service, but instead between the one entity responsible for ensuring that the job gets done and all other enterprises, regardless of their location. The ordinance thus falls outside that class of tariff or protectionist measures that the Commerce Clause has traditionally been thought to bar States from enacting against each other, and when the majority subsumes the ordinance within the class of laws this Court has struck down as facially discriminatory, the majority is in fact greatly extending the Clause's dormant reach.

There are, however, good and sufficient reasons against expanding the Commerce Clause's inherent capacity to trump exercises of state authority such as the ordinance at issue here. There is no indication in the record that any out-of-state trash processor has been harmed, or that the interstate movement or disposition of trash will be affected one whit. To the degree Local Law 9 affects the market for trash processing services, it does so only by subjecting Clarkstown residents and businesses to burdens far different from the burdens of local favoritism that dormant Commerce Clause jurisprudence seeks to root out. The town has found a way to finance a public improvement, not by transferring its cost to out-of-state economic interests, but by spreading it among the local generators of trash, an equitable result with tendencies that should not disturb the Commerce Clause and should not be disturbed by us.

HUNT v. WASHINGTON STATE APPLE ADVERTISING COMM'N

United States Supreme Court, 1977.
432 U.S. 333, 97 S.Ct. 2434, 53 L.Ed.2d 383.

Mr. Chief Justice BURGER delivered the opinion of the Court.

In 1973, North Carolina enacted a statute which required, inter alia, all closed containers of apples sold, offered for sale, or shipped into the State to bear "no grade other than the applicable U.S. grade or standard." In an action brought by the Washington State Apple Advertising Commission, a three-judge Federal District Court invalidated the statute insofar as it prohibited the display of Washington State apple grades on the ground that it unconstitutionally discriminated against interstate commerce.

The specific question[] presented on appeal [is] whether the challenged North Carolina statute constitutes an unconstitutional burden on interstate commerce.

Warren Burger

President Nixon appointed Burger Chief Justice in 1969, fulfilling a promise to appoint persons to the Court who were "strict constructionists." Previously, Burger had served on the United States Court of Appeals for the District of Columbia Circuit for thirteen years, where he enjoyed a solid if undistinguished reputation. While President Nixon undoubtedly wished him to undo the effects of the so-called liberal Warren Court, the Court under Chief Justice Burger in essence solidified the Warren Court jurisprudence, generally not extending it but also not overruling it. Indeed, in *Roe v. Wade*, Burger voted with the majority, finding a woman's constitutional right to obtain an abortion. Moreover, although he was appointed by President Nixon, it was Chief Justice Burger who wrote the unanimous opinion in *Nixon v. United States*, holding that Nixon was required to disclose the tapes recorded in the Oval Office to the grand jury investigating the Watergate conspiracy, which opinion inexorably led to Nixon's resignation. Burger retired in 1986, allowing President Reagan to appoint William Rehnquist Chief Justice.

Washington State is the Nation's largest producer of apples, its crops accounting for approximately 30% of all apples grown domestically and nearly half of all apples shipped in closed containers in interstate commerce. As might be expected, the production and sale of apples on this scale is a multimillion dollar enterprise which plays a significant role in Washington's economy. Because of the importance of the apple industry to the State, its legislature has undertaken to protect and enhance the reputation of Washington apples by establishing a stringent, mandatory inspection program, administered by the State's Department of Agriculture, which requires all apples shipped in interstate commerce to be tested under strict quality standards and graded accordingly. In all cases, the Washington State grades, which have gained substantial acceptance in the trade, are the equivalent of, or superior to, the comparable grades and standards adopted by the United States Department of Agriculture (USDA). Compliance with the Washington inspection scheme costs the State's growers approximately $1 million each year.

In addition to the inspection program, the state legislature has sought to enhance the market for Washington apples through the creation of a state agency, the Washington State Apple Advertising Commission, charged with the statutory duty of promoting and protecting the State's apple industry....

In 1972, the North Carolina Board of Agriculture adopted an administrative regulation, unique in the 50 States, which in effect required all closed containers of apples shipped into or sold in the State to display either the applicable USDA grade or none at all. State grades were expressly prohibited. In addition to its obvious consequence prohibiting the display of Washington State apple grades on containers of apples shipped into North Carolina, the regulation presented the Washington apple industry with a marketing problem of potentially nationwide significance. Washington apple growers annually ship in commerce approximately 40 million closed containers of apples, nearly 500,000 of which eventually find their way into North Carolina, stamped with the applicable Washington State variety and grade. It is the industry's practice to purchase these containers preprinted with the various apple varieties and grades, prior to harvest. After these containers are filled with apples of the appropriate type and grade, a substantial portion of them are placed in cold-storage warehouses where the grade labels identify the product and facilitate its handling. These apples are then shipped as needed throughout the year; after February 1 of each year, they constitute approximately two-thirds of all apples sold in fresh markets in this country. Since the ultimate destination of these apples is unknown at the time they are placed in storage, compliance with North Carolina's unique regulation would have required Washington growers to obliterate the printed labels on containers shipped to North Carolina, thus giving their product a damaged appearance. Alternatively, they could have changed their marketing practices to accommodate the needs of the North Carolina market, i. e., repack apples to be shipped to North Carolina in containers bearing only the USDA grade, and/or store the estimated portion of the harvest destined for that market in such special containers. As a last resort, they could discontinue the use of the preprinted containers entirely. None of these costly and less efficient options was very attractive to the industry. Moreover, in the event a number of other States followed North Carolina's lead, the resultant inability to display the Washington grades could force the Washington growers to abandon the State's expensive inspection and grading system which their customers had come to know and rely on over the 60–odd years of its existence....

Unsuccessful in its attempts to secure administrative relief, the Commission instituted this action challenging the constitutionality of the statute in the United States District Court for the Eastern District of North Carolina.... A three-judge Federal District Court was convened....

After a hearing, the District Court granted the requested relief.... This appeal followed....

We turn finally to the appellants' claim that the District Court erred in holding that the North Carolina statute violated the Commerce Clause insofar as it prohibited the display of Washington State grades on closed containers of apples shipped into the State. Appellants do not really contest the District Court's determination that the challenged statute burdened the Washington apple industry by increasing its costs of doing business in the North Carolina market and causing it to lose accounts there. Rather, they maintain that any such burdens on the interstate sale of Washington apples were far outweighed by the local benefits flowing from what they contend was a valid exercise of North Carolina's inherent police powers designed to protect its citizenry from fraud and deception in the marketing of apples.

Prior to the statute's enactment, appellants point out, apples from 13 different States were shipped into North Carolina for sale. Seven of those States, including the State of Washington, had their own grading systems which, while differing in their standards, used similar descriptive labels (e. g., fancy, extra fancy, etc.). This multiplicity of inconsistent state grades, as the District Court itself found, posed dangers of deception and confusion not only in the North Carolina market, but in the Nation as a whole. The North Carolina statute, appellants claim, was enacted to eliminate this source of deception and confusion by replacing the numerous state grades with a single uniform standard. Moreover, it is contended that North Carolina sought to accomplish this goal of uniformity in an evenhanded manner as evidenced by the fact that its statute applies to all apples sold in closed containers in the State without regard to their point of origin. Nonetheless, appellants argue that the District Court gave "scant attention" to the obvious benefits flowing from the challenged legislation and to the long line of decisions from this Court holding that the States possess "broad powers" to protect local purchasers from fraud and deception in the marketing of foodstuffs.

As the appellants properly point out, not every exercise of state authority imposing some burden on the free flow of commerce is invalid. Although the Commerce Clause acts as a limitation upon state power even without congressional implementation, our opinions have long recognized that, "in the absence of conflicting legislation by Congress, there is a residuum of power in the state to make laws governing matters of local concern which nevertheless in some measure affect interstate commerce or even, to some extent, regulate it."

Moreover, as appellants correctly note, that "residuum" is particularly strong when the State acts to protect its citizenry in matters pertaining to the sale of foodstuffs. By the same token, however, a finding that state legislation furthers matters of legitimate local concern, even in the health and consumer protection areas, does not end the inquiry.... Rather, when such state legislation comes into conflict with the Commerce Clause's overriding requirement of a national "common market," we are confronted with the task of effecting an accommodation of the competing national and local interests. *Pike v. Bruce Church, Inc.* We turn to that task.

As the District Court correctly found, the challenged statute has the practical effect of not only burdening interstate sales of Washington apples, but also discriminating against them. This discrimination takes various forms. The first, and most obvious, is the statute's consequence of raising the costs of doing business in the North Carolina market for Washington apple growers and dealers, while leaving those of their North Carolina counterparts unaffected. As previously noted, this disparate effect results from the fact that North Carolina apple producers, unlike their Washington competitors, were not forced to alter their marketing practices in order to comply with the statute. They were still free to market their wares under the USDA grade or none at all as they had done prior to the statute's enactment. Obviously, the increased costs imposed by the statute would tend to shield the local apple industry from the competition of Washington apple growers and dealers who are already at a competitive disadvantage because of their great distance from the North Carolina market.

Second, the statute has the effect of stripping away from the Washington apple industry the competitive and economic advantages it has earned for itself through its expensive inspection and grading system. The record demonstrates that the Washington apple-grading system has gained nationwide acceptance in the apple trade. Indeed, it contains numerous affidavits from apple brokers and dealers located both inside and outside of North Carolina who state their preference, and that of their customers, for apples graded under the Washington, as opposed to the USDA, system because of the former's greater consistency, its emphasis on color, and its supporting mandatory inspections. Once again, the statute had no similar impact on the North Carolina apple industry and thus operated to its benefit.

Third, by prohibiting Washington growers and dealers from marketing apples under their State's grades, the statute has a leveling effect which insidiously operates to the advantage of local apple producers. As noted earlier, the Washington State grades are equal or superior to the USDA grades in all corresponding categories. Hence, with free market forces at work, Washington sellers would normally enjoy a distinct market advantage vis-a-vis local producers in those categories where the Washington grade is superior. However, because of the statute's operation, Washington apples which would otherwise qualify for and be sold under the superior Washington grades will now have to be marketed under their inferior USDA counterparts. Such "downgrading" offers the North Carolina apple industry the very sort of protection against competing out-of-state products that the Commerce Clause was designed to prohibit. At worst, it will have the effect of an embargo against those Washington apples in the superior grades as Washington dealers withhold them from the North Carolina market. At best, it will deprive Washington sellers of the market premium that such apples would otherwise command.

Despite the statute's facial neutrality, the Commission suggests that its discriminatory impact on interstate commerce was not an unintended byproduct and there are some indications in the record to that effect. The most glaring is the response of the North Carolina Agriculture Commissioner to the Commission's request for an exemption following the statue's passage in which he indicated that before he could support such an exemption, he would "want to have the sentiment from our apple producers since they were mainly responsible for this legislation being passed...." Moreover, we find it somewhat suspect that North Carolina singled out only closed containers of apples, the very means by which apples are transported in commerce, to effectuate the statute's ostensible consumer protection purpose when apples are not generally sold at retail in their shipping containers. However, we need not ascribe an economic protection motive to the North Carolina Legislature to resolve this case; we conclude that the challenged statute cannot stand insofar as it prohibits the display of Washington State grades even if enacted for the declared purpose of protecting consumers from deception and fraud in the marketplace.

When discrimination against commerce of the type we have found is demonstrated, the burden falls on the State to justify it both in terms of the local benefits flowing from the statute and the unavailability of nondiscriminatory alternatives adequate to preserve the local interests at stake. North Carolina has failed to sustain that burden on both scores.

The several States unquestionably possess a substantial interest in protecting their citizens from confusion and deception in the marketing of foodstuffs, but the challenged statute does remarkably little to further that laudable goal at least with respect to Washington apples and grades. The statute, as already noted, permits the marketing of closed containers of apples under no grades at all. Such a result can hardly be thought to eliminate the problems of deception and confusion created by the multiplicity of differing state grades; indeed, it magnifies them by depriving purchasers of all information concerning the quality of the contents of closed apple containers. Moreover, although the statute is ostensibly a consumer protection measure, it directs its primary efforts, not at the consuming public at large, but at apple wholesalers and brokers who are the principal purchasers of closed containers of apples. And those individuals are presumably the most knowledgeable individuals in this area. Since the statute does nothing at all to purify the flow of information at the retail level, it does little to protect consumers against the problems it was designed to eliminate. Finally, we note that any potential for confusion and deception created by the Washington grades was not of the type that led to the statute's enactment. Since Washington grades are in all cases equal or superior to their USDA counterparts, they could only "deceive" or "confuse" a consumer to his benefit, hardly a harmful result.

In addition, it appears that nondiscrimnatory alternatives to the outright ban of Washington State grades are readily available. For example, North Carolina could effectuate its goal by permitting out-of-state growers to utilize state grades only if they also marked their shipments with the applicable USDA label. In that case, the USDA grade would serve as a benchmark against which the consumer could evaluate the quality of the various state grades. If this alternative was for some reason inadequate to eradicate problems caused by state grades inferior to those adopted by the USDA, North Carolina might consider banning those state grades which, unlike Washington's could not be demonstrated to be equal or superior to the corresponding USDA categories. Concededly, even in this latter instance, some potential for "confusion" might persist. However, it is the type of "confusion" that the national interest in the free flow of goods between the States demands be tolerated.

Mr. Justice REHNQUIST took no part in the consideration or decision of the case.

Comments and Questions

1. In *Philadelphia v. New Jersey*, *Dean Milk Co. v. Madison*, and *C & A Carbone, Inc. v. Clarkstown*, the state or local law had an explicit geographical restriction involved—out-of-state waste could not be brought into New Jersey, milk pasteurized outside a 5–mile limit of Madison could not be sold in Madison, and all waste in Clarkstown had to be processed in Clarkstown. Thus, there was a clear discrimination against the movement interstate of the commerce in question. We call this facial discrimination, because the discrimination can be found in the text of the law itself. *Hunt* is different. Here the law itself does not treat apples differently with respect to where they come from or where they go. Nevertheless, the Court finds that the law is discriminatory. We call this discriminatory in fact or in effect; that is, the discrimination or discriminatory effect depends on the particular facts. What facts does the Court identify as making this law discriminatory?

2. The Court in *Hunt* does not conclude that the purpose of the law is protectionism, although that is its effect, but the Court does make mention of something that might support a protectionist purpose behind the law. Why does the Court do that? Do you think it affected the Court's decision?

3. The only reason the North Carolina law is found unconstitutional is that it interferes with Washington apple growers obtaining the benefit of a Washington state law. That is, it is only because Washington state had already established its unique and special apple grading system that the North Carolina ban on out-of-state grades on apples crates interfered with interstate commerce. In the absence of the Washington law, the North Carolina law would be constitutional. Is it fair that Washington's law to benefit its apple growers can trump North Carolina's law that benefits its apple growers?

WEST LYNN CREAMERY, INC. v. HEALY

United States Supreme Court, 1994.
512 U.S. 186, 114 S.Ct. 2205, 129 L.Ed.2d 157.

Justice STEVENS delivered the opinion of the Court.

A Massachusetts pricing order imposes an assessment on all fluid milk sold by dealers to Massachusetts retailers. About two-thirds of that milk is produced out of State. The entire assessment, however, is distributed to Massachusetts dairy farmers. The question presented is whether the pricing order unconstitutionally discriminates against interstate commerce. We hold that it does.

Petitioner West Lynn Creamery, Inc., is a milk dealer licensed to do business in Massachusetts. It purchases raw milk, which it processes, packages, and sells to wholesalers, retailers, and other milk dealers. About 97% of the raw milk it purchases is produced by out-of-state farmers....

[I]n the 1980's and early 1990's, Massachusetts dairy farmers began to lose market share to lower cost producers in neighboring States. In response, the Governor of Massachusetts appointed a Special Commission to study the dairy industry. The commission found that many producers had sold their dairy farms during the past decade and that if prices paid to farmers for their milk were not significantly increased, a majority of the remaining farmers in Massachusetts would be "forced out of business within the year." ... [Consequently, Healy, the Commissioner of the Massachusetts Department of Food and Agriculture,] issued the pricing order that is challenged in this proceeding.

The order requires every "dealer"[4] in Massachusetts to make a monthly "premium payment" into the "Massachusetts Dairy Equalization Fund." ... Each month the fund is distributed to Massachusetts producers.[7] Each Massachusetts producer receives a share of the total fund equal to his proportionate contribution to the State's total production of raw milk.

[Petitioner West Lynn refused to make the premium payments, and respondent commenced license revocation proceedings. Petitioner] then filed an action in state court seeking an injunction against enforcement of the order on the ground that it violated the Commerce Clause of the Federal Constitution. The state court denied relief and ... the Supreme Judicial Court of Massachusetts ... affirmed, because it concluded that "the pricing order does not discriminate on its face, is evenhanded in its application, and only incidentally burdens interstate commerce." ... We granted certiorari and now reverse.

[T]he Commerce Clause ... limits the power of the Commonwealth of Massachusetts to adopt regulations that discriminate against interstate commerce. "This 'negative' aspect of the Commerce Clause prohibits economic protectionism—that is, regulatory measures designed to benefit in-state economic interests by burdening out-of-state competitors.... Thus, state statutes that clearly discriminate against interstate commerce are routinely struck down ... unless the discrimination is demonstrably justified by a valid factor unrelated to economic protectionism.

The paradigmatic example of a law discriminating against interstate commerce is the protective tariff or customs duty, which taxes goods imported from other States, but does not tax similar products pro-

4. A "dealer" is defined as "any person who is engaged within the Commonwealth in the business of receiving, purchasing, pasteurizing, bottling, processing, distributing, or otherwise handling milk, purchases or receives milk for sale as the consignee or agent of a producer, and shall include a producer-dealer, dealer-retailer, and sub-dealer."

7. A "producer" is defined as "any person producing milk from dairy cattle."

duced in State. A tariff is an attractive measure because it simultaneously raises revenue and benefits local producers by burdening their out-of-state competitors. Nevertheless, it violates the principle of the unitary national market by handicapping out-of-state competitors, thus artificially encouraging in-state production even when the same goods could be produced at lower cost in other States....

Under these cases, Massachusetts' pricing order is clearly unconstitutional. Its avowed purpose and its undisputed effect are to enable higher cost Massachusetts dairy farmers to compete with lower cost dairy farmers in other States. The "premium payments" are effectively a tax which makes milk produced out of State more expensive. Although the tax also applies to milk produced in Massachusetts, its effect on Massachusetts producers is entirely (indeed more than) offset by the subsidy provided exclusively to Massachusetts dairy farmers. Like an ordinary tariff, the tax is thus effectively imposed only on out-of-state products. The pricing order thus allows Massachusetts dairy farmers who produce at higher cost to sell at or below the price charged by lower cost out-of-state producers.... The Massachusetts pricing order thus will almost certainly "cause local goods to constitute a larger share, and goods with an out-of-state source to constitute a smaller share, of the total sales in the market." In fact, this effect was the motive behind the promulgation of the pricing order. This effect renders the program unconstitutional, because it, like a tariff, "neutraliz[es] advantages belonging to the place of origin."

In some ways, the Massachusetts pricing order is most similar to the law at issue in *Bacchus Imports, Ltd. v. Dias,* 468 U.S. 263 (1984). Both involve a broad-based tax on a single kind of good and special provisions for in-state producers. *Bacchus* involved a 20% excise tax on all liquor sales, coupled with an exemption for fruit wine manufactured in Hawaii and for okolehao, a brandy distilled from the root of a shrub indigenous to Hawaii. The Court held that Hawaii's law was unconstitutional because it "had both the purpose and effect of discriminating in favor of local products." By granting a tax exemption for local products, Hawaii in effect created a protective tariff. Goods produced out of State were taxed, but those produced in State were subject to no net tax. It is obvious that the result in *Bacchus* would have been the same if instead of exempting certain Hawaiian liquors from tax, Hawaii had rebated the amount of tax collected from the sale of those liquors....

Respondent's principal argument is that ... the payments to Massachusetts dairy farmers from the Dairy Equalization Fund are valid, because subsidies are constitutional exercises of state power, and that the order premium which provides money for the fund is valid, because it is a nondiscriminatory tax. Therefore the pricing order is constitutional, because it is merely the combination of two independently lawful regulations. In effect, respondent argues, if the State may impose a valid tax on dealers, it is free to use the proceeds of the tax as it chooses; and if it may independently subsidize its farmers, it is free to finance the subsidy by means of any legitimate tax.

Even granting respondent's assertion that both components of the pricing order would be constitutional standing alone,[15] the pricing order nevertheless must fall. A pure subsidy funded out of general revenue ordinarily imposes no burden on interstate commerce, but merely assists local business. The pricing order in this case, however, is funded principally from taxes on the sale of milk produced in other States. By so funding the subsidy, respondent not only assists local farmers, but burdens interstate commerce. The pricing order thus violates the cardinal principle that a State may not "benefit in-state economic interests by burdening out-of-state competitors."

[N]ondiscriminatory measures, like the evenhanded tax at issue here, are generally upheld, in spite of any adverse effects on interstate commerce, in part because "[t]he existence of major in-state interests adversely affected ... is a powerful safeguard against legislative abuse." However, when a nondiscriminatory tax is coupled with a subsidy to one of the groups hurt by the tax, a State's political processes can no longer be relied upon to prevent legislative abuse, because one of the in-state interests which would otherwise lobby against the tax has been mollified by the subsidy. So, in this case, one would ordinarily have expected at least three groups to lobby against the order premium, which, as a tax, raises the price (and hence lowers demand) for milk: dairy farmers, milk dealers, and consumers. But because the tax was coupled with a subsidy, one of the most powerful of these groups, Massachusetts dairy farmers, instead of exerting their influence against the tax, were in fact its primary supporters.

Respondent's argument would require us to analyze separately two parts of an integrated regulation, but we cannot divorce the premium payments from the use to which the payments are put. It is the entire program—not just the contributions to the fund or the distributions from that fund—that simultaneously burdens interstate commerce and discriminates in favor of local producers. The choice of constitutional means—nondiscriminatory tax and local subsidy—cannot guarantee the constitutionality of the program as a whole.... Similarly, the law held unconstitutional in *Bacchus Imports, Ltd. v. Dias,* 468 U.S. 263, 104 S.Ct. 3049, 82 L.Ed.2d 200 (1984), involved the exercise of Hawaii's undisputed power to tax and to grant tax exemptions.

Our Commerce Clause jurisprudence is not so rigid as to be controlled by the form by which a State erects barriers to commerce. Rather our cases have eschewed formalism for a sensitive, case-by-case analysis of purposes and effects. As the Court declared over 50 years ago: "The commerce clause forbids discrimination, whether forthright or ingenious. In each case it is our duty to determine whether the statute under

15. We have never squarely confronted the constitutionality of subsidies, and we need not do so now. We have, however, noted that "[d]irect subsidization of domestic industry does not ordinarily run afoul" of the negative Commerce Clause.

attack, whatever its name may be, will in its practical operation work discrimination against interstate commerce." ...

"Our system, fostered by the Commerce Clause, is that every farmer and every craftsman shall be encouraged to produce by the certainty that he will have free access to every market in the Nation, that no home embargoes will withhold his exports, and no foreign state will by customs duties or regulations exclude them. Likewise, every consumer may look to the free competition from every producing area in the Nation to protect him from exploitation by any. Such was the vision of the Founders; such has been the doctrine of this Court which has given it reality."

The judgment of the Supreme Judicial Court of Massachusetts is reversed.

Justice SCALIA, with whom Justice THOMAS joins, concurring in the judgment.

In my view the challenged Massachusetts pricing order is invalid under our negative-Commerce-Clause jurisprudence.... I do not agree with the reasons assigned by the Court, which seem to me ... a broad expansion of current law. Accordingly, I concur only in the judgment of the Court.

The purpose of the negative Commerce Clause, we have often said, is to create a national market. It does not follow from that, however, and we have never held, that every state law which obstructs a national market violates the Commerce Clause. Yet that is what the Court says today. It seems to have canvassed the entire corpus of negative-Commerce-Clause opinions, culled out every free-market snippet of reasoning, and melded them into the sweeping principle that the Constitution is violated by any state law or regulation that "artificially encourag[es] in-state production even when the same goods could be produced at lower cost in other States."

As the Court seems to appreciate by its eagerness expressly to reserve the question of the constitutionality of subsidies for in-state industry, this expansive view of the Commerce Clause calls into question a wide variety of state laws that have hitherto been thought permissible. It seems to me that a state subsidy would *clearly* be invalid under any formulation of the Court's guiding principle identified above. The Court guardedly asserts that a "pure subsidy funded out of general revenue *ordinarily* imposes no burden on interstate commerce, but merely assists local business," but under its analysis that must be taken to be true only because most local businesses (*e.g.,* the local hardware store) are not competing with businesses out of State. The Court notes that, in funding this subsidy, Massachusetts has taxed milk produced in other States, and thus "not only assists local farmers, but burdens interstate commerce." But the same could be said of almost all subsidies funded from general state revenues, which almost invariably include moneys from use taxes on out-of-state products. And even where the funding does not come in any part from taxes on out-of-state goods, "merely assist[ing]" in-State businesses, unquestionably neutralizes advantages possessed by out-of-state enterprises. Such subsidies, particularly where they are in the form of cash or (what comes to the same thing) tax forgiveness, are often admitted to have as their purpose—*indeed, are nationally advertised as having as their purpose*—making it more profitable to conduct business in-state than elsewhere, *i.e.,* distorting normal market incentives....

"The historical record provides no grounds for reading the Commerce Clause to be other than what it says—an authorization for Congress to regulate commerce." Nonetheless, we formally adopted the doctrine of the negative Commerce Clause 121 years ago, and since then have decided a vast number of negative-Commerce-Clause cases, engendering considerable reliance interests. As a result, I will, on *stare decisis* grounds, enforce a self-executing "negative" Commerce Clause in two situations: (1) against a state law that facially discriminates against interstate commerce, and (2) against a state law that is indistinguishable from a type of law previously held unconstitutional by this Court. Applying this approach—or at least the second part of it—is not always easy, since once one gets beyond facial discrimination our negative-Commerce-Clause jurisprudence becomes (and long has been) a "quagmire." The object should be, however, to produce a clear rule that honors the holdings of our past decisions but declines to extend the rationale that produced those decisions any further....

I would ... allow a State to subsidize its domestic industry so long as it does so from nondiscriminatory taxes that go into the State's general revenue fund. Perhaps, as some commentators contend, that line comports with an important economic reality: A State is less likely to maintain a subsidy when its citizens perceive that the money (in the general fund) is available for any number of competing, nonprotectionist, purposes. That is not, however, the basis for my position, for as THE CHIEF JUSTICE explains, "[a]nalysis of interest group participation in the political process may serve many useful purposes, but serving as a basis for interpreting the dormant Commerce Clause is not one of them." Instead, I draw the line where I do because it is a clear, rational line at the limits of our extant negative-Commerce-Clause jurisprudence.

Chief Justice REHNQUIST, with whom Justice BLACKMUN joins, dissenting.

The Court is less than just in its description of the reasons which lay behind the Massachusetts law which it strikes down. The law undoubtedly sought to aid struggling Massachusetts dairy farmers, beset by steady or declining prices and escalating costs.... The value of agricultural land located near metropolitan areas is driven up by the demand for housing and similar urban uses; distressed farmers eventually sell out to developers. Not merely farm produce is lost, as is the milk production in this case, but, as the Massachusetts Special Commission whose report was the basis for the order in question here found:

"Without the continued existence of dairy farmers, the Commonwealth will lose its supply of locally produced fresh milk, together with the open lands that are used as wildlife refuges, for recreation, hunting, fishing, tourism, and education."

Massachusetts has dealt with this problem by providing a subsidy to aid its beleaguered dairy farmers. In case after case, we have approved the validity under the Commerce Clause of such enactments.... But today the Court relegates these well-established principles to a footnote and, at the same time, gratuitously casts doubt on the validity of state subsidies, observing that "[w]e have never squarely confronted" their constitutionality....

The Court concludes that the combined effect of the milk order "simultaneously burdens interstate commerce and discriminates in favor of local producers." In support of this conclusion, the Court cites ... *Bacchus Imports, Ltd. v. Dias, supra,* as [an example] in which constitutional means were held to have unconstitutional effects on interstate commerce. But ... *Bacchus* [is] a far cry from this case....

In *Bacchus,* the State of Hawaii combined its undisputed power to tax and grant exemptions in a manner that the Court found violative of the Commerce Clause. There, the State exempted a local wine from the burdens of an excise tax levied on all other liquor sales. Despite the Court's strained attempt to compare the scheme in *Bacchus* to the milk order in this case, it is clear that the milk order does not produce the same effect on interstate commerce as the tax exemption in *Bacchus.* ... No decided case supports the Court's conclusion that the negative Commerce Clause prohibits the State from using money that it has lawfully obtained through a neutral tax on milk dealers and distributing it as a subsidy to dairy farmers....

Comments and Questions

1. As in *Hunt*, the Massachusetts pricing order does not distinguish between in-state and out-of-state milk or milk dealers; they all must pay the same assessment. Again, however, the Court finds that Massachusetts is discriminating against interstate commerce in milk. Do you agree with the majority that the Massachusetts' milk system is like Hawaii's tax exemption for Hawaiian made alcoholic beverages? Or do you agree with the dissent that Hawaii's tax exemption is totally distinguishable?

2. What is it about the majority's opinion that stops Justices Scalia and Thomas from concurring in the opinion, even though they both agree that the Massachusetts milk system violates the Commerce Clause? Do you read the majority's opinion to suggest that subsidies for a domestic industry paid from general state revenues would violate the Commerce Clause? If not, what is it about the subsidy here that is unconstitutional?

3. All of the above cases finding discrimination against interstate commerce involve regulatory systems. States can violate the Dormant

Commerce Clause through taxation as well, as the *Bacchus Imports* case discussed in *West Lynn Creamery, Inc. v. Healy* makes clear. Differential fees for assessed materials imported into a state, *see, e.g., Oregon Waste Systems, Inc. v. Department of Environmental Quality*, 511 U.S. 93 (1994), or special taxes imposed on items imported into the state are also facially discriminatory and almost *per se* a violation of the Dormant Commerce Clause. There is, however, one major exception to this general rule. That is a "compensatory use tax." In *Henneford v. Silas Mason Co.*, 300 U.S. 577 (1937), the Supreme Court upheld Washington's tax imposed on the use of goods imported into the state that had not been subject to the state's sales tax. The purpose of the tax was to equalize competition between in-state goods and out-of-state goods, rather than to give a particular benefit to in-state interests. Thus, although this use tax only applied to goods from out-of-state (or else they would already have paid the state sales tax) and thus was discriminatory on its face, the fact that it was intended to equalize competition between the states and was set at the same level as the state sales tax led the Court to view it as not discriminatory in effect.

b. Nondiscriminatory State Laws

Above we have considered discriminatory state laws, and while it is sometimes difficult to discern whether a law is or is not discriminatory, once it is determined to be discriminatory against interstate commerce, then it is usually not difficult to determinate the validity of the law, given the high hurdle it must overcome—there is no less discriminatory means to achieve a legitimate government interest. If a law is not discriminatory, as we have already seen described in cases above, the "test" announced in *Pike v. Bruce Church* is used:

> "Where the statute regulates even-handedly to effectuate a legitimate local public interest, and its effects on interstate commerce are only incidental, it will be upheld unless the burden imposed on such commerce is clearly excessive in relation to the putative local benefits."

MINNESOTA v. CLOVER LEAF CREAMERY CO.

United States Supreme Court, 1981.
449 U.S. 456, 101 S.Ct. 715, 66 L.Ed.2d 659.

Justice BRENNAN delivered the opinion of the Court:

In 1977, the Minnesota Legislature enacted a statute banning the retail sale of milk in plastic nonreturnable, nonrefillable containers, but permitting such sale in other nonreturnable, nonrefillable containers, such as paperboard milk cartons. Respondents[1] contend that the statute

1. Respondents, plaintiffs below, are a Minnesota dairy that owns equipment for producing plastic nonreturnable milk jugs, a Minnesota dairy that leases such equipment, a non-Minnesota company that manufactures such equipment, a Minnesota company that produces plastic nonreturnable milk jugs, a non-Minnesota dairy that

violates the Equal Protection and Commerce Clauses of the Constitution.

The purpose of the Minnesota statute is set out as § 1:

"The legislature finds that the use of nonreturnable, nonrefillable containers for the packaging of milk and other milk products presents a solid waste management problem for the state, promotes energy waste, and depletes natural resources. The legislature therefore, in furtherance of the policies stated in Minnesota Statutes, determines that the use of nonreturnable, nonrefillable containers for packaging milk and other milk products should be discouraged and that the use of returnable and reusable packaging for these products is preferred and should be encouraged."

Section 2 of the Act forbids the retail sale of milk and fluid milk products, other than sour cream, cottage cheese, and yogurt, in nonreturnable, nonrefillable rigid or semi-rigid containers composed at least 50% of plastic.[3]

The Act was introduced with the support of the state Pollution Control Agency, Department of Natural Resources, Department of Agriculture, Consumer Services Division, and Energy Agency, and debated vigorously in both houses of the state legislature. Proponents of the legislation argued that it would promote resource conservation, ease solid waste disposal problems, and conserve energy. Relying on the results of studies and other information, they stressed the need to stop introduction of the plastic nonreturnable container before it became entrenched in the market. Opponents of the Act, also presenting empirical evidence, argued that the Act would not promote the goals asserted by the proponents, but would merely increase costs of retail milk products and prolong the use of ecologically undesirable paperboard milk cartons.

After the Act was passed, respondents filed suit in Minnesota District Court, seeking to enjoin its enforcement. The court conducted extensive evidentiary hearings into the Act's probable consequences, and found the evidence "in sharp conflict." Nevertheless, finding itself "as factfinder ... obliged to weigh and evaluate this evidence," the court resolved the evidentiary conflicts in favor of respondents, and concluded that the Act "will not succeed in effecting the Legislature's published policy goals...." The court further found that, contrary to the statement of purpose in § 1, the "actual basis" for the Act "was to promote the economic interests of certain segments of the local dairy and pulpwood industries at the expense of the economic interests of other segments of the dairy industry and the plastics industry." The court therefore

sells milk products in Minnesota in plastic nonreturnable milk jugs, a Minnesota milk retailer, a non-Minnesota manufacturer of polyethylene resin that sells such resin in many States, including Minnesota, and a plastics industry trade association.

3. Minnesota is apparently the first State so to regulate milk containers.

declared the Act "null, void, and unenforceable" and enjoined its enforcement, basing the judgment on ... equal protection under the Fourteenth Amendment; and prohibition of unreasonable burdens on interstate commerce under Art. I, § 8, of the United States Constitution.

The State appealed to the Supreme Court of Minnesota, which affirmed the District Court on the federal equal protection ... grounds, without reaching the Commerce Clause ... issues. Unlike the District Court, the State Supreme Court found that the purpose of the Act was "to promote the state interests of encouraging the reuse and recycling of materials and reducing the amount and type of material entering the solid waste stream," and acknowledged the legitimacy of this purpose. Nevertheless, relying on the District Court's findings of fact, the full record, and an independent review of documentary sources, the State Supreme Court held that "the evidence conclusively demonstrates that the discrimination against plastic nonrefillables is not rationally related to the Act's objectives." We granted certiorari and now reverse....

[The Court held that it was improper under equal protection analysis for the courts to second-guess legislatures as to the facts underlying the legislative purposes for the statute. Therefore, the Court reversed the determination of the State Supreme Court that the facts did not support the conclusion that the law would further the statute's purposes.]

The District Court also held that the Minnesota statute is unconstitutional under the Commerce Clause because it imposes an unreasonable burden on interstate commerce.[14] We cannot agree.

When legislating in areas of legitimate local concern, such as environmental protection and resource conservation, States are nonetheless limited by the Commerce Clause. If a state law purporting to promote environmental purposes is in reality "simple economic protectionism," we have applied a "virtually *per se* rule of invalidity." *Philadelphia v. New Jersey*. Even if a statute regulates "evenhandedly," and imposes only "incidental" burdens on interstate commerce, the courts must nevertheless strike it down if "the burden imposed on such commerce is clearly excessive in relation to the putative local benefits." *Pike v. Bruce Church, Inc.*, 397 U.S. 137 (1970). Moreover, "the extent of the burden that will be tolerated will of course depend on the nature of the local interest involved, and on whether it could be promoted as well with a lesser impact on interstate activities."

Minnesota's statute does not effect "simple protectionism," but "regulates evenhandedly" by prohibiting all milk retailers from selling their products in plastic, nonreturnable milk containers, without regard to whether the milk, the containers, or the sellers are from outside the

14. The Minnesota Supreme Court did not reach the Commerce Clause issue. The parties and amici have fully briefed and argued the question, and because of the obvious factual connection between the rationality analysis under the Equal Protection Clause and the balancing of interests under the Commerce Clause, we will reach and decide the question.

State. This statute is therefore unlike statutes discriminating against interstate commerce, which we have consistently struck down....

Since the statute does not discriminate between interstate and intrastate commerce, the controlling question is whether the incidental burden imposed on interstate commerce by the Minnesota Act is "clearly excessive in relation to the putative local benefits." We conclude that it is not.

The burden imposed on interstate commerce by the statute is relatively minor. Milk products may continue to move freely across the Minnesota border, and since most dairies package their products in more than one type of containers, the inconvenience of having to conform to different packaging requirements in Minnesota and the surrounding States should be slight. Within Minnesota, business will presumably shift from manufacturers of plastic nonreturnable containers to producers of paperboard cartons, refillable bottles, and plastic pouches, but there is no reason to suspect that the gainers will be Minnesota firms, or the losers out-of-state firms. Indeed, two of the three dairies, the sole milk retailer, and the sole milk container producer challenging the statute in this litigation are Minnesota firms.

Pulpwood producers are the only Minnesota industry likely to benefit significantly from the Act at the expense of out-of-state firms. Respondents point out that plastic resin, the raw material used for making plastic nonreturnable milk jugs, is produced entirely by non-Minnesota firms, while pulpwood, used for making paperboard, is a major Minnesota product. Nevertheless, it is clear that respondents exaggerate the degree of burden on out-of-state interests, both because plastics will continue to be used in the production of plastic pouches, plastic returnable bottles, and paperboard itself, and because out-of-state pulpwood producers will presumably absorb some of the business generated by the Act.

Even granting that the out-of-state plastics industry is burdened relatively more heavily than the Minnesota pulpwood industry, we find that this burden is not "clearly excessive" in light of the substantial state interest in promoting conservation of energy and other natural resources and easing solid waste disposal problems.... We find these local benefits ample to support Minnesota's decision under the Commerce Clause. Moreover, we find that no approach with "a lesser impact on interstate activities," is available. Respondents have suggested several alternative statutory schemes, but these alternatives are either more burdensome on commerce than the Act (as, for example, banning all nonreturnables) or less likely to be effective (as, for example, providing incentives for recycling)....

The judgment of the Minnesota Supreme Court is *Reversed.*

Justice REHNQUIST took no part in the consideration or decision of this case.

Justice POWELL, concurring in part and dissenting in part.

The Minnesota statute at issue bans the retail sale of milk in plastic nonreturnable, nonrefillable containers, but permits such sale in paperboard milk cartons....

I would not ... reach the Commerce Clause issue, but would remand it for consideration by the Supreme Court of Minnesota. The District Court expressly found:

> "12. Despite the purported policy statement published by the legislature as its basis for enacting Chapter 268, the actual basis was to promote the economic interests of certain segments of the local dairy and pulpwood industries at the expense of the economic interests of other segments of the dairy industry and the plastics industry."

At a subsequent point in its opinion, and in even more explicit language, the District Court reiterated its finding that the purpose of the statute related to interstate commerce. These findings were highly relevant to the question whether the statute discriminated against interstate commerce. Indeed, the trial court's findings normally would require us to conclude that the Minnesota Legislature was engaging in such discrimination, as they were not rejected by the Minnesota Supreme Court. That court simply invalidated the statute on [other] grounds, and had no reason to consider the claim of discrimination against interstate commerce.

The Minnesota Supreme Court did accept the *avowed* legislative purpose of the statute.... The Court today reads this statement as an implied rejection of the trial court's specific finding that the "actual [purpose] was to promote the economic interests of certain segments of the local dairy and pulpwood industries at the expense of the economic interests" of the nonresident dairy and plastics industry. In my view, however, the Minnesota Supreme Court was merely assuming that the statute was intended to promote its stated purposes.... In drawing its conclusions, the court included no discussion whatever of the Commerce Clause issue and, certainly, no rejection of the trial court's express and repeated findings concerning the legislature's actual purpose.

I conclude therefore that this Court has no basis for *inferring* a rejection of the quite specific factfindings by the trial court. The Court's decision today, holding that Chapter 268 does not violate the Commerce Clause, is flatly contrary to the only relevant specific findings of fact. Although we are not *barred* from reaching the Commerce Clause issue, in doing so we also act without the benefit of a decision by the highest court of Minnesota on the question. In these circumstances, it is both unnecessary, and in my opinion inappropriate, for this Court to decide the Commerce Clause issue.

Justice STEVENS, dissenting.

[I]n my opinion the Court errs in undertaking to decide the Commerce Clause question at all. The state trial court addressed the question and found that the statute was designed by the Minnesota Legislature to promote the economic interests of the local dairy and pulpwood industries at the expense of competing economic groups. On appeal, the Minnesota Supreme Court expressly declined to consider this aspect of the trial court's decision, and accordingly made no comment at all upon the merits of the Commerce Clause question. Generally, when reviewing state-court decisions, this Court will not decide questions which the highest court of a State has properly declined to address. The majority offers no persuasive explanation for its unusual action in this case. In the absence of some substantial justification for this action, I would not deprive the Minnesota Supreme Court of the first opportunity to review this aspect of the decision of the Minnesota trial court....

Comments and Questions

1. The canonical test for whether a nondiscriminatory state law still violates the Dormant Commerce Clause is the statement in *Pike v. Bruce Church*:

> Where the statute regulates evenhandedly to effectuate a legitimate local public interest, and its effects on interstate commerce are only incidental, it will be upheld unless the burden imposed on such commerce is clearly excessive in relation to the putative local benefits.... If a legitimate local purpose is found, then the question becomes one of degree. And the extent of the burden that will be tolerated will of course depend on the nature of the local interest involved, and on whether it could be promoted as well with a lesser impact on interstate activities.

Applying this test is a less than exact science. As with many balancing tests, different people can end up with different predictions of how a court may rule. The one thing that is for sure is that this test places the burden on those challenging a law to show that the burden not only outweighs, but clearly outweighs, the legitimate benefits. If, however, the law were considered discriminatory, the burden would be on the person trying to uphold the law to show that there was indeed a legitimate local interest and that it could not be achieved in any less discriminatory way. This shift of burden in itself may be decisive. Moreover, courts have generally not given much consideration to whether the interest could be achieved in a less burdensome manner, so long as the law was found non-discriminatory.

2. In *Cloverleaf Creamery* the state trial court concluded in light of the effects of the statute that the purpose was protectionist and therefore invalid under both the Equal Protection Clause and the Commerce Clause. The state supreme court accepted the purported legitimate environmental purpose propounded by the state, but on the basis of the trial court's findings regarding the effects of the law held that the ban on plastic milk jugs would not further the law's purpose and therefore *under the Equal Protection Clause* was invalid. It did not reach the Com-

merce Clause issue. In the portion of the opinion edited out, the Supreme Court rejected the Minnesota Supreme Court's analysis essentially on the basis that in an equal protection challenge to economic regulation courts should not second guess debatable legislative factual determinations. Here, whether or not this law would in fact help to protect the environment was at least debatable. But how does this relate to the Supreme Court's determination of the Commerce Clause issue?

3. What do you think is most important to the Court's decision here—the benefit to the environment or the lack of adverse effect on interstate commerce?

4. Just as discriminatory state taxes can violate the Dormant Commerce Clause, nondiscriminatory state taxes can raise issues under the Clause. In *Complete Auto Transit, Inc. v. Brady*, 430 U.S. 274 (1977), the Court established a four-part test to determine the constitutionality of state taxes under the Commerce Clause:

- the tax must be applied to an activity with a substantial nexus with the taxing state;
- the tax must be fairly apportioned;
- the tax must be nondiscriminatory against interstate commerce; *and*
- the tax must be fairly related to the services provided by the state.

Like the *Pike v. Bruce Church* test, this test does not always lead to predictable results.

c. The Special Case of Transportation

BIBB v. NAVAJO FREIGHT LINES, INC.

United States Supreme Court, 1959.
359 U.S. 520, 79 S.Ct. 962, 3 L.Ed.2d 1003.

Mr. Justice DOUGLAS delivered the opinion of the Court.

We are asked in this case to hold that an Illinois statute requiring the use of a certain type of [contoured] rear fender mudguard on trucks and trailers operated on the highways of that State conflicts with the Commerce Clause of the Constitution....[3]

Appellees, interstate motor carriers holding certificates from the Interstate Commerce Commission, challenged the constitutionality of the Illinois Act. A specially constituted three-judge District Court* concluded that it unduly and unreasonably burdened and obstructed inter-

3. No contention is here made that the statute discriminates against interstate commerce, and it is clear that its provisions apply alike to vehicles in intrastate as well as in interstate commerce.

* At the time of this case, cases challenging the constitutionality of state laws in federal courts were held before a three-judge district court composed of two district court judges and one circuit court judge. Decisions from these court then could be appealed directly to the Supreme Court as of right (as opposed to by petition for certiorari). [author's note]

state commerce, because it made the conventional or straight mudflap, which is legal in at least 45 States, illegal in Illinois, and because the statute, taken together with a Rule of the Arkansas Commerce Commission requiring straight mudflaps, rendered the use of the same motor vehicle equipment in both States impossible. The statute was declared to be violative of the Commerce Clause and appellants were enjoined from enforcing it. An appeal was taken and we noted probable jurisdiction.

The power of the State to regulate the use of its highways is broad and pervasive. We have recognized the peculiarly local nature of this subject of safety, and have upheld state statutes applicable alike to interstate and intrastate commerce, despite the fact that they may have an impact on interstate commerce. The regulation of highways "is akin to quarantine measures, same laws, and like local regulations of rivers, harbors, piers, and docks, with respect to which the state has exceptional scope for the exercise of its regulatory power, and which, Congress not acting, have been sustained even though they materially interfere with interstate commerce."

These safety measures carry a strong presumption of validity when challenged in court. If there are alternative ways of solving a problem, we do not sit to determine which of them is best suited to achieve a valid state objective. Policy decisions are for the state legislature, absent federal entry into the field. Unless we can conclude on the whole record that "the total effect of the law as a safety measure in reducing accidents and casualties is so slight or problematical as not to outweigh the national interest in keeping interstate commerce free from interferences which seriously impede it" we must uphold the statute.

The District Court found that "since it is impossible for a carrier operating in interstate commerce to determine which of its equipment will be used in a particular area, or on a particular day, or days, carriers operating into or through Illinois * * * will be required to equip all their trailers in accordance with the requirements of the Illinois Splash Guard statute." With two possible exceptions the mudflaps required in those States which have mudguard regulations would not meet the standards required by the Illinois statute. The cost of installing the contour mudguards is $30 or more per vehicle. The District Court found that the initial cost of installing those mudguards on all the trucks owned by the appellees ranged from $4,500 to $45,840. There was also evidence in the record to indicate that the cost of maintenance and replacement of these guards is substantial.

Illinois introduced evidence seeking to establish that contour mudguards had a decided safety factor in that they prevented the throwing of debris into the faces of drivers of passing cars and into the windshields of a following vehicle. But the District Court in its opinion stated that it was "conclusively shown that the contour mud flap possesses no advantages over the conventional or straight mud flap previously required in Illinois and presently required in most of the states," and that "there is rather convincing testimony that use of the contour flap creates hazards previously unknown to those using the highways." These hazards were found to be occasioned by the fact that this new type of mudguard tended to cause an accumulation of heat in the brake drum, thus decreasing the effectiveness of brakes, and by the fact that they were susceptible of being hit and bumped when the trucks were backed up and of falling off on the highway.

These findings on cost and on safety are not the end of our problem.... State control of the width and weight of motor trucks and trailers sustained in *South Carolina State Highway Dept. v. Barnwell Bros.*, 303 U.S. 177 (1938), involved nice questions of judgment concerning the need of those regulations so far as the issue of safety was concerned. That case also presented the problem whether interstate motor carriers, who were required to replace all equipment or keep out of the State, suffered an unconstitutional restraint on interstate commerce. The matter of safety was said to be one essentially for the legislative judgment; and the burden of redesigning or replacing equipment was said to be a proper price to exact from interstate and intrastate motor carriers alike.... Cost taken into consideration with other factors might be relevant in some cases to the issue of burden on commerce. But it has assumed no such proportions here. If we had here only a question whether the cost of adjusting an interstate operation to these new local safety regulations prescribed by Illinois unduly burdened interstate commerce, we would have to sustain the law under the authority of [prior] cases. The same result would obtain if we had to resolve the much discussed issues of safety presented in this case.

This case presents a different issue. The equipment in the [prior] cases could pass muster in any State, so far as the records in those cases reveal. We were not faced there with the question whether one State could prescribe standards for interstate carriers that would conflict with the standards of another State, making it necessary, say, for an interstate carrier to shift its cargo to differently designed vehicles once another state line was reached. We had a related problem in *Southern Pacific Co. v. State of Arizona*, 325 U.S. 761 (1945), where the Court invalidated a statute of Arizona prescribing a maximum length of 70 cars for freight trains moving through that State. Those cases indicate the dimensions of our present problem.

An order of the Arkansas Commerce Commission, already mentioned, requires that trailers operating in that State be equipped with straight or conventional mudflaps. Vehicles equipped to meet the standards of the Illinois statute would not comply with Arkansas standards, and vice versa. Thus if a trailer is to be operated in both States, mudguards would have to be interchanged, causing a significant delay in an operation where prompt movement may be of the essence. It was found that from two to four hours of labor are required to install or remove a contour mudguard. Moreover, the contour guard is attached to the trailer by welding and if the trailer is conveying a cargo of explosives (e.g., for the United States Government) it would be exceedingly dangerous to attempt to weld on a contour mudguard without unloading the trailer.

It was also found that the Illinois statute seriously interferes with the "interline" operations of motor carriers—that is to say, with the interchanging of trailers between an originating carrier and another carrier when the latter serves an area not served by the former. These "interline" operations provide a speedy through-service for the shipper. Interlining contemplates the physical transfer of the entire trailer; there is no unloading and reloading of the cargo. The interlining process is particularly vital in connection with shipment of perishables, which would spoil if unloaded before reaching their destination, or with the movement of explosives carried under seal. Of course, if the originating carrier never operated in Illinois, it would not be expected to equip its trailers with contour mudguards. Yet if an interchanged trailer of that carrier were hauled to or through Illinois, the statute would require that it contain contour guards. Since carriers which operate in and through Illinois cannot compel the originating carriers to equip their trailers with contour guards, they may be forced to cease interlining with those who do not meet the Illinois requirements. Over 60 percent of the business of 5 of the 6 plaintiffs is interline traffic. For the other it constitutes 30 percent. All of the plaintiffs operate extensively in interstate commerce, and the annual mileage in Illinois of none of them exceeds 7 percent of total mileage.

This is [a] summary [of] the rather massive showing of burden on interstate commerce which appellees made at the hearing.

Appellants did not attempt to rebut the appellees' showing that the statute in question severely burdens interstate commerce. Appellants' showing was aimed at establishing that contour mudguards prevented the throwing of debris into the faces of drivers of passing cars and into the windshields of a following vehicle. They concluded that, because the Illinois statute is a reasonable exercise of the police power, a federal court is precluded from weighing the relative merits of the contour mudguard against any other kind of mudguard and must sustain the validity of the statute notwithstanding the extent of the burden it imposes on interstate commerce. They rely in the main on *South Carolina State Highway Dept. v. Barnwell Bros.* There is language in that opinion which, read in isolation from such later decisions as *Southern Pacific Co. v. State of Arizona*, would suggest that no showing of burden on interstate commerce is sufficient to invalidate local safety regulations in absence of some element of discrimination against interstate commerce.

The various exercises by the States of their police power stand, however, on an equal footing. All are entitled to the same presumption of validity ... when measured against the Commerce Clause.... Like any local law that conflicts with federal regulatory measures state regulations that run afoul of the policy of free trade reflected in the Commerce Clause must also bow.

This is one of those cases—few in number—where local safety measures that are nondiscriminatory place an unconstitutional burden on interstate commerce. This conclusion is especially underlined by the deleterious effect which the Illinois law will have on the "interline" operation of interstate motor carriers. The conflict between the Arkansas regulation and the Illinois regulation also suggests that this regulation of mudguards is not one of those matters "admitting of diversity of treatment, according to the special requirements of local conditions." ... A State which insists on a design out of line with the requirements of almost all the other States may sometimes place a great burden of delay and inconvenience on those interstate motor carriers entering or crossing its territory. Such a new safety device—out of line with the requirements of the other States—may be so compelling that the innovating State need not be the one to give way. But the present showing—balanced against the clear burden on commerce—is far too inconclusive to make this mudguard meet that test.

We deal not with absolutes but with questions of degree. The state legislatures plainly have great leeway in providing safety regulations for all vehicles—interstate as well as local. Our decisions so hold. Yet the heavy burden which the Illinois mudguard law places on the interstate movement of trucks and trailers seems to us to pass the permissible limits even for safety regulations.

Mr. Justice HARLAN, whom Mr. Justice STEWART joins, concurring.

The opinion of the Court clearly demonstrates the heavy burden, in terms of cost and interference with "interlining," which the Illinois statute here involved imposes on interstate commerce. In view of the findings of the District Court, summarized [in] the Court's opinion and fully justified by the record, to the effect that the contour mudflap "possesses no advantages" in terms of safety over the conventional flap permitted in all other States, and indeed creates certain safety hazards, this heavy burden cannot be justified on the theory that the Illinois statute is a necessary, appropriate, or helpful local safety measure. Accordingly, I concur in the judgment of the Court.

Comments and Questions

1. This section is entitled "the special case of transportation" because with respect to nondiscriminatory laws transportation cases raise special problems. *Bibb* is a good example. There is no suggestion by anyone that Illinois adopts its mudflap rule for any reason other than a good faith belief that it protects motorists from spray and objects thrown from tires on the trailers of large trucks. For whatever reason, its safety engineers believe that contoured mudflaps are preferable to straight mudflaps. If no other state had any mudflap rule, it is clear that Illinois's law would be constitutional, despite the unequivocal findings by the district court that the contoured flaps were less safe, rather than more safe, than straight flaps. However, other states do have mudflap rules. At the time Illinois adopts its rule, apparently 45 states have mudflap rules that allow straight mudflaps, with the result that virtually all large

trucks have straight mudflaps. However, all but two apparently would also allow the contoured mudflaps. Arkansas in particular requires the straight mudflaps. What is a trucker to do? He currently has straight mudflaps, but if he wants to take his trailer to Illinois he will have to replace them. That will be relatively expensive. Nevertheless, the Court suggests that, if this was all that was involved, the Illinois law would be upheld. However, Arkansas *requires* straight mudflaps, just as Illinois *requires* contoured mudflaps. Thus, the poor trucker will have to change mudflaps every time he goes between Arkansas and Illinois, and, even more important to the Court, it will make "interlining" very difficult, because it will be impossible to know which trailers will go where. This leads to an unacceptable burden on interstate commerce.

2. Note that Illinois's law is only unconstitutional because Arkansas has a directly contradictory law. Why is it that Illinois's law is unconstitutional rather than Arkansas's. Could Congress pass a law now requiring contoured mudflaps on all the nation's highways?

3. Obviously, what's special about transportation cases is that trucks, trains, ships, and airplanes are forever crossing state lines, and different state standards applicable to these modes of transportation could wreak havoc with an efficient national transportation system. What is not so obvious is why it is the courts that are supposed to sort out what are the appropriate standards when states disagree rather than Congress or some federal agency. Isn't that what the Commerce Clause was all about—empowering Congress to regulate commerce among the states? Why do you think the Court has taken up this responsibility?

3. THE MARKET PARTICIPANT DOCTRINE

In all of the above Dormant Commerce Clause cases, the state or locality acted as a market regulator. Does it make any difference if the state or locality's restriction on interstate commerce occurs as a market participant?

REEVES, INC. v. STAKE

United States Supreme Court, 1980.
447 U.S. 429, 100 S.Ct. 2271, 65 L.Ed.2d 244.

Mr. Justice BLACKMUN delivered the opinion of the Court.

The issue in this case is whether, consistent with the Commerce Clause, the State of South Dakota, in a time of shortage, may confine the sale of the cement it produces solely to its residents.

In 1919, South Dakota undertook plans to build a cement plant. The project, a product of the State's then prevailing Progressive political movement, was initiated in response to recent regional cement shortages that "interfered with and delayed both public and private enterprises," and that were "threatening the people of this state." In 1920, the South

Dakota Cement Commission anticipated "[t]hat there would be a ready market for the entire output of the plant within the state." The plant, however, ... soon produced more cement than South Dakotans could use. Over the years, buyers in no less than nine nearby States purchased cement from the State's plant. Between 1970 and 1977, some 40% of the plant's output went outside the State.

The plant's list of out-of-state cement buyers included petitioner Reeves, Inc.... For 20 years the relationship between Reeves and the South Dakota cement plant was amicable, uninterrupted, and mutually profitable.

As the 1978 construction season approached, difficulties at the plant slowed production. Meanwhile, a booming construction industry spurred demand for cement both regionally and nationally. The plant found itself unable to meet all orders. Faced with the same type of "serious cement shortage" that inspired the plant's construction, the Commission "reaffirmed its policy of supplying all South Dakota customers first and to honor all contract commitments, with the remaining volume allocated on a first come, first served basis."

Reeves, which had no pre-existing long-term supply contract, was hit hard and quickly by this development.... On July 19, Reeves brought this suit against the Commission, challenging the plant's policy of preferring South Dakota buyers, and seeking injunctive relief. [T]he District Court found no substantial issue of material fact and permanently enjoined the Commission's practice. The court reasoned that South Dakota's "hoarding" was inimical to the national free market envisioned by the Commerce Clause.

The United States Court of Appeals for the Eighth Circuit reversed.... We granted Reeves' petition for certiorari to consider once again. the impact of the Commerce Clause on state proprietary activity.

[In *Hughes v. Alexandria Scrap Corp.*, 426 U.S. 794 (1976) we considered] a Maryland program designed to remove abandoned automobiles from the State's roadways and junkyards. To encourage recycling, a "bounty" was offered for every Maryland-titled junk car converted into scrap.... [T]he ... law imposed more exacting documentation requirements on out-of-state than in-state processors.... Indeed, "[t]he practical effect was substantially the same as if Maryland had withdrawn altogether the availability of bounties on hulks delivered by ... suppliers to ... non-Maryland processors."

Invoking the Commerce Clause, a three-judge District Court struck down the legislation....

This Court reversed.... In the Court's view ... *Alexandria Scrap* did not involve "the kind of action with which the Commerce Clause is concerned." Unlike prior cases voiding state laws inhibiting interstate trade, "Maryland has not sought to prohibit the flow of hulks, or to regulate the conditions under which it may occur. Instead, it has entered into the market itself to bid up their price," "as a purchaser, in effect, of a potential article of interstate commerce," and has restricted "its trade to its own citizens or businesses within the State."

Having characterized Maryland as a market participant, rather than as a market regulator, the Court found no reason to "believe the Commerce Clause was intended to require independent justification for [the State's] action." The Court couched its holding in unmistakably broad terms. "Nothing in the purposes animating the Commerce Clause prohibits a State, in the absence of congressional action, from participating in the market and exercising the right to favor its own citizens over others."

The basic distinction drawn in *Alexandria Scrap* between States as market participants and States as market regulators makes good sense and sound law. As that case explains, the Commerce Clause responds principally to state taxes and regulatory measures impeding free private trade in the national marketplace. There is no indication of a constitutional plan to limit the ability of the States themselves to operate freely in the free market. The precedents comport with this distinction.

Restraint in this area is also counseled by considerations of state sovereignty, the role of each State " 'as guardian and trustee for its people,' " and "the long recognized right of trader or manufacturer, engaged in an entirely private business, freely to exercise his own independent discretion as to parties with whom he will deal."[12] Moreover, state proprietary activities may be, and often are, burdened with the same restrictions imposed on private market participants. Evenhandedness suggests that, when acting as proprietors, States should similarly share existing freedoms from federal constraints, including the inherent limits of the Commerce Clause. Finally, as this case illustrates, the competing considerations in cases involving state proprietary action often will be subtle, complex, politically charged, and difficult to assess under traditional Commerce Clause analysis. Given these factors, *Alexandria Scrap* wisely recognizes that, as a rule, the adjustment of interests in this context is a task better suited for Congress than this Court.

South Dakota, as a seller of cement, unquestionably fits the "market participant" label more comfortably than a State acting to subsidize local scrap processors. Thus, the general rule of *Alexandria Scrap* plainly applies here. Petitioner argues, however, that the exemption for marketplace participation necessarily admits of exceptions. While conceding that possibility, we perceive in this case no sufficient reason to depart from the general rule....

12. When a State buys or sells, it has the attributes of both a political entity and a private business. Nonetheless, the dissent would dismiss altogether the "private business" element of such activity and focus solely on the State's political character. The Court, however, heretofore has recognized that "[l]ike private individuals and businesses, the Government enjoys the unrestricted power to produce its own supplies, to determine those with whom it will deal, and to fix the terms and conditions upon which it will make needed purchases." While acknowledging that there may be limits on this sweepingly phrased principle, we cannot ignore the similarities of private businesses and public entities when they function in the marketplace.

Undaunted by these considerations, petitioner advances [other] arguments for reversal:

"If a state in this union, were allowed to hoard its commodities or resources for the use of their own residents only, a drastic situation might evolve. For example, Pennsylvania or Wyoming might keep their coal, the northwest its timber, and the mining states their minerals. The result being that embargo may be retaliated by embargo and commerce would be halted at state lines." This argument, although rooted in the core purpose of the Commerce Clause, does not fit the present facts. Cement is not a natural resource, like coal, timber, wild game, or minerals. It is the end product of a complex process whereby a costly physical plant and human labor act on raw materials. South Dakota has not sought to limit access to the State's limestone or other materials used to make cement. Nor has it restricted the ability of private firms or sister States to set up plants within its borders. Moreover, petitioner has not suggested that South Dakota possesses unique access to the materials needed to produce cement. Whatever limits might exist on a State's ability to invoke the *Alexandria Scrap* exemption to hoard resources which by happenstance are found there, those limits do not apply here....

Mr. Justice POWELL, with whom Mr. Justice BRENNAN, Mr. Justice WHITE, and Mr. Justice STEVENS join, dissenting.

The South Dakota Cement Commission has ordered that in times of shortage the state cement plant must turn away out-of-state customers until all orders from South Dakotans are filled. This policy represents precisely the kind of economic protectionism that the Commerce Clause was intended to prevent.[1] The Court, however, finds no violation of the Commerce Clause, solely because the State produces the cement. I agree with the Court that the State of South Dakota may provide cement for its public needs without violating the Commerce Clause. But I cannot agree that South Dakota may withhold its cement from interstate commerce in order to benefit private citizens and businesses within the State....

This case presents a novel constitutional question. The Commerce Clause would bar legislation imposing on private parties the type of restraint on commerce adopted by South Dakota.[2] Conversely, a private

1. By "protectionism," I refer to state policies designed to protect private economic interests within the State from the forces of the interstate market. I would exclude from this term policies relating to traditional governmental functions, such as education, and subsidy programs like the one at issue in *Hughes v. Alexandria Scrap Corp.*

2. The Court attempts to distinguish prior decisions that address the Commerce Clause limitations on a State's regulation of natural resource exploitation. The Court contends that cement production, unlike the activities involved in those cases, "is the end product of a complex proces[s] whereby a costly physical plant and human labor act on raw materials." The Court's distinction fails in two respects. First, the principles articulated in the natural resources cases also have been applied in decisions involving agricultural production, notably milk processing. More fundamentally, the Court's definition of cement production describes all sophisticated economic activity, including the exploitation of natural resources. The extraction of natural gas, for example, could hardly occur except through

business constitutionally could adopt a marketing policy that excluded customers who come from another State. This case falls between those polar situations. The State, through its Commission, engages in a commercial enterprise and restricts its own interstate distribution. The question is whether the Commission's policy should be treated like state regulation of private parties or like the marketing policy of a private business.

The application of the Commerce Clause to this case should turn on the nature of the governmental activity involved. If a public enterprise undertakes an "integral operatio[n] in areas of traditional governmental functions," *National League of Cities v. Usery*, the Commerce Clause is not directly relevant. If, however, the State enters the private market and operates a commercial enterprise for the advantage of its private citizens, it may not evade the constitutional policy against economic Balkanization.

This distinction derives from the power of governments to supply their own needs and from the purpose of the Commerce Clause itself, which is designed to protect "the natural functioning of the interstate market." In procuring goods and services for the operation of government, a State may act without regard to the private marketplace and remove itself from the reach of the Commerce Clause. But when a State itself becomes a participant in the private market for other purposes, the Constitution forbids actions that would impede the flow of interstate commerce....

The Court holds that South Dakota, like a private business, should not be governed by the Commerce Clause when it enters the private market. But precisely because South Dakota is a State, it cannot be presumed to behave like an enterprise " 'engaged in an entirely private business.' " A State frequently will respond to market conditions on the basis of political rather than economic concerns. To use the Court's terms, a State may attempt to act as a "market regulator" rather than a "market participant." In that situation, it is a pretense to equate the State with a private economic actor. State action burdening interstate trade is no less state action because it is accomplished by a public agency authorized to participate in the private market....

Unlike the market subsidies at issue in *Alexandria Scrap*, the marketing policy of the South Dakota Cement Commission has cut off interstate trade. The State can raise such a bar when it enters the market to supply its own needs. In order to ensure an adequate supply of cement for public uses, the State can withhold from interstate commerce the cement needed for public projects.

The State, however, has no parallel justification for favoring private, in-state customers over out-of-state customers. In response to political

a "complex process whereby a costly physical plant and human labor act on raw materials." ...

concerns that likely would be inconsequential to a private cement producer, South Dakota has shut off its cement sales to customers beyond its borders. That discrimination constitutes a direct barrier to trade "of the type forbidden by the Commerce Clause, and involved in previous cases...." The effect on interstate trade is the same as if the state legislature had imposed the policy on private cement producers. The Commerce Clause prohibits this severe restraint on commerce....

Comments and Questions

1. Both the majority and the dissent recognize that this case falls between the two endpoints of clear law—the Commerce Clause forbids states to enact protectionist regulatory laws, but the Commerce Clause imposes no limits on whom private companies can choose to deal with. The question in *Reeves* is which of these two endpoints is closer to the facts in that case. The dissent believes it is the former, while the majority believes it is the latter. Which do you think is closer?

2. The majority relies heavily on *Alexandria Scrap*, but the dissent distinguishes that case on the basis that there the state was using state funds to subsidize the scrapping of old automobiles, while here the state, at least by this time, is running the cement plant out of the plant's operating funds. Do you think that is relevant? The dissent also distinguishes producing cement for the state's own needs as opposed to being a market participant, citing *National League of Cities*. Do you recall that case under the Tenth Amendment portion of this chapter? It was overruled in *Garcia v. SAMTA*.

3. The petitioner tries to characterize the facts in *Reeves* as the state hoarding a natural resource, and the majority distinguishes a cement plant from a state's natural resources, such as coal, timber, wild game, or minerals. Do you think restricting the output of the state's cement plant is like hoarding the natural resources in the state? Consider the following case.

SOUTH-CENTRAL TIMBER DEVELOPMENT, INC. v. WUNNICKE

United States Supreme Court, 1984.
467 U.S. 82, 104 S.Ct. 2237, 81 L.Ed.2d 71.

Justice WHITE announced the judgment of the Court and delivered the opinion of the Court with respect to Parts I and II, and an opinion with respect to Parts III and IV, in which Justice BRENNAN, Justice BLACKMUN, and Justice STEVENS joined.

* * *

I

In September 1980, the Alaska Department of Natural Resources published a notice that it would sell approximately 49 million board-feet of timber in the area of Icy Cape, Alaska, on October 23, 1980. The notice of sale, the prospectus, and the proposed contract for the sale all provided, pursuant to [Alaska law] that "[p]rimary manufacture within the State of Alaska will be required as a special provision of the contract." Under the primary-manufacture requirement, the successful bidder must partially process the timber prior to shipping it outside of the State. The requirement is imposed by contract and does not limit the export of unprocessed timber not owned by the State.... When it imposes the requirement, the State charges a significantly lower price for the timber than it otherwise would.

Petitioner, South–Central Timber Development, Inc., is an Alaska corporation engaged in the business of purchasing standing timber, logging the timber, and shipping the logs into foreign commerce, almost exclusively to Japan.... [I]t brought an action in Federal District Court seeking an injunction, arguing that the requirement violated the negative implications of the Commerce Clause. The District Court agreed and issued an injunction. The Court of Appeals for the Ninth Circuit reversed, finding it unnecessary to reach the question whether, standing alone, the requirement would violate the Commerce Clause, because it found implicit congressional authorization in the federal policy of imposing a primary-manufacture requirement on timber taken from federal land in Alaska.

II

[The Court concluded that the fact that Congress imposed a primary-manufacture requirement on timber from federal land in Alaska did not implicitly authorize Alaska to impose a similar requirement with respect to state lands.]

III

We now turn to the issues left unresolved by the Court of Appeals. The first of these issues is whether Alaska's restrictions on export of unprocessed timber from state-owned lands are exempt from Commerce Clause scrutiny under the "market-participant doctrine."

Our cases make clear that if a State is acting as a market participant, rather than as a market regulator, the dormant Commerce Clause places no limitation on its activities. The precise contours of the market-participant doctrine have yet to be established, however, the doctrine having been applied in only three cases of this Court to date.

The first of the cases, *Hughes v. Alexandria Scrap Corp.*, involved a Maryland program designed to reduce the number of junked automobiles in the State. A "bounty" was established on Maryland-licensed junk cars, and the State imposed more stringent documentation requirements on out-of-state scrap processors than on in-state ones. The Court rejected a Commerce Clause attack on the program, although it noted that under traditional Commerce Clause analysis the program might well be invalid because it had the effect of reducing the flow of goods in interstate commerce....

In *Reeves, Inc. v. Stake*, the Court upheld a South Dakota policy of restricting the sale of cement from a state-owned plant to state residents, declaring that "[t]he basic distinction drawn in Alexandria Scrap between States as market participants and States as market regulators makes good sense and sound law." The Court relied upon " 'the long recognized right of trader or manufacturer, engaged in an entirely private business, freely to exercise his own independent discretion as to parties with whom he will deal.' " In essence, the Court recognized the principle that the Commerce Clause places no limitations on a State's refusal to deal with particular parties when it is participating in the interstate market in goods.

The most recent of this Court's cases developing the market-participant doctrine is *White v. Massachusetts Council of Construction Employers, Inc.*, 460 U.S. 204 (1983), in which the Court sustained against a Commerce Clause challenge an executive order of the Mayor of Boston that required all construction projects funded in whole or in part by city funds or city-administered funds to be performed by a work force of at least 50% city residents. The Court rejected the argument that the city was not entitled to the protection of the doctrine because the order had the effect of regulating employment contracts between public contractors and their employees. Recognizing that "there are some limits on a state or local government's ability to impose restrictions that reach beyond the immediate parties with which the government transacts business," the Court found it unnecessary to define those limits because "[e]veryone affected by the order [was], in a substantial if informal sense, 'working for the city.' " The fact that the employees were "working for the city" was "crucial" to the market-participant analysis in *White*.

The State of Alaska contends that its primary-manufacture requirement fits squarely within the market-participant doctrine, arguing that "Alaska's entry into the market may be viewed as precisely the same type of subsidy to local interests that the Court found unobjectionable in *Alexandria Scrap*." However, when Maryland became involved in the scrap market it was as a purchaser of scrap; Alaska, on the other hand, participates in the timber market, but imposes conditions downstream in the timber-processing market. Alaska is not merely subsidizing local timber processing in an amount "roughly equal to the difference between the price the timber would fetch in the absence of such a requirement and the amount the state actually receives." If the State directly subsidized the timber-processing industry by such an amount, the purchaser would retain the option of taking advantage of the subsidy by processing timber in the State or forgoing the benefits of the subsidy and exporting unprocessed timber. Under the Alaska requirement, however, the choice is made for him: if he buys timber from the State he is not free to take the timber out of state prior to processing.

The State also would have us find *Reeves* controlling. It states that

"*Reeves* made it clear that the Commerce Clause imposes no limitation on Alaska's power to choose the terms on which it will sell its timber." Such an unrestrained reading of *Reeves* is unwarranted. Although the Court in *Reeves* did strongly endorse the right of a State to deal with whomever it chooses when it participates in the market, it did not—and did not purport to—sanction the imposition of any terms that the State might desire. For example, the Court expressly noted in *Reeves* that Commerce Clause scrutiny may well be more rigorous when a restraint on foreign commerce is alleged; that a natural resource "like coal, timber, wild game, or minerals," was not involved, but instead the cement was "the end product of a complex process whereby a costly physical plant and human labor act on raw materials,"; and that South Dakota did not bar resale of South Dakota cement to out-of-state purchasers. In this case, all three of the elements that were not present in *Reeves*—foreign commerce, a natural resource, and restrictions on resale—are present.

Finally, Alaska argues that since the Court in *White* upheld a requirement that reached beyond "the boundary of formal privity of contract," then, a fortiori, the primary-manufacture requirement is permissible, because the State is not regulating contracts for resale of timber or regulating the buying and selling of timber, but is instead "a seller of timber, pure and simple." Yet it is clear that the State is more than merely a seller of timber. In the commercial context, the seller usually has no say over, and no interest in, how the product is to be used after sale; in this case, however, payment for the timber does not end the obligations of the purchaser, for, despite the fact that the purchaser has taken delivery of the timber and has paid for it, he cannot do with it as he pleases. Instead, he is obligated to deal with a stranger to the contract after completion of the sale.

That privity of contract is not always the outer boundary of permissible state activity does not necessarily mean that the Commerce Clause has no application within the boundary of formal privity. The market-participant doctrine permits a State to influence "a discrete, identifiable class of economic activity in which [it] is a major participant." *White*. Contrary to the State's contention, the doctrine is not carte blanche to impose any conditions that the State has the economic power to dictate, and does not validate any requirement merely because the State imposes it upon someone with whom it is in contractual privity.

The limit of the market-participant doctrine must be that it allows a State to impose burdens on commerce within the market in which it is a participant, but allows it to go no further. The State may not impose conditions, whether by statute, regulation, or contract, that have a substantial regulatory effect outside of that particular market. Unless the "market" is relatively narrowly defined, the doctrine has the potential of swallowing up the rule that States may not impose substantial burdens on interstate commerce even if they act with the permissible state purpose of fostering local industry....

There are sound reasons for distinguishing between a State's preferring its own residents in the initial disposition of goods when it is a market participant and a State's attachment of restrictions on dispositions subsequent to the goods coming to rest in private hands. First, simply as a matter of intuition a state market participant has a greater interest as a "private trader" in the immediate transaction than it has in what its purchaser does with the goods after the State no longer has an interest in them....

Second, downstream restrictions have a greater regulatory effect than do limitations on the immediate transaction. Instead of merely choosing its own trading partners, the State is attempting to govern the private, separate economic relationships of its trading partners; that is, it restricts the post-purchase activity of the purchaser, rather than merely the purchasing activity. In contrast to the situation in *White*, this restriction on private economic activity takes place after the completion of the parties' direct commercial obligations, rather than during the course of an ongoing commercial relationship in which the city retained a continuing proprietary interest in the subject of the contract. In sum, the State may not avail itself of the market-participant doctrine to immunize its downstream regulation of the timber-processing market in which it is not a participant....

IV

[Justice White then concluded that the primary-manufacture requirement substantially burdened foreign commerce and thus was prohibited by the Dormant Commerce Clause.]

Justice MARSHALL took no part in the decision of this case.

Justice BRENNAN, concurring.

I join Justice White's opinion in full because I believe Alaska's in-state processing requirement constitutes market regulation that is not authorized by Congress. In my view, Justice WHITE's treatment of the market-participant doctrine and the response of Justice REHNQUIST point up the inherent weakness of the doctrine.

Justice POWELL, with whom THE CHIEF JUSTICE joins, concurring in part and concurring in the judgment.

I join Parts I and II of Justice WHITE's opinion. I would remand the case to the Court of Appeals to allow that court to consider whether Alaska was acting as a "market participant" and whether Alaska's primary-manufacture requirement substantially burdened interstate commerce under the holding of *Pike v. Bruce Church, Inc.*

Justice REHNQUIST, with whom Justice O'CONNOR joins, dissenting.

In my view, the line of distinction drawn in the plurality opinion between the State as market participant and the State as market regulator is both artificial and unconvincing. The plurality draws this line "simply as a matter of intuition," but then seeks to bolster its intuition through a series of remarks more appropriate to antitrust law than to the Commerce Clause.[1] For example, the plurality complains that the State is using its "leverage" in the timber market to distort consumer choice in the timber-processing market, a classic example of a tying arrangement. And the plurality cites the common-law doctrine of restraints on alienation and the antitrust limits on vertical restraints in dismissing the State's claim that it could accomplish exactly the same result in other ways.

Perhaps the State's actions do raise antitrust problems. But what the plurality overlooks is that the antitrust laws apply to a State only when it is acting as a market participant. When the State acts as a market regulator, it is immune from antitrust scrutiny. Of course, the line of distinction in cases under the Commerce Clause need not necessarily parallel the line drawn in antitrust law. But the plurality can hardly justify placing Alaska in the market-regulator category, in this Commerce Clause case, by relying on antitrust cases that are relevant only if the State is a market participant.

The contractual term at issue here no more transforms Alaska's sale of timber into "regulation" of the processing industry than the resident-hiring preference imposed by the city of Boston in *White* constituted regulation of the construction industry. Alaska is merely paying the buyer of the timber indirectly, by means of a reduced price, to hire Alaska residents to process the timber. Under existing precedent, the State could accomplish that same result in any number of ways. For example, the State could choose to sell its timber only to those companies that maintain active primary-processing plants in Alaska. *Reeves*. Or the State could directly subsidize the primary-processing industry within the State. *Hughes v. Alexandria Scrap Corp*. The State could even pay to have the logs processed and then enter the market only to sell processed logs. It seems to me unduly formalistic to conclude that the one path chosen by the State as best suited to promote its concerns is the path forbidden it by the Commerce Clause.

Comments and Questions

1. Count the votes in this case. Is there an opinion for the Court on the Market Participant Doctrine? What does Justice Brennan mean by saying that Justice White's treatment of the Market Participant Doctrine and Justice Rehnquist's response point up the inherent weakness of the doctrine?

1. The plurality does offer one other reason for its demarcation of the boundary between these two concepts. "[D]ownstream restrictions have a greater regulatory effect than do limitations on the immediate transaction. Instead of merely choosing its own trading partners, the State is attempting to govern the private, separate economic relationships of its trading partners; that in it restricts the post-purchase activity of the purchaser, rather than merely the purchasing activity." But, of course, this is not a "reason" at all, but merely a restatement of the conclusion. The line between participation and regulation is what we are trying to determine. To invoke that very distinction in support of the line drawn is merely to fall back again on intuition.

2. Note that *Reeves* was a 5–4 decision, with Justice Blackmun writing the majority opinion, but in *Wunnicke* Justice Blackmun joins the *Reeves*' dissenters. Recall that it was Justice Blackmun who defected from the 5–4 majority of *National League of Cities v. Usery* to write the opinion in *Garcia v. SAMTA* overruling *National League of Cities*. Is this another signal of the judicial conversion of Justice Blackmun from a "conservative" to a "liberal" justice?

3. *Wunnicke* involves a state's natural resources. Is that what results in a different outcome from *Reeves*? When *Reeves* referred to a state's natural resources, was it referring to resources actually owned by the state, or was it referring to natural resources that simply happened to be found within the state? Here the timber was actually owned by the state.

4. Justice Rehnquist's dissent points out that private employers can, and sometimes do, impose "downstream conditions" on customers, although under certain circumstances such tying arrangements may run afoul of the antitrust laws. Why does the majority not treat Alaska like such a private employer?

5. Do you find it strange that the federal government by statute would restrict sales of federal timber in Alaska to persons who would process it in Alaska, and yet the Court finds no federal approval of Alaska making an identical restriction for state-owned timber?

6. Justice Rehnquist's last paragraph identifies certain ways Alaska could reach the same result without running afoul of the Dormant Commerce Clause. Why then should the Dormant Commerce Clause prohibit this particular way? In our past cases, have we ever seen before the Court strike down a law whose result could have been achieved through a different means?

UNITED HAULERS ASS'N v. ONEIDA–HERKIMER SOLID WASTE MANAGEMENT AUTHORITY

United States Supreme Court, 2007.
127 S.Ct. 1786, 167 L.Ed.2d 655.

Chief Justice ROBERTS delivered the opinion of the Court, except as to Part II–D.

"Flow control" ordinances require trash haulers to deliver solid waste to a particular waste processing facility. In *C & A Carbone, Inc. v. Clarkstown*, this Court struck down under the Commerce Clause a flow control ordinance that forced haulers to deliver waste to a particular *private* processing facility. In this case, we face flow control ordinances quite similar to the one invalidated in *Carbone*. The only salient difference is that the laws at issue here require haulers to bring waste to facilities owned and operated by a state-created public benefit corporation. We find this difference constitutionally significant. Disposing of trash has been a traditional government activity for years, and laws that favor the government in such areas—but treat every private business, whether in-state or out-of-state, exactly the same—do not discriminate against interstate commerce for purposes of the Commerce Clause. Applying the Commerce Clause test reserved for regulations that do not discriminate against interstate commerce, we uphold these ordinances because any incidental burden they may have on interstate commerce does not outweigh the benefits they confer on the citizens of Oneida and Herkimer Counties.

I

[R]esponding to [a number of local] problems involving the disposal of solid waste, the Counties requested and New York's Legislature and Governor created the Oneida–Herkimer Solid Waste Management Authority (Authority), a public benefit corporation....

In 1989, the Authority and the Counties entered into a Solid Waste Management Agreement, under which the Authority agreed to manage all solid waste within the Counties. Private haulers would remain free to pick up citizens' trash from the curb, but the Authority would take over the job of processing the trash, sorting it, and sending it off for disposal. To fulfill its part of the bargain, the Authority agreed to purchase and develop facilities for the processing and disposal of solid waste and recyclables generated in the Counties.

The Authority collected "tipping fees"[1] to cover its operating and maintenance costs for these facilities. The tipping fees significantly exceeded those charged for waste removal on the open market, but they allowed the Authority to do more than the average private waste disposer. In addition to landfill transportation and solid waste disposal, the fees enabled the Authority to provide recycling of 33 kinds of materials, as well as composting, household hazardous waste disposal, and a number of other services....

As described, the agreement had a flaw: Citizens might opt to have their waste hauled to facilities with lower tipping fees. To avoid being stuck with the bill for facilities that citizens voted for but then chose not to use, the Counties enacted "flow control" ordinances requiring that all solid waste generated within the Counties be delivered to the Authority's processing sites. Private haulers must obtain a permit from the Authority to collect waste in the Counties. Penalties for noncompliance with the ordinances include permit revocation, fines, and imprisonment.

Petitioners are United Haulers Association, Inc., a trade association made up of solid waste management companies, and six haulers that operated in Oneida and Herkimer Counties when this action was filed. In 1995, they sued the Counties and the Authority ..., alleging that the flow control laws violate the Commerce Clause by discriminating against

1. Tipping fees are disposal charges levied against collectors who drop off waste at a processing facility. They are called "tipping" fees because garbage trucks literally tip their back end to dump out the carried waste....

interstate commerce. They submitted evidence that without the flow control laws and the associated $86–per-ton tipping fees, they could dispose of solid waste at out-of-state facilities for between $37 and $55 per ton, including transportation.

The District Court read our decision in *Carbone* as categorically rejecting nearly all flow control laws. The court ruled in the haulers' favor, enjoining enforcement of the Counties' laws. The Second Circuit reversed.... Because the Sixth Circuit had recently issued a conflicting decision holding that a flow control ordinance favoring a public entity *does* facially discriminate against interstate commerce, we granted certiorari.

II

A

[T]o determine whether a law violates this so-called "dormant" aspect of the Commerce Clause, we first ask whether it discriminates on its face against interstate commerce. In this context, " 'discrimination' simply means differential treatment of in-state and out-of-state economic interests that benefits the former and burdens the latter." Discriminatory laws motivated by "simple economic protectionism" are subject to a "virtually *per se* rule of invalidity," which can only be overcome by a showing that the State has no other means to advance a legitimate local purpose.

B

[T]he haulers argue vigorously that the Counties' ordinances discriminate against interstate commerce under *Carbone*.... [There the] Court struck down the ordinance, holding that it discriminated against interstate commerce by "hoard[ing] solid waste, and the demand to get rid of it, for the benefit of the preferred processing facility." ...

The *Carbone* majority viewed Clarkstown's flow control ordinance as "just one more instance of local processing requirements that we long have held invalid." It then cited six local processing cases, every one of which involved discrimination in favor of *private* enterprise. The Court's own description of the cases acknowledges that the "offending local laws hoard a local resource—be it meat, shrimp, or milk—for the benefit of *local businesses* that treat it." If the Court were extending this line of local processing cases to cover discrimination in favor of local government, one would expect it to have said so....

C

The flow control ordinances in this case benefit a clearly public facility, while treating all private companies exactly the same. Because the question is now squarely presented on the facts of the case before us, we decide that such flow control ordinances do not discriminate against interstate commerce for purposes of the dormant Commerce Clause.

Compelling reasons justify treating these laws differently from laws favoring particular private businesses over their competitors. [S]tates and municipalities are not private businesses—far from it. Unlike private enterprise, government is vested with the responsibility of protecting the health, safety, and welfare of its citizens. These important responsibilities set state and local government apart from a typical private business.

Given these differences, it does not make sense to regard laws favoring local government and laws favoring private industry with equal skepticism. As our local processing cases demonstrate, when a law favors in-state business over out-of-state competition, rigorous scrutiny is appropriate because the law is often the product of "simple economic protectionism." Laws favoring local government, by contrast, may be directed toward any number of legitimate goals unrelated to protectionism. Here the flow control ordinances enable the Counties to pursue particular policies with respect to the handling and treatment of waste generated in the Counties, while allocating the costs of those policies on citizens and businesses according to the volume of waste they generate.

The contrary approach of treating public and private entities the same under the dormant Commerce Clause would lead to unprecedented and unbounded interference by the courts with state and local government. The dormant Commerce Clause is not a roving license for federal courts to decide what activities are appropriate for state and local government to undertake, and what activities must be the province of private market competition. In this case, the citizens of Oneida and Herkimer Counties have chosen the government to provide waste management services, with a limited role for the private sector in arranging for transport of waste from the curb to the public facilities. The citizens could have left the entire matter for the private sector, in which case any regulation they undertook could not discriminate against interstate commerce. But it was also open to them to vest responsibility for the matter with their government, and to adopt flow control ordinances to support the government effort. It is not the office of the Commerce Clause to control the decision of the voters on whether government or the private sector should provide waste management services.

We should be particularly hesitant to interfere with the Counties' efforts under the guise of the Commerce Clause because "[w]aste disposal is both typically and traditionally a local government function." ...

Finally, it bears mentioning that the most palpable harm imposed by the ordinances—more expensive trash removal—is likely to fall upon the very people who voted for the laws. Our dormant Commerce Clause cases often find discrimination when a State shifts the costs of regulation to other States, because when "the burden of state regulation falls on interests outside the state, it is unlikely to be alleviated by the operation of those political restraints normally exerted when interests within the state are affected." ...

We hold that the Counties' flow control ordinances, which treat in-state private business interests exactly the same as out-of-state ones, do not "discriminate against interstate commerce" for purposes of the dormant Commerce Clause.[7]

D

The Counties' flow control ordinances are properly analyzed under the test set forth in *Pike v. Bruce Church, Inc*.... Under the *Pike* test, we will uphold a nondiscriminatory statute like this one "unless the burden imposed on [interstate] commerce is clearly excessive in relation to the putative local benefits."

After years of discovery, both the Magistrate Judge and the District Court could not detect *any* disparate impact on out-of-state as opposed to in-state businesses.... We find it unnecessary to decide whether the ordinances impose any incidental burden on interstate commerce because any arguable burden does not exceed the public benefits of the ordinances.

The ordinances give the Counties a convenient and effective way to finance their integrated package of waste-disposal services. While "revenue generation is not a local interest that can justify *discrimination* against interstate commerce," we think it is a cognizable benefit for purposes of the *Pike* test.

At the same time, the ordinances are more than financing tools. They increase recycling ..., conferring significant health and environmental benefits upon the citizens of the Counties. For these reasons, any arguable burden the ordinances impose on interstate commerce does not exceed their public benefits....

Justice SCALIA, concurring in part.

I join Part I and Parts II–A through II–C of the Court's opinion. I write separately to reaffirm my view that "the so-called 'negative' Commerce Clause is an unjustified judicial invention, not to be expanded beyond its existing domain."

I am unable to join Part II–D of the principal opinion, in which the plurality performs so-called "*Pike* balancing." Generally speaking, the balancing of various values is left to Congress—which is precisely what the Commerce Clause (the *real* Commerce Clause) envisions.

Justice THOMAS, concurring in the judgment.

I concur in the judgment. Although I joined *C & A Carbone, Inc. v. Clarkstown,* I no longer believe it was correctly decided. The negative

7. The Counties and their amicus were asked at oral argument if affirmance would lead to the "Oneida–Herkimer Hamburger Stand," accompanied by a "flow control" law requiring citizens to purchase their burgers only from the state-owned producer. We doubt it.... Recognizing that local government may facilitate a customary and traditional government function such as waste disposal, without running afoul of the Commerce Clause, is hardly a prescription for state control of the economy. In any event, Congress retains authority under the Commerce Clause as written to regulate interstate commerce, whether engaged in by private or public entities....

Commerce Clause has no basis in the Constitution and has proved unworkable in practice. As the debate between the majority and dissent shows, application of the negative Commerce Clause turns solely on policy considerations, not on the Constitution. Because this Court has no policy role in regulating interstate commerce, I would discard the Court's negative Commerce Clause jurisprudence....

Because I believe that the power to regulate interstate commerce is a power given to Congress and not the Court, I concur in the judgment of the Court.

Justice ALITO, with whom Justice STEVENS and Justice KENNEDY join, dissenting.

In *C & A Carbone, Inc. v. Clarkstown,* we held that "a so-called flow control ordinance, which require[d] all solid waste to be processed at a designated transfer station before leaving the municipality," discriminated against interstate commerce and was invalid under the Commerce Clause because it "depriv[ed] competitors, including out-of-state firms, of access to a local market." Because the provisions challenged in this case are essentially identical to the ordinance invalidated in *Carbone,* I respectfully dissent....

This case cannot be meaningfully distinguished from *Carbone*. As the Court itself acknowledges, "[t]he only salient difference" between the cases is that the ordinance invalidated in *Carbone* discriminated in favor of a privately owned facility, whereas the laws at issue here discriminate in favor of "facilities owned and operated by a state-created public benefit corporation." The Court relies on the distinction between public and private ownership to uphold the flow-control laws, even though a straightforward application of *Carbone* would lead to the opposite result. The public-private distinction drawn by the Court is both illusory and without precedent.

The fact that the flow control laws at issue discriminate in favor of a government-owned enterprise does not meaningfully distinguish this case from *Carbone*. The preferred facility in *Carbone* was, to be sure, nominally owned by a private contractor who had built the facility on the town's behalf, but it would be misleading to describe the facility as private. In exchange for the contractor's promise to build the facility for the town free of charge and then to sell it to the town five years later for $1, the town guaranteed that, during the first five years of the facility's existence, the contractor would receive "a minimum waste flow of 120,000 tons per year" and that the contractor could charge an above-market tipping fee. If the facility "received less than 120,000 tons in a year, the town [would] make up the tipping fee deficit." To prevent residents, businesses, and trash haulers from taking their waste elsewhere in pursuit of lower tipping fees (leaving the town responsible for covering any shortfall in the contractor's guaranteed revenue stream), the town enacted an ordinance "requir[ing] all nonhazardous solid waste within the town to be deposited at" the preferred facility.

This Court observed that "[t]he object of this arrangement was to amortize the cost of the transfer station: The town would finance *its new facility* with the income generated by the tipping fees." "In other words," the Court explained, "the flow control ordinance [wa]s a financing measure," for what everyone—including the Court—regarded as *the town's* new transfer station.

The only real difference between the facility at issue in *Carbone* and its counterpart in this case is that title to the former had not yet formally passed to the municipality. The Court exalts form over substance in adopting a test that turns on this technical distinction, particularly since, barring any obstacle presented by state law, the transaction in *Carbone* could have been restructured to provide for the passage of title at the beginning, rather than the end, of the 5–year period.

In any event, we have never treated discriminatory legislation with greater deference simply because the entity favored by that legislation was a government-owned enterprise.... The Court has long subjected discriminatory legislation to strict scrutiny, and has never, until today, recognized an exception for discrimination in favor of a state-owned entity....

Nor has this Court ever suggested that discriminatory legislation favoring a state-owned enterprise is entitled to favorable treatment. To be sure, state-owned entities are accorded special status under the market-participant doctrine. But that doctrine is not applicable here.

Under the market-participant doctrine, a State is permitted to exercise " 'independent discretion as to parties with whom [it] will deal.' " The doctrine thus allows States to engage in certain otherwise-discriminatory practices (*e.g.,* selling exclusively to, or buying exclusively from, the State's own residents), so long as the State is "acting as a market participant, *rather than as a market regulator,*" *South-Central Timber Development, Inc. v. Wunnicke.*

Respondents are doing exactly what the market-participant doctrine says they cannot: While acting as market participants by operating a fee-for-service business enterprise in an area in which there is an established interstate market, respondents are also regulating that market in a discriminatory manner and claiming that their special governmental status somehow insulates them from a dormant Commerce Clause challenge.

Respondents insist that the market-participant doctrine has no application here because they are not asserting a defense under the market-participant doctrine, but that argument misses the point. Regardless of whether respondents can assert a defense under the market-participant doctrine, this Court's cases make clear that States cannot discriminate against interstate commerce unless they are acting solely as market participants. Today, however, the Court suggests, contrary to its prior holdings, that States can discriminate in favor of in-state interests while acting both as a market participant *and* as a market regulator.

Despite precedent condemning discrimination in favor of government-owned enterprises, the Court attempts to develop a logical justification for the rule it creates today. That justification rests on three principal assertions. First, the Court insists that it simply "does not make sense to regard laws favoring local government and laws favoring private industry with equal skepticism," because the latter are "often the product of 'simple economic protectionism,'" while the former "may be directed toward any number of legitimate goals unrelated to protectionism." Second, the Court reasons that deference to legislation discriminating in favor of a municipal landfill is especially appropriate considering that "'[w]aste disposal is both typically and traditionally a local government function.'" Third, the Court suggests that respondents' flow-control laws are not discriminatory because they "treat in-state private business interests exactly the same as out-of-state ones." I find each of these arguments unpersuasive....

Comments and Questions

1. *United Haulers* is not a Market Participant Doctrine case. The majority never refers to it. Instead, it is the dissent that raises the doctrine. Why does the dissent raise that issue?

2. Do you understand why the counties could not use the Market Participant Doctrine to defend their action despite the fact that they indeed were a market participant in supplying waste management services?

3. Justices Breyer, Ginsburg, and Souter, who are generally considered "liberals," were the justices who fully joined the opinion of Chief Justice Roberts, who is generally considered "conservative." Justice Stevens is definitely considered "liberal," but he joins the dissent authored by Justice Alito, who is generally considered "conservative." Does this suggest a problem with these labels?

4. Note that the majority holds that a facially discriminatory law favoring a "public" entity is exempt from the test applicable to discriminatory laws under the Dormant Commerce Clause. Four of these justices, however, hold that the *Pike v. Bruce Church* test for non-discriminatory laws still applies. What is it about the "publicness" of the entity receiving the benefit of the discrimination that exempts it from one Dormant Commerce Clause test but leaves it subject to another one?

5. Consider the dissent's discussion of *Wunnicke*. Does the majority essentially overrule the plurality opinion in *Wunnicke*? Does the dissent recognize that the language it quotes from *Wunnicke* was not subscribed to by a majority of the Court?

6. Justice Thomas would make a lot of law students happy by simply eliminating the Dormant Commerce Clause altogether, because, as he says, there is no textual basis for it in the Constitution. He is right on that score, is he not? If so, why is it that no other justice seems inclined to go along with him? Do they think there is a textual basis for it, or is there another reason?

B. THE PRIVILEGES AND IMMUNITIES CLAUSE

There are actually two Privileges and Immunities Clauses in the Constitution. One is Article IV, Section 2, Clause 1: The citizens of each state shall be entitled to all privileges and immunities of citizens in the several states. The other is the second sentence of Section 1 of the Fourteenth Amendment: No state shall make or enforce any law which shall abridge the privileges or immunities of citizens of the United States. In a course dealing with constitutional rights, the latter clause is addressed. Here we deal with the former clause, because of its similarity to the Dormant Commerce Clause in terms of judicial oversight of a national common market.

The Privileges and Immunities Clause of Article IV has its origin in an almost identical provision in the Articles of Confederation, and there as here it means that a state cannot deny to the citizens of another state the privileges and immunities enjoyed by its own citizens. Or, stated another way, one state cannot discriminate against the citizens of another state with respect to the privileges and immunities enjoyed by its own citizens. This prohibited discrimination against out-of-staters is one of the factors that makes this clause similar to the Dormant Commerce Clause. Another similarity is that a local ordinance discriminating against persons from outside that locality (and therefore necessarily someone from outside the state) can violate the Privileges and Immunities Clause. *See, e.g., United Building & Construction Trades Council v. Mayor and Council of Camden*, 465 U.S. 208 (1984) (local ordinance required city contractors to have at least 40% of their employees be residents of the city).

The two major issues that arise under the Privileges and Immunities Clause are: 1) what are privileges and immunities, and 2) what constitutes prohibited discrimination with respect to those privileges and immunities, as opposed to legitimate differentiation. Recall that under the Dormant Commerce Clause discrimination against interstate commerce is not necessarily unconstitutional, even though it imposes a very difficult test for the law to meet in order to save its constitutionality.

The Supreme Court often refers to a formulation of privileges and immunities made by Justice Bushrod Washington, sitting as a circuit judge in *Corfield v. Coryell*, 6 F. Cas. 546, 551 (C.C.E.D. Pa. 1823):

> We feel no hesitation in confining these expressions to those privileges and immunities which are, in their nature, fundamental; which belong, of right, to the citizens of all free governments; and which have, at all times, been enjoyed by the citizens of the several states which compose this Union, from the time of their becoming free, independent, and sovereign. What these fundamental principles are, it would perhaps be more tedious than difficult to enumerate. They may, however, be all comprehended under the following general heads: Protection by the government; the enjoyment of life and liberty, with the right

> to acquire and possess property of every kind, and to pursue and obtain happiness and safety; subject nevertheless to such restraints as the government may justly prescribe for the general good of the whole. The right of a citizen of one state to pass through, or to reside in any other state, for purposes of trade, agriculture, professional pursuits, or otherwise; to claim the benefit of the writ of habeas corpus; to institute and maintain actions of any kind in the courts of the state; to take, hold and dispose of property, either real or personal; and an exemption from higher taxes or impositions than are paid by the other citizens of the state; may be mentioned as some of the particular privileges and immunities of citizens, which are clearly embraced by the general description of privileges deemed to be fundamental.... These, and many others which might be mentioned, are, strictly speaking, privileges and immunities, and the enjoyment of them by the citizens of each state, in every other state, was manifestly calculated (to use the expressions of the preamble of the corresponding provision in the old articles of confederation) "the better to secure and perpetuate mutual friendship and intercourse among the people of the different states of the Union."

The Court has from time-to-time pointed to one or another of Justice Washington's examples to rule that something was a protected privilege or immunity, but the most common example referred to is "[t]he right of a citizen of one state to pass through, or to reside in any other state, for purposes of trade, agriculture, professional pursuits, or otherwise." Sometimes this is referred to as the right to engage in or pursue a "common calling." *See, e.g.*, *Hicklin v. Orbeck*, 437 U.S. 518 (1978) (Alaskan law giving preference to residents in hiring for work on oil or gas pipelines in the state discriminated against the right to engage in a common calling); *Toomer v. Witsell*, 334 U.S. 385 (1948) (South Carolina's restriction of commercial shrimp fishing to residents of the state discriminated against the right to engage in a common calling). *Compare Baldwin v. Fish & Game Commn. of Montana*, 436 U.S. 371 (1978) ("[w]hatever rights or activities may be 'fundamental' under the Privileges and Immunities Clause, ... [recreational] elk hunting by nonresidents in Montana is not one of them").

The following case addresses both what is a privilege and immunity and what circumstances might justify a state treating out-of-state citizens differently from its own citizens with respect to their "privileges and immunities."

SUPREME COURT OF NEW HAMPSHIRE v. PIPER

United States Supreme Court, 1985.
470 U.S. 274, 105 S.Ct. 1272, 84 L.Ed.2d 205.

Justice POWELL delivered the opinion of the Court.

The Rules of the Supreme Court of New Hampshire limit bar admission to state residents. We here consider whether this restriction violates the Privileges and Immunities Clause of the United States Constitution, Art. IV, § 2.

Kathryn Piper lives in Lower Waterford, Vermont, about 400 yards from the New Hampshire border. In 1979, she applied to take the February 1980 New Hampshire bar examination.... She was allowed to take, and passed, the examination. Piper was informed by the Board that she would have to establish a home address in New Hampshire prior to being sworn in.

On May 7, 1980, Piper requested from the Clerk of the New Hampshire Supreme Court a dispensation from the residency requirement.... On May 13, 1980, the Clerk informed Piper that her request had been denied....

On March 22, 1982, Piper filed this action in the United States District Court for the District of New Hampshire. She named as defendants the State Supreme Court, its five Justices, and its Clerk. She alleged that Rule 42 of the New Hampshire Supreme Court, that excludes nonresidents from the bar, violates the Privileges and Immunities Clause of Art. IV, § 2, of the United States Constitution.

On May 17, 1982, the District Court granted Piper's motion for summary judgment.... An evenly divided Court of Appeals for the First Circuit, sitting en banc, affirmed the judgment in favor of Piper....

The Supreme Court of New Hampshire filed a timely notice of appeal, and we noted probable jurisdiction. We now affirm the judgment of the court below.

Article IV, § 2, of the Constitution provides that the "Citizens of each State shall be entitled to all Privileges and Immunities of Citizens in the several States."[6] This Clause was intended to "fuse into one Nation a collection of independent, sovereign States." Recognizing this purpose, we have held that it is "[o]nly with respect to those 'privileges' and 'immunities' bearing on the vitality of the Nation as a single entity" that a State must accord residents and nonresidents equal treatment. *Baldwin v. Montana Fish & Game Comm'n*. In *Baldwin,* for example, we concluded that a State may charge a nonresident more than it charges a resident for the same elk-hunting license. Because elk hunting is "recreation" rather than a "means of a livelihood," we found that the right to a hunting license was not "fundamental" to the promotion of interstate harmony.

Derived ... from the fourth of the Articles of Confederation, the Privileges and Immunities Clause was intended to create a national economic union. It is therefore not surprising that this Court repeatedly has found that "one of the privileges which the Clause guarantees to citizens

6. Under this Clause, the terms "citizen" and "resident" are used interchangeably. Under the Fourteenth Amendment, of course, "[a]ll persons born or naturalized in the United States ... are citizens ... of the State wherein they reside."

of State A is that of doing business in State B on terms of substantial equality with the citizens of that State." In *Ward v. Maryland,* 12 Wall. 418 (1871), the Court invalidated a statute under which nonresidents were required to pay $300 per year for a license to trade in goods not manufactured in Maryland, while resident traders paid a fee varying from $12 to $150. Similarly, in *Toomer v. Witsell,* the Court held that nonresident fishermen could not be required to pay a license fee of $2,500 for each shrimp boat owned when residents were charged only $25 per boat. Finally, in *Hicklin v. Orbeck,* we found violative of the Privileges and Immunities Clause a statute containing a resident hiring preference for all employment related to the development of the State's oil and gas resources.[9]

There is nothing in *Ward, Toomer,* or *Hicklin* suggesting that the practice of law should not be viewed as a "privilege" under Art. IV, § 2. Like the occupations considered in our earlier cases, the practice of law is important to the national economy....

Appellant asserts that the Privileges and Immunities Clause should be held inapplicable to the practice of law because a lawyer's activities are "bound up with the exercise of judicial power and the administration of justice." Its contention is based on the premise that the lawyer is an "officer of the court," who "exercises state power on a daily basis." Appellant concludes that if the State cannot exclude nonresidents from the bar, its ability to function as a sovereign political body will be threatened.

Lawyers do enjoy a "broad monopoly ... to do things other citizens may not lawfully do." We do not believe, however, that the practice of law involves an "exercise of state power" justifying New Hampshire's residency requirement. [We have] held that the State could not exclude an alien from the bar on the ground that a lawyer is an " 'officer of the Court who' ... is entrusted with the 'exercise of actual governmental power.' " [H]e " 'makes his own decisions, follows his own best judgment, collects his own fees and runs his own business.' " Moreover, we held that the state powers entrusted to lawyers do not "involve matters of state policy or acts of such unique responsibility as to entrust them only to citizens."

Because ... a lawyer is not an "officer" of the State in any political sense, there is no reason for New Hampshire to exclude from its bar nonresidents. We therefore conclude that the right to practice law is protected by the Privileges and Immunities Clause.

The conclusion that Rule 42 deprives nonresidents of a protected privilege does not end our inquiry. The Court has stated that "[l]ike many other constitutional provisions, the privileges and immunities

9. In *United Building & Construction Trades Council v. Mayor & Council of Camden,* 465 U.S. 208 (1984), we stated that "the pursuit of a common calling is one of the most fundamental of those privileges protected by the Clause." We noted that "[m]any, if not most, of our cases expounding the Privileges and Immunities Clause have dealt with this basic and essential activity."

clause is not an absolute." The Clause does not preclude discrimination against nonresidents where (i) there is a substantial reason for the difference in treatment; and (ii) the discrimination practiced against nonresidents bears a substantial relationship to the State's objective. In deciding whether the discrimination bears a close or substantial relationship to the State's objective, the Court has considered the availability of less restrictive means.

The Supreme Court of New Hampshire offers several justifications for its refusal to admit nonresidents to the bar. It asserts that nonresident members would be less likely (i) to become, and remain, familiar with local rules and procedures; (ii) to behave ethically; (iii) to be available for court proceedings; and (iv) to do *pro bono* and other volunteer work in the State. We find that none of these reasons meets the test of "substantiality," and that the means chosen do not bear the necessary relationship to the State's objectives.[18]

There is no evidence to support appellant's claim that nonresidents might be less likely to keep abreast of local rules and procedures. Nor may we assume that a nonresident lawyer—any more than a resident—would disserve his clients by failing to familiarize himself with the rules. As a practical matter, we think that unless a lawyer has, or anticipates, a considerable practice in the New Hampshire courts, he would be unlikely to take the bar examination and pay the annual dues of $125.[19]

We also find the appellant's second justification to be without merit, for there is no reason to believe that a nonresident lawyer will conduct his practice in a dishonest manner....

There is more merit to the appellant's assertion that a nonresident member of the bar at times would be unavailable for court proceedings. In the course of litigation, pretrial hearings on various matters often are held on short notice. At times a court will need to confer immediately with counsel. Even the most conscientious lawyer residing in a distant State may find himself unable to appear in court for an unscheduled hearing or proceeding. Nevertheless, we do not believe that this type of problem justifies the exclusion of nonresidents from the state bar. One may assume that a high percentage of nonresident lawyers willing to take the state bar examination and pay the annual dues will reside in places reasonably convenient to New Hampshire. Furthermore, in those

18. A former president of the American Bar Association has suggested another possible reason for the rule: "Many of the states that have erected fences against out-of-state lawyers have done so primarily to protect their own lawyers from professional competition." This reason is not "substantial." The Privileges and Immunities Clause was designed primarily to prevent such economic protectionism.

19. Because it is markedly overinclusive, the residency requirement does not bear a substantial relationship to the State's objective. A less restrictive alternative would be to require mandatory attendance at periodic seminars on state practice.... New Hampshire's "simple residency" requirement is underinclusive as well, because it permits lawyers who move away from the State to retain their membership in the bar. There is no reason to believe that a former resident would maintain a more active practice in the New Hampshire courts than would a nonresident lawyer who had never lived in the State.

cases where the nonresident counsel will be unavailable on short notice, the State can protect its interests through less restrictive means. The trial court, by rule or as an exercise of discretion, may require any lawyer who resides at a great distance to retain a local attorney who will be available for unscheduled meetings and hearings.

The final reason advanced by appellant is that nonresident members of the state bar would be disinclined to do their share of *pro bono* and volunteer work. Perhaps this is true to a limited extent, particularly where the member resides in a distant location.... [However], a nonresident bar member, like the resident member, could be required to represent indigents and perhaps to participate in formal legal-aid work.

In summary, appellant neither advances a "substantial reason" for its discrimination against nonresident applicants to the bar, nor demonstrates that the discrimination practiced bears a close relationship to its proffered objectives ..

Justice WHITE, concurring in the result.

[I] have no doubt that the New Hampshire residency requirement is invalid as applied to appellee Piper. Except for the fact that she will commute from Vermont, she would be indistinguishable from other New Hampshire lawyers. There is every reason to believe that she will be as able as other New Hampshire lawyers to maintain professional competence, to stay abreast of local rules and procedures, to be available for sudden hearings, and to satisfy any requirements of a member of the New Hampshire bar to perform *pro bono* and volunteer work. It does not appear that her nonresidency presents a special threat to any of the State's interests that is not shared by lawyers living in New Hampshire. Hence, I conclude that the Privileges and Immunities Clause forbids her exclusion from the New Hampshire Bar.

The foregoing is enough to dispose of this case. I do not, and the Court itself need not, reach out to decide the facial validity of the New Hampshire residency requirement....

Justice REHNQUIST, dissenting.

Today the Court holds that New Hampshire cannot decide that a New Hampshire lawyer should live in New Hampshire. This may not be surprising to those who view law as just another form of business frequently practiced across state lines by interchangeable actors; the Privileges and Immunities Clause of Art. IV, § 2, has long been held to apply to States' attempts to discriminate against nonresidents who seek to ply their trade interstate. The decision will be surprising to many, however, because it so clearly disregards the fact that the practice of law is—almost by definition—fundamentally different from those other occupations that are practiced across state lines without significant deviation from State to State. The fact that each State is free, in a large number of areas, to establish *independently* of the other States its own laws for the governance of its citizens, is a fundamental precept of our Constitution that, I submit, is of equal stature with the need for the States to form a cohesive union. What is at issue here is New Hampshire's right to decide that those people who in many ways will intimately deal with New Hampshire's self-governance should reside within that State.

[T]he Framers ... created a system of federalism that deliberately allowed for the independent operation of many sovereign States, each with their own laws created by their own legislators and judges. The assumption from the beginning was that the various States' laws need not, and would not, be the same; the lawmakers of each State might endorse different philosophies and would have to respond to differing interests of their constituents, based on various factors that were of inherently local character....

It is but a small step from these facts to the recognition that a State has a very strong interest in seeing that its legislators and its judges come from among the constituency of state residents, so that they better understand the local interests to which they will have to respond. The Court does not contest this point; it recognizes that a State may require its lawmakers to be residents without running afoul of the Privileges and Immunities Clause of Art. IV, § 2.

Unlike the Court, I would take the next step, and recognize that the State also has a very "substantial" interest in seeing that its lawyers also are members of that constituency. I begin with two important principles that the Court seems to have forgotten: first, that in reviewing state statutes under this Clause "States should have considerable leeway in analyzing local evils and prescribing appropriate cures," and second, that regulation of the practice of law generally has been "left exclusively to the States...." My belief that the practice of law differs from other trades and businesses for Art. IV, § 2, purposes is not based on some notion that law is for some reason a superior profession. The reason that the practice of law should be treated differently is that law is one occupation that does not readily translate across state lines.[1] Certain aspects of legal practice are distinctly and intentionally *nonnational;* in this regard one might view this country's legal system as the antithesis of the norms embodied in the Art. IV Privileges and Immunities Clause. Put simply, the State has a substantial interest in creating its own set of laws responsive to its own local interests, and it is reasonable for a State to decide that those people who have been trained to analyze law and policy are better equipped to write those state laws and adjudicate cases arising under them....

It is no answer to these arguments that many lawyers simply will not perform these functions, or that out-of-state lawyers can perform them equally well, or that the State can devise less restrictive alterna-

1. I do not mean to suggest that the practice of law, unlike other occupations, is not a "fundamental" interest subject to the two-step analysis outlined by the Court. It makes little difference to me which prong of the Court's analysis is implicated, although the thrust of my position is that there are significant state interests justifying this type of interstate discrimination....

tives for accomplishing these goals. Conclusory second-guessing of difficult legislative decisions, such as the Court resorts to today, is not an attractive way for federal courts to engage in judicial review. Thus, whatever the reality of how much New Hampshire can expect to gain from having the members of its bar reside within that State, the point is that New Hampshire is entitled to believe and hope that its lawyers will provide the various unique services mentioned above, just as it is entitled to believe that the residency requirement is the appropriate way to that end....

In addition, I find the Court's "less restrictive means" analysis both ill-advised and potentially unmanageable. Initially I would note ... that such an analysis, when carried too far, will ultimately lead to striking down almost any statute on the ground that the Court could think of another "less restrictive" way to write it. This approach to judicial review, far more than the usual application of a standard of review, tends to place courts in the position of second-guessing legislators on legislative matters. Surely this is not a consequence to be desired....

Comments and Questions

1. The Court finds that to be a lawyer is to follow a common calling. As does Justice White. Justice Rehnquist appears to disagree. Do you think he is right to compare lawyers to judges and legislators?

2. What does the Court mean that a lawyer may be an "officer of the court" but "not an 'officer' of the State in any political sense"?

3. If Justice White agrees that lawyers are a common calling, why does he not concur in the Court's opinion?

4. After deciding that lawyers are a common calling, the Court first asks whether "(i) there is a substantial reason for the difference in treatment." Obviously, a substantial reason must also be a legitimate reason. Thus, the state cannot rely on impermissible reasons, such as protecting state jobs for state residents; this would be protectionism, as impermissible under the Privileges and Immunities Clause as under the Dormant Commerce Clause. In *Piper* the state argues that it has four legitimate purposes. The Court appears to dismiss two as not substantial.

5. Having found a substantial reason for a difference in treatment, the Court then asks whether "(ii) the discrimination practiced against nonresidents bears a substantial relationship to the State's objective. In deciding whether the discrimination bears a close or substantial relationship to the State's objective, the Court has considered the availability of less restrictive means." In other words, if there is a less discriminatory means available to achieve the substantial, legitimate purpose, that suggests that there is not a substantial relationship between the discrimination and the legitimate purpose. In *Piper* the Court finds that there are less discriminatory ways to achieve the two purposes deemed legitimate.

6. Justice Rehnquist takes issue with the "less restrictive means" test used by the Court to determine if the discrimination has a substantial relationship to the state's legitimate objective. He indicates it is unmanageable and will have terrible effects, but this is and was the test used for discriminatory laws under the Dormant Commerce Clause. Should it be any different for discrimination under the Privileges and Immunities Clause? Perhaps he objects because in an earlier case he had identified the appropriate inquiry to be whether it can be shown that the nonresidents "constitute a peculiar source of the evil at which the statute is aimed." *See United Building & Construction Trades Council v. Mayor and Council of Camden*, 465 U.S. 208, 222 (1984). How would one apply that test to the facts in *Piper* and would it result in any different outcome?

7. As you can see there are a number of similarities between Dormant Commerce Clause doctrine and Privileges and Immunities Clause doctrine. As a result, cases are often filed asserting a violation of both the Dormant Commerce Clause and the Privileges and Immunities Clause. There are, however, a few notable differences between the two doctrines:

- Corporations and other non-natural persons are not protected by the Privileges and Immunities Clause, because it only protects "citizens," and only natural persons can be citizens.

- There is no market participant exception to the Privileges and Immunities Clause prohibition on discriminatory state and local laws, *see United Building & Construction Trades Council v. Mayor and Council of Camden, supra.*

- While Congress can reverse a decision made by the Court under the Dormant Commerce Clause to authorize something the Court found unconstitutional or to prohibit something the Court found constitutional, Congress cannot reverse a decision by the Court under the Privileges and Immunities Clause.

Chapter 5

EXECUTIVE v. LEGISLATIVE POWER—THE SEPARATION OF POWERS

In Chapter 3 we surveyed the legislative powers vested in Congress by the Constitution. There we saw that the tension was between federal lawmaking and state lawmaking and the proper roles and responsibilities of the state and federal governments—or what is called federalism or sometimes the vertical separation of powers. In this chapter we survey the executive powers and privileges vested in the President by Article II of the Constitution. Here we will see that the tension is between executive powers and congressional powers and the proper roles and responsibilities of President and the Congress—or what is called the separation of powers (or horizontal separation of powers) and checks and balances. In addition, we will find that there are limitations on the ability of the President and Congress, even when acting together, to alter the roles and responsibilities the Court believes mandated by the Constitution.

As The Federalist papers recognized, "The accumulation of all powers legislative, executive and judiciary in the same hands, whether of one, a few or many, and whether hereditary, self-appointed, or elective, may justly be pronounced the very definition of tyranny." It is Civics 101 that to avoid tyranny the United States government is divided into three branches—the judicial, the legislative, and the executive. This division is called the separation of powers. At the same time, the branches are not hermetically sealed from one another. To the contrary, the Constitution mandates necessary interactions between them, what we call "checks and balances." For example, Congress is the legislative branch but the President is empowered to veto bills passed by Congress. The President is authorized to make treaties and appoint officers of the United States, but the former is subject to Senate ratification and the latter to Senate confirmation. The President appoints judges, but Congress can remove them through impeachment. The President is the Commander-in-Chief, but Congress raises and supports armies and provides the rules for the regulation of armed forces. These interactions provide a wealth of opportunities for clashes between the branches. During periods when the presidency and Congress are controlled by different political parties, the conflicts between them are sometimes partisan, rather than institutional, but even when the presidency and Congress are both controlled by the same party, with shared political orientations, there are often conflicts between the branches arising out of institutional concerns.

A. THE BACKGROUND

This chapter will begin with two canonical cases involving the power of the President.

UNITED STATES v. CURTISS–WRIGHT EXPORT CORP.

United States Supreme Court, 1936.
299 U.S. 304, 57 S.Ct. 216, 81 L.Ed. 255.

[This case needs some introduction. A longstanding border dispute between Paraguay and Bolivia over an area known as the Chaco broke out into war in 1932. The League of Nations imposed an international arms embargo to keep foreign weapons out of the war, and Congress passed a law authorizing the President by resolution to forbid the sale of weapons to persons involved in that dispute and provided criminal penalties for anyone violating such a Presidential resolution. This occurred during the period in which the Court was striking down various New Deal laws passed by Congress to deal with the Great Depression. Indeed, in the year prior to this case, the Court had in two cases found that laws authorizing the President to take certain actions were unconstitutional as an unconstitutional delegation of legislative power. *See Panama Refining Co. v. Ryan*, 293 U.S. 388 (1935); *A.L.A. Schechter Poultry Corporation v. United States*, 295 U.S. 495 (1935). The theory was that the Constitution vests the legislative authority in Congress, and Congress cannot delegate that authority to the President in a manner that gives him largely unfettered discretion. For example, imagine a law that said: the President may make all the laws for the next four years. Of course, the laws invalidated by the Court were not nearly so stark, and the law involved in *Panama Refining*, authorizing the President to ban from interstate commerce any oil produced in a state in violation of that state's law and creating criminal penalties for anyone violating that ban, looked much like the law in this case. Thus, Curtiss–Wright had some reason to believe that it might win on the argument that the law here was an unconstitutional delegation of legislative authority.]

Mr. Justice SUTHERLAND delivered the opinion of the Court.

On January 27, 1936, an indictment was returned in the court below, the first count of which charges that appellees, beginning with the 29th day of May, 1934, conspired to sell in the United States certain arms of war, namely, fifteen machine guns, to Bolivia, a country then engaged in armed conflict in the Chaco, in violation of the Joint Resolution of Congress approved May 28, 1934, and the provisions of a proclamation issued on the same day by the President of the United States pursuant to authority conferred by section 1 of the resolution....

Appellees severally demurred to the first count of the indictment.... [One point] urged in support of the demurrers [was] that the Joint Resolution effects an invalid delegation of legislative power to the executive....

Whether, if the Joint Resolution had related solely to internal affairs, it would be open to the challenge that it constituted an unlawful delegation of legislative power to the Executive, we find it unnecessary to determine. The whole aim of the resolution is to affect a situation entirely external to the United States, and falling within the category of foreign affairs. The determination which we are called to make, therefore, is whether the Joint Resolution, as applied to that situation, is vulnerable to attack under the rule that forbids a delegation of the lawmaking power. In other words, assuming (but not deciding) that the challenged delegation, if it were confined to internal affairs, would be invalid, may it nevertheless be sustained on the ground that its exclusive aim is to afford a remedy for a hurtful condition within foreign territory?

It will contribute to the elucidation of the question if we first consider the differences between the powers of the federal government in respect of foreign or external affairs and those in respect of domestic or internal affairs. That there are differences between them, and that these differences are fundamental, may not be doubted.

The two classes of powers are different, both in respect of their origin and their nature. The broad statement that the federal government can exercise no powers except those specifically enumerated in the Constitution, and such implied powers as are necessary and proper to carry into effect the enumerated powers, is categorically true only in respect of our internal affairs. In that field, the primary purpose of the Constitution was to carve from the general mass of legislative powers then possessed by the states such portions as it was thought desirable to vest in the federal government, leaving those not included in the enumeration still in the states. That this doctrine applies only to powers which the states had is self-evident. And since the states severally never possessed international powers, such powers could not have been carved from the mass of state powers but obviously were transmitted to the United States from some other source. During the Colonial period, those powers were possessed exclusively by and were entirely under the control of the Crown. By the Declaration of Independence, "the Representatives of the United States of America" declared the United (not the several) Colonies to be free and independent states, and as such to have "full Power to levy War, conclude Peace, contract Alliances, establish Commerce and to do all other Acts and Things which Independent States may of right do."

As a result of the separation from Great Britain by the colonies, acting as a unit, the powers of external sovereignty passed from the Crown not to the colonies severally, but to the colonies in their collective and corporate capacity as the United States of America. Even before the Declaration, the colonies were a unit in foreign affairs, acting through a common agency—namely, the Continental Congress, composed of delegates from the thirteen colonies. That agency exercised the powers of war and peace, raised an army, created a navy, and finally adopted the Declaration of Independence. Rulers come and go; governments end and forms of government change; but sovereignty survives. A political society cannot endure without a supreme will somewhere. Sovereignty is never held in suspense. When, therefore, the external sovereignty of Great Britain in respect of the colonies ceased, it immediately passed to the Union. That fact was given practical application almost at once. The treaty of peace, made on September 3, 1783, was concluded between his Brittanic Majesty and the "United States of America."

The Union existed before the Constitution, which was ordained and established among other things to form "a more perfect Union." Prior to that event, it is clear that the Union, declared by the Articles of Confederation to be "perpetual," was the sole possessor of external sovereignty, and in the Union it remained without change save in so far as the Constitution in express terms qualified its exercise. The Framers' Convention was called and exerted its powers upon the irrefutable postulate that though the states were several their people in respect of foreign affairs were one....

It results that the investment of the federal government with the powers of external sovereignty did not depend upon the affirmative grants of the Constitution. The powers to declare and wage war, to conclude peace, to make treaties, to maintain diplomatic relations with other sovereignties, if they had never been mentioned in the Constitution, would have vested in the federal government as necessary concomitants of nationality....

Not only, as we have shown, is the federal power over external affairs in origin and essential character different from that over internal affairs, but participation in the exercise of the power is significantly limited. In this vast external realm, with its important, complicated, delicate and manifold problems, the President alone has the power to speak or listen as a representative of the nation. He makes treaties with the advice and consent of the Senate; but he alone negotiates. Into the field of negotiation the Senate cannot intrude; and Congress itself is powerless to invade it. As Marshall said in his great argument of March 7, 1800, in the House of Representatives, "The President is the sole organ of the nation in its external relations, and its sole representative with foreign nations." The Senate Committee on Foreign Relations at a very early day in our history (February 15, 1816), reported to the Senate, among other things, as follows:

> "The President is the constitutional representative of the United States with regard to foreign nations. He manages our

> concerns with foreign nations and must necessarily be most competent to determine when, how, and upon what subjects negotiation may be urged with the greatest prospect of success. For his conduct he is responsible to the Constitution. The committee considers this responsibility the surest pledge for the faithful discharge of his duty. They think the interference of the Senate in the direction of foreign negotiations calculated to diminish that responsibility and thereby to impair the best security for the national safety. The nature of transactions with foreign nations, moreover, requires caution and unity of design, and their success frequently depends on secrecy and dispatch."

It is important to bear in mind that we are here dealing not alone with an authority vested in the President by an exertion of legislative power, but with such an authority plus the very delicate, plenary and exclusive power of the President as the sole organ of the federal government in the field of international relations—a power which does not require as a basis for its exercise an act of Congress, but which, of course, like every other governmental power, must be exercised in subordination to the applicable provisions of the Constitution. It is quite apparent that if, in the maintenance of our international relations, embarrassment—perhaps serious embarrassment—is to be avoided and success for our aims achieved, congressional legislation which is to be made effective through negotiation and inquiry within the international field must often accord to the President a degree of discretion and freedom from statutory restriction which would not be admissible were domestic affairs alone involved. Moreover, he, not Congress, has the better opportunity of knowing the conditions which prevail in foreign countries, and especially is this true in time of war. He has his confidential sources of information. He has his agents in the form of diplomatic, consular and other officials. Secrecy in respect of information gathered by them may be highly necessary, and the premature disclosure of it productive of harmful results. Indeed, so clearly is this true that the first President refused to accede to a request to lay before the House of Representatives the instructions, correspondence and documents relating to the negotiation of the Jay Treaty—a refusal the wisdom of which was recognized by the House itself and has never since been doubted. In his reply to the request, President Washington said:

> "The nature of foreign negotiations requires caution, and their success must often depend on secrecy; and even when brought to a conclusion a full disclosure of all the measures, demands, or eventual concessions which may have been proposed or contemplated would be extremely impolitic; for this might have a pernicious influence on future negotiations, or produce immediate inconveniences, perhaps danger and mischief, in relation to other powers. The necessity of such caution and secrecy was one cogent reason for vesting the power of making treaties in the President, with the advice and consent of the Senate, the prin-

ciple on which that body was formed confining it to a small number of members. To admit, then, a right in the House of Representatives to demand and to have as a matter of course all the papers respecting a negotiation with a foreign power would be to establish a dangerous precedent."

[W]hen the President is to be authorized by legislation to act in respect of a matter intended to affect a situation in foreign territory, the legislator properly bears in mind the important consideration that the form of the President's action—or, indeed, whether he shall act at all—may well depend, among other things, upon the nature of the confidential information which he has or may thereafter receive, or upon the effect which his action may have upon our foreign relations. This consideration, in connection with what we have already said on the subject discloses the unwisdom of requiring Congress in this field of governmental power to lay down narrowly definite standards by which the President is to be governed....

In the light of the foregoing observations, it is evident that this court should not be in haste to apply a general rule which will have the effect of condemning legislation like that under review as constituting an unlawful delegation of legislative power. The principles which justify such legislation find overwhelming support in the unbroken legislative practice which has prevailed almost from the inception of the national government to the present day.

Mr. Justice McREYNOLDS does not agree. He is of the opinion that the court below reached the right conclusion and its judgment ought to be affirmed.

Mr. Justice STONE took no part in the consideration or decision of this case.

Comments and Questions

1. Analytically, the outcome of this case is unremarkable—when Congress delegates power to the President, it can provide him more discretion regarding foreign affairs than would be the case in domestic affairs. Moreover, subsequent case law concerning even domestic delegations of legislative authority to the President has made clear that so long as there is any discernible standard to govern the President's actions, the delegation is not excessive. For example, the Clean Air Act's delegation of legislative authority to reduce air pollution "requisite to protect the public health" is easily an adequate standard. *See Whitman v. American Trucking Ass'ns*, 531 U.S. 457 (2001). In fact, no federal law has been found unconstitutional under the Delegation Doctrine since 1935.

2. However, *Curtiss-Wright* is not remembered for its discussion of the Delegation Doctrine. Instead, it is most often cited for the proposition that the President is "the sole organ of the nation in its external relations." This characterization, first made by John Marshall when he

was a member of Congress, is often mischaracterized as saying the President is solely or primarily responsible for our nation's foreign affairs. *See, e.g.*, the Wikipedia entry for *United States v. Curtiss–Wright Export Corp.* Marshall and the Court in *Curtiss-Wright* meant that the President is the actor through whom the nation's foreign affairs are conducted, not that the President is solely responsible for them. Recall the various provisions of Article I, Section 8, that authorize Congress to make laws regarding foreign and military affairs, not to mention the Senate's role in ratifying treaties.

3. *Curtiss-Wright* is also known for its historical analysis of the transfer of sovereignty from Great Britain directly to the United States as a nation, and not to the states separately and then from them to the United States through the Articles or the Constitution. While this history has been quite conclusively proven wrong, *see* Charles Lofgren, *United States v. Curtiss–Wright Export Corporation: A Historical Reassessment*, 83 Yale L.J. 1, 32 (1973), the theory that the United States possesses all the powers that any nation has under international law by reason of being a nation-state, even though some of these powers may not be mentioned in the Constitution, is largely unquestioned. To say that, however, is not necessarily to say that these unenumerated powers are possessed by the President, as opposed to possessed by the President and Congress together. Look back at the Court's opinion. Do you think it unequivocally states that these powers rest in the President?

YOUNGSTOWN SHEET & TUBE CO. v. SAWYER (THE STEEL SEIZURE CASE)

United States Supreme Court, 1952.
343 U.S. 579, 72 S.Ct. 863, 96 L.Ed. 1153.

Mr. Justice BLACK delivered the opinion of the Court.

We are asked to decide whether [President Truman] was acting within his constitutional power when he issued an order directing the Secretary of Commerce to take possession of and operate most of the Nation's steel mills. The mill owners argue that the President's order amounts to lawmaking, a legislative function which the Constitution has expressly confided to the Congress and not to the President. The Government's position is that the order was made on findings of the President that his action was necessary to avert a national catastrophe which would inevitably result from a stoppage of steel production, and that in meeting this grave emergency the President was acting within the aggregate of his constitutional powers as the Nation's Chief Executive and the Commander in Chief of the Armed Forces of the United States. The issue emerges here from the following series of events:

In the latter part of 1951, a dispute arose between the steel companies and their employees over terms and conditions that should be included in new collective bargaining agreements. Long-continued conferences failed to resolve the dispute.... On April 4, 1952, the Union gave notice of a nation-wide strike called to begin at 12:01 a.m. April 9. The indispensability of steel as a component of substantially all weapons and other war materials led the President to believe that the proposed work stoppage would immediately jeopardize our national defense and that governmental seizure of the steel mills was necessary in order to assure the continued availability of steel. Reciting these considerations for his action, the President, a few hours before the strike was to begin, issued Executive Order 10340.... The order directed the Secretary of Commerce to take possession of most of the steel mills and keep them running. The Secretary immediately issued his own possessory orders, calling upon the presidents of the various seized companies to serve as operating managers for the United States. They were directed to carry on their activities in accordance with regulations and directions of the Secretary. The next morning the President sent a message to Congress reporting his action.... Congress has taken no action.

Obeying the Secretary's orders under protest, the companies brought proceedings against him in the District Court.... [T]he District Court on April 30 issued a preliminary injunction restraining the Secretary from continuing the seizure and possession of the plant.... On the same day the Court of Appeals stayed the District Court's injunction. Deeming it best that the issues raised be promptly decided by this Court, we granted certiorari on May 3 and set the cause for argument on May 12....

The President's power, if any, to issue the order must stem either from an act of Congress or from the Constitution itself. There is no statute that expressly authorizes the President to take possession of property as he did here. Nor is there any act of Congress to which our attention has been directed from which such a power can fairly be implied. Indeed, we do not understand the Government to rely on statutory authorization for this seizure. There are two statutes which do authorize the President to take both personal and real property under certain conditions. However, the Government admits that these conditions were not met and that the President's order was not rooted in either of the statutes. The Government refers to the seizure provisions of one of these statutes (§ 201(b) of the Defense Production Act) as much too cumbersome, involved, and time-consuming for the crisis which was at hand.

Moreover, the use of the seizure technique to solve labor disputes in order to prevent work stoppages was not only unauthorized by any congressional enactment; prior to this controversy, Congress had refused to adopt that method of settling labor disputes. When the Taft–Hartley Act was under consideration in 1947, Congress rejected an amendment which would have authorized such governmental seizures in cases of emergency.... Instead, the plan sought to bring about settlements by use of the customary devices of mediation, conciliation, investigation by boards of inquiry, and public reports. In some instances temporary injunctions were authorized to provide cooling-off periods. All this failing, unions were left free to strike....

It is clear that if the President had authority to issue the order he did, it must be found in some provisions of the Constitution. And it is not claimed that express constitutional language grants this power to the President. The contention is that presidential power should be implied from the aggregate of his powers under the Constitution. Particular reliance is placed on provisions in Article II which say that the executive Power shall be vested in a President * * *; that he shall take Care that the Laws be faithfully executed; and that he shall be Commander in Chief of the Army and Navy of the United States.

The order cannot properly be sustained as an exercise of the President's military power as Commander in Chief of the Armed Forces. The Government attempts to do so by citing a number of cases upholding broad powers in military commanders engaged in day-to-day fighting in a theater of war. Such cases need not concern us here. Even though theater of war be an expanding concept, we cannot with faithfulness to our constitutional system hold that the Commander in Chief of the Armed Forces has the ultimate power as such to take possession of private property in order to keep labor disputes from stopping production. This is a job for the Nation's lawmakers, not for its military authorities.

Nor can the seizure order be sustained because of the several constitutional provisions that grant executive power to the President. In the framework of our Constitution, the President's power to see that the laws are faithfully executed refutes the idea that he is to be a lawmaker. The Constitution limits his functions in the lawmaking process to the recommending of laws he thinks wise and the vetoing of laws he thinks bad. And the Constitution is neither silent nor equivocal about who shall make laws which the President is to execute....

[T]he power of Congress to adopt such public policies as those proclaimed by the order is beyond question. It can authorize the taking of private property for public use. It can make laws regulating the relationships between employers and employees, prescribing rules designed to settle labor disputes, and fixing wages and working conditions in certain fields of our economy. The Constitution did not subject this law-making power of Congress to presidential or military supervision or control....

The Founders of this Nation entrusted the law making power to the Congress alone in both good and bad times. It would do no good to recall the historical events, the fears of power and the hopes for freedom that lay behind their choice. Such a review would but confirm our holding that this seizure order cannot stand.

Mr. Justice JACKSON, concurring in the judgment and opinion of the Court.

[T]he actual art of governing under our Constitution does not and cannot conform to judicial definitions of the power of any of its branches based on isolated clauses or even single Articles torn from context. While the Constitution diffuses power the better to secure liberty, it also contemplates that practice will integrate the dispersed powers into a workable government. It enjoins upon its branches separateness but interdependence, autonomy but reciprocity. Presidential powers are not fixed but fluctuate, depending upon their disjunction or conjunction with those of Congress. We may well begin by a somewhat over-simplified grouping of practical situations in which a President may doubt, or others may challenge, his powers, and by distinguishing roughly the legal consequences of this factor of relativity.

1. When the President acts pursuant to an express or implied authorization of Congress, his authority is at its maximum, for it includes all that he possesses in his own right plus all that Congress can delegate.[2] In these circumstances, and in these only, may he be said (for what it may be worth), to personify the federal sovereignty. If his act is held unconstitutional under these circumstances, it usually means that the Federal Government as an undivided whole lacks power. A seizure executed by the President pursuant to an Act of Congress would be supported by the strongest of presumptions and the widest latitude of judicial interpretation, and the burden of persuasion would rest heavily upon any who might attack it.

2. When the President acts in absence of either a congressional grant or denial of authority, he can only rely upon his own independent powers, but there is a zone of twilight in which he and Congress may have concurrent authority, or in which its distribution is uncertain. Therefore, congressional inertia, indifference or quiescence may sometimes, at least as a practical matter, enable, if not invite, measures on independent presidential responsibility. In this area, any actual test of power is likely to depend on the imperatives of events and contemporary imponderables rather than on abstract theories of law.[3]

3. When the President takes measures incompatible with the expressed or implied will of Congress, his power is at its lowest ebb, for then he can rely only upon his own constitutional powers minus any constitutional powers of Congress over the matter. Courts can sustain exclusive Presidential control in such a case only by disabling the Congress from acting upon the subject. Presidential claim to a power at once

2. It is in this class of cases that we find the broadest recent statements of presidential power, including those relied on here. *United States v. Curtiss–Wright Export Corp.* involved, not the question of the President's power to act without congressional authority, but the question of his right to act under and in accord with an Act of Congress.... That case does not solve the present controversy. It recognized internal and external affairs as being in separate categories, and held that the strict limitation upon congressional delegations of power to the President over internal affairs does not apply with respect to delegations of power in external affairs. It was intimated that the President might act in external affairs without congressional authority, but not that he might act contrary to an Act of Congress....

3. Since the Constitution implies that the writ of habeas corpus may be suspended in certain circumstances but does not say by whom, President Lincoln asserted and maintained it as an executive function in the face of judicial challenge and doubt. Congress eventually ratified his action.

so conclusive and preclusive must be scrutinized with caution, for what is at stake is the equilibrium established by our constitutional system.

Into which of these classifications does this executive seizure of the steel industry fit? It is eliminated from the first by admission, for it is conceded that no congressional authorization exists for this seizure. Can it then be defended under flexible tests available to the second category? It seems clearly eliminated from that class because Congress has not left seizure of private property an open field but has covered it by three statutory policies inconsistent with this seizure. In cases where the purpose is to supply needs of the Government itself, two courses are provided: one, seizure of a plant which fails to comply with obligatory orders placed by the Government, another, condemnation of facilities, including temporary use under the power of eminent domain. The third is applicable where it is the general economy of the country that is to be protected rather than exclusive governmental interests. None of these were invoked. In choosing a different and inconsistent way of his own, the President cannot claim that it is necessitated or invited by failure of Congress to legislate upon the occasions, grounds and methods for seizure of industrial properties.

This leaves the current seizure to be justified only by the severe tests under the third grouping, where it can be supported only by any remainder of executive power after subtraction of such powers as Congress may have over the subject. In short, we can sustain the President only by holding that seizure of such strike-bound industries is within his domain and beyond control by Congress. Thus, this Court's first review of such seizures occurs under circumstances which leave Presidential power most vulnerable to attack and in the least favorable of possible constitutional postures.

I did not suppose, and I am not persuaded, that history leaves it open to question, at least in the courts, that the executive branch, like the Federal Government as a whole, possesses only delegated powers. The purpose of the Constitution was not only to grant power, but to keep it from getting out of hand. However, because the President does not enjoy unmentioned powers does not mean that the mentioned ones should be narrowed by a niggardly construction. Some clauses could be made almost unworkable, as well as immutable, by refusal to indulge some latitude of interpretation for changing times. I have heretofore, and do now, give to the enumerated powers the scope and elasticity afforded by what seem to be reasonable practical implications instead of the rigidity dictated by a doctrinaire textualism.

The Solicitor General seeks the power of seizure in three clauses of the Executive Article, the first reading, The executive Power shall be vested in a President of the United States of America. Lest I be thought to exaggerate, I quote the interpretation which his brief puts upon it: In our view, this clause constitutes a grant of all the executive powers of which the Government is capable. If that be true, it is difficult to see why the forefathers bothered to add several specific items, including some trifling ones.

The example of such unlimited executive power that must have most impressed the forefathers was the prerogative exercised by George III, and the description of its evils in the Declaration of Independence leads me to doubt that they were creating their new Executive in his image. Continental European examples were no more appealing. And if we seek instruction from our own times, we can match it only from the executive powers in those governments we disparagingly describe as totalitarian. I cannot accept the view that this clause is a grant in bulk of all conceivable executive power but regard it as an allocation to the presidential office of the generic powers thereafter stated.

The clause on which the Government next relies is that The President shall be Commander in Chief of the Army and Navy of the United States * * *. These cryptic words have given rise to some of the most persistent controversies in our constitutional history. Of course, they imply something more than an empty title. But just what authority goes with the name has plagued Presidential advisers who would not waive or narrow it by nonassertion yet cannot say where it begins or ends. It undoubtedly puts the Nation's armed forces under Presidential command. Hence, this loose appellation is sometimes advanced as support for any Presidential action, internal or external, involving use of force, the idea being that it vests power to do anything, anywhere, that can be done with an army or navy.

That seems to be the logic of an argument tendered at our bar—that the President having, on his own responsibility, sent American troops abroad derives from that act "affirmative power" to seize the means of producing a supply of steel for them. To quote, "Perhaps the most forceful illustrations of the scope of Presidential power in this connection is the fact that American troops in Korea, whose safety and effectiveness are so directly involved here, were sent to the field by an exercise of the President's constitutional powers." Thus, it is said he has invested himself with "war powers."

I cannot foresee all that it might entail if the Court should indorse this argument. Nothing in our Constitution is plainer than that declaration of a war is entrusted only to Congress. Of course, a state of war may in fact exist without a formal declaration. But no doctrine that the Court could promulgate would seem to me more sinister and alarming than that a President whose conduct of foreign affairs is so largely uncontrolled, and often even is unknown, can vastly enlarge his mastery over the internal affairs of the country by his own commitment of the Nation's armed forces to some foreign venture. I do not, however, find it necessary or appropriate to consider the legal status of the Korean enterprise to discountenance argument based on it.

Assuming that we are in a war de facto, whether it is or is not a war de jure, does that empower the Commander-in-Chief to seize industries he thinks necessary to supply our army? The Constitution expressly places in Congress power "to raise and support Armies" and "to provide and maintain a Navy." This certainly lays upon Congress primary responsibility for supplying the armed forces. Congress alone controls the raising of revenues and their appropriation and may determine in what manner and by what means they shall be spent for military and naval procurement....

There are indications that the Constitution did not contemplate that the title Commander-in-Chief of the Army and Navy will constitute him also Commander-in-Chief of the country, its industries and its inhabitants. He has no monopoly of "war powers," whatever they are. While Congress cannot deprive the President of the command of the army and navy, only Congress can provide him an army or navy to command. It is also empowered to make rules for the Government and Regulation of land and naval forces, by which it may to some unknown extent impinge upon even command functions....

While broad claims under this rubric often have been made, advice to the President in specific matters usually has carried overtones that powers, even under this head, are measured by the command functions usual to the topmost officer of the army and navy. Even then, heed has been taken of any efforts of Congress to negative his authority.

We should not use this occasion to circumscribe, much less to contract, the lawful role of the President as Commander-in-Chief. I should indulge the widest latitude of interpretation to sustain his exclusive function to command the instruments of national force, at least when turned against the outside world for the security of our society. But, when it is turned inward, not because of rebellion but because of a lawful economic struggle between industry and labor, it should have no such indulgence. His command power is not such an absolute as might be implied from that office in a militaristic system but is subject to limitations consistent with a constitutional Republic whose law and policy-making branch is a representative Congress. The purpose of lodging dual titles in one man was to insure that the civilian would control the military, not to enable the military to subordinate the presidential office. No penance would ever expiate the sin against free government of holding that a President can escape control of executive powers by law through assuming his military role. What the power of command may include I do not try to envision, but I think it is not a military prerogative, without support of law, to seize persons or property because they are important or even essential for the military and naval establishment.

The third clause in which the Solicitor General finds seizure powers is that he shall take Care that the Laws be faithfully executed * * *. That authority must be matched against words of the Fifth Amendment that No person shall be * * * deprived of life, liberty, or property, without due process of law * * *. One gives a governmental authority that reaches so far as there is law, the other gives a private right that authority shall go no farther. These signify about all there is of the principle that ours is a government of laws, not of men, and that we submit ourselves to rulers only if under rules.

The Solicitor General lastly grounds support of the seizure upon nebulous, inherent powers never expressly granted but said to have accrued to the office from the customs and claims of preceding administrations. The plea is for a resulting power to deal with a crisis or an emergency according to the necessities of the case, the unarticulated assumption being that necessity knows no law.

Loose and irresponsible use of adjectives colors all non-legal and much legal discussion of presidential powers. "Inherent" powers, "implied" powers, "incidental" powers, "plenary" powers, "war" powers and "emergency" powers are used, often interchangeably and without fixed or ascertainable meanings.

The vagueness and generality of the clauses that set forth presidential powers afford a plausible basis for pressures within and without an administration for presidential action beyond that supported by those whose responsibility it is to defend his actions in court. The claim of inherent and unrestricted presidential powers has long been a persuasive dialectical weapon in political controversy. While it is not surprising that counsel should grasp support from such unadjudicated claims of power, a judge cannot accept self-serving press statements of the attorney for one of the interested parties as authority in answering a constitutional question, even if the advocate was himself. But prudence has counseled that actual reliance on such nebulous claims stop short of provoking a judicial test....

The appeal, however, that we declare the existence of inherent powers *ex necessitate* to meet an emergency asks us to do what many think would be wise, although it is something the forefathers omitted. They knew what emergencies were, knew the pressures they engender for authoritative action, knew, too, how they afford a ready pretext for usurpation. We may also suspect that they suspected that emergency powers would tend to kindle emergencies. Aside from suspension of the privilege of the writ of habeas corpus in time of rebellion or invasion, when the public safety may require it, they made no express provision for exercise of extraordinary authority because of a crisis. I do not think we rightfully may so amend their work, and, if we could, I am not convinced it would be wise to do so....

In the practical working of our Government we already have evolved a technique within the framework of the Constitution by which normal executive powers may be considerably expanded to meet an emergency. Congress may and has granted extraordinary authorities which lie dormant in normal times but may be called into play by the Executive in war or upon proclamation of a national emergency.... Under this procedure we retain Government by law—special, temporary law, perhaps, but law nonetheless. The public may know the extent and limitations of the powers that can be asserted, and persons affected may be informed from the statute of their rights and duties.

In view of the ease, expedition and safety with which Congress can grant and has granted large emergency powers, certainly ample to embrace this crisis, I am quite unimpressed with the argument that we should affirm possession of them without statute. Such power either has no beginning or it has no end. If it exists, it need submit to no legal restraint. I am not alarmed that it would plunge us straightway into dictatorship, but it is at least a step in that wrong direction....

But I have no illusion that any decision by this Court can keep power in the hands of Congress if it is not wise and timely in meeting its problems. A crisis that challenges the President equally, or perhaps primarily, challenges Congress.... We may say that power to legislate for emergencies belongs in the hands of Congress, but only Congress itself can prevent power from slipping through its fingers....

With all its defects, delays and inconveniences, men have discovered no technique for long preserving free government except that the Executive be under the law, and that the law be made by parliamentary deliberations. Such institutions may be destined to pass away. But it is the duty of the Court to be last, not first, to give them up.

Mr. Justice BURTON, concurring in both the opinion and judgment of the Court. [Opinion omitted].

Mr. Justice CLARK, concurring in the judgment of the Court.

One of this Court's first pronouncements upon the powers of the President under the Constitution was made by Chief Justice John Marshall some one hundred and fifty years ago. In *Little v. Barreme*, [2 Cranch 170 (1804)] he used this characteristically clear language in discussing the power of the President to instruct the seizure of the "Flying–Fish," a vessel bound from a French port: It is by no means clear that the President of the United States whose high duty it is to take care that the laws be faithfully executed, and who is commander in chief of the armies and navies of the United States, might not, without any special authority for that purpose, in the then existing state of things, have empowered the officers commanding the armed vessels of the United States, to seize and send into port for adjudication, American vessels which were forfeited by being engaged in this illicit commerce. But when it is observed that (an act of Congress) gives a special authority to seize on the high seas, and limits that authority to the seizure of vessels bound or sailing to a French port, the legislature seem to have prescribed that the manner in which this law shall be carried into execution, was to exclude a seizure of any vessel not bound to a French port. Accordingly, a unanimous Court held that the President's instructions had been issued without authority and that they could not legalize an act which without those instructions would have been a plain trespass. I know of no subsequent holding of this Court to the contrary.

The limits of presidential power are obscure. However, Article II, no less than Article I, is part of a constitution intended to endure for ages to come, and, consequently, to be adapted to the various crises of human affairs. Some of our Presidents, such as Lincoln, felt that measures otherwise unconstitutional might become lawful by becoming indispensable to the preservation of the Constitution through the preservation of the nation. Others, such as Theodore Roosevelt, thought the President to be capable, as a "steward" of the people, of exerting all power save that which is specifically prohibited by the Constitution or the Congress. In my view—taught me not only by the decision of Chief Justice Marshall in *Little v. Barreme*, but also by a score of other pronouncements of distinguished members of this bench—the Constitution does grant to the President extensive authority in times of grave and imperative national emergency. In fact, to my thinking, such a grant may well be necessary to the very existence of the Constitution itself. As Lincoln aptly said, (is) it possible to lose the nation and yet preserve the Constitution? In describing this authority I care not whether one calls it "residual," "inherent," "moral," "implied," "aggregate," "emergency," or otherwise. I am of the conviction that those who have had the gratifying experience of being the President's lawyer have used one or more of these adjectives only with the utmost of sincerity and the highest of purpose.

I conclude that where Congress has laid down specific procedures to deal with the type of crisis confronting the President, he must follow those procedures in meeting the crisis; but that in the absence of such action by Congress, the President's independent power to act depends upon the gravity of the situation confronting the nation. I cannot sustain the seizure in question because here, as in *Little v. Barreme*, Congress had prescribed methods to be followed by the President in meeting the emergency at hand....

Mr. Justice DOUGLAS, concurring.

There can be no doubt that the emergency which caused the President to seize these steel plants was one that bore heavily on the country. But the emergency did not create power; it merely marked an occasion when power should be exercised. And the fact that it was necessary that measures be taken to keep steel in production does not mean that the President, rather than the Congress, had the constitutional authority to act. The Congress, as well as the President, is trustee of the national welfare. The President can act more quickly than the Congress. The President with the armed services at his disposal can move with force as well as with speed. All executive power—from the reign of ancient kings to the rule of modern dictators—has the outward appearance of efficiency.

Legislative power, by contrast, is slower to exercise. There must be delay while the ponderous machinery of committees, hearings, and debates is put into motion. That takes time; and while the Congress slowly moves into action, the emergency may take its toll.... Legislative action may indeed often be cumbersome, time-consuming, and apparently inefficient....

We therefore cannot decide this case by determining which branch of government can deal most expeditiously with the present crisis. The answer must depend on the allocation of powers under the Constitution....

The legislative nature of the action taken by the President seems to me to be clear. When the United States takes over an industrial plant to settle a labor controversy, it is condemning property....

The power of the Federal Government to condemn property is well established.... The command of the Fifth Amendment is that no private property be taken for public use, without just compensation."

The President has no power to raise revenues. That power is in the Congress by Article I, Section 8 of the Constitution. The President might seize and the Congress by subsequent action might ratify the seizure.[1] But until and unless Congress acted, no condemnation would be lawful. The branch of government that has the power to pay compensation for a seizure is the only one able to authorize a seizure or make lawful one that the President had effected.

Mr. Justice FRANKFURTER, concurring.

[T]he Founders of this Nation were not imbued with the modern cynicism that the only thing that history teaches is that it teaches nothing. They acted on the conviction that the experience of man sheds a good deal of light on his nature. It sheds a good deal of light not merely on the need for effective power, if a society is to be at once cohesive and civilized, but also on the need for limitations on the power of governors over the governed.

[T]he content of the three authorities of government is not to be derived from an abstract analysis. The areas are partly interacting, not wholly disjointed. The Constitution is a framework for government. Therefore the way the framework has consistently operated fairly establishes that it has operated according to its true nature. Deeply embedded traditional ways of conducting government cannot supplant the Constitution or legislation, but they give meaning to the words of a text or supply them. It is an inadmissibly narrow conception of American constitutional law to confine it to the words of the Constitution and to disregard the gloss which life has written upon them. In short, a systematic, unbroken, executive practice, long pursued to the knowledge of the Congress and never before questioned, engaged in by Presidents who have also sworn to uphold the Constitution, making as it were such exercise of power part of the structure of our government, may be treated as a gloss on "executive Power" vested in the President....

[Justice Frankfurter then considered executive practice from the beginning of the Republic.] Down to the World War II period, then, the

1. What a President may do as a matter of expediency or extremity may never reach a definitive constitutional decision. For example, President Lincoln suspended the writ of habeas corpus, claiming the constitutional right to do so. Congress ratified his action.

record is barren of instances comparable to the one before us. Of twelve seizures by President Roosevelt prior to the enactment of the War Labor Disputes Act in June, 1943, three were sanctioned by existing law, and six others were effected after Congress, on December 8, 1941, had declared the existence of a state of war. In this case, reliance on the powers that flow from declared war has been commendably disclaimed by the Solicitor General. Thus the list of executive assertions of the power of seizure in circumstances comparable to the present reduces to three in the six-month period from June to December of 1941. We need not split hairs in comparing those actions to the one before us, though much might be said by way of differentiation. Without passing on their validity, as we are not called upon to do, it suffices to say that these three isolated instances do not add up, either in number, scope, duration or contemporaneous legal justification, to the kind of executive construction of the Constitution [often exercised over a long period of time with full acquiesence of Congress].

Mr. Chief Justice VINSON, with whom Mr. Justice REED and Mr. Justice MINTON join, dissenting.

The President of the United States directed the Secretary of Commerce to take temporary possession of the Nation's steel mills during the existing emergency because a work stoppage would immediately jeopardize and imperil our national defense and the defense of those joined with us in resisting aggression, and would add to the continuing danger of our soldiers, sailors and airmen engaged in combat in the field....

Some members of the Court are of the view that the President is without power to act in time of crisis in the absence of express statutory authorization. Other members of the Court affirm on the basis of their reading of certain statutes. Because we cannot agree that affirmance is proper on any ground, and because of the transcending importance of the questions presented not only in this critical litigation but also to the powers the President and of future Presidents to act in time of crisis, we are compelled to register this dissent.

In passing upon the question of Presidential powers in this case, we must first consider the context in which those powers were exercised.

Those who suggest that this is a case involving extraordinary powers should be mindful that these are extraordinary times. A world not yet recovered from the devastation of World War II has been forced to face the threat of another and more terrifying global conflict.

Accepting in full measure its responsibility in the world community, the United States was instrumental in securing adoption of the United Nations Charter, approved by the Senate by a vote of 89 to 2. The first purpose of the United Nations is to maintain international peace and security, and to that end: to take effective collective measures for the prevention and removal of threats to the peace, and for the suppression of acts of aggression or other breaches of the peace, * * *. In 1950, when the United Nations called upon member nations "to render every assistance" to repel aggression in Korea, the United States furnished its vigorous support. For almost two full years, our armed forces have been fighting in Korea, suffering casualties of over 108,000 men. Hostilities have not abated. The determination of the United Nations to continue its action in Korea to meet the aggression has been reaffirmed. Congressional support of the action in Korea has been manifested by provisions for increased military manpower and equipment and for economic stabilization, as hereinafter described....

Our treaties represent not merely legal obligations but show congressional recognition that mutual security for the free world is the best security against the threat of aggression on a global scale. The need for mutual security is shown by the very size of the armed forces outside the free world. Defendant's brief informs us that the Soviet Union maintains the largest air force in the world and maintains ground forces much larger than those presently available to the United States and the countries joined with us in mutual security arrangements. Constant international tensions are cited to demonstrate how precarious is the peace....

Congress also directed the President to build up our own defenses. Congress, recognizing the grim fact * * * that the United States is now engaged in a struggle for survival and that it is imperative that we now take those necessary steps to make our strength equal to the peril of the hour, granted authority to draft men into the armed forces. As a result, we now have over 3,500,000 men in our armed forces....

Secretary of Defense Lovett swore that a work stoppage in the steel industry will result immediately in serious curtailment of production of essential weapons and munitions of all kinds. He illustrated by showing that 84% of the national production of certain alloy steel is currently used for production of military-end items and that 35% of total production of another form of steel goes into ammunition, 80% of such ammunition now going to Korea. The Secretary of Defense stated that: We are holding the line (in Korea) with ammunition and not with the lives of our troops....

[T]he central fact of this case [is] that the Nation's entire basic steel production would have shut down completely if there had been no Government seizure. Even ignoring for the moment whatever confidential information the President may possess as the Nation's organ for foreign affairs, the uncontroverted affidavits in this record amply support the finding that a work stoppage would immediately jeopardize and imperil our national defense....

Accordingly, if the President has any power under the Constitution to meet a critical situation in the absence of express statutory authorization, there is no basis whatever for criticizing the exercise of such power in this case....

A review of executive action demonstrates that our Presidents have on many occasions exhibited the leadership contemplated by the Framers when they made the President Commander in Chief, and imposed upon him the trust to take Care that the Laws be faithfully executed. With or without explicit statutory authorization, Presidents have at such times dealt with national emergencies by acting promptly and resolutely to enforce legislative programs, at least to save those programs until Congress could act. Congress and the courts have responded to such executive initiative with consistent approval.

Our first President displayed at once the leadership contemplated by the Framers. When the national revenue laws were openly flouted in some sections of Pennsylvania, President Washington, without waiting for a call from the state government, summoned the militia and took decisive steps to secure the faithful execution of the laws. When international disputes engendered by the French revolution threatened to involve this country in war, and while congressional policy remained uncertain, Washington issued his Proclamation of Neutrality. Hamilton, whose defense of the Proclamation has endured the test of time, invoked the argument that the Executive has the duty to do that which will preserve peace until Congress acts and, in addition, pointed to the need for keeping the Nation informed of the requirements of existing laws and treaties as part of the faithful execution of the laws....

Without declaration of war, President Lincoln took energetic action with the outbreak of the War Between the States. He summoned troops and paid them out of the Treasury without appropriation therefor. He proclaimed a naval blockade of the Confederacy and seized ships violating that blockade. Congress, far from denying the validity of these acts, gave them express approval. The most striking action of President Lincoln was the Emancipation Proclamation, issued in aid of the successful prosecution of the War Between the States, but wholly without statutory authority.

[The dissent then details a large number of circumstances in which a President took action in response to one crisis or another, which action was not previously authorized by Congress.]

This is but a cursory summary of executive leadership. But it amply demonstrates that Presidents have taken prompt action to enforce the laws and protect the country whether or not Congress happened to provide in advance for the particular method of execution. At the minimum, the executive actions reviewed herein sustain the action of the President in this case. And many of the cited examples of Presidential practice go far beyond the extent of power necessary to sustain the President's order to seize the steel mills. The fact that temporary executive seizures of industrial plants to meet an emergency have not been directly tested in this Court furnishes not the slightest suggestion that such actions have been illegal. Rather, the fact that Congress and the courts have consistently recognized and given their support to such executive action indicates that such a power of seizure has been accepted throughout our history.

History bears out the genius of the Founding Fathers, who created a Government subject to law but not left subject to inertia when vigor and initiative are required....

Much of the argument in this case has been directed at straw men. We do not now have before us the case of a President acting solely on the basis of his own notions of the public welfare. Nor is there any question of unlimited executive power in this case. The President himself closed the door to any such claim when he sent his Message to Congress stating his purpose to abide by any action of Congress, whether approving or disapproving his seizure action. Here, the President immediately made sure that Congress was fully informed of the temporary action he had taken only to preserve the legislative programs from destruction until Congress could act....

There is no statute prohibiting seizure as a method of enforcing legislative programs....

Whatever the extent of Presidential power on more tranquil occasions, and whatever the right of the President to execute legislative programs as he sees fit without reporting the mode of execution to Congress, the single Presidential purpose disclosed on this record is to faithfully execute the laws by acting in an emergency to maintain the status quo, thereby preventing collapse of the legislative programs until Congress could act. The President's action served the same purposes as a judicial stay entered to maintain the status quo in order to preserve the jurisdiction of a court. In his Message to Congress immediately following the seizure, the President explained the necessity of his action in executing the military procurement and anti-inflation legislative programs and expressed his desire to cooperate with any legislative proposals approving, regulating or rejecting the seizure of the steel mills. Consequently, there is no evidence whatever of any Presidential purpose to defy Congress or act in any way inconsistent with the legislative will....

The broad executive power granted by Article II to an officer on duty 365 days a year cannot, it is said, be invoked to avert disaster. Instead, the President must confine himself to sending a message to Congress recommending action. Under this messenger-boy concept of the Office, the President cannot even act to preserve legislative programs from destruction so that Congress will have something left to act upon. There is no judicial finding that the executive action was unwarranted because there was in fact no basis for the President's finding of the existence of an emergency for, under this view, the gravity of the emergency and the immediacy of the threatened disaster are considered irrelevant as a matter of law....

Comments and Questions

1. Consider the timeline of this case. The President issues his proclamation on April 8, 1952. Within a half hour attorneys from leading New York law firms filed an action in federal district court in the District of Columbia seeking a temporary restraining order. That request was

denied, and the case was heard on an expedited basis, with the district court rendering an opinion on April 30 enjoining the seizure of the steel mills. The government immediately sought a stay of the order, which was denied by the district court but granted by the *en banc* United States Court of Appeals for the District of Columbia Circuit on the same day. Rather than have the case go through the normal process of an appeal to a court of appeals, the Supreme Court granted certiorari three days later, with briefs due in one week and oral argument two days later. The government in its week filed a 175 page brief, with much of it devoted to listing all the examples of Presidential actions taken without statutory authorization in the history of the nation. The Court allowed five hours for oral argument, and on June 2, three weeks later, rendered its decision in six separate opinions. And all of this was done without Westlaw or word processing.

2. After the decision, President Truman immediately ordered the Secretary of Commerce to return the steel mills to their owners, and shortly thereafter the strike began. While it went on for 50 days, there was no apparent effect on the "war" effort, as there had been a significant stockpile of steel created beforehand.

3. One might wonder why the steelworkers who went on strike would come back to work just because the government seized the mills. The answer is simple; the first act of the Secretary of Commerce after seizing the mills was to grant the workers the wage demands they had sought before going on strike. Indeed, the owners' first argument in court was not to overturn the seizure but to overturn the requirement to pay the higher wages. That is, the owners' real objection was not to the seizure, but to the requirement to pay the increased wages.

4. One might also wonder why President Truman did not use one of the three statutory mechanisms alluded to. The two statutory systems for seizing factories would have taken more time and had not been created to deal with labor/management problems. The Taft–Hartley Act, which specifically dealt with labor/management problems and which would have allowed the President to delay the strike, had been passed over President Truman's veto, so he did not wish to utilize it. Moreover, because it would have maintained the status quo as to wages, it would have disadvantaged the workers, and Truman believed that in the labor/management dispute labor was in the right.

5. While Justice Black's opinion is for the Court, it is not the opinion that has become the canonical opinion. That place is reserved for Justice Jackson's concurrence. While Justice Black's opinion is what scholars would call "formalistic," because it draws bright lines based on the Constitution's text, Justice Jackson's opinion is what scholars would call "functional," because it tries to accommodate the realities of governing in modern times with the ambiguous constitutional commands. Justice Black's approach provides clear answers—the President's action is unlawful because no statute authorizes it and there is no constitutional text authorizing it. The "functional" approach, however, is less determi-

native; it requires balancing. Justice Jackson's three groupings, which have become a standard approach to assessing the constitutionality of Presidential actions, provide guidance but no firm answer. For example, even after he determines that the seizure of the steel mills is in the third category—contrary to Congress's commands—that still does not by itself determine that the action is unconstitutional.

6. Justice Douglas's opinion appears to take the same formalistic approach as Justice Black's, except that Douglas appears to allow for the possibility that Congress can ratify after-the-fact a Presidential action that would have been unconstitutional without it, and in that sense approving of a President taking action without authority but in the expectation (or hope) that Congress will ratify it later—as indeed President Truman obviously hoped here.

7. Justice Frankfurter's opinion stresses the relevance of historical practice in assessing the constitutionality of Presidential action, where the Constitution is unclear. Here, he finds no historical practice justifying the seizure. The dissent, by contrast, reads the history just the opposite—as a clear justification for the seizure. Inasmuch as they are both using the same history, does this suggest the indeterminancy of history as a guide to constitutional decisionmaking? Of course, that is not to say that other guides are not indeterminate as well.

8. Justice Clark's opinion reflects an approach much like Justice Jackson's, but a bit more categorical. He is willing to accept a broad executive power in the absence of congressional action, but when Congress has spoken, the President must comply. It is interesting that John Marshall even had something to say about this, and that it remains on point today.

9. Justices Jackson, Clark, Frankfurter, and Burton all characterize the statutes in issue as reflecting a congressional decision that the President could not seize the mills as he did. The dissent, however, correctly notes that none of these laws or any other state that the President may not do what he did. They all provide other means to accomplish the same end but do not in terms forbid other means. Who do you think is right?

10. Do you see any correspondence between Truman's action in this case and some of President Bush's actions under the "War on Terror"?

B. WARS AND EMERGENCIES

The text of the Constitution would not seem to give much power or responsibility to the President with respect to wars and national emergencies. The President is the Commander-in-Chief of the army and navy and of the militia, when called into national service, a not inconsiderable power, but nonetheless a relatively subordinate role when compared to Congress's power and authority to declare war; to grant letters of marque and reprisal; to make rules for captures on land and water; to raise and support armies; to provide and maintain a navy; to make rules for the government and regulation of the land and naval forces; to provide for calling forth the militia to execute the laws, suppress insurrections, and repel invasions; and to provide for the organizing, arming, disciplining, and governing the militia when called into national service. In other words, it would appear that the President is to be the top General, but always subject to congressional control.

The Federalist papers do not provide much support for expansive Presidential authority in wars or emergencies. Reflecting their purpose to convince people to ratify the Constitution, the Federalist papers had to tread a narrow line. On the one hand, they needed to portray the powers of the President as less than those of the king of Great Britain and not dissimilar to those of some state governors. This would reassure people that the President would not be too strong. *See* The Federalist, No. 69. On the other hand, The Federalist papers needed to justify why the executive power was to be lodged in one person's hands, rather than a Council, which had been an alternative recommendation. Here, The Federalist papers stress the importance of energy and vigor in the executive, and they argue that "unity" is a necessity for such energy and vigor. *See* The Federalist, No. 70. Another necessity for energy and vigor, The Federalist papers state, is the provision of adequate powers. In Numbers 73–77, Hamilton identifies the various powers provided the President. The discussion of the powers of Commander-in-Chief is amazingly short.

> The propriety of this provision is so evident in itself, and it is, at the same time, so consonant to the precedents of the State constitutions in general, that little need be said to explain or enforce it. Even those of them which have, in other respects, coupled the chief magistrate with a council, have for the most part concentrated the military authority in him alone. Of all the cares or concerns of government, the direction of war most peculiarly demands those qualities which distinguish the exercise of power by a single hand. The direction of war implies the direction of the common strength; and the power of directing and employing the common strength, forms a usual and essential part in the definition of the executive authority.

The Federalist, No. 74. He explains that the President's authority as Commander-in-Chief is:

> nominally the same with that of the king of Great Britain, but in substance much inferior to it. It would amount to nothing more than the supreme command and direction of the military and naval forces, as first General and admiral of the Confederacy; while that of the British king extends to the declaring of war and to the raising and regulating of fleets and armies, all which, by the Constitution under consideration, would appertain to the legislature.

The Federalist, No. 69. Nowhere do The Federalist papers suggest any authority in the President beyond the listed powers. Instead, Hamilton finishes his discussion of the powers of the President by explaining the safeguards against a misuse or abuse of those powers: the limited term of office, possible impeachment, and possible subsequent criminal prosecution. Then Hamilton concludes:

> But these precautions, great as they are, are not the only ones which the plan of the convention has provided in favor of the public security. In the only instances in which the abuse of the executive authority was materially to be feared, the Chief Magistrate of the United States would, by that plan, be subjected to the control of a branch of the legislative body. What more could be desired by an enlightened and reasonable people?

The Federalist, No. 77.

Perhaps, however, Hamilton had his fingers crossed, because, after all, he was trying to reassure potential ratifiers that the President was not to be feared. Later, defending President Washington's declaration of neutrality in the war between France and Great Britain against claims that the President had no authority to make such a determination, Hamilton wrote that such a declaration clearly is not for the legislative branch, because it "is not the organ of intercourse between the United States and foreign nations." Equally clearly, it was not an appropriate exercise of judicial functions. Thus, because this power did not belong to the legislative or the judicial branches, it "of course, must belong to the executive." That is, all residual powers of the government not expressly granted to the legislative and judicial branches must reside in the executive. Moreover, Hamilton wrote,

> It deserves to be remarked, that as the participation of the senate in the making of treaties, and the power of the legislature to declare war, are exceptions out of the general "executive power" vested in the President, they are to be construed strictly, and ought to be extended no further than is essential to their execution.

The "general 'executive power' " Hamilton refers to here was the executive power that historically resided in the king of Great Britain, who alone could declare war and make treaties. Here Hamilton tells us what he really thinks.

Hamilton's view was not unopposed at the time. Madison, then a member of Congress, wrote in opposition, reflecting the views of the Democratic–Republicans of a more limited executive authority than envisaged by the Federalists.

Whoever one believes has the better argument in theory or from the constitutional text, historical practice has definitely reflected the notion of a strong executive, especially in wars, emergencies, and foreign affairs. From Washington's declaration of neutrality and Jefferson's action against the Barbary pirates to Lincoln's actions during the Civil

War, Wilson's actions preceding and during the First World War, and Roosevelt's actions preceding and during the Second World War, presidents did not shy from using their military and diplomatic powers to protect the nation and its interests—as understood by those presidents. Although the United States has only declared war on five occasions, the President has dispatched Americans armed forces abroad on more than 200 occasions. For various reasons, almost all of these actions escaped judicial review. Some, however, did not.

THE PRIZE CASES

United States Supreme Court, 1862.
67 U.S. 635, 17 L.Ed. 459.

Mr. Justice GRIER.

[On April 12, 1861, Confederate batteries in Charleston, South Carolina, opened fire on Fort Sumter, a fort located in the harbor, when it refused to surrender. This was the first outbreak of hostilities between the Union and the Confederacy. One week later, President Lincoln announced a naval blockade of the Confederate States, and pursuant to it a number of ships were seized by the U.S. Navy. The practice at the time was to sell the captured ships and any goods thereon as "prizes" at auction, with a portion of the funds being used to reward the crew of the capturing ship. The owners of these ships challenged the lawfulness of their seizure on the grounds that the blockade was unlawful, because there was as a matter of law no "war" then existing that would authorize a blockade.]

[H]ad the President a right to institute a blockade of ports in possession of persons in armed rebellion against the Government, on the principles of international law, as known and acknowledged among civilized States? ... Let us enquire whether, at the time this blockade was instituted, a state of war existed which would justify a resort to these means of subduing the hostile force....

Insurrection against a government may or may not culminate in an organized rebellion, but a civil war always begins by insurrection against the lawful authority of the Government. A civil war is never solemnly declared; it becomes such by its accidents—the number, power, and organization of the persons who originate and carry it on. When the party in rebellion occupy and hold in a hostile manner a certain portion of territory; have declared their independence; have cast off their allegiance; have organized armies; have commenced hostilities against their former sovereign, the world acknowledges them as belligerents, and the contest a *war*. *They* claim to be in arms to establish their liberty and independence, in order to become a sovereign State, while the sovereign party treats them as insurgents and rebels who owe allegiance, and who should be punished with death for their treason.

The laws of war, as established among nations, have their foundation in reason, and all tend to mitigate the cruelties and misery produced by the scourge of war. Hence the parties to a civil war usually concede to each other belligerent rights. They exchange prisoners, and adopt the other courtesies and rules common to public or national wars.

"A civil war," says Vattel, "breaks the bands of society and government, or at least suspends their force and effect; it produces in the nation two independent parties, who consider each other as enemies, and acknowledge no common judge. Those two parties, therefore, must necessarily be considered as constituting, at least for a time, two separate bodies, two distinct societies. Having no common superior to judge between them, they stand in precisely the same predicament as two nations who engage in a contest and have recourse to arms. This being the case, it is very evident that the common laws of war—those maxims of humanity, moderation, and honor—ought to be observed by both parties in every civil war....

As a civil war is never publicly proclaimed, *eo nomine*, against insurgents, its actual existence is a fact in our domestic history which the Court is bound to notice and to know.

The true test of its existence, as found in the writings of the sages of the common law, may be thus summarily stated: "When the regular course of justice is interrupted by revolt, rebellion, or insurrection, so that the Courts of Justice cannot be kept open, *civil war exists* and hostilities may be prosecuted on the same footing as if those opposing the Government were foreign enemies invading the land."

By the Constitution, Congress alone has the power to declare a national or foreign war. It cannot declare war against a State, or any number of States, by virtue of any clause in the Constitution. The Constitution confers on the President the whole Executive power. He is bound to take care that the laws be faithfully executed. He is Commander-in-chief of the Army and Navy of the United States, and of the militia of the several States when called into the actual service of the United States. He has no power to initiate or declare a war either against a foreign nation or a domestic State. But by the Acts of Congress of February 28th, 1795, and 3d of March, 1807, he is authorized to call out the militia and use the military and naval forces of the United States in case of invasion by foreign nations, and to suppress insurrection against the government of a State or of the United States.

If a war be made by invasion of a foreign nation, the President is not only authorized but bound to resist force by force. He does not initiate the war, but is bound to accept the challenge without waiting for any special legislative authority. And whether the hostile party be a foreign invader, or States organized in rebellion, it is none the less a war, although the declaration of it be "*unilateral*." ... It is not the less a war on *that account*, for war may exist without a declaration on either side. It is so laid down by the best writers on the law of nations. A declaration of war by one country only, is not a mere challenge to be accepted or refused at pleasure by the other....

This greatest of civil wars was not gradually developed by popular commotion, tumultuous assemblies, or local unorganized insurrections. However long may have been its previous conception, it nevertheless sprung forth suddenly from the parent brain, a Minerva in the full panoply of *war*. The President was bound to meet it in the shape it presented itself, without waiting for Congress to baptize it with a name; and no name given to it by him or them could change the fact....

Whether the President in fulfilling his duties, as Commander-in-chief, in suppressing an insurrection, has met with such armed hostile resistance, and a civil war of such alarming proportions as will compel him to accord to them the character of belligerents, is a question to be decided *by him*, and this Court must be governed by the decisions and acts of the political department of the Government to which this power was entrusted. "He must determine what degree of force the crisis demands." The proclamation of blockade is itself official and conclusive evidence to the Court that a state of war existed which demanded and authorized a recourse to such a measure, under the circumstances peculiar to the case....

If it were necessary to the technical existence of a war, that it should have a legislative sanction, we find it in almost every act passed at the extraordinary session of the Legislature of 1861, which was wholly employed in enacting laws to enable the Government to prosecute the war with vigor and efficiency. And finally, in 1861, we find Congress "*ex majore cautela*" and in anticipation of such astute objections, passing an act "approving, legalizing, and making valid all the acts, proclamations, and orders of the President, &c., as if they had been *issued and done under the previous express authority* and direction of the Congress of the United States." ...

On this first question therefore we are of the opinion that the President had a right, *jure belli*, to institute a blockade of ports in possession of the States in rebellion, which neutrals are bound to regard....

Mr. Justice NELSON, dissenting.

* * *

Another objection taken to the seizure of this vessel and cargo is, that there was no existing war between the United States and the States in insurrection within the meaning of the law of nations, which drew after it the consequences of a public or civil war. A contest by force between independent sovereign States is called a public war; and, when duly commenced by proclamation or otherwise, it entitles both of the belligerent parties to all the rights of war against each other, and as respects neutral nations. Chancellor Kent observes, "Though a solemn declaration, or previous notice to the enemy, be now laid aside, it is essential that some formal public act, proceeding directly from the competent source, should announce to the people at home their new relations and duties growing out of a state of war, and which should equally apprize neutral nations of the fact, to enable them to conform their conduct to the rights belonging to the new state of things." "Such an official act operates from its date to legalize all hostile acts, in like manner as a treaty of peace operates from its date to annul them." He further observes, "as war cannot lawfully be commenced on the part of the United States without an act of Congress, such act is, of course, a formal notice to all the world, and equivalent to the most solemn declaration." ...

This great and pervading change in the existing condition of a country, and in the relations of all her citizens or subjects, external and internal, from a state of peace, is the immediate effect and result of a state of war: and hence the same code which has annexed to the existence of a war all these disturbing consequences has declared that the right of making war belongs exclusively to the supreme or sovereign power of the State.

This power in all civilized nations is regulated by the fundamental laws or municipal constitution of the country.

By our constitution this power is lodged in Congress. Congress shall have power "to declare war, grant letters of marque and reprisal, and make rules concerning captures on land and water." ...

In the case of a rebellion or resistance of a portion of the people of a country against the established government, there is no doubt, if in its progress and enlargement the government thus sought to be overthrown sees fit, it may by the competent power recognize or declare the existence of a state of civil war, which will draw after it all the consequences and rights of war between the contending parties as in the case of a public war.... But before this insurrection against the established Government can be dealt with on the footing of a civil war, within the meaning of the law of nations and the Constitution of the United States, and which will draw after it belligerent rights, it must be recognized or declared by the war-making power of the Government. No power short of this can change the legal status of the Government or the relations of its citizens from that of peace to a state of war, or bring into existence all those duties and obligations of neutral third parties growing out of a state of war. The war power of the Government must be exercised before this changed condition of the Government and people and of neutral third parties can be admitted. There is no difference in this respect between a civil or a public war....

An idea seemed to be entertained that all that was necessary to constitute a war was organized hostility in the district of country in a state of rebellion—that conflicts on land and on sea—the taking of towns and capture of fleets—in fine, the magnitude and dimensions of the resistance against the Government—constituted war with all the belligerent rights belonging to civil war. With a view to enforce this idea, we had, during the argument, an imposing historical detail of the several measures adopted by the Confederate States to enable them to resist the authority of the general Government, and of many bold and daring acts of resistance and of conflict. It was said that war was to be ascertained by looking at the armies and navies or public force of the contending parties, and the battles lost and won—that in the language of one of the learned counsel, "Whenever the situation of opposing hostilities has assumed the proportions and pursued the methods of war, then peace is driven out, the ordinary authority and administration of law are suspended, and war in fact and by necessity is the *status* of the nation until peace is restored and the laws resumed their dominion."

Now, in one sense, no doubt this is war, and may be a war of the most extensive and threatening dimensions and effects, but it is a statement simply of its existence in a material sense, and has no relevancy or weight when the question is what constitutes war in a legal sense, in the sense of the law of nations, and of the Constitution of the United States? For it must be a war in this sense to attach to it all the consequences that belong to belligerent rights. Instead, therefore, of inquiring after armies and navies, and victories lost and won, or organized rebellion against the general Government, the inquiry should be into the law of nations and into the municipal fundamental laws of the Government. For we find there that to constitute a civil war in the sense in which we are speaking, before it can exist, in contemplation of law, it must be recognized or declared by the sovereign power of the State, and which sovereign power by our Constitution is lodged in the Congress of the United States–civil war, therefore, under our system of government, can exist only by an act of Congress, which requires the assent of two of the great departments of the Government, the Executive and Legislative.

We have thus far been speaking of the war power under the Constitution of the United States, and as known and recognized by the law of nations. But we are asked, what would become of the peace and integrity of the Union in case of an insurrection at home or invasion from abroad if this power could not be exercised by the President in the recess of Congress, and until that body could be assembled?

The framers of the Constitution fully comprehended this question, and provided for the contingency. Indeed, it would have been surprising if they had not, as a rebellion had occurred in the State of Massachusetts while the Convention was in session, and which had become so general that it was quelled only by calling upon the military power of the State. The Constitution declares that Congress shall have power "to provide for calling forth the militia to execute the laws of the Union, suppress insurrections, and repel invasions."Another clause, "that the President shall be Commander-in-chief of the Army and Navy of the United States, and of the militia of the several States when called into the actual service of United States;" and, again, "He shall take care that the laws shall be faithfully executed."Congress passed laws on this subject in 1792 and 1795.

The last Act provided that whenever the United States shall be invaded or be in imminent danger of invasion from a foreign nation, it shall be lawful for the President to call forth such number of the militia most convenient to the place of danger, and in case of insurrection in any State against the Government thereof, it shall be lawful for the President, on the application of the Legislature of such State, if in session, or if not, of the Executive of the State, to call forth such number of militia of any other State or States as he may judge sufficient to suppress such insurrection. [A]nd by the Act 3 March, 1807, it is provided that in case of insurrection or obstruction of the laws, either in the United States or of any State of Territory, where it is lawful for the President to call forth the militia for the purpose of suppressing such insurrection, and causing the laws to be executed, it shall be lawful to employ for the same purpose such part of the land and naval forces of the United States as shall be judged necessary.

It will be seen, therefore, that ample provision has been made under the Constitution and laws against any sudden and unexpected disturbance of the public peace from insurrection at home or invasion from abroad. The whole military and naval power of the country is put under the control of the President to meet the emergency.

It has been argued that the authority conferred on the President by the Act of 1795 invests him with the war power. But the obvious answer is, that it proceeds from a different clause in the Constitution and which is given for different purposes and objects, namely, to execute the laws and preserve the public order and tranquillity of the country in a time of peace by preventing or suppressing any public disorder or disturbance by foreign or domestic enemies. Certainly, if there is any force in this argument, then we are in a state of war with all the rights of war, and all the penal consequences attending it every time this power is exercised by calling out a military force to execute the laws or to suppress insurrection or rebellion; for the nature of the power cannot depend upon the numbers called out. If so, what numbers will constitute war and what numbers will not? It has also been argued that this power of the President from necessity should be construed as vesting him with the war power, or the Republic might greatly suffer or be in danger from the attacks of the hostile party before the assembling to Congress. But we have seen that the whole military and naval force are in his hands under the municipal laws of the country. He can meet the adversary upon land and water with all the forces of the Government. The truth is, this idea of the existence of any necessity for clothing the President with the war power, under the Act of 1795, is simply a monstrous exaggeration; for, besides having the command of the whole of the army and navy, Congress can be assembled within any thirty days, if the safety of the country requires that the war power shall be brought into operation....

Congress assembled on the call for an extra session the 4th of July, 1861, and among the first acts passed was one in which the President was authorized by proclamation to interdict all trade and intercourse between all the inhabitants of States in insurrection and the rest of the United States, subjecting vessel and cargo to capture and condemnation as prize, and also to direct the capture of any ship or vessel belonging in whole or in part to any inhabitant of a State whose inhabitants are declared by the proclamation to be in a state of insurrection, found at sea or in any part of the rest of the United States. Act of Congress of 13th of July, 1861, secs. 5, 6....

This Act of Congress, we think, recognized a state of civil war between the Government and the Confederate States, and made it territorial.... We agree, therefore, that the Act 13th July, 1861, recognized a state of civil war between the Government and the people of the State described in that proclamation....

Upon the whole, after the most careful consideration of this case which the pressure of other duties has admitted, I am compelled to the conclusion that no civil war existed between this Government and the States in insurrection till recognized by the Act of Congress 13th of July, 1861; that the President does not possess the power under the Constitution to declare war or recognize its existence within the meaning of the law of nations, which carries with it belligerent rights, and thus change the country and all its citizens from a state of peace to a state of war; that this power belongs exclusively to the Congress of the United States, and, consequently, that the President had no power to set on foot a blockade under the law of nations, and that the capture of the vessel and cargo in this case, and in all cases before us in which the capture occurred before the 13th of July, 1861, for breach of blockade, or as enemies' property, are illegal and void, and that the decrees of condemnation should be reversed and the vessel and cargo restored.

Mr. Chief Justice TANEY, Mr. Justice CATRON and Mr. Justice CLIFFORD, concurred in the dissenting opinion of Mr. Justice Nelson.

Comments and Questions

1. Everyone on the Court agrees that a civil war can be a "war" within the meaning of international law and the Constitution, just as they all agree that hostilities between nations can be a war within the meaning of international law and the Constitution. The disagreement between the majority and the dissent is what it takes to transform a state of hostilities, whether between nations or within a nation, into a "war" for legal purposes. What does the majority say? What does the dissent say?

2. If the President can characterize any given state of hostilities as a "war" for legal purposes, what does the Constitution mean that Congress has the power to declare war?

3. Do you agree with the dissent that the only way hostilities can be a "war" for legal purposes is for Congress to so declare it? What difference does it make today whether something is a "war" for legal purposes as opposed to for practical purposes? After all, we don't take "prizes" anymore.

4. The dissent seems to think it is important that the President can call out the militia as well as utilize all the armed forces on his own

say so pursuant to the several militia acts. If these did not exist, would it make a difference to the dissent's analysis?

5. Both the majority and dissent agree that the Act of 13 July, 1861, had the effect of declaring war, although it did not say so in so many words. What does it take to characterize a legislative act as a declaration of war? Is it enough that it authorizes action that would be illegal (domestically or internationally) but for a state of war?

EX PARTE QUIRIN

United States Supreme Court, 1942.
317 U.S. 1, 63 S.Ct. 2, 87 L.Ed. 3.

Mr. Chief Justice STONE delivered the opinion of the Court.

[On the night of June 13, 1942, a German submarine deposited on Amagansett Beach on Long Island, New York, four persons equipped with explosives, fuses and incendiary and timing devices. Four nights later a German submarine deposited four more persons similarly equipped on Ponte Vedra Beach, near Jacksonville, Florida. All proceeded in civilian clothes with orders to destroy war industries and war facilities in the United States. Two of the persons who landed in New York turned themselves into the Federal Bureau of Investigation, and as a result the remainder were taken into custody shortly thereafter in New York or Chicago by FBI agents. All of these persons had been born in Germany, lived for some period in the United States, but had returned to Germany between 1933 and 1941. All but one were German citizens. One claimed to be an American citizen. All had received training at a sabotage school near Berlin, Germany, where they were instructed in the use of explosives and in methods of secret writing.

Pursuant to an order of President Roosevelt, they were charged before a military commission for spying in violation of the laws of war. They sought habeas corpus review in a federal district court, which denied review. They sought immediate review of that decision in the Supreme Court, which the Court granted. It heard argument on July 29 and 30, while their trial before the Military Commission was still underway, but denied the writ on July 31 with a brief *per curiam* opinion, stating that a full opinion would come later. They were all convicted and sentenced to death, but President Roosevelt commuted the sentences for the two who had turned themselves in, requiring instead a life sentence for one and 30 years for the other. On August 8, the remaining six were executed. On October 29, the Supreme Court filed its full opinion, which follows.]

[T]he question for decision is whether the detention of petitioners by respondent for trial by Military Commission, appointed by Order of the President of July 2, 1942, on charges preferred against them purporting to set out their violations of the law of war and of the Articles of War, is in conformity to the laws and Constitution of the United States....

The President, as President and Commander in Chief of the Army and Navy, by Order of July 2, 1942, appointed a Military Commission and directed it to try petitioners for offenses against the law of war and the Articles of War, and prescribed regulations for the procedure on the trial and for review of the record of the trial and of any judgment or sentence of the Commission. On the same day, by Proclamation, the President declared that "all persons who are subjects, citizens or residents of any nation at war with the United States or who give obedience to or act under the direction of any such nation, and who during time of war enter or attempt to enter the United States * * * through coastal or boundary defenses, and are charged with committing or attempting or preparing to commit sabotage, espionage, hostile or warlike acts, or violations of the law of war, shall be subject to the law of war and to the jurisdiction of military tribunals."

The Proclamation also stated in terms that all such persons were denied access to the courts....

Petitioners' main contention is that the President is without any statutory or constitutional authority to order the petitioners to be tried by military tribunal for offenses with which they are charged; that in consequence they are entitled to be tried in the civil courts with the safeguards, including trial by jury, which the Fifth and Sixth Amendments guarantee to all persons charged in such courts with criminal offenses. In any case it is urged that the President's Order, in prescribing the procedure of the Commission and the method for review of its findings and sentence, and the proceedings of the Commission under the Order, conflict with Articles of War adopted by Congress—particularly Articles 38, 43, 46, 50 1/2 and 70—and are illegal and void.

The Government challenges each of these propositions. But regardless of their merits, it also insists that petitioners must be denied access to the courts, both because they are enemy aliens or have entered our territory as enemy belligerents, and because the President's Proclamation undertakes in terms to deny such access to the class of persons defined by the Proclamation, which aptly describes the character and conduct of petitioners. It is urged that if they are enemy aliens or if the Proclamation has force no court may afford the petitioners a hearing. But there is certainly nothing in the Proclamation to preclude access to the courts for determining its applicability to the particular case. And neither the Proclamation nor the fact that they are enemy aliens forecloses consideration by the courts of petitioners' contentions that the Constitution and laws of the United States constitutionally enacted forbid their trial by military commission....

We are not here concerned with any question of the guilt or innocence of petitioners. Constitutional safeguards for the protection of all who are charged with offenses are not to be disregarded in order to inflict merited punishment on some who are guilty. But the detention and trial of petitioners—ordered by the President in the declared exercise of his powers as Commander in Chief of the Army in time of war and of grave public danger—are not to be set aside by the courts without the clear conviction that they are in conflict with the Constitution or laws of Congress constitutionally enacted.

Congress and the President, like the courts, possess no power not derived from the Constitution. But one of the objects of the Constitution, as declared by its preamble, is to "provide for the common defence". As a means to that end the Constitution gives to Congress [a number of powers.]

The Constitution confers on the President the "executive Power," and imposes on him the duty to "take Care that the Laws be faithfully executed." It makes him the Commander in Chief of the Army and Navy, and empowers him to appoint and commission officers of the United States.

The Constitution thus invests the President as Commander in Chief with the power to wage war which Congress has declared, and to carry into effect all laws passed by Congress for the conduct of war and for the government and regulation of the Armed Forces, and all laws defining and punishing offences against the law of nations, including those which pertain to the conduct of war.

By the Articles of War, Congress has provided rules for the government of the Army. [T]he Articles ... recognize the "military commission" appointed by military command as an appropriate tribunal for the trial and punishment of offenses against the law of war not ordinarily tried by court martial. Articles 38 and 46 authorize the President, with certain limitations, to prescribe the procedure for military commissions. Articles 81 and 82 authorize trial, either by court martial or military commission, of those charged with relieving, harboring or corresponding with the enemy and those charged with spying....

Similarly the Espionage Act of 1917, which authorizes trial in the district courts of certain offenses that tend to interfere with the prosecution of war, provides that nothing contained in the act "shall be deemed to limit the jurisdiction of the general courts-martial, military commissions, or naval courts-martial."

From the very beginning of its history this Court has recognized and applied the law of war as including that part of the law of nations which prescribes, for the conduct of war, the status, rights and duties of enemy nations as well as of enemy individuals. By the Articles of War, ... Congress has explicitly provided, so far as it may constitutionally do so, that military tribunals shall have jurisdiction to try offenders or offenses against the law of war in appropriate cases. Congress, in addition to making rules for the government of our Armed Forces, has thus exercised its authority to define and punish offenses against the law of nations by sanctioning, within constitutional limitations, the jurisdiction of military commissions to try persons for offenses which, according to the rules and precepts of the law of nations, and more particularly the law of war, are cognizable by such tribunals. And the President, as Commander in Chief, by his Proclamation in time of war has invoked that law. By his Order creating the present Commission he has undertaken to exercise the authority conferred upon him by Congress, and also such authority as the Constitution itself gives the Commander in Chief, to direct the performance of those functions which may constitutionally be performed by the military arm of the nation in time of war.

[I]t is unnecessary for present purposes to determine to what extent the President as Commander in Chief has constitutional power to create military commissions without the support of Congressional legislation. For here Congress has authorized trial of offenses against the law of war before such commissions. We are concerned only with the question whether it is within the constitutional power of the national government to place petitioners upon trial before a military commission for the offenses with which they are charged. We must therefore first inquire whether any of the acts charged is an offense against the law of war cognizable before a military tribunal, and if so whether the Constitution prohibits the trial. We may assume that there are acts ... which would not be triable by military tribunal here, ... because they are of that class of offenses constitutionally triable only by a jury. It was upon such grounds that the Court denied the right to proceed by military tribunal in Ex parte Milligan. But as we shall show, these petitioners were charged with an offense against the law of war which the Constitution does not require to be tried by jury....

By universal agreement and practice the law of war draws a distinction between the armed forces and the peaceful populations of belligerent nations and also between those who are lawful and unlawful combatants. Lawful combatants are subject to capture and detention as prisoners of war by opposing military forces. Unlawful combatants are likewise subject to capture and detention, but in addition they are subject to trial and punishment by military tribunals for acts which render their belligerency unlawful. The spy who secretly and without uniform passes the military lines of a belligerent in time of war, seeking to gather military information and communicate it to the enemy, or an enemy combatant who without uniform comes secretly through the lines for the purpose of waging war by destruction of life or property, are familiar examples of belligerents who are generally deemed not to be entitled to the status of prisoners of war, but to be offenders against the law of war subject to trial and punishment by military tribunals....

Our Government, by thus defining lawful belligerents entitled to be treated as prisoners of war, has recognized that there is a class of unlawful belligerents not entitled to that privilege, including those who though combatants do not wear "fixed and distinctive emblems". And by Article 15 of the Articles of War Congress has made provision for their trial and punishment by military commission, according to "the law of war." ...

Citizenship in the United States of an enemy belligerent does not relieve him from the consequences of a belligerency which is unlawful because in violation of the law of war. Citizens who associate themselves with the military arm of the enemy government, and with its aid, guidance and direction enter this country bent on hostile acts are enemy belligerents within the meaning of the Hague Convention and the law of war....

But petitioners insist that even if the offenses with which they are charged are offenses against the law of war, their trial is subject to the requirement of the Fifth Amendment that no person shall be held to answer for a capital or otherwise infamous crime unless on a presentment or indictment of a grand jury, and that such trials by Article III, § 2, and the Sixth Amendment must be by jury in a civil court....

Presentment by a grand jury and trial by a jury of the vicinage where the crime was committed were at the time of the adoption of the Constitution familiar parts of the machinery for criminal trials in the civil courts. But they were procedures unknown to military tribunals, which are not courts in the sense of the Judiciary Article.... In the light of this long-continued and consistent interpretation we must conclude that § 2 of Article III and the Fifth and Sixth Amendments cannot be taken to have extended the right to demand a jury to trials by military commission, or to have required that offenses against the law of war not triable by jury at common law be tried only in the civil courts.

Since the Amendments, like § 2 of Article III, do not preclude all trials of offenses against the law of war by military commission without a jury when the offenders are aliens not members of our Armed Forces, it is plain that they present no greater obstacle to the trial in like manner of citizen enemies who have violated the law of war applicable to enemies....

We conclude that the Fifth and Sixth Amendments did not restrict whatever authority was conferred by the Constitution to try offenses against the law of war by military commission, and that petitioners, charged with such an offense not required to be tried by jury at common law, were lawfully placed on trial by the Commission without a jury.

Petitioners, and especially petitioner Haupt, stress the pronouncement of this Court in the *Milligan* case, that the law of war "can never be applied to citizens in states which have upheld the authority of the government, and where the courts are open and their process unobstructed." Elsewhere in its opinion, the Court was at pains to point out that Milligan, a citizen twenty years resident in Indiana, who had never been a resident of any of the states in rebellion, was not an enemy belligerent either entitled to the status of a prisoner of war or subject to the penalties imposed upon unlawful belligerents. We construe the Court's statement as to the inapplicability of the law of war to Milligan's case as having particular reference to the facts before it. From them the Court concluded that Milligan, not being a part of or associated with the armed forces of the enemy, was a non-belligerent, not subject to the law of war save as—in circumstances found not there to be present and not involved here—martial law might be constitutionally established.

The Court's opinion is inapplicable to the case presented by the present record. We have no occasion now to define with meticulous care the ultimate boundaries of the jurisdiction of military tribunals to try persons according to the law of war. It is enough that petitioners here, upon the conceded facts, were plainly within those boundaries, and were held in good faith for trial by military commission, charged with being enemies who, with the purpose of destroying war materials and utilities, entered or after entry remained in our territory without uniform—an offense against the law of war. We hold only that those particular acts constitute an offense against the law of war which the Constitution authorizes to be tried by military commission....

There remains the contention that the President's Order of July 2, 1942, so far as it lays down the procedure to be followed on the trial before the Commission and on the review of its findings and sentence, and the procedure in fact followed by the Commission, are in conflict with Articles of War 38, 43, 46, 50 1/2 and 70....

Petitioners do not argue and we do not consider the question whether the President is compelled by the Articles of War to afford unlawful enemy belligerents a trial before subjecting them to disciplinary measures. Their contention is that, if Congress has authorized their trial by military commission upon the charges preferred—violations of the law of war and the 81st and 82nd Articles of War—it has by the Articles of War prescribed the procedure by which the trial is to be conducted; and that since the President has ordered their trial for such offenses by military commission, they are entitled to claim the protection of the procedure which Congress has commanded shall be controlling.

We need not inquire whether Congress may restrict the power of the Commander in Chief to deal with enemy belligerents. For the Court is unanimous in its conclusion that the Articles in question could not at any stage of the proceedings afford any basis for issuing the writ. But a majority of the full Court are not agreed on the appropriate grounds for decision. Some members of the Court are of opinion that Congress did not intend the Articles of War to govern a Presidential military commission convened for the determination of questions relating to admitted enemy invaders and that the context of the Articles makes clear that they should not be construed to apply in that class of cases. Others are of the view that—even though this trial is subject to whatever provisions of the Articles of War Congress has in terms made applicable to "commissions"—the particular Articles in question, rightly construed, do not foreclose the procedure prescribed by the President or that shown to have been employed by the Commission in a trial of offenses against the law of war and the 81st and 82nd Articles of War, by a military commission appointed by the President.

Accordingly, we conclude that Charge I, on which petitioners were detained for trial by the Military Commission, alleged an offense which the President is authorized to order tried by military commission; that his Order convening the Commission was a lawful order and that the

Commission was lawfully constituted; that the petitioners were held in lawful custody and did not show cause for their discharge. It follows that the orders of the District Court should be affirmed, and that leave to file petitions for habeas corpus in this Court should be denied.

Mr. Justice MURPHY took no part in the consideration or decision of these cases.

Comments and Questions

1. Here there is no question that there is a declared war. Rather the question is what power the President has to detain, try, and execute a sentence with regard to persons alleged to be unlawful enemy combatants acting in violation of the laws of war. The alternative, sought by the petitioners, is that they be tried by civilian courts for violations of the criminal law. They cite the Civil War case of *Ex Parte Milligan*, 71 U.S. 2 (1866), in which the Court set Milligan free from military custody and held that he could not be tried by military commission. The Court in *Quirin* finds the facts in *Milligan* distinguishable, but the language in *Milligan* is unconditional: "[the laws of war] can never be applied to citizens in states which have upheld the authority of the government [*i.e.*, not Confederate states], and where the courts are open and their process unobstructed." Haupt, the saboteur who claimed American citizenship, argued this language applied to him, because he was found in a state upholding the authority of the government and where the courts were open and unobstructed. And there were (and are) federal laws criminalizing sabotage and conspiracy to commit sabotage, not to mention treason. Do you think the *Quirin* Court's factual distinction is sufficient?

2. How important is it in *Quirin* that Congress had authorized the use of military commissions in such cases? What is the disagreement on the Court regarding the claim that the commission did not follow the procedures required by the Articles of War?

3. *Quirin* has become very topical because of the "War on Terror," the federal military detention of a large number of alleged unlawful combatants, and the desire by the government to try them by military commission. How would *Quirin*'s analysis of who can be subjected to military commissions apply to Jose Padilla, the citizen arrested by the FBI in Chicago for allegedly being involved in a plot to detonate a "dirty bomb," who was then turned over to the military and held in military custody as an alleged unlawful enemy combatant? Could he be tried by military commission? The government at first took the position that he could, but when the case looked like it would go to the Supreme Court, the government released him from military custody, took him into civilian custody, and charged him with several federal criminal violations. In August 2007 he was convicted on all charges by a federal jury.

HAMDI v. RUMSFELD

United States Supreme Court, 2004.
542 U.S. 507, 124 S.Ct. 2633, 159 L.Ed.2d 578.

Justice O'CONNOR announced the judgment of the Court and delivered an opinion, in which THE CHIEF JUSTICE, Justice KENNEDY, and Justice BREYER join.

At this difficult time in our Nation's history, we are called upon to consider the legality of the Government's detention of a United States citizen on United States soil as an "enemy combatant" and to address the process that is constitutionally owed to one who seeks to challenge his classification as such.... We hold that although Congress authorized the detention of combatants in the narrow circumstances alleged here, due process demands that a citizen held in the United States as an enemy combatant be given a meaningful opportunity to contest the factual basis for that detention before a neutral decisionmaker.

On September 11, 2001, the al Qaeda terrorist network used hijacked commercial airliners to attack prominent targets in the United States.... One week later, ... Congress passed a resolution authorizing the President to "use all necessary and appropriate force against those nations, organizations, or persons he determines planned, authorized, committed, or aided the terrorist attacks" or "harbored such organizations or persons, in order to prevent any future acts of international terrorism against the United States by such nations, organizations or persons." Authorization for Use of Military Force (AUMF). Soon thereafter, the President ordered United States Armed Forces to Afghanistan, with a mission to subdue al Qaeda and quell the Taliban regime that was known to support it.

This case arises out of the detention of a man whom the Government alleges took up arms with the Taliban during this conflict. His name is Yaser Esam Hamdi. Born in Louisiana in 1980, Hamdi moved with his family to Saudi Arabia as a child. By 2001, the parties agree, he resided in Afghanistan. At some point that year, he was seized by members of the Northern Alliance, a coalition of military groups opposed to the Taliban government, and eventually was turned over to the United States military.... The Government contends that Hamdi is an "enemy combatant," and that this status justifies holding him in the United States indefinitely—without formal charges or proceedings—unless and until it makes the determination that access to counsel or further process is warranted.

The threshold question before us is whether the Executive has the authority to detain citizens who qualify as "enemy combatants." There is some debate as to the proper scope of this term, and the Government has never provided any court with the full criteria that it uses in classifying individuals as such. It has made clear, however, that, for purposes of this case, the "enemy combatant" that it is seeking to detain is an individual who, it alleges, was " 'part of or supporting forces hostile to the United States or coalition partners' " in Afghanistan and who " 'engaged in an armed conflict against the United States' " there. We therefore answer only the narrow question before us: whether the detention of citizens falling within that definition is authorized.

The Government maintains that no explicit congressional authorization is required, because the Executive possesses plenary authority to detain pursuant to Article II of the Constitution. We do not reach the question whether Article II provides such authority, however, because we agree with the Government's alternative position, that Congress has in fact authorized Hamdi's detention, through the AUMF.

[F]or the reasons that follow, we conclude that the AUMF is explicit congressional authorization for the detention of individuals in the narrow category we describe (assuming, without deciding, that such authorization is required)....

The AUMF authorizes the President to use "all necessary and appropriate force" against "nations, organizations, or persons" associated with the September 11, 2001, terrorist attacks. There can be no doubt that individuals who fought against the United States in Afghanistan as part of the Taliban, an organization known to have supported the al Qaeda terrorist network responsible for those attacks, are individuals Congress sought to target in passing the AUMF. We conclude that detention of individuals falling into the limited category we are considering, for the duration of the particular conflict in which they were captured, is so fundamental and accepted an incident to war as to be an exercise of the "necessary and appropriate force" Congress has authorized the President to use.

The capture and detention of lawful combatants and the capture, detention, and trial of unlawful combatants, by "universal agreement and practice," are "important incident[s] of war." *Ex parte Quirin.* The purpose of detention is to prevent captured individuals from returning to the field of battle and taking up arms once again.

There is no bar to this Nation's holding one of its own citizens as an enemy combatant. In *Quirin,* one of the detainees, Haupt, alleged that he was a naturalized United States citizen. We held that "[c]itizens who associate themselves with the military arm of the enemy government, and with its aid, guidance and direction enter this country bent on hostile acts, are enemy belligerents within the meaning of ... the law of war." ...

In light of these principles, it is of no moment that the AUMF does not use specific language of detention. Because detention to prevent a combatant's return to the battlefield is a fundamental incident of waging war, in permitting the use of "necessary and appropriate force," Congress has clearly and unmistakably authorized detention in the narrow circumstances considered here.

Hamdi objects, nevertheless, that Congress has not authorized the *indefinite* detention to which he is now subject.... We take Hamdi's objection to be not to the lack of certainty regarding the date on which the conflict will end, but to the substantial prospect of perpetual detention. We recognize that the national security underpinnings of the "war on terror," although crucially important, are broad and malleable. As the Government concedes, "given its unconventional nature, the current conflict is unlikely to end with a formal cease-fire agreement." The prospect Hamdi raises is therefore not farfetched. If the Government does not consider this unconventional war won for two generations, and if it maintains during that time that Hamdi might, if released, rejoin forces fighting against the United States, then the position it has taken throughout the litigation of this case suggests that Hamdi's detention could last for the rest of his life.

It is a clearly established principle of the law of war that detention may last no longer than active hostilities.

Hamdi contends that the AUMF does not authorize indefinite or perpetual detention. Certainly, we agree that indefinite detention for the purpose of interrogation is not authorized. Further, we understand Congress' grant of authority for the use of "necessary and appropriate force" to include the authority to detain for the duration of the relevant conflict, and our understanding is based on longstanding law-of-war principles. If the practical circumstances of a given conflict are entirely unlike those of the conflicts that informed the development of the law of war, that understanding may unravel. But that is not the situation we face as of this date. Active combat operations against Taliban fighters apparently are ongoing in Afghanistan. The United States may detain, for the duration of these hostilities, individuals legitimately determined to be Taliban combatants who "engaged in an armed conflict against the United States." If the record establishes that United States troops are still involved in active combat in Afghanistan, those detentions are part of the exercise of "necessary and appropriate force," and therefore are authorized by the AUMF....

Even in cases in which the detention of enemy combatants is legally authorized, there remains the question of what process is constitutionally due to a citizen who disputes his enemy-combatant status.... Though they reach radically different conclusions on the process that ought to attend the present proceeding, the parties begin on common ground. All agree that, absent suspension, the writ of habeas corpus remains available to every individual detained within the United States....

The [Government argues] that further factual exploration is unwarranted and inappropriate in light of the extraordinary constitutional interests at stake. Under the Government's most extreme rendition of this argument, "[r]espect for separation of powers and the limited institutional capabilities of courts in matters of military decision-making in connection with an ongoing conflict" ought to eliminate entirely any individual process, restricting the courts to investigating only whether legal authorization exists for the broader detention scheme. At most, the Government argues, courts should review its determination that a citizen is an enemy combatant under a very deferential "some evidence" standard. Under this review, a court would assume the accuracy of the Government's articulated basis for Hamdi's detention....

In response, Hamdi emphasizes that this Court consistently has recognized that an individual challenging his detention may not be held at the will of the Executive without recourse to some proceeding before a neutral tribunal to determine whether the Executive's asserted justifications for that detention have basis in fact and warrant in law....

Both of these positions highlight legitimate concerns. And both emphasize the tension that often exists between the autonomy that the Government asserts is necessary in order to pursue effectively a particular goal and the process that a citizen contends he is due before he is deprived of a constitutional right....

We ... hold that a citizen-detainee seeking to challenge his classification as an enemy combatant must receive notice of the factual basis for his classification, and a fair opportunity to rebut the Government's factual assertions before a neutral decisionmaker....

At the same time, the exigencies of the circumstances may demand that, aside from these core elements, enemy-combatant proceedings may be tailored to alleviate their uncommon potential to burden the Executive at a time of ongoing military conflict. Hearsay, for example, may need to be accepted as the most reliable available evidence from the Government in such a proceeding. Likewise, the Constitution would not be offended by a presumption in favor of the Government's evidence, so long as that presumption remained a rebuttable one and fair opportunity for rebuttal were provided. Thus, once the Government puts forth credible evidence that the habeas petitioner meets the enemy-combatant criteria, the onus could shift to the petitioner to rebut that evidence with more persuasive evidence that he falls outside the criteria. A burden-shifting scheme of this sort would meet the goal of ensuring that the errant tourist, embedded journalist, or local aid worker has a chance to prove military error while giving due regard to the Executive once it has put forth meaningful support for its conclusion that the detainee is in fact an enemy combatant....

In so holding, we necessarily reject the Government's assertion that separation of powers principles mandate a heavily circumscribed role for the courts in such circumstances.... We have long since made clear that a state of war is not a blank check for the President when it comes to the rights of the Nation's citizens. *Youngstown Sheet & Tube*. Whatever power the United States Constitution envisions for the Executive in its exchanges with other nations or with enemy organizations in times of conflict, it most assuredly envisions a role for all three branches when individual liberties are at stake....

The judgment of the [court of appeals] is vacated, and the case is remanded for further proceedings.

Justice SOUTER, with whom Justice GINSBURG joins, concurring in part, dissenting in part, and concurring in the judgment.

According to Yaser Hamdi's petition for writ of habeas corpus, brought on his behalf by his father, the Government of the United States is detaining him, an American citizen on American soil, with the explanation that he was seized on the field of battle in Afghanistan, having been on the enemy side. It is undisputed that the Government has not charged him with espionage, treason, or any other crime under domestic law. It is likewise undisputed that for one year and nine months, on the basis of an Executive designation of Hamdi as an "enemy combatant," the Government denied him the right to send or receive any communication beyond the prison where he was held and, in particular, denied him access to counsel to represent him. The Government asserts a right to hold Hamdi under these conditions indefinitely, that is, until the Government determines that the United States is no longer threatened by the terrorism exemplified in the attacks of September 11, 2001....

The Government [argues] that Hamdi's incommunicado imprisonment as an enemy combatant seized on the field of battle falls within the President's power as Commander in Chief under the laws and usages of war, and is in any event authorized by two statutes. Accordingly, the Government contends that Hamdi has no basis for any challenge by petition for habeas except to his own status as an enemy combatant; and even that challenge may go no further than to enquire whether "some evidence" supports Hamdi's designation; if there is "some evidence," Hamdi should remain locked up at the discretion of the Executive. At the argument of this case, in fact, the Government went further and suggested that as long as a prisoner could challenge his enemy combatant designation when responding to interrogation during incommunicado detention he was accorded sufficient process to support his designation as an enemy combatant. ("[H]e has an opportunity to explain it in his own words" "[d]uring interrogation"). Since on either view judicial enquiry so limited would be virtually worthless as a way to contest detention, the Government's concession of jurisdiction to hear Hamdi's habeas claim is more theoretical than practical, leaving the assertion of Executive authority close to unconditional.

The plurality rejects any such limit on the exercise of habeas jurisdiction and so far I agree with its opinion. The plurality does, however, accept the Government's position that if Hamdi's designation as an enemy combatant is correct, his detention (at least as to some period) is authorized by an Act of Congress ... , that is, by the Authorization for Use of Military Force. Here, I disagree and respectfully dissent. The Government has failed to demonstrate that the Force Resolution authorizes the detention complained of here even on the facts the Government claims....

[T]here is the Government's claim, accepted by the plurality, that the terms of the Force Resolution are adequate to authorize detention of an enemy combatant under the circumstances described.... Since the

Force Resolution was adopted one week after the attacks of September 11, 2001, it naturally speaks with some generality, but its focus is clear, and that is on the use of military power. It is fairly read to authorize the use of armies and weapons, whether against other armies or individual terrorists. But, ... it never so much as uses the word detention, and there is no reason to think Congress might have perceived any need to augment Executive power to deal with dangerous citizens within the United States, given the well-stocked statutory arsenal of defined criminal offenses covering the gamut of actions that a citizen sympathetic to terrorists might commit....

Subject to these qualifications, I join with the plurality in a judgment of the Court vacating the Fourth Circuit's judgment and remanding the case.

Justice SCALIA, with whom Justice STEVENS joins, dissenting.

Petitioner Yaser Hamdi, a presumed American citizen, has been imprisoned without charge or hearing in the Norfolk and Charleston Naval Brigs for more than two years, on the allegation that he is an enemy combatant who bore arms against his country for the Taliban. His father claims to the contrary, that he is an inexperienced aid worker caught in the wrong place at the wrong time. This case brings into conflict the competing demands of national security and our citizens' constitutional right to personal liberty. Although I share the plurality's evident unease as it seeks to reconcile the two, I do not agree with its resolution.

Where the Government accuses a citizen of waging war against it, our constitutional tradition has been to prosecute him in federal court for treason or some other crime. Where the exigencies of war prevent that, the Constitution's Suspension Clause, Art. I, § 9, cl. 2, allows Congress to relax the usual protections temporarily. Absent suspension, however, the Executive's assertion of military exigency has not been thought sufficient to permit detention without charge.... Accordingly, I would reverse the judgment below.

The very core of liberty secured by our Anglo–Saxon system of separated powers has been freedom from indefinite imprisonment at the will of the Executive....

To be sure, certain types of permissible *non* criminal detention—that is, those not dependent upon the contention that the citizen had committed a criminal act—did not require the protections of criminal procedure. However, these fell into a limited number of well-recognized exceptions—civil commitment of the mentally ill, for example, and temporary detention in quarantine of the infectious. It is unthinkable that the Executive could render otherwise criminal grounds for detention noncriminal merely by disclaiming an intent to prosecute, or by asserting that it was incapacitating dangerous offenders rather than punishing wrongdoing....

The allegations here, of course, are no ordinary accusations of criminal activity. Yaser Esam Hamdi has been imprisoned because the Government believes he participated in the waging of war against the United States. The relevant question, then, is whether there is a different, special procedure for imprisonment of a citizen accused of wrongdoing *by aiding the enemy in wartime.*

Justice O'CONNOR, writing for a plurality of this Court, asserts that captured enemy combatants (other than those suspected of war crimes) have traditionally been detained until the cessation of hostilities and then released. That is probably an accurate description of wartime practice with respect to enemy *aliens.* The tradition with respect to American citizens, however, has been quite different. Citizens aiding the enemy have been treated as traitors subject to the criminal process....

There are times when military exigency renders resort to the traditional criminal process impracticable.... Where the Executive has not pursued the usual course of charge, committal, and conviction, it has historically secured the Legislature's explicit approval of a suspension.... Our Federal Constitution contains a provision explicitly permitting suspension, but limiting the situations in which it may be invoked....

The Suspension Clause was by design a safety valve, the Constitution's only "express provision for exercise of extraordinary authority because of a crisis," *Youngstown Sheet & Tube Co. v. Sawyer* (Jackson, concurring).

The Government argues that our more recent jurisprudence ratifies its indefinite imprisonment of a citizen within the territorial jurisdiction of federal courts. It places primary reliance upon *Ex parte Quirin,* a World War II case upholding the trial by military commission of eight German saboteurs, one of whom, Herbert Haupt, was a U.S. citizen. The case was not this Court's finest hour....

But ... *Quirin* would still not justify denial of the writ here. In *Quirin* it was uncontested that the petitioners were members of enemy forces.... The specific holding of the Court was only that, "upon the *conceded* facts," the petitioners were "plainly within [the] boundaries" of military jurisdiction. But where those jurisdictional facts are *not* conceded where the petitioner insists that he is *not* a belligerent—*Quirin* left the pre-existing law in place: Absent suspension of the writ, a citizen held where the courts are open is entitled either to criminal trial or to a judicial decree requiring his release....

Several limitations give my views in this matter a relatively narrow compass. They apply only to citizens, accused of being enemy combatants, who are detained within the territorial jurisdiction of a federal court. This is not likely to be a numerous group; currently we know of only two, Hamdi and Jose Padilla. Where the citizen is captured outside and held outside the United States, the constitutional requirements may be different. Moreover, even within the United States, the accused citizen-enemy combatant may lawfully be detained once prosecution is in progress or in contemplation.... If civil rights are to be curtailed during wartime, it must be done openly and democratically, as the Constitution requires, rather than by silent erosion through an opinion of this Court.

The Founders well understood the difficult tradeoff between safety and freedom. "Safety from external danger," Hamilton declared,

> "is the most powerful director of national conduct. Even the ardent love of liberty will, after a time, give way to its dictates. The violent destruction of life and property incident to war; the continual effort and alarm attendant on a state of continual danger, will compel nations the most attached to liberty, to resort for repose and security to institutions which have a tendency to destroy their civil and political rights. To be more safe, they, at length, become willing to run the risk of being less free."

The Founders warned us about the risk, and equipped us with a Constitution designed to deal with it.

Many think it not only inevitable but entirely proper that liberty give way to security in times of national crisis—that, at the extremes of military exigency, *inter arma silent leges*. Whatever the general merits of the view that war silences law or modulates its voice, that view has no place in the interpretation and application of a Constitution designed precisely to confront war and, in a manner that accords with democratic principles, to accommodate it. Because the Court has proceeded to meet the current emergency in a manner the Constitution does not envision, I respectfully dissent.

Justice THOMAS, dissenting.

The Executive Branch, acting pursuant to the powers vested in the President by the Constitution and with explicit congressional approval, has determined that Yaser Hamdi is an enemy combatant and should be detained. This detention falls squarely within the Federal Government's war powers, and we lack the expertise and capacity to second-guess that decision. As such, petitioners' habeas challenge should fail, and there is no reason to remand the case. The plurality reaches a contrary conclusion by failing adequately to consider basic principles of the constitutional structure as it relates to national security and foreign affairs....

The Founders intended that the President have primary responsibility—along with the necessary power—to protect the national security and to conduct the Nation's foreign relations. They did so principally because the structural advantages of a unitary Executive are essential in these domains....

These structural advantages are most important in the national-security and foreign-affairs contexts....

This Court has long recognized these features and has accordingly held that the President has *constitutional* authority to protect the national security and that this authority carries with it broad discretion.

"If a war be made by invasion of a foreign nation, the President

> is not only authorized but bound to resist force by force. He does not initiate the war, but is bound to accept the challenge without waiting for any special legislative authority.... Whether the President in fulfilling his duties, as Commander in-chief, in suppressing an insurrection, has met with such armed hostile resistance ... is a question to be decided *by him.*" *Prize Cases.*

[W]ith respect to foreign affairs as well, the Court has recognized the President's independent authority and need to be free from interference. See, *e.g., United States v. Curtiss–Wright Export Corp.*

Congress, to be sure, has a substantial and essential role in both foreign affairs and national security. But it is crucial to recognize that *judicial* interference in these domains destroys the purpose of vesting primary responsibility in a unitary Executive.... First, with respect to certain decisions relating to national security and foreign affairs, the courts simply lack the relevant information and expertise to second-guess determinations made by the President based on information properly withheld. Second, even if the courts could compel the Executive to produce the necessary information, such decisions are simply not amenable to judicial determination because "[t]hey are delicate, complex, and involve large elements of prophecy." Third, the Court ... has correctly recognized the primacy of the political branches in the foreign-affairs and national-security contexts....

I acknowledge that the question whether Hamdi's executive detention is lawful is a question properly resolved by the Judicial Branch, though the question comes to the Court with the strongest presumptions in favor of the Government. The plurality agrees that Hamdi's detention is lawful if he is an enemy combatant. But the question whether Hamdi is actually an enemy combatant is "of a kind for which the Judiciary has neither aptitude, facilities nor responsibility and which has long been held to belong in the domain of political power not subject to judicial intrusion or inquiry." That is, although it is appropriate for the Court to determine the judicial question whether the President has the asserted authority, we lack the information and expertise to question whether Hamdi is actually an enemy combatant, a question the resolution of which is committed to other branches....

I agree with the plurality that the Federal Government has power to detain those that the Executive Branch determines to be enemy combatants. But I do not think that the plurality has adequately explained the breadth of the President's authority to detain enemy combatants, an authority that includes making virtually conclusive factual findings. In my view, the structural considerations discussed above, as recognized in our precedent, demonstrate that we lack the capacity and responsibility to second-guess this determination.

For these reasons, I would affirm the judgment of the Court of Appeals.

Comments and Questions

1. Hamdi was eventually released on condition that he give up his American citizenship and leave the United States to return to Saudi Arabia.

2. As you can see, there is no majority opinion, but eight of the nine justices reject the government's arguments that the Court should simply defer to the President's determinations as to the need to keep an American citizen in custody indefinitely simply because he was captured in a country in which the United States was engaged in hostilities. The plurality reads the AUMF as authorization to detain captured combatants for the duration of the hostilities. Does the plurality read the AUMF as the equivalent of a declaration of war? Does Justice Souter or Justice Scalia or Justice Thomas?

3. Based upon the plurality's opinion, the government created "Combat Status Review Tribunals" (CSRTs) to hold hearings to determine whether detainees were really enemy combatants. These are not military commissions, because they do not assess whether the detainee committed any violation of the laws of war and do not impose any punishment; they merely determine whether the detainee is properly kept in custody until the "war" in Afghanistan is over. Hearings and determinations based upon them are ongoing.

4. The government did, however, also create military commissions to try alleged war criminals. Ahmed Hamdan, a Yemeni national and not a United States citizen, was captured during fighting in Afghanistan, brought to Guantanamo, and ultimately charged with "conspiracy to commit war crimes." Hamdan petitioned for habeas corpus, which was granted by the district court but then reversed by the Court of Appeals for the D.C. Circuit. Justice Stevens in an opinion for the Court on most issues held that the military commissions that had been established were not in accordance with statutory authorization and therefore were unauthorized, citing the *Steel Seizure* case. *Hamdan v. Rumsfeld*, 548 U.S. 557 (2006). Congress responded by enacting the Military Commissions Act of 2006, which among other things prohibited the exclusion of the defendant from the proceedings (which the presidentially created commissions could do) but also limited judicial review of the outcomes of the proceedings. This Act was challenged by another person designated to be tried by commission, but the D.C. Circuit by a 2–1 vote found the act constitutional. The Supreme Court, after first denying certiorari, in a most unusual move vacated the denial of certiorari, granted certiorari, and scheduled the case to be heard in December of 2007.

5. If you were writing the Constitution today, how would you address these issues?

C. THE UNITARY EXECUTIVE

The "unitary executive" should not be confused with the "imperial presidency." However, they often are. The latter term is a derogatory term used to characterize the claim that "the executive power" extends to everything that is not expressly legislative or judicial—that is, it is a derogatory term for a broad reading of "executive power." Presidents from Andrew Jackson to Theodore Roosevelt to Franklin Roosevelt to George W. Bush have made such claims. Often, although not always, the claimed power is in the foreign affairs or national security realm. Thus, such a characterization might be made if the President claimed a constitutional authority to commit American troops abroad without the approval of Congress and even contrary to congressional enactments. The cases we have been considering might be said to address this concept.

The term "unitary executive" refers instead to the idea that the "executive power" (whatever it is) resides in the President alone and cannot be divested from him. For example, those who believe in the "unitary executive" would say that Congress cannot by law place the responsibility for executing a particular law in the head of an agency as opposed to the President. This has been an area of active legal scholarship in recent years. *Compare, e.g.*, Peter Strauss, *Overseer, or "The Decider"? The President in Administrative Law*, 75 Geo. Wash. L.Rev. 696 (2007)(critiquing the unitary executive) *with* Christopher Yoo, Steven Calabresi, and Anthony Colangelo, *The Unitary Executive in the Modern Era, 1945–2004*, 90 Iowa L. Rev. 601 (2005)(defending unitary executive). The issue has often come up in the context of legislative restrictions on appointments to positions in the government and on the removal of persons from such positions.

1. APPOINTMENTS

The Appointments Clause, Article II, Section 2, Clause 2, provides that the President, with the advice and consent of the Senate, "shall appoint ... officers of the United States ..., but the Congress may by law vest the appointment of such inferior officers, as they think proper, in the President alone, in the courts of law, or in the heads of departments." It is, however, not uncommon for statutes creating agencies and specifying the officers to administer them to place some limits on whom the President may appoint. For example, the Solicitor General, who assists the Attorney General and by regulation is responsible for the position of the United States in litigation in courts, must be "learned in the law." 28 U.S.C. § 505. The Secretary of Defense must be (and have been for the last ten years) a civilian. 10 U.S.C. § 113. The Administrator of the Federal Emergency Management Agency (as a result of the Katrina disaster) is now required to have "a demonstrated ability in and knowledge of emergency management and homeland security and not less than 5 years of executive leadership and management experience in the public or private sector." 6 U.S.C. § 313 (c)(2). Statutes creating agencies headed by multiple members, rather than a single administrator, such as the Federal Communications Commission (FCC), the Federal Trade Commission (FTC), the Securities Exchange Commission, the Federal

Energy Regulatory Commission, and the Federal Reserve Board, typically require that no more than a simple majority of the members be from one political party (meaning, for example, that of the five members of the FCC, no more than three can be Republicans (or Democrats)). While none of these restrictions have been subject to any judicial challenge, in a case involving statutory restrictions on the President's use of advisory committees, Justice Kennedy (joined by Chief Justice Rehnquist and Justice O'Connor) opined that any statutory limitation on the President's power to nominate and, with Senate confirmation, to appoint officers of the United States would be unconstitutional. Moreover, Presidents since Ronald Reagan have regularly stated that such restrictions are an unconstitutional restriction on the President's authority (subject to the Senate's confirmation) to appoint officers of the United States. Others suggest that qualifications for an office are different from limitations on whom the President may appoint. However, if the qualifications for the office are that the holder must be a law professor who has taught constitutional law for at least 25 years, is at least 60 years old, is at least 5' 9" tall and 180 pounds in weight, with blue eyes and a bad back, then this author is a shoo-in. In other words, it may be difficult to distinguish between "qualifications for an office" and limitations on whom the President might appoint.

On occasion, Congress has by statute specified the actual individuals to hold certain positions (*see, e.g.*, 20 U.S.C. 42 (naming the Vice President and the Chief Justice of the United States as the Regents of the Smithsonian Institution)) or required that the persons be appointed by the President Pro Tem* of the Senate or the Speaker of the House, rather than by the President. The latter appointment process has been challenged in court. In the Federal Election Campaign Act of 1971, the first federal statute regulating campaign contributions, Congress created the Federal Elections Commission (FEC) and provided that it would be composed of six members: two appointed by the President, subject to confirmation by both the House and Senate; two appointed by the President Pro Tem of the Senate; and two appointed by the Speaker of the House. Because this appointment process did not comply with the requirements of the Appointments Clause, the question was whether the commissioners were officers at all. If not, then their appointments would be constitutional, but if they had to be "officers" in order to perform their statutory functions, then their appointments would be unconstitutional. The Court held that persons "exercising significant authority pursuant to the laws of the United States" must be officers. Because Congress itself can investigate and issue reports as incident to its legislative function, the Court did not believe those activities would constitute "exercising significant authority" and thus did not require officers to perform them. However, the FEC did more than just investigate and make reports; it also had the authority to make rules and regulations with the force of law, as

* The President Pro Tempore of the Senate, usually referred to as the President Pro Tem., is elected by the Senate and traditionally has been the senior-most Senator of the majority party.

well as to prosecute persons for violating the Federal Election Campaign Act. These were the exercise of significant authority requiring their performance by officers, so the Court held the appointments unconstitutional. See *Buckley v. Valeo*, 424 U.S. 1 (1976).

Compare the Federal Election Commission to the United States Commission on Civil Rights. The latter has eight commissioners, four appointed by the President without Senate confirmation, two appointed by the President Pro Tem of the Senate, and two appointed by the Speaker of the House. Clearly, the latter four cannot be officers of the United States in light of the way they are appointed. Therefore, either the Commission does not exercise significant authority of the United States, or the appointment of these commissioners is unconstitutional. The mission and powers of the Commission are:

- To investigate complaints alleging that citizens are being deprived of their right to vote by reason of their race, color, religion, sex, age, disability, or national origin, or by reason of fraudulent practices.

- To study and collect information relating to discrimination or a denial of equal protection of the laws under the Constitution because of race, color, religion, sex, age, disability, or national origin, or in the administration of justice.

- To appraise federal laws and policies with respect to discrimination or denial of equal protection of the laws because of race, color, religion, sex, age, disability, or national origin, or in the administration of justice.

- To serve as a national clearinghouse for information in respect to discrimination or denial of equal protection of the laws because of race, color, religion, sex, age, disability, or national origin.

- To submit reports, findings, and recommendations to the President and Congress.

- To issue public service announcements to discourage discrimination or denial of equal protection of the laws.

Is the Commission constitutional?

The Appointments Clause provides that, if Congress thinks proper, it may vest the appointment of inferior officers in the President alone, the courts of law, or the heads of departments. Of course, if Congress does not so specify, inferior officers would be appointed in the same manner as principal officers—by the President with the advice and consent of the Senate. Because the methods of appointment may differ between inferior and principal officers, it is important to be able to distinguish between them. In *Morrison v. Olson*, 487 U.S. 654 (1988), the Court addressed this issue. Under provisions of the Ethics in Government Act of 1978, upon a report by the Attorney General that there were sufficient grounds to investigate possible violations of federal criminal laws by federal officials, a Special Division of the United States Court of Appeals for the District of Columbia Circuit was required to appoint an independent counsel to investigate those possible violations. Thus, if the independent counsel was a principal officer, her appointment was unconstitutional, because it would be made by a court of law, rather than by the President with the advice and consent of the Senate.

The Court said that the line between principal and inferior officers is unclear, but that the independent counsel was "clearly" an inferior officer in light of four factors. First, the counsel was subject to removal by a higher executive branch official but someone below the President (the Attorney General); thus, she was inferior to a principal officer. Second, she was authorized only to perform certain limited duties—the investigation and possible prosecution of certain specified offenses. This distinguished her from United States Attorneys, for example, who have the authority, among other things, to investigate and prosecute any federal crimes by any person. Third, her jurisdiction was limited to what is granted to her by the Special Division, which like the second factor distinguished her from other federal prosecutors. Finally, her tenure was limited to accomplishing the particular task she was assigned. Thus, in a real sense, her appointment was a temporary one. These factors can, therefore, be applied in other circumstances to discern whether a particular officer is inferior or principal.

There remained a question whether "interbranch appointments" were constitutional. The claim was that a court of law could only appoint inferior officers in the judicial branch, because it was inappropriate for courts of law to appoint executive officers, as the independent counsel concededly was. The Court rejected this argument as well. It noted that the Appointments Clause contained no such limitation and indeed by its terms seemed to leave the issue to the discretion of Congress ("as [Congress] think[s] proper"). The Court did leave open the possibility of some constitutional limitation if "there was some 'incongruity' between the functions normally performed by the courts" and the functions of the officer they were to appoint. But, the Court said, "This is not a case in which judges are given power to appoint an officer in an area in which they have no special knowledge or expertise, as in, for example, a statute authorizing the courts to appoint officials in the Department of Agriculture or the Federal Energy Regulatory Commission."

Finally, "officers" must be distinguished from "employees" of the executive branch. The Constitution does not address the appointment, or more accurately the hiring, of employees. In *Buckley*, the Court said that "employees are lesser functionaries subordinate to officers of the United States." Employees are not authorized to make policy; they merely carry it out. Nevertheless, some inferior officers may be fairly indistinguishable from an employee. For example, the clerk of a district court is an inferior officer.

2. REMOVAL

While Article II has a specific clause governing appointments that is fairly clear as constitutional provisions go, the Constitution nowhere says anything about who may remove officers, other than that Congress may remove them through impeachment. The history is clear, however, that impeachment was intended to be an extraordinary power to be exercised in rare circumstances demanding a check by the legislative branch over the executive or judicial branches; it was not to be the means by which to manage executive or judicial personnel.

The Constitution states that federal judges hold their offices "during good behavior," but again it says nothing about who should determine when a judge fails to behave well. Historically, there has never been an attempt to remove a judge except through impeachment, but from time-to-time there have been suggestions of institutionalizing a system within the judicial branch by which it would be able to remove judges upon a determination that they no longer are in "good behavior." These suggestions, however, have not had traction.

Again, historically, appointment to federal office was often patronage bestowed on political supporters. One would be hard pressed to say that some appointments today are not made on that basis. Because they were based on patronage, the assumption was that the person who hired you could fire you and replace you with a new supporter, and the assumption was that a new administration would replace virtually all the principal officers and many, if not most, of the inferior officers. It is standard practice today for principal officers in the executive branch to offer their resignations to the new incoming President.

There are and have been exceptions to this standard practice, however. For example, when Andrew Johnson became President after Lincoln's assassination, and the Congress controlled by radical Republicans wished to limit his power, it passed the Tenure in Office Act, which prohibited the removal of any principal officer without the consent of the Senate. The theory was that, if such an officer could only be appointed with the consent of the Senate, that officer should only be able to be removed with the consent of the Senate. Johnson, however, did not abide by the law and fired the Secretary of War, who was in league with the radical Republicans against Johnson. This violation of the Tenure in Office Act became one of the articles of impeachment against Johnson.

That Act remained in effect until it was repealed in 1887, but an 1876 law provided that Postmasters "shall be appointed and may be removed by the President with the advice and consent of the Senate," and in 1920 President Woodrow Wilson fired the Postmaster of Portland, Oregon, without seeking the advice and consent of the Senate, and the Postmaster sued for his salary.

MYERS v. UNITED STATES

United States Supreme Court, 1926.
272 U.S. 52, 47 S.Ct. 21, 71 L.Ed. 160

William Howard Taft

Taft was a protégé of President Theodore Roosevelt, serving in several positions in his administration. Roosevelt anointed him as his successor, but after Taft's election as President, while continuing the generally progressive policies of his predecessor, Taft took his own course, alienating Roosevelt who ran as a third party candidate against him in the next election, assuring Taft's defeat by Wilson. Taft retreated to Yale Law School as a professor, but the next Republican President, Warren G. Harding, appointed him to the Supreme Court as Chief Justice in 1921, a position he always said he desired more than the presidency. Although he authored over 200 opinions before his retirement in 1930, Taft's legacy is not in his jurisprudence but in the Supreme Court building which he lobbied to have built.

Mr. Chief Justice TAFT delivered the opinion of the Court.

This case presents the question whether under the Constitution the President has the exclusive power of removing executive officers of the United States whom he has appointed by and with the advice and consent of the Senate....

The Senate did not consent to the President's removal of Myers during his term. If this statute in its requirement [that he can be removed by the President only] with the consent of the Senate is valid, the appellant, Myers' administratrix,* is entitled to recover his unpaid salary for his full term.... The government maintains that the requirement is invalid, for the reason that under article 2 of the Constitution the President's power of removal of executive officers appointed by him with the advice and consent of the Senate is full and complete without consent of the Senate. If this view is sound, the removal of Myers by the President without the Senate's consent was legal.... We are therefore confronted by the constitutional question and cannot avoid it....

There is no express provision respecting removals in the Constitution, except as section 4 of article 2 provides for removal from office by impeachment. The subject was not discussed in the Constitutional Convention. Under the Articles of Confederation, Congress was given the power of appointing certain executive officers of the Confederation, and during the Revolution and while the articles were given effect, Congress exercised the power of removal....

In the House of Representatives of the First Congress, ... Mr. Madison moved in the committee of the whole that there should be established three executive departments, one of Foreign Af-

* An administratrix is a female administrator. The term is no longer in use; both males and females are now called administrators. An administrator in this context is a person appointed by a court to handle the affairs of a person who has died without a will. Here, Myers, the Postmaster, had died without a will, and his wife was the administrator of his affairs, including continuing this lawsuit. [author's note]

fairs, another of the Treasury, and a third of War, at the head of each of which there should be a Secretary, to be appointed by the President by and with the advice and consent of the Senate, and to be removable by the President. [The Court then provides an extensive history of the debates over the provision that the heads of these departments would removable by the President.]

It is very clear from this history that the exact question which the House voted upon was whether it should recognize and declare the power of the President under the Constitution to remove the Secretary of Foreign Affairs without the advice and consent of the Senate. That was what the vote was taken for. Some effort has been made to question whether the decision carries the result claimed for it, but there is not the slightest doubt, after an examination of the record, that the vote was, and was intended to be, a legislative declaration that the power to remove officers appointed by the President and the Senate vested in the President alone, and until the Johnson impeachment trial in 1868 its meaning was not doubted, even by those who questioned its soundness....

It is convenient in the course of our discussion of this case to review the reasons advanced by Mr. Madison and his associates for their conclusion, supplementing them, so far as may be, by additional considerations which lead this court to concur therein....

Mr. Madison and his associates in the discussion in the House dwelt at length upon the necessity there was for construing article 2 to give the President the sole power of removal in his responsibility for the conduct of the executive branch, and enforced this by emphasizing his duty expressly declared in the third section of the article to "take care that the laws be faithfully executed."

The vesting of the executive power in the President was essentially a grant of the power to execute the laws. But the President alone and unaided could not execute the laws. He must execute them by the assistance of subordinates.... As he is charged specifically to take care that they be faithfully executed, the reasonable implication, even in the absence of express words, was that as part of his executive power he should select those who were to act for him under his direction in the execution of the laws. The further implication must be, in the absence of any express limitation respecting removals, that as his selection of administrative officers is essential to the execution of the laws by him, so must be his power of removing those for whom he cannot continue to be responsible....

Second. The view of Mr. Madison and his associates was that not only did the grant of executive power to the President in the first section of article 2 carry with it the power of removal, but the express recognition of the the power of appointment in the second section enforced this view on the well-approved principle of constitutional and statutory construction that the power of removal of executive officers was incident to the power of appointment.... The reason for the principle is that those in charge of and responsible for administering functions of government, who select their executive subordinates, need in meeting their responsibility to have the power to remove those whom they appoint....

Fourth. Mr. Madison and his associates pointed out with great force the unreasonable character of the view that the convention intended, without express provision, to give to Congress or the Senate, in case of political or other differences, the means of thwarting the executive in the exercise of his great powers and in the bearing of his great responsibility by fastening upon him, as subordinate executive officers, men who by their inefficient service under him, by their lack of loyalty to the service, or by their different views of policy might make his taking care that the laws be faithfully executed most difficult or impossible.

Made responsible under the Constitution for the effective enforcement of the law, the President needs as an indispensable aid to meet it the disciplinary influence upon those who act under him of a reserve power of removal. But it is contended that executive officers appointed by the President with the consent of the Senate are bound by the statutory law, and are not his servants to do his will, and that his obligation to care for the faithful execution of the laws does not authorize him to treat them as such. The degree of guidance in the discharge of their duties that the President may exercise over executive officers varies with the character of their service as prescribed in the law under which they act. The highest and most important duties which his subordinates perform are those in which they act for him. In such cases they are exercising not their own but his discretion. This field is a very large one. It is sometimes described as political. Each head of a department is and must be the President's alter ego in the matters of that department where the President is required by law to exercise authority....

The duties which are thus imposed upon him he is further enabled to perform by the recognition in the Constitution, and the creation by Acts of Congress, of executive departments, which have varied in number from four or five to seven or eight, the heads of which are familiarly called Cabinet ministers. These aid him in the performance of the great duties of his office, and represent him in a thousand acts to which it can hardly be supposed his personal attention is called, and thus he is enabled to fulfill the duty of his great department, expressed in the phrase that "he shall take care that the laws be faithfully executed."

In ... cases [in which the President acts under his constitutional powers], the discretion to be exercised is that of the President in determining the national public interest and in directing the action to be taken by his executive subordinates to protect it. In this field his cabinet officers must do his will. He must place in each member of his official family, and his chief executive subordinates, implicit faith. The moment that he loses confidence in the intelligence, ability, judgment, or loyalty of any one of them, he must have the power to remove him without delay. To require him to file charges and submit them to the consideration of the Senate might make impossible that unity and coordination in executive administration essential to effective action....

But this is not to say that there are not strong reasons why the President should have a like power to remove his appointees charged with other duties than those above described. The ordinary duties of officers prescribed by statute come under the general administrative control of the President by virtue of the general grant to him of the executive power, and he may properly supervise and guide their construction of the statutes under which they act in order to secure that unitary and uniform execution of the laws which article 2 of the Constitution evidently contemplated in vesting general executive power in the President alone. Laws are often passed with specific provision for adoption of regulations by a department or bureau head to make the law workable and effective. The ability and judgment manifested by the official thus empowered, as well as his energy and stimulation of his subordinates, are subjects which the President must consider and supervise in his administrative control. Finding such officers to be negligent and inefficient, the President should have the power to remove them. Of course there may be duties so peculiarly and specifically committed to the discretion of a particular officer as to raise a question whether the President may overrule or revise the officer's interpretation of his statutory duty in a particular instance. Then there may be duties of a quasi judicial character imposed on executive officers and members of executive tribunals whose decisions after hearing affect interests of individuals, the discharge of which the President cannot in a particular case properly influence or control. But even in such a case he may consider the decision after its rendition as a reason for removing the officer, on the ground that the discretion regularly entrusted to that officer by statute has not been on the whole intelligently or wisely exercised. Otherwise he does not discharge his own constitutional duty of seeing that the laws be faithfully executed.

We have devoted much space to this discussion and decision of the question of the presidential power of removal in the First Congress, not because a congressional conclusion on a constitutional issue is conclusive, but first because of our agreement with the reasons upon which it was avowedly based, second because this was the decision of the First Congress on a question of primary importance in the organization of the government made within two years after the Constitutional Convention and within a much shorter time after its ratification, and third because that Congress numbered among its leaders those who had been members of the convention, it must necessarily constitute a precedent upon which many future laws supplying the machinery of the new government would be based and, if erroneous, would be likely to evoke dissent and departure in future Congresses....

The power to remove inferior executive officers, like that to remove superior executive officers, is an incident of the power to appoint them, and is in its nature an executive power. The authority of Congress given by the excepting clause to vest the appointment of such inferior officers in the heads of departments carries with it authority incidentally to invest the heads of departments with power to remove. It has been the practice of Congress to do so and this court has recognized that power.... But the court never has held, nor reasonably could hold, although it is argued to the contrary on behalf of the appellant, that the excepting clause enables Congress to draw to itself, or to either branch of it, the power to remove or the right to participate in the exercise of that power. To do this would be to go beyond the words and implications of that clause, and to infringe the constitutional principle of the separation of governmental powers....

For the reasons given, we must therefore hold that the provision of the law of 1876 by which the unrestricted power of removal of first-class postmasters is denied to the President is in violation of the Constitution and invalid....

The separate opinion of Mr. Justice McREYNOLDS.

May the President oust at will all postmasters appointed with the Senate's consent for definite terms under an act which inhibits removal without consent of that body? ... I think there is no such power. Certainly it is not given by any plain words of the Constitution; and the argument advanced to establish it seems to me forced and unsubstantial....

Again and again Congress has enacted statutes prescribing restrictions on removals, and by approving them many Presidents have affirmed its power therein. The following are some of the officers who have been or may be appointed with consent of the Senate under such restricting statutes: Members of the Interstate Commerce Commission, Board of General Appraisers, Federal Reserve Board, Federal Trade Commission, Tariff Commission, Shipping Board, Federal Farm Loan Board, Railroad Labor Board; officers of the Army and Navy; Comptroller General; Postmaster General and his assistants; Postmasters of the first, second, and third classes; judge of the United States Court for China; judges of the Court of Claims, established in 1855, the judges to serve "during good behavior"; judges of territorial (statutory) courts; judges of the Supreme Court and Court of Appeals for the District of Columbia (statutory courts), appointed to serve "during good behavior." ...

Every one of these officers, we are now told in effect, holds his place subject to the President's pleasure or caprice....

Nothing short of language clear beyond serious disputation should be held to clothe the President with authority wholly beyond congressional control arbitrarily to dismiss every officer whom he appoints except a few judges. There are no such words in the Constitution, and the asserted inference conflicts with the heretofore accepted theory that this government is one of carefully enumerated powers under an intelligible charter....

For the United States it is asserted: Except certain judges, the President may remove all officers whether executive or judicial appointed by him with the Senate's consent, and therein he cannot be limited or restricted by Congress. The argument runs thus: The Constitution gives the President all executive power of the national government, except as this is checked or controlled by some other definite provision; power to remove is executive and unconfined; accordingly, the President may remove at will. Further, the President is required to take care that the laws be faithfully executed; he cannot do this unless he may remove at will all officers whom he appoints; therefore he has such authority.

The argument assumes far too much. Generally, the actual ouster of an officer is executive action; but to prescribe the conditions under which this may be done is legislative. The act of hanging a criminal is executive; but to say when and where and how he shall be hanged is clearly legislative....

The Legislature may create post offices and prescribe qualifications, duties, compensation, and term. And it may protect the incumbent in the enjoyment of his term unless in some way restrained therefrom. The real question, therefore, comes to this: Does any constitutional provision definitely limit the otherwise plenary power of Congress over postmasters, when they are appointed by the President with the consent of the Senate? The question is not the much-mooted one whether the Senate is part of the appointing power under the Constitution and therefore must participate in removals....

If the framers of the Constitution had intended "the executive power," in article 2, § 1, to include all power of an executive nature, they would not have added the carefully defined grants of section 2.... Why say, the President shall be commander-in-chief [etc] if all of these things and more had already been vested in him by the general words? ... That the general words of a grant are limited, when followed by those of special import, is an established canon; and an accurate writer would hardly think of emphasizing a general grant by adding special and narrower ones without explanation....

Mr. Justice BRANDEIS, dissenting.

[P]ostmasters are inferior officers. Congress might have vested their appointment in the head of the department.... May the President, having acted under the statute in so far as it creates the office and authorizes the appointment, ignore, while the Senate is in session, the provision which prescribes the condition under which a removal may take place?

It is this narrow question, and this only, which we are required to decide. We need not consider what power the President, being Commander-in-Chief, has over officers in the Army and the Navy. We need not determine whether the President, acting alone, may remove high political officers.... The sole question is whether, in respect to inferior offices, Congress may impose upon the Senate both responsibilities, as it may deny to it participation in the exercise of either function....

Over removal from inferior civil offices, Congress has, from the foundation of our government, exercised continuously some measure of control by legislation. The instances of such laws are many....

The practice of Congress to control the exercise of the executive power of removal from inferior offices is evidenced by many statutes which restrict it in many ways besides the removal clause here in question. Each of these restrictive statutes became law with the approval of the President. Every President who has held office since 1861, except President Garfield, approved one or more of such statutes. Some of these statutes, prescribing a fixed term, provide that removal shall be made only for one of several specified causes. Some provide a fixed term, subject generally to removal for cause. Some provide for removal only after hearing. Some provide a fixed term, subject to removal for reasons to be communicated by the President to the Senate. Some impose the restriction in still other ways....

The assertion that the mere grant by the Constitution of executive power confers upon the President as a prerogative the unrestricted power of appointment and of removal from executive offices, except so far as otherwise expressly provided by the Constitution, is clearly inconsistent also with those statutes which restrict the exercise by the President of the power of nomination. There is not a word in the Constitution which in terms authorizes Congress to limit the President's freedom of choice in making nominations for executive offices.... But a multitude of laws have been enacted which limit the President's power to make nominations, and which through the restrictions imposed, may prevent the selection of the person deemed by him best fitted. Such restriction upon the power to nominate has been exercised by Congress continuously since the foundation of the government. Every President has approved one or more of such acts. Every President has consistently observed them. This is true of those offices to which he makes appointments without the advice and consent of the Senate as well as of those for which its consent is required....

The separation of the powers of government did not make each branch completely autonomous. It left each in some measure, dependent upon the others, as it left to each power to exercise, in some respects, functions in their nature executive, legislative and judicial. Obviously the President cannot secure full execution of the laws, if Congress denies to him adequate means of doing so. Full execution may be defeated because Congress declines to create offices indispensable for that purpose; or because Congress, having created the office, declines to make the indispensable appropriation; or because Congress, having both created the office and made the appropriation, prevents, by restrictions which it imposes, the appointment of officials who in quality and character are indispensable to the efficient execution of the law. If, in any such way, adequate means are denied to the President, the fault will lie with Congress. The President performs his full constitutional duty, if, with the means and instruments provided by Congress and within the limitations prescribed by it, he uses his best endeavors to secure the faithful execution of the laws enacted.

Mr. Justice HOLMES, dissenting.

[T]he arguments drawn from the executive power of the President, and from his duty to appoint officers of the United States (when Congress does not vest the appointment elsewhere), to take care that the laws be faithfully executed, and to commission all officers of the United States, seem to me spiders' webs inadequate to control the dominant facts.

We have to deal with an office that owes its existence to Congress and that Congress may abolish tomorrow. Its duration and the pay attached to it while it lasts depend on Congress alone. Congress alone confers on the President the power to appoint to it and at any time may transfer the power to other hands. With such power over its own creation, I have no more trouble in believing that Congress has power to prescribe a term of life for it free from any interference than I have in accepting the undoubted power of Congress to decree its end. I have equally little trouble in accepting its power to prolong the tenure of an incumbent until Congress or the Senate shall have assented to his removal. The duty of the President to see that the laws be executed is a duty that does not go beyond the laws or require him to achieve more than Congress sees fit to leave within his power.

Comments and Questions

1. The opinion for the Court is written by Chief Justice Taft, who had been President of the United States from 1909–13. Thus, it is perhaps not surprising that he comes out on the side of presidential power rather than congressional power.

2. It is well to keep in mind that the law in question in *Myers* did not impose just any restriction on the power of the President to remove postmasters; it required the approval of the Senate. That is, it did not just restrict the President's absolute power to remove, as, for example, a limitation that he could remove someone only for good cause; it subjected his decisions to the approval of a portion of a different branch of government. In the First Congress, this too was the issue; could Congress subject the President's removal power to the supervision of a portion of Congress? While aspects of the Court's opinion do recognize the nature of the specific limitation in the case before it, much of the rhetoric is not so restricted, and it is that rhetoric that Presidents subsequently have drawn on.

3. Justice McReynolds' dissent likewise makes little of the nature of the particular restriction on the President's removal authority in *Myers*. Rather he treats it like any other restriction, of which he notes there had been many in many statutes.

4. What is the focus of Justice Brandeis' dissent? How does the majority opinion respond to Brandeis' argument?

5. What about Justice Holmes' dissent? Under his interpretation of the Constitution could Congress prohibit the President from either directing or removing any officer of the United States? If so, how could the President take care that the laws are faithfully executed? Could Congress place the entire removal power in the Senate under Holmes' theory? If so, what would be the purpose of the Impeachment Clause of the Constitution?

6. *Myers* is important not just for its interpretation of the President's removal authority, and the basis for it, but also for its imposition of limitations on Congress's powers as a result of structural implications implied by the Constitution. Implications from the structure of the Constitution can extend much more broadly than questions regarding removal.

HUMPHREY'S EXECUTOR v. UNITED STATES

United States Supreme Court, 1935.
295 U.S. 602, 55 S.Ct. 869, 79 L.Ed. 1611.

Mr. Justice SUTHERLAND delivered the opinion of the Court.

Plaintiff brought suit in the Court of Claims against the United States to recover a sum of money alleged to be due the deceased for salary as a Federal Trade Commissioner from October 8, 1933, when the President undertook to remove him from office, to the time of his death on February 14, 1934. [William E. Humphrey, the decedent, on December 10, 1931, was appointed by President Hoover as a member of the Federal Trade Commission for a term of seven years. In July 1933, President Roosevelt asked for his resignation, on the ground "that the aims and purposes of the Administration with respect to the work of the Commission can be carried out most effectively with personnel of my own selection." Later, the President wrote the commissioner saying: "You will, I know, realize that I do not feel that your mind and my mind go along together on either the policies or the administering of the Federal Trade Commission, and, frankly, I think it is best for the people of this country that I should have a full confidence." The commissioner declined to resign; and on October 7, 1933, the President removed him.] The court below has certified to this court two questions in respect of the power of the President to make the removal....

1. Do the provisions of section 1 of the Federal Trade Commission Act, stating that "any commissioner may be removed by the President for inefficiency, neglect of duty, or malfeasance in office", restrict or limit

the power of the President to remove a commissioner except upon one or more of the causes named?

If the foregoing question is answered in the affirmative, then-

2. If the power of the President to remove a commissioner is restricted or limited as shown by the foregoing interrogatory and the answer made thereto, is such a restriction or limitation valid under the Constitution of the United States?

The Federal Trade Commission Act creates a commission of five members to be appointed by the President by and with the advice and consent of the Senate, and section 1 provides: " ... Any commissioner may be removed by the President for inefficiency, neglect of duty, or malfeasance in office. * * * "

First. The question first to be considered is whether, by the provisions of section 1 of the Federal Trade Commission Act already quoted, the President's power is limited to removal for the specific causes enumerated therein.... [The government argued that the listed bases for removal were not exclusive, and the President might remove commissioners at will.]

The commission is to be nonpartisan; and it must, from the very nature of its duties, act with entire impartiality. It is charged with the enforcement of no policy except the policy of the law. Its duties are neither political nor executive, but predominantly quasi judicial and quasi legislative. Like the Interstate Commerce Commission, its members are called upon to exercise the trained judgment of a body of experts "appointed by law and informed by experience."

The legislative reports in both houses of Congress clearly reflect the view that a fixed term was necessary to the effective and fair administration of the law.... [The Senate report states:] "It is manifestly desirable that the terms of the commissioners shall be long enough to give them an opportunity to acquire the expertness in dealing with these special questions concerning industry that comes from experience."

The report declares that one advantage which the commission possessed over the Bureau of Corporations (an executive subdivision in the Department of Commerce which was abolished by the act) lay in the fact of its independence, and that it was essential that the commission should not be open to the suspicion of partisan direction....

The debates in both houses demonstrate that the prevailing view was that the Commission was not to be "subject to anybody in the government but * * * only to the people of the United States"; free from "political domination or control" or the "probability or possibility of such a thing"; to be "separate and apart from any existing department of the government—not subject to the orders of the President."

Thus, the language of the act, the legislative reports, and the general purposes of the legislation as reflected by the debates, all combine to demonstrate the congressional intent to create a body of experts who shall gain experience by length of service; a body which shall be independent of executive authority, except in its selection, and free to exercise its judgment without the leave or hindrance of any other official or any department of the government. To the accomplishment of these purposes, it is clear that Congress was of opinion that length and certainty of tenure would vitally contribute. And to hold that, nevertheless, the members of the commission continue in office at the mere will of the President, might be to thwart, in large measure, the very ends which Congress sought to realize by definitely fixing the term of office.

We conclude that the intent of the act is to limit the executive power of removal to the causes enumerated, the existence of none of which is claimed here; and we pass to the second question.

Second. To support its contention that the removal provision of section 1, as we have just construed it, is an unconstitutional interference with the executive power of the President, the government's chief reliance is *Myers v. United States*. That case has been so recently decided, and the prevailing and dissenting opinions so fully review the general subject of the power of executive removal, that further discussion would add little of value to the wealth of material there collected. These opinions examine at length the historical, legislative, and judicial data bearing upon the question, beginning with what is called "the decision of 1789" in the first Congress and coming down almost to the day when the opinions were delivered. They occupy 243 pages of the volume in which they are printed. Nevertheless, the narrow point actually decided was only that the President had power to remove a postmaster of the first class, without the advice and consent of the Senate as required by act of Congress. In the course of the opinion of the court, expressions occur which tend to sustain the government's contention, but these are beyond the point involved and, therefore, do not come within the rule of *stare decisis*. In so far as they are out of harmony with the views here set forth, these expressions are disapproved.

The office of a postmaster is so essentially unlike the office now involved that the decision in the *Myers Case* cannot be accepted as controlling our decision here. A postmaster is an executive officer restricted to the performance of executive functions. He is charged with no duty at all related to either the legislative or judicial power. The actual decision in the *Myers Case* finds support in the theory that such an officer is merely one of the units in the executive department and, hence, inherently subject to the exclusive and illimitable power of removal by the Chief Executive, whose subordinate and aid he is. Putting aside dicta, which may be followed if sufficiently persuasive but which are not controlling, the necessary reach of the decision goes far enough to include all purely executive officers. It goes no farther; much less does it include an officer who occupies no place in the executive department and who exercises no part of the executive power vested by the Constitution in the President.

The Federal Trade Commission is an administrative body created by

Congress to carry into effect legislative policies embodied in the statute in accordance with the legislative standard therein prescribed, and to perform other specified duties as a legislative or as a judicial aid. Such a body cannot in any proper sense be characterized as an arm or an eye of the executive. Its duties are performed without executive leave and, in the contemplation of the statute, must be free from executive control. In administering the provisions of the statute in respect of "unfair methods of competition," that is to say, in filling in and administering the details embodied by that general standard, the commission acts in part quasi legislatively and in part quasi judicially.... To the extent that it exercises any executive function, as distinguished from executive power in the constitutional sense, it does so in the discharge and effectuation of its quasi legislative or quasi judicial powers, or as an agency of the legislative or judicial departments of the government.

If Congress is without authority to prescribe causes for removal of members of the trade commission and limit executive power of removal accordingly, that power at once becomes practically all-inclusive in respect of civil officers with the exception of the judiciary provided for by the Constitution....

[T]he authority of Congress, in creating quasi legislative or quasi judicial agencies, to require them to act in discharge of their duties independently of executive control cannot well be doubted; and that authority includes, as an appropriate incident, power to fix the period during which they shall continue, and to forbid their removal except for cause in the meantime. For it is quite evident that one who holds his office only during the pleasure of another cannot be depended upon to maintain an attitude of independence against the latter's will.

The fundamental necessity of maintaining each of the three general departments of government entirely free from the control or coercive influence, direct or indirect, of either of the others, has often been stressed and is hardly open to serious question. So much is implied in the very fact of the separation of the powers of these departments by the Constitution; and in the rule which recognizes their essential coequality. The sound application of a principle that makes one master in his own house precludes him from imposing his control in the house of another who is master there....

The power of removal here claimed for the President falls within this principle, since its coercive influence threatens the independence of a commission, which is not only wholly disconnected from the executive department, but which, as already fully appears, was created by Congress as a means of carrying into operation legislative and judicial powers, and as an agency of the legislative and judicial departments.

In the light of the question now under consideration, we have re-examined the precedents referred to in the *Myers Case*, and find nothing in them to justify a conclusion contrary to that which we have reached. The so-called "decision of 1789" had relation to a bill proposed by Mr. Madison to establish an executive Department of Foreign Affairs.... We shall not discuss the subject further, since it is so fully covered by the opinions in the *Myers Case*, except to say that the office under consideration by Congress was not only purely executive, but the officer one who was responsible to the President, and to him alone, in a very definite sense. A reading of the debates shows that the President's illimitable power of removal was not considered in respect of other than executive officers....

The result of what we now have said is this: Whether the power of the President to remove an officer shall prevail over the authority of Congress to condition the power by fixing a definite term and precluding a removal except for cause will depend upon the character of the office; the *Myers* decision, affirming the power of the President alone to make the removal, is confined to purely executive officers; and as to officers of the kind here under consideration, we hold that no removal can be made during the prescribed term for which the officer is appointed, except for one or more of the causes named in the applicable statute.

To the extent that, between the decision in the *Myers Case*, which sustains the unrestrictable power of the President to remove purely executive officers, and our present decision that such power does not extend to an office such as that here involved, there shall remain a field of doubt, we leave such cases as may fall within it for future consideration and determination as they may arise

Mr. Justice McREYNOLDS [concurs in the judgment.] A separate opinion in *Myers v. United States* states his views concerning the power of the President to remove appointees.

Comments and Questions

1. The first issue in the case is whether the specified grounds for removal are the exclusive grounds for removal, or whether the President can also remove commissioners for other reasons, like lack of confidence. This does not appear to be a hard question. What techniques does the Court use to decide this statutory issue?

2. On the second question, the constitutionality of the limitation on the President's ability to remove commissioners, what's happened? The Court's opinion in *Myers* declaring a broad immunity of the President from limitations on his power of removal has changed to a unanimous decision that creating a "for cause" removal requirement for principal officers of the United States is fully within the power of Congress. First, the composition of the Court has changed. McReynolds, Brandeis, and Holmes, all of whom dissented in *Myers*, are all still on the Court, but Taft, the presidentially oriented Chief Justice, has been replaced by Charles Evans Hughes, a Republican from New York. Second, the year is 1935, the year in which the Court found two statutes unconstitutional delegations of legislative authority to the President, and in which it was imposing judicial barriers to the New Deal. In other words, the Court

was strongly hostile to President Roosevelt and his policies. Strengthening the independence of certain agencies was a way of thwarting Roosevelt's attempt to take control of the government to achieve his policies. Third, *Humphreys* is a different case from *Myers*, whether *Myers* is viewed as involving a purely executive officer (the point of distinction relied upon by the *Humphreys* Court), an inferior officer, or a removal subject to approval by a portion of Congress as opposed to simply a limitation on the President's unfettered discretion.

3. The Court suggests that the Federal Trade Commission is not part of the executive branch because it is "an administrative body created by Congress to carry into effect legislative policies embodied in the statute in accordance with the legislative standard therein prescribed." But why would that be so? First, all administrative agencies are created by Congress; the Constitution neither creates nor identifies any department or agency. Second, wouldn't this description equally fit the Department of Interior, the Department of Commerce, the Department of Labor, and the Department of Agriculture—to mention some of the departments then in existence? Indeed, other than perhaps the Department of State, the Department of Defense, and the Department of Justice, are not all departments and agencies of the United States created by Congress exclusively to carry into effect legislative policies embodied in the statute creating them? And certainly the Departments of State, Defense, and Justice at least in part are created to carry out legislative policies. Does this mean that it is a matter of congressional policy, discretion, or whim whether a department or agency is "within the executive branch" or instead must be able to act "without executive leave and ... free from executive control"?

4. The Court says that if the Federal Trade Commission performs any executive function, it does it in the discharge of its "quasi-legislative" and "quasi-judicial" functions. What does the Court mean by "quasi-legislative" and "quasi-judicial" functions? If you take Administrative Law, you will learn that when agencies adopt rules or regulations, they engage in quasi-legislative functions, and when they perform adjudication, they engage in quasi-judicial functions. But virtually all departments and agencies perform these functions. Again, could Congress make them all independent of the President? What would this mean with respect to the President's constitutional duty to take care that the laws are faithfully executed?

MORRISON v. OLSON

United States Supreme Court, 1988.
487 U.S. 654, 108 S.Ct. 2597, 101 L.Ed.2d 569.

Chief Justice REHNQUIST delivered the opinion of the Court

[In 1982, during the Reagan administration, two Subcommittees of the House of Representatives issued subpoenas directing the Environmental Protection Agency (EPA) to produce certain documents relating to actions by the EPA under the "Superfund Law," an environmental law requiring persons whose hazardous waste was a threat to the environment to clean that waste up. There were allegations that EPA was making sweetheart deals with industry contrary to the requirements of the law. Acting on the advice of the Justice Department, the President ordered the Administrator of EPA to invoke executive privilege to withhold certain of the documents on the ground that they contained "enforcement sensitive information." The Administrator obeyed this order and withheld the documents. In response, the House voted to hold the Administrator in contempt. The conflict abated when the administration agreed to give the House Subcommittees limited access to the documents. The following year, the House Judiciary Committee began an investigation into the Justice Department's role in the controversy over the EPA documents. During this investigation, Assistant Attorney General Theodore Olson testified before a House Subcommittee. Later, the majority members of the Judiciary Committee published a lengthy report on the Committee's investigation. The report not only criticized various officials in the Department of Justice for their role in the EPA executive privilege dispute, but it also suggested that Olson had given false and misleading testimony to the Subcommittee. The Chairman of the Judiciary Committee forwarded a copy of the report to the Attorney General with a request that he seek the appointment of an independent counsel to investigate the allegations pursuant to the independent counsel provisions of the Ethics in Government Act of 1978. As a result, the Special Division of the United States Court of Appeals for the District of Columbia Circuit appointed Alexia Morrison independent counsel. She in turn subpoenaed various documents from Olson. He moved to quash the subpoenas on the ground that the independent counsel provisions of the Act were unconstitutional. Recall from the discussion of this case in the previous section on Appointments that one of the claims was that the independent counsel was a principal officer and therefore had to be appointed by the President with the advice and consent of the Senate. The Court rejected that claim, finding the independent counsel an inferior officer. In addition, Olson argued that because the statute provided that the independent counsel could only be removed by the Attorney General "for good cause," the statute was unconstitutional under *Myers v. United States*.]

We now turn to consider whether the Act is invalid under the constitutional principle of separation of powers. Two related issues must be addressed: The first is whether the provision of the Act restricting the Attorney General's power to remove the independent counsel to only those instances in which he can show "good cause," taken by itself, impermissibly interferes with the President's exercise of his constitutionally appointed functions. The second is whether, taken as a whole, the Act violates the separation of powers by reducing the President's ability to control the prosecutorial powers wielded by the independent counsel.

Two Terms ago we had occasion to consider whether it was consistent with the separation of powers for Congress to pass a statute that authorized a Government official who is removable only by Congress to participate in what we found to be "executive powers." *Bowsher v. Synar,* 478 U.S. 714 (1986). We held in *Bowsher* that "Congress cannot reserve for itself the power of removal of an officer charged with the execution of the laws except by impeachment." A primary antecedent for this ruling was our 1926 decision in *Myers v. United States*.... There too, Congress' attempt to involve itself in the removal of an executive official was found to be sufficient grounds to render the statute invalid. As we observed in *Bowsher,* the essence of the decision in *Myers* was the judgment that the Constitution prevents Congress from "draw[ing] to itself ... the power to remove or the right to participate in the exercise of that power." ...

Unlike both *Bowsher* and *Myers,* this case does not involve an attempt by Congress itself to gain a role in the removal of executive officials other than its established powers of impeachment and conviction. The Act instead puts the removal power squarely in the hands of the Executive Branch; an independent counsel may be removed from office, "only by the personal action of the Attorney General, and only for good cause." ... In our view, the removal provisions of the Act make this case more analogous to *Humphrey's Executor v. United States* ... than to *Myers* or *Bowsher.*

In *Humphrey's Executor,* [w]e stated that whether Congress can "condition the [President's power of removal] by fixing a definite term and precluding a removal except for cause, will depend upon the character of the office." At least in regard to "quasi-legislative" and "quasi-judicial" agencies such as the FTC, "[t]he authority of Congress, in creating [such] agencies, to require them to act in discharge of their duties independently of executive control ... includes, as an appropriate incident, power to fix the period during which they shall continue in office, and to forbid their removal except for cause in the meantime." ...

Appellees contend that *Humphrey's Executor* [is] distinguishable from this case because [it] did not involve officials who performed a "core executive function." They argue that our decision in *Humphrey's Executor* rests on a distinction between "purely executive" officials and officials who exercise "quasi-legislative" and "quasi-judicial" powers. In their view, when a "purely executive" official is involved, the governing precedent is *Myers,* not *Humphrey's Executor.* And, under *Myers,* the President must have absolute discretion to discharge "purely" executive officials at will.

We undoubtedly did rely on the terms "quasi-legislative" and "quasi-judicial" to distinguish the officials involved in *Humphrey's Executor* and *Wiener* from those in *Myers,* but our present considered view is that the determination of whether the Constitution allows Congress to impose a "good cause"-type restriction on the President's power to remove an official cannot be made to turn on whether or not that official is classified as "purely executive." The analysis contained in our removal cases is designed not to define rigid categories of those officials who may or may not be removed at will by the President,[28] but to ensure that Congress does not interfere with the President's exercise of the "executive power" and his constitutionally appointed duty to "take care that the laws be faithfully executed" under Article II. *Myers* was undoubtedly correct in its holding, and in its broader suggestion that there are some "purely executive" officials who must be removable by the President at will if he is to be able to accomplish his constitutional role....

At the other end of the spectrum from *Myers,* the characterization of the agencies in *Humphrey's Executor* ... as "quasi-legislative" or "quasi-judicial" in large part reflected our judgment that it was not essential to the President's proper execution of his Article II powers that these agencies be headed up by individuals who were removable at will. We do not mean to suggest that an analysis of the functions served by the officials at issue is irrelevant. But the real question is whether the removal restrictions are of such a nature that they impede the President's ability to perform his constitutional duty, and the functions of the officials in question must be analyzed in that light.

Considering for the moment the "good cause" removal provision in isolation from the other parts of the Act at issue in this case, we cannot say that the imposition of a "good cause" standard for removal by itself unduly trammels on executive authority. There is no real dispute that the functions performed by the independent counsel are "executive" in the sense that they are law enforcement functions that typically have been undertaken by officials within the Executive Branch. As we noted above, however, the independent counsel is an inferior officer under the Appointments Clause, with limited jurisdiction and tenure and lacking policymaking or significant administrative authority. Although the counsel exercises no small amount of discretion and judgment in deciding how to carry out his or her duties under the Act, we simply do not see how the President's need to control the exercise of that discretion is so central to the functioning of the Executive Branch as to require as a matter of constitutional law that the counsel be terminable at will by the President.

28. The difficulty of defining such categories of "executive" or "quasi-legislative" officials is illustrated by a comparison of our decisions in cases such as *Humphrey's Executor*, *Buckley v. Valeo*, and *Bowsher*. In *Buckley*, we indicated that the functions of the Federal Election Commission are "administrative," and "more legislative and judicial in nature," and are "of kinds usually performed by independent regulatory agencies or by some department in the Executive Branch under the direction of an Act of Congress." In *Bowsher*, we found that the functions of the Comptroller General were "executive" in nature, in that he was required to exercise judgment concerning facts that affect the application of the Act, and he must "interpret the provisions of the Act to determine precisely what budgetary calculations are required." Compare this with the description of the FTC's powers in *Humphrey's Executor*, which we stated "occupie[d] no place in the executive department": "The [FTC] is an administrative body created by Congress to carry into effect legislative policies embodied in the statute in accordance with the legislative standard therein prescribed, and to perform other specified duties as a legislative or as a judicial aid." As Justice WHITE noted in his dissent in *Bowsher*, it is hard to dispute that the powers of the FTC at the time of *Humphrey's Executor* would at the present time be considered "executive," at least to some degree.

Nor do we think that the "good cause" removal provision at issue here impermissibly burdens the President's power to control or supervise the independent counsel, as an executive official, in the execution of his or her duties under the Act. This is not a case in which the power to remove an executive official has been completely stripped from the President, thus providing no means for the President to ensure the "faithful execution" of the laws. Rather, because the independent counsel may be terminated for "good cause," the Executive, through the Attorney General, retains ample authority to assure that the counsel is competently performing his or her statutory responsibilities in a manner that comports with the provisions of the Act. Although we need not decide in this case exactly what is encompassed within the term "good cause" under the Act, the legislative history of the removal provision also makes clear that the Attorney General may remove an independent counsel for "misconduct." Here, as with the provision of the Act conferring the appointment authority of the independent counsel on the special court, the congressional determination to limit the removal power of the Attorney General was essential, in the view of Congress, to establish the necessary independence of the office. We do not think that this limitation as it presently stands sufficiently deprives the President of control over the independent counsel to interfere impermissibly with his constitutional obligation to ensure the faithful execution of the laws.

The final question to be addressed is whether the Act, taken as a whole, violates the principle of separation of powers by unduly interfering with the role of the Executive Branch. Time and again we have reaffirmed the importance in our constitutional scheme of the separation of governmental powers into the three coordinate branches....

We observe first that this case does not involve an attempt by Congress to increase its own powers at the expense of the Executive Branch. Unlike some of our previous cases, most recently *Bowsher v. Synar,* this case simply does not pose a "dange[r] of congressional usurpation of Executive Branch functions." ...

Finally, we do not think that the Act "impermissibly undermine[s]" the powers of the Executive Branch or "disrupts the proper balance" between the coordinate branches [by] prevent [ing] the Executive Branch from accomplishing its constitutionally assigned functions. It is undeniable that the Act reduces the amount of control or supervision that the Attorney General and, through him, the President exercises over the investigation and prosecution of a certain class of alleged criminal activity. The Attorney General is not allowed to appoint the individual of his choice; he does not determine the counsel's jurisdiction; and his power to remove a counsel is limited. Nonetheless, the Act does give the Attorney General several means of supervising or controlling the prosecutorial powers that may be wielded by an independent counsel. Most importantly, the Attorney General retains the power to remove the counsel for "good cause," a power that we have already concluded provides the Executive with substantial ability to ensure that the laws are "faithfully executed" by an independent counsel. No independent counsel may be appointed without a specific request by the Attorney General, and the Attorney General's decision not to request appointment if he finds "no reasonable grounds to believe that further investigation is warranted" is committed to his unreviewable discretion. The Act thus gives the Executive a degree of control over the power to initiate an investigation by the independent counsel. In addition, the jurisdiction of the independent counsel is defined with reference to the facts submitted by the Attorney General, and once a counsel is appointed, the Act requires that the counsel abide by Justice Department policy unless it is not "possible" to do so. Notwithstanding the fact that the counsel is to some degree "independent" and free from executive supervision to a greater extent than other federal prosecutors, in our view these features of the Act give the Executive Branch sufficient control over the independent counsel to ensure that the President is able to perform his constitutionally assigned duties....

Justice KENNEDY took no part in the consideration or decision of this case.

Justice SCALIA, dissenting....

The Court concedes that "[t]here is no real dispute that the functions performed by the independent counsel are 'executive' " ... Governmental investigation and prosecution of crimes is a quintessentially executive function....

The utter incompatibility of the Court's approach with our constitutional traditions can be made more clear, perhaps, by applying it to the powers of the other two branches. Is it conceivable that if Congress passed a statute depriving itself of less than full and entire control over some insignificant area of legislation, we would inquire whether the matter was "so central to the functioning of the Legislative Branch" as really to require complete control, or whether the statute gives Congress "sufficient control over the surrogate legislator to ensure that Congress is able to perform its constitutionally assigned duties"? Of course we would have none of that. Once we determined that a purely legislative power was at issue we would require it to be exercised, wholly and entirely, by Congress....

The Court has, nonetheless, replaced the clear constitutional prescription that the executive power belongs to the President with a "balancing test." What are the standards to determine how the balance is to be struck, that is, how much removal of Presidential power is too much? ... Once we depart from the text of the Constitution, just where short of that do we stop? The most amazing feature of the Court's opinion is that it does not even purport to give an answer. It simply announces, with no analysis, that the ability to control the decision whether to investigate and prosecute the President's closest advisers, and indeed the President himself, is not "so central to the functioning of the Executive Branch" as to be constitutionally required to be within the President's control.

Apparently that is so because we say it is so. Having abandoned as the basis for our decision-making the text of Article II that "the executive Power" must be vested in the President, the Court does not even attempt to craft a substitute criterion—a "justiciable standard," however remote from the Constitution—that today governs, and in the future will govern, the decision of such questions. Evidently, the governing standard is to be what might be called the unfettered wisdom of a majority of this Court, revealed to an obedient people on a case-by-case basis. This is not only not the government of laws that the Constitution established; it is not a government of laws at all....

Comments and Questions

1. After three years and $2 million, the independent counsel closed its investigation with no charges brought.

2. The Court says that the outcomes in both *Myers* and *Humphreys* were correct, but it rejects the analyses of both. What does the Court mean in footnote 28?

3. The Court discusses the case of *Bowsher v. Synar*, decided two years before. There Congress had passed a statute designed to change the federal budgeting process in order to try to rein in the consistent deficits. An integral part of the statute was the ability of the Comptroller General to make a report assessing the proposed income and expenditures of the government, and if the expenditures exceeded the income by specified amounts, the Comptroller General would direct the President to cut expenditures to bring the difference within the specified figures. Such power, the Court held, could only be performed by an officer of the executive branch of government, and the question was whether the Comptroller General could be such an officer in light of the manner in which he could be removed—by an act of Congress finding any of the following: permanent disability, inefficiency, neglect of duty, malfeasance, or a felony or conduct involving moral turpitude. The Court held that by assigning the removal power to Congress, Congress made the Comptroller General subservient to it, allowing Congress to play a role in the execution of the laws. This, the Court held, Congress could not do. Consequently, the role assigned to the Comptroller General was unconstitutional. Recall that *Myers* to a large extent was about the role the Senate would play in the removal of the postmaster.

4. In *Bowsher* the Court discussed the grounds upon which the Comptroller General could be removed. "The statute permits removal for 'inefficiency,' 'neglect of duty,' or 'malfeasance.' These terms are very broad and, as interpreted by Congress, could sustain removal of a Comptroller General for any number of actual or perceived transgressions of the legislative will." 478 U.S. at 729. Recall, however, the grounds upon which a commissioner of the Federal Trade Commission may be removed by the President: inefficiency, neglect of duty, or malfeasance in office. If these terms are so broad that the President could interpret them to sustain removal of a commissioner for any number of transgressions of the

President's will, how "independent" are the so-called independent regulatory agencies? Is this a reason why such limitations might not interfere with the President's responsibility to take care that the laws are faithfully executed?

5. Justice Scalia is alone in his fulminations against the majority's "balancing test." Would Justice Scalia overrule *Humphreys*?

6. Note that in footnote 28 the Court acknowledges that today the so-called independent regulatory agencies, like the Federal Trade Commission, are considered "executive" agencies, "at least to some degree."

D. ATTEMPTS TO ADDRESS STRUCTURAL ISSUES

The next two cases involve attempts by Congress and the President to address structural difficulties encountered in modern government.

IMMIGRATION AND NATURALIZATION SERVICE v. CHADHA

United States Supreme Court, 1983.
462 U.S. 919, 103 S.Ct. 2764, 77 L.Ed.2d 317.

[Historically, if an illegal alien was found, he was subject to deportation, no matter how long he had managed to stay in the United States and no matter what ties he had established, such as a wife and family and steady job. One way of avoiding the harshness of deportation in such cases was by way of a "private bill." A private bill is a bill introduced into Congress for the relief of a particular individual (or company), as opposed to being for the good of the general public. If the alien's lawyer or congressman could convince enough members of the House and Senate, they could pass a law and submit it to the President for signature, in order to adjust the alien's status from deportable to immigrant. In order to replace this very cumbersome and inadequate process, which relied more on influence and contacts than justice, Congress eventually passed the Immigration and Nationality Act in 1952.]

[Under Section 244 of that Act, an alien who was ordered deported could apply to the Attorney General for a "suspension" of deportation on the grounds that he had been physically present in the United States for a continuous period of not less than seven years, that he was of good moral character, and that he or his immediate family would suffer "extreme hardship" if he was deported. If the Attorney General in his discretion granted the "suspension," the Act required the Attorney General to report the "suspension" with a detailed statement of facts and reasons to both houses of Congress. If before the end of the next session of Congress either house of Congress voted a resolution of disapproval, the "suspension" would be terminated, and the alien would have to be deported. If, however, neither house voted such a resolution before the end of the next session of Congress, then the Attorney General would cancel the deportation proceedings, and the alien was allowed to remain in the United States.]

[Jagdish Rai Chadha was an East Indian from Kenya admitted into the United States on a student visa in 1966. His visa expired in 1972, and the following year the Immigration and Naturalization Service, the agency then responsible for immigration matters, ordered him to show cause why he should not be deported. At the immigration hearing the following year, Chadha conceded his deportability, but the hearing was stayed to enable him to file an application for a suspension of deportation in light of the fact that neither Kenya nor India recognized him as a citizen, because he carried a British passport from before Kenya was an independent nation. In June 1974, an immigration judge, operating under a delegation of authority from the Attorney General, granted Chadha a suspension of deportation. The suspension was reported to Congress, and in December 1975 the House of Representatives without debate or recorded vote, on the basis of the recommendation of the House Committee on the Judiciary, passed a resolution of disapproval.]

[Chadha, unlike numerous other aliens in identical circumstances, challenged the constitutionality of this process. The Board of Immigration Appeals held it had no authority to rule on the constitutionality of the law. Chadha then appealed to the Ninth Circuit. Before the Ninth Circuit the Immigration and Naturalization Service agreed with Chadha that the one-house veto provision of § 244(c)(2) of the Act was unconstitutional. The House and Senate sought to intervene in the case, and the court granted them intervention but, nonetheless, held the one-house veto provision unconstitutional in an opinion by then-Judge Anthony Kennedy. The House and Senate petitioned the Supreme Court for certiorari, which was granted.]

Chief Justice BURGER delivered the opinion of the Court.

[W]e turn now to the question whether action of one House of Congress under § 244(c)(2) violates strictures of the Constitution.... Its wisdom is not the concern of the courts; if a challenged action does not violate the Constitution, it must be sustained....

By the same token, the fact that a given law or procedure is efficient, convenient, and useful in facilitating functions of government, standing alone, will not save it if it is contrary to the Constitution. Convenience and efficiency are not the primary objectives—or the hallmarks—of democratic government and our inquiry is sharpened rather than blunted by the fact that Congressional veto provisions are appearing with increasing frequency in statutes which delegate authority to executive and independent agencies:

> "Since 1932, when the first veto provision was enacted into law, 295 congressional veto-type procedures have been inserted in 196 different statutes as follows: from 1932 to 1939, five statutes were affected; from 1940–49, nineteen statutes; between

1950–59, thirty-four statutes; and from 1960–69, forty-nine. From the year 1970 through 1975, at least one hundred sixty-three such provisions were included in eighty-nine laws."

[E]xplicit and unambiguous provisions of the Constitution prescribe and define the respective functions of the Congress and of the Executive in the legislative process.... These provisions of Art. I are integral parts of the constitutional design for the separation of powers....

The decision to provide the President with a limited and qualified power to nullify proposed legislation by veto was based on the profound conviction of the Framers that the powers conferred on Congress were the powers to be most carefully circumscribed. It is beyond doubt that lawmaking was a power to be shared by both Houses and the President....

The President's role in the lawmaking process also reflects the Framers' careful efforts to check whatever propensity a particular Congress might have to enact oppressive, improvident, or ill-considered measures.... The Court also has observed that the Presentment Clauses serve the important purpose of assuring that a "national" perspective is grafted on the legislative process: "The President is a representative of the people just as the members of the Senate and of the House are, and it may be, at some times, on some subjects, that the President elected by all the people is rather more representative of them all than are the members of either body of the Legislature whose constituencies are local and not countrywide...." *Myers v. United States.*

The bicameral requirement of Art. I, §§ 1, 7 was of scarcely less concern to the Framers than was the Presidential veto and indeed the two concepts are interdependent. By providing that no law could take effect without the concurrence of the prescribed majority of the Members of both Houses, the Framers reemphasized their belief, already remarked upon in connection with the Presentment Clauses, that legislation should not be enacted unless it has been carefully and fully considered by the Nation's elected officials....

We see therefore that the Framers were acutely conscious that the bicameral requirement and the Presentment Clauses would serve essential constitutional functions. The President's participation in the legislative process was to protect the Executive Branch from Congress and to protect the whole people from improvident laws. The division of the Congress into two distinctive bodies assures that the legislative power would be exercised only after opportunity for full study and debate in separate settings. The President's unilateral veto power, in turn, was limited by the power of two thirds of both Houses of Congress to overrule a veto thereby precluding final arbitrary action of one person. It emerges clearly that the prescription for legislative action in Art. I, §§ 1, 7 represents the Framers' decision that the legislative power of the Federal government be exercised in accord with a single, finely wrought and exhaustively considered, procedure.

The Constitution sought to divide the delegated powers of the new federal government into three defined categories, legislative, executive and judicial, to assure, as nearly as possible, that each Branch of government would confine itself to its assigned responsibility. The hydraulic pressure inherent within each of the separate Branches to exceed the outer limits of its power, even to accomplish desirable objectives, must be resisted.

Although not "hermetically" sealed from one another, the powers delegated to the three Branches are functionally identifiable. When any Branch acts, it is presumptively exercising the power the Constitution has delegated to it. When the Executive acts, it presumptively acts in an executive or administrative capacity as defined in Art. II. And when, as here, one House of Congress purports to act, it is presumptively acting within its assigned sphere.

Beginning with this presumption, we must nevertheless establish that the challenged action under § 244(c)(2) is of the kind to which the procedural requirements of Art. I, § 7 apply. Not every action taken by either House is subject to the bicameralism and presentment requirements of Art. I. Whether actions taken by either House are, in law and fact, an exercise of legislative power depends not on their form but upon "whether they contain matter which is properly to be regarded as legislative in its character and effect."

Examination of the action taken here by one House pursuant to § 244(c)(2) reveals that it was essentially legislative in purpose and effect. [T]he House took action that had the purpose and effect of altering the legal rights, duties and relations of persons, including the Attorney General, Executive Branch officials and Chadha, all outside the legislative branch.... The one-House veto operated in this case to overrule the Attorney General and mandate Chadha's deportation; absent the House action, Chadha would remain in the United States. Congress has *acted* and its action has altered Chadha's status.

The legislative character of the one-House veto in this case is confirmed by the character of the Congressional action it supplants. Neither the House of Representatives nor the Senate contends that, absent the veto provision in § 244(c)(2), either of them, or both of them acting together, could effectively require the Attorney General to deport an alien once the Attorney General, in the exercise of legislatively delegated authority, had determined the alien should remain in the United States. Without the challenged provision in § 244(c)(2), this could have been achieved, if at all, only by legislation requiring deportation....

The nature of the decision implemented by the one-House veto in this case further manifests its legislative character. After long experience with the clumsy, time consuming private bill procedure, Congress made a deliberate choice to delegate to the Executive Branch, and specifically to the Attorney General, the authority to allow deportable aliens to remain in this country in certain specified circumstances. It is not disputed that this choice to delegate authority is precisely the kind of decision that can be implemented only in accordance with the procedures set out in Art. I. Disagreement with the Attorney General's decision on Chadha's deportation—that is, Congress' decision to deport Chadha—no less than Congress' original choice to delegate to the Attorney General the authority to make that decision, involves determinations of policy that Congress can implement in only one way; bicameral passage followed by presentment to the President. Congress must abide by its delegation of authority until that delegation is legislatively altered or revoked.

Finally, we see that when the Framers intended to authorize either House of Congress to act alone and outside of its prescribed bicameral legislative role, they narrowly and precisely defined the procedure for such action. There are but four provisions in the Constitution, explicit and unambiguous, by which one House may act alone with the unreviewable force of law, not subject to the President's veto:

(a) The House of Representatives alone was given the power to initiate impeachments. Art. I, § 2, cl. 6;

(b) The Senate alone was given the power to conduct trials following impeachment on charges initiated by the House and to convict following trial. Art. I, § 3, cl. 5;

(c) The Senate alone was given final unreviewable power to approve or to disapprove presidential appointments. Art. II, § 2, cl. 2;

(d) The Senate alone was given unreviewable power to ratify treaties negotiated by the President. Art. II, § 2, cl. 2.

Clearly, when the Draftsmen sought to confer special powers on one House, independent of the other House, or of the President, they did so in explicit, unambiguous terms. These carefully defined exceptions from presentment and bicameralism underscore the difference between the legislative functions of Congress and other unilateral but important and binding one-House acts provided for in the Constitution. These exceptions are narrow, explicit, and separately justified; none of them authorize the action challenged here. On the contrary, they provide further support for the conclusion that Congressional authority is not to be implied and for the conclusion that the veto provided for in § 244(c)(2) is not authorized by the constitutional design of the powers of the Legislative Branch.

Since it is clear that the action by the House under § 244(c)(2) was not within any of the express constitutional exceptions authorizing one House to act alone, and equally clear that it was an exercise of legislative power, that action was subject to the standards prescribed in Article I....

Justice POWELL, concurring in the judgment.

The Court's decision, based on the Presentment Clauses, Art. I, § 7, cls. 2 and 3, apparently will invalidate every use of the legislative veto. The breadth of this holding gives one pause. Congress has included the veto in literally hundreds of statutes, dating back to the 1930s. Congress clearly views this procedure as essential to controlling the delegation of power to administrative agencies. One reasonably may disagree with Congress' assessment of the veto's utility, but the respect due its judgment as a coordinate branch of Government cautions that our holding should be no more extensive than necessary to decide this case. In my view, the case may be decided on a narrower ground. When Congress finds that a particular person does not satisfy the statutory criteria for permanent residence in this country it has assumed a judicial function in violation of the principle of separation of powers. Accordingly, I concur only in the judgment.

Justice WHITE, dissenting.

Today the Court not only invalidates § 244(c)(2) of the Immigration and Nationality Act, but also sounds the death knell for nearly 200 other statutory provisions in which Congress has reserved a "legislative veto." For this reason, the Court's decision is of surpassing importance. And it is for this reason that the Court would have been well-advised to decide the case, if possible, on the narrower grounds of separation of powers, leaving for full consideration the constitutionality of other congressional review statutes operating on such varied matters as war powers and agency rulemaking, some of which concern the independent regulatory agencies.

The prominence of the legislative veto mechanism in our contemporary political system and its importance to Congress can hardly be overstated. It has become a central means by which Congress secures the accountability of executive and independent agencies. Without the legislative veto, Congress is faced with a Hobson's choice: either to refrain from delegating the necessary authority, leaving itself with a hopeless task of writing laws with the requisite specificity to cover endless special circumstances across the entire policy landscape, or in the alternative, to abdicate its law-making function to the executive branch and independent agencies. To choose the former leaves major national problems unresolved; to opt for the latter risks unaccountable policymaking by those not elected to fill that role. Accordingly, over the past five decades, the legislative veto has been placed in nearly 200 statutes. The device is known in every field of governmental concern: reorganization, budgets, foreign affairs, war powers, and regulation of trade, safety, energy, the environment and the economy....

[T]he legislative veto is more than "efficient, convenient, and useful." It is an important if not indispensable political invention that allows the President and Congress to resolve major constitutional and policy differences, assures the accountability of independent regulatory agencies, and preserves Congress' control over lawmaking. Perhaps there are other means of accommodation and accountability, but the increasing reliance of Congress upon the legislative veto suggests that the alternatives to which Congress must now turn are not entirely satisfactory.[10] ...

If the legislative veto were as plainly unconstitutional as the Court strives to suggest, its broad ruling today would be more comprehensible. But, the constitutionality of the legislative veto is anything but clearcut. The issue divides scholars, courts, attorneys general, and the two other branches of the National Government. If the veto devices so flagrantly disregarded the requirements of Article I as the Court today suggests, I find it incomprehensible that Congress, whose members are bound by oath to uphold the Constitution, would have placed these mechanisms in nearly 200 separate laws over a period of 50 years.

The reality of the situation is that the constitutional question posed today is one of immense difficulty over which the executive and legislative branches—as well as scholars and judges—have understandably disagreed. That disagreement stems from the silence of the Constitution on the precise question: The Constitution does not directly authorize or prohibit the legislative veto. Thus, our task should be to determine whether the legislative veto is consistent with the purposes of Art. I and the principles of Separation of Powers which are reflected in that Article and throughout the Constitution.... Only within the last half century has the complexity and size of the Federal Government's responsibilities grown so greatly that the Congress must rely on the legislative veto as the most effective if not the only means to insure their role as the nation's lawmakers. But the wisdom of the Framers was to anticipate that the nation would grow and new problems of governance would require different solutions. Accordingly, our Federal Government was intentionally chartered with the flexibility to respond to contemporary needs without losing sight of fundamental democratic principles....

This is the perspective from which we should approach the novel constitutional questions presented by the legislative veto. In my view, neither Article I of the Constitution nor the doctrine of separation of powers is violated by this mechanism by which our elected representatives preserve their voice in the governance of the nation....

[T]he power to exercise a legislative veto is not the power to write new law without bicameral approval or presidential consideration. The veto must be authorized by statute and may only negative what an Executive department or independent agency has proposed. On its face, the legislative veto no more allows one House of Congress to make law than does the presidential veto confer such power upon the President....

The wisdom and the constitutionality of these broad delegations [of

10. While Congress could write certain statutes with greater specificity, it is unlikely that this is a realistic or even desirable substitute for the legislative veto.... Oversight hearings and congressional investigations have their purpose, but unless Congress is to be rendered a think tank or debating society, they are no substitute for the exercise of actual authority.... Finally, the passage of corrective legislation after agency regulations take effect or Executive Branch officials have acted entail the drawbacks endemic to a retroactive response.

legislative authority to the President] are matters that still have not been put to rest. But for present purposes, these cases establish that by virtue of congressional delegation, legislative power can be exercised by independent agencies and Executive departments without the passage of new legislation....

If Congress may delegate lawmaking power to independent and executive agencies, it is most difficult to understand Article I as forbidding Congress from also reserving a check on legislative power for itself. Absent the veto, the agencies receiving delegations of legislative or quasi-legislative power may issue regulations having the force of law without bicameral approval and without the President's signature. It is thus not apparent why the reservation of a veto over the exercise of that legislative power must be subject to a more exacting test. In both cases, it is enough that the initial statutory authorizations comply with the Article I requirements....

Justice REHNQUIST, with whom Justice WHITE joins, dissenting.

[B]ecause I believe that Congress did not intend the one-House veto provision of § 244(c)(2) to be severable, I dissent....

Comments and Questions

1. Unlike many constitutional law cases, *Chadha* establishes a clear rule of law—one-house vetoes and two-house vetoes of executive action are unconstitutional, the former because it lacks both bicameralism and presentment and the latter because it lacks presentment. Some laws have provided for a single congressional committee to be able to veto executive action, but of course those provisions would likewise be unconstitutional for the same reason.

2. What happens to § 244(c)(2) of the Act after *Chadha*? Justice Rehnquist argued that the one-house veto provision was not "severable" from the other portions of the provision allowing for suspension of deportation by the Attorney General. In his view, shared by Justice White, Congress would not have granted the Attorney General the authority to suspend deportation without retaining the ability to veto that decision. Thus, if the one-house veto provision was unconstitutional, so was the entire section, meaning that Chadha would have to be deported, because the Attorney General's suspension of deportation itself would be part of the provision declared unconstitutional. For this reason, Justice Rehnquist said, Chadha did not have standing to bring this action, because his injury would not be redressed by a favorable court decision—he would still have to be deported. The Court, however, found that the one-house veto provision was severable. The general presumption is that Congress would intend its acts to remain in effect even if one provision was found unconstitutional, and the Act here contained a severability provision stating explicitly that if any provision of the Act was found unconstitutional, the remainder of the Act should stay in effect. As a result, those portions of the statute that provide for the Attorney Gen-

eral to suspend deportation and to report it to Congress remain in effect. At the end of the next session of Congress, the temporary suspension of deportation is ended but the alien's deportation proceedings are also terminated, so he or she may remain in the United States.

3. *Chadha* is often cited as an example of formalistic, as opposed to functional, constitutional analysis. Recall Justice Black's decision for the majority in the *Steel Seizure Case*, another formalistic opinion. There as here the Court states that what is being done is "legislative action." In the *Steel Seizure Case* that made the seizure unconstitutional, because the President is not a lawmaker. In *Chadha* the fact that the action is legislative action makes the one-house veto unconstitutional, because lawmaking must go through both houses and be presented to the President. In both cases the characterization of the action as legislative action dictates the outcome, but what makes the one-house veto "legislative action"? Is it that it is action by a branch of the legislature? Or is it that the action has legal effect? Or is it both together? Why does Justice Powell think it is judicial action rather than legislative action?

4. Justice White's opinion in *Chadha*, on the other hand, is a functional opinion. That is, rather than dealing with the issue on a formalistic basis of deciding what box the action falls within, he discusses how the provision acts in the real world—as a balance to broad delegations to the executive, thereby serving the checks and balances of the separation of powers. No one agrees with him, however.

5. Imagine that Congress amended the Act to provide that instead of the Attorney General reporting the temporary suspension to Congress, the Attorney General must report the suspension to the Secretary of State, and if the Secretary of State does nothing for 18 months, then the suspension is permanent, but if the Secretary of State vetoes the suspension, then the alien must be deported. Would this be constitutional? It certainly would not be legislative action.

6. Imagine that both houses of Congress pass a bill containing a one-house veto provision and submit it to the President. Imagine further that but for that provision, the President supports the policies in the bill. Must the President veto the bill, because he believes it to be unconstitutional, or may he sign the bill with the caveat that he will not recognize the validity of any one-house veto that might be made pursuant to the law? Congress has in fact passed such bills subsequent to *Chadha*, and Presidents have signed them while announcing that they will not give effect to the one-house veto provisions.

7. Statements made by Presidents when signing bills into law are known as signing statements. Generally, they enable the President to make politically suitable remarks, and they have never had any particular legal effect. President George W. Bush has received a fair amount of press regarding his signing statements, because in many he has announced his views relating to constitutionality of certain aspects of the legislation he is signing. In his statements he has expressed an intention either to interpret the law to avoid what he views as its uncon-

stitutionality or to ignore those portions of the law he views as unconstitutional. While President Bush has used signing statements in this way more frequently than any other President, virtually every President since James Monroe has made signing statements of like effect. Do you see anything wrong with a President making such a signing statement, if be believes the law he signs has a constitutional problem? Would it be better if he just kept it a secret what his views were? Do you think he is required by the Constitution to veto any bill that he believes contains an unconstitutional provision? Is it constitutional for a President to enforce a law he believes is unconstitutional?

8. In 1996, Congress enacted the Congressional Review Act. That Act requires the executive to send to Congress each regulation adopted by a federal agency before it becomes effective. "Major" regulations, generally those with more than $100 million effect on the economy, may not go into effect until at least 60 days after it has been reported to Congress. During that period the Act provides an expedited procedure by which Congress may enact a joint resolution of disapproval of the regulation. The joint resolution is sent to the President for his signature or veto (as are all joint resolutions).* This is constitutional. Do you see how this is different from what was involved in *Chadha*?

CLINTON v. NEW YORK

United States Supreme Court, 1998.
524 U.S. 417, 118 S.Ct. 2091, 141 L.Ed.2d 393.

[The Presentment Clause refers to "every bill" passed by the House and Senate being presented to the President before it becomes a law. It then states that the President shall sign "it" if he approves, but if not, he shall return "it" with his objections. Then Congress may reconsider "it," and if two thirds approve, "it" becomes law. This language has been interpreted by every President since George Washington as requiring the President to accept or veto the entire bill presented to him. He is not allowed to veto a particular article, section, or provision. This makes possible a particular legislative strategy for Congress, allowing it to include in a bill, which for various reasons a President feels the need to approve, a provision that otherwise the President would veto, a provision that may have nothing to do with the rest of the bill and that is included solely for the purpose of attaching it to a veto-proof bill. This strategy can be used particularly in the appropriations area. Congress may include various appropriations that the President thinks are inappropriate or unnecessary in an appropriation bill that is otherwise abso-

* A "joint resolution" is the equivalent of a "bill," in that it is voted on by both houses and sent to the President for his approval or veto, and the result is the same—they become law. The only distinction is a parliamentary one. Bills may be amended on the floor of either house, but resolutions cannot be amended on the floor of either house; they must be voted on as they are introduced. Joint resolutions are distinct from "concurrent resolutions." These are voted on by both houses but not sent to the President. Therefore, they do not become law.

lutely necessary—e.g., salaries for military forces.]

[Recognizing the problems created by this arrangement, especially in the context of federal deficits in part created by unnecessary expenditures, Congress passed with the President's support the Line Item Veto Act in 1996, effective on January 1, 1997. That Act authorized the President to "cancel" three types of provisions that may be signed into law: "(1) any dollar amount of discretionary budget authority; (2) any item of new direct spending; or (3) any limited tax benefit." In August, President Clinton "cancelled" an "item of new direct spending"—approximately $2.6 billion for the City of New York—contained in the Balanced Budget Act of 1997. As a result, New York sued, arguing that the Line Item Veto Act was unconstitutional.]

Justice STEVENS delivered the opinion of the Court.

The Act requires the President to adhere to precise procedures whenever he exercises his cancellation authority. In identifying items for cancellation he must consider the legislative history, the purposes, and other relevant information about the items. He must determine, with respect to each cancellation, that it will "(i) reduce the Federal budget deficit; (ii) not impair any essential Government functions; and (iii) not harm the national interest." Moreover, he must transmit a special message to Congress notifying it of each cancellation within five calendar days (excluding Sundays) after the enactment of the canceled provision. It is undisputed that the President meticulously followed these procedures in these cases.

A cancellation takes effect upon receipt by Congress of the special message from the President. If, however, a "disapproval bill" pertaining to a special message is enacted into law, the cancellations set forth in that message become "null and void." The Act sets forth a detailed expedited procedure for the consideration of a "disapproval bill," but no such bill was passed for either of the cancellations involved in these cases. A majority vote of both Houses is sufficient to enact a disapproval bill. The Act does not grant the President the authority to cancel a disapproval bill, but he does, of course, retain his constitutional authority to veto such a bill.

The effect of a cancellation is plainly stated … in the Act. With respect to … an item of new direct spending … , the cancellation prevents the item "from having legal force or effect." Thus, under the plain text of the statute, … the action[] of the President that [is] challenged in these cases prevented one section of the Balanced Budget Act of 1997 … "from having legal force or effect." …

In both legal and practical effect, the President has amended [an Act] of Congress by repealing a portion of [it]. "[R]epeal of statutes, no less than enactment, must conform with Art. I." *INS v. Chadha*. There is no provision in the Constitution that authorizes the President to enact, to amend, or to repeal statutes. Both Article I and Article II assign responsibilities to the President that directly relate to the lawmaking process, but neither addresses the issue presented by these cases. The President "shall from time to time give to the Congress Information on the State of the Union, and recommend to their Consideration such Measures as he shall judge necessary and expedient...." Art. II, § 3. Thus, he may initiate and influence legislative proposals. Moreover, after a bill has passed both Houses of Congress, but "before it become[s] a Law," it must be presented to the President. If he approves it, "he shall sign it, but if not he shall return it, with his Objections to that House in which it shall have originated, who shall enter the Objections at large on their Journal, and proceed to reconsider it." His "return" of a bill, which is usually described as a "veto," is subject to being overridden by a two-thirds vote in each House.

There are important differences between the President's "return" of a bill pursuant to Article I, § 7, and the exercise of the President's cancellation authority pursuant to the Line Item Veto Act. The constitutional return takes place *before* the bill becomes law; the statutory cancellation occurs *after* the bill becomes law. The constitutional return is of the entire bill; the statutory cancellation is of only a part. Although the Constitution expressly authorizes the President to play a role in the process of enacting statutes, it is silent on the subject of unilateral Presidential action that either repeals or amends parts of duly enacted statutes.

There are powerful reasons for construing constitutional silence on this profoundly important issue as equivalent to an express prohibition. The procedures governing the enactment of statutes set forth in the text of Article I were the product of the great debates and compromises that produced the Constitution itself. Familiar historical materials provide abundant support for the conclusion that the power to enact statutes may only "be exercised in accord with a single, finely wrought and exhaustively considered, procedure." Our first President understood the text of the Presentment Clause as requiring that he either "approve all the parts of a Bill, or reject it in toto." What has emerged in these cases from the President's exercise of his statutory cancellation powers, however, are truncated versions of two bills that passed both Houses of Congress. They are not the product of the "finely wrought" procedure that the Framers designed.

The Government advances two related arguments to support its position that despite the unambiguous provisions of the Act, cancellations do not amend or repeal properly enacted statutes in violation of the Presentment Clause. First, relying primarily on *Field v. Clark,* 143 U.S. 649 (1892), the Government contends that the cancellations were merely exercises of discretionary authority granted to the President by the Balanced Budget Act and the Taxpayer Relief Act read in light of the previously enacted Line Item Veto Act. Second, the Government submits that the substance of the authority to cancel tax and spending items "is, in practical effect, no more and no less than the power to 'decline to spend' specified sums of money, or to 'decline to implement' specified tax measures." Neither argument is persuasive.

In *Field v. Clark,* the Court upheld the constitutionality of the Tariff Act of 1890. That statute contained a "free list" of almost 300 specific articles that were exempted from import duties "unless otherwise specially provided for in this act." Section 3 was a special provision that directed the President to suspend that exemption for sugar, molasses, coffee, tea, and hides "whenever, and so often" as he should be satisfied that any country producing and exporting those products imposed duties on the agricultural products of the United States that he deemed to be "reciprocally unequal and unreasonable ..." The section then specified the duties to be imposed on those products during any such suspension. The Court provided this explanation for its conclusion that § 3 had not delegated legislative power to the President:

> "Nothing involving the expediency or the just operation of such legislation was left to the determination of the President.... [W]hen he ascertained the fact that duties and exactions, reciprocally unequal and unreasonable, were imposed upon the agricultural or other products of the United States by a country producing and exporting sugar, molasses, coffee, tea or hides, it became his duty to issue a proclamation declaring the suspension, as to that country, which Congress had determined should occur. He had no discretion in the premises except in respect to the duration of the suspension so ordered. But that related only to the enforcement of the policy established by Congress. As the suspension was absolutely required when the President ascertained the existence of a particular fact, it cannot be said that in ascertaining that fact and in issuing his proclamation, in obedience to the legislative will, he exercised the function of making laws.... It was a part of the law itself as it left the hands of Congress that the provisions, full and complete in themselves, permitting the free introduction of sugars, molasses, coffee, tea and hides, from particular countries, should be suspended, in a given contingency, and that in case of such suspensions certain duties should be imposed."

This passage identifies three critical differences between the power to suspend the exemption from import duties and the power to cancel portions of a duly enacted statute. First, the exercise of the suspension power was contingent upon a condition that did not exist when the Tariff Act was passed: the imposition of "reciprocally unequal and unreasonable" import duties by other countries. In contrast, the exercise of the cancellation power within five days after the enactment of the Balanced Budget and Tax Reform Acts necessarily was based on the same conditions that Congress evaluated when it passed those statutes. Second, under the Tariff Act, when the President determined that the contingency had arisen, he had a duty to suspend; in contrast, while it is true that the President was required by the Act to make three determinations before he canceled a provision, those determinations did not qualify his discretion to cancel or not to cancel. Finally, whenever the President suspended an exemption under the Tariff Act, he was executing the policy that Congress had embodied in the statute. In contrast, whenever the President cancels an item of new direct spending or a limited tax benefit he is rejecting the policy judgment made by Congress and relying on his own policy judgment. Thus, the conclusion in *Field v. Clark* that the suspensions mandated by the Tariff Act were not exercises of legislative power does not undermine our opinion that cancellations pursuant to the Line Item Veto Act are the functional equivalent of partial repeals of Acts of Congress that fail to satisfy Article I, § 7.

The cited statutes all relate to foreign trade, and this Court has recognized that in the foreign affairs arena, the President has "a degree of discretion and freedom from statutory restriction which would not be admissible were domestic affairs alone involved." *United States v. Curtiss–Wright Export Corp.* "Moreover, he, not Congress, has the better opportunity of knowing the conditions which prevail in foreign countries." More important, when enacting the statutes discussed in *Field,* Congress itself made the decision to suspend or repeal the particular provisions at issue upon the occurrence of particular events subsequent to enactment, and it left only the determination of whether such events occurred up to the President. The Line Item Veto Act authorizes the President himself to effect the repeal of laws, for his own policy reasons, without observing the procedures set out in Article I, § 7. The fact that Congress intended such a result is of no moment. Although Congress presumably anticipated that the President might cancel some of the items in the Balanced Budget Act and in the Taxpayer Relief Act, Congress cannot alter the procedures set out in Article I, § 7, without amending the Constitution.

Neither are we persuaded by the Government's contention that the President's authority to cancel new direct spending ... is no greater than his traditional authority to decline to spend appropriated funds. The Government has reviewed in some detail the series of statutes in which Congress has given the Executive broad discretion over the expenditure of appropriated funds. For example, the First Congress appropriated "sum[s] not exceeding" specified amounts to be spent on various Government operations. In those statutes, as in later years, the President was given wide discretion with respect to both the amounts to be spent and how the money would be allocated among different functions. It is argued that the Line Item Veto Act merely confers comparable discretionary authority over the expenditure of appropriated funds. The critical difference between this statute and all of its predecessors, however, is that unlike any of them, this Act gives the President the unilateral power to change the text of duly enacted statutes. None of the Act's predecessors could even arguably have been construed to authorize such a change.

Although they are implicit in what we have already written, the profound importance of these cases makes it appropriate to emphasize three points.

First, we express no opinion about the wisdom of the procedures authorized by the Line Item Veto Act....

Second, although appellees challenge the validity of the Act on alternative grounds, the only issue we address concerns the "finely wrought" procedure commanded by the Constitution. We have been favored with extensive debate about the scope of Congress' power to delegate lawmaking authority, or its functional equivalent, to the President[,] but [it] does not really bear on the narrow issue that is dispositive of these cases.

Third, our decision rests on the narrow ground that the procedures authorized by the Line Item Veto Act are not authorized by the Constitution.... If the Line Item Veto Act were valid, it would authorize the President to create a different law—one whose text was not voted on by either House of Congress or presented to the President for signature. Something that might be known as "Public Law 105–33 as modified by the President" may or may not be desirable, but it is surely not a document that may "become a law" pursuant to the procedures designed by the Framers of Article I, § 7, of the Constitution....

Justice KENNEDY, concurring.

[I] write to respond to my colleague Justice BREYER, who observes that the statute does not threaten the liberties of individual citizens, a point on which I disagree. The argument is related to his earlier suggestion that our role is lessened here because the two political branches are adjusting their own powers between themselves. To say the political branches have a somewhat free hand to reallocate their own authority would seem to require acceptance of two premises: first, that the public good demands it, and second, that liberty is not at risk. The former premise is inadmissible. The Constitution's structure requires a stability which transcends the convenience of the moment. The latter premise, too, is flawed. Liberty is always at stake when one or more of the branches seek to transgress the separation of powers.

Separation of powers was designed to implement a fundamental insight: Concentration of power in the hands of a single branch is a threat to liberty....

In recent years, perhaps, we have come to think of liberty as defined by that word in the Fifth and Fourteenth Amendments and as illuminated by the other provisions of the Bill of Rights. The conception of liberty embraced by the Framers was not so confined. They used the principles of separation of powers and federalism to secure liberty in the fundamental political sense of the term, quite in addition to the idea of freedom from intrusive governmental acts....

Justice SCALIA, with whom Justice O'CONNOR joins, and with whom Justice BREYER joins as to Part III, concurring in part and dissenting in part.

* * *

III

[T]he Presentment Clause requires, in relevant part, that "[e]very Bill which shall have passed the House of Representatives and the Senate, shall, before it become a Law, be presented to the President of the United States; If he approve he shall sign it, but if not he shall return it." There is no question that enactment of the Balanced Budget Act complied with these requirements: the House and Senate passed the bill, and the President signed it into law. It was only *after* the requirements of the Presentment Clause had been satisfied that the President exercised his authority under the Line Item Veto Act to cancel the spending item. Thus, the Court's problem with the Act is not that it authorizes the President to veto parts of a bill and sign others into law, but rather that it authorizes him to "cancel"—prevent from "having legal force or effect"—certain parts of duly enacted statutes.

Article I, § 7, of the Constitution obviously prevents the President from canceling a law that Congress has not authorized him to cancel. Such action cannot possibly be considered part of his execution of the law, and if it is legislative action, as the Court observes, " 'repeal of statutes, no less than enactment, must conform with Art. I.' " But that is not this case. It was certainly arguable, as an original matter, that Art. I, § 7, also prevents the President from canceling a law which itself *authorizes* the President to cancel it. But as the Court acknowledges, that argument has long since been made and rejected.... The Tariff Act of 1890 authorized the President to "suspend, by proclamation to that effect" certain of its provisions if he determined that other countries were imposing "reciprocally unequal and unreasonable" duties. This Court upheld the constitutionality of that Act in *Field v. Clark*, reciting the history since 1798 of statutes conferring upon the President the power to "discontinue the prohibitions and restraints hereby enacted and declared," "suspend the operation of the aforesaid act," and "declare the provisions of this act to be inoperative."

As much as the Court goes on about Art. I, § 7, therefore, that provision does not demand the result the Court reaches. It no more categorically prohibits the Executive *reduction* of congressional dispositions in the course of implementing statutes that authorize such reduction, than it categorically prohibits the Executive *augmentation* of congressional dispositions in the course of implementing statutes that authorize such augmentation—generally known as substantive rulemaking. There are, to be sure, limits upon the former just as there are limits upon the latter—and I am prepared to acknowledge that the limits upon the former may be much more severe. Those limits are established, however, not by some categorical prohibition of Art. I, § 7, which our cases conclusively disprove, but by what has come to be known as the doctrine of unconstitutional delegation of legislative authority: When authorized Executive reduction or augmentation is allowed to go too far, it usurps the nondelegable function of Congress and violates the separation of powers.

It is this doctrine, and not the Presentment Clause, that was discussed in the *Field* opinion, and it is this doctrine, and not the Presentment Clause, that is the issue presented by the statute before us here....

I turn, then, to the crux of the matter: whether Congress's authorizing the President to cancel an item of spending gives him a power that our history and traditions show must reside exclusively in the Legislative Branch. I may note, to begin with, that the Line Item Veto Act is not the first statute to authorize the President to "cancel" spending items. In *Bowsher v. Synar,* we addressed the constitutionality of the Balanced Budget and Emergency Deficit Control Act of 1985, which required the President, if the federal budget deficit exceeded a certain amount, to issue a "sequestration" order mandating spending reductions specified by the Comptroller General. The effect of sequestration was that "amounts sequestered ... shall be *permanently cancelled.*" We held that the Act was unconstitutional, not because it impermissibly gave the Executive legislative power, but because it gave the Comptroller General, an officer of the Legislative Branch over whom Congress retained removal power, "the ultimate authority to determine the budget cuts to be made," "functions ... plainly entailing execution of the law in constitutional terms." The President's discretion under the Line Item Veto Act is certainly broader than the Comptroller General's discretion was under the 1985 Act, but it is no broader than the discretion traditionally granted the President in his execution of spending laws.

Insofar as the degree of political, "lawmaking" power conferred upon the Executive is concerned, there is not a dime's worth of difference between Congress's authorizing the President to *cancel* a spending item, and Congress's authorizing money to be spent on a particular item at the President's discretion. And the latter has been done since the founding of the Nation....

Certain Presidents have claimed Executive authority to withhold appropriated funds even *absent* an express conferral of discretion to do so.... President Nixon, the Mahatma Gandhi of all impounders, asserted at a press conference in 1973 that his "constitutional right" to impound appropriated funds was "absolutely clear." Our decision two years later in *Train v. City of New York,* 420 U.S. 35 (1975), proved him wrong, but it implicitly confirmed that Congress may confer discretion upon the Executive to withhold appropriated funds, even funds appropriated for a specific purpose.... This Court held, as a matter of statutory interpretation, that the statute *did not grant* the Executive discretion to withhold the funds, but required allotment of the full amount authorized.

The short of the matter is this: Had the Line Item Veto Act authorized the President to "decline to spend" any item of spending contained in the Balanced Budget Act of 1997, there is not the slightest doubt that authorization would have been constitutional. What the Line Item Veto

Act does instead—authorizing the President to "cancel" an item of spending—is technically different. But the technical difference does *not* relate to the technicalities of the Presentment Clause, which have been fully complied with; and the doctrine of unconstitutional delegation, which *is* at issue here, is preeminently *not* a doctrine of technicalities. The title of the Line Item Veto Act, which was perhaps designed to simplify for public comprehension, or perhaps merely to comply with the terms of a campaign pledge, has succeeded in faking out the Supreme Court. The President's action it authorizes in fact is not a line-item veto and thus does not offend Art. I, § 7; and insofar as the substance of that action is concerned, it is no different from what Congress has permitted the President to do since the formation of the Union.

Justice BREYER, with whom Justice O'CONNOR and Justice SCALIA join as to Part III, dissenting.

I

[I]n my view the Line Item Veto Act (Act) does not violate any specific textual constitutional command, nor does it violate any implicit separation-of-powers principle. Consequently, I believe that the Act is constitutional.

II

I approach the constitutional question before us with three general considerations in mind. *First,* the Act represents a legislative effort to provide the President with the power to give effect to some, but not to all, of the expenditure and revenue-diminishing provisions contained in a single massive appropriations bill. And this objective is constitutionally proper....

Second, the case in part requires us to focus upon the Constitution's generally phrased structural provisions, provisions that delegate all "legislative" power to Congress and vest all "executive" power in the President....

Third, we need not here referee a dispute among the other two branches....

The background circumstances also mean that we are to interpret nonliteral separation-of-powers principles in light of the need for "workable government." *Youngstown Sheet and Tube Co.* If we apply those principles in light of that objective, as this Court has applied them in the past, the Act is constitutional.

III

The Court believes that the Act violates the literal text of the Constitution. A simple syllogism captures its basic reasoning:

Major Premise: The Constitution sets forth an exclusive method for enacting, repealing, or amending laws.

Minor Premise: The Act authorizes the President to "repea[l] or amen[d]" laws in a different way, namely by announcing a cancellation of a portion of a previously enacted law.

Conclusion: The Act is inconsistent with the Constitution.

I find this syllogism unconvincing, however, because its Minor Premise is faulty. When the President "canceled" the ... appropriation measure[] now before us, he did not *repeal* any law nor did he *amend* any law. He simply *followed* the law, leaving the statutes, as they are literally written, intact.

To understand why one cannot say, *literally speaking,* that the President has repealed or amended any law, imagine how the provisions of law before us might have been, but were not, written. Imagine that the canceled New York health care tax provision at issue here had instead said the following:

> "Section One. Taxes ... that were collected by the State of New York from a health care provider before June 1, 1997, and for which a waiver of the provisions [requiring payment] have been sought ... are deemed to be permissible health care related taxes ... *provided however that the President may prevent the just-mentioned provision from having legal force or effect if he determines x, y, and z.* (Assume x, y and z to be the same determinations required by the Line Item Veto Act).

Whatever a person might say, or think, about the constitutionality of this imaginary law, there is one thing the English language would prevent one from saying. One could not say that a President who "prevent[s]" the deeming language from "having legal force or effect" has either *repealed* or *amended* this particular hypothetical statute. Rather, the President has *followed* that law to the letter. He has exercised the power it explicitly delegates to him. He has executed the law, not repealed it.

It could make no significant difference to this linguistic point were the italicized proviso to appear, not as part of what I have called Section One, but, instead, at the bottom of the statute page, say, referenced by an asterisk, with a statement that it applies to every spending provision in the Act next to which a similar asterisk appears. And that being so, it could make no difference if that proviso appeared, instead, in a different, earlier enacted law, along with legal language that makes it applicable to every future spending provision picked out according to a specified formula.

But, of course, this last mentioned possibility is this very case.... In sum, I recognize that the Act before us is novel. In a sense, it skirts a constitutional edge. But that edge has to do with means, not ends. The means chosen do not amount literally to the enactment, repeal, or amendment of a law. Nor, for that matter, do they amount literally to the "line item veto" that the Act's title announces. Those means do not violate any basic separation-of-powers principle. They do not improperly shift the constitutionally foreseen balance of power from Congress to the President. Nor, since they comply with separation-of-powers principles, do they threaten the liberties of individual citizens. They represent an experiment that may, or may not, help representative government work better. The Constitution, in my view, authorizes Congress and the President to try novel methods in this way. Consequently, with respect, I dissent.

Comments and Questions

1. Is the majority not correct that the Line Item Veto Act allows the President to do precisely what he could not do under the Presentment Clause, at least with respect to the three specific types of laws that the Act covers? That is, is there any distinction between the effect of an actual line-item veto, that is not provided for in the Presentment Clause, and what the President can do with respect to specific appropriations within one appropriations law?

2. Even if this is so, is there a reason for finding something unconstitutional just because it allows something that the Constitution did not provide for? That is, did the requirement in the Constitution for the President to veto a whole bill or none of the bill constitute a prohibition on Congress allowing him to veto a part of a bill? There would seem to be a difference between what the Constitution allows in all circumstances and establishes beyond congressional interference (the President's power to veto entire bills) and what the Constitution might allow Congress to permit in specified circumstances. Does the latter really threaten the constitutional arrangement?

3. If the Constitution really does prohibit that which it did not allow with respect to line-item vetoes, how is it that everyone agrees that Congress can write an appropriation bill that leaves to the President's discretion whether particular appropriations in that bill will be spent? What is it about *Field v. Clark* that would distinguish it from the line-item veto in the *Clinton* case? What would *Field v. Clark* say about a law that authorized the President not to spend certain line items within that law?

4. Is the problem in the Line Item Veto Act that one Congress, the one that passed the Line Item Veto Act, is authorizing the President to reduce the spending contained in a subsequent law passed by a possibly different Congress? Can one Congress pass a law binding a subsequent Congress? If not, presumably Congress also cannot delegate a power to the President that would bind a subsequent Congress. Is that what the Line Item Veto Act does?

5. Would this explain why this is not simply a delegation issue, as argued by Justice Scalia?

6. In the two cases of *Chadha* and *Clinton*, we see that attempts by Congress to structure relations between the executive and legislative

branches in ways not explicitly authorized by constitutional text, even with presidential support, are struck down by the Court. In the discussion of Removals, there was also mention of *Bowsher v. Synar*, in which Congress also attempted a structural solution to chronic deficits, providing the Comptroller General authority over total spending, which solution also was found unconstitutional. Nevertheless, not all such structural solutions are struck down. For example, in order to address complaints of radically inconsistent sentencing by federal judges, Congress enacted the Sentencing Reform Act of 1984, which created the United States Sentencing Commission and tasked it with developing rules to guide sentencing discretion in federal courts. The Commission was composed of seven members appointed by the President with the advice and consent of the Senate, at least three of whom had to be federal judges "selected after considering a list of six judges recommended to the President by the Judicial Conference of the United States." The commission was described as "an independent commission in the judicial branch." This structure was challenged as unconstitutional under the separation of powers, in that it delegated legislative authority to the judicial branch. In *Mistretta v. United States*, 488 U.S. 361 (1989), the Court upheld the structure, although acknowledging that the Commission was a "peculiar institution." The Court recognized that normally it was inappropriate for the judicial branch to perform administrative duties of a nonjudicial nature, but placement of the Commission in the judicial branch for the purpose of adopting rules governing sentencing—a paradigmatic judicial function—was not inconsistent with the duties and responsibilities of the judicial branch. Moreover, utilizing judges on the Commission for such work did not impermissibly involve judges in nonjudicial activities in ways that would undermine their independence. Justice Scalia, as in *Morrison*, was the lone dissenter. Reflecting his belief in a unitary executive, he did not believe it was constitutional to assign this function to the judicial branch.

7. *Clinton* is an example of a law that would fit in Justice Jackson's first category in the *Steel Seizure case*—Presidential actions authorized by statute—the category in which the President's authority is at its greatest. Nevertheless, the Court finds the action unconstitutional.

E. PRIVILEGES AND IMMUNITIES OF THE CONGRESS AND PRESIDENT

When we considered federalism issues, we identified the two Privileges and Immunities Clauses in the Constitution: Article IV, Section 2, Clause 1 and the Fourteenth Amendment, Section 1. Both those clauses deal with the privileges and immunities of ordinary persons or, as we might say, individual rights. Here the "privileges" and "immunities" are special privileges and immunities arising out of the office of President or membership in the House of Representatives or the Senate. They have no relationship to "privileges and immunities" enjoyed by ordinary persons.

1. CONGRESSIONAL PRIVILEGES AND IMMUNITIES

Article I, Section 6, Clause 1 of the Constitution, provides that Senators and Representatives:

> shall in all cases, except treason, felony and breach of the peace, be privileged from arrest during their attendance at the session of their respective houses, and in going to and returning from the same; and for any speech or debate in either house, they shall not be questioned in any other place.

The privilege from arrest sounds like something Senator Larry Craig* should have known about, but in fact it would not have helped him, because the Supreme Court has interpreted this privilege to apply only to arrests in civil cases, which were common in 1789 but no longer exist, because the phrase "treason, felony and breach of the peace" were read to mean all criminal laws. *See Williamson v. United States*, 207 U.S. 425 (1908). In other words, this privilege is meaningless today. Is that disturbing? It means that the executive branch can criminally prosecute members of the legislative branch, and the only protection is the same protection afforded any member of the public. Is that consistent with the separation of powers? Moreover, it means that a local prosecutor, a local district attorney, for example, might be able to incapacitate a member of the House or a Senator, depriving the state or a district of representation.

However, the prohibition against questioning Senators and Representatives "for any speech or debate in either house," known as the "Speech and Debate Clause," is alive and well.

GRAVEL v. UNITED STATES

United States Supreme Court, 1972.
408 U.S. 606, 92 S.Ct. 2614, 33 L.Ed.2d 583.

[On June 13, 1971, during the height of the antiwar sentiment against the war in Vietnam, the New York Times began publishing excerpts from a leaked, highly classified history of the war that had been prepared by the Defense Department, known today as the Pentagon Papers. The excerpts indicated that President Lyndon Johnson had systematically misled the public in order to drum up support for beginning United States military intervention in Vietnam. The Nixon administration sought and obtained a preliminary injunction against the Times to stop the publication on June 15, the only time in the nation's history when the federal government sought to restrain the publication of information in a newspaper. The court of appeals affirmed that decision on June 23, and the Supreme Court granted certiorari on June 25, heard argument on June 26, and rendered its decision on June 30, overturning

* Senator Craig was arrested for disorderly conduct in an airport restroom when returning home from Congress.

the injunction. *See New York Times Co. v. United States*, 403 U.S. 713 (1971).

On the eve of the Supreme Court decision, with its outcome still unknown, Senator Mike Gravel of Alaska called a meeting of the Subcommittee on Buildings and Grounds of the Senate Public Works Committee, of which he was chair, and proceeded to read from the Pentagon Papers, which had also been leaked to him after the injunction against the Times' publication.]

Opinion of the Court by Mr. Justice WHITE, announced by Mr. Justice BLACKMUN.

These cases arise out of the investigation by a federal grand jury into possible criminal conduct with respect to the release and publication of a classified Defense Department study entitled History of the United States Decision-Making Process on Viet Nam Policy. This document, popularly known as the Pentagon Papers, bore a Defense security classification of Top Secret-Sensitive....

Among the witnesses subpoenaed were Leonard S. Rodberg, an assistant to Senator Mike Gravel of Alaska and a resident fellow at the Institute of Policy Studies.... Senator Gravel, as intervenor,[2] filed motions to quash the subpoenas.... He asserted that requiring these witnesses to appear and testify would violate his privilege under the Speech or Debate Clause of the United States Constitution, Art. I, § 6, cl. 1.

It appeared that on the night of June 29, 1971, Senator Gravel, as Chairman of the Subcommittee on Buildings and Grounds of the Senate Public Works Committee, convened a meeting of the subcommittee and there read extensively from a copy of the Pentagon Papers. He then placed the entire 47 volumes of the study in the public record. Rodberg had been added to the Senator's staff earlier in the day and assisted Gravel in preparing for and conducting the hearing.[3] Some weeks later there were press reports that Gravel had arranged for the papers to be published by Beacon Press....

The District Court [held that the Speech and Debate Clause protected whatever the Senator did in the committee meeting as well anything done by his assistant that would have been protected if done by the Senator. However, the trial court held the private publication of the documents was not privileged by the Speech or Debate Clause.]

2. The District Court permitted Senator Gravel to intervene in the proceeding on Dr. Rodberg's motion to quash the subpoena ordering his appearance before the grand jury and accepted motions from Gravel to quash the subpoena and to specify the exact nature of the questions to be asked Rodberg.

3. The District Court found that "as personal assistant to movant (Gravel), Dr. Rodberg assisted movant in preparing for disclosure and subsequently disclosing to movant's colleagues and constituents, at a hearing of the Senate Subcommittee on Public Buildings and Grounds, the contents of the so-called 'Pentagon Papers,' which were critical of the Executive's conduct in the field of foreign relations...."

The Court of Appeals affirmed the [trial court's rulings under the Speech and Debate Clause.]....

The United States petitioned for certiorari challenging the ruling that aides and other persons may not be questioned with respect to legislative acts. ... Senator Gravel also petitioned for certiorari seeking reversal of the Court of Appeals insofar as it held private publication unprotected by the Speech or Debate Clause.... We granted both petitions.

Because the claim is that a Member's aide shares the Member's constitutional privilege, we consider first whether and to what extent Senator Gravel himself is exempt from process or inquiry by a grand jury investigating the commission of a crime. Our frame of reference is Art. I, § 6, cl. 1, of the Constitution....

Senator Gravel ... points out that the last portion of § 6 affords Members of Congress [a] vital privilege—they may not be questioned in any other place for any speech or debate in either House. [H]is insistence is that the Speech or Debate Clause at the very least protects him from criminal or civil liability and from questioning elsewhere than in the Senate, with respect to the events occurring at the subcommittee hearing at which the Pentagon Papers were introduced into the public record. To us this claim is incontrovertible. The Speech or Debate Clause was designed to assure a co-equal branch of the government wide freedom of speech, debate, and deliberation without intimidation or threats from the Executive Branch. It thus protects Members against prosecutions that directly impinge upon or threaten the legislative process. We have no doubt that Senator Gravel may not be made to answer—either in terms of questions or in terms of defending himself from prosecution—for the events that occurred at the subcommittee meeting. Our decision is made easier by the fact that the United States appears to have abandoned whatever position it took to the contrary in the lower courts.

Even so, the United States strongly urges that because the Speech or Debate Clause confers a privilege only upon "Senators and Representatives," Rodberg himself has no valid claim to constitutional immunity from grand jury inquiry. In our view, both courts below correctly rejected this position. We agree with the Court of Appeals that for the purpose of construing the privilege a Member and his aide are to be "treated as one," [T]he "Speech or Debate Clause prohibits inquiry into things done by Dr. Rodberg as the Senator's agent or assistant which would have been legislative acts, and therefore privileged, if performed by the Senator personally." [I]t is literally impossible, in view of the complexities of the modern legislative process, with Congress almost constantly in session and matters of legislative concern constantly proliferating, for Members of Congress to perform their legislative tasks without the help of aides and assistants; that the day-to-day work of such aides is so critical to the Members' performance that they must be treated as the latter's alter egos; and that if they are not so recognized, the central role of the Speech or Debate Clause—to prevent intimidation of legislators by the Executive and accountability before a possibly hostile judiciary—will inevitably be diminished and frustrated....

It is true that the Clause itself mentions only "Senators and Representatives," but prior cases have plainly not taken a literalistic approach in applying the privilege. The Clause also speaks only of "Speech or Debate," but the Court's consistent approach has been that to confine the protection of the Speech or Debate Clause to words spoken in debate would be an unacceptably narrow view. Committee reports, resolutions, and the act of voting are equally covered; "(i)n short, ... things generally done in a session of the House by one of its members in relation to the business before it." Rather than giving the clause a cramped construction, the Court has sought to implement its fundamental purpose of freeing the legislator from executive and judicial oversight that realistically threatens to control his conduct as a legislator. We have little doubt that we are neither exceeding our judicial powers nor mistakenly construing the Constitution by holding that the Speech or Debate Clause applies not only to a Member but also to his aides insofar as the conduct of the latter would be a protected legislative act if performed by the Member himself....

The United States fears the abuses that history reveals have occurred when legislators are invested with the power to relieve others from the operation of otherwise valid civil and criminal laws. But these abuses, it seems to us, are for the most part obviated if the privilege applicable to the aide is viewed, as it must be, as the privilege of the Senator, and invocable only by the Senator or by the aide on the Senator's behalf, and if in all events the privilege available to the aide is confined to those services that would be immune legislative conduct if performed by the Senator himself. This view places beyond the Speech or Debate Clause a variety of services characteristically performed by aides for Members of Congress, even though within the scope of their employment. It likewise provides no protection for criminal conduct threatening the security of the person or property of others, whether performed at the direction of the Senator in preparation for or in execution of a legislative act or done without his knowledge or direction. Neither does it immunize Senator or aide from testifying at trials or grand jury proceedings involving third-party crimes where the questions do not require testimony about or impugn a legislative act. Thus our refusal to distinguish between Senator and aide in applying the Speech or Debate Clause does not mean that Rodberg is for all purposes exempt from grand jury questioning.

We are convinced also that the Court of Appeals correctly determined that Senator Gravel's alleged arrangement with Beacon Press to publish the Pentagon Papers was not protected speech or debate within the meaning of Art. I, § 6, cl. 1, of the Constitution.

Historically, the English legislative privilege was not viewed as protecting republication of an otherwise immune libel on the floor of the House....

Prior cases have read the Speech or Debate Clause "broadly to effectuate its purposes," and have included within its reach anything "generally done in a session of the House by one of its members in relation to the business before it." Thus, voting by Members and committee reports are protected; and we recognize today—as the Court has recognized before—that a Member's conduct at legislative committee hearings, although subject to judicial review in various circumstances, as is legislation itself, may not be made the basis for a civil or criminal judgment against a Member because that conduct is within the "sphere of legitimate legislative activity."

But the Clause has not been extended beyond the legislative sphere. That Senators generally perform certain acts in their official capacity as Senators does not necessarily make all such acts legislative in nature. Members of Congress are constantly in touch with the Executive Branch of the Government and with administrative agencies—they may cajole, and exhort with respect to the administration of a federal statute—but such conduct, though generally done, is not protected legislative activity....

Legislative acts are not all-encompassing. The heart of the Clause is speech or debate in either House. Insofar as the Clause is construed to reach other matters, they must be an integral part of the deliberative and communicative processes by which Members participate in committee and House proceedings with respect to the consideration and passage or rejection of proposed legislation or with respect to other matters which the Constitution places within the jurisdiction of either House. As the Court of Appeals put it, the courts have extended the privilege to matters beyond pure speech or debate in either House, but "only when necessary to prevent indirect impairment of such deliberations."

Here, private publication by Senator Gravel through the cooperation of Beacon Press was in no way essential to the deliberations of the Senate; nor does questioning as to private publication threaten the integrity or independence of the Senate by impermissibly exposing its deliberations to executive influence. The Senator had conducted his hearings; the record and any report that was forthcoming were available both to his committee and the Senate. Insofar as we are advised, neither Congress nor the full committee ordered or authorized the publication. We cannot but conclude that the Senator's arrangements with Beacon Press were not part and parcel of the legislative process.[16]

There are additional considerations. Article I, § 6, cl. 1, as we have emphasized, does not purport to confer a general exemption upon Mem-

16. The sole constitutional claim asserted here is based on the Speech or Debate Clause. We need not address issues that may arise when Congress or either House, as distinguished from a single Member, orders the publication and/or public distribution of committee hearings, reports, or other materials....

bers of Congress from liability or process in criminal cases. Quite the contrary is true. While the Speech or Debate Clause recognizes speech, voting, and other legislative acts as exempt from liability that might otherwise attach, it does not privilege either Senator or aide to violate an otherwise valid criminal law in preparing for or implementing legislative acts. If republication of these classified papers would be a crime under an Act of Congress, it would not be entitled to immunity under the Speech or Debate Clause. It also appears that the grand jury was pursuing this very subject in the normal course of a valid investigation. The Speech or Debate Clause does not in our view extend immunity to Rodberg, as a Senator's aide, from testifying before the grand jury about the arrangement between Senator Gravel and Beacon Press or about his own participation, if any, in the alleged transaction, so long as legislative acts of the Senator are not impugned.

Mr. Justice DOUGLAS, dissenting.

I would construe the Speech or Debate Clause to insulate Senator Gravel and his aides from inquiry concerning the Pentagon Papers, and Beacon Press from inquiry concerning publication of them, for that publication was but another way of informing the public as to what had gone on in the privacy of the Executive Branch concerning the conception and pursuit of the so-called "war" in Vietnam. Alternatively, I would hold that Beacon Press is protected by the First Amendment from prosecution or investigations for publishing or undertaking to publish the Pentagon Papers.

Mr. Justice BRENNAN, with whom Mr. Justice DOUGLAS, and Mr. Justice MARSHALL, join, dissenting.

The facts of this litigation, which are detailed by the Court, and the objections to overclassification of documents by the Executive, detailed by my Brother DOUGLAS, need not be repeated here. My concern is with the narrow scope accorded the Speech or Debate Clause by today's decision. I fully agree with the Court that a Congressman's immunity under the Clause must also be extended to his aides if it is to be at all effective.... The scope of that immunity, however, is as important as the persons to whom it extends. In my view, today's decision so restricts the privilege of speech or debate as to endanger the continued performance of legislative tasks that are vital to the workings of our democratic system.

In holding that Senator Gravel's alleged arrangement with Beacon Press to publish the Pentagon Papers is not shielded from extra-senatorial inquiry by the Speech or Debate Clause, the Court adopts what for me is a far too narrow view of the legislative function. The Court seems to assume that words spoken in debate or written in congressional reports are protected by the Clause, so that if Senator Gravel had recited part of the Pentagon Papers on the Senate floor or copied them into a Senate report, those acts could not be questioned "in any other Place." Yet because he sought a wider audience, to publicize information deemed relevant to matters pending before his own committee, the Senator suddenly loses his immunity and is exposed to grand jury investigation and possible prosecution for the republication. The explanation for this anomalous result is the Court's belief that "Speech or Debate" encompasses only acts necessary to the internal deliberations of Congress concerning proposed legislation....

Thus, the Court excludes from the sphere of protected legislative activity a function that I had supposed lay at the heart of our democratic system. I speak, of course, of the legislator's duty to inform the public about matters affecting the administration of government. That this "informing function" falls into the class of things "generally done in a session of the House by one of its members in relation to the business before it," [has been] explicitly acknowledged by the Court....

We need look no further than Congress itself to find evidence supporting the Court's observation.... Congress has provided financial support for communications between its Members and the public, including the franking privilege for letters, telephone and telegraph allowances, stationery allotments, and favorable prices on reprints from the Congressional Record. Congressional hearings, moreover, are not confined to gathering information for internal distribution, but are often widely publicized, sometimes televised, as a means of alerting the electorate to matters of public import and concern....

Though I fully share these and related views on the educational values served by the informing function, there is yet another, and perhaps more fundamental, interest at stake. It requires no citation of authority to state that public concern over current issues—the war, race relations, governmental invasions of privacy—has transformed itself in recent years into what many believe is a crisis of confidence, in our system of government and its capacity to meet the needs and reflect the wants of the American people. Communication between Congress and the electorate tends to alleviate that doubt by exposing and clarifying the workings of the political system, the policies underlying new laws and the role of the Executive in their administration. To the extent that the informing function succeeds in fostering public faith in the responsiveness of Government, it is not only an "ordinary" task of the legislator but one that is essential to the continued vitality of our democratic institutions.

Unlike the Court, therefore, I think that the activities of Congressmen in communicating with the public are legislative acts protected by the Speech or Debate Clause. I agree with the Court that not every task performed by a legislator is privileged; intervention before Executive departments is one that is not. But the informing function carries a far more persuasive claim to the protections of the Clause.... To say in the face of these facts that the informing function is not privileged merely because it is not necessary to the internal deliberations of Congress is to give the Speech or Debate Clause an artificial and narrow reading unsupported by reason....

[T]he dialogue between Congress and people has been recognized, from the days of our founding, as one of the necessary elements of a representative system. We should not retreat from that view merely because, in the course of that dialogue, information may be revealed that is embarrassing to the other branches of government or violates their notions of necessary secrecy. A Member of Congress who exceeds the bounds of propriety in performing this official task may be called to answer by the other Members of his chamber. We do violence to the fundamental concepts of privilege, however, when we subject that same conduct to judicial scrutiny at the instance of the Executive.... The Nation as a whole benefits from the congressional investigation and exposure of official corruption and deceit. It likewise suffers when that exposure is replaced by muted criticism, carefully hushed behind congressional walls....

Mr. Justice STEWART, dissenting in part. [Opinion omitted.]

Comments and Questions

1. This case gives a good sense of the judicial approach to the Speech or Debate Clause—a functional, rather than formalist view, even though there is clear text that could be used for strict line drawing. The difficulty with a functional approach is also apparent in this case, because it does not provide a clear answer where to draw the line. The majority draws the line at what happens in the context of the committee hearing, an official, congressional function, whereas three of the justices would extend protection to the private publication of information by the congressman, inasmuch as informing the public is in their view an important and recognized function of Congress, Senators, and Representatives. One justice addresses an issue the others do not, whether the Senator is protected from questions as to how he obtained the leaked material.

2. Ultimately, Beacon Press did publish the Pentagon Papers without legal incident. The administration determined that Daniel Ellsberg, a former Defense Department employee, had leaked the papers and prosecuted him for various criminal acts. The trial court, however, dismissed the charges because of prosecutorial misconduct—the illegal burglarizing of Ellsberg's psychiatrist's office (by the same people who later burglarized the Watergate).

3. Not all congressional acts of making information public seem as public spirited as Senator Gravel's. For example, in 1970, a special select subcommittee of the House Committee on the District of Columbia published a report critical of the District's school system. The report included some 45 pages of supporting documents, including: absentee lists identifying by name "frequent class cutters," actual test papers with student names that bore failing grades, and letters, memoranda, and other documents relating to disciplinary problems of specifically named students. The parents of the named children sued seeking an injunction against further publication of this and other information about the students and seeking damages. The defendants to the suit included the

members of the House committee; the Clerk, Staff Director, and Counsel of the Committee; a consultant and an investigator for the Committee; and the Superintendent of Documents and the Public Printer. The Court in *Doe v. McMillan*, 412 U.S. 306 (1973), held that all the congressional actors, including the consultant and investigator, were immune from suit, but that the Superintendent of Documents and Public Printer were subject to suit for the publication of the report "beyond the reasonable bounds of the legislative task." To a great extent, this seems quite consistent with *Gravel*. However, while *Gravel* found no protection for the private publishers of the Pentagon Papers, in *McMillan* the government printers found no protection under the Speech and Debate Clause even for the official publication to the public at large of the committee report, although the congressional actors and publication for legislative purposes were still protected.

4. In *Hutchinson v. Proxmire*, 443 U.S. 111 (1979), a Senator found he had no Speech and Debate Clause protection when he personally published derogatory information about a person in press releases and constituent newsletters. In dictum, the Court repeated what it had said in *Gravel*: that the Clause would not protect a congressperson in communications with executive branch agencies in which the congressperson was trying to influence the agency's conduct.

5. A recurring issue under the Speech and Debate Clause is to what extent the government may use evidence of a Senator's or Representative's official actions in a criminal prosecution of the Senator or Representative for bribery or similar crime. For example, in *United States v. Johnson*, 383 U.S. 169 (1966), a congressman was convicted for taking money for the purpose of making a speech on the floor of the House defending certain indicted savings and loan companies, so that the companies could use the speech to reassure customers. The Court held that the use of his speech against him in the prosecution violated the Speech and Debate Clause. In *United States v. Helstoski*, 442 U.S. 477 (1979), a congressman was prosecuted for accepting bribes to introduce private bills to allow illegal aliens to remain in the United States. The Court held that the government could not introduce into evidence either the bills he introduced or any reference to them after the fact. The Court distinguished between promises to perform a legislative act (not protected) and references to a past legislative act (protected). Thus, the government may enter into evidence a tape recorded promise to introduce a bill in consideration for a bribe, but it may not introduce into evidence the fact—available in public records for all to see—that the congressman did indeed introduce the bill.

6. In *Gravel* Justice Stewart dissented in part because the majority (in an edited portion of the opinion) allowed for questioning of the Senator and his aide regarding actions "in preparation of the subcommittee meeting" that were not themselves criminal, if "it proves relevant to investigating possible third-party crime." Justice Stewart interpreted that to mean that the grand jury could question them as to where they

obtained the Pentagon Papers, but the Solicitor General had specifically conceded in oral argument that the grand jury could not question the Senator as to where he obtained the papers, and the majority clearly provided the aide with the same protection as the Senator himself. Accordingly, it is not clear that Justice Stewart's interpretation was correct. And, in fact, neither Senator Gravel nor his aide were ever questioned by the grand jury concerning where they obtained the papers.

7. Remember that even if members of Congress are protected by the Speech and Debate Clause from being questioned "in any other place," their respective houses are fully able to question and sanction members, including expulsion from the House or Senate, for speech and acts performed in their legislative capacities.

2. EXECUTIVE PRIVILEGES AND IMMUNITIES

Unlike members of Congress, nothing in the Constitution mentions or even hints at any privilege or immunity arising out of the office of the President. That, however, like the absence of any mention of the President's removal powers, has not stopped the Court from inferring privileges and immunities from the Constitution's text and structure.

UNITED STATES v. NIXON

United States Supreme Court, 1974.
418 U.S. 683, 94 S.Ct. 3090, 41 L.Ed.2d 1039.

[On June 17, 1972, during the presidential campaign between incumbent President Richard Nixon and the Democratic Party nominee, George McGovern, there was a burglary at the headquarters of the National Committee of the Democratic Party, located in the Watergate apartment building in Washington, D.C. The burglars, who were attempting to install listening devices in the office to replace malfunctioning devices they had earlier installed, were caught on the scene as a result of their own incompetence. The five men were former contract personnel for the Central Intelligence Agency but were presently associated with the Committee to ReElect the President (CREEP, as it was known at the time). They implicated two others, E. Howard Hunt, Jr. and Gordon Liddy, both of whom were directly employed by CREEP. All seven were convicted of conspiracy, burglary, and violation of federal wiretapping laws. One of the seven, who felt betrayed because he was not "taken care of," wrote a letter to the sentencing judge stating that the conspiracy went much further.

This led to the appointment of a Special Prosecutor, Archibald Cox, a professor at Harvard Law School. His aggressive investigation of White House involvement in a conspiracy to obstruct justice by covering up White House involvement led to indictments of John N. Mitchell, the former Attorney General and director of CREEP; H. R. Haldeman, the White House Chief of Staff; John D. Ehrlichman, the Advisor to the President for Domestic Affairs; Charles W. Colson, Special Counsel to the President; Robert C. Mardian, Assistant Attorney General for the Internal Security Division; Kenneth W. Parkinson, Counsel to CREEP; and Gordon Strachan, an aide to H.R. Haldeman. The grand jury named President Nixon an unindicted co-conspirator.

Revelations in congressional testimony that President Nixon had bugged the Oval Office to record the conversations there led Cox to subpoena President Nixon for copies of the tapes of those conversations in order to obtain further evidence against the indicted individuals. Nixon refused and instead ordered Attorney General Elliot Richardson to fire Cox. Richardson resigned rather than carry out the order, as did Deputy Attorney General William Ruckelshaus. This event, because it happened on a Saturday night, is known as the "Saturday Night Massacre." The next in line of succession at the Justice Department was Solicitor General Robert Bork, who carried out the order, firing Cox. The political firestorm that followed led to the appointment of a new Special Prosecutor, Leon Jaworski, a Texas lawyer who had supported Nixon in the previous election. Nevertheless, Jaworski continued the subpoena for the tapes. The President's personal counsel filed a motion to quash the subpoena on the grounds that the information sought was constitutionally privileged that the President was bound to maintain confidential. At the same time the House Judiciary Committee began hearings into the possible impeachment of the President. The district court denied the President's motion to quash and ordered the President to produce the tapes in court. The President appealed to the court of appeals, but the United States (i.e., the Special Prosecutor) petitioned for certiorari directly to the Supreme Court, and the President cross-petitioned. The Court granted the petition.]

Mr. Chief Justice BURGER delivered the opinion of the Court.

[W]e turn to the claim that the subpoena should be quashed because it demands "confidential conversations between a President and his close advisors that it would be inconsistent with the public interest to produce." The first contention is a broad claim that the separation of powers doctrine precludes judicial review of a President's claim of privilege. The second contention is that if he does not prevail on the claim of absolute privilege, the court should hold as a matter of constitutional law that the privilege prevails over the subpoena duces tecum.

In the performance of assigned constitutional duties each branch of the Government must initially interpret the Constitution, and the interpretation of its powers by any branch is due great respect from the others. The President's counsel, as we have noted, reads the Constitution as providing an absolute privilege of confidentiality for all Presidential communications. Many decisions of this Court, however, have unequivocally reaffirmed the holding of *Marbury v. Madison*, that "(i)t is emphatically the province and duty of the judicial department to say what the law is." ...

In support of his claim of absolute privilege, the President's counsel urges two grounds, one of which is common to all governments and one of which is peculiar to our system of separation of powers. The first ground is the valid need for protection of communications between high Government officials and those who advise and assist them in the performance of their manifold duties; the importance of this confidentiality is too plain to require further discussion. Human experience teaches that those who expect public dissemination of their remarks may well temper candor with a concern for appearances and for their own interests to the detriment of the decisionmaking process.[15] Whatever the nature of the privilege of confidentiality of Presidential communications in the exercise of Art. II powers, the privilege can be said to derive from the supremacy of each branch within its own assigned area of constitutional duties. Certain powers and privileges flow from the nature of enumerated powers; the protection of the confidentiality of Presidential communications has similar constitutional underpinnings.

The second ground asserted by the President's counsel in support of the claim of absolute privilege rests on the doctrine of separation of powers. Here it is argued that the independence of the Executive Branch within its own sphere insulates a President from a judicial subpoena in an ongoing criminal prosecution, and thereby protects confidential Presidential communications.

However, neither the doctrine of separation of powers, nor the need for confidentiality of high-level communications, without more, can sustain an absolute, unqualified Presidential privilege of immunity from judicial process under all circumstances. The President's need for complete candor and objectivity from advisers calls for great deference from the courts. However, when the privilege depends solely on the broad, undifferentiated claim of public interest in the confidentiality of such conversations, a confrontation with other values arises. Absent a claim of need to protect military, diplomatic, or sensitive national security secrets, we find it difficult to accept the argument that even the very important interest in confidentiality of Presidential communications is significantly diminished by production of such material for in camera inspection with all the protection that a district court will be obliged to provide.

The impediment that an absolute, unqualified privilege would place in the way of the primary constitutional duty of the Judicial Branch to do justice in criminal prosecutions would plainly conflict with the function of the courts under Art. III....

To read the Art. II powers of the President as providing an absolute privilege as against a subpoena essential to enforcement of criminal statutes on no more than a generalized claim of the public interest in

15. There is nothing novel about governmental confidentiality. The meetings of the Constitutional Convention in 1787 were conducted in complete privacy. Moreover, all records of those meetings were sealed for more than 30 years after the Convention. Most of the Framers acknowledge that without secrecy no constitution of the kind that was developed could have been written.

confidentiality of nonmilitary and nondiplomatic discussions would upset the constitutional balance of "a workable government" and gravely impair the role of the courts under Art. III.

Since we conclude that the legitimate needs of the judicial process may outweigh Presidential privilege, it is necessary to resolve those competing interests in a manner that preserves the essential functions of each branch....

The expectation of a President to the confidentiality of his conversations and correspondence, like the claim of confidentiality of judicial deliberations, for example, has all the values to which we accord deference for the privacy of all citizens and, added to those values, is the necessity for protection of the public interest in candid, objective, and even blunt or harsh opinions in Presidential decisionmaking. A President and those who assist him must be free to explore alternatives in the process of shaping policies and making decisions and to do so in a way many would be unwilling to express except privately. These are the considerations justifying a presumptive privilege for Presidential communications. The privilege is fundamental to the operation of Government and inextricably rooted in the separation of powers under the Constitution....

But this presumptive privilege must be considered in light of our historic commitment to the rule of law. This is nowhere more profoundly manifest than in our view that "the twofold aim (of criminal justice) is that guilt shall not escape or innocence suffer." We have elected to employ an adversary system of criminal justice in which the parties contest all issues before a court of law. The need to develop all relevant facts in the adversary system is both fundamental and comprehensive. The ends of criminal justice would be defeated if judgments were to be founded on a partial or speculative presentation of the facts. The very integrity of the judicial system and public confidence in the system depend on full disclosure of all the facts, within the framework of the rules of evidence. To ensure that justice is done, it is imperative to the function of courts that compulsory process be available for the production of evidence needed either by the prosecution or by the defense.

Only recently the Court restated the ancient proposition of law, albeit in the context of a grand jury inquiry rather than a trial, "that 'the public ... has a right to every man's evidence,' except for those persons protected by a constitutional, common-law, or statutory privilege."

The privileges referred to by the Court are designed to protect weighty and legitimate competing interests.... Whatever their origins, these exceptions to the demand for every man's evidence are not lightly created nor expansively construed, for they are in derogation of the search for truth.

In this case the President challenges a subpoena served on him as a third party requiring the production of materials for use in a criminal prosecution; he does so on the claim that he has a privilege against disclosure of confidential communications. He does not place his claim of privilege on the ground they are military or diplomatic secrets. As to these areas of Art. II duties the courts have traditionally shown the utmost deference to Presidential responsibilities....

No case of the Court, however, has extended this high degree of deference to a President's generalized interest in confidentiality. Nowhere in the Constitution ... is there any explicit reference to a privilege of confidentiality, yet to the extent this interest relates to the effective discharge of a President's powers, it is constitutionally based.

The right to the production of all evidence at a criminal trial similarly has constitutional dimensions. The Sixth Amendment explicitly confers upon every defendant in a criminal trial the right "to be confronted with the witnesses against him" and "to have compulsory process for obtaining witnesses in his favor." Moreover, the Fifth Amendment also guarantees that no person shall be deprived of liberty without due process of law. It is the manifest duty of the courts to vindicate those guarantees, and to accomplish that it is essential that all relevant and admissible evidence be produced.

In this case we must weigh the importance of the general privilege of confidentiality of Presidential communications in performance of the President's responsibilities against the inroads of such a privilege on the fair administration of criminal justice.[19] The interest in preserving confidentiality is weighty indeed and entitled to great respect. However, we cannot conclude that advisers will be moved to temper the candor of their remarks by the infrequent occasions of disclosure because of the possibility that such conversations will be called for in the context of a criminal prosecution.

On the other hand, the allowance of the privilege to withhold evidence that is demonstrably relevant in a criminal trial would cut deeply into the guarantee of due process of law and gravely impair the basic function of the courts. A President's acknowledged need for confidentiality in the communications of his office is general in nature, whereas the constitutional need for production of relevant evidence in a criminal proceeding is specific and central to the fair adjudication of a particular criminal case in the administration of justice....

We conclude that when the ground for asserting privilege as to subpoenaed materials sought for use in a criminal trial is based only on the generalized interest in confidentiality, it cannot prevail over the fundamental demands of due process of law in the fair administration of criminal justice. The generalized assertion of privilege must yield to the demonstrated, specific need for evidence in a pending criminal trial.

19. We are not here concerned with the balance between the President's generalized interest in confidentiality and the need for relevant evidence in civil litigation, nor with that between the confidentiality interest and congressional demands for information, nor with the President's interest in preserving state secrets. We address only the conflict between the President's assertion of a generalized privilege of confidentiality and the constitutional need for relevant evidence in criminal trials.

We have earlier determined that the District Court did not err in authorizing the issuance of the subpoena. If a President concludes that compliance with a subpoena would be injurious to the public interest he may properly, as was done here, invoke a claim of privilege on the return of the subpoena. Upon receiving a claim of privilege from the Chief Executive, it became the further duty of the District Court to treat the subpoenaed material as presumptively privileged and to require the Special Prosecutor to demonstrate that the Presidential material was "essential to the justice of the (pending criminal) case." Here the District Court treated the material as presumptively privileged, proceeded to find that the Special Prosecutor had made a sufficient showing to rebut the presumption, and ordered an in camera examination of the subpoenaed material. On the basis of our examination of the record we are unable to conclude that the District Court erred in ordering the inspection. Accordingly we affirm the order of the District Court that subpoenaed materials be transmitted to that court. We now turn to the important question of the District Court's responsibilities in conducting the in camera examination of Presidential materials or communications delivered under the compulsion of the subpoena duces tecum.

[S]tatements that meet the test of admissibility and relevance must be isolated; all other material must be excised. At this stage the District Court is not limited to representations of the Special Prosecutor as to the evidence sought by the subpoena; the material will be available to the District Court. It is elementary that in camera inspection of evidence is always a procedure calling for scrupulous protection against any release or publication of material not found by the court, at that stage, probably admissible in evidence and relevant to the issues of the trial for which it is sought. That being true of an ordinary situation, it is obvious that the District Court has a very heavy responsibility to see to it that Presidential conversations, which are either not relevant or not admissible, are accorded that high degree of respect due the President of the United States.

Mr. Justice REHNQUIST took no part in the consideration or decision of these cases.

Comments and Questions

1. Prior to the Court's opinion there was some question whether President Nixon would comply with an adverse decision, especially if it was a split decision. Apparently the Court felt some need to have a unanimous opinion, and it was rendered in some haste given the unfolding political events. The President did comply with the Court's decision, and information on the tapes confirming Nixon's complicity in the cover up, as well as an unexplained 18 minute gap where the tapes had been mysteriously erased, made impeachment a certainty and a conviction in the Senate a near certainty. As a result, President Nixon resigned two and a half weeks after the Court's decision.

2. On what basis does the Court find a constitutionally based executive privilege? How is the privilege for confidential advice different

from an executive privilege based on national security secrets?

3. Inasmuch as the President loses the case, what does it mean that the Court found an executive privilege? What good is it?

4. What does the Court mean by the "constitutional duty of the Judicial Branch to do justice in criminal prosecutions"? Reliable, probative evidence is inadmissible in criminal prosecutions for a variety of reasons. Would a prosecutor have a right to obtain common-law privileged information, such as attorney-client, doctor-patient, priest-penitent, or husband-wife communications? If these common law privileges are "absolute," why is the President's constitutionally based privilege only a "qualified" privilege.

5. Would the Court's analysis be any different if it were a local prosecutor investigating a local crime?

6. A case should always be viewed in light of its historical circumstances, and *Nixon* is a good example of how a case might be driven more by those circumstances than by legal logic. Hopefully, a similar circumstance will not arise again. However, executive privilege issues arise with some frequency with respect to congressional demands for information. Recall that the event that triggered the appointment of the independent counsel involved in *Morrison v. Olson* was an invocation of executive privilege by the Administrator of the Environmental Protection Agency on the legal advice of the Olson, the Assistant Attorney General for the Office of Legal Counsel in the Justice Department, with regard to subpoenas from House subcommittees.

7. In George W. Bush's administration, the House Judiciary Committee subpoenaed certain testimony and information from executive branch officials regarding the highly publicized firing of several U.S. Attorneys, allegedly for political reasons. The President invoked executive privilege, instructing those subject to the subpoenas to ignore them. As a result, in 2008 the House voted contempt against the persons to whom the subpoenas were directed and forwarded the contempt citations to the U.S. Attorney for the District of Columbia for prosecution under the contempt of Congress criminal provisions, 2 U.S.C. §§ 192, 194. The Attorney General then directed the U.S. Attorney not to prosecute, stating "that the contempt of Congress statute was not intended to apply and could not constitutionally be applied to an Executive Branch official who asserts the President's claim of executive privilege." Consequently, the House filed a civil suit against the persons to whom the subpoenas were directed, seeking a judicial resolution of the validity of the claim of executive privilege. Historically, courts have been very reluctant to decide these disputes between the executive and legislative branches, finding various excuses to avoid decision. As a result no court has yet ruled on the power of the President to invoke executive privilege with regard to a congressional investigation. It seems unlikely that courts will change their approach in this case. Is this a "political question"?

8. Imagine that this issue drags into the next Presidential administration, which seems highly likely. Could the new President waive the executive privilege invoked by President Bush? Or can only the President who invoked executive privilege waive it, even if he is no longer President?

NIXON v. FITZGERALD

United States Supreme Court, 1982.
457 U.S. 731, 102 S.Ct. 2690, 73 L.Ed.2d 349.

[In 1970, A. Ernest Fitzgerald lost his job as a management analyst with the Department of the Air Force pursuant to an alleged reduction in force. Because he had recently exposed embarrassing cost-overruns on a major Air Force Contract, including testifying before a Senate committee on the subject, however, there was general speculation that he had instead been terminated in retaliation for causing the administration embarrassment. He sought review of his termination by the Civil Service Commission in 1970. After hearing over 4,000 pages of testimony, the Chief Examiner for the Civil Service Commission issued his decision in 1973, finding that Fitzgerald's dismissal had offended applicable civil service regulations. Following the Commission's order, respondent ultimately was reassigned to his former position, but Fitzgerald also filed a suit for damages in the United States District Court, alleging a continuing conspiracy to deprive him of his job, to deny him reemployment, and to besmirch his reputation. This suit was dismissed because of a 3–year statute of limitations, but on appeal the court held that the statute had not run as to one of the several original defendants. After remand and extensive discovery, Fitzgerald filed a second amended complaint in 1978. In this complaint he included as a defendant former President Nixon, who sought dismissal on the grounds that he was absolutely immune from suit for actions taken in his official capacity as President. The trial court rejected the immunity claim, and its decision was affirmed by the court of appeals.]

Justice POWELL delivered the opinion of the Court.

[A]s this Court has not ruled on the scope of immunity available to a President of the United States, we granted certiorari to decide this important issue....

This Court consistently has recognized that government officials are entitled to some form of immunity from suits for civil damages....

In *Scheuer v. Rhodes*, 416 U.S. 232 (1974), the Court considered the immunity available to state executive officials in a § 1983 suit alleging the violation of constitutional rights. In that case we rejected the officials' claim to absolute immunity ... , finding instead that state executive officials possessed a good faith immunity from § 1983 suits alleging constitutional violations.* Balancing the purposes of § 1983 against the imperatives of public policy, the Court held that in varying scope, a qualified immunity is available to officers of the executive branch of government, the variation being dependent upon the scope of discretion and responsibilities of the office and all the circumstances as they reasonably appeared at the time of the action on which liability is sought to be based.

As construed by subsequent cases, *Scheuer* established a two-tiered division of immunity defenses in § 1983 suits. To most executive officers *Scheuer* accorded qualified immunity. For them the scope of the defense varied in proportion to the nature of their official functions and the range of decisions that conceivably might be taken in good faith. This functional approach also defined a second tier, however, at which the especially sensitive duties of certain officials—notably judges and prosecutors—required the continued recognition of absolute immunity.

This approach was reviewed in detail in *Butz v. Economou*, 438 U.S. 478 (1978), when we considered for the first time the kind of immunity possessed by *federal* executive officials who are sued for constitutional violations. In *Butz* the Court rejected an argument, based on decisions involving federal officials charged with common-law torts, that all high federal officials have a right to absolute immunity from constitutional damages actions. Concluding that a blanket recognition of absolute immunity would be anomalous in light of the qualified immunity standard applied to state executive officials, we held that federal officials generally have the same qualified immunity possessed by state officials in cases under § 1983. In so doing we reaffirmed our holdings that some officials, notably judges and prosecutors, because of the special nature of their responsibilities, require a full exemption from liability....

This case now presents the claim that the President of the United States is shielded by absolute immunity from civil damages liability. In the case of the President the inquiries into history and policy, though mandated independently by our cases, tend to converge. Because the Presidency did not exist through most of the development of common law, any historical analysis must draw its evidence primarily from our constitutional heritage and structure. Historical inquiry thus merges almost at its inception with the kind of public policy analysis appropriately undertaken by a federal court. This inquiry involves policies and principles that may be considered implicit in the nature of the President's office in a system structured to achieve effective government under a constitutionally mandated separation of powers.

Here a former President asserts his immunity from civil damages claims of two kinds. He stands named as a defendant in a direct action under the Constitution and in two statutory actions under federal laws

* 42 U.S.C. § 1983 provides a private right of action for injunctive relief or damages against any person acting under color of law to deprive another person of their rights under the Constitution or any federal law. [author's note].

of general applicability. In neither case has Congress taken express legislative action to subject the President to civil liability for his official acts.[27]

Applying the principles of our cases to claims of this kind, we hold that petitioner, as a former President of the United States, is entitled to absolute immunity from damages liability predicated on his official acts. We consider this immunity a functionally mandated incident of the President's unique office, rooted in the constitutional tradition of the separation of powers and supported by our history....

The President occupies a unique position in the constitutional scheme. [T]he President [is] the chief constitutional officer of the Executive Branch, entrusted with supervisory and policy responsibilities of utmost discretion and sensitivity. These include the enforcement of federal law ... ; the conduct of foreign affairs ... ; and management of the Executive Branch....

In arguing that the President is entitled only to qualified immunity, the respondent relies on cases in which we have recognized immunity of this scope for governors and cabinet officers. We find these cases to be inapposite. The President's unique status under the Constitution distinguishes him from other executive officials.[31]

Because of the singular importance of the President's duties, diversion of his energies by concern with private lawsuits would raise unique risks to the effective functioning of government. As is the case with prosecutors and judges—for whom absolute immunity now is established—a President must concern himself with matters likely to arouse the most intense feelings. Yet, as our decisions have recognized, it is in precisely such cases that there exists the greatest public interest in providing an official the maximum ability to deal fearlessly and impartially with the duties of his office. This concern is compelling where the officeholder must make the most sensitive and far-reaching decisions entrusted to any official under our constitutional system.[32] Nor can the sheer prominence of the President's office be ignored. In view of the visibility of his office and the effect of his actions on countless people, the President would be an easily identifiable target for suits for civil damages. Cognizance of this personal vulnerability frequently could distract a President from his public duties, to the detriment of not only the President and his

27. In the present case we therefore are presented only with implied causes of action, and we need not address directly the immunity question as it would arise if Congress expressly had created a damages action against the President of the United States....

31. Noting that the Speech and Debate Clause provides a textual basis for congressional immunity, respondent argues that the Framers must be assumed to have rejected any similar grant of executive immunity. This argument is unpersuasive. First, a specific textual basis has not been considered a prerequisite to the recognition of immunity. No provision expressly confers judicial immunity. Yet the immunity of judges is well settled....

32. Among the most persuasive reasons supporting official immunity is the prospect that damages liability may render an official unduly cautious in the discharge of his official duties....

office but also the Nation that the Presidency was designed to serve....

In defining the scope of an official's absolute privilege, this Court has recognized that the sphere of protected action must be related closely to the immunity's justifying purposes. Frequently our decisions have held that an official's absolute immunity should extend only to acts in performance of particular functions of his office. But the Court also has refused to draw functional lines finer than history and reason would support. In view of the special nature of the President's constitutional office and functions, we think it appropriate to recognize absolute Presidential immunity from damages liability for acts within the outer perimeter of his official responsibility....

A rule of absolute immunity for the President will not leave the Nation without sufficient protection against misconduct on the part of the Chief Executive. There remains the constitutional remedy of impeachment. In addition, there are formal and informal checks on Presidential action that do not apply with equal force to other executive officials. The President is subjected to constant scrutiny by the press. Vigilant oversight by Congress also may serve to deter Presidential abuses of office, as well as to make credible the threat of impeachment. Other incentives to avoid misconduct may include a desire to earn reelection, the need to maintain prestige as an element of Presidential influence, and a President's traditional concern for his historical stature.

The existence of alternative remedies and deterrents establishes that absolute immunity will not place the President above the law. For the President, as for judges and prosecutors, absolute immunity merely precludes a particular private remedy for alleged misconduct in order to advance compelling public ends.

Chief Justice BURGER, concurring. [Opinion omitted.]

Justice WHITE, with whom Justice BRENNAN, Justice MARSHALL, and Justice BLACKMUN join, dissenting.

The four dissenting Members of the Court in *Butz v. Economou* argued that all federal officials are entitled to absolute immunity from suit for any action they take in connection with their official duties. That immunity would extend even to actions taken with express knowledge that the conduct was clearly contrary to the controlling statute or clearly violative of the Constitution. Fortunately, the majority of the Court rejected that approach: We held that although public officials perform certain functions that entitle them to absolute immunity, the immunity attaches to particular functions—not to particular offices. Officials performing functions for which immunity is not absolute enjoy qualified immunity; they are liable in damages only if their conduct violated well-established law and if they should have realized that their conduct was illegal.

The Court now applies the dissenting view in *Butz* to the Office of the President: A President, acting within the outer boundaries of what

Presidents normally do, may, without liability, deliberately cause serious injury to any number of citizens even though he knows his conduct violates a statute or tramples on the constitutional rights of those who are injured. Even if the President in this case ordered Fitzgerald fired by means of a trumped-up reduction in force, knowing that such a discharge was contrary to the civil service laws, he would be absolutely immune from suit. By the same token, if a President, without following the statutory procedures which he knows apply to himself as well as to other federal officials, orders his subordinates to wiretap or break into a home for the purpose of installing a listening device, and the officers comply with his request, the President would be absolutely immune from suit. He would be immune regardless of the damage he inflicts, regardless of how violative of the statute and of the Constitution he knew his conduct to be, and regardless of his purpose.[1]

The Court intimates that its decision is grounded in the Constitution. If that is the case, Congress cannot provide a remedy against Presidential misconduct and the criminal laws of the United States are wholly inapplicable to the President. I find this approach completely unacceptable. I do not agree that if the Office of President is to operate effectively, the holder of that Office must be permitted, without fear of liability and regardless of the function he is performing, deliberately to inflict injury on others by conduct that he knows violates the law....

Attaching absolute immunity to the Office of the President, rather than to particular activities that the President might perform, places the President above the law. It is a reversion to the old notion that the King can do no wrong. Until now, this concept had survived in this country only in the form of sovereign immunity.... Now, however, the Court clothes the Office of the President with sovereign immunity, placing it beyond the law....

The functional approach to the separation-of-powers doctrine and the Court's more recent immunity decisions converge on the following principle: The scope of immunity is determined by function, not office. The wholesale claim that the President is entitled to absolute immunity in all of his actions stands on no firmer ground than did the claim that all Presidential communications are entitled to an absolute privilege, which was rejected in favor of a functional analysis, by a unanimous Court in *United States v. Nixon*. Therefore, whatever may be true of the necessity of such a broad immunity in certain areas of executive responsibility,[30] the only question that must be answered here is whether the dismissal of employees falls within a constitutionally assigned executive function, the performance of which would be substantially impaired by the possibility of a private action for damages. I believe it does not.

1. This, of course, is not simply a hypothetical example. *See Halperin v. Kissinger*, 606 F.2d 1192 (1979), *aff'd by an equally divided Court*, 452 U.S. 713 (1981).

30. I will not speculate on the Presidential functions which may require absolute immunity, but a clear example would be instances in which the President participates in prosecutorial decisions.

Justice BLACKMUN, with whom Justice BRENNAN and Justice MARSHALL join, dissenting. [Opinion omitted.]

Comments and Questions

1. The dispute in this case is whether the President should enjoy absolute immunity for his official acts, as found by the five member majority, or only qualified immunity, as argued by the four person dissent. Absolute immunity means what it sounds like; any suit filed against the President for an "official act," broadly construed, will be subject to a motion to dismiss. Judges and prosecutors, as the Court notes, enjoy absolute immunity for their official acts. Qualified immunity, which is what most executive officials in state and federal government enjoy, means that they enjoy immunity if their conduct "does not violate clearly established statutory or constitutional rights of which a reasonable person would have known." *Harlow v. Fitzgerald*, 457 U.S. 800, 818 (1982). The *Harlow* case was a companion case to *Nixon v. Fitzgerald*. Harlow was an adviser to the President and was sued by Fitzgerald as being involved in the conspiracy to fire him in violation of the Civil Service Laws as well as the Constitution.

2. In setting this standard for qualified immunity, the Court balanced the need to vindicate the violation of a person's individual rights against the need to avoid requiring government officials to go to trial on insubstantial claims. Accordingly, the Court altered the prior standard for establishing qualified immunity, which included a subjective, "good faith" element, which almost necessarily called for a trial on that issue, with what it said was a wholly objective standard—the reasonable person standard. The problem with even this "objective" standard for qualified immunity is that it often cannot be determined what the official actually did—a necessary precondition to deciding if it violated a clearly established right—before there has been substantial discovery or even a trial. For example, in the *Harlow* case, Harlow denied that he had any role whatsoever in Fitzgerald's firing, but that is a factual question, not a legal question. Fitzgerald alleged that Harlow had been involved in firing him in retaliation for providing Congress with truthful information simply because that information was embarrassing to the administration, and that firing a protected civil servant for such a reason was clearly unlawful. Such an allegation would survive the motion to dismiss, because in a motion to dismiss the alleged facts are presumed to be true. Consequently, there would have to be discovery to determine whether there was any basis to the allegations. Indeed, in the *Harlow* case, discovery went on for eight years, at which point the trial court found that there were disputed facts that would need to go to trial. In short, the qualified immunity standard is not very successful at "permit[ting] the defeat of insubstantial claims without resort to trial," one of the goals that the Court sought to achieve.

3. What is it about the Presidency that leads the Court to grant the President absolute immunity, unlike other executive officers? Should

it be a relevant consideration that Nixon was no longer President when he was sued?

4. What kind of immunity do you think the Vice President should enjoy? Vice President Cheney has been sued by Valerie Plame, the Central Intelligence Agency, employee allegedly outed by the administration to discredit a report undermining the administration's claim that Iraq was developing nuclear weapons.

CLINTON v. JONES

United States Supreme Court, 1997.
520 U.S. 681, 117 S.Ct. 1636, 137 L.Ed.2d 945.

Justice STEVENS delivered the opinion of the Court.

This case raises a constitutional and a prudential question concerning the Office of the President of the United States. Respondent, a private citizen, seeks to recover damages from the current occupant of that office based on actions allegedly taken before his term began. The President submits that in all but the most exceptional cases the Constitution requires federal courts to defer such litigation until his term ends and that, in any event, respect for the office warrants such a stay. Despite the force of the arguments supporting the President's submissions, we conclude that they must be rejected.

Petitioner, William Jefferson Clinton, was elected to the Presidency in 1992, and re-elected in 1996. His term of office expires on January 20, 2001. In 1991 he was the Governor of the State of Arkansas. Respondent, Paula Corbin Jones, is a resident of California. In 1991 she lived in Arkansas, and was an employee of the Arkansas Industrial Development Commission.

On May 6, 1994, she commenced this action in the United States District Court for the Eastern District of Arkansas by filing a complaint naming petitioner and Danny Ferguson, a former Arkansas State Police officer, as defendants. The complaint alleges two federal claims, and two state-law claims over which the federal court has jurisdiction because of the diverse citizenship of the parties. As the case comes to us, we are required to assume the truth of the detailed—but as yet untested—factual allegations in the complaint.

Those allegations principally describe events that are said to have occurred on the afternoon of May 8, 1991, during an official conference held at the Excelsior Hotel in Little Rock, Arkansas. The Governor delivered a speech at the conference; respondent—working as a state employee—staffed the registration desk. She alleges that Ferguson persuaded her to leave her desk and to visit the Governor in a business suite at the hotel, where he made abhorrent sexual advances that she vehemently rejected. She further claims that her superiors at work subsequently dealt with her in a hostile and rude manner, and changed her duties to punish her for rejecting those advances. Finally, she alleges that after petitioner was elected President, Ferguson defamed her by making a statement to a reporter that implied she had accepted petitioner's alleged overtures, and that various persons authorized to speak for the President publicly branded her a liar by denying that the incident had occurred.

Respondent seeks actual damages of $75,000 and punitive damages of $100,000. Her complaint contains four counts. The first charges that petitioner, acting under color of state law, deprived her of rights protected by the Constitution, in violation of Rev. Stat. § 1979, 42 U.S.C. § 1983. The second charges that petitioner and Ferguson engaged in a conspiracy to violate her federal rights, also actionable under federal law ... The third is a state common law claim for intentional infliction of emotional distress, grounded primarily on the incident at the hotel. The fourth count, also based on state law, is for defamation, embracing both the comments allegedly made to the press by Ferguson and the statements of petitioner's agents. Inasmuch as the legal sufficiency of the claims has not yet been challenged, we assume, without deciding, that each of the four counts states a cause of action as a matter of law. With the exception of the last charge, which arguably may involve conduct within the outer perimeter of the President's official responsibilities, it is perfectly clear that the alleged misconduct of petitioner was unrelated to any of his official duties as President of the United States and, indeed, occurred before he was elected to that office.

In response to the complaint, petitioner ... filed a motion to dismiss ... without prejudice and to toll any statutes of limitation [that may be applicable] until he is no longer President, at which time the plaintiff may refile the instant suit....

The District Judge denied the motion to dismiss on immunity grounds and ruled that discovery in the case could go forward, but ordered any trial stayed until the end of petitioner's Presidency....

Both parties appealed. A divided panel of the Court of Appeals affirmed the denial of the motion to dismiss, but because it regarded the order postponing the trial until the President leaves office as the functional equivalent of a grant of temporary immunity, it reversed that order.... The majority specifically rejected the argument that, unless immunity is available, the threat of judicial interference with the Executive Branch through scheduling orders, potential contempt citations, and sanctions would violate separation-of-powers principles. Judge Bowman suggested that judicial case management sensitive to the burdens of the presidency and the demands of the President's schedule would avoid the perceived danger....

The President, represented by private counsel, filed a petition for certiorari. The Acting Solicitor General, representing the United States, supported the petition, arguing that the decision of the Court of Appeals was fundamentally mistaken and created serious risks for the institution of the Presidency....

[It is] appropriate to identify two important constitutional issues not encompassed within the questions presented by the petition for certiorari that we need not address today.

First, because the claim of immunity is asserted in a federal court and relies heavily on the doctrine of separation of powers that restrains each of the three branches of the Federal Government from encroaching on the domain of the other two, it is not necessary to consider or decide whether a comparable claim might succeed in a state tribunal. If this case were being heard in a state forum, instead of advancing a separation-of-powers argument, petitioner would presumably rely on federalism and comity concerns, as well as the interest in protecting federal officials from possible local prejudice that underlies the authority to remove certain cases brought against federal officers from a state to a federal court. Whether those concerns would present a more compelling case for immunity is a question that is not before us.

Second, our decision rejecting the immunity claim and allowing the case to proceed does not require us to confront the question whether a court may compel the attendance of the President at any specific time or place. We assume that the testimony of the President, both for discovery and for use at trial, may be taken at the White House at a time that will accommodate his busy schedule, and that, if a trial is held, there would be no necessity for the President to attend in person, though he could elect to do so.[14]

Petitioner's principal submission—that in all but the most exceptional cases, the Constitution affords the President temporary immunity from civil damages litigation arising out of events that occurred before he took office—cannot be sustained on the basis of precedent.

Only three sitting Presidents have been defendants in civil litigation involving their actions prior to taking office. Complaints against Theodore Roosevelt and Harry Truman had been dismissed before they took office; the dismissals were affirmed after their respective inaugurations. Two companion cases arising out of an automobile accident were filed against John F. Kennedy in 1960 during the Presidential campaign. After taking office, he unsuccessfully argued that his status as Commander in Chief gave him a right to a stay under the Soldiers' and Sailors' Civil Relief Act of 1940. The motion for a stay was denied by the District Court, and the matter was settled out of court. Thus, none of those cases sheds any light on the constitutional issue before us.

The principal rationale for affording certain public servants immunity from suits for money damages arising out of their official acts is inapplicable to unofficial conduct. In cases involving prosecutors, legislators, and judges we have repeatedly explained that the immunity serves the public interest in enabling such officials to perform their des-

14. Although Presidents have responded to written interrogatories, given depositions, and provided videotaped trial testimony, no sitting President has ever testified, or been ordered to testify, in open court.

ignated functions effectively without fear that a particular decision may give rise to personal liability.

That rationale provided the principal basis for our holding that a former President of the United States was entitled to absolute immunity from damages liability predicated on his official acts, *Nixon v. Fitzgerald*. Our central concern was to avoid rendering the President unduly cautious in the discharge of his official duties.[19]

This reasoning provides no support for an immunity for *unofficial* conduct. As we explained in *Fitzgerald,* the sphere of protected action must be related closely to the immunity's justifying purposes. Because of the President's broad responsibilities, we recognized in that case an immunity from damages claims arising out of official acts extending to the outer perimeter of his authority. But we have never suggested that the President, or any other official, has an immunity that extends beyond the scope of any action taken in an official capacity....

Petitioner's effort to construct an immunity from suit for unofficial acts grounded purely in the identity of his office is unsupported by precedent.

We are also unpersuaded by the evidence from the historical record to which petitioner has called our attention.... Respondent, in turn, has called our attention to conflicting historical evidence....

In the end, as applied to the particular question before us, we reach the same conclusion about these historical materials that Justice Jackson described when confronted with an issue concerning the dimensions of the President's power.... They largely cancel each other.

Petitioner's strongest argument supporting his immunity claim is based on the text and structure of the Constitution. He does not contend that the occupant of the Office of the President is above the law, in the sense that his conduct is entirely immune from judicial scrutiny. The President argues merely for a postponement of the judicial proceedings that will determine whether he violated any law. His argument is grounded in the character of the office that was created by Article II of the Constitution, and relies on separation-of-powers principles that have structured our constitutional arrangement since the founding.

As a starting premise, petitioner contends that he occupies a unique

19. Petitioner draws our attention to dicta in *Fitzgerald*, which he suggests are helpful to his cause. We noted there that [b]ecause of the singular importance of the President's duties, diversion of his energies by concern with private lawsuits would raise unique risks to the effective functioning of government, and suggested further that [c]ognizance of ... personal vulnerability frequently could distract a President from his public duties. Petitioner argues that in this aspect the Court's concern was parallel to the issue he suggests is of great importance in this case, the possibility that a sitting President might be distracted by the need to participate in litigation during the pendency of his office. In context, however, it is clear that our dominant concern was with the diversion of the President's attention during the decisionmaking process caused by needless worry as to the possibility of damages actions stemming from any particular official decision. Moreover, *Fitzgerald* did not present the issue raised in this case because that decision involved claims against a former President.

office with powers and responsibilities so vast and important that the public interest demands that he devote his undivided time and attention to his public duties. He submits that—given the nature of the office—the doctrine of separation of powers places limits on the authority of the Federal Judiciary to interfere with the Executive Branch that would be transgressed by allowing this action to proceed.

We have no dispute with the initial premise of the argument....

It does not follow, however, that separation-of-powers principles would be violated by allowing this action to proceed.... The litigation of questions that relate entirely to the unofficial conduct of the individual who happens to be the President poses no perceptible risk of misallocation of either judicial power or executive power.

Rather than arguing that the decision of the case will produce either an aggrandizement of judicial power or a narrowing of executive power, petitioner contends that—as a byproduct of an otherwise traditional exercise of judicial power—burdens will be placed on the President that will hamper the performance of his official duties. We have recognized that [e]ven when a branch does not arrogate power to itself ... the separation-of-powers doctrine requires that a branch not impair another in the performance of its constitutional duties. As a factual matter, petitioner contends that this particular case—as well as the potential additional litigation that an affirmance of the Court of Appeals judgment might spawn—may impose an unacceptable burden on the President's time and energy, and thereby impair the effective performance of his office.

Petitioner's predictive judgment finds little support in either history or the relatively narrow compass of the issues raised in this particular case. As we have already noted, in the more than 200–year history of the Republic, only three sitting Presidents have been subjected to suits for their private actions. If the past is any indicator, it seems unlikely that a deluge of such litigation will ever engulf the Presidency. As for the case at hand, if properly managed by the District Court, it appears to us highly unlikely to occupy any substantial amount of petitioner's time.

Of greater significance, petitioner errs by presuming that interactions between the Judicial Branch and the Executive, even quite burdensome interactions, necessarily rise to the level of constitutionally forbidden impairment of the Executive's ability to perform its constitutionally mandated functions. The fact that a federal court's exercise of its traditional Article III jurisdiction may significantly burden the time and attention of the Chief Executive is not sufficient to establish a violation of the Constitution. Two long-settled propositions, first announced by Chief Justice Marshall, support that conclusion.

First, we have long held that when the President takes official action, the Court has the authority to determine whether he has acted within the law....

Second, it is also settled that the President is subject to judicial process in appropriate circumstances. Although Thomas Jefferson apparently thought otherwise, Chief Justice Marshall, when presiding in the treason trial of Aaron Burr, ruled that a subpoena *duces tecum* could be directed to the President. We unequivocally and emphatically endorsed Marshall's position when we held that President Nixon was obligated to comply with a subpoena commanding him to produce certain tape recordings of his conversations with his aides.

Sitting Presidents have responded to court orders to provide testimony and other information with sufficient frequency that such interactions between the Judicial and Executive Branches can scarcely be thought a novelty. President Ford complied with an order to give a deposition in a criminal trial, and President Clinton has twice given videotaped testimony in criminal proceedings. Moreover, sitting Presidents have also voluntarily complied with judicial requests for testimony. President Grant gave a lengthy deposition in a criminal case under such circumstances, and President Carter similarly gave videotaped testimony for use at a criminal trial.

In sum, [i]t is settled law that the separation-of-powers doctrine does not bar every exercise of jurisdiction over the President of the United States. If the Judiciary may severely burden the Executive Branch by reviewing the legality of the President's official conduct, and if it may direct appropriate process to the President himself, it must follow that the federal courts have power to determine the legality of his unofficial conduct. The burden on the President's time and energy that is a mere byproduct of such review surely cannot be considered as onerous as the direct burden imposed by judicial review and the occasional invalidation of his official actions.[40] We therefore hold that the doctrine of separation of powers does not require federal courts to stay all private actions against the President until he leaves office.

[W]e turn to the question whether the District Court's decision to stay the trial until after petitioner leaves office was an abuse of discretion....

Strictly speaking the stay was not the functional equivalent of the constitutional immunity that petitioner claimed, because the District Court ordered discovery to proceed. Moreover, a stay of either the trial or discovery might be justified by considerations that do not require the recognition of any constitutional immunity. The District Court has broad discretion to stay proceedings as an incident to its power to control its own docket. As we have explained, [e]specially in cases of extraordinary public moment, [a plaintiff] may be required to submit to delay not immoderate in extent and not oppressive in its consequences if the pub-

40. [W]e recognize that a President, like any other official or private citizen, may become distracted or preoccupied by pending litigation. Presidents and other officials face a variety of demands on their time, however, some private, some political, and some as a result of official duty. While such distractions may be vexing to those subjected to them, they do not ordinarily implicate constitutional separation-of-powers concerns.

lic welfare or convenience will thereby be promoted. Although we have rejected the argument that the potential burdens on the President violate separation-of-powers principles, those burdens are appropriate matters for the District Court to evaluate in its management of the case. The high respect that is owed to the office of the Chief Executive, though not justifying a rule of categorical immunity, is a matter that should inform the conduct of the entire proceeding, including the timing and scope of discovery.

Nevertheless, we are persuaded that it was an abuse of discretion for the District Court to defer the trial until after the President leaves office. Such a lengthy and categorical stay takes no account whatever of the respondent's interest in bringing the case to trial....

The decision to postpone the trial was, furthermore, premature.... We think the District Court may have given undue weight to the concern that a trial might generate unrelated civil actions that could conceivably hamper the President in conducting the duties of his office. If and when that should occur, the court's discretion would permit it to manage those actions in such fashion (including deferral of trial) that interference with the President's duties would not occur. But no such impingement upon the President's conduct of his office was shown here....

Justice BREYER, concurring in the judgment.

I agree with the majority that the Constitution does not automatically grant the President an immunity from civil lawsuits based upon his private conduct. Nor does the doctrine of separation of powers ... require federal courts to stay virtually all private actions against the President until he leaves office. To obtain a postponement the President must bea[r] the burden of establishing its need.

In my view, however, once the President sets forth and explains a conflict between judicial proceeding and public duties, the matter changes. At that point, the Constitution permits a judge to schedule a trial in an ordinary civil damages action (where postponement normally is possible without overwhelming damage to a plaintiff) only within the constraints of a constitutional principle—a principle that forbids a federal judge in such a case to interfere with the President's discharge of his public duties. I have no doubt that the Constitution contains such a principle applicable to civil suits, based upon Article II's vesting of the entire executive Power in a single individual, implemented through the Constitution's structural separation of powers, and revealed both by history and case precedent....

Comments and Questions

1. Subsequent to the Court's decision, the plaintiff's attorneys sought to depose the President regarding all past extramarital affairs for the purpose of showing a pattern of behavior. The judge, over the objection of Clinton's lawyers, required President Clinton to answer these questions. As part of that deposition, Clinton denied having "sexual rela-

tions" with Monica Lewinsky. Later the judge decided that evidence regarding past affairs was not admissible and ultimately ruled against Jones on all claims. While the case was on appeal, Clinton settled with Jones for $850,000.

2. His denial of sexual relations with Monica Lewinsky in the *Jones* deposition led Independent Counsel Ken Starr to broaden his investigation of the President regarding certain real estate transactions the Clintons had made while he was Governor of Arkansas to include possible perjury in the *Jones* case. As part of this new investigation, the President was required to testify before a grand jury regarding his relationship with Monica Lewinsky, and there he testified that he did not have sexual intercourse with her and that he believed his responses in the *Jones* case were truthful, because he understood the questions there to have related to sexual intercourse. As to whether there was oral intercourse, the President refused to answer, admitting only to an inappropriate intimate relationship. While Starr did not bring any criminal charges against the President, he referred the matter to the House of Representatives for use in possible impeachment proceedings. Alleged perjury in the *Jones* suit and before the grand jury constituted two of the four counts considered by the House. On party lines, the House voted to impeach the President for the alleged grand jury perjury as well as for obstruction of justice in impeding the grand jury investigation. The Senate acquitted him on both counts, with 10 Republicans joining all the Democrats on the perjury charge and five Republicans joining all the Democrats on the obstruction of justice charge. The judge in the *Jones* case, however, held Clinton in civil contempt for lying in the deposition, fined him $90,000, and referred the matter to the Arkansas Supreme Court, for possible disciplinary action. Later, as part of a deal with Starr's successor to avoid criminal prosecution, Clinton admitted to giving false testimony in the *Jones* case and agreed to a five-year suspension of his bar membership. Subsequently, he resigned his membership to avoid permanent disbarment.

3. Given the fallout from the *Jones* deposition, what do you think of the Supreme Court's statement that "if properly managed by the District Court, it appears to us highly unlikely [that the case will] occupy any substantial amount of petitioner's time"? Does this suggest the case was *not* properly managed by the trial judge? Given the stakes involved, do you think it appropriate to leave the fate of the Presidency to the judgment of one of almost 700 federal district court judges? Or is what happened simply Bill Clinton's fault for lying in the deposition? How many people in public life would want to be asked under oath about all their extramarital affairs?

4. One might ask why the Independent Counsel did not bring any criminal charges. The final report of the Independent Counsel explained:

> In the Independent Counsel's judgment, there was sufficient evidence to prosecute President Clinton for violating federal criminal laws within this Office's jurisdiction. Nonetheless, in

> light of: (1) President Clinton's admission of providing false testimony that was knowingly misleading, evasive, and prejudicial to the administration of justice before the United States District Court for the Eastern District of Arkansas; (2) his acknowledgement that his conduct violated the Rules of Professional Conduct of the Arkansas Supreme Court; (3) the five-year suspension of his license to practice law and $25,000 fine imposed on him by the Circuit Court of Pulaski County, Arkansas; (4) the civil contempt penalty of more than $90,000 imposed on President Clinton by the federal court for violating its orders; (5) the payment of more than $850,000 in settlement to Paula Jones; (6) the express finding by the federal court that President Clinton had engaged in contemptuous conduct; and (7) the substantial public condemnation of President Clinton arising from his impeachment, the Independent Counsel concluded, consistent with the Principles of Federal Prosecution, that further proceedings against President Clinton for his conduct should not be initiated.

5. There is substantial dispute concerning whether a sitting President may be prosecuted criminally. This undoubtedly affected the Independent Counsel in the Clinton case as well as the Special Prosecutor in the Nixon case. Recall that the grand jury named Nixon as an *unindicted* co-conspirator in the obstruction of justice charges. It was even an issue with respect to Nixon's Vice President, Spiro Agnew, who, in light of evidence that he had accepted bribes when he was governor of Maryland and continuing while he was Vice President, was induced to resign the Vice Presidency in return for a plea agreement to income tax evasion and money laundering charges that imposed only a $10,000 fine and three years probation.

Appendix I

The Constitution of the United States

PREAMBLE

We the People of the United States, in Order to form a more perfect Union, establish Justice, insure domestic Tranquility, provide for the common defence, promote the general Welfare, and secure the Blessings of Liberty to ourselves and our Posterity, do ordain and establish this Constitution for the United States of America.

ARTICLE I

Section 1. All legislative Powers herein granted shall be vested in a Congress of the United States, which shall consist of a Senate and House of Representatives.

Section 2. [1] The House of Representatives shall be composed of Members chosen every second Year by the People of the several States, and the Electors in each State shall have the Qualifications requisite for Electors of the most numerous Branch of the State Legislature.

[2] No Person shall be a Representative who shall not have attained to the Age of twenty five Years, and been seven Years a Citizen of the United States, and who shall not, when elected, be an Inhabitant of that State in which he shall be chosen.

[3] Representatives and direct Taxes shall be apportioned among the several States which may be included within this Union, according to their respective Numbers, which shall be determined by adding to the whole Number of free Persons, including those bound to Service for a Term of Years, and excluding Indians not taxed, three fifths of all other Persons. The actual Enumeration shall be made within three Years after the first Meeting of the Congress of the United States, and within every subsequent Term of ten Years, in such Manner as they shall by Law direct. The Number of Representatives shall not exceed one for every thirty Thousand, but each State shall have at Least one Representative; and until such enumeration shall be made, the State of New Hampshire shall be entitled to chuse three, Massachusetts eight, Rhode Island and Providence Plantations one, Connecticut five, New York six, New Jersey four, Pennsylvania eight, Delaware one, Maryland six, Virginia ten, North Carolina five, South Carolina five, and Georgia three.

[4] When vacancies happen in the Representation from any State, the Executive Authority thereof shall issue Writs of Election to fill such Vacancies.

[5] The House of Representatives shall chuse their Speaker and other Officers; and shall have the sole Power of Impeachment.

Section 3. [1] The Senate of the United States shall be composed of two Senators from each State, chosen by the Legislature thereof, for six Years; and each Senator shall have one Vote.

[2] Immediately after they shall be assembled in Consequence of the first Election, they shall be divided as equally as may be into three Classes. The Seats of the Senators of the first Class shall be vacated at the Expiration of the Second Year, of the second Class at the Expiration of the fourth Year, and of the third Class at the Expiration of the sixth Year, so that one third may be chosen every second Year; and if Vacancies happen by Resignation, or otherwise, during the Recess of the Legislature of any State, the Executive thereof may make temporary Appointments until the next Meeting of the Legislature, which shall then fill such Vacancies.

[3] No Person shall be a Senator who shall not have attained to the Age of thirty Years, and been nine Years a Citizen of the United States, and who shall not, when elected, be an Inhabitant of that State for which he shall be chosen.

[4] The Vice President of the United States shall be President of the Senate, but shall have no Vote, unless they be equally divided.

[5] The Senate shall chuse their other Officers, and also a President pro tempore, in the Absence of the Vice President, or when he shall exercise the Office of President of the United States.

[6] The Senate shall have the sole Power to try all Impeachments. When sitting for that Purpose, they shall be on Oath or Affirmation. When the President of the United States is tried, the Chief Justice shall preside: And no Person shall be convicted without the Concurrence of two thirds of the Members present.

[7] Judgment in Cases of Impeachment shall not extend further than to removal from Office, and disqualification to hold and enjoy any Office of honor, Trust, or Profit under the United States: but the Party convicted shall nevertheless be liable and subject to Indictment, Trial, Judgment, and Punishment, according to Law.

Section 4. [1] The Times, Places and Manner of holding Elections for Senators and Representatives, shall be prescribed in each State by the Legislature thereof; but the Congress may at any time by Law make or alter such Regulations, except as to the Places of chusing Senators.

[2] The Congress shall assemble at least once in every Year, and such Meeting shall be on the first Monday in December, unless they shall by Law appoint a different Day.

Section 5. [1] Each House shall be the Judge of the Elections, Returns, and Qualifications of its own Members, and a Majority of each shall constitute a Quorum to do Business; but a smaller Number may adjourn from day to day, and may be authorized to compel the Attendance of absent Members, in such Manner, and under such Penalties as each House may provide.

[2] Each House may determine the Rules of its Proceedings, punish its Members for disorderly Behavior, and, with the Concurrence of two thirds, expel a Member.

[3] Each House shall keep a Journal of its Proceedings, and from time to time publish the same, excepting such Parts as may in their Judgment require Secrecy; and the Yeas and Nays of the Members of either House on any question shall, at the Desire of one fifth of those Present, be entered on the Journal.

[4] Neither House, during the Session of Congress, shall without the Consent of the other, adjourn for more than three days, nor to any other Place than that in which the two Houses shall be sitting.

Section 6. [1] The Senators and Representatives shall receive a Compensation for their Services, to be ascertained by Law, and paid out of the Treasury of the United States. They shall in all Cases, except Treason, Felony and Breach of the Peace, be privileged from Arrest during their Attendance at the Session of their respective Houses, and in going to and returning from the same; and for any Speech or Debate in either House, they shall not be questioned in any other Place.

[2] No Senator or Representative shall, during the Time for which he was elected, be appointed to any civil Office under the Authority of the United States, which shall have been created, or the Emoluments whereof shall have been increased during such time; and no Person holding any Office under the United States, shall be a Member of either House during his Continuance in Office.

Section 7. [1] All Bills for raising Revenue shall originate in the House of Representatives; but the Senate may propose or concur with Amendments as on other Bills.

[2] Every Bill which shall have passed the House of Representatives and the Senate, shall, before it become a Law, be presented to the President of the United States; If he approve he shall sign it, but if not he shall return it, with his Objections to the House in which it shall have originated, who shall enter the Objections at large on their Journal, and proceed to reconsider it. If after such Reconsideration two thirds of that House shall agree to pass the Bill, it shall be sent together with the Objections, to the other House, by which it shall likewise be reconsidered, and if approved by two thirds of that House, it shall become a Law. But in all such Cases the Votes of both Houses shall be determined by yeas and Nays, and the Names of the Persons voting for and against the Bill shall be entered on the Journal of each House respectively. If any Bill shall not be returned by the President within ten Days (Sundays excepted) after it shall have been presented to him, the Same shall be a Law, in like Manner as if he had signed it, unless the Congress by their Adjournment prevent its Return in which Case it shall not be a Law.

[3] Every Order, Resolution, or Vote, to Which the Concurrence of the Senate and House of Representatives may be necessary (except on a question of Adjournment) shall be presented to the President of the United States; and before the Same shall take Effect, shall be approved by him, or being disapproved by him, shall be repassed by two thirds of the Senate and House of Representatives, according to the Rules and Limitations prescribed in the Case of a Bill.

Section 8. [1] The Congress shall have Power To lay and collect Taxes, Duties, Imposts and Excises, to pay the Debts and provide for the common Defence and general Welfare of the United States; but all Duties, Imposts and Excises shall be uniform throughout the United States;

[2] To borrow money on the credit of the United States;

[3] To regulate Commerce with foreign Nations, and among the several States, and with the Indian Tribes;

[4] To establish an uniform Rule of Naturalization, and uniform Laws on the subject of Bankruptcies throughout the United States;

[5] To coin Money, regulate the Value thereof, and of foreign Coin, and fix the Standard of Weights and Measures;

[6] To provide for the Punishment of counterfeiting the Securities and current Coin of the United States;

[7] To Establish Post Offices and Post Roads;

[8] To promote the Progress of Science and useful Arts, by securing for limited Times to Authors and Inventors the exclusive Right to their respective Writings and Discoveries;

[9] To constitute Tribunals inferior to the supreme Court;

[10] To define and punish Piracies and Felonies committed on the high Seas, and Offenses against the Law of Nations;

[11] To declare War, grant Letters of Marque and Reprisal, and make Rules concerning Captures on Land and Water;

[12] To raise and support Armies, but no Appropriation of Money to that Use shall be for a longer Term than two Years;

[13] To provide and maintain a Navy;

[14] To make Rules for the Government and Regulation of the land and naval Forces;

[15] To provide for calling forth the Militia to execute the Laws of the Union, suppress Insurrections and repel Invasions;

[16] To provide for organizing, arming, and disciplining, the Militia, and for governing such Part of them as may be employed in the Service of the United States, reserving to the States respectively, the Appointment of the Officers, and the Authority of training the Militia according to the discipline prescribed by Congress;

[17] To exercise exclusive Legislation in all Cases whatsoever, over such District (not exceeding ten Miles square) as may, by Cession of particular States, and the Acceptance of Congress, become the Seat of the Government of the United States, and to exercise like Authority over all Places purchased by the Consent of the Legislature of the State in which the Same shall be, for the Erection of Forts, Magazines, Arsenals, dock-Yards, and other needful Buildings;—And

[18] To make all Laws which shall be necessary and proper for carrying into Execution the foregoing Powers, and all other Powers vested by this Constitution in the Government of the United States, or in any Department or Officer thereof.

Section 9. [1] The Migration or Importation of Such Persons as any of the States now existing shall think proper to admit, shall not be prohibited by the Congress prior to the Year one thousand eight hundred and eight, but a Tax or duty may be imposed on such Importation, not exceeding ten dollars for each Person.

[2] The privilege of the Writ of Habeas Corpus shall not be suspended, unless when in Cases of Rebellion or Invasion the public Safety may require it.

[3] No Bill of Attainder or ex post facto Law shall be passed.

[4] No Capitation, or other direct, Tax shall be laid, unless in Proportion to the Census or Enumeration herein before directed to be taken.

[5] No Tax or Duty shall be laid on Articles exported from any State.

[6] No Preference shall be given by any Regulation of Commerce or Revenue to the Ports of one State over those of another: nor shall Vessels bound to, or from, one State be obliged to enter, clear, or pay Duties in another.

[7] No money shall be drawn from the Treasury, but in Consequence of Appropriations made by Law; and a regular Statement and Account of the Receipts and Expenditures of all public Money shall be published from time to time.

[8] No Title of Nobility shall be granted by the United States: And no Person holding any Office of Profit or Trust under them, shall, without the Consent of the Congress, accept of any present, Emolument, Office, or Title, of any kind whatever, from any King, Prince, or foreign State.

Section 10. [1] No State shall enter into any Treaty, Alliance, or Confederation; grant Letters of Marque and Reprisal; coin Money; emit Bills of Credit; make any Thing but gold and silver Coin a Tender in Payment of Debts; pass any Bill of Attainder, ex post facto Law, or Law impairing the Obligation of Contracts, or grant any Title of Nobility.

[2] No State shall, without the Consent of the Congress, lay any Imposts or Duties on Imports or Exports, except what may be absolutely

necessary for executing it's inspection Laws: and the net Produce of all Duties and Imposts, laid by any State on Imports or Exports, shall be for the Use of the Treasury of the United States; and all such Laws shall be subject to the Revision and Control of the Congress.

[3] No State shall, without the Consent of Congress, lay any Duty of Tonnage, keep Troops, or Ships of War in time of Peace, enter into any Agreement or Compact with another State, or with a foreign Power, or engage in War, unless actually invaded, or in such imminent Danger as will not admit of delay.

Article II

Section 1. [1] The executive Power shall be vested in a President of the United States of America. He shall hold his Office during the Term of four Years, and, together with the Vice President, chosen for the same Term, be elected, as follows:

[2] Each State shall appoint, in such Manner as the Legislature thereof may direct, a Number of Electors, equal to the whole Number of Senators and Representatives to which the State may be entitled in the Congress; but no Senator or Representative, or Person holding an Office of Trust or Profit under the United States, shall be appointed an Elector.

[3] The Electors shall meet in their respective States, and vote by Ballot for two Persons, of whom one at least shall not be an Inhabitant of the same State with themselves. And they shall make a List of all the Persons voted for, and of the Number of Votes for each; which List they shall sign and certify, and transmit sealed to the Seat of the Government of the United States, directed to the President of the Senate. The President of the Senate shall, in the Presence of the Senate and House of Representatives, open all the Certificates, and the Votes shall then be counted. The Person having the greatest Number of Votes shall be the President, if such Number be a Majority of the whole Number of Electors appointed; and if there be more than one who have such Majority, and have an equal Number of Votes, then the House of Representatives shall immediately chuse by Ballot one of them for President; and if no Person have a Majority, then from the five highest on the List the said House shall in like Manner chuse the President. But in chusing the President, the Votes shall be taken by States, the Representation from each State having one Vote; A quorum for this Purpose shall consist of a Member or Members from two thirds of the States, and a Majority of all the States shall be necessary to a Choice. In every Case, after the Choice of the President, the Person having the greater Number of Votes of the Electors shall be the Vice President. But if there should remain two or more who have equal Votes, the Senate shall chuse from them by Ballot the Vice President.

[4] The Congress may determine the Time of chusing the Electors, and the Day on which they shall give their Votes; which Day shall be the same throughout the United States.

[5] No person except a natural born Citizen, or a Citizen of the United States, at the time of the Adoption of this Constitution, shall be eligible to the Office of President; neither shall any Person be eligible to that Office who shall not have attained to the Age of thirty five Years, and been fourteen Years a Resident within the United States.

[6] In case of the removal of the President from Office, or of his Death, Resignation or Inability to discharge the Powers and Duties of the said Office, the Same shall devolve on the Vice President, and the Congress may by Law provide for the Case of Removal, Death, Resignation or Inability, both of the President and Vice President, declaring what Officer shall then act as President, and such Officer shall act accordingly, until the Disability be removed, or a President shall be elected.

[7] The President shall, at stated Times, receive for his Services, a Compensation, which shall neither be increased nor diminished during the Period for which he shall have been elected, and he shall not receive within that Period any other Emolument from the United States, or any of them.

[8] Before he enter on the Execution of his Office, he shall take the following Oath or Affirmation: "I do solemnly swear (or affirm) that I will faithfully execute the Office of President of the United States, and will to the best of my Ability, preserve, protect and defend the Constitution of the United States."

Section 2. [1] The President shall be Commander in Chief of the Army and Navy of the United States, and of the militia of the several States, when called into the actual Service of the United States; he may require the Opinion, in writing, of the principal Officer in each of the Executive Departments, upon any Subject relating to the Duties of their respective Offices, and he shall have Power to grant Reprieves and Pardons for Offenses against the United States, except in Cases of Impeachment.

[2] He shall have Power, by and with the Advice and Consent of the Senate, to make Treaties, provided two thirds of the Senators present concur; and he shall nominate, and by and with the Advice and Consent of the Senate, shall appoint Ambassadors, other public Ministers and Consuls, Judges of the supreme Court, and all other Officers of the United States, whose Appointments are not herein otherwise provided for, and which shall be established by Law; but the Congress may by Law vest the Appointment of such inferior Officers, as they think proper, in the President alone, in the Courts of Law, or in the Heads of Departments.

[3] The President shall have Power to fill up all Vacancies that may happen during the Recess of the Senate, by granting Commissions which shall expire at the End of their next Session.

Section 3. He shall from time to time give to the Congress Information of the State of the Union, and recommend to their Consideration such Measures as he shall judge necessary and expedient; he may, on extraordinary Occasions, convene both Houses, or either of them, and in Case of Disagreement between them, with Respect to the Time of Adjournment, he may adjourn them to such Time as he shall think proper; he shall receive Ambassadors and other public Ministers; he shall take Care that the Laws be faithfully executed, and shall Commission all the Officers of the United States.

Section 4. The President, Vice President and all civil Officers of the United States, shall be removed from Office on Impeachment for, and Conviction of, Treason, Bribery, or other high Crimes and Misdemeanors.

Article III

Section 1. The judicial Power of the United States, shall be vested in one supreme Court, and in such inferior Courts as the Congress may from time to time ordain and establish. The Judges, both of the supreme and inferior Courts, shall hold their Offices during good Behaviour, and shall, at stated Times, receive for their Services a Compensation, which shall not be diminished during their Continuance in Office.

Section 2. [1] The judicial Power shall extend to all Cases, in Law and Equity, arising under this Constitution, the Laws of the United States, and Treaties made, or which shall be made, under their Authority;—to all Cases affecting Ambassadors, other public Ministers and Consuls;—to all Cases of admiralty and maritime Jurisdiction;—to Controversies to which the United States shall be a Party;—to Controversies between two or more States;—between a State and Citizens of another State;—between Citizens of different States;—between Citizens of the same State claiming Lands under the Grants of different States, and between a State, or the Citizens thereof, and foreign States, Citizens or Subjects.

[2] In all Cases affecting Ambassadors, other public Ministers and Consuls, and those in which a State shall be a Party, the supreme Court shall have original Jurisdiction. In all the other Cases before mentioned, the supreme Court shall have appellate Jurisdiction, both as to Law and Fact, with such Exceptions, and under such Regulations as the Congress shall make.

[3] The trial of all Crimes, except in Cases of Impeachment, shall be by Jury; and such Trial shall be held in the State where the said Crimes shall have been committed; but when not committed within any State, the Trial shall be at such Place or Places as the Congress may by Law have directed.

Section 3. [1] Treason against the United States, shall consist only in levying War against them, or, in adhering to their Enemies, giving them Aid and Comfort. No Person shall be convicted of Treason unless on the Testimony of two Witnesses to the same overt Act, or on Confession in open Court.

[2] The Congress shall have Power to declare the Punishment of Treason, but no Attainder of Treason shall work Corruption of Blood, or Forfeiture except during the Life of the Person attainted.

Article IV

Section 1. Full Faith and Credit shall be given in each State to the public Acts, Records, and judicial Proceedings of every other State. And the Congress may by general Laws prescribe the Manner in which such Acts, Records and Proceedings shall be proved, and the Effect thereof.

Section 2. [1] The Citizens of each State shall be entitled to all Privileges and Immunities of Citizens in the several States.

[2] A Person charged in any State with Treason, Felony, or other Crime, who shall flee from Justice, and be found in another State, shall on demand of the executive Authority of the State from which he fled, be delivered up, to be removed to the State having Jurisdiction of the Crime.

[3] No Person held to Service or Labour in one State, under the Laws thereof, escaping into another, shall, in Consequence of any Law or Regulation therein, be discharged from such Service or Labour, but shall be delivered up on Claim of the Party to whom such Service or Labour may be due.

Section 3. [1] New States may be admitted by the Congress into this Union; but no new State shall be formed or erected within the Jurisdiction of any other State; nor any State be formed by the Junction of two or more States, or Parts of States, without the Consent of the Legislatures of the States concerned as well as of the Congress.

[2] The Congress shall have Power to dispose of and make all needful Rules and Regulations respecting the Territory or other Property belonging to the United States; and nothing in this Constitution shall be so construed as to Prejudice any Claims of the United States, or of any particular State.

Section 4. The United States shall guarantee to every State in this Union a Republican Form of Government, and shall protect each of them against Invasion; and on Application of the Legislature, or of the Executive (when the Legislature cannot be convened) against domestic Violence.

Article V

The Congress, whenever two thirds of both Houses shall deem it necessary, shall propose Amendments to this Constitution, or, on the Application of the Legislatures of two thirds of the several States, shall call a Convention for proposing Amendments, which, in either Case, shall be valid to all Intents and Purposes, as part of this Constitution, when ratified by the Legislatures of three fourths of the several States, or by Conventions in three fourths thereof, as the one or the other Mode of Ratification may be proposed by the Congress; Provided that no

Amendment which may be made prior to the Year One thousand eight hundred and eight shall in any Manner affect the first and fourth Clauses in the Ninth Section of the first Article; and that no State, without its Consent, shall be deprived of its equal Suffrage in the Senate.

Article VI

[1] All Debts contracted and Engagements entered into, before the Adoption of this Constitution shall be as valid against the United States under this Constitution, as under the Confederation.

[2] This Constitution, and the Laws of the United States which shall be made in Pursuance thereof; and all Treaties made, or which shall be made, under the Authority of the United States, shall be the supreme Law of the Land; and the Judges in every State shall be bound thereby, any Thing in the Constitution or Laws of any State to the Contrary notwithstanding.

[3] The Senators and Representatives before mentioned, and the Members of the several State Legislatures, and all executive and judicial Officers, both of the United States and of the several States, shall be bound by Oath or Affirmation, to support this Constitution; but no religious Test shall ever be required as a Qualification to any Office or public Trust under the United States.

Article VII

The Ratification of the Conventions of nine States shall be sufficient for the Establishment of this Constitution between the States so ratifying the Same.

AMENDMENTS OF THE CONSTITUTION OF THE UNITED STATES OF AMERICA, PROPOSED BY CONGRESS AND RATIFIED BY THE LEGISLATURES OF THE SEVERAL STATES PURSUANT TO THE FIFTH ARTICLE OF THE ORIGINAL CONSTITUTION.

Amendment I [1791]

Congress shall make no law respecting an establishment of religion, or prohibiting the free exercise thereof; or abridging the freedom of speech, or of the press; or the right of the people peaceably to assemble, and to petition the Government for a redress of grievances.

Amendment II [1791]

A well regulated Militia, being necessary to the security of a free State, the right of the people to keep and bear Arms, shall not be infringed.

Amendment III [1791]

No Soldier shall, in time of peace be quartered in any house, without the consent of the Owner, nor in time of war, but in a manner to be prescribed by law.

Amendment IV [1791]

The right of the people to be secure in their persons, houses, papers, and effects, against unreasonable searches and seizures, shall not be violated, and no Warrants shall issue, but upon probable cause, supported by Oath or affirmation and particularly describing the place to be searched, and the persons or things to be seized.

Amendment V [1791]

No person shall be held to answer for a capital, or otherwise infamous crime, unless on a presentment or indictment of a Grand Jury, except in cases arising in the land or naval forces, or in the Militia, when in actual service in time of War or public danger; nor shall any person be subject for the same offence to be twice put in jeopardy of life or limb; nor shall be compelled in any criminal case to be a witness against himself, nor be deprived of life, liberty, or property, without due process of law; nor shall private property be taken for public use, without just compensation.

Amendment VI [1791]

In all criminal prosecutions, the accused shall enjoy the right to a speedy and public trial, by an impartial jury of the State and district wherein the crime shall have been committed, which district shall have been previously ascertained by law, and to be informed of the nature and cause of the accusation; to be confronted with the witnesses against him; to have compulsory process for obtaining witnesses in his favor, and to have the Assistance of Counsel for his defence.

Amendment VII [1791]

In Suits at common law, where the value in controversy shall exceed twenty dollars, the right of trial by jury shall be preserved, and no fact tried by jury, shall be otherwise re-examined in any Court of the United States, than according to the rules of the common law.

Amendment VIII [1791]

Excessive bail shall not be required, nor excessive fines imposed, nor cruel and unusual punishments inflicted.

Amendment IX [1791]

The enumeration in the Constitution, of certain rights, shall not be construed to deny or disparage others retained by the people.

Amendment X [1791]

The powers not delegated to the United States by the Constitution, nor prohibited by it to the States, are reserved to the States respectively, or to the people.

Amendment XI [1798]

The Judicial power of the United States shall not be construed to extend to any suit in law or equity, commenced or prosecuted against one of the United States by Citizens of another State, or by Citizens or Subjects of any Foreign State.

Amendment XII [1804]

The Electors shall meet in their respective states and vote by ballot for President and Vice-President, one of whom, at least, shall not be an inhabitant of the same state with themselves; they shall name in their ballots the person voted for as President, and in distinct ballots the person voted for as Vice-President, and they shall make distinct lists of all persons voted for as President, and of all persons voted for as Vice-President, and of the number of votes for each, which lists they shall sign and certify, and transmit sealed to the seat of the government of the United States, directed to the President of the Senate;—The President of the Senate shall, in the presence of the Senate and House of Representatives, open all the certificates and the votes shall then be counted;—The person having the greatest number of votes for President, shall be the President, if such number be a majority of the whole number of Electors appointed; and if no person have such majority, then from the persons having the highest numbers not exceeding three on the list of those voted for as President, the House of Representatives shall choose immediately, by ballot, the President. But in choosing the President, the votes shall be taken by states, the representation from each state having one vote; a quorum for this purpose shall consist of a member or members from two-thirds of the states, and a majority of all the states shall be necessary to a choice. And if the House of Representatives shall not choose a President whenever the right of choice shall devolve upon them before the fourth day of March next following, then the Vice-President shall act as President, as in the case of the death or other constitutional disability of the President.—The person having the greatest number of votes as Vice-President, shall be the Vice-President, if such number be a majority of the whole number of Electors appointed, and if no person have a majority, then from the two highest numbers on the list, the Senate shall choose the Vice-President; a quorum for the purpose shall consist of two-thirds of the whole number of Senators, and a majority of the whole number shall be necessary to a choice. But no person constitutionally ineligible to the office of President shall be eligible to that of Vice-President of the United States.

Amendment XIII [1865]

Section 1. Neither slavery nor involuntary servitude, except as a punishment for crime whereof the party shall have been duly convicted, shall exist within the United States, or any place subject to their jurisdiction.

Section 2. Congress shall have power to enforce this article by appropriate legislation.

Amendment XIV [1868]

Section 1. All persons born or naturalized in the United States, and subject to the jurisdiction thereof, are citizens of the United States and of the State wherein they reside. No State shall make or enforce any law which shall abridge the privileges or immunities of citizens of the United States; nor shall any State deprive any person of life, liberty, or property, without due process of law; nor deny to any person within its jurisdiction the equal protection of the laws.

Section 2. Representatives shall be apportioned among the several States according to their respective numbers, counting the whole number of persons in each State, excluding Indians not taxed. But when the right to vote at any election for the choice of electors for President and Vice President of the United States, Representatives in Congress, the Executive and Judicial officers of a State, or the members of the Legislature thereof, is denied to any of the male inhabitants of such State, being twenty-one years of age, and citizens of the United States, or in any way abridged, except for participation in rebellion, or other crime, the basis of representation therein shall be reduced in the proportion which the number of such male citizens shall bear to the whole number of male citizens twenty-one years of age in such State.

Section 3. No person shall be a Senator or Representative in Congress, or elector of President and Vice President, or hold any office, civil or military, under the United States, or under any State, who having previously taken an oath, as a member of Congress, or as an officer of the United States, or as a member of any State legislature, or as an executive or judicial officer of any State, to support the Constitution of the United States, shall have engaged in insurrection or rebellion against the same, or given aid or comfort to the enemies thereof. But Congress may by a vote of two-thirds of each House, remove such disability.

Section 4. The validity of the public debt of the United States, authorized by law, including debts incurred for payment of pensions and bounties for services in suppressing insurrection or rebellion, shall not be questioned. But neither the United States nor any State shall assume or pay any debt or obligation incurred in aid of insurrection or rebellion against the United States, or any claim for the loss or emancipation of any slave; but all such debts, obligations and claims shall be held illegal and void.

Section 5. The Congress shall have power to enforce, by appropriate legislation, the provisions of this article.

Amendment XV [1870]

Section 1. The right of citizens of the United States to vote shall not be denied or abridged by the United States or by any State on account of race, color, or previous condition of servitude.

Section 2. The Congress shall have power to enforce this article by appropriate legislation.

Amendment XVI [1913]

The Congress shall have power to lay and collect taxes on incomes, from whatever source derived, without apportionment among the several States, and without regard to any census or enumeration.

AMENDMENT XVII [1913]

[1] The Senate of the United States shall be composed of two Senators from each State, elected by the people thereof, for six years; and each Senator shall have one vote. The electors in each State shall have the qualifications requisite for electors of the most numerous branch of the State legislatures.

[2] When vacancies happen in the representation of any State in the Senate, the executive authority of such State shall issue writs of election to fill such vacancies: *Provided,* That the legislature of any State may empower the executive thereof to make temporary appointments until the people fill the vacancies by election as the legislature may direct.

[3] This amendment shall not be so construed as to affect the election or term of any Senator chosen before it becomes valid as part of the Constitution.

AMENDMENT XVIII [1919]

Section 1. After one year from the ratification of this article the manufacture, sale, or transportation of intoxicating liquors within, the importation thereof into, or the exportation thereof from the United States and all territory subject to the jurisdiction thereof for beverage purposes is hereby prohibited.

Section 2. The Congress and the several States shall have concurrent power to enforce this article by appropriate legislation.

Section 3. This article shall be inoperative unless it shall have been ratified as an amendment to the Constitution by the legislatures of the several States, as provided in the Constitution, within seven years from the date of the submission hereof to the States by the Congress.

AMENDMENT XIX [1920]

[1] The right of citizens of the United States to vote shall not be denied or abridged by the United States or by any State on account of sex.

[2] Congress shall have power to enforce this article by appropriate legislation.

AMENDMENT XX [1933]

Section 1. The terms of the President and Vice President shall end at noon on the 20th day of January, and the terms of Senators and Representatives at noon on the 3d day of January, of the years in which such terms would have ended if this article had not been ratified; and the terms of their successors shall then begin.

Section 2. The Congress shall assemble at least once in every year, and such meeting shall begin at noon on the 3d day of January, unless they shall by law appoint a different day.

Section 3. If, at the time fixed for the beginning of the term of the President, the President elect shall have died, the Vice President elect shall become President. If the President shall not have been chosen before the time fixed for the beginning of his term, or if the President elect shall have failed to qualify, then the Vice President elect shall act as President until a President shall have qualified; and the Congress may by law provide for the case wherein neither a President elect nor a Vice President elect shall have qualified, declaring who shall then act as President, or the manner in which one who is to act shall be selected, and such person shall act accordingly until a President or Vice President shall have qualified.

Section 4. The Congress may by law provide for the case of the death of any of the persons from whom the House of Representatives may choose a President whenever the right of choice shall have devolved upon them, and for the case of the death of any of the persons from whom the Senate may choose a Vice President whenever the right of choice shall have devolved upon them.

Section 5. Sections 1 and 2 shall take effect on the 15th day of October following the ratification of this article.

Section 6. This article shall be inoperative unless it shall have been ratified as an amendment to the Constitution by the legislatures of three-fourths of the several States within seven years from the date of its submission.

Amendment XXI [1933]

Section 1. The eighteenth article of amendment to the Constitution of the United States is hereby repealed.

Section 2. The transportation or importation into any State, Territory, or possession of the United States for delivery or use therein of intoxicating liquors, in violation of the laws thereof, is hereby prohibited.

Section 3. This article shall be inoperative unless it shall have been ratified as an amendment to the Constitution by conventions in the several States, as provided in the Constitution, within seven years from the date of the submission hereof to the States by the Congress.

Amendment XXII [1951]

Section 1. No person shall be elected to the office of the President more than twice, and no person who has held the office of President, or acted as President, for more than two years of a term to which some other person was elected President shall be elected to the office of President more than once. But this Article shall not apply to any person holding the office of President when this Article was proposed by the Congress, and shall not prevent any person who may be holding the office of President, or acting as President, during the term within which this Article becomes operative from holding the office of President or acting as President during the remainder of such term.

Section 2. This article shall be inoperative unless it shall have been ratified as an amendment to the Constitution by the legislatures of three-fourths of the several States within seven years from the date of its submission to the States by the Congress.

Amendment XXIII [1961]

Section 1. The District constituting the seat of Government of the United States shall appoint in such manner as the Congress may direct:

A number of electors of President and Vice President equal to the whole number of Senators and Representatives in Congress to which the District would be entitled if it were a State, but in no event more than the least populous state; they shall be in addition to those appointed by the states, but they shall be considered, for the purposes of the election of President and Vice President, to be electors appointed by a state; and they shall meet in the District and perform such duties as provided by the twelfth article of amendment.

Section 2. The Congress shall have power to enforce this article by appropriate legislation.

Amendment XXIV [1964]

Section 1. The right of citizens of the United States to vote in any primary or other election for President or Vice President, for electors for President or Vice President, or for Senator or Representative in Congress, shall not be denied or abridged by the United States or any State by reason of failure to pay any poll tax or other tax.

Section 2. The Congress shall have power to enforce this article by appropriate legislation.

Amendment XXV [1967]

Section 1. In case of the removal of the President from office or of his death or resignation, the Vice President shall become President.

Section 2. Whenever there is a vacancy in the office of the Vice President, the President shall nominate a Vice President who shall take office upon confirmation by a majority vote of both Houses of Congress.

Section 3. Whenever the President transmits to the President pro tempore of the Senate and the Speaker of the House of Representatives his written declaration that he is unable to discharge the powers and duties of his office, and until he transmits to them a written declaration to the contrary, such powers and duties shall be discharged by the Vice President as Acting President.

Section 4. Whenever the Vice President and a majority of either the principal officers of the executive departments or of such other body as Congress may by law provide, transmit to the President pro tempore of the Senate and the Speaker of the House of Representatives their written declaration that the President is unable to discharge the powers and duties of his office, the Vice President shall immediately assume the powers and duties of the office as Acting President.

Thereafter, when the President transmits to the President pro tempore of the Senate and the Speaker of the House of Representatives his written declaration that no inability exists, he shall resume the powers and duties of his office unless the Vice President and a majority of either the principal officers of the executive department or of such other body as Congress may by law provide, transmit within four days to the President pro tempore of the Senate and the Speaker of the House of Representatives their written declaration that the President is unable to discharge the powers and duties of his office. Thereupon Congress shall decide the issue, assembling within forty-eight hours for that purpose if not in session. If the Congress, within twenty-one days after receipt of the latter written declaration, or, if Congress is not in session, within twenty-one days after Congress is required to assemble, determines by two-thirds vote of both Houses that the President is unable to discharge the powers and duties of his office, the Vice President shall continue to discharge the same as Acting President; otherwise, the President shall resume the powers and duties of his office.

Amendment XXVI [1971]

Section 1. The right of citizens of the United States, who are eighteen years of age or older, to vote shall not be denied or abridged by the United States or by any State on account of age.

Section 2. The Congress shall have power to enforce this article by appropriate legislation.

Amendment XXVII [1992]*

No law, varying compensation for the services of Senators and Representatives, shall take effect, until an election of Representatives shall have intervened.

*

* On May 7, 1992, more than 200 years after it was first proposed by James Madison, the Twenty-Seventh Amendment was ratified by a 38th State (Michigan). Although Congress set no time limit for ratification of this amendment, ten of the *other* amendments proposed at the same time (1789)—now known as the Bill of Rights—were ratified in a little more than two years. After all this time, is the ratification of the Twenty–Seventh Amendment valid? Does it matter that many of the states that ratified the amendment did not exist at the time it was first proposed?

Appendix II

Declaration and Resolves of the First Continental Congress

October 14, 1774

Whereas, since the close of the last war, the British parliament, claiming a power, of right, to bind the people of America by statutes in all cases whatsoever, hath, in some acts, expressly imposed taxes on them, and in others, under various presences, but in fact for the purpose of raising a revenue, hath imposed rates and duties payable in these colonies, established a board of commissioners, with unconstitutional powers, and extended the jurisdiction of courts of admiralty, not only for collecting the said duties, but for the trial of causes merely arising within the body of a county:

And whereas, in consequence of other statutes, judges, who before held only estates at will in their offices, have been made dependant on the crown alone for their salaries, and standing armies kept in times of peace: And whereas it has lately been resolved in parliament, that by force of a statute, made in the thirty-fifth year of the reign of King Henry the Eighth, colonists may be transported to England, and tried there upon accusations for treasons and misprisions, or concealments of treasons committed in the colonies, and by a late statute, such trials have been directed in cases therein mentioned:

And whereas, in the last session of parliament, three statutes were made; one entitled, "An act to discontinue, in such manner and for such time as are therein mentioned, the landing and discharging, lading, or shipping of goods, wares and merchandise, at the town, and within the harbour of Boston, in the province of Massachusetts–Bay in New England;" another entitled, "An act for the better regulating the government of the province of Massachusetts–Bay in New England;" and another entitled, "An act for the impartial administration of justice, in the cases of persons questioned for any act done by them in the execution of the law, or for the suppression of riots and tumults, in the province of the Massachusetts–Bay in New England;" and another statute was then made, "for making more effectual provision for the government of the province of Quebec, etc." All which statutes are impolitic, unjust, and cruel, as well as unconstitutional, and most dangerous and destructive of American rights:

And whereas, assemblies have been frequently dissolved, contrary to the rights of the people, when they attempted to deliberate on grievances;

and their dutiful, humble, loyal, and reasonable petitions to the crown for redress, have been repeatedly treated with contempt, by his Majesty's ministers of state:

The good people of the several colonies of New–Hampshire, Massachusetts–Bay, Rhode Island and Providence Plantations, Connecticut, New–York, New–Jersey, Pennsylvania, Newcastle, Kent, and Sussex on Delaware, Maryland, Virginia, North-Carolina and South–Carolina, justly alarmed at these arbitrary proceedings of parliament and administration, have severally elected, constituted, and appointed deputies to meet, and sit in general Congress, in the city of Philadelphia, in order to obtain such establishment, as that their religion, laws, and liberties, may not be subverted: Whereupon the deputies so appointed being now assembled, in a full and free representation of these colonies, taking into their most serious consideration, the best means of attaining the ends aforesaid, do, in the first place, as Englishmen, their ancestors in like cases have usually done, for asserting and vindicating their rights and liberties, DECLARE,

That the inhabitants of the English colonies in North–America, by the immutable laws of nature, the principles of the English constitution, and the several charters or compacts, have the following RIGHTS:

Resolved, N.C.D. 1. That they are entitled to life, liberty and property: and they have never ceded to any foreign power whatever, a right to dispose of either without their consent.

Resolved, N.C.D. 2. That our ancestors, who first settled these colonies, were at the time of their emigration from the mother country, entitled to all the rights, liberties, and immunities of free and natural-born subjects, within the realm of England.

Resolved, N.C.D. 3. That by such emigration they by no means forfeited, surrendered, or lost any of those rights, but that they were, and their descendants now are, entitled to the exercise and enjoyment of all such of them, as their local and other circumstances enable them to exercise and enjoy.

Resolved, 4. That the foundation of English liberty, and of all free government, is a right in the people to participate in their legislative council: and as the English colonists are not represented, and from their local and other circumstances, cannot properly be represented in the British parliament, they are entitled to a free and exclusive power of legislation in their several provincial legislatures, where their right of representation can alone be preserved, in all cases of taxation and internal polity, subject only to the negative of their sovereign, in such manner as has been heretofore used and accustomed: But, from the necessity of the case, and a regard to the mutual interest of both countries, we cheerfully consent to the operation of such acts of the British parliament, as are bonfide, restrained to the regulation of our external commerce, for the purpose of securing the commercial advantages of the whole empire to the mother country, and the commercial benefits of its respective members; excluding every idea of taxation internal or external, for raising a revenue on the subjects, in America, without their consent.

Resolved, N.C.D. 5. That the respective colonies are entitled to the common law of England, and more especially to the great and inestimable privilege of being tried by their peers of the vicinage, according to the course of that law.

Resolved, N.C.D. 6. That they are entitled to the benefit of such of the English statutes, as existed at the time of their colonization; and which they have, by experience, respectively found to be applicable to their several local and other circumstances.

Resolved, N.C.D. 7. That these, his Majesty's colonies, are likewise entitled to all the immunities and privileges granted and confirmed to them by royal charters, or secured by their several codes of provincial laws.

Resolved, N.C.D. 8. That they have a right peaceably to assemble, consider of their grievances, and petition the king; and that all prosecutions, prohibitory proclamations, and commitments for the same, are illegal.

Resolved, N.C.D. 9. That the keeping a standing army in these colonies, in times of peace, without the consent of the legislature of that colony, in which such army is kept, is against law.

Resolved, N.C.D. 10. It is indispensably necessary to good government, and rendered essential by the English constitution, that the constituent branches of the legislature be independent of each other; that, therefore, the exercise of legislative power in several colonies, by a council appointed, during pleasure, by the crown, is unconstitutional, dangerous and destructive to the freedom of American legislation.

All and each of which the aforesaid deputies, in behalf of themselves, and their constituents, do claim, demand, and insist on, as their indubitable rights and liberties, which cannot be legally taken from them, altered or abridged by any power whatever, without their own consent, by their representatives in their several provincial legislature.

In the course of our inquiry, we find many infringements and violations of the foregoing rights, which, from an ardent desire, that harmony and mutual intercourse of affection and interest may be restored, we pass over for the present, and proceed to state such acts and measures as have been adopted since the last war, which demonstrate a system formed to enslave America.

Resolved, N.C.D. That the following acts of parliament are infringements and violations of the rights of the colonists; and that the repeal of them is essentially necessary, in order to restore harmony between Great Britain and the American colonies, viz.

The several acts of Geo. III. ch. 15, and ch. 34.–5 Geo. III. ch.25.–6 Geo. ch. 52.–7 Geo.III. ch. 41 and ch. 46.–8 Geo. III. ch. 22. which impose duties for the purpose of raising a revenue in America, extend the power of the admiralty courts beyond their ancient limits, deprive the American subject of trial by jury, authorize the judges certificate to indemnify the prosecutor from damages, that he might otherwise be liable to, requiring oppressive security from a claimant of ships and goods seized, before he shall be allowed to defend his property, and are subversive of American rights.

Also 12 Geo. III. ch. 24, intituled, “An act for the better securing his majesty’s dockyards, magazines, ships, ammunition, and stores,” which declares a new offence in America, and deprives the American subject of a constitutional trial by jury of the vicinage, by authorizing the trial of any person, charged with the committing any offence described in the said act, out of the realm, to be indicted and tried for the same in any shire or county within the realm.

Also the three acts passed in the last session of parliament, for stopping the port and blocking up the harbour of Boston, for altering the charter and government of Massachusetts–Bay, and that which is entitled, “An act for the better administration of justice, etc.”

Also the act passed in the same session for establishing the Roman Catholic religion, in the province of Quebec, abolishing the equitable system of English laws, and erecting a tyranny there, to the great danger (from so total a dissimilarity of religion, law and government) of the neighboring British colonies, by the assistance of whose blood and treasure the said country was conquered from France.

Also the act passed in the same session, for the better providing suitable quarters for officers and soldiers in his majesty’s service, in North–America.

Also, that the keeping a standing army in several of these colonies, in time of peace, without the consent of the legislature of that colony, in which such army is kept, is against law.

To these grievous acts and measures, Americans cannot submit, but in hopes their fellow subjects in Great Britain will, on a revision of them, restore us to that state, in which both countries found happiness and prosperity, we have for the present, only resolved to pursue the following peaceable measures: 1. To enter into a non-importation, non-consumption, and non-exportation agreement or association. 2. To prepare an address to the people of Great–Britain, and a memorial to the inhabitants of British America: and 3. To prepare a loyal address to his majesty, agreeable to resolutions already entered into.

Appendix III

The Declaration of Independence

IN CONGRESS, July 4, 1776.

The unanimous Declaration of the thirteen united States of America,

When in the Course of human events, it becomes necessary for one people to dissolve the political bands which have connected them with another, and to assume among the powers of the earth, the separate and equal station to which the Laws of Nature and of Nature's God entitle them, a decent respect to the opinions of mankind requires that they should declare the causes which impel them to the separation.

We hold these truths to be self-evident, that all men are created equal, that they are endowed by their Creator with certain unalienable Rights, that among these are Life, Liberty and the pursuit of Happiness.—That to secure these rights, Governments are instituted among Men, deriving their just powers from the consent of the governed,—That whenever any Form of Government becomes destructive of these ends, it is the Right of the People to alter or to abolish it, and to institute new Government, laying its foundation on such principles and organizing its powers in such form, as to them shall seem most likely to effect their Safety and Happiness. Prudence, indeed, will dictate that Governments long established should not be changed for light and transient causes; and accordingly all experience hath shewn, that mankind are more disposed to suffer, while evils are sufferable, than to right themselves by abolishing the forms to which they are accustomed. But when a long train of abuses and usurpations, pursuing invariably the same Object evinces a design to reduce them under absolute Despotism, it is their right, it is their duty, to throw off such Government, and to provide new Guards for their future security.—Such has been the patient sufferance of these Colonies; and such is now the necessity which constrains them to alter their former Systems of Government. The history of the present King of Great Britain is a history of repeated injuries and usurpations, all having in direct object the establishment of an absolute Tyranny over these States. To prove this, let Facts be submitted to a candid world.

He has refused his Assent to Laws, the most wholesome and necessary for the public good.

He has forbidden his Governors to pass Laws of immediate and pressing importance, unless suspended in their operation till his Assent should be obtained; and when so suspended, he has utterly neglected to attend to them.

He has refused to pass other Laws for the accommodation of large districts of people, unless those people would relinquish the right of Representation in the Legislature, a right inestimable to them and formidable to tyrants only.

He has called together legislative bodies at places unusual, uncomfortable, and distant from the depository of their public Records, for the sole purpose of fatiguing them into compliance with his measures.

He has dissolved Representative Houses repeatedly, for opposing with manly firmness his invasions on the rights of the people.

He has refused for a long time, after such dissolutions, to cause others to be elected; whereby the Legislative powers, incapable of Annihilation, have returned to the People at large for their exercise; the State remaining in the mean time exposed to all the dangers of invasion from without, and convulsions within.

He has endeavoured to prevent the population of these States; for that purpose obstructing the Laws for Naturalization of Foreigners; refusing to pass others to encourage their migrations hither, and raising the conditions of new Appropriations of Lands.

He has obstructed the Administration of Justice, by refusing his Assent to Laws for establishing Judiciary powers.

He has made Judges dependent on his Will alone, for the tenure of their offices, and the amount and payment of their salaries.

He has erected a multitude of New Offices, and sent hither swarms of Officers to harrass our people, and eat out their substance.

He has kept among us, in times of peace, Standing Armies without the Consent of our legislatures.

He has affected to render the Military independent of and superior to the Civil power.

He has combined with others to subject us to a jurisdiction foreign to our constitution, and unacknowledged by our laws; giving his Assent to their Acts of pretended Legislation:

For Quartering large bodies of armed troops among us:

For protecting them, by a mock Trial, from punishment for any Murders which they should commit on the Inhabitants of these States:

For cutting off our Trade with all parts of the world:

For imposing Taxes on us without our Consent:

For depriving us in many cases, of the benefits of Trial by Jury:

For transporting us beyond Seas to be tried for pretended offences:

For abolishing the free System of English Laws in a neighbouring Province, establishing therein an Arbitrary government, and enlarging its Boundaries so as to render it at once an example and fit instrument for introducing the same absolute rule into these Colonies:

For taking away our Charters, abolishing our most valuable Laws, and altering fundamentally the Forms of our Governments:

For suspending our own Legislatures, and declaring themselves invested with power to legislate for us in all cases whatsoever.

He has abdicated Government here, by declaring us out of his Protection and waging War against us.

He has plundered our seas, ravaged our Coasts, burnt our towns, and destroyed the lives of our people.

He is at this time transporting large Armies of foreign Mercenaries to compleat the works of death, desolation and tyranny, already begun with circumstances of Cruelty & perfidy scarcely paralleled in the most barbarous ages, and totally unworthy the Head of a civilized nation.

He has constrained our fellow Citizens taken Captive on the high Seas to bear Arms against their Country, to become the executioners of their friends and Brethren, or to fall themselves by their Hands.

He has excited domestic insurrections amongst us, and has endeavoured to bring on the inhabitants of our frontiers, the merciless Indian Savages, whose known rule of warfare, is an undistinguished destruction of all ages, sexes and conditions.

In every stage of these Oppressions We have Petitioned for Redress in the most humble terms: Our repeated Petitions have been answered only by repeated injury. A Prince whose character is thus marked by every act which may define a Tyrant, is unfit to be the ruler of a free people.

Nor have We been wanting in attentions to our Brittish brethren. We have warned them from time to time of attempts by their legislature to extend an unwarrantable jurisdiction over us. We have reminded them of the circumstances of our emigration and settlement here. We have appealed to their native justice and magnanimity, and we have conjured them by the ties of our common kindred to disavow these usurpations, which would inevitably interrupt our connections and correspondence. They too have been deaf to the voice of justice and of consanguinity. We must, therefore, acquiesce in the necessity, which denounces our Separation, and hold them, as we hold the rest of mankind, Enemies in War, in Peace Friends.

We, therefore, the Representatives of the united States of America, in General Congress, Assembled, appealing to the Supreme Judge of the world for the rectitude of our intentions, do, in the Name, and by Authority of the good People of these Colonies, solemnly publish and declare, That these United Colonies are, and of Right ought to be Free and Independent States; that they are Absolved from all Allegiance to the British Crown, and that all political connection between them and the State of Great Britain, is and ought to be totally dissolved; and that as Free and Independent States, they have full Power to levy War, conclude Peace, contract Alliances, establish Commerce, and to do all other Acts and Things which Independent States may of right do. And for the support of this Declaration, with a firm reliance on the protection of divine Providence, we mutually pledge to each other our Lives, our Fortunes and our sacred Honor.

Appendix IV

The Articles of Confederation

To all to whom these Presents shall come, we the undersigned Delegates of the States affixed to our Names send greeting.

Articles of Confederation and perpetual Union between the states of New Hampshire, Massachusetts Bay, Rhode Island and Providence Plantations, Connecticut, New York, New Jersey, Pennsylvania, Delaware, Maryland, Virginia, North Carolina, South Carolina and Georgia.

I.

The style of this confederacy shall be "The United States of America".

II.

Each state retains its sovereignty, freedom, and independence, and every power, jurisdiction, and right, which is not by this confederation expressly delegated to the United States, in Congress assembled.

III.

The said states hereby severally enter into a firm league of friendship with each other, for their common defense, the security of their liberties, and their mutual and general welfare, binding themselves to assist each other, against all force offered to, or attacks made upon them, or any of them, on account of religion, sovereignty, trade, or any other pretense whatever.

IV.

The better to secure and perpetuate mutual friendship and intercourse among the people of the different states in this union, the free inhabitants of each of these states, paupers, vagabonds, and fugitives from justice excepted, shall be entitled to all privileges and immunities of free citizens in the several states; and the people of each state shall have free ingress and regress to and from any other state, and shall enjoy therein all the privileges of trade and commerce, subject to the same duties, impositions, and restrictions as the inhabitants thereof respectively. Provided that such restrictions shall not extend so far as to prevent the removal of property imported into any state to any other state of which the owner is an inhabitant; provided also, that no imposition, duties, or restriction, shall be laid by any state on the property of the United States, or either of them.

If any person guilty of or charged with treason, felony, or other high misdemeanor, in any state, shall flee from justice, and be found in any of the United States, he shall, upon demand of the Governor or executive power of the state from which he fled, be delivered up, and removed to the state having jurisdiction of his offense.

Full faith and credit shall be given in each of these states to the records, acts, and judicial proceedings, of the courts and magistrates of every other state.

V.

For the most convenient management of the general interests of the United States, delegates shall be annually appointed in such manner as the legislatures of each state shall direct, to meet in Congress on the first Monday in November, in every year, with a power reserved to each state to recall its delegates, or any of them, at any time within the year, and to send others in their stead for the remainder of the year.

No state shall be represented in Congress by less than two, nor more than seven members; and no person shall be capable of being a delegate for more than three years in any term of six years; nor shall any person, being a delegate, be capable of holding any office under the United States, for which he, or another for his benefit, receives any salary, fees or emolument of any kind.

Each state shall maintain its own delegates in a meeting of the states, and while they act as members of the committee of the states.

In determining questions in the United States in Congress assembled, each state shall have one vote.

Freedom of speech and debate in Congress shall not be impeached or questioned in any court or place out of Congress, and the members of Congress shall be protected in their persons from arrests or imprisonments, during the time of their going to and from, and attendance on Congress, except for treason, felony, or breach of the peace.

VI.

No state, without the consent of the United States in Congress assembled, shall send any embassy to, or receive any embassy from, or enter into any conference, agreement, alliance or treaty with any king, prince or state; nor shall any person holding any office of profit or trust under the United States, or any of them, accept any present, emolument, office or title of any kind whatever from any king, prince or foreign state; nor shall the United States in Congress assembled, or any of them, grant any title of nobility.

No two or more states shall enter into any treaty, confederation or alliance whatever between them, without the consent of the United States in Congress assembled, specifying accurately the purposes for which the same is to be entered into, and how long it shall continue.

No state shall lay any imposts or duties, which may interfere with any stipulations in treaties, entered into by the United States in Congress assembled, with any king, prince or state, in pursuance of any treaties already proposed by Congress, to the courts of France and Spain.

No vessel of war shall be kept up in time of peace by any state, except such number only, as shall be deemed necessary by the United States in Congress assembled, for the defense of such state, or its trade; nor shall any body of forces be kept up by any state in time of peace, except such number only, as in the judgement of the United States in Congress assembled, shall be deemed requisite to garrison the forts necessary for the defense of such state; but every state shall always keep up a well-regulated and disciplined militia, sufficiently armed and accoutered, and shall provide and constantly have ready for use, in public stores, a due number of field pieces and tents, and a proper quantity of arms, ammunition and camp equipage.

No state shall engage in any war without the consent of the United States in Congress assembled, unless such state be actually invaded by enemies, or shall have received certain advice of a resolution being formed by some nation of Indians to invade such state, and the danger is so imminent as not to admit of a delay till the United States in Congress assembled can be consulted; nor shall any state grant commissions to any ships or vessels of war, nor letters of marque or reprisal, except it be after a declaration of war by the United States in Congress assembled, and then only against the kingdom or state and the subjects thereof, against which war has been so declared, and under such regulations as shall be established by the United States in Congress assembled, unless such state be infested by pirates, in which case vessels of war may be fitted out for that occasion, and kept so long as the danger shall continue, or until the United States in Congress assembled shall determine otherwise.

VII.

When land forces are raised by any state for the common defense, all officers of or under the rank of colonel shall be appointed by the legislature of each state respectively by whom such forces shall be raised, or in such manner as such state shall direct, and all vacancies shall be filled up by the state which first made the appointment.

VIII.

All charges of war, and all other expenses that shall be incurred for the common defense or general welfare, and allowed by the United States in Congress assembled, shall be defrayed out of a common treasury, which shall be supplied by the several states in proportion to the value of all land within each state, granted or surveyed for any person, as such land and the buildings and improvements thereon shall be estimated according to such mode as the United States in Congress assembled, shall from time to time direct and appoint.

The taxes for paying that proportion shall be laid and levied by the authority and direction of the legislatures of the several states within the time agreed upon by the United States in Congress assembled.

IX.

The United States in Congress assembled shall have the sole and exclusive right and power of determining on peace and war, except in the cases mentioned in the sixth article—of sending and receiving ambassadors—entering into treaties and alliances, provided that no treaty of commerce shall be made whereby the legislative power of the respective states shall be restrained from imposing such imposts and duties on foreigners, as their own people are subjected to, or from prohibiting the exportation or importation of any species of goods or commodities whatsoever—of establishing rules for deciding in all cases, what captures on land or water shall be legal, and in what manner prizes taken by land or naval forces in the service of the United States shall be divided or appropriated—of granting letters of marque and reprisal in times of peace—appointing courts for the trial of piracies and felonies committed on the high seas and establishing courts for receiving and determining finally appeals in all cases of captures, provided that no member of Congress shall be appointed a judge of any of the said courts. The United States in Congress assembled shall also be the last resort on appeal in all disputes and differences now subsisting or that hereafter may arise between two or more states concerning boundary, jurisdiction, or any other causes whatever; which authority shall always be exercised in the manner following. Whenever the legislative or executive authority or lawful agent of any state in controversy with another shall present a petition to Congress, stating the matter in question, and praying for a hearing, notice thereof shall be given by order of Congress to the legislative or executive authority of the other state in controversy, and a day assigned for the appearance of the parties by their lawful agents, who shall then be directed to appoint, by joint consent, commissioners or judges to constitute a court for hearing and determining the matter in question; but if they cannot agree, Congress shall name three persons out of each of the United States, and from the list of such persons each party shall alternately strike out one, the petitioners beginning, until the number shall be reduced to thirteen, and from that number not less than seven, nor more than nine names, as Congress shall direct, shall in the presence of Congress be drawn out by lot, and the persons whose names shall be so drawn, or any five of them, shall be commissioners, or judges, to hear and finally determine the controversy, so always as a major part of the judges who shall hear the cause shall agree in the determination. And if either party shall neglect to attend at the day appointed, without showing reasons which Congress shall judge sufficient, or being present shall refuse to strike, the Congress shall proceed to nominate three persons out of each state, and the secretary of Congress shall strike in behalf of such party absent or refusing; and the judgement and sentence of the court to be appointed, in the manner before prescribed, shall be final and conclusive. And if any of the parties shall refuse to submit to the authority of such court, or to appear or defend their claim or cause, the court shall nevertheless proceed to pronounce sentence, or judgement, which shall in like manner be final and decisive, the judgement or sentence and other proceedings being in either case transmitted to Congress, and lodged among the acts of Congress for the security of the parties concerned. Provided, that every commissioner, before he sits in judgement, shall take an oath to be administered by one of the judges of the supreme or superior court of the state where the cause shall be tried, "well and truly to hear and determine the matter in question, according to the best of his judgement, without favor, affection or hope of reward." Provided also, that no state shall be deprived of territory for the benefit of the United States.

All controversies concerning the private right of soil claimed under different grants of two or more states, whose jurisdictions as they may respect such lands, and the states which passed such grants are adjusted, the said grants or either of them being at the same time claimed to have originated antecedent to such settlement of jurisdiction, shall on the petition of either party to the Congress of the United States, be finally determined as near as may be in the same manner as is before prescribed for deciding disputes respecting territorial jurisdiction between different states.

The United States in Congress assembled shall also have the sole and exclusive right and power of regulating the alloy and value of coin struck by their own authority, or by that of the respective states—fixing the standards of weights and measures throughout the United States—regulating the trade and managing all affairs with the Indians, not members of any of the states, provided that the legislative right of any state within its own limits be not infringed or violated—establishing or regulating post offices from one state to another, throughout all the United States, and exacting such postage on the papers passing through the same as may be requisite to defray the expenses of the said office—appointing all officers of the land forces in the service of the United States, excepting regimental officers—appointing all the officers of the naval forces, and commissioning all officers whatever in the service of the United States—making rules for the government and regulation of the said land and naval forces, and directing their operations.

The United States in Congress assembled shall have authority to appoint a committee to sit in the recess of Congress, to be denominated "A committee of the states," and to consist of one delegate from each state, and to appoint such other committees and civil officers as may be necessary for managing the general affairs of the United States under their direction—to appoint one of their members to preside, provided that no person be allowed to serve in the office of president more than one year in any term of three years; to ascertain the necessary sums of money to be raised for the service of the United States, and to appropriate and apply the same for defraying the public expenses—to borrow money, or emit bills on the credit of the United States, transmitting every half-year to the respective states an account of the sums of money so borrowed or emitted—to build and equip a navy—to agree upon the number of land forces, and to make requisitions from each state for its quota, in proportion to the number of white inhabitants in such state; which requisition shall be binding, and thereupon the legislature of each state shall appoint the regimental officers, raise the men and clothe, arm and equip them in a solid-like manner, at the expense of the United States; and the officers and men so clothed, armed and equipped shall march to the place appointed, and within the time agreed on by the United States in Congress assembled. But if the United States in Congress assembled shall, on consideration of circumstances, judge proper that any state should not raise men, or should raise a smaller number of men than the quota thereof, such extra number shall be raised, officered, clothed, armed and equipped in the same manner as the quota of each state, unless the legislature of such state shall judge that such extra number cannot be safely spread out in the same, in which case they shall raise, officer, clothe, arm and equip as many of such extra number as they judge can be safely spared. And the officers and men so clothed, armed, and equipped, shall march to the place appointed, and within the time agreed on by the United States in Congress assembled.

The United States in Congress assembled shall never engage in a war, nor grant letters of marque or reprisal in time of peace, nor enter into any treaties or alliances, nor coin money, nor regulate the value thereof, nor ascertain the sums and expenses necessary for the defense and welfare of the United States, or any of them, nor emit bills, nor borrow money on the credit of the United States, nor appropriate money, nor agree upon the number of vessels of war to be built or purchased, or the number of land or sea forces to be raised, nor appoint a commander in chief of the army or navy, unless nine states assent to the same; nor shall a question on any other point, except for adjourning from day to day be determined, unless by the votes of the majority of the United States in Congress assembled.

The Congress of the United States shall have power to adjourn to any time within the year, and to any place within the United States, so that no period of adjournment be for a longer duration than the space of six months, and shall publish the journal of their proceedings monthly, except such parts thereof relating to treaties, alliances or military operations, as in their judgement require secrecy; and the yeas and nays of the delegates of each state on any question shall be entered on the journal, when it is desired by any delegates of a state, or any of them, at his or their request shall be furnished with a transcript of the said journal, except such parts as are above excepted, to lay before the legislatures of the several states.

X.

The committee of the states, or any nine of them, shall be authorized to execute, in the recess of Congress, such of the powers of Congress as the United States in Congress assembled, by the consent of the nine states, shall from time to time think expedient to vest them with; provided that no power be delegated to the said committee, for the exercise of which, by the articles of confederation, the voice of nine states in the Congress of the United States assembled be requisite.

XI.

Canada acceding to this confederation, and adjoining in the measures of the United States, shall be admitted into, and entitled to all the advantages of this union; but no other colony shall be admitted into the same, unless such admission be agreed to by nine states.

XII.

All bills of credit emitted, monies borrowed, and debts contracted by, or under the authority of Congress, before the assembling of the United States, in pursuance of the present confederation, shall be deemed and considered as a charge against the United States, for payment and satisfaction whereof the said United States, and the public faith are hereby solemnly pledged.

XIII.

Every State shall abide by the determination of the United States in Congress assembled on all questions which by this confederation are submitted to them. And the articles of this confederation shall be inviolably observed by every state, and the union shall be perpetual; nor shall any alteration at any time hereafter be made in any of them; unless such alteration be agreed to in a Congress of the United States, and be afterwards confirmed by the legislatures of every state.

Agreed to by Congress 15 November 1777. In force after ratification by Maryland, 1 March 1781.

*

Appendix V

Timeline of Historic Events and Judicial Decisions

Historical Event	Supreme Court Chief Justice	Famous Case
(1607) Jamestown settled		
(1619) First slaves imported to Jamestown		
(1620) Pilgrims land at Plymouth Rock		
(1623) New Hampshire colony formed		
(1634) Maryland is founded as a British colony for Catholics		
(1636) Roger Williams founds the Providence Plantation (Rhode Island); Connecticut Colony formed		
(1663) The King of England grants the Carolinas to 8 noblemen		
(1664) New York and New Jersey become British colonies after seizure from the Dutch		
(1681) William Penn founds the Pennsylvania colony as a haven for Quakers		
(1729) The Carolinas split into North and South Carolina, the former largely poor tobacco farmers and the latter largely rich plantation owners		
(1732) The Georgia colony founded by James Oglethorpe		
(1754) French and Indian War begins		
(1763) French and Indian War ends; Canada becomes a British possession		

Historical Event	Supreme Court Chief Justice	Famous Case
(1770) Boston Massacre; population of colonies reaches 2 million (1773) Boston Tea Party (1774) First Continental Congress meets (1775) Battles of Lexington and Concord; Revolutionary War begins (1777) Articles of Confederation drafted (1781) Articles of Confederation ratified; British General Cornwallis surrenders to the Americans at Yorktown (1783) The Treaty of Paris signed, thus initiating the end of the Revolutionary War (1784) Continental Congress ratifies the Treaty of Paris (1785) Land Ordinance of 1785 passed (1787) Constitutional Convention; Delaware first to ratify the Constitution, followed by Pennsylvania, and New Jersey		

Historical Event	Supreme Court Chief Justice	Famous Case
(1788) Georgia, Connecticut, Massachusetts, Maryland, South Carolina, New Hampshire, Virginia and New York ratify the Constitution making it the law of the land, replacing the Articles of Confederation		
(1789) George Washington inaugurated as first President; North Carolina ratifies the Constitution; Judiciary Act of 1789	1789 John Jay appointed Chief Justice by George Washington	
(1790) Rhode Island ratifies the constitution; U.S. population reaches 3.9 million (including slaves)		
(1791) The Bill of Rights is ratified; First Bank of the United States chartered; The Republic of Vermont becomes the 14th state		
(1792) Kentucky (formerly part of Virginia) becomes the 15th state		
(1793) Fugitive Slave Act passed		

Historical Event	Supreme Court Chief Justice	Famous Case
(1795) 11th Amendment		
(1796) Tennessee (formerly part of North Carolina) becomes a state	1796 Oliver Ellsworth appointed Chief Justice by George Washington	
(1797) John Adams inaugurated President with Jefferson as Vice President		
(1800) Library of Congress founded		
(1801) Thomas Jefferson becomes President	1801 John Marshall appointed Chief Justice by John Adams	
(1803) Louisiana Purchase Treaty; Ohio becomes a state		*Marbury v. Madison*, 5 U.S. 137 (1803)
(1804) 12th Amendment; Lewis and Clark set out		

Historical Event	Supreme Court Chief Justice	Famous Case
(1808) U.S. slave trade with Africa ends		
(1809) James Madison becomes President		
(1814) British burn Washington; the *Star Spangled Banner* composed by Francis Scott Key while captive aboard a British ship		
(1816) Indiana becomes a state; Second Bank of the United States chartered		
(1817) James Monroe becomes President; Mississippi becomes a state		
(1818) Illinois becomes a state		
(1819) Alabama becomes a state		*McCulloch v. Maryland*, 17 U.S. 316 (1819)
(1820) Missouri Compromise; Maine becomes a state		
(1821) Missouri becomes a state		
(1829) Andrew Jackson becomes President		*Gibbons v. Ogden*, 22 U.S. 1 (1824)
(1831) Nat Turner's revolt		
(1835) Texas War for Independence begins		
(1836) Battle of the Alamo; Arkansas becomes a state	1836 Roger Taney appointed Chief Justice by Andrew Jackson	

Historical Event	Supreme Court Chief Justice	Famous Case
(1837) Michigan becomes a state; first coeducation in the United States occurs at Oberlin College		
(1845) Florida and Texas become states		
(1846) The United States declares war on Mexico; Iowa becomes a state		
(1848) Treaty of Guadalupe Hidalgo ends war; Mexico cedes California, Nevada, Utah, and parts of Colorado, Arizona, and New Mexico; Wisconsin becomes a state		
(1849) California Gold Rush begins		
(1850) California becomes a state		
		Dred Scott v. Sandford, 60 U.S. 393 (1857)
(1858) Minnesota becomes a state; Lincoln–Douglas Debates		
(1859) Oregon becomes a state		
(1861) Abraham Lincoln becomes President; the Confederacy is established; Civil War begins at Fort Sumter, South Carolina		
(1862) Battle of Antietam; Lincoln issues Emancipation Proclamation		
(1863) Battle of Gettysburg; West Virginia joins the Union		

Historical Event	Supreme Court Chief Justice	Famous Case
(1864) Nevada becomes a state	 1864 Salmon P. Chase appointed Chief Justice by Abraham Lincoln	
(1865) Abraham Lincoln assassinated; Andrew Johnson becomes President; Civil War ends; 13th Amendment		
(1866) Civil Rights Act of 1866; Ku Klux Klan founded		
(1867) Reconstruction Acts; Alaska Purchase from Russia; Nebraska becomes a state		
(1868) 14th Amendment		
(1869) Wyoming grants voting rights to women		
(1870) 15th Amendment		*Slaughterhouse Cases*, 83 U.S. 36 (1873)

Historical Event	Supreme Court Chief Justice	Famous Case
	1874 Morrison Waite appointed Chief Justice by Ulysses S. Grant	
(1875) Civil Rights Act of 1875		
(1876) Colorado becomes a state; telephone invented by Alexander Graham Bell		
(1879) Light bulb invented by Thomas Edison		
(1880) U.S. population exceeds 50 million		
		Civil Rights Cases, 109 U.S. 3 (1883)
(1887) Interstate Commerce Commission created		
	1888 Melville Fuller appointed Chief Justice by Grover Cleveland	

Historical Event	Supreme Court Chief Justice	Famous Case
(1889) North Dakota, South Dakota, Montana, and Washington become states		
(1890) Sherman Antitrust Act; Idaho and Wyoming become states		
(1892) Sierra Club founded		
(1896) Utah becomes a state		*Plessy v. Ferguson*, 163 U.S. 537 (1896)
(1898) Spanish-American War; the United States obtains Guam, Puerto Rico, and the Philippines and grants Cuba independence		
(1900) U.S. population exceeds 75 million		
(1901) Theodore Roosevelt becomes President		
(1903) Ford Motor Company formed; Department of Commerce and Labor created		
		Lochner v. New York, 198 U.S. 45 (1905)
(1907) Oklahoma becomes a state		
(1908) Federal Bureau of Investigation established		
(1909) William Howard Taft becomes President; NAACP founded by W. E. B. DuBois		

Historical Event	Supreme Court Chief Justice	Famous Case
	1910 Edward Douglass White appointed Chief Justice by William Howard Taft	
(1912) New Mexico and Arizona become states		
(1913) Woodrow Wilson becomes President		
(1914) Ludlow Massacre		
(1917) U.S. enters World War I; Espionage and Sedition Acts		
(1919) World War I ends but United States Senate rejects Treaty of Versailles creating League of Nations		*Schenck v. United States*, 249 U.S. 47 (1919)
(1920) 19th Amendment; U.S. population tops 100 million; First radio broadcast		
	1921 William Howard Taft appointed Chief Justice by Warren G. Harding	

Historical Event	Supreme Court Chief Justice	Famous Case
		Pennsylvania Coal v. Mahon, 260 U.S. 393 (1922)
(1929) Great Depression begins		
	1930 Charles Evans Hughes appointed Chief Justice by Herbert Hoover	
(1933) Franklin Delano Roosevelt becomes President; Agricultural Adjustment Act; 21st Amendment		*Nebbia v. New York*, 291 U.S. 502 (1934) *United States v. Curtiss Wright Export Corp*, 299 U.S. 304 (1936)
(1941) Attack on Pearl Harbor; U.S. enters World War II; Japanese–American internment begins		

Historical Event	Supreme Court Chief Justice	Famous Case
	1941 Harlan Fiske Stone appointed Chief Justice by Franklin Delano Roosevelt	
		Chaplinsky v. New Hampshire, 315 U.S. 368 (1942) *Wickard v. Filburn*, 317 U.S. 111 (1942)
(1944) D–Day; Battle of the Bulge		
(1945) Franklin Delano Roosevelt dies; Harry S. Truman becomes President; atomic bomb dropped on Hiroshima and Nagasaki; World War II ends as Germany and Japan surrender; United Nations created		
	1946 Fred M. Vinson appointed Chief Justice by Harry S. Truman	

Historical Event	Supreme Court Chief Justice	Famous Case
(1948) Truman desegregates armed forces		
(1949) North Atlantic Treaty Organization (NATO) formed		
(1950) Korean War begins		
		Youngstown Sheet & Tube Co. v. Sawyer, 343 U.S. 579 (1952)
(1953) Dwight D. Eisenhower becomes President		
	1953 Earl Warren appointed Chief Justiceby Dwight D. Eisenhower	
		Brown v. Board of Education of Topeka, 347 U.S. 483 (1954)
(1957) School desegregation in Little Rock, Arkansas; Russians launch first space satellite		
(1959) Alaska and Hawaii become states		
(1961) John F. Kennedy becomes President; Peace Corps founded; Bay of Pigs Invasion; Vietnam War officially begins		
(1962) Cuban Missile Crisis		

Historical Event	Supreme Court Chief Justice	Famous Case
(1963) John F. Kennedy assassinated; Lyndon Johnson becomes President; Martin Luther King, Jr. "I have a dream" speech during the March on Washington (1964) Civil Rights Act of 1964 (1965) Voting Rights Act (1968) Martin Luther King Jr. assassinated; Robert F. Kennedy assassinated		*New York Times v. Sullivan*, 376 U.S. 254 (1964) *Reynolds v. Sims*, 377 U.S. 533 (1964) *Griswold v. Connecticut*, 381 U.S. 479 (1965) *United States v. O'Brien*, 391 U.S. 367(1968)
(1969) Richard Nixon becomes President; Neil Armstrong walks on the moon (1970) Environmental Protection Agency created	1969 Warren E. Burger appointed Chief Justice by Richard Nixon	*Brandenburg v. Ohio*, 395 U.S. 444 (1969) *Lemon v. Kurtzman*, 403 U.S. 602 (1971) *Swann v. Charlotte–Mecklenburg Board of Education*, 402 U.S. 1 (1971) *Cohen v. California*, 403 U.S. 15 (1971) *Miller v. California*, 413 U.S. 15 (1973) *Roe v. Wade* 410 U.S. 113 (1973)

Historical Event	Supreme Court Chief Justice	Famous Case
(1974) Richard Nixon resigns Presidency; Gerald R. Ford becomes President		*United States v. Nixon*, 418 U.S. 683 (1974)
(1975) Last American troops leave Vietnam		
		Buckley v. Valeo, 424 U.S. 1 (1976) *Washington v. Davis*, 426 U.S. 229 (1976)
(1977) Jimmy Carter becomes President		
		Penn Central Transportation Co. v. New York City, 438 U.S. 104 (1978) *Regents of the University of California v. Bakke*, 438 U.S. 265 (1978)
(1979) Three Mile Island nuclear accident		
(1980) John Lennon assassinated		*Central Hudson Gas v. Public Service Commission of New York*, 447 U.S. 557 (1980)
(1981) Ronald Reagan becomes President		
		Immigration and Naturalization Service v. Chadha, 462 U.S. 919 (1983) *Garcia v. San Antonio Metropolitan Transit Authority*, 469 U.S. 528 (1984)
(1986) Space Shuttle Challenger accident		

Historical Event	Supreme Court Chief Justice	Famous Case
	1986 William Rehnquist appointed Chief Justice by Ronald Reagan	*Bowers v. Hardwick*, 478 U.S. 186 (1986)
(1989) George H. W. Bush becomes President; Exxon Valdez oil spill		*Morrison v. Olson*, 487 U.S. 654 (1988) *Richmond v. J.A. Croson Co.*, 488 U.S. 469 (1989) *Employment Division v. Smith*, 494 U.S. 872 (1990)
(1991) Gulf War		*Lucas v. South Carolina Coastal Council*, 505 U.S. 1003 (1992) *New York v. United States*, 505 U.S. 144 (1992) *Planned Parenthood of Southeastern Pennsylvania v. Casey*, 505 U.S. 833 (1992)
(1993) Bill Clinton becomes President; World Trade Center bombing		*United States v. Lopez*, 514 U.S. 549 (1995)
(1999) Senate acquits Bill Clinton in impeachment trial		*Bush v. Gore*, 531 U.S. 98 (2000)
(2001) George W. Bush becomes President; Terrorists attack World Trade Center and The Pentagon; Invasion of Afghanistan		

Historical Event	Supreme Court Chief Justice	Famous Case
(2003) Invasion of Iraq (2005) Hurricane Katrina	2005 John Roberts appointed Chief Justice by George W. Bush	*Grutter and Gratz v. Bollinger*, 539 U.S. 306 (2003) *Lawrence v. Texas*, 539 U.S. 558 (2003)

*

Appendix VI

Membership of Supreme Court

(Bolded names reflect newly appointed members of Court)

Appendix VI – Membership of Supreme Court
(Bolded names reflect newly appointed members of Court)

Court Term	President	Chief Justice	Seat 2	Seat 3	Seat 4	Seat 5	Seat 6	Seat 7	Seat 8	Seat 9	Seat 10
1789	George Washington	**Jay**	**Rutledge**	**Cushing**	**Wilson**	**Blair**					
1790-91	George Washington	Jay	Rutledge	Cushing	Wilson	Blair	**Iredell**				
1791-93	George Washington	Jay	**Johnson**	Cushing	Wilson	Blair	Iredell				
1793-95	George Washington	Jay	**Patterson**	Cushing	Wilson	Blair	Iredell				
1795-96	George Washington	**Rutledge**	Patterson	Cushing	Wilson	Blair	Iredell				
1796-99	George Washington	**Ellsworth**	Patterson	Cushing	Wilson	**Chase**	Iredell				
1799-1800	John Adams	Ellsworth	Patterson	Cushing	**Washington**	Chase	Iredell				
1800-01	John Adams	Ellsworth	Patterson	Cushing	Washington	Chase	**Moore**				
1801-04	John Adams	**Marshall, J.**	Patterson	Cushing	Washington	Chase	Moore				
1804-07	Thomas Jefferson	Marshall, J.	Patterson	Cushing	Washington	Chase	**Johnson, W.**				
1807-11	Thomas Jefferson	Marshall, J.	**Livingston**	Cushing	Washington	Chase	Johnson, W.	**Todd**			
1811-24	James Madison	Marshall, J.	Livingston	**Story**	Washington	**Duvall**	Johnson, W.	Todd			
1824-26	James Monroe	Marshall, J.	**Thompson**	Story	Washington	Duvall	Johnson, W.	Todd			
1826-29	John Quincy Adams	Marshall, J.	Thompson	Story	Washington	Duvall	Johnson, W.	**Trimble**			
1829-30	Andrew Jackson	Marshall, J.	Thompson	Story	Washington	Duvall	Johnson, W.	**McLean**			

Court Term	President	Chief Justice	Seat 2	Seat 3	Seat 4	Seat 5	Seat 6	Seat 7	Seat 8	Seat 9	Seat 10
1830-36	Andrew Jackson	Marshall, J.	Thompson	Story	**Baldwin**	Duvall	Johnson, W.	McLean			
1835-36	Andrew Jackson	Marshall, J.	Thompson	Story	Baldwin	Duvall	**Wayne**	McLean			
1836-37	Andrew Jackson	**Taney**	Thompson	Story	Baldwin	**Barbour**	Wayne	McLean			
1837-41	Martin Van Buren	Taney	Thompson	Story	Baldwin	Barbour	Wayne	McLean	**Catron**	**McKinley**	
1841-44	Martin Van Buren	Taney	Thompson	Story	Baldwin	**Daniel**	Wayne	McLean	Catron	McKinley	
1845-46	John Tyler	Taney	**Nelson**	Story	**(vacant)**	Daniel	Wayne	McLean	Catron	McKinley	
1846-52	James K. Polk	Taney	Nelson	**Woodbury**	**Grier**	Daniel	Wayne	McLean	Catron	McKinley	
1852-53	Millard Fillmore	Taney	Nelson	**Curtis**	Grier	Daniel	Wayne	McLean	Catron	McKinley	
1853-58	Franklin Pierce	Taney	Nelson	Curtis	Grier	Daniel	Wayne	McLean	Catron	**Campbell**	
1858-61	James Buchanan	Taney	Nelson	**Clifford**	Grier	Daniel	Wayne	McLean	Catron	Campbell	
1861-62	Abraham Lincoln	Taney	Nelson	Clifford	Grier	**(vacant)**	Wayne	McLean	Catron	Campbell	
1862-63	Abraham Lincoln	Taney	Nelson	Clifford	Grier	Miller	Wayne	**Swayne**	Catron	**Davis**	
1863-65	Abraham Lincoln	Taney	Nelson	Clifford	Grier	Miller	Wayne	Swayne	Catron	Davis	**Field**
1865-66	Abraham Lincoln	**Chase, S.P.**	Nelson	Clifford	Grier	Miller	Wayne	Swayne	Catron	Davis	Field
1866-68	Andrew Johnson	Chase, S.P.	Nelson	Clifford	Grier	Miller	Wayne	Swayne	[Catron not replaced; SCt returns to 9 justices	Davis	Field
1868-70	Johnson/ Grant	Chase, S.P.	Nelson	Clifford	Grier	Miller	**(vacant)**	Swayne	Field	Davis	

Court Term	President	Chief Justice	Seat 2	Seat 3	Seat 4	Seat 5	Seat 6	Seat 7	Seat 8	Seat 9	Seat 10
1870-73	Ulysses S. Grant	Chase, S.P.	Nelson	Clifford	**Strong**	Miller	**Bradley**	Swayne	Field	Davis	
1873-74	Ulysses S. Grant	Chase, S.P.	**Hunt**	Clifford	Strong	Miller	Bradley	Swayne	Field	Davis	
1874-77	Ulysses S. Grant	**Waite**	Hunt	Clifford	Strong	Miller	Bradley	Swayne	Field	Davis	
1877-81	Rutherford B. Hayes	Waite	Hunt	Clifford	Strong	Miller	Bradley	Swayne	Field	**Harlan I**	
1881-82	Rutherford B. Hayes / James Garfield	Waite	Hunt	Clifford	**Woods**	Miller	Bradley	**Mathews**	Field	Harlan I	
1882-88	Chester A. Arthur	Waite	**Blatchford**	Gray	Woods	Miller	Bradley	Mathews	Field	Harlan I	
1888	Grover Cleveland	Waite	Blatchford	Gray	**Lamar, L.**	Miller	Bradley	Mathews	Field	Harlan I	
1888-89	Grover Cleveland	**Fuller**	Blatchford	Gray	Lamar, L.	Miller	Bradley	Mathews	Field	Harlan I	
1889-92	Benjamin Harrison	Fuller	Blatchford	Gray	Lamar, L.	Miller	Bradley	**Brewer**	Field	Harlan I	
1892-93	Benjamin Harrison	Fuller	Blatchford	Gray	Lamar, L.	**Brown**	**Shiras**	Brewer	Field	Harlan I	
1893-94	Benjamin Harrison	Fuller	Blatchford	Gray	**Jackson, H.**	Brown	Shiras	Brewer	Field	Harlan I	
1894-96	Grover Cleveland	Fuller	**White, E.**	Gray	Jackson, H.	Brown	Shiras	Brewer	Field	Harlan I	
1896-98	Grover Cleveland	Fuller	White, E.	Gray	**Peckham**	Brown	Shiras	Brewer	Field	Harlan I	
1898-1903	William McKinley	Fuller	White, E.	Gray	Peckham	Brown	Shiras	Brewer	**McKenna**	Harlan I	
1903-07	Theodore Roosevelt	Fuller	White, E.	**Holmes**	Peckham	Brown	**Day**	Brewer	McKenna	Harlan I	
1907-10	Theodore Roosevelt	Fuller	White, E.	Holmes	Peckham	**Moody**	Day	Brewer	McKenna	Harlan I	

Court Term	President	Chief Justice	Seat 2	Seat 3	Seat 4	Seat 5	Seat 6	Seat 7	Seat 8	Seat 9	Seat 10
1910	William Howard Taft	Fuller	White, E.	Holmes	**Lurton**	Moody	Day	Brewer	McKenna	Harlan I	
1910-12	William Howard Taft	**White, E.**	**Van Devanter**	Holmes	Lurton	**Lamar, J.**	Day	**Hughes**	McKenna	Harlan I	
1912-14	William Howard Taft	White, E.	Van Devanter	Holmes	Lurton	Lamar, J.	Day	Hughes	McKenna	**Pitney**	
1914-16	Woodrow Wilson	White, E.	Van Devanter	Holmes	**McReynolds**	Lamar, J.	Day	Hughes	McKenna	Pitney	
1916-22	Woodrow Wilson	White, E.	Van Devanter	Holmes	McReynolds	**Brandeis**	Day	**Clarke**	McKenna	Pitney	
1922-25	Warren G. Harding	**Taft**	Van Devanter	Holmes	McReynolds	Brandeis	**Butler**	**Sutherland**	McKenna	Pitney	
1925-30	Calvin Coolidge	Taft	Van Devanter	Holmes	McReynolds	Brandeis	Butler	Sutherland	**Stone**	**Sanford**	
1930-32	Herbert Hoover	**Hughes**	Van Devanter	Holmes	McReynolds	Brandeis	Butler	Sutherland	Stone	**Roberts**	
1932-37	Herbert Hoover	Hughes	Van Devanter	**Cardozo**	McReynolds	Brandeis	Butler	Sutherland	Stone	Roberts	
1937-38	Franklin Delano Roosevelt	Hughes	**Black**	Cardozo	McReynolds	Brandeis	Butler	Sutherland	Stone	Roberts	
1938-39	Franklin Delano Roosevelt	Hughes	Black	Cardozo	McReynolds	Brandeis	Butler	**Reed**	Stone	Roberts	
1939-40	Franklin Delano Roosevelt	Hughes	Black	**Frankfurter**	McReynolds	**Douglas**	Butler	Reed	Stone	Roberts	
1940-41	Franklin Delano Roosevelt	Hughes	Black	Frankfurter	McReynolds	Douglas	**Murphy**	Reed	Stone	Roberts	
1941-42	Franklin Delano Roosevelt	**Stone**	Black	Frankfurter	**Byrnes**	Douglas	Murphy	Reed	Stone	Roberts	

Court Term	President	Chief Justice	Seat 2	Seat 3	Seat 4	Seat 5	Seat 6	Seat 7	Seat 8	Seat 9	Seat 10
1942-43	Franklin Delano Roosevelt	Stone	Black	Frankfurter	Byrnes	Douglas	Murphy	Reed	**Jackson, R.**	Roberts	
1943-45	Franklin Delano Roosevelt	Stone	Black	Frankfurter	**Rutledge, W.**	Douglas	Murphy	Reed	Jackson, R.	Roberts	
1945-46	Harry S. Truman	Stone	Black	Frankfurter	Rutledge, W.	Douglas	Murphy	Reed	Jackson, R.	**Burton**	
1946-49	Harry S. Truman	**Vinson**	Black	Frankfurter	Rutledge, W.	Douglas	Murphy	Reed	Jackson, R.	Burton	
1949-53	Harry S. Truman	Vinson	Black	Frankfurter	**Minton**	Douglas	**Clark**	Reed	Jackson, R.	Burton	
1953-54	Dwight D. Eisenhower	**Warren**	Black	Frankfurter	Minton	Douglas	Clark	Reed	Jackson, R.	Burton	
1955-57	Dwight D. Eisenhower	Warren	Black	Frankfurter	Minton	Douglas	Clark	Reed	**Harlan II**	Burton	
1957-59	Dwight D. Eisenhower	Warren	Black	Frankfurter	**Brennan**	Douglas	Clark	**Whittaker**	Harlan II	Burton	
1959-62	Dwight D. Eisenhower	Warren	Black	Frankfurter	Brennan	Douglas	Clark	Whittaker	Harlan II	**Stewart**	
1962-65	John F. Kennedy	Warren	Black	**Goldberg**	Brennan	Douglas	Clark	**White**	Harlan II	Stewart	
1965-67	Lyndon B. Johnson	Warren	Black	**Fortas**	Brennan	Douglas	Clark	White	Harlan II	Stewart	
1967-68	Lyndon B. Johnson	Warren	Black	Fortas	Brennan	Douglas	**Marshall**	White	Harlan II	Stewart	
1968-69	Richard Nixon	**Burger**	Black	Fortas	Brennan	Douglas	Marshall	White	Harlan II	Stewart	
1970-71	Richard Nixon	Burger	Black	**Blackmun**	Brennan	Douglas	Marshall	White	Harlan II	Stewart	
1971-75	Richard Nixon	Burger	**Powell**	Blackmun	Brennan	Douglas	Marshall	White	**Rehnquist**	Stewart	
1975-81	Gerald Ford	Burger	Powell	Blackmun	Brennan	**Stevens**	Marshall	White	Rehnquist	Stewart	

Court Term	President	Chief Justice	Seat 2	Seat 3	Seat 4	Seat 5	Seat 6	Seat 7	Seat 8	Seat 9	Seat 10
1981-87	Ronald Reagan	Burger	Powell	Blackmun	Brennan	Stevens	Marshall	White	Rehnquist	**O'Connor**	
1986-87	Ronald Reagan	**Rehnquist**	Powell	Blackmun	Brennan	Stevens	Marshall	White	**Scalia**	O'Connor	
1988-90	Ronald Reagan	Rehnquist	**Kennedy**	Blackmun	Brennan	Stevens	Marshall	White	Scalia	O'Connor	
1990-91	George H.W. Bush	Rehnquist	Kennedy	Blackmun	**Souter**	Stevens	Marshall	White	Scalia	O'Connor	
1991-93	George H.W. Bush	Rehnquist	Kennedy	Blackmun	Souter	Stevens	**Thomas**	White	Scalia	O'Connor	
1993-94	Bill Clinton	Rehnquist	Kennedy	Blackmun	Souter	Stevens	Thomas	**Ginsburg**	Scalia	O'Connor	
1994-2005	Bill Clinton	Rehnquist	Kennedy	**Breyer**	Souter	Stevens	Thomas	Ginsburg	Scalia	O'Connor	
2005-08	George W. Bush	**Roberts**	Kennedy	Breyer	Souter	Stevens	Thomas	Ginsburg	Scalia	**Alito**	

Index

References are to Pages

References are to Pages

References are to Pages

O

P

R

S

T

V

W

†